ESSENTIALS OF MARKETING RESEARCH

NARESH K. MALHOTRA
DAVID F. BIRKS
PETER A. WILLS

ESSENTIALS OF MARKETING RESEARCH

PEARSON

Harlow, England • London • New York • Boston • San Francisco • Toronto • Sydney • Auckland • Singapore • Hong Kong
Tokyo • Seoul • Taipei • New Delhi • Cape Town • São Paulo • Mexico City • Madrid • Amsterdam • Munich • Paris • Milan

Pearson Education Limited
Edinburgh Gate
Harlow
Essex CM20 2JE
England

and Associated Companies throughout the world

Visit us on the World Wide Web at:

www.pearson.com/uk

First published 2013 (print and electronic)

© Pearson Education Limited 2013 (print and electronic)

ISBN: 978-0-273-72433-9 (print)
       978-0-273-72437-7 (PDF)
       978-0-273-78109-7 (eText)

British Library Cataloguing-in-Publication Data
A catalogue record for the print edition is available from the British Library

Library of Congress Cataloging-in-Publication Data
A catalog record for the print edition is available from the Library of Congress

10 9 8 7 6 5 4 3 2 1
17 16 15 14 13

Print edition typeset in 10/12 pt Minion by 73
Printed and bound by Rotolito Lombarda, Italy

NOTE THAT ANY PAGE CROSS REFERENCES REFER TO THE PRINT EDITION

Brief contents

Contents

Companion Website

For open-access **student resources** specifically written to complement this textbook and support your learning, please visit **www.pearsoned.co.uk/malhotra-euro**

Lecturer Resources

For password-protected online resources tailored to support the use of this textbook in teaching, please visit **www.pearsoned.co.uk/malhotra-euro**

Preface

Our 4th European edition of *Marketing Research: An Applied Approach* (2012) presents a comprehensive view of the thinking and practice of marketing research. However, we recognise that the aims and design of many marketing and research based degrees does not enable a full evaluation and use of this text. Many colleges and universities deliver excellent marketing research modules where advanced quantitative data analyses chapters are not addressed. It is for such marketing research modules, primarily at an introductory level, that this book was written. The aim in writing this book was to distil the essence and best examples from our 4th Edition of *Marketing Research: An Applied Approach*. This book was written in a manner that is easy to read, understand and apply. It includes an array of European and international examples, practices and illustrations. It portrays a balance of qualitative and quantitative research approaches and how these approaches work together. These approaches demonstrate the nature and value of marketing research in delivering creative support to decision makers. Marketing researchers must also be able to cope with the mass of digital developments that are changing the manner in which established research methods are conducted and are creating new research methods. Digital developments are fundamentally shaping how researchers plan, gather, analyse and interpret information. This book addresses the impact of digital developments upon the thinking and practice of marketing research. It includes a chapter that addresses the nature and use of social media in marketing research. *The Essentials of Marketing Research* will guide the reader through the challenges faced in conducting marketing research of the highest quality. This is achieved through an appropriate blend of scholarship with a highly applied and managerial orientation.

Pedagogical features

The book is written for use in introductory marketing research modules at both the undergraduate and post-graduate levels. The coverage is comprehensive and the depth and breadth of topics are well suited to both levels. There are numerous diagrams, tables and examples to help explain and illustrate basic concepts. If a chapter does not cover a particular topic in sufficient depth, there are numerous references to follow a line of enquiry. The web addresses presented throughout allow for further illustration of ideas and, in many instances, demonstration versions of software. The companion website presents a thorough evaluation of important marketing research organisations, web and software links.

The Essentials of Marketing Research delivers the following features:

1 *Balanced orientation.* We have blended scholarship with a highly applied and managerial orientation showing how researchers apply concepts and techniques and how managers use their findings to improve marketing practice. In each chapter, we discuss real marketing research challenges to support a great breadth of marketing decisions.

2 *Real-life examples.* Real-life examples ('Real research') describe the kind of marketing research that organisations use to address specific managerial problems and how they implement research to great effect.

3 *Hands-on approach.* We present real-life scenarios and exercises in every chapter. The end of chapter exercises set online research challenges, role play as a researcher and a marketing manager. Real-life marketing situations can be tackled in which the role of a consultant can be assumed whose role it is to recommend research and marketing management decisions.

4 *International focus.* Every chapter has a section entitled 'International marketing research' (except for the two quantitative data analysis chapters). As digital developments are breaking down many cultural and communication barriers, many of the examples used throughout each chapter address international research challenges.

5 *Ethics focus.* Ethical issues are pervasive in marketing research. The development and implementation of research codes of practice gives integrity to the marketing research profession and distinguishes the practice from many other forms of data gathering. Every chapter has a section entitled 'Ethics in marketing research' (except for the two quantitative data analysis chapters). Additional examples that address ethical issues are presented throughout the text.

6 *Digital development focus.* This book has a chapter entitled 'Social media research methods'. This brings together much of the thinking and practice of new and developing research methods. Throughout the book we will show how online research activities have impacted upon the thinking, planning and practice of marketing research. Technological and digital developments are continually shaping the nature and value of research practice. Every chapter has a section entitled 'Digital developments in marketing research' (except for the two quantitative data analysis chapters).

7 *Contemporary focus.* We apply marketing research to current challenges such as customer value, experiential marketing, satisfaction, loyalty, customer equity, brand equity and management, innovation, entrepreneurship, relationship marketing, creativity and design, and socially responsible marketing throughout the text.

8 *Statistical software.* We illustrate data analysis procedures with emphasis upon a student edition of SNAP FMS. Seven of the fourteen chapters present guidance to use SNAP FMS. This will enable students to plan, design, deliver, analyse and report the findings of their own surveys with a sound theoretical basis. Any number of questions can be tackled with SNAP FMS, with responses from up to 100 participants. The guidance presented will enable students to search for and use the functions of many other survey design and data analysis packages, such as SPSS and SAS.

9 *Companion website.* The companion website has a comprehensive list of:

- Marketing Research Associations worldwide
- Statistical bodies throughout Europe and beyond
- The largest marketing research companies in the world
- A selection of inspiring marketing research companies
- Marketing research magazines and journals
- A selection of excellent marketing research blogs
- A selection of excellent marketing research apps
- More general sources of support for marketing researchers.

10 *Instructor's manual.* The instructor's manual is very closely tied to the text, but is not prescriptive in how the material should be handled in the classroom. The manual offers teaching suggestions, answers to all end-of-chapter questions, Professional perspective discussion points, and case study exercises. Also included are PowerPoint slides, incorporating all the figures and tables.

11 *Photography.* With the growth of social media, consumers are expressing characteristics of their behaviour, attitudes and emotions through the use of photographs. Marketing research students benefit enormously from a development of visual awareness, both in engaging with research participants and with research users, especially in the visualisation of data. To support a visual awareness, we see the photographs in this text as a means to encapsulate the essence of marketing research and its challenges. Some of the images in this edition have a serious intent, linking a particular image to concepts and aiding the recall of a concept. Others are there to lighten the sometimes difficult technical passages. In their own right, each image has many technical and artistic merits.

Acknowledgements

Many people have been most generous in helping to write *The Essentials of Marketing Research*.

In developing the critical approach I take in marketing research practice and writing, I must thank my Consumer Behaviour teacher and PhD supervisor John Southan of the University of Salford. My friend and former work colleague, the late Kevin Fogarty, retains a special distinction for his humour, creativity and for shaping many of the values I hold dear.

In working through the 'Digital developments in marketing research', colleagues and associates of the Association for Survey Computing (ASC) have been of great help. In particular, I have had excellent support and advice from ASC member Tim Macer, Honorary Research Fellow at the University of Winchester. In evaluating the emergent skills and development of future researchers I have had excellent support from Danny Wain, Honorary Knowledge Exchange Fellow at the University of Winchester.

I am most grateful to Peter Wills in joining Naresh Malhotra and myself as co-author for this edition. Peter is the Chair of the Association for Survey Computing. His support has come in helping to articulate the relevance and importance of technological, digital and social media research developments for marketing research. Peter is also the Chair of Snap Surveys Ltd, and along with Managing Director Dr Stephen Jenkins, has made possible the development and integration of a student learning edition of SNAP for this book. Thank you so much, Pete and Steve, for your inspiring and generous support.

My students and colleagues at Winchester Business School have helped enormously in the development of this text. The values and culture of the University of Winchester and Winchester Business School help enormously to engage, reflect upon and apply research ideas. In particular, many of the ideas and approaches in this text were developed in the MSc Marketing modules of Marketing Research and Analysis, and Research Methods in Business. I must thank my students for their patience and kindness in responding to my ideas.

To Rachel Gear at Pearson Education, I have so much to thank you for. I have really enjoyed our working relationship and your totally positive outlook. Also, David Cox, formerly at Pearson Education, my thanks to you; you gave me so much encouragement to get started on this book. My thanks too, to Rufus Curnow for his hard work in conjunction with the Marketing and Sales teams.

At Pearson Education the book has also come together with the help of Kay Holman in Production, Kelly Miller as Designer, Philippa Fiszzon as Project Editor, Christopher Kingston as Editorial Assistant, and Summa Verbeek and Mary Nisbet in Marketing. I would also like to thank Paul Silk and George White who introduced and tutored me in the use of the Pearson Online Database (POD). POD is a rich resource of visuals; I enjoyed learning how to use this database and especially working with the amazing images that were available to me.

Last, but by no means least, to be able to find the time and space to write, the love, support and understanding of your family is vital. To my partner Helen, enormous thanks and love for all that you give to me and to my beautiful son Jesse, who with Helen brings me so much laughter, inspiration and light.

David F. Birks

About the authors

Dr Naresh K. Malhotra is Regents' Professor, DuPree College of Management, Georgia Institute of Technology. He is listed in *Marquis Who's Who in America*, 51st Edition (1997), 52nd Edition (1998), 53rd Edition (1999), and in the *National Registry of Who's Who* (1999).

In an article by Wheatley and Wilson (1987 AMA Educators' Proceedings), Professor Malhotra was ranked number one in the country based on articles published in the *Journal of Marketing Research* from 1980 to 1985. He also holds the all-time record for the most publications in the *Journal of Health Care Marketing*. He is ranked number one based on publications in the *Journal of the Academy of Marketing Science* (JAMS) from its inception through volume 23, 1995. He is also number one based on publications in JAMS from 1986 to 1995. He is listed as one of the best researchers in marketing in John Fraedrich, 'The best researchers in marketing', Marketing Educator (Summer 1997), p. 5.

He has published more than 75 papers in major refereed journals including the *Journal of Marketing Research*, *Journal of Consumer Research, Marketing Science, Journal of Marketing, Journal of Academy of Marketing Science, Journal of Retailing, Journal of Health Care Marketing*, and leading journals in statistics, management science and psychology. In addition, he has also published numerous refereed articles in the proceedings of major national and international conferences. Several articles have received research awards.

He was Chairman, Academy of Marketing Science Foundation, 1996–1998, and was President, Academy of Marketing Science, 1994–1996, and Chairman of the Board of Governors from 1990 to 1992. He is a Distinguished Fellow of the Academy and Fellow of the Decision Sciences Institute. He serves as an Associate Editor of *Decision Sciences Journal* and has served as Section Editor, Health Care Marketing Abstracts, *Journal of Health Care Marketing*. Also, he serves on the Editorial Boards of eight journals.

His book entitled *Marketing Research: An Applied Orientation*, Sixth Edition, was published by Prentice Hall, Inc in 2010. An International Edition and an Australian Edition of his book have also been published, along with a Spanish translation. The book has received widespread adoption at both the graduate and undergraduate levels with more than 100 schools using it in the USA.

Dr Malhotra has consulted for business, non-profit and government organisations in the USA and abroad and has served as an expert witness in legal and regulatory proceedings. He is the winner of numerous awards and honours for research, teaching and service to the profession.

Dr Malhotra is a member and Deacon, First Baptist Church of Atlanta. He lives in the Atlanta area with his wife, Veena, and children, Ruth and Paul.

Dr David Frederick Birks is a Professor of Marketing at Winchester Business School, the University of Winchester, England. He teaches quantitative and qualitative marketing research and is leading developments across the University in digital marketing research. David moved to Winchester Business School after a period of four years working at Winchester School of Art, the University of Southampton. With the growth and impact of social media research upon marketing research thinking and practice, the School of Art played a major role in his thoughts on emerging data capture, analysis and presentation techniques in marketing research. David has lectured at the School of Management at the University of Southampton where he designed and was Programme Director for their MSc in Marketing Analytics. He has also lectured at the Universities of Bath, Strathclyde and Salford. In the School of Management at the University of Bath he was the Director of Studies for their Executive MBAs in Malaysia and China, and their Postgraduate Research Programme. David's publications have covered the fields of Housing, Statistics, Marketing and Information Systems. In the field of Information Systems he has co-edited a 2012 special edition on the use of Grounded Theory in Information Systems Research, for the European Journal of Information Systems. In 2011 David co-chaired and edited the Association of Survey Computing's (ASC) 6th International Conference, 'Shifting the Boundaries of Research', at the University of Bristol. He is an active committee member of the ASC, being committed to their agenda of sharing best thinking and practice in the use of technology in research.

 **Peter A. Wills** is the Chairman of Snap Surveys and Honorary Knowledge Exchange Fellow at the University of Winchester. He brings his distinguished expert knowledge of technology within the marketing research industry to this new edition. Peter founded Snap Surveys in 1981 to develop software products for desktop computers. Snap Surveys were the first company to create a desktopbased system for analysing surveys. From this point he led the expansion of their product line into areas such as web based surveys, scanning, and multimode data capture, along with additional services to provide outsourced data processing services, consultancy and training. Peter set up a US operation in 1995 to support North and South American Snap Survey users. He now oversees a staff of 70 in the UK and the US, with a client base of 30,000 users in both the public and private sector across the globe. Peter was responsible in 1992 for proposing an industry standard for the interchange of survey information between competing software products. This initiative has flourished and continues to operate as triple-s www.triple-s.org. He is the Chairman of the Association for Survey Computing, the world's leading society for the advancement of knowledge in software and technology for research surveys and statistics.

Publisher's acknowledgements

We are grateful to the following for permission to reproduce copyright material:

Figures

Figures on page 418, images courtesy of Snap Surveys, advanced survey software and service solutions, www.snapsurveys.com

Screenshots

Screenshots on pages 152, 153, 154, 155, 224, 225, 226, 259, 260, 261, 296, 297, 298, 299, 355, 356, 357, 391, 392, 393, 420, 421, 422 and 423, images courtesy of Snap Surveys, advanced survey software and service solutions, www.snapsurveys.com

Tables

Table on page 19 adapted from *From consumer connection to consumer insight: a Nestlé case study*, ESOMAR Consumer Insights Conference, Milan, May 2007 (Blachowska, M.); Table 4.2 adapted from 'Online audio group discussions: a comparison with face-to-face methods', *International Journal of Market Research*, Vol. 51 (2), pp. 219–241 (Cheng, C.C., Krumwiede, D. and Sheu, C. 2009); Table on page 204 adapted from www.fifa.com; Table on page 389 from 'The incidence of unethical practices in marketing research: An empirical investigation', *Journal of the Academy of Marketing Science*, Vol. 18, pp. 143–152 (Akaah, I.P. and Riordon, E.A. 1990), Table 3, p. 148, Copyright © Springer 1990, with kind permission from Springer Science + Business Media.

Text

Interview on pages 273–4 from 'How was it for you?', *Research*, pp. 8–9 (Park, C. 2000), Fieldwork Supplement, July. Originally published in Research magazine – www.research-live.com., republished with permission.

Photographs

Pearson Education Ltd: Don Farrall/Photodisc 417, Geoff Manasse/Photodisc 1, H. Wiesenhofer/Photolink/Photodisc 194, 381, Harnett/Hanzon/Photodisc 362, Ian Hooton/Image Source 273, Image Source 79, Image Source/Alamy 101, Imagemore Co., Ltd 53, Ingram Collection 293, Ingram Publishing/Alamy 28, 36, 200, 277, Jack Star/Photolink/Photodisc 34, 149, James Hardy/PhotoAlto/Getty Images 108, John Foxx Collection/Imagestate 6, 18, 59, 89, 119, 160, 163, 184, 233, 246, 304, 306, 322, 329, 337, 413, 433, 439, Jupiterimages/Comstock Images 145, Lord and Leverett 182, 377, Naki Kouyioumtzis 249, Neil Beer/Photodisc 238, Nigel Riches/Image Source 176, Philip Parkhouse 74, Photodisc 427, 431, Photolink/Photodisc 171, 330, 388, S. Wanke/Photolink/Photodisc 87, Sozaijiten 420, Steve Cole/Photodisc 139, 266, 340, 399, SuperStock/Ingram Publishing/Alamy 319, Sverre Haugland/Image Source/photolibrary.com 80, Tudor Photography 21.

In some instances we have been unable to trace the owners of copyright material, and we would appreciate any information that would enable us to do so.

1

Management decisions and the marketing research problem

Stage 1

Problem definition

Stage 2

Research approach developed

Stage 3

Research design developed

Stage 4

Fieldwork or data collection

Stage 5

Data integrity and analysis

Stage 6

Report preparation and presentation

Researchers support decision makers by bringing creativity, integrity and a scientific approach to the resolution of marketing problems.

Objectives

After reading this chapter, you should be able to:

1 understand the nature and scope of marketing research and its role in supporting successful marketing decisions;

2 describe a conceptual framework for conducting marketing research;

3 understand why some decision makers may be sceptical of the value of marketing research;

4 describe how marketing research may be applied to problem identification and problem solving;

5 describe the types and roles of research suppliers;

6 describe the steps of the marketing research process;

7 understand the nature and value of the research brief and research proposal in planning research projects;

8 appreciate the complexities involved in conducting international marketing research;

9 appreciate the basis of ethical challenges in conducting marketing research;

10 appreciate how digital developments and social media research techniques are shaping marketing research.

Overview

Marketing research comprises one of the most important and fascinating facets of marketing. In this chapter, we describe the nature and scope of marketing research, emphasising its role of supporting successful marketing decision making. We set out a conceptual framework that helps to encapsulate the value of marketing research support. There are many successful marketing decisions that have been founded upon sound marketing research: however, marketing research does not replace decision making. We set out why some decision makers may be sceptical of the value of marketing research. Marketing research can be applied to many forms of marketing decision, and we present a classification to demonstrate how research can help to identify and/or solve problems. The marketing research industry encompasses a vast range of skill sets and qualities. We set out a framework to classify marketing research organisations and describe the types of services they offer.

The six steps involved in the marketing research process are described. The most important step of this process is problem definition. This forms the foundation upon which creative and effective marketing research is planned and implemented. Defining the marketing research problem sets the course of an entire research project. We set out the means by which decision makers may articulate the research support they need in the form of a research brief. This is followed by the means by which the researcher may respond to a brief in the form of a research proposal.

A final section of the chapter is devoted to contemporary issues in marketing research. The topic of international marketing research is introduced. The role of researchers in addressing the challenges and opportunities of the globalisation of markets is introduced. The ethical challenges of marketing research and the responsibilities that marketing research stakeholders have to themselves, to each other and to the research project are introduced. A general introduction to the impact of digital applications in marketing practices upon marketing research thinking and practice is made.

What is marketing research?

The term 'marketing research' is broad in meaning and application. This breadth will be explored and illustrated throughout this book. What will become apparent is that it is related to supporting marketing decision making in many traditional and new digital manners. The following examples illustrate the use and decision support offered by conventional quantitative and qualitative marketing research methods.

| Real research | Online market research at the International Data Group[1] |

The International Data Group (IDG) (**www.idg.com**) was one of the world's leading providers of IT media, IT research and specialist conferences and exhibitions for the IT industry. The publishing group had more than 300 newspaper and magazine titles in 85 countries with more than 100 million readers. The trend towards declining circulations for print titles has had an impact on IDG's business. Besides magazine titles, the group offered its customers wide ranging Internet publications, including a number of titles that were only available online. IDG's marketing research team changed from paper and telephone-based surveys to online survey methods. Their surveys were used for an ever wider range of applications. For example, readers were questioned on an ongoing basis about their satisfaction with editorial content, their preferences and their requirements. The surveys delivered vital insights into the demographic structure of their readership, which was fundamentally important to advertising customers. IDG also offered its advertising customers online surveys into the impact of advertisements. In these surveys, readers indicated which advertisements they remembered and what they thought of them. This enabled the success of individual advertisements and advertising campaigns to be measured and assessed.

| Real research | Using qualitative research to design better phones for the elderly[2] |

BT Freestyle was a range of fixed line telephones sold with/without an answering machine, and in bundles of 1/2/3 phones together. The range was targeted at elderly users or those who had physical impairments, but was also widely used by people who wish to own an easy to use home telephone. The design company TheAlloy (**http://thealloy.com**) had worked with BT teams for over 15 years to design hundreds of consumer devices. The design team was made aware that the Freestyle range needed to be improved into a new Freestyle 700 range and an outline brief was provided of key attributes and market segments. The core elements of the design brief were: **Key product attributes:** clear controls, clear display, simple operation and comfort. **Consumer types (or potential markets):** partiality sighted, dexterity problems, technophobes, older segment of the population, less design conscious, comfort orientated, ease of use oriented. The design solution was driven by TheAlloy's proprietary *Experience Mapping* process that sought to create better user experiences. Their understanding of user experiences were based upon 15 individual in-depth interviews with elderly users. These interviews played a major part in helping the designers to create and launch a new range of Freestyle phones. Within two years of its launch, the Freestyle 700 range gained a value market share of 6 per cent, in a market with around 500 individual products from global brands such as Panasonic, Siemens, Motorola and Philips and with no single product commanding a value market share greater than 8 per cent; this was seen as an excellent return. Within a year of launch, the Freestyle 700 family had gained 42 per cent more market share than the previous Freestyle 600 range.

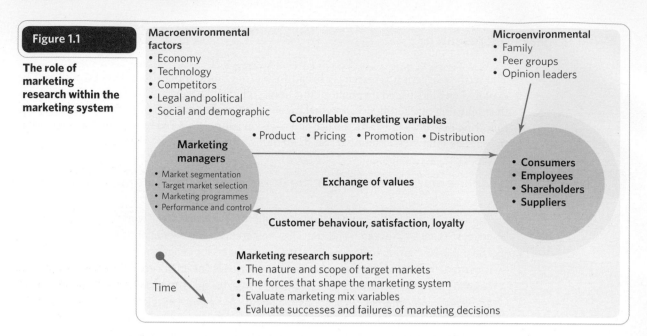

Figure 1.1

The role of marketing research within the marketing system

Macroenvironmental factors
• Economy
• Technology
• Competitors
• Legal and political
• Social and demographic

Microenvironmental
• Family
• Peer groups
• Opinion leaders

Controllable marketing variables
• Product • Pricing • Promotion • Distribution

Marketing managers
• Market segmentation
• Target market selection
• Marketing programmes
• Performance and control

Exchange of values

• **Consumers**
• **Employees**
• **Shareholders**
• **Suppliers**

Customer behaviour, satisfaction, loyalty

Time

Marketing research support:
• The nature and scope of target markets
• The forces that shape the marketing system
• Evaluate marketing mix variables
• Evaluate successes and failures of marketing decisions

These examples illustrate just a few of the many methods used to conduct marketing research, which may range from highly structured surveys with large samples to open-ended in-depth interviews with small samples; from the collection and analysis of readily available data to the generation of 'new' quantitative and qualitative data; from personal face-to-face interactions to remote observations and interactions with consumers online; from small local studies to large global studies. This book will introduce you to the full complement of marketing research techniques and challenges. These examples also illustrate the crucial role played by marketing research in designing and implementing successful marketing plans.[3]

The role of marketing research can be better understood in light of a basic marketing paradigm depicted in Figure 1.1. The emphasis in marketing, as illustrated in the BT telephone example above, is on understanding customer experiences and the delivery of satisfaction. To understand customer experiences and to implement marketing strategies and plans aimed at delivering satisfying experiences, marketing managers need information about customers, competitors and other forces in the marketplace. In recent years, many factors have increased the need for more accurate and timely information. As firms have become national and international in scope, the need for information on larger and more distant markets has increased. As consumers have become more affluent, discerning and sophisticated, marketing managers need better information on how they will respond with new products and other new experiences. As competition has become more intense, managers need information on the effectiveness of their marketing tools. As the environment is changing more rapidly, marketing managers need more timely information to cope with the impact of changes.[4]

Marketers make decisions about what they see as potential opportunities and problems, i.e. a process of identifying issues. They go on to devise the most effective ways to realise these opportunities and overcome problems they have identified. They do this based on a 'vision' of the distinct characteristics of the target markets and customer groups. From this 'vision' they develop, implement and control marketing programmes. This 'vision' of markets and subsequent marketing decisions may be complicated by the interactive effects of an array of environmental forces that shape the nature and scope of target markets. These forces also affect the marketers' ability to deliver experiences that will satisfy their chosen target markets. Within this framework of decision making, marketing research helps the marketing manager link the marketing variables with their environment and customer groups. It helps remove some of the uncertainty by providing relevant information about marketing variables, environment and consumers.

The role of the researcher in supporting the marketing decision maker can therefore be summarised as helping to:

- describe the nature and scope of customer groups;
- understand the nature of forces that shape customer groups;
- understand the nature of forces that shape the marketer's ability to satisfy targeted customer groups;
- test individual and interactive variables that shape consumer experiences;
- monitor and reflect upon past successes and failures in marketing decisions.

Definition of marketing research

Marketing research

Marketing research is the function that links the consumer, customer, and public to the marketer through information – information used to identify and define marketing opportunities and problems; generate, refine, and evaluate marketing actions; monitor marketing performance; and improve understanding of marketing as a process. Marketing research specifies the information required to address these issues, designs the method for collecting information, manages and implements the data collection process, analyses the results, and communicates the findings and their implications.

Marketing research process

A set of six steps which define the tasks to be accomplished in conducting a marketing research study. These include problem definition, developing an approach to the problem, research design formulation, fieldwork, data integrity and analysis, and report generation and presentation.

The European Society for Opinion and Marketing Research (ESOMAR) (**www.esomar.org**) base their view of marketing research on the definition approved by the American Marketing Association. For the purpose of this book, which emphasises the need for information of the highest integrity in the support of decision making, marketing research is defined as:

the function that links the consumer, customer, and public to the marketer through information – information used to identify and define marketing opportunities and problems; generate, refine, and evaluate marketing actions; monitor marketing performance; and improve understanding of marketing as a process. Marketing research specifies the information required to address these issues, designs the method for collecting information, manages and implements the data collection process, analyses the results, and communicates the findings and their implications.

Several aspects of this definition are noteworthy. It stresses the role of 'linking' the marketer to the consumer, customer and public to help improve the whole process of marketing decision making. It also sets out the challenges faced by marketing decision makers and thus where research support can help them make better decisions and/or decisions with lower risks.

One of the major qualities of the American Marketing Association's definition of marketing research is its encapsulation of the marketing research process. The process is founded upon an understanding of the marketing decision(s) needing support. From this understanding, research aims and objectives are defined. To fulfil defined aims and objectives, an approach to conducting the research is established. Next, relevant information sources are identified and a range of data collection methods are evaluated for their appropriateness, forming a research design. The data are collected using the most appropriate method; they are analysed and interpreted, and inferences are drawn. Finally, the findings, implications and recommendations are provided in a format that allows the information to be used for marketing decision making and to be acted upon directly.

In order to attain the highest integrity, marketing research should aim to be objective. It should attempt to provide accurate information in an impartial manner. Although research is always influenced by the researcher's social, cultural and educational background, it should be free from personal or political biases of the researcher or decision makers. Research motivated by personal or political gain involves a breach of professional standards. Such research is deliberately biased to result in predetermined findings. The motto of every researcher should be 'find it and tell it like it is'. Second, it is worth noting the term 'total field of information'. This recognises that marketing decisions are not exclusively supported by marketing research. There are other means of information support for marketers from management consultants, raw data providers such as call centres, direct marketing, database marketing telebusinesses and social media.[5] These alternative forms of support are now competing with a 'traditional' view of marketing research. The methods of these competitors may not be administered with the same scientific rigour and/or ethical standards applied in the marketing research industry. Nonetheless, many marketing decision makers are increasingly using these other sources which collectively are changing the demands placed upon researchers.

Justifying the value of marketing research

It must be recognised that if decision makers use researchers, even if the best theories and practice of the marketing research process are followed 'to the letter', there is no guarantee that a marketing decision supported by research will be successful. The act of decision making and conducting marketing research are distinctive activities and there are examples where the vital link between these activities has resulted in failure. If decision makers have gaps in their knowledge, if they perceive risk and uncertainty in their decision making and cannot find support at hand within their organisation, they can gain support from marketing research. However, many decision makers can recount cases where the use of marketing research has resulted in failure or where decisions based upon gut feeling or intuition have proved to be successful. Such cases present a challenge to researchers, especially in light of the competition faced by the industry from alternative data sources.[6] Reflecting upon such cases should remind researchers to maintain a focus of offering real and valuable support to decision makers. Understanding what real and valuable support means should underpin the whole array of creative data collection and analysis procedures available to the researcher. The following example starts this reflection process with a case that was very close to home!

Real research | **What's this marketing research then, Dave?**

James Birks founded and successfully ran a kiln construction company for over 40 years. He designed, built and maintained kilns for some of the most demanding porcelain and ceramics manufacturers worldwide, including Wedgwood, Royal Doulton and Spode. At retirement age he sold his company as a going concern – a very wealthy man. James was presented with a copy of *Marketing Research: An Applied Approach* by his nephew, David Birks. He was very pleased with the present but was intrigued by the title and asked, 'What's this marketing research then, Dave?' He certainly had a clear idea of what marketing meant to his business and what was involved in being a successful marketer in his industry, but the notion of researching marketing activities and spending money on research was alien to him.

The intriguing aspect of this question is that James Birks had run a successful business on an international basis for over 40 years without the need to be aware of or to use marketing research. Had he used marketing research, could he have been even more successful, or would it have been a wasted investment? Could he have been practising marketing research 'activities' in a very informal manner to support marketing decisions? In his business-to-business marketing situation, he knew his customers and competitors well, and knew what shaped their demands. He understood the networks and relationships within those networks that were vital to the running and development of his business. This knowledge he acquired on a day-to-day basis, nurturing a curiosity about opportunities and how to realise them – without resorting to support from formal ad hoc marketing research. The example of James Birks shows that decision makers do not rely solely upon marketing research and in certain circumstances can survive and perform well without it.

In defending the nature and value of marketing research, there are two key misconceptions that should be clarified:[7]

Marketing research does not make decisions. The role of marketing research is not to make decisions. Rather, research replaces hunches, impressions or a total lack of knowledge with information that can be trusted.

Marketing research does not guarantee success. Research, at best, can improve the odds of making a correct decision. Anyone who expects to eliminate the possibility of failure by doing research is both unrealistic and likely to be disappointed. The real value of research can be seen over a long period where increasing the percentage of good decisions should be manifested in improved bottom-line performance and in the occasional revelation that arises from research.

The latter point shows the long-term benefits of conducting marketing research, i.e. that the results of a study may help decision makers with an immediate problem, but by building their knowledge they can also have long-term benefits. Researchers and decision makers must be aware that out of the array of research and information support approaches, there is no one guaranteed approach, research design or technique that can create the perfect means to support a decision. If decision makers complain that research is misleading or is only telling them what they already know, the researcher may argue that the fault lies with managers who pose the wrong questions or problem in the first place. If one takes the narrow view that the decision maker poses the questions and the researcher finds the answers, there may be some validity in such an argument. It does not hold if one considers that the decision maker and the researcher have a joint commitment to solve problems. In this joint commitment they have quite distinct but complementary creative skills that they can bring together to understand what problem they should be researching, how they conduct the research and how they interpret their findings.

Can researchers survive in an age of increasing competition from other information providers? Can they cope with the threats of growth of in-house research, new entrants to the industry that adopt new technologies and techniques, especially in the use of social media? Can the industry fend off the challenge from the armies of consultants and avoid research being seen as a commodity?[8] To achieve this, the industry has to offer marketers insights that have integrity and can be trusted rather than just 'robust' data collection and analysis. Such insights should lead to fresh perspectives to business problems and/or a competitively advantaged solution.[9] The researcher's input must be seen to benefit the bottom line.

A classification of marketing research

The ESOMAR definition encapsulates two key reasons for undertaking marketing research: (1) to identify opportunities and problems, and (2) to generate and refine marketing actions. This distinction serves as a basis for classifying marketing research into problem identification research and problem-solving research, as shown in Figure 1.2. Linking this classification to the basic marketing paradigm in Figure 1.1, problem identification research can be linked to: the description of the nature and scope of customer groups, understanding the nature of forces that shape customer groups, and understanding the nature of forces that shape the marketer's ability to satisfy targeted customer groups. Problem-solving research can be

Figure 1.2

A classification of marketing research

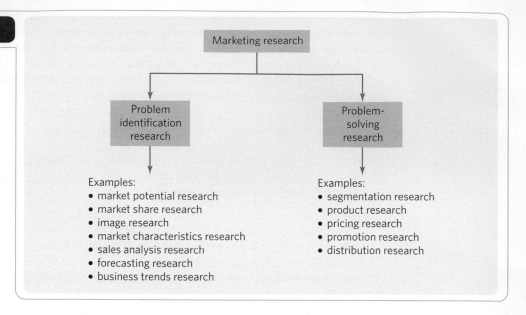

linked: to test individual and interactive marketing mix variables that create consumer experiences, and to monitor and reflect upon past successes and failures in marketing decisions.

Problem identification research is undertaken to help identify problems that are, perhaps, not apparent on the surface and yet exist or are likely to arise in the future. Examples of problem identification research include market potential, market share, brand or company image, market characteristics, sales analysis, short-range forecasting, long-range forecasting and business trends research. Research of this type provides information about the marketing environment and helps diagnose a problem. For example, a declining market potential indicates that the firm is likely to have a problem achieving its growth targets. Similarly, a problem exists if the market potential is increasing but the firm is losing market share. The recognition of economic, social or cultural trends, such as changes in consumer behaviour, may point to underlying problems or opportunities.

Once a problem or opportunity has been identified, **problem-solving research** may be undertaken to help develop a solution. The findings of problem-solving research are used to support decisions that tackle specific marketing problems. Problem-solving research linked to problem identification research is illustrated by the following example of developing a new cereal at Kellogg's.

Problem identification research

Research undertaken to help identify problems that are not necessarily apparent on the surface, yet exist or are likely to arise in the future.

Problem-solving research

Research undertaken to help solve specific marketing problems.

Real research

Crunchy Nut Red adds colour to Kellogg's sales[10]

Kellogg's (**www.kelloggs.com**), experienced a slump in the market and faced the challenge of reviving low cereal sales. Through problem identification research, Kellogg's was able to identify the problem and through problem-solving research, develop several solutions to increase cereal sales. Kellogg's performed several tasks to identify the problem. Researchers spoke to decision makers within the company, interviewed industry experts, conducted analysis of available data, performed some qualitative research, and surveyed consumers about their perceptions and preferences for cereals. Several important issues or problems were identified by this research. Current products were being targeted to children, bagels and muffins were winning for favoured breakfast foods, and high prices were turning consumers to generic brands. Other information also came to light during the research. Adults wanted quick foods that required very little or no preparation.

Collectively, these issues helped Kellogg's identify the problem. The company were not being creative in introducing new products to meet the needs of the adult market. After defining the problem, Kellogg's went to work on solutions. The company developed and tested several new flavours of cereals based upon the results of survey interviews with adult consumers. Based on the results, Kellogg's introduced new flavours that were more suited to the adult palate but were not the tasteless varieties of the past. For example, it introduced Kellogg's Nutri-Grain Cereal Bar Blackberry. The new cereal bar was supported by an advertising campaign and major in-store promotions. Through creative problem identification research followed by problem-solving research, Kellogg's not only saw an increase in sales, but also increased consumption of cereal at times other than breakfast.

This example illustrates how the careful crafting of problem identification research can help to develop a clear focus to problem-solving research. The outcome was research that supported marketing decisions in many ways. A problem-solving perspective enabled Kellogg's decision makers to focus on issues of product development and an integrated communications campaign. Table 1.1 shows the different types of issue that can be addressed using problem-solving research.

Problem identification research and problem-solving research can go hand in hand as seen in the Kellogg's case, and a given marketing research project may combine both types of research.

Table 1.1	Examples of problem-solving research
Segmentation research	Determine basis of segmentation Establish market potential and responsiveness for various segments Select target markets and create lifestyle profiles: demography, media, and product image characteristics
Experiential design research	Determine the process of consuming products and services Online consumption experiences Social media engagement Sensory tests
Product research	Determine optimal product design Test concept Package tests Product modification Brand positioning and repositioning Test marketing
Pricing research	Importance of price in brand selection Pricing policies Product line pricing Price elasticity of demand Initiating and responding to price changes
Promotions research	Optimal promotional budget Optimal promotion mix Copy decisions Creative advertising testing Evaluation of advertising effectiveness
Distribution research	Attitudes of channel members Intensity of wholesale and retail coverage Channel margins Retail and wholesale locations

An overview of the marketing research industry

External suppliers
Outside marketing research companies hired to supply marketing research services.

Full-service suppliers
Companies that offer the full range of marketing research activities.

Syndicated services
Companies that collect and sell common pools of data designed to serve information needs shared by a number of clients.

Customised services
Companies that tailor research procedures to best meet the needs of each client.

The marketing research industry consists of suppliers that provide marketing research services. Figure 1.3 broadly categorises research suppliers as either external or internal. **External suppliers** range from small (one or a few persons) operations to very large global corporations. We now examine the nature of services that may be supplied by external suppliers. External suppliers can be classified as full-service or limited-service suppliers.

Full-service suppliers offer the entire range of marketing research services: for example, defining a problem, developing a research design, conducting focus group interviews, designing questionnaires, sampling, collecting, analysing and interpreting data, and presenting reports. They may also address the marketing implications of the information they present, i.e. have the management skills to interpret and communicate the impact of their research findings at the highest levels. They may also manage customer database analyses, being able to integrate the management and analyses databases with the management and analyses of conventional marketing research techniques.

The services provided by these suppliers can be further broken down into syndicated services, customised services, online services and market research reports and advisory service (see Figure 1.3). Examples of these companies include Kantar (**www.kantar.com**) and Synovate (**www.synovate.com**).

Syndicated services collect information of known commercial value that they provide to multiple clients on a subscription basis. Surveys, diary panels, scanners and audits are the main means by which these data are collected. Examples of these companies include Nielsen (**www.nielsen.com**) and GfK (**www.gfk.com**).

Customised services offer a variety of marketing research services specifically designed to suit a client's particular needs. Each marketing research project is treated uniquely.

Figure 1.3

Marketing research suppliers

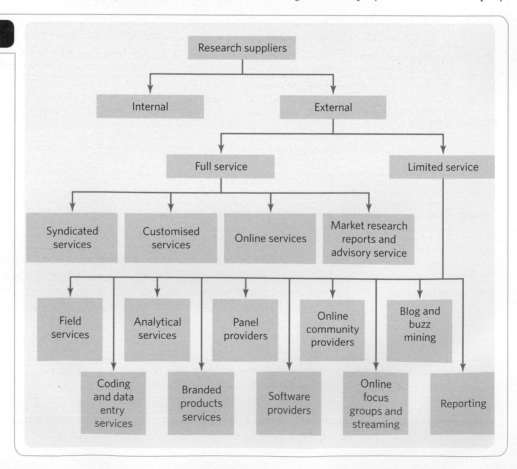

Online services

Companies that specialise in the use of the Internet to collect, analyse and distribute marketing research information.

Market research reports and advisory services

Companies that provide off-the-shelf reports as well as data and briefs on a range of markets, consumer types and issues.

Limited-service suppliers

Companies that specialise in one or a few phases of a marketing research project.

Field services

Companies whose primary service offering is their expertise in collecting data for research projects.

Coding and data entry services

Companies whose primary service offering is their expertise in converting completed surveys or interviews into a usable database for conducting statistical analysis.

Analytical services

Companies that provide guidance in the development of research design.

Branded marketing research products

Specialised data collection and analysis procedures developed to address specific types of marketing research problems.

Panel providers

Provide access to consumer, B2B and specialist panels of participants alongside scripting and hosting surveys.

Software providers

Provide software packages that create platforms to script, host and analyse surveys, or Software as a Service (SaaS) options.

Online community providers

Build online research communities where researchers can employ a wide variety of quantitative and qualitative techniques to connect to consumers.

Online focus groups and streaming

Provide platforms for running online focus groups and streaming the results.

Examples of these companies include TNS (**www.tnsglobal.com**) and Ipsos MORI (**www.ipsos-mori.com**).

Online services offer a combination or variety of secondary data and intelligence gathering, survey or qualitative interviewing, social media engagement and the analysis and publication of research findings, exclusively online. Examples of these companies include YouGov (**www.yougov.com**) and OnePoll (**www.onepoll.com**).

Market research reports and advisory services provide off-the-shelf reports as well as data and briefs on a range of markets, consumer types and issues; as such they are thought of as part of the broader information market and not necessarily part of the traditional marketing research industry. Examples of these companies include Euromonitor (**www.euromonitor.com**) and Mintel (**www.mintel.com**).

Limited-service suppliers specialise in one or a few phases of a marketing research project. Services offered by such suppliers are classified as field services, coding and data entry, analytical services, branded products, viewing facilities, panel providers, software providers, web analytics, online community providers, online focus groups and streaming, blog and buzz mining, and reporting.[11]

Field services collect data through postal, face-to-face interviews, telephone interviews and the Internet. Firms that specialise in interviewing are called field service organisations. These organisations may range from small proprietary companies that operate locally to large multinationals. Some organisations maintain extensive interviewing facilities across the country for interviewing shoppers. Many offer qualitative data collection services such as focus group interviewing. Examples of these companies include GMI (Global Market Insite) (**www.gmi-mr.com**) and Indiefield (**www.indiefield.co.uk**).

Coding and data entry services include editing completed questionnaires, developing a coding scheme and transcribing the data for input into a computer. Examples of these companies include Eurodata Computer Services Limited (**www.data-entry-service.co.uk**) and The Analysis Solution (**www.plus4.co.uk/analysis_solution**).

Analytical services include designing and pretesting questionnaires, determining the best means of collecting data, and designing sampling plans, as well as other aspects of the research design. Some complex marketing research projects require knowledge of sophisticated procedures, including specialised experimental designs and analytical techniques such as conjoint analysis and multidimensional scaling. This kind of expertise can be obtained from firms and consultants specialising in analytical services. Examples of these companies include Cobalt Sky Ltd (**www.cobalt-sky.com**) and Digitab (**www.digitab.uk.com**).

Branded marketing research products and services are specialised data collection and analysis procedures developed to address specific types of marketing research problems. These procedures may be patented, given brand names, and marketed like any other branded product. Examples of these companies include Comparisat® at FDS (**www.fds.co.uk/about_comparisat.asp**) and Millward Brown's Optimor (**www.millwardbrown.com/mboptimor**).

Panel providers offer researchers the opportunity to access consumer, B2B and specialist panels of participants alongside scripting and hosting surveys. Examples of these companies include e-Rewards (**www.e-rewards.co.uk**) and Toluna (**www.toluna.com**).

Software providers offer software packages that create platforms to script, host and analyse surveys, or Software as a Service (SaaS) options. Examples of these companies include Confirmit (**www.confirmit.com**) and SNAP (**www.snapsurveys.com**).

Online community providers build online research communities where researchers can employ a wide variety of quantitative and qualitative techniques to connect to consumers. Examples of these companies include Communispace (**www.communispace.com**) and FreshMinds (**www.freshminds.co.uk**).

Online focus groups and streaming provide platforms for running online focus groups and streaming the results. Examples of these companies include ActiveGroup (**www.activegroup.net**) and FocusVision (**www.focusvision.com**).

Blog and buzz mining
Provide the means
to observe, track or
initiate views in research
communities, social
networks and anywhere else
that people post comments,
visuals, music and other
forms of art on the Internet.

Reporting
Offers research companies
reporting solutions that
seek to engage clients
in oral and electronic
presentations beyond
conventional reporting
methods such as hard copy
reports and PowerPoint.

Blog and buzz mining provide the means to observe, track or initiate views in research communities, social networks and anywhere else that people post comments, visuals, music and other forms of art on the Internet. Examples of these companies include Nielsen's Buzzmetrics (**http://en-us.nielsen.com/content/nielsen/en_us/product_families/nielsen_buzzmetrics.html**) and SimplyZesty (**www.simplyzesty.com**).

Reporting offers research companies reporting solutions that seek to engage clients in oral and electronic presentations beyond conventional reporting methods such as hard copy reports and PowerPoint. They utilise specialist art and graphic design services to create static data presentation formats and data dashboards that can be interrogated. Examples of these companies include E-Tabs (**www.e-tabs.org**) and Wordle (**www.wordle.net**).

The marketing research process

The marketing research process consists of six broad stages as illustrated in Figure 1.4. Each of these stages is developed in more detail in subsequent chapters; thus, the discussion here is brief.

Step 1: Problem definition The logical starting point in wishing to support the decision maker is trying to understand the nature of the marketing problem that requires research support. The process of writing a research brief and research proposal will be shortly outlined. The process of writing a brief and a proposal should demonstrate that marketing decision problems are not simple 'givens', much work may be needed to properly diagnose a problem. The symptoms and causes of a problem may emerge from discussions with decision makers, in-depth interviews with industry experts, and the collection and analysis of readily available published information (from both inside and outside an organisation commission-

Figure 1.4

The marketing research process

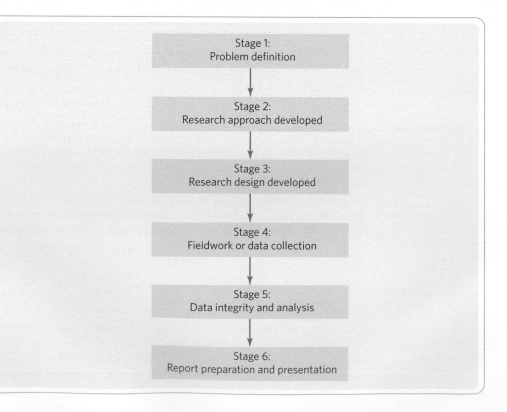

Stage 1:
Problem definition

Stage 2:
Research approach developed

Stage 3:
Research design developed

Stage 4:
Fieldwork or data collection

Stage 5:
Data integrity and analysis

Stage 6:
Report preparation and presentation

ing research). Once the problem has been precisely defined, the researcher can move on to designing and conducting the research process with confidence.

Step 2: Development of an approach to the problem The development of an approach to the problem involves identifying factors that influence research design. A key element of this step involves the selection, adaptation and development of an appropriate theoretical framework to underpin a research design. Understanding the interrelated characteristics of the nature of target participants, the issues to be elicited from them and the context in which this will happen rely upon 'sound' theory. 'Sound' theory helps the researcher to decide 'what should be measured or understood' and 'how best to encapsulate and communicate the measurements or understandings'. In deciding what should be either measured or encapsulated, the researcher also develops a broad appreciation of how the data collected will be analysed.

Step 3: Research design developed A research design is a framework or plan for conducting a marketing research project. It details the procedures necessary for obtaining the required information. Its purpose is to establish a study design that will either test the hypotheses of interest or determine possible answers to set research questions, and ultimately provide the information needed for decision making. Conducting any exploratory techniques, precisely defining variables to be measured, and designing appropriate scales to measure variables can also be part of the research design. The issue of how the data should be obtained from the participants (e.g. by conducting a survey or an experiment) must be addressed. These steps are discussed in detail in the text.

Step 4: Fieldwork or data collection Data collection is accomplished using a staff that operates in the field. Fieldwork involves the planning and administration of research techniques for online, telephone, face-to-face and postal studies.

Step 5: Data integrity and analysis Data integrity focuses upon ensuring the quality of data and includes editing, coding, transcription and verification. The process of data integrity and analysis is essentially the same for both quantitative and qualitative techniques, for data collected from both secondary and primary sources. Considerations of data analysis do not occur after data have been collected; such considerations are an integral part of the development of an approach, the development of a research design, and the implementation of individual quantitative or qualitative methods.

Step 6: Report preparation and presentation The entire project should be documented in a written report that addresses the specific research questions identified, describes the approach, research design, data collection and data analysis procedures adopted, and presents the results and major findings. Research findings should be presented in a comprehensible format so that they can be readily used in the decision making process. In addition, an oral presentation to decision makers should be made using tables, figures and graphs to enhance clarity and impact.

Defining the marketing research problem

Problem definition
A broad statement of the general problem and identification of the specific components of the marketing research problem.

Although each step in a marketing research project is important, the first step of problem definition is the most important. **Problem definition** involves stating the general problem and identifying the specific components of the marketing research problem. Only when the marketing research problem has been clearly defined can research be designed and conducted properly:

> *Of all the tasks in a marketing research project, none is more vital to the ultimate fulfilment of a client's needs than an accurate and adequate definition of the research problem. All the effort, time, and money spent from this point on will be wasted if the problem is misunderstood and ill-defined.*[12]

An analogy to this is the medical doctor prescribing treatment after a cursory examination of a patient; the medicine may be even more dangerous than the condition it is supposed to cure! The truly serious mistakes are made not as a result of wrong answers but because of asking the wrong questions. This point is worth remembering because inadequate problem definition is a leading cause of failure of marketing research projects. Further, better communication and more involvement in problem definition are the most frequently mentioned ways of improving the usefulness of research. The following example illustrates how the iconic American motorbike brand Harley-Davidson has achieved a remarkable turnaround in their performance and brand positioning. Marketing research played a major role in supporting the decisions that achieved this turnaround. The example further illustrates how they established focus for their marketing research and developed a clear set of research questions.

Real research | **Marketing an American icon[13]**

The motorcycle manufacturer Harley-Davidson (**www.harleydavidson.com**) made such an important comeback in the early 2000s that there was a long waiting list to get a bike. Although distributors urged Harley-Davidson to build more motorcycles, the company was sceptical about investing in new production facilities. Many years of declining sales taught top management to be more risk averse than risk prone. Harley-Davidson was performing well again, and investing in new facilities meant taking risks. Would the demand follow in the long term or would customers stop wanting Harleys when the next fashion came along? The decrease in motorcycles' quality linked to Harley's fast growth had cost the company all its bad years. Top management was afraid that the decision to invest was too early. On the other hand, investing would help Harley-Davidson expand and possibly become the clear market leader in the heavyweight bike segment. Discussions with industry experts indicated that brand loyalty was a major factor influencing the sales and repeat sales of motorcycles. Secondary data revealed that the vast majority of motorcycle owners also owned other vehicles. Forecasts predicted an increase in consumer spending on entertainment and recreation up to the year 2015. Focus groups with motorcycle owners further indicated that motorcycles were not used primarily as a means of basic transportation but as a means of recreation.

This process and the findings that emerged define the management decision problem and the marketing research problem. The management decision problem was: Should Harley-Davidson invest to produce more motorcycles? The marketing research problem was to determine if customers would be loyal buyers of Harley-Davidson in the long term. Specifically, the research had to address the following questions:

1 Who are the customers? What are their demographic and psychographic characteristics?
2 Can different types of customers be distinguished? Is it possible to segment the market in a meaningful way?
3 How do customers feel about their Harleys? Are all customers motivated by the same appeal?
4 Are customers loyal to Harley-Davidson? What is the extent of brand loyalty?

One of the research questions (RQs) was examined and its associated hypotheses were:

RQ: Can the motorcycle buyers be segmented based on psychographic characteristics?
H1: There are distinct segments of motorcycle buyers
H2: Each segment is motivated to own a Harley for a different reason
H3: Brand loyalty is high among Harley-Davidson customers in all segments.

This research was guided by the theory that brand loyalty is the result of brand beliefs, attitudes, affect and experience with the brand. Both qualitative and quantitative research were subsequently conducted. First, focus groups of current owners, would-be owners, and owners of other brands were conducted to understand their feelings about Harley-Davidson. Then 16,000 questionnaires were posted to customers to determine their psychological, sociological and demographic profiles and their perceptions of Harley-Davidson.

Key findings included the following.

Seven categories of customers could be distinguished: (1) the adventure-loving traditionalist (2) the sensitive pragmatist (3) the stylish status seeker (4) the laid-back camper (5) the classy capitalist (6) the cool-headed loner (7) the cocky misfit. Thus H1 was supported.

All customers, however, had the same desire to own a Harley: it was a symbol of independence, freedom and power. This uniformity across segments was suprising, contradicting H2.

All customers were long-term loyal customers of Harley-Davidson, supporting H3.

Based on these findings, the decision was taken to invest and in this way to increase the number of Harley's built in the future.

The importance of clearly identifying and defining the research problem cannot be overstated. The foundation of defining a research problem is the communication that develops between marketing decision makers and researchers. In some form or another, marketing decision makers must communicate what they see as being the problems they face and what research support they need. This communication usually comes in the form of a research brief. The researcher responds to the research brief with a research proposal, which encapsulates the researcher's vision of a practical solution to the set research problem.

The marketing research brief

Research brief
A document produced by the users of research findings or the buyers of a piece of marketing research. The brief is used to communicate the perceived requirements of a marketing research study.

The marketing **research brief** is a document produced by the users of research findings or the buyers of a marketing research study. The brief may be used to communicate the perceived requirements of a marketing research study to external agencies or internally within an organisation to research professionals. It should act as the first step for decision makers to express the nature of a marketing and research problem as they see it. This first step is vital in developing an agreement of an appropriate research approach. As a first step of problem diagnosis and negotiation, *the marketing research brief should not be carved in tablets of stone!*

It has been contended that the greatest form of potential error in marketing research lies in the initial relationship between marketing decision makers and researchers.[14] In developing a sound initial relationship, the research brief plays a vital role. Without some formal method of communicating the nature of a marketing problem, there is great potential for ambiguities, illogical actions (by both parties), misunderstandings and even forgetfulness.

The purpose of a written marketing research brief may be summarised as:

- It makes the initiator of the brief more certain of how the information to be collected will support decision making.
- It ensures an amount of agreement or cohesion among all parties who may benefit from the research findings.
- It helps both the marketer and the researcher to plan and implement the research design.
- It helps to reduce disputes that can occur when the gaps in decision makers' knowledge are not 'filled' as intended.
- It can form the basis for negotiation with a variety of research organisations.

In all, the research brief saves resources in time and money by helping to ensure that the nature of the problem or opportunity under investigation has been thought through.

Components of the marketing research brief

The rationale for a marketing research brief may seem logical, but actually generating a brief from marketing decision makers can be extremely difficult. If a decision maker has a very clear idea of the nature of decision support needed *and* can define the research objectives that will create such support *and* define the research design that will fulfil the research objectives, the decision maker could write a research brief that is highly structured. A structured brief created in these conditions would basically be a tender document, allowing a number of research suppliers to pitch for business on a like-for-like basis. Not all marketing decision makers have such clarity of the marketing research support they need. Even if they do, by sticking to highly structured and prescriptive marketing research briefs, they can under utilise the experience and creativity of researchers. This is illustrated by the following quote, based upon the experiences of a researcher who has seen many research problems misdiagnosed:

> When a client calls for a meeting on a research brief, quite often the tendency is for a methodology meeting: 'I'd like to have a product test done on three new flavours that we have developed.' Off goes the researcher, conducts the test, identifies the winning flavour, the client launches it and finds to their dismay that it fails dismally. Why? It turns out the flavours were developed to try and revitalise an ageing product category and brand. In the product test, the familiar flavours orange and lemon won over the more exotic flavour to boost the category image. Had the researcher been allowed to look beyond the brief and ask one simple question on why the flavours were being made, it may have led to a clearer brief which in turn would have led to a research design which was more appropriately designed to cull out the real insight, which was that the consumers were bored and something rather more than flavour extensions were needed to revitalise the category.[15]

The following format for a research brief helps to make the most of the experience and creativity of both the marketing decision maker and the researcher and has clear advantages for both parties. First, it does not demand that decision makers have a great deal of technical knowledge about research. Their focus can remain upon the gaps in their knowledge, the nature of support they need, not the technicalities of how data are to be collected and analysed. Second, it allows the researchers the opportunity to demonstrate their creative abilities and awareness of the latest research and analysis techniques. Using their experiences from problems faced by other decision makers, perhaps from a great variety of contexts and industries, researchers have the possibility of examining the marketing and research problem from many different perspectives. They can create, develop and adapt a research design to the research problem that supports the marketing decision maker within clear time and cost parameters (Figure 1.5):

1 *Background information.* The background serves to put research objectives into context, helping the researcher to understand why certain decisions and research objectives are being pursued. Decision makers would detail what they see as being the main events that have caused or contributed to the problem under study. Such a background gives a framework for the researcher to investigate other potential events, contributory factors or causes.

2 *Objectives.* The first part of this section would detail which marketing decisions are to be completed once the research has been undertaken. This requires decision makers to explain what they see as the focus of the decisions they plan to make. They then go on to explain what gap(s) they see in their knowledge. Those gaps create the focus to planned research activities and set the research objectives. The formulation of the marketing objectives can encompass two areas: organisational objectives and personal objectives of the decision

Figure 1.5

**Components of the
marketing research
brief**

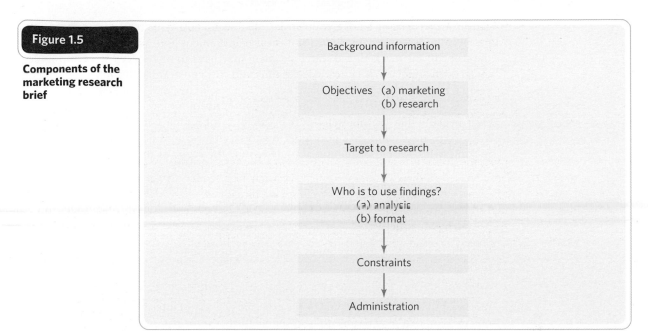

maker. For a research project to be successful, it must serve the objectives of the organisation and of the decision maker. For the researcher, this may not be explicit or obvious to discern. It may take some time working with a decision maker or a particular organisation to see potential conflicts in organisational and personal objectives. The problem faced by researchers is that decision makers may not formulate marketing objectives clearly. Rather, it is likely that objectives tend to be stated in terms that have no operational significance, such as 'to improve corporate image'. Ultimately this does not matter, as this 'first-step' brief offers the opportunity for the researcher to draw out and develop a much clearer vision of marketing and research objectives. Drawing out and developing decision makers' perspectives of objectives, even if they have no operational significance, helps the process of developing a common understanding of what the decision maker is trying to achieve.

3   *Target to research.* Any marketing research project will measure, understand or observe a target group of individuals. These may be distinct groups of consumers, channel members such as retailers or competitors, or company employees. In this section, details of the characteristics of the target group(s) can help in many research design decisions. These cover areas of identification, gaining access to potential participants, understanding which techniques are appropriate to measure or understand these individuals, and the best environment or context in which to conduct research.

4   *Who is to use the findings?* This section would outline brief details of the decision makers who will use the research findings. For example, certain decision makers may be entrepreneurial and introspective, looking for short-term tactical advantages. Presenting research findings that make tactical advantages apparent would be the best way to communicate to such managers. Managers with a background and training in statistics may expect results to be analysed and presented in a particular manner to have any credibility. Other managers, e.g. those responsible for many product and/or communications design decisions, may not have such training or may even be distrustful of statistical analyses and seek a more qualitative interpretation. These issues have an impact upon the nature and extent of analysis conducted upon the data collected and the style and format in which research findings will be presented.

5   *Constraints.* The main limitation to researchers carrying out what they may perceive as being the correct way to research a problem is the time and money that decision makers

can afford. Proposing a large-scale project that would cost €200,000 when only €50,000 has been budgeted obviously will not meet management approval. In many instances, the scope of the marketing research problem may have to be reduced to accommodate budget constraints. With knowledge of time and cost constraints, the researcher can develop a research design to suit these needs. The researcher may also demonstrate other courses of action that could demand greater amounts of money or time, but could have clear benefits that the marketer may be unaware of. Other constraints, such as those imposed by the client firm's personnel, organisational structure and culture, or decision making styles, should be identified to determine the scope of the research project. Yet, constraints should not be allowed to diminish the value of the research to the decision maker or to compromise the integrity of the research process. In instances where the resources are too limited to allow a project of sufficient quality, the firm should be advised not to undertake formal marketing research. In the following example, researcher Malgorzata Blachowska of Nestlé in Poland describes how she helped to develop a research brief that facilitated creative input from researchers, marketers and their communications agency.

6   *Administrative considerations.* These would lay out administrative details in completing the research project. Examples could be the expected delivery of interim reports, contacts in an organisation that may be able to help supply further information, or reference to sources of materials and individuals that are needed to complete the research successfully.

Real research

Can marketing research support effective communication ideas for children?[16]

The marketing team of the ice cream division of Nestlé in Poland wished to brief their creative agency. They turned to their marketing research team to see what support they could give to develop strong communications with their target market of children. The researchers seized the opportunity to be part of the process of advertising development, rather than simply delivering data or consumer test results. They decided to try a new way of cross-functional team cooperation to the challenge, which started with the preparation of a research brief. Their short brief described:

1   Clear and straightforward project objectives, including details of the target group they would be addressing. In this particular case the research objective was to '*reconstruct consumer insights, which help to build the most relevant and effective communication for children in the ice cream category in Poland'*. The core target group was children aged 6 to 11 years old.

2   Details of participant characteristics.

3   A detailed plan of the project:

What?	Who is responsible?
a Short brief with the objective	Marketing team
b Prepare and conduct the training from Consumer Insight Process at Nestlé and how to talk with consumers	Marketing research team
c Preparation and conduct of the training for 'consumer connection' – what this is, how to talk to your consumer and how to obtain knowledge in the connection process	Marketing research team and agency
d Meeting with consumers at their homes	Marketing research agency and everyone
e Preparation of guide (how to talk to the consumers)	Marketing research team and marketing research agency
f Affinity groups – just before their workshop – to put everyone in the 'mood of consumers'	Everyone
g Final workshop	Marketing research team and agency
h Analyses: information about the product and consumer habits	Marketing team
i Analyses: communications for children	Creative team
j Knowledge from the meetings with the consumers (pictures, toys, verbatims)	Everyone
k Reports; required at distinct stages throughout the whole project	Marketing research team

Three of the best ideas were tested in the research study, one was chosen, filmed and aired. The outcome was a success for the new business in Poland (Nestlé was a relatively new brand which did not really exist in consumers' minds as they had taken over the Scholler brand). They increased awareness of the Nestlé brand and the BluMis brand (hero of the Nestlé children's ice creams in Poland); they sold much more than their operational plan and they began building the image of their brand.

With a formal marketing research brief and perhaps preliminary discussion with the organisation that is to commission the research, the researcher has the necessary material to develop a research proposal. In many instances, however, the researcher does not enjoy the luxury of a written research brief.[17] The marketing decision maker may outline ideas in an oral manner, perhaps on an informal basis. This can happen if the decision maker is not aware of the personal benefits of producing a written research brief detailed above. Decision makers may see the brief as a time-consuming process that really is the job of the researcher. If researchers are faced with an oral brief, they can use the proposed brief outline above as a guideline to the issues they should elicit in informal discussions in order to develop an effective proposal.

The marketing research proposal

Research proposal
The official layout of the planned marketing research activity.

In response to a research brief, the researcher will develop a research plan and will develop a **research proposal** to communicate this plan. The marketing research proposal contains the essence of the project and, in its final format, can serve as a contract between the researcher and decision makers.[18] The research proposal covers all phases of the marketing research process. It allows the researcher to present an interpretation of the problems faced by management and to be creative in developing a research solution that will effectively support decision makers. Although the format of a research proposal may vary considerably, most proposals address all the steps of the marketing research process and contain the elements shown in Figure 1.6:

1 *Executive summary.* The proposal should begin with a summary of the major points from each of the other sections, presenting an overview of the entire proposal.

Figure 1.6

The marketing research proposal

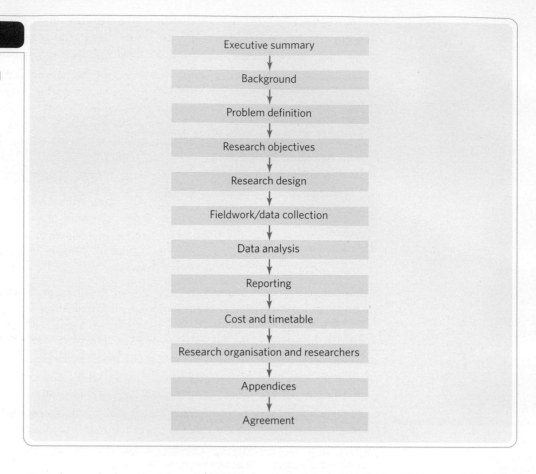

Executive summary

↓

Background

↓

Problem definition

↓

Research objectives

↓

Research design

↓

Fieldwork/data collection

↓

Data analysis

↓

Reporting

↓

Cost and timetable

↓

Research organisation and researchers

↓

Appendices

↓

Agreement

2 *Background*. The researcher would be expected to have researched and developed ideas beyond those presented in the brief 'background'. Other potential causes of the problems faced or alternative interpretations of the factors that shape the background in an environmental context should be presented. The extent of developmental work on the background to a research project will depend mostly upon how much past work researchers have done for the decision makers. In projects where researchers and decision makers are working together for the first time, much exploratory work may be undertaken by the researcher to understand an industry, organisation, decision makers, and planned campaigns. After working together on a number of projects, much of this may be understood and not need restating.

3 *Problem definition*. Again, if necessary, the researcher may go beyond the problem definition presented in the brief. If the researcher sees potential to add value for the marketer through alternative diagnoses of the problem presented in the brief, then these should be shown. If the researcher sees a problem in the brief that is ambiguous or unattainable, other alternative diagnoses should be presented. From this section, the marketer's gaps in knowledge should be apparent.

4 *Research objectives*. These may be presented in the form of clear hypotheses that may be tested. They may also cover broader areas in terms of 'research questions' that are to be explored rather than formally measured in a conclusive manner.

5 *Research design*. The research design to be adopted, classified in broad terms as exploratory, descriptive or causal, should be specified. Beyond such a broad classification should be details of the individual techniques that will be adopted and how they will unfold and connect to each other. This means that the reader will clearly see methods of collecting the desired data, justification for these methods, and a sampling plan to include details of sample size(s). This applies to both quantitative and qualitative approaches.

6 *Fieldwork/data collection.* The proposal should discuss how the data will be collected and who will collect them. If the fieldwork is to be subcontracted to another supplier, this should be stated. Control mechanisms to ensure the quality of data collected should be described.

7 *Data analysis.* This should describe the kind of data analysis that will be conducted, e.g. content analysis, simple cross-tabulations, univariate analysis or multivariate analysis. If software packages are to be used in these analyses, they should be specified, as they will be indicative of the potential analyses that can be conducted. There should be further description of the extent to which the results will be interpreted in light of the set marketing objectives, beyond the specified analysis techniques.

8 *Reporting.* The proposal should specify the nature of any intermediate reports to be presented, what will be the form of the final report, and whether an oral presentation of the results will be made.

9 *Cost and timetable.* The cost of the project and a time schedule, broken down by phases, should be presented. A critical path method chart might be included. In large projects, a payment schedule is also worked out in advance.

10 *Research organisation* The qualities and value of the research organisation and key researchers that will work on a project should be presented. When an organisation is working with researchers for the first time, some idea of past research projects and clients should be displayed. This can help the marketer to trust the researcher in problem diagnosis, research design and implementation (e.g. how credible the researchers may be seen by the individuals they are to research and how this may affect participant openness and honesty), and interpretation of the findings.

11 *Appendices.* Any statistical or other information of interest to perhaps only a few people should be contained in appendices.

12 *Agreement.* All parties concerned with fulfilling the research plan should sign and date their agreement to the proposal.

Preparing a research proposal has several advantages. It ensures that the researcher and management agree about the nature of the project, and it helps sell the project to a wider array of decision makers who may contribute to and benefit from the research findings. As preparation of the proposal entails planning; it helps the researcher conceptualise and execute the marketing research project.

Chapter 2 will further develop the challenges of defining a research problem. It will set out a structure and process that could underpin the writing of well-crafted research proposals.

International marketing research

With the globalisation of markets and forms of communication, marketing research has assumed a truly international character. The international nature of marketing research can mean reaching out to decision makers, researchers and participants in distant lands with many communication and logistical challenges. International marketing research tends to be more complex and demanding when compared to domestic marketing research. However, with the growth of many multicultural societies, domestic marketing research can demand that researchers

appreciate the cultural and language challenges of participants within their own country.

The marketing, government, legal, economic, structural, socio-cultural and informational environments prevailing in target international markets, and the characteristics of target participants that are being studied, influence the manner in which marketing research problems should be addressed. Most decision makers and researchers are aware that there are different and equally legitimate ways

to approach research problems and that no one school of thought has absolute authority for all types of problem. This greater flexibility has made multi-country coordinated projects much more feasible though not easier, as they represent intellectually, logistically and diplomatically the most demanding of problems. The following example illustrates some of the research design and operational challenges faced by researchers working in international markets.

Real research   A world of chicken flavours[19]

A study was conducted to support the development of 'new chicken flavours', sponsored by flavour consultants Givaudan (**www.givaudan.com**) and delivered by QualiData (**www.qualidataresearch.com**). With the cooperation of local research agencies, the study was conducted within multiple regions in eight countries: United States, Mexico, Colombia, Brazil, France, Spain, China and Indonesia. A critical idea underlying the study was that the experience of flavour was more than just sensory; it was also deeply cultural. To fulfil the study's objectives, the researchers devised a research design based on ethnographic methods, across the regions explored. In each case, they accompanied shoppers as they purchased chickens and other ingredients used in the creation of various dishes. This took them to local markets, shops and supermarkets where they often discussed chicken production methods with vendors. They then went home with the consumers to observe in painstaking detail how dishes were prepared and then served to their households. At mealtimes, they paid attention to other foods and beverages prepared alongside chicken, how dishes were served with respect to household hierarchies and how leftovers were saved and stored for future usage. At every step, they considered the impact of the process upon flavour creation and discussed flavour with all household members. A critical element in the study was the selection of appropriate participants. The key family cook they were seeking was someone who regularly prepared meals consistent with local cooking styles and used fresh ingredients. Their participants were typically, but not exclusively, female. These cooks did not need to use cookbooks but confidently relied instead upon sensory cues, memory and intuition while preparing meals. The most challenging aspects of this project were the large scale logistics involved in an eight-country project and the emerging knowledge integration and use of that knowledge. The global presentation of the study's findings was a major feat of logistics. They had sites in Singapore, China, Mexico, Brazil, USA and several European cities scheduled on a six-hour conference call and web-based slide presentation. The first hour was a summary presentation starting at 7.00 a.m., the best time to obtain attendance from every country. This was followed by more detailed presentations of countries rolling from Indonesia, to China, European countries, and finally Mexico, Colombia, Brazil and the United States. Part of knowledge integration was creating insight and innovation by weaving the ethnography results into the other sources of consumer insight that were ongoing and related to chicken flavour. This would include the use of consumer surveys, product testing and other forms of insight generation which varied by country and by the key issues in the local markets. As a consequence, the process of extracting, integrating and utilising the information from this project fell out over a period of about a year, as other related projects were completed.

Ethics in marketing research

Marketing research often involves contact with the participants, usually by way of data collection, dissemination of the research findings and marketing activities such as advertising campaigns based on these findings. There is the potential to abuse or misuse marketing research by taking advantage of these people. If participants feel that they or their views are being abused or misrepresented, they either will not take part in future studies or may do so without honesty or full engagement in the issues being researched. They may also lobby politicians to protect them from what they see as intrusions into their privacy and liberties. In short, unethical research practices can severely impair the quality of the research process, undermine the validity of research findings and ultimately inflict serious damage upon the body of professional researchers. If participants cannot distinguish between genuine marketing research and unethical telemarketing or direct marketing where surveys are used to gain access to participants to deliver a sales pitch or to generate sales, there can be severe repercussions for the marketing research industry through legislation designed to protect the privacy of citizens.

ESOMAR distinguishes marketing research from other competitive forms of data gathering, primarily through the issue of the anonymity of participants. It stresses that in marketing research the identity of the provider of information is not disclosed. It makes a clear distinction between marketing research and other forms of data gathering where the names and addresses of the people contacted are to be used for individual selling, promotional, fundraising or other non-research purposes. ESOMAR has eight principles that encapsulate the scientific aim and character of marketing research as well as its special responsibility towards participants, clients and the public.

The eight principles incorporated into the ESOMAR code of conduct are:[20]

1 Researchers will conform to all relevant national and international laws.

2 Researchers will behave ethically and will not do anything which might damage the reputation of marketing research.

3 Researchers will take special care when carrying out research among children and other vulnerable groups of the population.

4 Participants' cooperation is voluntary and must be based on adequate, and not misleading, information about the general purpose and nature of the project when their agreement to participate is being obtained and all such statements must be honoured.

5 The rights of participants as private individuals will be respected by researchers and they will not be harmed or disadvantaged as the result of cooperating in a marketing research project.

6 Researchers will never allow personal data they collect in a marketing research project to be used for any purpose other than marketing research.

7 Researchers will ensure that projects and activities are designed, carried out, reported and documented accurately, transparently, objectively and to appropriate quality.

8 Researchers will conform to the accepted principles of fair competition.

The basic principles of the ESOMAR code of conduct and the full array of ESOMAR codes of conduct can be viewed at: (**http://www.esomar.org/index.php/codes-guidelines.html**).

Digital developments in marketing research

Millions of people across the globe are actively engaging in online discussions, giving their opinions, meeting new people, showing their activities, preferences, uses and attitudes, talking about brands, services, music and films. Social media developments are creating opportunities to reach and observe participants in novel ways, changing the dynamics of the research process. These changes are resulting in the emergence of new research methods and the adaptation of more traditional approaches. The rise in social media has shown researchers how open participants can be with their thoughts, opinions and data. There are a number of pioneering individuals and 'new wave' research agencies that are inspiring advances in thinking and application in marketing research. These newer agencies are creating a healthy competitive environment, stimulating the development of innovative products and services.[21] The following example illustrates how the European research company Insites Consulting is developing new marketing research techniques. It illustrates how social media is being used to supplement and integrate with techniques that have been described as 'traditional marketing research'. This example illustrates the use of emerging research techniques that can dovetail with traditional marketing research techniques or in some cases be a replacement.

Real research **Stop asking questions and start listening[22]**

RTL Netherlands and its innovative research agency Insites Consulting (**www.insites.eu**) illustrated the power of buzz mining in the Dutch version of the *X Factor*. Because the *X Factor* lasts for several weeks, from auditions, to boot camp, to the knockout rounds, the show was particularly suitable for an iterative research process. In this case, the iterative research used searching and web scraping online conversations during the show. During the project, over 70,000 comments were captured from a variety of Dutch language online communities. In a version of online ethnography or discourse analysis, Insites Consulting analysed what people were saying about the show, its contestants, the songs, and the way the show was shaping. RTL Netherlands was able to use this information to make week-by-week alterations to the show and the acccompanying website to make the show 'sharper' and increase the interest of the audience. The show was broadcast on Fridays, so the agency did its web scraping on Mondays, reporting back to RTL on Wednesdays, which allowed the information to impact the show on Friday.

Summary

Marketing research provides support to marketing decision makers by helping to describe the nature and scope of customer groups, understand the nature of forces that shape the needs of customer groups and the marketer's ability to satisfy those groups, test individual and interactive controllable marketing variables, and monitor and reflect upon past successes and failures in marketing decisions. The overall purpose of marketing research is to assess information needs and provide the relevant information in a systematic and objective manner to improve marketing decision making. Conducting marketing research does not guarantee the success of decision making. However, well-crafted research should support decision makers to reduce the risks inherent in decision making.

Marketing research may be classified into problem identification research and problem-solving research. In general terms, problem identification uncovers the potential that may be exploited in markets, and problem-solving uncovers the means to realise that potential. Marketing research may be conducted internally (by internal suppliers) or may be purchased from external suppliers. Full-service suppliers provide the entire range of marketing research services, from problem definition to report preparation and presentation. They may also manage customer database analyses and social media research, being able to integrate the management and analyses databases with the management and analyses of conventional marketing research techniques. Limited-service suppliers specialise in one or a few phases of the marketing research project.

The marketing research process consists of six broad steps that must be followed creatively and systematically. The process involves problem definition, research approach development, research design formulation, fieldwork or data collection, data preparation and analysis, and report preparation and presentation. Defining the marketing research problem is the most important step in a research project. Problem definition is a difficult step because frequently decision makers have not determined the actual problem or only have a vague notion about it. The researcher's role is to help decision makers identify and define their marketing research problem. The formal ways in which decision makers and researchers communicate their perspectives on a research problem and how to solve it are through the development of a research brief and a research proposal.

International marketing research can be much more complex than domestic research because the researcher must consider the environments prevailing in the international markets being researched. Research is founded upon the willing co-operation, of the public and of business organisations. Ethical marketing research practices nurture that cooperation, allowing a more professional approach and more accurate research information. There are many competitive threats to the marketing research industry that have been exacerbated by the development of social media interactions. However, there are many great opportunities for researchers are afforded by social media interactions and digital developments. New types of participant can be reached across global markets, with new forms of engagement that may be integrated with more traditional forms of marketing research.

Questions

1 Describe the purpose of marketing research.
2 What decisions are made by marketing decision makers? How does marketing research help in supporting these decisions?
3 Why is it not possible to guarantee the success of marketing decisions supported by marketing research?
4 What arguments would you use to defend investment in marketing research?
5 How may the sound practice of problem identification research enhance the sound practice of problem-solving research?
6 What is the main difference between a full-service and a limited-service research supplier?
7 Describe the steps in the marketing research process.
8 Why is it vital to define the marketing research problem correctly?
9 What is the role of the researcher in the problem definition process?
10 Describe the components of a marketing research brief?
11 Describe the components of a marketing research proposal?
12 How may a researcher be creative in interpreting a research brief and developing a research proposal?

Exercises

1 Examine the business sections of newspapers and magazines to identify and compile five examples of problem identification research and five examples of problem-solving research.

2   Describe how marketing research could support decision makers in:

(a)   Your university or college

(b)   A shoe brand

(c)   An advertising agency commissioned by a toy manufaturer

(d)   A designer of a fashion store, responsible for creating the right 'atmosphere' for a store.

3   Visit the website of the Market Research Society, **www.mrs.org.uk**. Work through the array of publications and support it gives to its members. Specifically examine and register for **www.research-live.com/** and examine the published code of conduct. Compare the MRS code of conduct with that available on the ESOMAR website, **www.esomar.org**. Are there any differences in their respective approaches to maintaining professional standards in the marketing research industry?

4   Imagine that you are the Marketing Director of easyJet.

(a)   Make a list of potential marketing objectives whose fulfilment could improve the performance of easyJet.

(b)   Select what you feel would be the most important marketing objective. Develop a set of marketing research objectives that you consider would support the decisions needed to fulfil that marketing objective.

5   In a small group discuss the following issues:

(a)   What is the ideal educational background for someone seeking a career in marketing research?

(b)   Is it possible to enforce ethical standards within the marketing research industry?

(c)   Is it feasible that marketing decision makers may not conceive of or be able to express the nature of decision support they need? What are the implications of such a possibility in the development of research proposals?

Notes

1. EFS Survey, 'IDG Business Media uses online market research to optimize its print and online publications', *GlobalPark Case Study* (2011), **www.globalpark.co.uk** (accessed 23 March 2011).

2. Design Business Association, BT Freestyle 700 Family, *Bronze, Design Effectiveness Awards* (2010).

3. For the strategic role of marketing research, see Methner, T. and Frank, D., 'Welcome to the house of research: Achieving new insights and better brand knowledge through courageous ways of collaboration in what is usually a competitive environment', ESOMAR, *Congress Odyssey*, Athens (September 2010); Bakken, D.G., 'Riding the value shift in market research: Only the paranoid survive', ESOMAR, *Congress Odyssey*, Athens (September 2010); Kaufmann, R. and Wakenhut, G., 'Crossing the frontier – the fusion of research, consulting and creativity', ESOMAR, *Annual Congress*, Montreal (September 2008).

4. For relationships between information processing, marketing decisions and performance, see Roberts, D. and Adams, R., 'Agenda development for marketing research: the user's voice', *International Journal of Market Research*, 52 (3) (2010).

5. Casteleyn, J., Mottart, A. and Rutten, K., 'How to use Facebook in your market research', *International Journal of Market Research*, 51 (4) (2009).

6. ESOMAR, *Global Market Research*, ESOMAR Industry Report (2010), 48.

7. Lehmann, D.R., *Market Research and Analysis*, 3rd edn (Homewood, IL: Irwin, 1994), 14.

8. ESOMAR, *Global Market Research*, ESOMAR Industry Report (2010) 48.

9. Srivatsa, A., Puri, A. and Raj, S., 'The case of the elusive insight: lessons from the greatest researcher of them all', *Consumer Insights Conference*, Milan (May 2005).

10. Boal, C., 'Kellogg rolls out new cereal and snacking options', *Bakery & Snacks* (12 February 2007); Anon, 'Kellogg's Crunchy Nuts gets ready for adult breakfast', *Grocer*, 224 (7524) (October 6 2001), 53 and **www.kelloggs.com**.

11. ESOMAR, *Global Market Research*, ESOMAR Industry Report (2010), 28.

12. 'Marketing profs knowledge exchange: money spent, marketing research, decision-making', **www.marketingprofs.com/ea/qst_question.asp?qstID=11527**, accessed 4 November 2010; Sheth, J.N. and Sisodia, R.S., 'Marketing productivity: issues and analysis', *Journal of Business Research*, 55 (5) (May 2002), A9; Butler, P., 'Marketing problem: from analysis to decision', *Marketing Intelligence & Planning* 12 (2) (1994), 4–12.

13. Corporate Design Foundation, 'Harley-Davidson: Marketing an American Icon,' **www.cdf.org/issue_journal/harley-davidson_marketing_an_american_icon.html**, accessed 2 November 2010; Alva, M., 'Hog maker gets (Financial) motor running', *Investor's Business Daily* (28 January 2002).

14. John, C.F., 'From Iliad to Odyssey: the odyssey of our profession', ESOMAR, *Congress Odyssey*, Athens (Sept. 2010); Greenhalgh, C., 'How should we initiate effective research?' The Market Research Society Conference, 1983.

15. Srivatsa, A., Puri, A. and Raj, S., 'The case of the elusive insight: lessons from the greatest researcher of them all', ESOMAR, *Consumer Insights Conference*, Milan (May 2007).

16. Blachowska, M., 'From consumer connection to consumer insight: a Nestlé case study', ESOMAR, *Consumer Insights Conference*, Milan (May 2007).

17. Methner, T. and Frank, D., 'Welcome to the house of research: Achieving new insights and better brand knowledge through courageous ways of collaboration in what is usually a competitive environment,' ESOMAR, *Congress Odyssey*, Athens (Sept. 2010).

18. Pagani, P., Raubik, P. and May, J., 'Coca-Cola Europe and the Philosopher's Stone: Crafting a rare win-win-win situation,' ESOMAR, *Congress Odyssey*, Athens (Sept. 2010).

19. Mariampolski, H., 'A world of chicken flavours – using ethnography in multi-country studies', ESOMAR, *Annual Congress*, Montreal (September 2008).

20. Havermans, J., 'New international MR practice in 8 principles', *Research World* (May 2004), 20–21.

21. ESOMAR, *Global Market Research*, ESOMAR Industry Report (2010), 42–46.

22. Poynter, R., 'Stop asking questions and start listening', *Admap Magazine* (July/August 2010).

Stage 1

Problem definition

Stage 2

Research approach developed

Stage 3

Research design developed

Stage 4

Fieldwork or data collection

Stage 5

Data integrity and analysis

Stage 6

Report preparation and presentation

Defining the research problem correctly is fundamental in crafting a research design and delivering information of value to decision makers

Objectives

After reading this chapter, you should be able to:

1 understand the importance of, and the process used, in defining marketing research problems;

2 discuss the environmental factors affecting the definition of the research problem;

3 explain the structure of a well-defined marketing research problem, including the broad statement and the specific components;

4 understand the nature and significance of a research approach;

5 compare and contrast the basic research designs: exploratory, descriptive and causal;

6 understand how participants or the subjects of research design affect research design choices;

7 describe the major sources of errors in a research design, including random sampling error and the various sources of non-sampling error;

8 appreciate the challenges involved in developing a research design in international marketing research;

9 appreciate ethical issues and conflicts that arise in defining research problems and a research approach;

10 appreciate ways in which digital applications can support the development of a research design.

Overview

This chapter covers the first three of the six steps of the marketing research process as described in Chapter 1: problem definition, developing an approach to the problem and developing a research design. In Chapter 1 we set out how researchers and decision makers may communicate their views of these three steps through the presentation of a research brief and research proposal. In this chapter we evaluate the process of these three steps in detail. Problem definition is the most important step, since only when a problem has been clearly evaluated can a research project be properly conducted. Defining the marketing research problem sets the course of the entire project. Regardless of how well a research plan is designed and subsequent stages are carried out, if the problem is not correctly diagnosed, research findings could be misleading or even dangerous. We discuss the factors that influencing a research approach to resolve a diagnosed problem. The nature of a research approach is evaluated as are the components that shape an approach in terms of theoretical frameworks, analytical models, research questions and hypotheses.

We examine the nature of research design from the perspectives of decision makers and participants. Two major types of research design are then discussed: exploratory and conclusive. We further classify conclusive research designs as descriptive or causal and discuss both types. The differences between the two types of descriptive designs are considered (cross-sectional and longitudinal) and sources of errors are identified.

The special considerations involved in defining research problems and the development of a research design in international marketing research are discussed. Several ethical issues that arise at this stage of the marketing research process are considered. The chapter concludes by examining how digital developments can help in the crafting of creative research design. A better appreciation of the concepts presented in this chapter can be gained by first considering the following example.

Real research

Understand women's health issues through consumer and cultural insights[1]

The pharmaceutical company Pfizer (**www.pfizer.com**) worked with the research company Truth (**www.truth.ms**) on a project to innovate within the subject of 'women's health'. With many of Pfizer's product patents coming to an end, it was critical for them to understand how they could develop existing brands as well creating and/or buying new products and services. There were three key questions they needed to answer: (1) How could Pfizer make their existing products/brands more successful? (2) How could Pfizer successfully launch pharmaceutical products/brands into the areas of women's health? (3) How could Pfizer create new growth opportunities, adjacent to the core Pfizer business, to meet the unmet needs of women in relation to health? In addressing these questions, their biggest challenge was how to develop a research approach that would not only allow them to understand the needs of women and healthcare professionals now and, in the broader area of women's health, how such needs would evolve in the future. Their research approach integrated two critical perspectives: (1) **Cultural perspective:** Drawing insight, inspiration and direction from immediate and adjacent categories in health, as well as wider popular culture. (2) **Consumer perspective:** Grounding and informing the study in women's attitudes towards health and well-being in general, and women's conditions specifically. As a result, the project involved an integration of cultural and semiotic analysis of both women and health contexts, as well as ethnographic observations, interviews and group discussions with consumers and healthcare professionals across Europe: in France, Germany, Italy, Spain, Sweden and the United Kingdom.

In this example Pfizer broadly set out marketing problems and opportunities for which they need marketing research support. They set out a research approach that brings together two critical perspectives. Examining these perspectives enabled them to work through a research design based upon a series of qualitative research methods conducted in a number of European countries.

The process of defining the problem and developing a research approach

By formally developing and exchanging a marketing research brief and research proposal, the marketing decision maker and the researcher utilise their distinctive skills. They ensure that the marketing problem and research problems have been correctly defined and an appropriate research approach is developed. The research brief and the research proposal are the formal documents that ensure each party is clear about the nature and scope of the research task. These documents allow decision makers and researchers formally to present their perspective of the task in hand. The detail of defining the nature of problems and developing an appropriate research approach to the point of creating a research design is shown in Figure 2.1.

The tasks involved in problem definition consist of discussions with decision makers, qualitative interviews with industry experts and other knowledgeable individuals, and analysis of readily available **secondary data**. These tasks help the researcher to understand the background of the problem by analysing the environmental context. An understanding of the environmental context facilitates the identification of the marketing decision problem. Then, the marketing decision problem is translated into a marketing research problem. Based on

Secondary data
Data collected for some purpose other than the problem at hand.

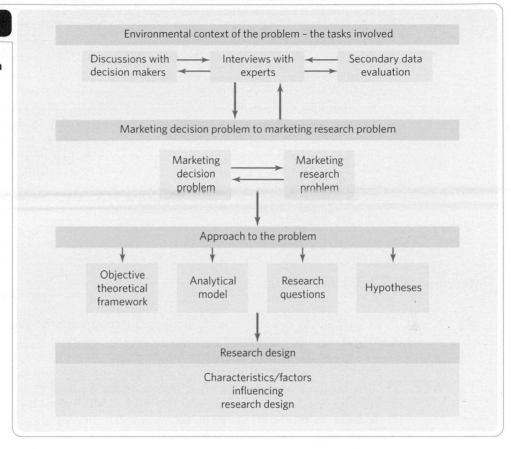

Figure 2.1

The process of defining the problem and developing an approach

the definition of the marketing research problem, an approach to the problem is established and an appropriate research design is developed. Further explanation of the problem definition process begins with a discussion of the tasks involved.

Environmental context of the problem

The tasks involved in understanding the environmental context of the marketing and research problem can include discussions with decision makers, qualitative interviews with industry experts, and secondary data collection and analysis. The purposes of these tasks are to develop an understanding of forces that may affect the nature of decision makers' problems and related research problems.

Discussions with decision makers

Discussions with the decision makers beyond the formal presentation of a research brief and research proposal can be of enormous value. The decision maker needs to understand the capabilities and limitations of research.[2] Research provides information relevant to management decisions, but it cannot provide solutions because solutions require managerial creativity and judgement. Conversely, the researcher needs to understand the nature of the decision that managers face, and what they hope to learn from research. In these discussions the researcher attempts to elicit further explanations of what may have been presented in a research brief. In the case where no formal or written research brief has been presented, the researcher would use a research brief structure as a means to elicit why decision makers are seeking research support. In this process it is essential that the researcher gets a clear sense of why research is to be conducted and what its value is to decision makers.

To identify the marketing problem, the researcher must possess considerable skill in interacting with the decision maker. Several factors may complicate this interaction. Access to certain decision makers may be difficult. The organisational status of the researcher or the research department may make it difficult to reach the key decision maker in the early stages of the project. Finally, there may be more than one key decision maker, and meeting collectively or individually may be difficult. These problems can make it difficult to develop decision makers' perspective of an environmental context. Despite these problems, it is necessary that the researcher attempts to interact directly with key decision makers.[3]

Interviews with industry experts

In addition to discussions with decision makers, qualitative interviews with industry experts can help enormously in understanding an environmental context. These experts are individuals with knowledge about an organisation that is seeking research support and the industry they compete in.[4] These experts may be found both inside and outside a client organisation. Typically, expert information is obtained by unstructured face-to-face interviews or using online methods. The order in which these topics are covered and the questions to ask should not be predetermined. The list of topics to cover and the type of expert sought should evolve as the researcher becomes more attuned to the nature of the marketing problem.

The purpose of interviewing experts is to explore ideas, make new connections between ideas, and create new perspectives in exploring an environmental context and defining the marketing research problem. If the technique works well by identifying an appropriate individual with the qualities to give insight upon a particular topic, and an amount of trust and rapport is developed, the potential to generate and test ideas can be immense. Experts may have other contacts that the researcher may not be aware of or may not be able to get access to. They may also have secondary data which, again, the researcher may not be aware of or have access to.

Initial secondary data analyses

Secondary data collection and analysis will be addressed in detail subsequently (Chapter 3). Here it can be seen in a broad context to include data generated within organisations, externally generated data and business intelligence. A brief introduction here will demonstrate the worth of secondary data at the stage of problem diagnosis. Secondary data are data collected for some purpose other than the problem at hand. **Primary data**, on the other hand, are originated by the researcher for the specific purpose of addressing the research problem. Secondary data include data generated within an organisation, including customer databases, information made available by business and government sources, commercial marketing research firms, and the vast resources available online. Secondary data are an economical and quick source of background information. Past information, forecasts and commentary on trends with respect to sales, market share, profitability, technology, population, demographics and lifestyle can help the researcher to understand the environmental

Primary data
Data originated by the researcher specifically to address the research problem.

context and marketing research problem. Where appropriate, this kind of analysis should be carried out at the industry and organisation levels. For example, if a organisation's sales have decreased but industry sales have increased, the problems will be very different than if the industry sales have also decreased. In the former case, the problems are likely to be specific to the firm.

Marketing decision problem and marketing research problem

Marketing decision problem
The problem confronting the marketing decision maker, which asks what the decision maker needs to do.

Marketing research problem
A problem that entails determining what information is needed and how it can be obtained in the most feasible way.

The **marketing decision problem** asks what the decision maker needs to do, whereas the **marketing research problem** asks what information is needed and how it can best be obtained.[5] The marketing decision problem is action oriented. It is concerned with the possible actions the decision maker can take. How should the loss of market share be arrested? Should the market be segmented differently? Should a new product be introduced? Should the promotional budget be increased?

In contrast, the marketing research problem is information oriented. It involves determining what information is needed and how that information can be obtained effectively and efficiently. Consider, for example, the loss of market share for a particular product line. The decision maker's problem is how to recover this loss. Alternative courses of action can include modifying existing products, introducing new products, changing other elements in the marketing mix, and segmenting the market. Suppose that the decision maker and the researcher believe that the problem is caused by inappropriate segmentation of the market and want research to provide information on this issue; the research problem would then become the identification and evaluation of an alternative basis for segmenting the market. Note that this process requires much interaction, in the sense that both parties critically evaluate, develop and defend each other's ideas to clarify the nature of decision and research problems, and to ensure there is a clear and logical connection between them. The following example further illustrates the distinction between the marketing decision problem and the marketing research problem. It also illustrates the interactive nature of identifying the marketing decision problem and the research problem, each one unfolding and informing the understanding of the other.

Real research — Defining the problem

Shoe retailer X: We are experiencing a loss of market share in our French stores.
Researcher: Is it just France?
Shoe retailer X: No, but as we conduct the majority of our business there, the loss is causing us the greatest amount of concern.
Researcher: Why do you think you are losing market share?
Shoe retailer X: We wish we knew!
Researcher: How are your competitors coping?
Shoe retailer X: We suspect that other French stores are also suffering, and that online shoe stores are capturing market share.
Researcher: How do your customers feel about the quality of services you deliver?
Shoe retailer X: We recently attained our ISO 9001 for service quality, which we are proud of!
Researcher: But how does your service delivery and customer experience compare with your competitors?

After a series of discussions with key decision makers, analysis of secondary data and business intelligence sources within the retailer and from other sources, many possible problems were evaluated including shoe designs, pricing and sales policies. Eventually the problem was identified as follows:

• *Marketing decision problem.* To improve the relationship experience with in-store customers in order to arrest the decline in market share.

• *Marketing research problem.* Determine the relative strengths and weaknesses in terms of shopping experiences of Shoe Retailer X, vis-à-vis other major competitors in France. This would be done with respect to factors that influence consumers in their choice of a shoe retailer.

| **Table 2.1** | **Marketing decision problem versus the marketing research problem** |

Marketing decision problem	Marketing research problem
Evaluates what the decision maker needs to do	Evaluates what information is needed to support the identified marketing decision
Action orientated	Information orientated
Focuses upon symptoms	Focuses on the underlying causes
The following examples further distinguish between the marketing decision problem and the marketing research problem	
Which product line extension should we invest in?	To determine consumer perceptions of the qualities and fit to existing products of a selection of product line extensions.
Should we invest in celebrity X to endorse our brand in Europe?	To determine consumer perceptions of the qualities and fit to a brand of a selection of celebrities.
Should we reposition our brand with an emphasis upon raising prices?	To determine the price elasticity of demand and impact on sales and profits of various levels of price changes.

Defining the marketing research problem

The general rule to be followed in defining the research problem is that the definition should:

1   allow the researcher to obtain all the information needed to address the marketing decision problem;

2   guide the researcher in maintaining focus and proceeding with the project in a consistent manner.

Figure 2.2

Proper definition of the marketing research problem

Marketing research problem

Broad statement

Specific components

Researchers make two common errors in problem definition. The first arises when the research problem is defined too broadly. A broad definition does not provide clear guidelines for the subsequent steps involved in the project. Some examples of excessively broad marketing research problem definitions are: developing a marketing strategy for a brand, improving the competitive position of the firm, or improving the company's image. These are not specific enough to suggest an approach to the problem or a research design. The second type of error is just the opposite: the marketing research problem is defined too narrowly. A narrow focus may preclude consideration of some courses of action, particularly those that are innovative and not obvious. It may also prevent the researcher from addressing important components of the marketing decision problem.

The likelihood of committing either error of problem definition can be reduced by stating the marketing research problem in broad, general terms and identifying its specific components (see Figure 2.2). The broad statement of the problem provides perspective and acts as a safeguard against committing the second type of error. The specific components of the problem focus on the key aspects and provide clear guidelines on how to proceed further, and act as a safeguard against committing the first type of error.

Broad statement of the problem
The initial statement of the marketing research problem that provides an appropriate perspective on the problem.

Specific components of the problem
The second part of the marketing research problem definition that focuses on the key aspect of the problem and provides clear guidelines on how to proceed further.

Developing a research approach

Paradigm
A set of assumptions consisting of agreed upon knowledge, criteria of judgement, problem fields and ways to consider them.

Once the marketing decision maker and researcher have clarified the decision problem and established the research problem they face, it has to be decided how to approach the research problem. The research problem may be very clear in the sense that there are strong established theories of what should be measured and how to conduct the measurements. Conversely, the research problem may lack theoretical foundation, with the researcher trying to cope with a broad set of issues that have not been sufficiently researched beforehand and unable to trust existing theories. The manner in which the researcher perceives the research problem will affect the paradigm they will adopt. The paradigm may be adopted in either an implicit or explicit manner and is built upon a set of assumptions. These assumptions consist of 'agreed upon' knowledge, criteria of judgement, problem fields and ways to consider them.[6] What is 'agreed upon' refers to how strong the theories are in defining and encapsulating the issues that make up a research problem.[7] Bringing together the 'agreed upon' knowledge, criteria of judgement, problem fields and ways to consider them can be undertaken by considering: a objective/theoretical framework, analytical models, research questions and hypotheses. Each of these components is discussed in the following sections. Collectively they may be considered to be the 'approach' that a researcher will take.

Objective/theoretical framework

Theory
A conceptual scheme based on foundational statements, or axioms, that are assumed to be true.

Objective evidence
Perceived to be unbiased evidence, supported by empirical findings.

In general, researchers should aim to base their investigations upon objective evidence, supported by **theory**. A theory is a conceptual scheme based on foundational statements called axioms that are assumed to be true. **Objective evidence** is gathered by compiling relevant findings from secondary sources. Likewise, an appropriate theory to guide the research might be identified by reviewing academic literature contained in books, journals, conference proceedings and monographs. Researchers should rely on theory to help them to measure or understand the variables they are investigating. Academic sources of new developments to measure, understand and analyse consumers should be constantly evaluated; the following example illustrates why.

Real research | **Using faces: measuring emotional engagement: FaceTrace™[8]**

The research company Brainjuicer (**www. brainjuicer.com**) tested a number of adverts that had won awards from the Institute of Practioners in Advertising, and had therefore been shown to deliver against their business objectives. Alongside these, they tested a set of adverts from each of the same categories, with what might commonly be termed as having the same kind of advertising objective (i.e. direct message, relaunch, brand building). An experiment was conducted online, and each advert was tested with 150 participants. The emotional scale they developed was able to tell them how many viewers felt each emotion, having viewed the adverts, and also the intensity with which they felt any emotion. A review of methods used to measure emotion led them to the conclusion that they needed to develop a self-report technique (it needed to be easy to administer and user-friendly) that overcame some of the criticisms of self-report, namely that identified the emotion felt without the need for a great deal of cognitive processing on the part of the participant.

Brainjuicer turned to the work of Paul Ekman[9] a respected psychologist, who puts a case for a set of seven basic emotions: *happiness, surprise, sadness, fear, anger, contempt and disgust,* all of which are universally conveyed by and recognisable in the face. Ekman's research on reading emotion in people's faces had two important implications:

1 It gave them a framework for understanding which emotions they should be looking to capture.

2 It provided a means of accessing what participants feel, with minimal cognitive processing on their part.

Ekman's research findings served as Brainjuicer's theoretical framework for measuring emotional response. They were fundamental in helping to set out important new findings for the measurement of emotion in advertising.

Table 2.2	The role of theory in applied marketing research
Research task	**Role of theory**
Conceptualising and identifying key variables	Provides a conceptual foundation and understanding of the basic processes underlying the problem situation. These processes will suggest key dependent and independent variables
Operationalising key variables	Provides guidance for the practical means to measure or encapsulate the concepts or key variables identified
Selecting a research design	Causal or associative relationships suggested by the theory may indicate whether a causal, descriptive or exploratory research design should be adopted
Selecting a sample	Helps in defining the nature of a population, characteristics that may be used to stratify populations or to validate samples
Analysing and interpreting data	The theoretical framework and the models, research questions and hypotheses based on it guide the selection of a data analysis strategy and the interpretation of results
Integrating findings	The findings obtained in the research project can be interpreted in the light of previous research and integrated with the existing body of knowledge

Analytical model
An explicit specification of a set of variables and their interrelationships designed to represent some real system or process in whole or in part.

Verbal models
Analytical models that provide a written representation of the relationships between variables.

Researchers should also rely on theory to determine which variables should be investigated. Past research on theory development and testing can provide important guidelines on determining dependent variables (variables that depend on the values of other variables) and independent variables (variables whose values affect the values of other variables). Furthermore, theoretical considerations provide information on how the variables should be operationalised and measured, as well as how the research design and sample should be selected. A theory also serves as a foundation on which the researcher can organise and interpret the findings.[10] Conversely, by neglecting theory, researchers increase the likelihood that they will fail to understand the data obtained or be unable to interpret and integrate the findings of the project with findings obtained by others. The role of theory in the various phases of an applied marketing research project is summarised in Table 2.2.

Applying a theory to a marketing research problem requires creativity on the part of the researcher. A theory may not specify adequately how variables can be embodied in a real-world phenomenon. Researchers must therefore take the best of what they believe to be the most novel theories to represent and encapsulate consumer thinking and behaviour. It is also vital for researchers to recognise that theories are incomplete; they deal with only a subset of variables that exist in the real world. Hence, the researcher must also identify and examine other variables that have yet to be published as theories.

Analytical model

Graphical models
Analytical models that provide a visual picture of the relationships between variables.

Mathematical models
Analytical models that explicitly describe the relationships between variables, usually in equation form.

An **analytical model** is a set of variables and their interrelationships designed to represent, in whole or in part, some real system or process. Models can have many different forms. The most common are verbal, graphical and mathematical structures. In **verbal models**, the variables and their relationships are stated in prose form. Such models may be mere restatements of the main tenets of a theory. **Graphical models** are visual. They are used to isolate variables and to suggest directions of relationships but are not designed to provide numerical results. They are logical, preliminary steps to developing mathematical models.[11] **Mathematical models** explicitly specify the relationships among variables, usually in equation form.[12] These models can be used as guides for formulating the research design and have the advantage of being amenable to manipulation.[13] The different models are illustrated in the following example.

| **Model building in shoe retailing**

Verbal model

A consumer first becomes aware of a shoe store. That person then gains an understanding of the store by evaluating it in terms of factors making up the choice criteria. Based on the evaluation, the consumer forms a degree of preference for the store. If the preference is strong enough, the customer will patronise the store.

Graphical model

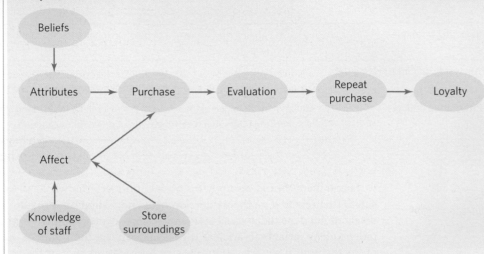

Mathematical model

Shoe store loyalty $= b_0 + b_1$ Beliefs $+ b_2$ Liking $+ b_3$ Purchase $+ b_4$ Repeat purchase

where b_0 is base level of loyalty and b_0, b_1, b_2, b_3, b_4, are weightings applied to relevant factors.

The verbal, graphical and mathematical models depict the same phenomenon or theoretical framework in different ways. The phenomenon of 'shoe store loyalty', stated verbally, is represented for clarity through a figure (graphical model) and is put in equation form (mathematical model) for ease of statistical estimation and testing. Graphical models are particularly helpful in clarifying the concept or approach to the problem. The verbal, graphical and mathematical models complement each other and help the researcher identify relevant research questions and hypotheses.

Research questions

Research questions
Refined statements of the specific components of the problem.

Research questions are refined statements of the components of the problem. Although the components of the problem define the problem in specific terms, further detail may be needed to develop an approach. Each component of the problem may have to be broken down into subcomponents or research questions. Research questions ask what specific information is required with respect to the problem components. If the research questions are answered by the research, then the information obtained should aid the decision maker. The formulation of the research questions should be guided not only by the problem definition, but also by the theoretical framework and the analytical model adopted. For a given problem component, there are likely to be several research questions.

Hypothesis

Hypothesis
An unproven statement or proposition about a factor or phenomenon that is of interest to a researcher.

A **hypothesis** is an unproven statement or proposition about a factor or phenomenon that is of interest to the researcher. For example, it may be a tentative statement about relationships between two or more variables as stipulated by the theoretical framework or the analytical model. Often, a hypothesis is a possible answer to the research question.[14] Hypotheses go beyond research questions because they are statements of relationships or propositions rather than merely questions to which answers are sought. Research questions are interrogative; hypotheses are declarative and can be tested empirically. An important role of a hypothesis is to suggest variables to be included in the research design.[15] The relationship between the marketing research problem, research questions and hypotheses, along with the influence of the objective/theoretical framework and analytical models, is described in Figure 2.3.[16]

Hypotheses are an important part of the approach to a research problem. When stated in operational terms, they provide guidelines on what, and how, data are to be collected and analysed. When operational hypotheses are stated using symbolic notation, they are commonly referred to as statistical hypotheses.

It is important to note that not all research questions can be developed into hypotheses that can be tested. Certain research questions may be exploratory in nature, with the researcher having no preconceived notions of possible answers to the research questions, nor the ability to produce statements of relationships or propositions. If the researcher is faced with such a situation, it does not mean that the investigation will not be as valid as one where hypotheses are clearly established. It means that the researcher may have to adopt a different approach or paradigm to establish its validity.

Figure 2.3

Development of research questions and hypotheses

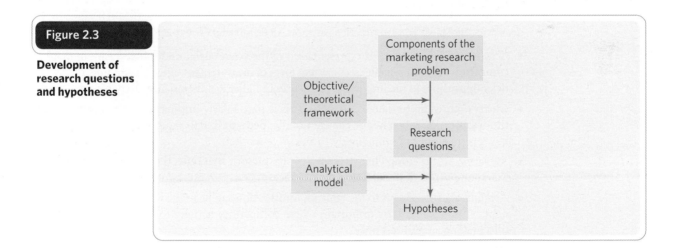

Developing a research design

Research design
A framework or blueprint for conducting the marketing research project. It specifies the details of the procedures necessary for obtaining the information needed to structure or solve marketing research problems.

Once the research approach has been developed to address a specific research problem, researchers must develop a **research design**. A research design is a framework or plan for conducting a marketing research project. It details the procedures necessary for obtaining the information needed to structure or solve marketing research problems. Although a broad approach to the problem has already been developed, the research design specifies the details and practical aspects of implementing that approach. A research design lays the foundation for conducting the project. A good research design will ensure that the marketing research project is conducted effectively and efficiently. Typically, a research design involves the following components or tasks, which will be discussed in detail in the text:

1 Define the information needed.

2 Decide whether the overall design is to be exploratory or conclusive.

3 Design the sequence of method to understand and/or measure to the phenomena under study.

4 Construct and pretest an appropriate means to capture data.

5 Specify the qualitative and/or quantitative sampling process and sample size.

6 Develop a plan of qualitative and/or quantitative data analysis.

In formulating a research design, the researcher has to balance the perspectives of marketing decision makers and target participants. Marketing decision makers may have certain techniques that they believe to be the most effective and in which they subsequently have more confidence. There is no problem with this, providing the technique is the best means to measure or understand the issue under investigation, from the perspective of participants. Thus, research design involves the researchers developing an understanding of the type of data decision makers have confidence in, plus an understanding of how participants may respond to different techniques. The first part of this balancing act involves understanding research design from the decision makers' perspective; the second part involves understanding the participants' perspective.

Research design from the decision makers' perspective

Marketing decision makers seek support from researchers that is of practical relevance to the decisions they face. To give practical support, decision makers expect information that is:

- *Accurate*, i.e. the most valid representation of the phenomena under investigation, that has come from the most reliable or consistent form of measurement or understanding, that is sufficiently sensitive to the important differences in individuals being measured or understood.
- *Current*, i.e. as up to date as possible. This is particularly important where consumer attitudes, lifestyle or behaviour change rapidly, perhaps due to rapid technology changes or new product offerings in a highly competitive market.
- *Sufficient*, i.e. the completeness or clarity of a 'picture' that reflects the characteristics of the marketing problem the decision makers face.
- *Available*, i.e. that access to the relevant information can be made when a decision is imminent. This is particularly important where competitive activity forces the decision maker into making a rapid response.
- *Relevant*, i.e. that the support given 'makes sense' to decision makers and is felt to be credible.

Generating information that fulfils all the above characteristics is extremely difficult, if not impossible to achieve in marketing research. The evaluation of sources of error (see below) and the restrictions of budget and timescales mean that this list represents 'ideals'. Realistically, trade-offs must be made among the above characteristics. Of all the potential trade-offs, if one were to remove *relevance* then the whole rationale of supporting the marketing decision maker would be removed. Therefore this characteristic can never be compromised. Relevance embraces, *inter alia*, the ability to plan and forecast from research findings, to be able to distinguish real differences in consumer traits, and to know that characteristics are representative of groups of individuals. With relevant information such as this, the decision maker can build up a stronger understanding or awareness of markets and the forces that shape them. In building up this understanding, the decision maker cannot turn to a single technique or even body of techniques that may be deemed 'ideal' in ensuring that information is relevant.[17] In different types of decision making scenarios, different techniques will offer the best support for that decision maker. Establishing the best form of support is the essence of research design. A fundamental starting point in deciding an appropriate design is viewing the process from the point of view of the potential research participants.

Research design from the participants' perspective

Potential participants to any marketing research study play a vital role in deciding which research design will work in practice. A subject of study may be complex and need time for participants to reflect upon and put words to any questions posed. Certain techniques are more likely to build up a rapport and trust, in these circumstances putting the participants in the right frame of mind, and getting them to respond in a full and honest manner. Figure 2.4 is a framework that serves to remind how participants may be accessed, and what kinds of response may be generated.[18]

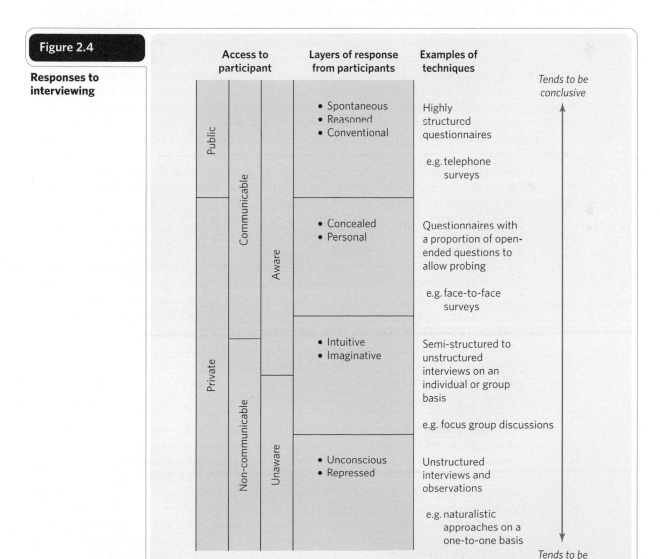

Figure 2.4

Responses to interviewing

In Figure 2.4 the box under the heading 'Layers of response from participants' represents how participants may react to questions posed to them. In the first layer of 'Spontaneous, Reasoned, Conventional' are questions that participants can express a view about quickly, and that are simple for them to reflect upon, relating to common everyday occurrences that are at the forefront of their minds. In such circumstances, simple structured questioning (or self-reporting) in a standardised manner is possible. Further, the same procedure can be conducted in a consistent manner to a whole array of 'types' of participant such as age groups, social class and intellectual levels. For example, if questions were posed on which yogurts someone eats, it is a reasonable assumption that participants are aware of the yogurt brand(s) they eat. Further, it may be assumed that views on these brand(s) can be communicated and the topic of eating yogurt is not a sensitive issue. In these circumstances, where answers to questions on eating yogurt are relatively easy to access and respond to, highly structured questionnaires are appropriate. Clearly, in such situations, quantitative techniques are applicable that allow very detailed descriptions or experiments to be conducted.

Progressing down Figure 2.4, at the second level are questions that are more personal and more sensitive. There are two characteristics that can turn otherwise mundane topics into sensitive ones.[19] The first involves any private, sacred or stressful aspect of a participant's life. The second is the real or perceived stigma associated with specific thoughts or actions. A great amount of business-to-business research can be added to these in terms of commercially sensitive information. An example of a sensitive question could be on the subject of alcohol consumption. Certain participants may views questions on their alcohol consumption as sensitive and may either not respond or not be truthful. Structured questionnaires could measure relevant issues on alcohol consumption but an amount of rapport may be needed to induce participants to trust the interviewer and reveal their 'more personal' attitudes and behaviour. Where the presence of the interviewer causes discomfort or bias, the method of computer assisted personal interviewing (CAPI) may be used[20] or, far more frequently, the anonymity of online research methods can facilitate more honest and open responses.[21] Such techniques combine the higher response rates of personal interviews with the privacy of self-administered questionnaires.

At the third level are questions that require participants to be creative. For example, if participants were to be asked about their attitudes and behaviour towards eating yogurt, this could be done in a very structured manner. Questions could be set to determine when it was eaten, favourite flavours and brands, where it was bought, how much was spent. The same can be said of alcohol consumption, though as discussed, this could well be a sensitive issue for many participants. Now imagine a new product idea that mixes yogurt and alcohol. What combinations of alcohol and yogurt would work, and what types of consumer would be attracted to them? Would they be a dessert liqueur such as Baileys Irish Cream or frozen yogurt to compete with the Häagen-Dazs luxury ice creams? Would champagne, advocaat, whisky or beer be the best alcoholic ingredient? Should any fruits be added? Individually? Forest fruits? Tropical fruits? How would the product be packaged? What name would best suit it? What price level would it sell at? On what occasions would it be consumed?

Answering these questions demands a great amount of creativity and imagination. It demands that participants reflect upon ideas, can play with ideas and words and dig deep to draw out ideas in a relaxed manner. Structured questionnaires cannot do this; such a scenario would work best with the use of focus groups. One of the major participant access challenges that participants face at this level relates to how they articulate their views and feelings, especially their emotional states related to brands.

At the fourth level may be questions that participants may not be able to conceptualise, never mind be able and willing to express what they feel about particular views and feelings. Consumers may absorb masses of marketing related stimuli, react to them and 'intend' to behave without really knowing why or even being aware of the true drivers of their intentions or behaviour.[22] An example may be trying to understand the childhood influences of family and friends on an individual's perception and loyalty to brands that they may purchase perhaps on a habitual basis, an example being washing-up liquid. Another example may be understanding the image consumers have of themselves and an image they wish to portray by spending €20,000 on a Rolex wristwatch. Participants do not normally have to think through such issues or articulate reasons for buying expensive luxury or fashion brands, until a researcher asks them.

In circumstances where the researcher is digging deep into topics that participants do not normally think about or articulate, polite responses to questions may be very misleading. The characteristics of the individual participant may determine what is the best way to probe and elicit appropriate responses. Nothing is standardised or consistent in these circumstances, the researchers having to shape the questions, probes and observations as they see fit in each situation.

As well as understanding how participants may react to particular issues, researchers should also understand how the context or environment may affect participants (Figure 2.5). The following example illustrates why 'context' is so important when thinking about where participants are questioned and/or observed.

Figure 2.5

Understanding participants – to help choose optimum research techniques

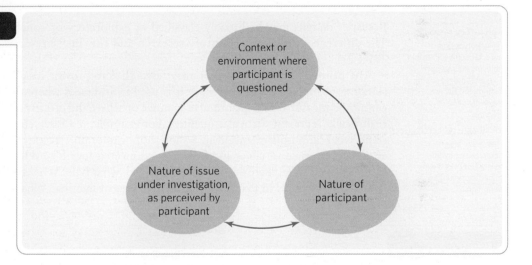

Real research

Engaging participants in remote locations with mobile devices[23]

In China, TNS (**www.tnsglobal.com**) and the digital market research company Mobile-Measure (**http://mobile-measure.com**) successfully ran qualitative and quantitative projects in both urban and rural settings using non-Smart Java enabled phones. Mobile-Measure's Text, Photo and Video platform (TPV) provided a low cost, fun and easy to use mechanism for researchers to leverage mobile phones and get closer to consumers' lives. This enabled research participants to use their non-Smart (Java enabled phones) to blog, text and upload photos and videos in real time – capturing real time 'in-the-moment' behaviour instantly. Specially trained moderators were provided with a live data online dashboard to monitor the study in real time. The moderators, often located remotely in other parts of the country, could monitor the live feeds coming in. Additionally they could comment, communicate and elicit responses from the group or individual participants in real time or in a pre-planned manner – all done remotely. In a study that focused on snacking behaviour, researchers tapped into the impulse and planned snacking consumption cycle of participants real time without having to be physically present. A great depth of data was realised, demonstrating that consumers (even in rapid growth and emerging markets) were extremely comfortable utilising their mobile devices to capture information and provide commentary (even in a 2G environment). On average TNS recorded 20–25 text blogs per week, 18–25 photos per week and 3–5 videos per week per participant, highlighting the validity and robustness of this technique and above all its natural fit with consumers' day-to-day lives. The MobileMeasure–TNS partnership successfully demonstrated the ability and benefits of mobile devices as research tools, particularly when the research application works effectively on non-Smart phone devices. The value of a mobile device as a research tool was that participants enjoyed utilising it! There was a clear fit between the research design and participants' everyday behaviour and, as such, participant response was high in terms of both frequency and depth.

Research design classification

Exploratory research
A research design characterised by a flexible and evolving approach to understand marketing phenomena that are inherently difficult to measure.

Conclusive research
A research design characterised by the measurement of clearly defined marketing phenomena.

Research designs may be broadly classified as exploratory or conclusive (see Figure 2.6). The differences between **exploratory research** and **conclusive research** are summarised in Table 2.3.

The primary objective of exploratory research is to provide insights into and an understanding of marketing phenomena.[24] It is used in instances where the subject of the study cannot be measured in a quantitative manner or where the process of measurement cannot realistically represent particular qualities. For example, if a researcher was trying to understand what 'atmosphere' meant in a shoe shop, exploratory research may help to establish all the appropriate variables and how they connected together. What role do the smells of leather play? Should there be any music and if so, what type? What types of furniture? What colours and textures in that furniture? What types of lighting? What architectural features?

Figure 2.6

A classification of marketing research designs

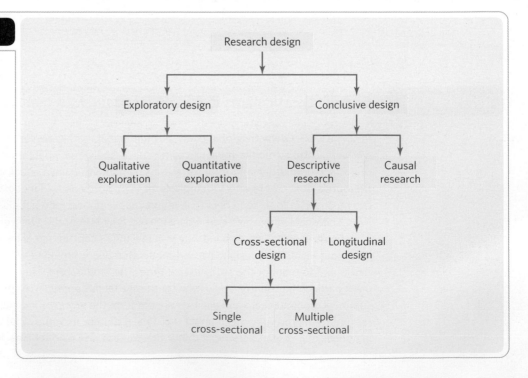

Table 2.3	Differences between exploratory and conclusive research	
	Exploratory	**Conclusive**
Objectives	To provide insights and understanding of the nature of marketing phenomena	To test specific hypotheses and examine relationships
	To understand	To measure
Characteristics	Information needed may be loosely defined	Information needed is clearly defined
	Research process is flexible, unstructured and may evolve	Research process is formal and structured
	Samples are small	Sample is large and aims to be representative
	Data analysis can be qualitative or quantitative	Data analysis is quantitative
Findings/results	Can be used in their own right	Can be used in their own right
	May feed into conclusive research	May feed into exploratory research
	May illuminate specific conclusive findings	May set a context to exploratory findings
Methods	Expert surveys	Surveys
	Pilot surveys	Secondary data
	Secondary data	Databases
	Qualitative interviews	Panels
	Unstructured observations	Structured observations
	Quantitative exploratory multivariate methods	Experiments

This list could go on to consider what 'atmosphere' may mean in the context of a shoe shopping experience for particular types of consumer. 'Atmosphere' may not be measurable from the participant's perspective. From the perspective of the creative director in an advertising agency, quantitative measurements of the individual components of 'atmosphere' may not create the holistic feel of a shoe shop in a manner the creative director can relate to.

Exploratory research may also be used in cases where researchers must define the problem more precisely, identify relevant courses of action, or gain additional insights before going on to confirm findings using a conclusive design. Exploratory research is meaningful in any situation where the researcher is open to new ideas and insights as they proceed with a study. Thus, the creativity and ingenuity of the researcher play a major role in exploratory research.

The objective of conclusive research is to describe specific phenomena, to test specific hypotheses and to examine specific relationships. This requires that the information needed is clearly specified.[25] Conclusive research is typically more formal and structured than exploratory research. It is based on large, representative samples, and the data obtained are subjected to quantitative analysis. As shown in Figure 2.6, conclusive research designs may be either descriptive or causal, and descriptive research designs may be either cross-sectional or longitudinal. Each of these classifications is discussed further, beginning with descriptive research.

Descriptive research

Descriptive research
A type of conclusive research that has as its major objective the description of something, usually market characteristics or functions

As the name implies, the major objective of **descriptive research** is to describe something, usually market characteristics or functions.[26] A major difference between exploratory and descriptive research is that descriptive research is characterised by the prior formulation of specific research questions and hypotheses. Thus, the information needed is clearly defined. As a result, descriptive research is preplanned and structured. It is typically based on large samples. A descriptive research design specifies the methods for selecting the sources of information and for collecting data from those sources.

Examples of descriptive studies in marketing research are as follows:

- Market studies describing the size of the market, buying power of the consumers, availability of distributors, and consumer profiles.
- Product usage studies describing consumption patterns.
- Distribution studies determining traffic flow patterns and the number and location of distributors.
- Advertising studies describing media consumption habits and audience profiles for specific TV programmes and magazines.

These examples demonstrate the range and diversity of descriptive research studies. Descriptive research can be further classified into cross-sectional and longitudinal research (Figure 2.6).

Cross-sectional designs

The cross-sectional study is the most frequently used descriptive design in marketing research. Cross-sectional designs involve the collection of information from any given sample of population elements only once. They may be either single cross-sectional or multiple cross-sectional (Figure 2.6). In single cross-sectional designs, only one sample of participants is drawn from the target population, and information is obtained from this sample only once. In multiple cross-sectional designs, there are two or more samples of participants, and information from each sample is obtained only once. Often, information from different samples is obtained at different times.

Cohort analysis consists of a series of surveys conducted at appropriate time intervals, where the cohort serves as the basic unit of analysis. A cohort is a group of participants who experience the same event within the same time interval.[27] For example, a birth (or age) cohort is a group of people who were born during the same time interval, such as 1961–1970. The term 'cohort analysis' refers to any study in which characteristics are measured of one or more cohorts at two or more points in time.

Longitudinal designs

The other type of descriptive design is longitudinal design. In longitudinal designs, a fixed sample (or samples) of population elements is measured repeatedly. A longitudinal design differs from a cross-sectional design in that the sample or samples remain the same over time. In other words, the same people are studied over time. In contrast to the typical cross-sectional design, which gives a snapshot of the variables of interest at a single point in time, a longitudinal study provides a series of 'pictures'. These 'pictures' give an in-depth view of the situation and the changes that take place over time. For example, the question 'How did the Danish people rate the performance of Prime Minister Lars Løkke Rasmussen immediately after the 2009 United Nations Climate Conference?' (**www.en.cop15.dk**) would be addressed using a cross-sectional design. A longitudinal design, however, would be used to address the question 'How did the Danish people change their view of Rasmussen's performance during his term of office?'

Often, the term panel is used in conjunction with the term 'longitudinal design'. A panel consists of a sample of participants, generally households, who have agreed to provide general or specific information at set intervals over an extended period. The emphasis of the panel is on measuring facts, e.g. who in the household bought what, where they bought it, when, and other aspects of their behaviour. Panels are really only established when observations or measurements over an extended period are meaningful. The observations

Cross-sectional design
A type of research design involving the collection of information from any given sample of population elements only once.

Single cross-sectional design
A cross-sectional design in which one sample of participants is drawn from the target population and information is obtained from this sample once.

Multiple cross-sectional design
A cross-sectional design in which there are two or more samples of participants, and information from each sample is obtained only once.

Cohort analysis
A multiple cross-sectional design consisting of surveys conducted at appropriate time intervals. The cohort refers to the group of participants who experience the same event within the same interval.

Longitudinal design
A type of research design involving a fixed sample of population elements measured repeatedly. The sample remains the same over time, thus providing a series of pictures that, when viewed together, vividly illustrate the situation and the changes that are taking place.

Panel
A sample of participants who have agreed to provide information at specified intervals over an extended period.

are usually gathered through questionnaires or increasingly through social media methods. Panels are maintained by syndicated firms such as TNS (**www.tnsglobal.com**) and panel members are compensated for their participation with gifts, coupons, information or cash.[28]

Causal research

Causal research
A type of conclusive research where the major objective is to obtain evidence regarding cause-and-effect (causal) relationships.

Causal research is used to obtain evidence of cause-and-effect (causal) relationships. Marketing managers continually make decisions based on assumed causal relationships. These assumptions may not be justifiable, and the validity of the causal relationships should be examined via formal research.[29] For example, the common assumption that a decrease in price will lead to increased sales and market share does not hold in certain competitive environments. Causal research is appropriate for the following purposes:

1 To understand which variables are the cause (independent variables) and which variables are the effect (dependent variables) of marketing phenomena.

2 To determine the nature of the relationship between the causal variables and the effect to be predicted.

3 To test hypotheses.

Like descriptive research, causal research requires a planned and structured design. Although descriptive research can determine the degree of association between variables, it is not appropriate for examining causal relationships. Such an examination requires a causal design, in which the causal or independent variables are manipulated in a relatively controlled environment. Such an environment is one in which the other variables that may affect the dependent variable are controlled or checked as much as possible. The effect of this manipulation on one or more dependent variables is then measured to infer causality. The main method of causal research is experimentation.[30]

Relationships between exploratory, descriptive and causal research

Exploratory, descriptive and causal research are major classifications of research designs, but the distinctions among these classifications are not absolute. A given research project may involve more than one type of research design and thus serve several purposes. Which combination of research designs to employ depends on the nature of the research problem. The following are general guidelines for choosing research designs.

1 When little is known about the problem situation, it is desirable to begin with exploratory research. Exploratory research is appropriate for the following:
    (a) When the nature of the topic under study cannot be measured in a structured, quantifiable manner.
    (b) When the problem needs to be defined more precisely.
    (c) When alternative courses of action need to be identified.
    (d) When research questions or hypotheses need to be developed.
    (e) When key variables need to be isolated and classified as dependent or independent.

2 Exploratory research may be an initial step in a research design. It may be followed by descriptive or causal research. For example, hypotheses developed via exploratory research can be statistically tested using descriptive or causal research.

3 It is not necessary to begin every research design with exploratory research. It depends on the precision with which the problem has been defined and the researcher's degree of certainty about the approach to the problem. A research design could well begin with descriptive or causal research.

4 Although exploratory research is generally the initial step, it need not be. Exploratory research may follow descriptive or causal research. For example, descriptive or causal research results in findings that are hard for managers to interpret. Exploratory research may provide more insights to help understand these findings.

Potential sources of error in research designs

Total error
The variation between the true mean value in the population of the variable of interest and the observed mean value obtained in the marketing research project.

Several potential sources of error can affect a research design. A good research design attempts to control the various sources of error. Where the focus of a study is a quantitative measurement, the **total error** is the variation between the true mean value in the population of the variable of interest and the observed mean value obtained in the marketing research project. For example, the annual average income of a target population may be €85,650, as determined from census information via tax returns, but a marketing research project estimates it at €62,580 based upon a sample survey. As shown in Figure 2.7, the total error (in the above case €23,070) is composed of random sampling error and non-sampling error.

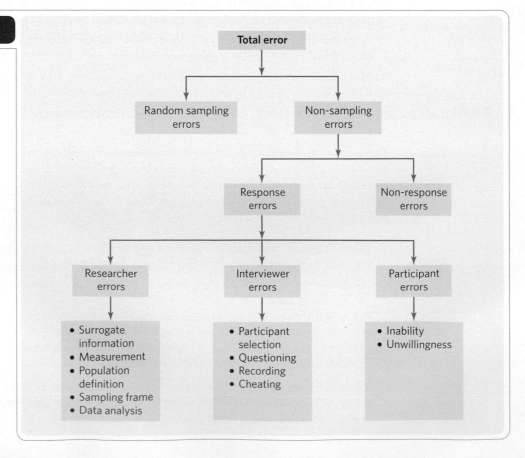

Figure 2.7

Potential sources of error in research designs

Random sampling error

Random sampling error
The error arising because the particular sample selected is an imperfect representation of the population of interest. It may be defined as the variation between the true mean value for the sample and the true mean value of the population.

Random sampling error occurs because the particular sample selected is an imperfect representation of the population of interest. Random sampling error is the variation between the true mean value for the sample and the true mean value for the population.

Non-sampling error

Non-sampling error
An error that can be attributed to sources other than sampling and that can be random or non-random.

Non-response error
A type of non-sampling error that occurs when some of the participants included in the sample do not respond. This error may be defined as the variation between the true mean value of the variable in the original sample and the true mean value in the net sample.

Response error
A type of non-sampling error arising from participants who do respond but who give inaccurate answers or whose answers are mis-recorded or mis-analysed. It may be defined as a variation between the true mean value of the variable in the net sample and the observed mean value obtained in the market research project.

Non-sampling errors can be attributed to sources other than sampling, and may be random or non-random. They result from a variety of reasons, including errors in problem definition, approach, scales, questionnaire design, interviewing methods, and data preparation and analysis. Non-sampling errors consist of non-response errors and response errors.

A non-response error arises when some of the participants included in the sample simply do not respond. The primary causes of non-response are refusals and not-at-homes. Non-response will cause the net or resulting sample to be different in size or composition from the original sample. Non-response error is defined as the variation between the true mean value of the variable in the original sample and the true mean value in the net sample.

Response error arises when participants give inaccurate answers or their answers are mis-recorded or mis-analysed. Response error is defined as the variation between the true mean value of the variable in the net sample and the observed mean value obtained in the marketing research project. Response error is determined not only by the non-response percentage but also by the difference between participants and those who failed to cooperate, for whatever reason, as response errors can be made by researchers, interviewers or participants.[31] A central question in evaluating response error is whether those who participated in a survey differ from those who did not take part, in characteristics relevant to the content of the survey.[32]

Errors made by the researcher include surrogate information, measurement, population definition, sampling frame and data analysis errors:

- *Surrogate information error* may be defined as the variation between the information needed for the marketing research problem and the information sought by the researcher. For example, instead of obtaining information on consumer choice of a new brand (needed for the marketing research problem), the researcher obtains information on consumer preferences because the choice process cannot be easily measured.

- *Measurement error* may be defined as the variation between the information sought and information generated by the measurement process employed by the researcher. While seeking to measure consumer preferences, the researcher employs a scale that measures perceptions rather than preferences.

- *Population definition error* may be defined as the variation between the actual population relevant to the problem at hand and the population as defined by the researcher. The problem of appropriately defining the population may be far from trivial, as illustrated by the following example of affluent households. Their number and characteristics varied depending on the definition, underscoring the need to avoid population definition error. Depending upon the way the population of affluent households was defined, the results of this study would have varied markedly.

Real research   **How affluent is affluent?**

The population of the affluent households was defined in four different ways in a study:

1   Households with income of €80,000 or more.

2   The top 20% of households, as measured by income.

3   Households with net worth over €450,000.

4   Households with discretionary income to spend being 30% higher than that of comparable households.

- *Sampling frame error* may be defined as the variation between the population defined by the researcher and the population as implied by the sampling frame (list) used. For example, the telephone directory used to generate a list of telephone numbers does not accurately represent the population of potential landline consumers due to unlisted, disconnected and new numbers in service. It also misses out the great number of consumers that choose not to have landlines, exclusively using mobile phones

- *Data analysis error* encompasses errors that occur while raw data from questionnaires are transformed into research findings. For example, an inappropriate statistical procedure is used, resulting in incorrect interpretation and findings.

Response errors made by the interviewer include participant selection, questioning, recording and cheating errors:

- *Participant selection error* occurs when interviewers select participants other than those specified by the sampling design or in a manner inconsistent with the sampling design.

- *Questioning error* denotes errors made in asking questions of the participants or in not probing when more information is needed. For example, while asking questions an interviewer does not use the exact wording or prompts as set out in the questionnaire.

- *Recording error* arises due to errors in hearing, interpreting and recording the answers given by the participants. For example, a participant indicates a neutral response (undecided) but the interviewer misinterprets that to mean a positive response (would buy the new brand).

- *Cheating error* arises when the interviewer fabricates answers to a part or the whole of the interview. For example, an interviewer does not ask the sensitive questions related to a participant's debt but later fills in the answers based on personal assessment.

Response errors made by the participant comprise errors of inability and unwillingness:

- *Inability error* results from the participant's inability to provide accurate answers. Participants may provide inaccurate answers because of unfamiliarity, fatigue, boredom, question format, question content or because the topic is buried deep in the participant's mind.

- *Unwillingness error* arises from the participant's unwillingness to provide accurate information. Participants may intentionally misreport their answers because of a desire to provide socially acceptable answers, because they cannot see the relevance of the survey and/or a question posed, to avoid embarrassment, to please the interviewer.[33] For example, to impress the interviewer, a participant intentionally says that they read *The Economist* magazine.

In formulating a research design, the researcher should attempt to minimise the total error, not just a particular source. This caution is warranted by a tendency of some researchers to control sampling error by using large samples. Increasing the sample size does decrease sampling error, but it may also increase non-sampling error, e.g. by increasing interviewer errors. Non-sampling error is likely to be more problematic than sampling error. Sampling error can be calculated, whereas many forms of non-sampling error defy estimation. Moreover, non-sampling error has been found to be the major contributor to total error, whereas random sampling error is relatively small in magnitude. The point is that the researcher must not lose sight of the impact of total error upon the integrity of their research design and the findings they present. A particular type of error is important only in that it contributes to total error.

Sometimes, researchers deliberately increase a particular type of error to decrease the total error by reducing other errors. For example, suppose that a postal survey is being conducted to determine consumer preferences in purchasing shoes from a shoe retailer.

A large sample size has been selected to reduce sampling error. A response rate of 30% may be expected. Given the limited budget for the project, the selection of a large sample size does not allow for follow-up mailings. Past experience, however, indicates that the response rate could be increased to 45% with one follow-up mailing and to 55% with two follow-up mailings. Given the subject of the survey, non-participants are likely to differ from participants in many features. Therefore it may be wise to reduce the sample size to make money available for follow-up mailings. While decreasing the sample size will increase random sampling error, the two follow-up mailings will more than offset this loss by decreasing non-response error.[34]

International marketing research

The precise definition of the marketing research problem is more difficult in international marketing research than in domestic marketing research. Unfamiliarity with the environmental factors of the country where the research is being conducted can greatly increase the difficulty of defining market decision problems and research problems. Many international marketing efforts fail not because research was not conducted, but because the relevant environmental factors were not taken into account and fully appreciated. While developing theoretical frameworks, models, research questions and hypotheses, differences in the environmental factors, especially the socio-cultural environment, may lead to differences in the formation of perceptions, attitudes, preferences and choice behaviour. In developing an approach to a research problem, researchers should consider the equivalence of consumer behaviour across the cultures being investigated. This is critical to the identification of the correct research questions, hypotheses and characteristics/factors that influence the research design.

When developing a research design for international marketing research, it is important to realise that, given environmental differences, what may be appropriate for one country may not be suitable in another. An understanding of cultural influences can affect the choice and application of individual research methods. The following example illustrates cultural differences in international research and how this may impact upon what may be seen as a sensitive issue.

Real research | **Sanitary napkins: Building the idea of intimacy[35]**

What is a sanitary napkin? It is a female 'protection pad' whose functional value is based on its absorption capacity, its maximum thinness and its anatomical adaptability. Saul Feldman of FOCOS Latinoamerica (**www.focoslatin.com.ar**) has conducted qualitative research throughout Latin America for a number of product categories that include the sensitive nature of buying and using sanitary napkins. Using focus groups, ethnographic interviews, creative workshops and semiotic analysis of advertisements, Saul has built up a strong understanding of cultural differences in the region. Far from having the same meanings in every culture, there were differences as evidenced in his work in Colombia (Bogotá), Costa Rica (San José) and Argentina. In Colombia, with more rigid and and traditional in terms of gender roles, women felt the need to look the same in 'those days' without breakdowns and trying obsessively to hide their condition. In Costa Rica, the period was accepted from the standpoint that there was no difference with men, as something 'natural' with no reason to change behaviour. In Argentina, tolerance of 'those days' was greater and it was allowed to be different; to search for pleasure, and treats. One aspect studied was the organisation of the product on supermarket shelves, and the way in which women 'navigated' to buy them. Saul wanted to understand how they managed to pick what they wanted in a category with a lot of different varieties, but also with small packs, full of 'objective' information, with multiple details, lots of descriptions and little differentiation. In Colombia, with fast, effective and determined attitudes at the shelves (a public place for something so intimate) such products should not be shown. Costa Rica showed the opposite; women took more time to observe, find new products, choose what was best, it was just another purchase. Argentinians demanded more feminine rhetoric for presentations and moved around shelves with apparent certainty as if they already knew what they wanted to find, with the idea that having to choose was superfluous.

Ethics in marketing research

Identifying the correct marketing research problem is crucial to the success of the project. This process can, however, be compromised by the personal agendas of the researcher or the decision maker. For example, the researcher, after performing the tasks involved in problem definition and analysing the environmental context of the problem, realises that the correct marketing research problem may be defined in a way that makes primary research unnecessary. This could reduce the cost of the project and the researcher's profit margin. Does the researcher define the problem correctly, fabricate a research problem that involves primary data collection, or refuse to proceed with this project in lieu of those more profitable?

Ethical situations affecting the researcher and the client may also arise in developing an approach to the problem. When researchers conduct studies for different clients in related industries (e.g. fashion and jewellery) or in similar research areas (e.g. customer satisfaction) they may be tempted to cut corners in theoretical framework and model development. Take an example where a fashion brand client has

on its board of directors the Chair of a major jewellery brand. The jewellery brand recently conducted customer satisfaction research using a model specifically developed for their needs. The Chair has access to this research. The researcher feels that the customer satisfaction model for the jeweller could be easily adapted to work for the fashion brand and would like to approach the Chair. The client from the fashion brand feels that even though it may help enormously with their study, it would not be a good business decision to have access to this information and guides the researcher not to approach the Chair. There is an underlying trust between the researcher and the client that the research firm is honour bound not to reuse client-specific models or findings for other projects.

In creating a research design, every precaution should be taken to ensure the participants' right to safety, right to privacy, or right to choose. With the rise in social media research methods, protecting the privacy of participants has become more challenging for researchers.

Digital developments in marketing research

The development of digital social media has opened up great opportunities for marketing decision makers and researchers to listen to consumers. It is likely that through listening to consumers via social media sources, a richer environmental context of a problem, together with a greater understanding of a marketing decision problem and marketing research problem, can all be developed.

Online research methods including social media research techniques are delivering more opportunities to researchers to be creative in crafting research designs. These opportunities are not just traditional research techniques that can be facilitated online, but entirely new techniques. Digital applications are enabling marketing research techniques to be more engaging, making the process of questioning, debate and sharing views more fun.

Exploratory research

If an exploratory research design is to be utilised, discussion groups, chat rooms, blogs or newsgroups can be used to discuss a particular topic to great depth. Files can be exchanged that can include moving images and sounds, allowing questions and probes to be built around this material. Formal online focus groups may be conducted with experts or individuals representing target groups, all on a global basis if needed. Digital applications can help to gain access to individuals that previously could not be accessed, or if they could be accessed it would be at great cost or take much time. They can also facilitate accessing individual in contexts where they feel comfortable to engage in research.

Conclusive research

Conclusive online quantitative research has grown year on year in both expenditure terms and as a proportion of all marketing research spend. It is expected that this will grow, not just in its own right but also in integrated forms that allow other techniques to be applied. The following example illustrates this form of integration where a series of conclusive online surveys were supported by participants photographing the context in which they were experiencing the World Cup.

Real research	World Cup 2010 – Redefining 'multi-modal' research to understand audience engagement[36]

The 2010 FIFA World Cup in South Africa showcased athletic prowess, compelling stories of players and teams, national pride and many unexpected moments. The event bridged nations, languages, cultures and passions. The Nielsen Life360 project (**www.nielsen.com**) was a new research approach to measure the effects of the World Cup via three multi-media screens; TV, Internet and mobile devices. The project was built upon set a clear objective: capture the 'day in the life' behaviour of sample participants and their interactions with the World Cup anytime, anywhere they occurred. The Nielsen researchers equipped a panel of 420 South African adults (ages 16+ years) with web-enabled BlackBerry devices running the Techneos SODA (**www.techneos.com**) mobile research application in four main tournament cities: Johannesburg, Pretoria, Durban and Cape Town.

Each participant carried the mobile phone for the full four and a half weeks of the tournament and completed a series of prompted surveys that asked them to share 'in-the-moment' behaviour, moods and location, plus retrospective media usage along with photos. Surveys were delivered five times daily in a choice of languages: Afrikaans, English, Tswana and Zulu. Question formats included multiple-choice, open-ended responses and extended to brand awareness and select daily expenditures. For games watched, details such as platform, channel and participating teams could be recorded. Data from the sample was weighted for age, gender, language and economic status in proportion to South Africa's total population and reported on a daily, weekly and full-round basis via a proprietary online dashboard. In all, 61,000 data records and more than 54,000 images were collected during the month-long tournament. The method delivered abundant rich data garnered from multiple screens, platforms, countries and demographics supplanted by a plethora of photos shared by participants. Its key capacity for capturing on-the-ground and 'in-the-moment' engagement with the tournament delivered new insights and previously unattainable figures. One immediate benefit of the complex research undertaking identified a core advantage: being able to measure 'out-of-home' enabled a new capacity to engage and understand the experiences of the fans across Johannesburg, Pretoria, Durban and Cape Town watching television at work, friends' homes, entertainment facilities and at fan parks.

Summary

Defining the marketing research problem is the most important step in a research project. The formal ways in which decision makers and researchers communicate their perspectives on a research problem and how to solve it are through the development of a research brief and a research proposal. To develop these documents fully, researchers should be proactive in communicating with key decision makers, which should include a problem audit whenever possible. They should also conduct, where necessary, interviews with relevant experts, and secondary data collection and analyses. These tasks should lead to an analysis of the environmental context. This analysis should assist in the identification of the marketing decision problem, which should then be translated into a marketing research problem. The marketing decision asks what the decision maker needs to do, whereas the marketing research problem asks what information is needed and how it can be obtained effectively and efficiently.

Developing an approach to the problem is the second step in the marketing research process. The components of an approach may consist of an objective/theoretical framework, analytical models, research questions and hypotheses. It is necessary that the approach developed be based upon objective evidence or empirical evidence and be grounded in theory as far as it is appropriate. The relevant variables and their interrelationships may be neatly summarised in an analytical model. The most common kinds of model structures are verbal, graphical and mathematical. The research questions are refined statements of the specific components of the problem that ask what specific information is required with respect to the problem components. Research questions may be further refined into hypotheses.

A research design is a plan for conducting a marketing research project. It specifies the details of how a project should be conducted in order to fulfil set marketing research problems. The challenge faced by researchers in developing a research design is that they need to balance an understanding of research design from the decision makers' perspective with an understanding of potential participants' reactions to issues researched using different methods, applied in differing contexts. Research designs may be broadly classified as exploratory or conclusive. The primary purpose of exploratory research is to develop understanding and provide insights. Conclusive research is conducted to measure and describe phenomena, test specific hypotheses and examine specific relationships. Conclusive research may be either descriptive or causal. The findings from both exploratory and conclusive research can be used as input into marketing decision making.

The major objective of descriptive research is to describe market characteristics or functions. Descriptive research can be classified into cross-sectional and longitudinal research. Cross-sectional designs involve the collection of information from a sample of population elements at a single point in time. These designs can be further classified as single cross-sectional or multiple cross-sectional designs. In contrast, in longitudinal designs repeated measurements are taken on a fixed sample. Causal research is designed for the primary purpose of obtaining evidence about cause-and-effect (causal) relationships. Many research designs combine techniques that can be classified as exploratory, descriptive and causal. A research design consists of six components and errors can be associated with any of these components. The total error is composed of random sampling error and non-sampling error. Non-sampling error consists of non-response and response errors. Response error encompasses errors made by researchers, interviewers and participants.

When defining the marketing research problem in international research, researchers must take into account relevant environmental factors. When developing a research design for international marketing research, it is important to realise that what may be appropriate for one country may not be suitable in another. An understanding of cultural influences can affect the choice and application of individual research methods. In terms of ethical issues, the researchers must ensure that the research design used will provide the information sought and that the information sought is the information needed by the client. In creating a research design, every precaution should be taken to ensure the participants' right to safety, right to privacy, or right to choose. With the rise in social media research methods, protecting the privacy of participants has become more challenging for researchers. Online research methods including social media research techniques are delivering more opportunities for researchers to be creative in crafting research designs. These opportunities are not just traditional research methods that can be facilitated online, but entirely new methods.

Questions

1 Why is it vital to define the marketing research problem correctly?
2 What is the role of the researcher in the problem definition process?
3 What interrelated events occur in the environmental context of a research problem?
4 Describe the factors that may affect the approach to a research problem.
5 What is the role of theory in the development of a research approach?
6 What are the differences between research questions and hypotheses?

7   Define research design in your own words.

8   How does the subject of a study as seen by potential research participants affect research design?

9   Differentiate between exploratory and conclusive research.

10   What are the major purposes for which exploratory research is conducted?

11   What are the major purposes for which descriptive research is conducted?

12   What potential sources of error can affect a research design?

Exercises

1   You are a consultant working on a project for Aston Martin.

    (a)   Use online databases to compile a list of articles related to Aston Martin and the global high-performance luxury car market in the past year.

    (b)   Visit the Aston Martin and Ferrari websites and evaluate the extent of competitive information available at each.

    (c)   Based upon the information collected from 1(a) and 1(b), write a report on the environmental context surrounding Aston Martin.

2   Visit **www.fabindia.com**. In particular, look at the sections that describe the philosophy behind this business. Gather online secondary data and business intelligence from both online sources, especially your library's online databases. If Fabindia were to further develop their brand in selected European countries what would their key challenges be? Write a brief report of 1,000 words that sets out Fabindia's challenges, identify five experts who may have a view of capitalising upon these challenges, and give brief details of why these individuals may be seen as experts.

3   Imagine that you are the researcher appointed by BMW and that you have been hired to conduct a study of its corporate image.

    (a)   Discuss the potential issues that may affect your choice of context in which to interview female executives that buy the 7-series cars.

    (b)   Discuss the potential issues that may affect your choice of context in which to interview teenagers whose parent(s) own a BMW.

4   Visit the website of the Market Research Society. Browse through their Research Buyers Guide (**www.rbg.org.uk**) to get a feel for the nature of industries and marketing issues that may be supported by exploratory studies. Find the agency Brainjuicer and examine the work this research company (**www.brainjuicer.com**). In what manner(s) does this agency link exploratory designs to conclusive designs?

5   In a small group discuss the following issues: 'Is it feasible that marketing decision makers may not conceive of or be able to express the nature of decision support they need? What are the implications of such a possibility in the development of research proposals?' and 'There are many potential sources of error in a research project. It is impossible to control all of them. Hence, all marketing research contains errors and we cannot be confident of findings.'

Notes

1. Curphey, J., Dexter, A. and Tomasevic, L., 'Culture: Insight's third space = Conducting and integrating cultural analysis to drive brand value', ESOMAR, *Qualitative Conference*, Vienna (Nov. 2011).

2. Cooke, M. and Buckley, N., 'Web 2.0, social networks and the future of market research' *International Journal of Market Research*, 50 (2) (2008) 267–92; Marshall, G.W., 'Selection decision making by sales managers and human resource managers: decision impact, decision frame and time of valuation', *Journal of Personal Selling and Sales Management* (Winter 2001), 19–28.

3. Anon., 'How to decide who should get what data', *HR Focus* (May 2001), 7; Cronin, M.J., 'Using the web to push key data to decision makers', *Fortune*, 36 (6) (29 September 1997), 254.

4. Grisham, T., 'The Delphi technique: a method for testing complex and multifaceted topics', *International Journal of Managing Projects in Business*, 2 (1) (2009) 112–30; Malo, K., 'Corporate strategy requires market research', *Marketing News* 36 (2) (21 January 2001), 14; Winett, R., 'Guerilla marketing research outsmarts the competition', *Marketing News*, 29 (1) (January 1995), 33.

5. Ganeshasundaram, R. and Henley, N., 'The prevalence and usefulness of market research: an empirical investigation into "background" versus "decision" research', *International Journal of Market Research*, 48 (5) (2006) 525–50; Roe, M. and Vervoot, J., 'A Market Research Training Simulation – Bringing market research closer to decision makers', ESOMAR, *Innovate! Conference*, Paris (Feb 2005); Gordon, A., 'Linking marketing decisions with consumer decision making. Closing the gap between feelings and behaviour', ESOMAR, *Annual Congress*, Lisbon (Sept. 2004).

6. Potter, G., *The Philosophy of Social Science: New Perspectives* (Harlow: Pearson, 2000), 242.

7. Saren, M. and Pels, J., 'A comment on paradox and middle-range theory: universality, synthesis and supplement', *Journal of Business & Industrial Marketing*, 23 (2) (2008) 105–107.

8. Wood, O., 'Using faces: measuring emotional engagement for early stage creative', ESOMAR, *Annual Congress*, Berlin, (Sept. 2007).

9. Ekman, P., *Emotions Revealed, Understanding Faces and Feelings*, Phoenix, London (2003).

10. Nyilasy, G. and Reid, L.N., 'The academician-practitioner gap in advertising', *International Journal of Advertising*, 26 (4), (2007) 425–445; Lilien, G.L., 'Bridging the marketing theory', *Journal of Business Research* 55 (2) (February 2002), 111; Hunt, S.D., 'For reason and realism in marketing', *Journal of Marketing*, 56 (April 1992), 89–102.

11. For an illustration of a graphical model, see Nauckhoff, F., Asberg. P. and Hemmingsson, C., 'Managing media planning and brand positioning across media platforms', ESOMAR, *Worldwide Media Measurement*, Stockholm (May 2009).

12. For an illustration of a mathematical model based on it, see Suher, J. and Sorenson, H., 'The Power of Atlas: Why In-Store Shopping Behavior Matters', *Journal of Advertising Research*, 50 (1) (2010), 21–29.

13. Patwardhan, P. and Ramaprasad, J., 'Rational integrative model of online consumer decision making', *The Journal of Interactive Advertising*, 6 (1) (Fall 2005); Malhotra, N.K. and Wu, L., 'Decision models and descriptive models: complementary roles', *Marketing Research*, 13 (4) (December 2001), 43–44.

14. For an example of hypothesis formulation, see Bian, X. and Moutinho, L., 'The Role of Brand Image, Product Involvement, and Knowledge in Explaining Consumer Purchase Behaviour of Counterfeits: Direct and Indirect Effects', *European Journal of Marketing*, 45 (1/2) (2010).

15. For an example of model development and hypothesis formulation see Heath, R.G., Nairn, A.C. and Bottomley, P.A., 'How Effective is Creativity? Emotive Content in TV Advertising Does Not Increase Attention', *Journal of Advertising Research*, 49 (4) (Dec. 2009), 450–63.

16. The integrated role of theory, models, research questions and hypotheses in marketing research can be seen in Nygaard, A. and Dahlstrom, R., 'Role stress and effectiveness in horizontal alliances', *Journal of Marketing*, 66 (April 2002), 61–82; Nunes, J.C., 'A cognitive model of people's usage estimations', *Journal of marketing Research*, 37 (4) (November 2000), 397–409.

17. Roberts, D. and Adams, R., 'Agenda development for marketing research: the user's voice', *International Journal of Market Research*, 52 (3) (2010), 329–52.

18. Cooper, P., 'In search of excellence: the evolution and future of qualitative research', ESOMAR, *Annual Congress*, Berlin (Sept. 2007); Figure adapted from Cooper, P. and Braithwaite, A., 'Qualitative technology – new perspectives on measurement and meaning through qualitative research', Market Research Society Conference, 2nd pre-conference workshop, 1979.

19. Examples of research conducted on sensitive topics include: Kouznetsov, A. and Dass, M., 'Does size matter? A qualitative study into areas of corruption where a firm's size influences prospects for distributors of foreign-made goods in Russia', *Baltic Journal of Management*, 5 (1) (2010), 51–67; Vasconcelos, A.F., 'Intuition, prayer, and managerial decision making processes: a religion-based framework', *Management Decision*, 47 (6) (2009) 930–49; Matthew, H.T., Yap, M.H.T. and Ineson, E.M., 'HIV-infected employees in the Asian hospitality industry', *Journal of Service Management*, 20 (5) (2009), 503–20.

20. Chambers, K., 'Lies, damn lies and sensitive topics', *Imprints* (July 2004), 6.

21. Brüggen, E. and Willems, P., 'A critical comparison of offline focus groups, online focus groups and e-Delphi', *International Journal of Market Research*, 51 (3) (2009), 363–81.

22. Heath, R. and Feldwick, P., 'Fifty years using the wrong model of advertising', *International Journal of Market Research*, 50 (1)(2008), 29–59; Gordon, W. 'Consumer decision making', *Admap* (October 2004), 74.

23. Williams, N and Fergusson, J., 'Bridging the digital divide in qualitative research in emerging markets: Smart qual using Smart and non-Smart phones in developing markets', ESOMAR, *Asia Pacific*, Melbourne (2011).

---

24. Yaman, H.R. and Shaw, R.N., 'Marketing research and small travel agents: An exploratory study', *Journal of Vacation Marketing*, 8 (2) (2002), 127–40; Halman, I.M., 'Evaluating effectiveness of project start-ups: An exploratory study', *International Journal of Project Management*, 20 (January 2002), 81.

25. Kover, A.J., Carlson, L. and Ford, J., 'Comments – the quant-qual debate: where are we in advertising?' *International Journal of Advertising*, 27 (4) (2008) 659–69; Creswell, J.W., *Research Design: Qualitative, quantitative, and mixed method approaches*, 2nd edn (Thousand Oaks, CA: Sage, 2002); Lee, H., Lindquist, J.D. and Acito, F., 'Managers' evaluation of research design and its impact on the use of research: an experimental approach', *Journal of Business Research*, 39 (3) (July 1997), 231–40; Wilson, R.D., 'Research design: qualitative and quantitative approaches', *Journal of Marketing Research*, 33 (2) (May 1996), 252–55.

26. For examples of descriptive research, see Lindstrand, A. and Lindbergh, J., 'SMEs' dependency on banks during international expansion', *International Journal of Bank Marketing*, 29 (1) (2010); Robinson, W.Y., 'Is the first to market the first to fail?' *Journal of Marketing Research*, 39 (1) (February 2002), 120–28; Song, S.M. and Perry, M.E., 'The determinants of Japanese new product success', *Journal of Marketing Research*, 34 (February 1997), 64–76.

27. Yang, K. and Jolly, L.D., 'Age cohort analysis in adoption of mobile data services: gen Xers versus baby boomers', *Journal of Consumer Marketing*, 25 (5) (2008), 272–80; Creswell, J., *Research Design: Qualitative, quantitative and mixed method approaches*, 2nd edn (Thousand Oaks CA, Sage, 2002); Misra, R. and Panigrahi, B., 'Changes in attitudes toward women: a cohort analysis', *International Journal of Sociology & Social Policy*, 15 (6) (1995), 1–20; Glenn, N.D., *Cohort Analysis* (Beverly Hills, CA: Sage, 1981).

28. For example, see Tinson, J., Nancarrow, C. and Brace, I., 'Purchase decision making and the increasing significance of family types', *Journal of Consumer Marketing*, 25 (1) (2008), 45–56; Elrod, T. and Keane, M.P., 'A factor-analytic profit model for representing the market structure in panel data', *Journal of Marketing Research*, 32 (February 1995), 1–16.

29. Huertas-Garcia, R. and Consolación-Segura, C., 'Using statistical design experiment methodologies to identify customers' needs', *International Journal of Market Research*, 51 (1) (2009), 115–36; Gould, G.F. and Gould, J.L., '*Chance and Causation: To experimental design and statistics*' (New York: W.H. Freeman, 2001); Hulland, J., Ho, Y. and Lam, S., 'Use of causal models in marketing research: a review', *International Journal of Research in Marketing*, 13 (2) (April 1996), 181–197. See also Cox, K.K. and Enis, B.M., *Experimentation for Marketing Decisions* (Scranton, PA: International Textbook, 1969), 5.

30. Ryals, L. and Wilson, H., 'Experimental methods in market research: From information to insight', *International Journal of Market Research*, 47 (4) (2005), 345–64; Winer, R.S., 'Experimentation in the 21st century: The importance of external validity', *Journal of the Academy of Marketing Science* (Summer 1999), 349–58.

31. Poynter, R., 'A Taxonomy of New MR', Market Research Society, *Annual Conference* (2010); Lee, E., 'Are consumer survey results distorted? Systematic impact of behavioural frequency and duration on survey response errors', *Journal of Marketing Research* (February 2000), 125–33; Dutka, S. and Frankel, L.R., 'Measuring response error', *Journal of Advertising Research*, 37 (1) (January/February 1997), 33–39.

32. van Meurs, L., van Ossenbruggen, R. and Nekkers, L., 'Do rotten apples spoil the whole barrel? Exploring quality issues in panel data', ESOMAR, *Panel Research*, Orlando (Oct. 2007); Loosveldt, G., Carton, A. and Billiet, J., 'Assessment of survey data quality: a pragmatic approach focused on interviewer tasks', *International Journal of Market Research*, 46 (1) (2004), 68.

33. Blyth, B., 'Mixed mode: the only "fitness" regime?' *International Journal of Market Research*, 50 (2) (2008), 241–66; Brooks, D.V. 'A hands on approach to response rates', *Imprints* (October 2003), 24.

34. Manfreda, K.L., Bosnjak, M., Berzelak, J., Haas, I. and Vehovar, V., 'Web surveys versus other survey modes: a meta-analysis comparing response rates', *International Journal of Market Research*, 50 (1) (2008), 79–104; Sinha, P., 'Determination of reliability of estimations obtained with survey research: A method of simulation', *International Journal of Market Research*, 42 (3) (Summer 2000), 311–18; Rollere, M.R., 'Control is elusive in research design', *Marketing News*, 31 (19) (15 September 1997), 17; Corlett, T. , 'Sampling errors in practice', *Journal of the Market Research Society*, 38 (4) (April 1997), 307–318.

35. Feldman, S., 'Building market paradoxes – cross-cultural experiences in different categories', ESOMAR, *Latin America Conference*, Mexico City (May 2008).

36. Benezra, K., Conry, S. and Singh, S., '3 Screen Measurement: Soccer World Cup 2010 – Redefining "Multi-Modal" Research to Understand Audience Engagement', ESOMAR, *Congress Odyssey*, Athens, (Sept. 2010).

3

Secondary data collection and analysis: internal and external sources

Stage 1

Problem definition

Stage 2

Research approach developed

Stage 3

Research design developed

Stage 4

Fieldwork or data collection

Stage 5

Data integrity and analysis

Stage 6

Report preparation and presentation

Sourcing, evaluating and analysing secondary data in a critical and creative manner is vital to the planning and delivery of effective marketing research.

Objectives

After reading this chapter, you should be able to:

1 define the nature of secondary data and distinguish secondary data from primary data;

2 analyse the advantages and disadvantages of secondary data and their uses in the various stages of the marketing research process;

3 evaluate secondary data using the criteria of specifications, error, currency, objectives, nature and dependability;

4 distinguish different sources of secondary data, from internal to external sources;

5 appreciate how company databases have developed into powerful means to understand customer behaviour;

6 describe the nature of different sources of externally generated secondary data;

7 discuss the syndicated sources of secondary data, including household and consumer data obtained via surveys, purchase and media panels, and scanner services, as well as institutional data related to retailers and industrial or service firms;

8 understand the challenges of using secondary data in international marketing research;

9 explain the ethical issues involved in the use of secondary data;

10 appreciate how social media research techniques are integrating with traditional forms of research and how this integration may impact upon what may be defined as secondary data.

Overview

The collection and analysis of secondary data can help to define the marketing research problem and develop effective research designs. In addition, before collecting primary data, researchers should locate and analyse relevant secondary data. Secondary data can help in sample designs and in the detail of primary research methods. In some projects, research may be largely confined to the analysis of secondary data because some marketing problems may be resolved using only secondary data.

This chapter discusses the distinction between primary data and secondary data. The advantages and disadvantages of secondary data are considered, and criteria for evaluating secondary data are presented, along with a classification of secondary data. Internal secondary data are described along with the use of customer databases and customer relationship management systems. The major sources of external secondary data, such as published materials, online and offline databases, and syndicated services, are also described. The use and relative advantages and disadvantages of external secondary data sources are evaluated.

Using secondary data in international marketing research is discussed. Several ethical issues that arise in the use of secondary data are identified especially in the use of internally generated customer data and the use of databases. The impact of the growth and development of secondary data sources through the development of social media research and the growth of database and analytics technology will be evaluated. To begin with, we present an example that illustrates how secondary data was used in a research design on the nature of globalisation.

Has globalisation stalled?[1]

As a result of the Asian economic crisis in 1997–1998 and the global financial crisis in 2008–2009, there has been increasing speculation that 'globalisation' may have stalled. It has been argued that a new form of post-globalisation has emerged where the world is organised around regions such as Europe, North America and Asia, thus making a case for 'regionalisation'. A study was designed to evaluate these conjectures through a two-stage design. The *first stage* applied an exploratory approach to provide a market overview of China, India, Indonesia and South Korea. This stage drew upon secondary data to appraise the assertions that underpinned the study. The countries chosen for analysis had experienced substantial economic growth in the past with projections for continued growth in the future. China and India were the two most populous countries in the world with a growing middle class and a small, but very rich, upper class. Indonesia was an emerging economy with a population of 238 million and potential for substantial future economic growth. Korea, a former emerging economy, joined the ranks of the OECD in 1997 and was thus a developed country with well-established global brands, e.g. Samsung, LG, Hyundai and Kia. The *second stage* sought to test convergence and divergence hypotheses on a consumer sample. This enabled the researchers to analyse consumer attitude and behaviour and compare these findings with the secondary data sources used in the first stage of the project. Secondary data was also used in the sample design in China, India, Indonesia and South Korea. A consumer panel with consumers of identical profiles was built to enable valid comparison analyses. Stratified data ensured that different segments of society were equally represented, e.g. age and income groups.

Defining primary data and secondary data

Primary data
Data originated by the researcher specifically to address the research problem.

Secondary data
Data collected for some purpose other than the problem at hand.

Primary data are data originated by a researcher for the specific purpose of addressing the problem at hand. They are individually tailored for the decision makers of organisations that pay for well-focused and exclusive support. Compared with readily available data from a variety of sources, this exclusivity can mean higher costs and a longer time frame in collecting and analysing the data.

Secondary data are data that have already been collected for purposes other than the problem at hand. These data can be located relatively quickly and inexpensively.[2]

In the development of credible support for decision makers, researchers need to be thorough and creative in their collection and evaluation of secondary data. This requires researchers to connect and validate different data sources, ultimately leading to decision maker support in its own right and support of more focused primary data collection.

Advantages and uses of secondary data

Secondary data offer several advantages over primary data. Secondary data have become more easily accessible, relatively inexpensive and quickly obtained. Some secondary data sources can be accessed free of charge, but many sources do charge fees to reflect the investment made to gather, analyse and present accurate information. Although it is rare for secondary data to provide all the answers to a non-routine research problem, such data can be useful in a variety of ways.[3] Secondary data can help researchers to:

1 Diagnose the research problem.

2 Develop an approach to the problem.

3   Develop a sampling plan.

4   Formulate an appropriate research design (e.g. by identifying the key variables to measure or understand).

5   Answer certain research questions and test some hypotheses.

6   Interpret primary data with more insight.

7   Validate qualitative research findings.

Given these advantages and uses of secondary data, we state the following general rule:

> *Examination of available secondary data is a prerequisite to the collection of primary data. Start with secondary data. Proceed to primary data only when the secondary data sources have been exhausted or yield marginal returns.*

The rich dividends obtained by following this rule are illustrated in the example at the start of this chapter. It shows that the collection and analysis of even one relevant secondary data source can provide valuable insights. The decision maker and researcher can use the ideas generated in secondary data as a very strong foundation to primary data design and collection. However, the researcher should be cautious in using secondary data, because they have some limitations and disadvantages.

Disadvantages of secondary data

Because secondary data have been collected for purposes other than the problem at hand, their usefulness to the current problem may be limited in several important ways, including relevance and accuracy. The objectives, nature and methods used to collect the secondary data may not be appropriate to the present situation. Also, secondary data may be lacking in accuracy or may not be completely current or dependable. Before using secondary data, it is important to evaluate them according to a series of factors. These factors are discussed in more detail in the following section.

Criteria for evaluating secondary data

The quality of secondary data should be routinely evaluated, using the criteria presented in Table 3.1 and the discussion in the following sections.

Specifications: research design and how the data was collected

The specifications of the research design used to collect the data should be critically examined to identify possible sources of bias. Such design considerations include size and nature of the sample, response rate and quality, questionnaire design and administration, procedures used for fieldwork and data analysis and reporting procedures. These checks provide information on the reliability and validity of the data and help determine whether they can be generalised to the problem at hand. The reliability and validity can be further ascertained by an examination of the error, currency, objectives, nature and dependability associated with the secondary data.

Error: accuracy of the data

The researcher must determine whether the data are accurate enough for the purposes of the present study. Secondary data can have a number of sources of error or inaccuracy, including errors in the approach, research design, sampling, data collection, analysis, and reporting

Table 3.1	Criteria for evaluating secondary data	
Criteria	**Issues**	**Remarks**
Specifications and research design	• Data collection method • Response rate • Population definition • Sampling method • Sample size • Questionnaire design • Fieldwork • Data analysis	Data should be reliable, valid and generalisable to the problem at hand
Error and accuracy	Examine errors in: • Approach • Research design • Sampling • Data collection • Data analysis • Reporting	Assess accuracy by comparing data from different sources
Currency	Time lag between collection and publication. Frequency of updates	Census data are periodically updated by syndicated firms
Objective	Why the data were collected	The objective will determine the relevance of data
Nature	• Definition of key variables • Units of measurement • Categories used • Relationships examined	Reconfigure the data to increase their usefulness, if possible
Dependability	Source: • Expertise • Credibility • Reputation • Trustworthiness	Preference should be afforded to an original rather than an acquired source

stages of the project. Moreover, it is difficult to evaluate the accuracy of secondary data because the researcher did not participate in the research. One approach is to find multiple sources of data if possible, and compare them using standard statistical procedures.

The accuracy of secondary data can vary in the following ways: What is being measured? What rules apply to those measurements? What happens if there are rapid changes in what is being measured? With different researchers potentially measuring the 'same' phenomena, data obtained from different sources may not agree. In these cases, the researcher should verify the accuracy of secondary data by conducting pilot studies or by other exploratory work that verifies the analytical framework used to arrive at certain figures.

Currency: when the data were collected

Secondary data may not be current and the time lag between data collection and publication may be long, as is the case with much census data which may take over two years from collection to publication. Moreover, the data may not be updated frequently enough for the purpose of the problem at hand. Decision makers require current data; therefore, the value of secondary data is diminished as they become dated.

Objective: the purpose for which the data were collected

Data are invariably collected with some objective in mind, and a fundamental question to ask is why the data were collected in the first place. The objective for collecting data will ultimately determine the purpose for which that information is relevant and useful. Data collected with a specific objective in mind may not be appropriate in another situation.

Nature: the content of the data

The nature, or content, of the data should be examined with special attention to the definition of key variables, the units of measurement, the categories used and the relationships examined. If the key variables have not been defined or are defined in a manner inconsistent with the researcher's definition, then the usefulness of the data is limited. Consider, for example, secondary data on consumer preferences for TV programmes. To use this information, it is important to know how preference for programmes was defined. Was it defined in terms of the programme watched most often, the one considered most needed, most enjoyable, most informative, or the programme of greatest service to the community?

Likewise, secondary data may be measured in units that may not be appropriate for the current problem. For example, income may be measured by individual, family, household or spending unit and could be gross or net after taxes and deductions. Income may be classified into categories that are different from research needs. If the researcher is interested in high-income consumers with gross annual household incomes of over €120,000, secondary data with income categories of less than €20,000, €20,001–€50,000, €50,001–€75,000 and more than €75,000 will not be of much use. Determining the measurement of variables such as income may be a complex task, requiring the wording of the definition of income to be precise. Finally, the relationships examined should be taken into account in evaluating the nature of data. If, for example, actual behaviour is of interest, then data inferring behaviour from self-reported attitudinal information may have limited usefulness. Sometimes it is possible to reconfigure the available data, for example to convert the units of measurement, so that the resulting data are more useful to the problem at hand.

Dependability: how dependable are the data?

An overall indication of the dependability of data may be obtained by examining the expertise, credibility, reputation and trustworthiness of the source. This information can be obtained by checking with others who have used the information provided by the source. Data published to promote sales, to advance specific interests, or to carry on propaganda should be viewed with suspicion. The same may be said of data published anonymously or in a form that attempts to hide the details of the data collection research design and process. It is also pertinent to examine whether the secondary data came from an original source, one that generated the data, or an acquired source, one that procured the data from an original source and published it in a different context. Generally, secondary data should be secured from an original rather than an acquired source. There are at least two reasons for this rule: first, an original source is the one that specifies the details of the data collection research design; and, second, an original source is likely to be more accurate and complete than a acquired source.

Classification of secondary data

Internal data

Data available within the organisation for whom the research is being conducted.

Figure 3.1 presents a classification of secondary data. Secondary data may be classified as either internal or external. Internal data are those generated within the organisation for which the research is being conducted. This information may be available on a ready to use format, such as information routinely reported in decision support systems. On the other hand, these data may exist within the organisation but may require considerable processing

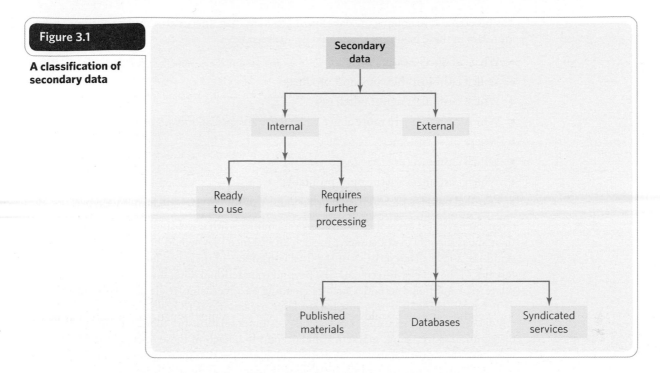

Figure 3.1

A classification of secondary data

External data
Data that originate outside the organisation.

before they are useful to the researcher. **External data**, on the other hand, are those generated by sources outside the organisation. These data may exist in the form of published material, databases, or information made available by syndicated services. Externally generated secondary data may be more difficult to access, more expensive and more difficult to evaluate for accuracy, in comparison with internal secondary data. These factors mean that, before collecting external secondary data, it is vital to gather, analyse and interpret any readily available internal secondary data and intelligence.

Internal secondary data

Operational data
Data generated about an organisation's customers, through day-to-day transactions.

Internal secondary data are generally seen as being drawn from **operational data**, i.e. data that represent the daily activities, transactions and enquiries of an organisation.

Daily transactions may be held in different departments such as sales, accounts or human resources and stored in different manners. The use of operational data has presented opportunities to researchers for as long as businesses have been recording their daily transactions. Even in the days of transactions being recorded manually, it was invaluable for researchers to track down different sources of data and analyse them. The value of internal secondary data at all stages of the research process means that locating and analysing this data should be the starting point in any research project. The main values they hold are in defining: the nature of a marketing decision problem; which individuals should be questioned or observed; the nature of questions and observations to be directed at these individuals. These reasons are fundamental to the quality, action orientation and perceived value of marketing research. In addition, as these data have already been collected, there are no additional data collection costs, there should be fewer access problems and the quality of the data should be easier to establish (in comparison with externally generated data).

Most organisations have a wealth of in-house information even if they are not marketing or customer focused, so some data may be readily available. For example, imagine a shoe manufacturer that has traditionally sold shoes to retailers e.g. Grenson (**www.grenson.co.uk**). It creates invoices for all its sales to these business accounts. Its accounts department handles this process and maintains the data that it generates. Yet, there exists much consumer behaviour data in these invoices. They could be analysed by:

- What products customers buy.
- Which customers buy the most products.
- Which customers repeat purchases.
- Which customers are more active when there are special offers.
- Where these customers are located.
- Which customers are the most loyal.
- Which customers are the most profitable.
- Seasonal patterns of purchasing behaviour by product types and customer types.

Grenson have also developed e-business capabilities, with a website that enables them to sell their shoes directly to consumers. In such an instance they would have the ability to understand the above characteristics of the final consumers of their products, rather than characteristics of the retailer intermediaries. Beyond transactional data, there may also be data that relate to promotional activities such as spending on advertising, trade fairs, sponsorship deals or personal selling. It is not unusual for large organisations to have a multiplicity of different data sources, for example, sales orders, customer relationship management, assets, stock, distribution, advertising, marketing and accounting. Each of these operational data systems may have their own databases but there is no guarantee that these systems and databases are linked.[4] Thus the researcher may be faced with many discrete and/or integrated internal data sources from which characteristics of customers, their past behaviour and potential behaviour may be discerned. The norm for many companies is to formally integrate data about their customers and invest in developing and maintaining a **customer database**.

Customer database
A database that details characteristics of customers and prospects that can include names and addresses, geographic, demographic and buying behaviour data.

The customer database can be used to design and deliver marketing activities and strategies, and the response from these activities is fed back to improve and update it. Databases support techniques, such as segmentation analysis, which at one time were developed from data gathered from relatively small samples collected at considerable expense. With a customer database, insights can be developed from larger samples obtained at almost no marginal cost as the data usually were gathered in the course of normal business operations.[5] A major development in how customer insight may be generated is through the use of a customer relationship management system (CRM). Such an example of a CRM and how it may integrate with marketing research is illustrated in the following example.

Real research   **Creation of a pan-European online customer panel for Nintendo[6]**

Nintendo wished to develop a platform to integrate online customer surveys with data stored in its CRM system. Globalpark (**www.globalpark.com**) worked in close cooperation with Nintendo to develop a workflow that networked their existing CRM system with Globalpark survey software. As a result, almost 1 million registered Nintendo customers could be managed and surveyed with their EFS (Enterprise Feedback System) Panel. An interface in EFS Panel made it possible to extract samples from the customer database according to specific criteria such as socio-demographic features. The master data could be used to identify suitable participants for a specific survey. Collected data from the survey was then fed back into the integrated system. The entire survey process, from the development of the survey, the recruitment of participants from the Nintendo CRM system, and the invitation via e-mail, to field control and the delivery of rewards at the end of the survey, could be coordinated using the EFS Panel. This process allowed Nintendo to conduct online product tests, customer satisfaction analyses, communications campaigns and ad-hoc marketing research projects.

From the researchers' perspective, many benefits also accrue from the internally generated secondary data from databases and a CRM system. The following list summarises the benefits to the researcher:

1 *Profiles of customers can be built up.* The types of individual that are being attracted to a business, particular types of product and responses to different types of promotion can be monitored. The returns and contributions made by particular types of customer can be measured. Profiles of the 'ideal' customer type can be built up, and plans developed to attract potential customers based upon these profiles.

2 *One big laboratory.* The monitoring of customers, markets and interrelated marketing mix activities allows for many causal inferences to be established. For example, what is the effect, and upon whom, of raising the price of Häagen Dazs ice cream by 10 per cent? What is the effect of inserting a cut-out coupon to give a discount on after-sun lotion, placed in *Cosmopolitan* magazine?

3 *Refining the marketing process.* With time series of responses to planned marketing activities, statistical models of consumer response can be built with associated probabilities of a particular outcome. Likewise, models of the consumers over their lifetimes can be built. Again, statistical models can be built with associated probabilities of particular types of product being bought at different stages of a consumer's life.

4 *Developing a clear understanding of 'gaps' in the knowledge of consumers.* The customer database records observed behaviour but do not encapsulate attitudinal data. The nature and levels of satisfaction, what is perceived as good-quality service, or what image is associated with a particular brand are examples of attitudinal data. The use of the database helps to identify target populations to measure and the attitudinal data that need to be collected. In all, there can be a much greater clarity in the nature of primary marketing research that tackles attitudinal issues.

5 *Linking behavioural and attitudinal data.* If attitudinal data are elicited from consumers, the data gathered can be analysed in their own right. It is possible, however, to link the gathered data back to the behavioural data in the database. The notion of linking together databases and survey data from different sources is at the heart of building a strong understanding of both the behaviour and motivation of consumers.

In the development of good research designs, the customer database can be seen as a vital resource to the researcher when conducting internal secondary data searches. The idea of accessing a customer database represents a clear opportunity for researchers, but such a resource may not be singular and can be integrated with many other databases and systems. There are a whole array of different means to electronically capture customer transaction behaviour and even potential customers through their search for information to buy services and products.

External secondary data

Sources of published external secondary data include local authorities, regional and national governments, the EU, non-profit organisations (e.g. Chambers of Commerce), trade associations and professional organisations, commercial publishers, investment brokerage firms and professional marketing research firms.[7] Such a quantity of data is available that the researcher can be overwhelmed. Therefore, it is important to classify published sources (see Figure 3.2). Published external sources may be broadly classified as general business data or government data. General business sources comprise guides, directories, indexes and statistical data. Government sources may be broadly categorised as census data and other publications.

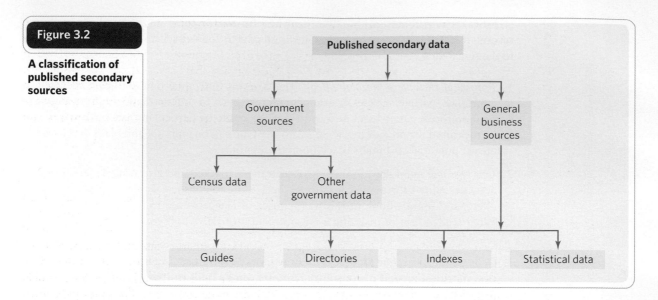

Figure 3.2

A classification of published secondary sources

General business sources

Businesses publish a lot of information in the form of books, periodicals, journals, newspapers, magazines, reports and trade literature. This information can be located in hard copy and electronically by using guides, directories and indexes. Sources are also available to identify statistical data.

Guides Guides are an excellent source of standard or recurring information. A guide may help identify other important sources of directories, trade associations and trade publications. Guides are one of the first sources a researcher should consult. Commercial guides can be used to assist decision makers or researchers to current issues and sources regarding individual industries or countries. An example of one of these would be the Datamonitor guides; search for 'guides' on (**www.datamonitor.com**).

Directories Directories are helpful for identifying individuals or organisations that collect specific data. An example is Europages, a reference business directory in Europe that classifies 23 million companies in 35 European countries, in 26 languages (**www.europages.com**). Another directory worth exploring is ESOMAR's *Directory of Research Organisations* (**http://directory.esomar.org**).

Indexes It is possible to locate information on a particular topic in several different publications by using an index and abstracts. Indexes and abstracts, therefore, can increase the efficiency of the search process. Several indexes and abstracts are available for both academic and business sources. Examples of newspaper indexes include the *Financial Times Index* (**www.ft.com**), *Le Monde Index* (**www.le-monde.fr**) and the Japanese Business News online, *The Nikkei Weekly* (**www.nikkei.co.jp**). These indexes allow researchers to identify sources of particular topics, industries and individuals.

Non-government statistical data Business research often involves compiling statistical data reflecting market or industry factors. Market statistics related to population demographics, purchasing levels, television viewership, and product usage are some of the types of non-governmental statistics available from secondary sources. As well any published commentary presented in these resources, further statistical analyses and graphical manipulations can be performed on these data to draw important insights. Examples of non-governmental statistical data include Euromonitor (**www.euromonitor.com**), which publishes monthly market research journals covering a great breadth of industries and countries across the world. The United Nations provides an example of an organisation with a Statistics Division that provides a wide range of statistical outputs on a global basis (**http://unstats.un.org**). The Statistics Division produces printed publications of statistics and statistical methods in the fields of international merchandise trade, national accounts, demography and population, social indicators, gender, industry, energy, environment, human settlements and disability.

Government sources

European governments and the EU also produce large amounts of secondary data. Each European country has its own statistical office which produces lists of the publications available (and the costs involved). Examples of national statistical offices include the Centraal Bureau voor de Statistiek Nederlands (**www.cbs.nl**), Danmarks Statistik (**www.dst.dk**), the Federal Statistical Office of Germany (**www.destatis.de**), the French Institut National de la Statistique et des Études Economiques (**www.insee.fr**) and the British Office for National Statistics (**www.statistics.gov.uk**). All of these links allow you to examine quickly the array of publications that they produce. Their publications may be divided into census data and other publications.

Census data Most European countries produce either catalogues or newsletters that describe the array of census publications available and the plans for any forthcoming census. In the UK, for example, **www.ons.gov.uk/census** contains the latest information about the 2011 Census in England and Wales. Census Marketing in Britain can supply unpublished data from the 1961, 1971, 1981, 1991, 2001 Censuses in the form of Small Area Statistics (SAS). SAS are available for standard census areas within England and Wales, such as counties, local government districts, London boroughs, wards, civil parishes and enumeration districts. Maps can also be purchased to complement the data.

Other government publications In addition to the census, national statistical offices collect and publish a great deal of statistical data. As well as general population censuses, national statistical offices produce an array of nationally relevant statistics. The value of these may lie in evaluating and describing markets, environments and the challenges and opportunities these hold. To examine any of the national statistics offices in Europe and global regions, visit the excellent Central Statistics Office Ireland website (**www.cso.ie/links**) and follow the country links. There are also links to many other important organisations with relevant statistics such as the European Central Bank (**www.ccb.int**) and the International Monetary Fund (**www.imf.org**).

Databases

A major category of secondary data is available in the form of browsable online databases.[8] From the 1980s to date, the number of databases, as well as the vendors providing these services, has grown enormously. Browsable online databases offer a number of advantages over printed data, including:[9]

1 **Current information.** The data can be current, up to date, and even 'live'.

2 **Faster data search.** Online vendors can provide ready access to hundreds of databases. Moreover, this information can be accessed instantaneously, and the search process is simplified as the vendors provide uniform search protocols and commands for accessing the database.

3 **Low cost.** The cost of accessing these is relatively low, because of the accuracy of searching for the right data, and the speed of location and transfer of data.

4 **Convenience.** It is convenient to access these data using many forms of working online, including mobile devices.

Although online database information can be helpful, it is not necessarily free. It is vital to consider what costs are incurred in generating, presenting and updating quality and dependable information databases. The number of database vendors and the breadth of subjects covered can be vast and confusing, especially at the commencement of a project. Thus a classification of online databases is helpful.

Classification of online databases

Online databases

Databases that can be accessed, searched and analysed via the Internet.

Bibliographic databases

Databases composed of citations to articles in journals, magazines, newspapers, marketing research studies, technical reports, government documents and the like. They often provide summaries or abstracts of the material cited.

Numeric databases

Databases containing numerical and statistical information that may be important sources of secondary data.

Online databases may be classified as bibliographic, numeric, full-text, directory or special-purpose databases, as shown in Figure 3.3.

Bibliographic databases are composed of citations to articles in journals, magazines, newspapers, marketing research studies, technical reports, government documents and the like.[10] They often provide summaries or abstracts of the material cited. The IMRI database is a good example of this (**www.imriresearch.com**). The IMRI database includes over 50,000 abstracts of market research reports and sources (including journals, databases, audits, published surveys, etc.). This is a comprehensive directory of marketing research agencies, publishers and associations in over 100 countries. Besides country listings, agencies appear in regions (e.g. Asia), specialist fields (e.g. quantitative) and market sectors (e.g. healthcare and pharmaceutical). The IMRI database is hosted on Datastar, Thompson/Dialog's collection of information databases (**www.dialog.com**).

Numeric databases contain numerical and statistical information. For example, some numeric databases provide time series data about the economy and specific industries. The earlier examples of census-based numeric databases using data over a series of censuses provide an example of a numeric database. The Experian MOSAIC database is a good example of a numeric database (**www.experian.co.uk/business-strategies**). Experian data includes business and consumer demographics and classifications, mapping, economic forecasts and statistics, local area data and retail and business information. It is delivered in a range of formats, including databases, reports and products such as Experian's MOSAIC consumer classification.

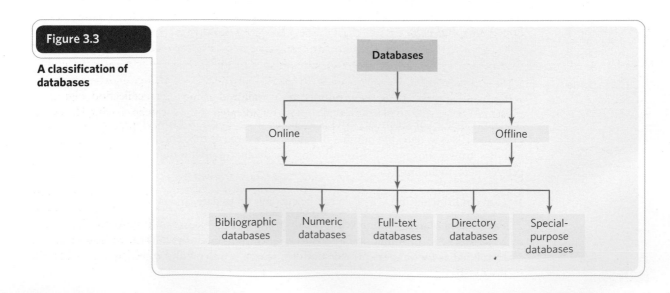

Figure 3.3

A classification of databases

Full-text databases
Databases that contain the complete text of secondary source documents comprising the database.

Full-text databases contain the complete text of the source documents held in the database. They usually have the ability to conduct advanced searches for topics, authors, phrases, words and interconnections between these. Examples include Emerald Insight (**www .emeraldinsight.com**) and the Gale Newspaper Database (**www.gale.cengage.com**). Emerald is an independent publisher of global research with impact in business, society, public policy and education. Its database provides access to more than 68,000 articles, some dating back as far as 1898. It has backfiles of over 120 business and management titles in one unified platform and access to 217 business and management e-journals.

Directory databases
Databases that provide information on individuals, organisations and services.

Directory databases provide information on individuals, organisations and services. European Directories (**www.europeandirectories.com**) is an example of a directory database. European Directories is a pan-European local search and lead generation company. It provides local search services to help customers find, evaluate and connect with local businesses across multiple media including print, online and mobile. It can help advertisers ensure they have a strong presence wherever consumers might be searching for local businesses.

Special-purpose databases
Databases that contain information of a specific nature, e.g. data on a specialised industry.

Finally, there are **special-purpose databases**. A good example of a special-purpose database is the fashion trend forecasting service WGSN (**www.wgsn.com**). WGSN is a leading online trend-analysis and research service providing creative and marketing intelligence for the apparel, style, design and retail industries. Its data supports all business functions, including design, production, manufacturing, purchasing, merchandising, marketing, product development and general management. WGSN has a 12-year archive with more than 5 million images and 650,000 pages of information.

Virtually all libraries of major educational institutions maintain special-purpose databases of research activities that reflect their distinct specialisms. Beyond the internally generated, special-purpose databases, university libraries and reference libraries maintain online databases with instructions relating to what may be accessed and how it may be accessed. Another library source worth examining for online sources is the European Commission's 'Libraries' site (**http://europa.eu**). The site, which is multilingual, is distributed by the EUROPA server, the portal site of the EU. It provides up-to-date coverage of European affairs and essential information on European integration. Users can access websites of each of the EU institutions.

Syndicated sources of secondary data

Syndicated sources (services)
Information services offered by marketing research organisations that provide information from a common database to different firms that subscribe to their services.

In addition to published data or data available in the form of online databases, syndicated sources constitute the other major source of external secondary data. **Syndicated sources**, also referred to as **syndicated services**, are companies that collect and sell common pools of data designed to serve information needs shared by a number of clients. These data are not collected with a focus on a specific marketing problem, but the data and reports supplied to client companies can be personalised to fit specific needs. For example, reports could be organised based on the clients' sales territories or product lines. Using syndicated services is frequently less expensive than commissioning tailored primary data collection. Figure 3.4 presents a classification of syndicated sources. Syndicated sources can be classified based on the unit of measurement (households and consumers or institutions). Household and consumer data may be obtained from surveys, purchase and media panels or electronic scanner services. Information obtained through surveys consists of values and lifestyles, advertising evaluation, or general information related to preferences, purchase, consumption and other aspects of behaviour. Diary panels can focus upon information on purchases or media consumption. Electronic scanner services might provide scanner data only, scanner data linked to panels, or scanner data linked to panels and pay TV. When institutions are the unit of measurement, the data may be obtained from retailers, wholesalers or industrial firms. An overview of the various syndicated sources is given in Table 3.2. Each of these sources will be discussed.

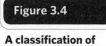

Figure 3.4

A classification of syndicated services

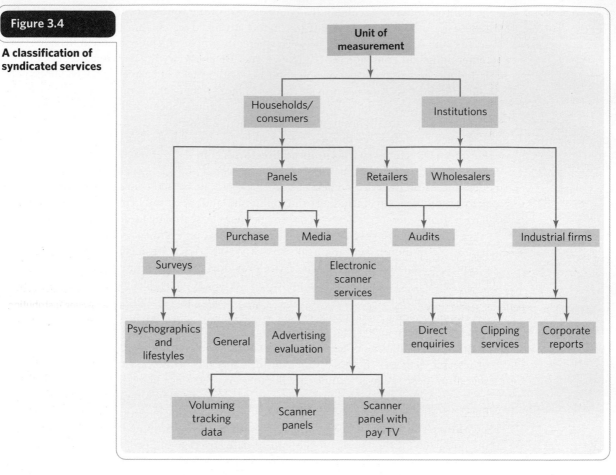

Table 3.2   **Overview of syndicated services**

Type	Characteristics	Advantages	Disadvantages	Uses
Surveys	Surveys conducted at regular intervals	Most flexible way of obtaining data; information on underlying motives	Interviewer errors, participant errors, response rate challenges	Market segmentation, advertising theme selection and advertising effectiveness
Purchase panels	Households provide specific information regularly over an extended period of time; participants asked to record specific behaviour as it occurs	Recorded purchase behaviour can be linked to demographic/ psychographic characteristics	Lack of representativeness; response bias; maturation	Forecasting sales, market share and trends; establishing consumer profiles, brand loyalty and switching; evaluating test markets, advertising and distribution
Media panels	Electronic devices automatically recording behaviour, supplemented by a diary or blog	Same as purchase panel	Same as purchase panel	Establishing advertising; selecting media programme or air time; establishing viewer profiles

Table 3.2	Continued			
Type	**Characteristics**	**Advantages**	**Disadvantages**	**Uses**
Scanner volume tracking data	Household purchases recorded through electronic scanners in supermarkets	Data reflect actual purchases; timely data, less expensive	Data may not be representative; errors in recording purchases; difficult to link purchases to elements of marketing mix other than price	Price tracking, modelling effectiveness of in-store promotions
Scanner panels with pay TV	Scanner panels of households that subscribe to pay TV	Data reflect actual purchases; sample control; ability to link panel data to household characteristics	Data may not be representative; quality of data limited	Promotional mix analyses, copy testing, new product testing, positioning
Audit services	Verification of product movement by examining physical records or performing inventory analysis	Relatively precise information at retail and wholesale levels	Coverage may be incomplete; matching of data on competitive activity may be difficult	Measurement of consumer sales and market share; competitive activity; analysing distribution patterns; tracking of new products
Industrial product syndicated services	Data banks on industrial establishments created through direct enquiries of companies, clipping services and corporate reports	Important source of information in industrial firms; particularly useful in initial phases of research projects	Data can be lacking in terms of content, quantity and quality, i.e. this equates more with business and competitor intelligence services	Determining market potential by geographic area, defining sales territories, allocating advertising budget

Syndicated data from households

Surveys

Surveys
Interviews with a large number of participants using a questionnaire.

Omnibus survey
A distinctive form of survey that serves the needs of a syndicated group. The omnibus survey targets particular types of participants such as those in specific locations, e.g. Luxembourg residents, or customers of particular types of product, e.g. business air travellers. With that target group of participants, a core set of questions can be asked, with other questions added as syndicate members wish.

Many research companies offer syndicated services by conducting **surveys** and **omnibus surveys**. As with any survey, the process involves interviews with a large number of participants using a pre-designed questionnaire. Survey design and the relative advantages and disadvantages of different survey types will be discussed in detail later in the text (Chapter 5). The distinction made here is that rather than designing a survey for the specific needs of a client company, the syndicated survey is designed for a number of client companies. The needs of sometimes quite a disparate array of client companies can be met by a syndicated survey. The key benefits of the syndicated survey lie combining the resources of a number of clients to craft a survey of high quality and the economies of scale this may bring to individual clients. The downside may be that not all the information needs of an individual client may be met, and additional primary data may need to be collected. One of the most prolific forms of syndicated survey is the omnibus survey. The distinction of the omnibus survey compared to ad-hoc surveys is that they target particular types of participants such as those in certain geographic locations, e.g. Luxembourg residents, or consumers of particular types of products, e.g. business air travellers.

With a defined target group of participants, a core set of questions can be asked with other questions added as syndicate members wish. Other syndicate members can 'jump on the omnibus' and buy the answers to all the questionnaire responses or to specific questions of their choice. Surveys and omnibus surveys may be broadly classified based on their content as psychographics and lifestyles, advertising evaluation, or general surveys.

Psychographics
Quantified profiles of individuals based upon lifestyle characteristics.

Lifestyles
Distinctive patterns of living described by the activities people engage in, the interests they have, and the opinions they hold of themselves and the world around them.

Psychographics and lifestyles Psychographics refer to the psychological profiles of individuals and to psychologically based measures of lifestyle. Lifestyles refer to the distinctive modes of living of a society or some of its segments. Together, these measures are generally referred to as activities, interests and opinions.[11] Companies may wish to buy syndicated data that describes the lifestyles of consumers as this can help them to further understand the characteristics of their existing and especially potential customers. A good example of a marketing research agency that works upon the measurement and marketing applications of lifestyles can be found at the Natural Marketing Institute (**www.nmisolutions.com**).

Advertising evaluation The purpose of using surveys to evaluate advertising is to assess the effectiveness of advertising that may be delivered through print, broadcast, online, outdoors and social media.[12] The sums involved in planning, creating and delivering effective advertising mean that research has long played a part in supporting advertising decisions, and surveys continue to play a major role in that evaluation process. The subject of advertising research has a long history and very large literature base with strong academic and practitioner viewpoints.[13] One of the main contemporary challenges in measuring the impact of advertising is in isolating a specific medium, as illustrated in the following example. This example illustrates that creative research designs can be used to isolate and measure the impact of a single communications medium.

Real research	**It can be measured**[14]

Radio Ad Effectiveness Lab (RAEL, **www.radioadlab.org**) was founded in 2001 and is dedicated to providing research about how radio advertising works. One of its first studies was dedicated to the return on investment (ROI) on radio advertising. With the help of Millward Brown (**www .millwardbrown.com**) and Information Resources (IRI, **www .symphonyiri.com**) and four adventurous advertisers, RAEL

created a 'real-world' test. It used IRI's BehaviorScan Targetable TV test market capabilities to control the delivery of TV advertisements household by household, while simultaneously using test and control markets to deliver or not deliver radio advertising. This involved a six-month test of actual advertising campaigns for multiple advertisers. RAEL created four matching test cells: one with no local radio or national TV advertising; one with only the national TV ads, one with only an equivalent weight of local radio advertising; and one with equivalent weights of both national TV and local radio advertising. Alongside the survey data collected, RAEL also had corresponding scanner shopping data from IRI for four national advertisers. At the end of the six-month period, RAEL looked at the cell-by-cell details for each advertiser. On a sales lift basis, the radio campaigns for the four advertisers aquitted themselves very well. The radio campaigns were linked to a statistically significant sales lift of 4.1 per cent. Meanwhile, TV with a much higher spend level accounted for 7.5 per cent in additional sales. When advertising costs were considered, radio delivered 49 per cent better ROI than the corresponding (and similar weights of) national TV advertising.

General surveys Syndicated surveys are also conducted for a variety of other purposes, including examination of purchase and consumption behaviour. Because a variety of data can be obtained, survey data have numerous uses. They can be used for market segmentation, as with psychographic and lifestyle data, and for establishing consumer profiles. Surveys are also useful for determining product image, measurement and positioning, and conducting price perception analysis.

The advantage of surveys lies in their flexibility in eliciting data from participants. The researcher can focus on only a certain segment of the population, e.g. teenagers, owners of holiday homes or students aged 18 to 20. Surveys are the primary means of obtaining information about consumers' motives, attitudes and preferences. A variety of questions can be asked and visual aids, packages, products or other props can be used during interviews. Properly analysed, survey data can be manipulated in many ways so that the researcher can look at inter-group differences, examine the effects of independent variables, such as age or income, or even predict future behaviour. On the other hand, survey data may be limited in several significant ways. The researcher has to rely primarily upon participants' self-reports. There can be a gap between what people say and what they actually do. Errors may occur because participants remember incorrectly or give socially desirable responses. Furthermore, samples may be biased, questions poorly phrased, interviewers not properly instructed or supervised and results misinterpreted.

Purchase and media panels

About a fifth of all research budgets are spent on panels in their various formats, among the largest investors in this format in Europe being Switzerland at 38 per cent, Germany 34 per cent and the Netherlands 31 per cent.[15] Panels are samples of participants who provide specified information at regular intervals over an extended period of time. These participants may be organisations, households or individuals, although household panels are most common. The distinguishing feature of panels is that the participants record specific behaviours as they occur. Previously, behaviour was recorded in a handwritten diary, and the diary returned to the research organisation every one to four weeks. Panel diaries have been gradually replaced by electronic diaries and blog diaries.[16] Now, most panels are online and consumption and media behaviour is recorded electronically, either entered online by the participants or recorded automatically by electronic devices.

In media panels, electronic devices automatically record viewing behaviour, thus supplementing a diary. Media panels yield information helpful for establishing advertising rates by radio and TV networks, selecting appropriate programming, and profiling viewer or listener subgroups. Advertisers, media planners and buyers find panel information particularly useful. Another media vehicle that competes heavily for advertising budgets is the Internet. The following example illustrates how TNS use media panels to understand the likelihood of viewers responding to advertisements.

Media panels
A data gathering technique composed of samples of participants whose TV viewing behaviour is automatically recorded by electronic devices, supplementing the purchase information recorded in a diary or blog.

Real research | **Targeting ad responders[17]**

The Skyview panel, conceived and developed by BSkyB (**www.sky.com**) and TNS (**www.tnsglobal.com**), comprises 33,000 Sky households, from which detailed second-by-second TV viewing data covering all television channels is collected via a set-top box. Of these homes, 6,000 are also members of Worldpanel, the service operated by TNS which provides detail on each household's purchasing of grocery products on a continuous basis. Sky Media (**www.skymedia.co.uk**) is the media sales arm of BSkyB and it wanted to use data from Worldpanel to identify which households are the most responsive to advertising. Having identified these 'high responders', Sky Media could then go on to examine their viewing patterns and thus find ways in which advertising could be more effectively targeted at the most responsive buyers through the better use of timing advertisements throughout the day, channels and specific programmes. Worldpanel data reveals when each household made a purchase of a product category and whether the advertised brand or another brand was bought. It was possible to count the number of times the advertised brand was bought when the household was exposed to the brand's advertising. Skymedia built upon this relationship to help predict the likelihood of someone responding to an advertisement. To investigate this it studied 33 brands across three categories: breakfast cereals, shampoo and yogurts. In each case it identified the 'ad responders'. For each panelist it added a description of their demographics, together with their scores on 137 attitudinal statements and their propensity to view TV. On average, 13 per cent of panelists were classified as 'ad responders'. Those with the highest propensity to be ad responders were people who liked advertising, were heavy consumers of commercial TV, and had two or more people in the household. By contrast, the least responsive were those that claimed not to like advertising, were living on their own and working full-time.

Purchase panels
A data gathering technique in which participants record their purchases, either online, in a diary or in a blog.

With **purchase panels**, participants record their purchases of a variety of products. This type of longitudinal data would be hard to ascertain from a cross-sectional study as it would rely on participants recalling past purchases over a long period of time. These panels provide information useful for forecasting sales, estimating market shares, assessing brand loyalty and brand-switching behaviour, establishing profiles of specific user groups, measuring promotional effectiveness, and conducting controlled store tests.

Compared with sample surveys, panels offer certain distinct advantages.[18] Panels can provide longitudinal data (data can be obtained from the same participants repeatedly). They enable specific types of consumer to be targeted for study, relatively quicker than generating a tailored sample. People who are willing to serve on panels may be more motivated to engage in a particular study and thus provide more and higher quality data than one-off sample participants. In purchase panels, information is recorded at the time of purchase, eliminating recall errors.[19] If information is recorded by electronic devices, it is generally more accurate as it eliminates recall errors.

The disadvantages of panels include lack of representativeness, maturation and response biases.[20] This problem is further compounded by refusal to respond and attrition of panel members. Over time, maturation sets in, and the panel members should be replaced. Response biases may occur, since simply being on the panel may alter behaviour. There has been much debate on the challenges of creating representative and/or probability based samples, with some researchers claiming that panels are an unsustainable research method.[21] In spite of these disadvantages, purchase panels are extensively used in marketing research.

Electronic scanner services

Scanner data
Data obtained by passing merchandise over a laser scanner that reads the UPC from the packages.

Although information provided by surveys and purchase and media panels are useful, electronic scanner services have continued to deliver great value to decision makers. **Scanner data** are collected by passing merchandise over a laser scanner that optically reads the bar-coded description (Universal Product Code, or UPC) printed on the merchandise. This code is then linked to the current price held on the computer and used to prepare a sales slip. Information printed on the sales slip includes descriptions as well as prices of all items purchased. Checkout scanners have revolutionised packaged goods marketing research. A simplified version of electronic scanning is the HomeScan service provided by ACNielsen. For this system the recruited panel members use a barcode scanner at home to record their purchases after each shopping trip.

Three types of scanner data are available: **volume tracking data**, **scanner panels** and **scanner panels with pay TV**. Volume tracking data provide information on purchases by brand, size, price and flavour or formulation, based on sales data collected from the check-out scanner. This information is collected nationally from a sample of supermarkets (rather than individual supermarkets tracking their customers' purchases using loyalty cards) with electronic scanners. In scanner panels, each household member is given an ID card. Panel members present their ID card at the checkout counter each time they shop. The checker scans their ID and each item of that customer's order. The information is stored by day of week and time of day.

Scanner panels with pay TV combine panels with new technologies growing out of the pay TV industry. Households on these panels subscribe to one of the pay TV systems in their market. By means of a pay TV 'split', the researcher targets different advertisements into the homes of the panel members. For example, half the households may view test advertisement A during the 6 p.m. newscast while the other half view test advertisement B. These panels allow researchers to conduct fairly controlled experiments in a relatively natural environment. It is possible to combine store-level scanner data with scanner panel data to do integrated analyses of consumer behaviour.

Scanner data are useful for a variety of purposes.[22] National volume tracking data can be used for tracking sales, prices and distribution, for modelling, and for analysing early warning signals. Scanner panels with pay TV can be used for testing new products, repositioning products, analysing promotional mixes, and making advertising decisions, including budget, copy and media, and pricing. These panels provide researchers with a unique controlled environment for the manipulation of marketing variables.

Scanner data have an obvious advantage over surveys and panels: they reflect purchasing behaviour that is not subject to interviewing, recording, memory or expert biases. The record of purchases obtained by scanners is complete and unbiased by price sensitivity, because the panelist is not required to be particularly conscious of price levels and changes. Another advantage is that in-store variables such as pricing, promotions and displays are part of the dataset. The data are also likely to be current and can be obtained quickly. Finally, scanner panels with pay TV provide a highly controlled testing environment.

A major weakness of scanner data can be a lack of representativeness. National volume tracking data may not be projectable on to the total population. Not all purchases are scanned in the manner of large supermarkets. Many types of retail and wholesale outlets, which consumers may physically or virtually shop at, may well be excluded. Scanner data provide product and media behavioural and sales information; they do not provide information on underlying attitudes and preferences and the reasons for specific choices. The following example illustrates how panel and scanning organisations like Nielsen make panels work.

Volume tracking data
Scanner data that provide information on purchases by brand, size, price and flavour or formulation.

Scanner panels
Scanner data where panel members are identified by an ID card, allowing information about each panel member's purchases to be stored with respect to the individual shopper.

Scanner panels with pay TV
The combination of a scanner panel with manipulations of the advertising that is being broadcast by pay TV companies.

Real research | **ACNielsen Worldwide Consumer Panel Services**

ACNielsen Homescan was launched in 1989, the first continuous consumer panel in Europe to use in-home barcode scanners to collect data. The panel is regionally and demographically balanced to represent the household population and captures consumer package goods purchases brought back into the home, including variable weight and non bar-coded fresh products. Each household provides daily information on their purchases of consumer goods for in-home use. Collected on a continuous basis, it is possible to measure the ongoing changes and interactions of households' purchasing behaviour across all grocery and fresh foods products. Homescan incorporates both descriptive and diagnostic information. Consumer panel data provides information on purchaser attributes, purchase behaviour, market penetration, share of category requirements, brand loyalty, brand switching and parallel consumption plus a wide range of other powerful analytics. The database provides insights into why consumers behave the way they do. Subscribers can get answers to questions specific to their brand such as: How many households purchased a product on a trial basis? Did they return later to purchase again? What did buyers purchase before a marketing campaign, what did they purchase subsequently? Where did buyers of a brand come from? What else do buyers purchase? Where else do buyers shop? How store-loyal are shoppers? What is the demographic composition of buyers? How do lifestyles and attitudes impact purchasing behaviour?

Syndicated data from institutions

Retail audits

As Figure 3.4 shows, syndicated data are available from retailers as well as industrial firms. A retail audit is a regular survey that monitors sales of products via a sample of retail outlets. Retail audit data allows decision makers to analyse their product structure, pricing and distribution policy, and their position in relation to their competition. (See the example of the work of German marketing research company GfK at **http://wwwqs.gfk.com** which conducts retail and wholesale audits in the following sectors: consumer electronics, IT and office equipment, telecommunications, domestic appliances, photographic equipment, DIY/gardening products and entertainment hardware/software.)

Audit
A data collection process derived from physical records or performing inventory analysis. Data are collected personally by the researcher, or by representatives of the researcher, and are based on counts usually of physical objects rather than people.

The most popular means of obtaining data from retailers is an **audit**, a formal examination and verification of product movement carried out by examining physical records or analysing inventory. Retailers who participate in the audit receive basic reports and cash payments from the audit service, but the main beneficiary is the brand owner who wishes to monitor the sales of their brand through many retail outlets. Audit data focus on the products or services sold through the outlets or the characteristics of the outlets themselves.

The uses of retail audit data include: (1) determining the size of the total market and the distribution of sales by type of outlet, region or city; (2) assessing brand shares and competitive activity; (3) identifying shelf space allocation and inventory problems; (4) analysing distribution problems; (5) developing sales potentials and forecasts; (6) developing and monitoring promotional allocations based on sales volume. Thus, audit data can be particularly helpful in understanding and developing the environmental context should further stages of research need to be administered.

Audits provide relatively accurate information on the movement of many different products. Furthermore, this information can be broken down by a number of important variables, such as brand, type of outlet and size of market. Audits may have limited coverage; not all categories of particular products or brands are necessarily included. In addition, audit information may not be timely or current, particularly compared with scanner data. At one time, there could be a two-month gap between the completion of the audit cycle and the publication of reports. Another disadvantage is that, unlike scanner data, audit data cannot be linked to consumer characteristics. In fact, there may even be a problem in relating audit data to advertising expenditures and other marketing efforts. Some of these limitations are overcome in online audit panels. GfK Retail and Technology (**www.gfkrt.com**) performs online tracking in over 80 countries and covers markets such as tourism, optics and fashion. The following example illustrates the nature and value of its work for fashion brands.

GfK FashionLife

GfK FashionLife offers market figures and the fast, fact-based delivery of detailed information to allow companies to steer their performance accordingly. The power to benchmark products and markets allows fashion companies to maintain a firm grip on insights by channel. Reporting includes information on sales volume, sales value and average prices and forms the basis for a continuous service for both retailers and suppliers within the fashion industry. Reports are available from top level aggregation down to single product level and are customisable according to individual client needs. Delivery is on a monthly or weekly basis. Fashion products

tracked by GfK FashionLife include: watches, luggage, jewellery, clothing and shoes, leisure, home textiles. GfK pitches the benefits of its online retail audit for fashion businesses as: fast weekly data directly from retailers; high levels of granularity in reporting; a basis for decisions on product assortments and ranges; a platform for understanding performance against competitors and the impact price has on market share; additional information to help target advertising and promotional activities; help in maximising stock efficiency.

Industry services

These provide syndicated data about industrial firms, businesses and other institutions. Examples of these include Datamonitor, Bureau Van Dijk and Dun and Bradstreet. The Datamonitor Group (**www.datamonitor.com**) is a provider of global business information, delivering data, analysis and opinion across the automotive, consumer packaged goods, energy and sustainability, financial services, logistics and express, pharmaceutical and healthcare, retail, sourcing, technology and telecoms industries. It supports over 6000 of the world's leading companies in strategic and operational decision making. Its market intelligence products and services are delivered online. Bureau Van Dijk (**www.bvdinfo.com**) provides a range of company information products that is co-published with many information providers. Its product range includes databases of company information and marketing intelligence for individual countries, regions and the world. Van Dijk's global database, ORBIS (**www.BvDInfo.com/Orbis**), combines information from around 100 sources and covers approaching 65 million companies. It also provides e-publishing solutions, based on open and flexible platforms, and offers features such as search, secure delivery, e-commerce, rendering systems and hosting. Van Dijk's clients include publishers of books, scientific, technological and medical journals, news, directories and reference guides. Dun and Bradstreet (**www.dnb.com**, but also look for specific countries e.g. Netherlands **http://dbnetherlands .dnb.com**) has a global commercial database that contains more than 151 million business records. Through the D&B Worldwide Network its clients gain access to perhaps the world's largest global commercial business information database. It has global data coverage on business records in over 190 countries. To help ensure the accuracy and completeness of its information, it updates its database over 1.5 million times a day.

Information provided by industrial services is useful for sales management decisions, including identifying potential target markets, defining territories and measuring market potential by geographic areas. It can also support communications decisions such as targeting prospects, allocating communications budgets, selecting media and measuring communications effectiveness. Given the rich competitive intelligence available, these sources of information are also useful for segmentation and positioning decisions. Industry services represent an important contextual source of support in defining the environmental context for management decisions and any subsequent bespoke marketing research. They are particularly valuable for researchers who aim to measure and understand the networks and relationships of industrial firms.

International marketing research

A wide variety of secondary data are available for international marketing research.[23] As in the case of domestic research, the problem is not a lack of data but the potential overabundance of information. The international researcher has to work through an array of potential sources to find accurate, up-to-date and relevant information. Evaluation of secondary data is even more critical for international than for domestic projects. Different sources report different values for a given statistic, such as the GDP, because of differences in the way the unit is defined. Measurement units may not be equivalent across countries. In France, for example, some workers are still paid a 13-monthly salary each year as an automatic bonus, resulting in a measurement construct that is different from those in other countries.[24] The accuracy of secondary data may also vary from country to country. Data from highly industrialised countries in Europe tend to be more accurate than those from developing nations.

One of the more significant developments in international research relates to how research companies in fast growing economies are using advanced technological solutions. For example, one of the

staple methods in traditional syndicated research has been the consumer diary. Encouraging participants to fully engage in and complete their diaries has always been a challenge. In the following example, the diary is completed as a blog and is enhanced with images, allowing participants to express their feelings in novel and enjoyable ways. Though this example delivered information support to an individual client, the approach could be used to great effect in syndicated research.

| Real research | **Chinese real estate product development[25]** |

Vanke (**www.vanke.com**), founded in 1984, is one of the leading real estate developers in China. Vanke used to be designer-orientated with its product-developing process. What Vanke hoped would make its properties stand out was its designers' capabilities in design. Vanke felt that targeting potential customers after the product had been shaped posed a substantial risk. Therefore, Vanke selected Horizon Research (**www.horizon-china.com**) to cooperate in exploring a customer-orientated development model in residential properties. The Horizon and Vanke research team started its research by observing the 'high-powered, high-stress' young generation. The team started the project by understanding the needs of designers, rather than consumers. Designers typically were frustrated that marketing research findings do not communicate to them in ways that they find useful. What are useful to designers are not direct questions, such as how large should an apartment be, how many bathrooms or bedrooms, but how they are going to live in the apartment, what furniture and decorations they are going to use, how they relate themselves to each space and what they dream for the apartment. In order to visualise such needs, 40 young people in Beijing, Shanghai and Guangzhou were asked to keep diaries in the following format:

- To write two blogs on the topics of 'ideal life' and 'ideal home'.
- To take photographs of their favourite surroundings and products, and provide brief comments on each photograph.

Following the diary, the most enjoyable environment for participants was chosen to conduct a relaxed in-depth interview to learn of their ideal choice and preferences from their blogs and photos. The researchers took photos and conducted interviews whilst visiting the participant's current home; this helped them to understand their lives and unmet needs. The participants' needs were translated into the language that designers could understand for a more precise concept-generation process. The concepts based on this research were adopted and localised in many cities, and finally became homes, sold with more competitive advantage. This project not only demonstrated a customer-orientated product development process but also helped Vanke to form a customer-orientated design culture. Horizon continued to work with Vanke on a series of product development projects such as 'Little Kid Family' and 'Active Adult'.

Linking the array of databases that may be held within organisations with survey data and/or other forms of quantitative and qualitative data has transformed international marketing research. Within individual companies, customers may be analysed from CRM systems within individual countries, showing different patterns of behaviour between different regions or cities and relating that behaviour to their marketing activities. When a company operates across borders, country differences become just another geographical variable.

Ethics in marketing research

The ethical issues related to the growth of digital measurement of consumers in creating secondary data should be considered. A lot of attention has been focused on the array of digital measurement tools and how much secondary data is collected, analysed and reported online. Relatively less consideration has been given to people's acceptance of these devices and processes. The challenge that researchers face is overcoming the perception, and in many case the practices, that digital measurements pose as a privacy threat.[26]

From the emergence of marketing research as a discipline, researchers have been confronted by ethical challenges related to the use of customer data. Research associations such as ESOMAR have been very clear in their codes of conduct to draw a distinction between direct marketing activities (e.g. using customer data in CRM systems) and bona fide marketing research. With the growth of social networking, blogging and online communities, protecting the anonymity of research participants has become far more problematic.[27] Technological advances in computing power, mobile devices and storage media carry many benefits, but they too add risk that must be mitigated. The risks posed by online and social media research include identity theft, harassment, defamation of character, and maintaining client confidentiality.

Given the phenomenal growth and power of CRM, and other databases used in marketing and the support they offer to decision makers, they are here to stay. They can be seen as competing with marketing research approaches to deliver what may be seen as more relevant and better value consumer insights, or they can be seen as complementary. With well-planned traditional marketing research integrated with database analyses, the strategic power of consumer and market analyses can be phenomenal. If marketers abuse their knowledge of consumers, they stand to do great harm to their brands and corporate image. Consumers are now more aware of how valuable knowledge of their behaviour is and how it is used by marketers.[28] They are willing to trade this knowledge for specific rewards and mutual respect. Decision makers and researchers should be aware of the rewards and respect expected by consumers and the dangers of abusing the knowledge that is imparted to them.

Digital developments in marketing research

Secondary data can be obtained from an ever increasing number of vendors. More data sources can be accessed online with excellent indexing facilities to locate particular subjects, companies and individuals. Government data for the European Community and for individual countries through to regional and city councils can be accessed online. The sources and quantity of data have grown, but this should be clearly distinguished from the quality of data. Being able to evaluate the quality of secondary data is vital in understanding what may be used to support specific decisions and/or the design and implementation of further primary data collection and analyses.

It is not only the quantity and quality of data that should concern the researcher but also how Internet developments have shaped the expectations of decision makers. More analytics, insights and future outlooks are demanded by decision makers to help them better understand their customers, the marketplace and the overall business environment. Researchers can be expected to help understand the macro business operating environment, monitor market trends, conduct competitive analyses, answer business questions, identify business opportunities and assess potential risks.[29] Given this wider

job scope, gathering and validating good secondary data and marketing intelligence is seen as a vital skill for researchers. Conducting quality desk research, gathering syndicated reports, news clippings, key performance indicators and customer behaviour data and being able to integrate and interpret these sources are vital to actionable marketing research. Researchers may have to see themselves as 'data curators' or aggregators of data, integrating disparate types of data with our more traditional lines of enquiry and make strategic sense of it for decision makers.[30]

Researchers also now have access to powerful tools and techniques enabling them to: engage consumers via social media tools; listen to audiences by mining social media; reach an increasingly more sought after, younger generation of consumers through social media, and be able to do this across international markets. With the advent of Twitter and social networks including Facebook, user-generated content (UGC) is becoming increasingly accessible and intertwined with the daily lives of consumers across the globe. Consequently, the way researchers can tap into consumer views online has changed enormously. Social media research is not a fad, but a fundamental shift in the way researchers can communicate and gather information. Thanks to the exceptionally rapid growth of social media, the Internet offers limitless opportunities for researchers to connect with vast populations of diverse people who are spending more of their free time online every day. Blogs, communities and various Web 2.0 mechanisms are empowering the transformation of marketing research into an engaging and iterative process. Using these techniques as secondary data sources enables researchers to gather more in-depth insights in real time while observing consumers in their natural habitat and enhancing the innovation process.[31] In the context of evaluating internally generated secondary data, it is worth considering, for example, the extent to which the content of a company's Facebook page would constitute a valuable secondary data resource for the researcher.

Summary

In contrast to primary data, which originate with the researcher for the specific purpose of the problem at hand, secondary data are data originally collected for other purposes. Secondary data can be obtained quickly and are relatively inexpensive though not free, especially for accurate, high quality data. Secondary data have limitations, and should be carefully evaluated to determine their appropriateness for the problem at hand. The evaluation criteria consist of specifications, error, currency, objectivity, nature and dependability.

A wealth of information exists within organisations that commission research. This information constitutes internal secondary data. Internal secondary data in the form of databases and CRM data are radically changing how marketing decision making is supported. There is much debate as to whether the use of databases is compatible with traditional techniques of marketing research. Handled with the professional acumen that researchers have displayed for many years, the database presents great opportunities for the researcher. For the researcher, databases help to build profiles of consumers, linked to the products, communications and distribution methods those consumers favour. Databases present opportunities to experiment in 'one big laboratory', build models of consumer behaviour, develop an understanding of the gaps in knowledge of consumers and make links between behavioural and attitudinal data.

External data are generated by sources outside the organisation. These data exist in the form of published (printed) material, online and offline databases, or information made available by syndicated services. Published external sources may be broadly classified as general business data or government data. General business sources comprise guides, directories, indexes and statistical data. Government sources may be broadly categorised as census data and other data. Online databases may be online or offline. Both online and offline databases may be further classified as bibliographic, numeric, full-text, directory or specialised databases.

Syndicated sources are companies that collect and sell common pools of data designed to serve a number of clients. Syndicated sources can be classified based on the unit of measurement (households and consumers or institutions). Household and consumer data may be obtained via surveys, purchase or media panels, or electronic scanner services. When institutions are the unit of measurement, the data may be obtained from retailers or industrial units. It is desirable to combine information obtained from different secondary sources.

Several specialised sources of secondary data are useful for conducting international marketing research. The evaluation of secondary data becomes even more critical, however, because the usefulness and accuracy of these data can vary widely. The ethics of using databases provokes much debate in the marketing research industry. As many research practitioners grow more accustomed to using databases, marketing research guidelines and codes of practice are being developed to reflect the good practices that exist in many companies. These codes of practice are being constantly updated to reflect technological developments and the changing expectations of consumers, decision makers and researchers. The growth of online sources of externally generated secondary data has exerted demands upon researchers to be able to access, integrate and interpret this data. The emergence of social media research techniques has generated not only new research techniques but also new forms of data that could raise questions about what constitutes 'secondary data'.

Questions

1   What are the differences between primary data and secondary data?

2   What are the relative advantages and disadvantages of secondary data?

3   At what stages of the marketing research process can secondary data be used?

4   Why is it important to locate and analyse secondary data before progressing to primary data?

5   What is the difference between internal and external secondary data?

6   What is a customer database? Why may a researcher wish to analyse the data held in a customer database?

7   If you had two sources of secondary data for a project, the first being dependable but out of date, the second not dependable but up to date, which would you prefer?

8   Explain what an online panel is, giving examples of different types of panel. What are the advantages and disadvantages of online panels?

9   What is an audit? Describe the uses, advantages and disadvantages of audits.

10 How does the compilation of different types of data help researchers engaged in international research projects?

11 What are the ethical challenges and dilemmas for researchers using data from customer databases?

12 In what way may the use of data generated through social media sources be considered as secondary data?

Exercises

1   Select an industry of your choice. Using secondary sources, obtain industry sales and the sales of the major firms in that industry for the past year. Estimate the market shares of each major firm. From another source where this work may have already been completed, e.g. Mintel, compare and contrast the estimates:

(a) To what extent do they agree?

(b) If there are differences in the estimates, what may account for these differences?

2   Select an industry of your choice. Write a report on the potential growth in that industry and the factors that are driving that growth. Use both secondary data and intelligence sources to build your case.

3 Call in at a supermarket or store that operates a reward or loyalty card scheme that requires you to apply for membership. Pick up an application form and examine the nature of questions you are expected to answer.

(a) What marketing research use can be made of the data collected from this application form?

(b) Evaluate the design of this form and make recommendations on how the nature of questions could be improved.

4 Visit the Central Statistics Office Ireland website (**www.cso.ie/links**) and follow a link to the national statistics office in a country of your choice. Write a report about the secondary data available from this office that would be useful to a national housing developer for the purpose of formulating its marketing strategy.

5 In a small group discuss the following issues: 'What is the significance and limitations of government census data for researchers?' and 'If, on ethical grounds, researchers refused to utilise the benefits of marketing databases, what inherent weaknesses may exist in their research designs?'

Notes

1. Baumann, C., Hamin, R.T. and Toll, R., 'Convergence or divergence of the Asian market: Is regionalism leading to regionalisation', ESOMAR, *Asia Pacific* Melbourne (2011).

2. Patzer, G.L., *Using Secondary Data in Marketing Research* (Westport, CT: Greenwood Publishing Group, 1995); Stewart, D.W. *Secondary Research: Information Sources and Methods* (Beverley Hills: Sage Publications, 1984) 23–33.

3. For applications of secondary data, see Allen, L. and Spencer, N., 'Managing knowledge, maximising returns – Revolutions in business information management', ESOMAR, *Congress,* Montreux (Sept. 2009); Houston, M. B., 'Assessing the validity of secondary data proxies for marketing constructs', *Journal of Business Research,* 57 (2) (2004) 154–161; Kotabe, M., 'Using Euromonitor database in international marketing research', *Journal of the Academy of Marketing Science,* 30 (2) (Spring 2002), 172.

4. Macer, T., 'Conference notes – Making technology decisions in combining attitudinal and behavioural data', *International Journal of Market Research,* 51 (4) (2009).

5. Bakken, D.G., 'Riding the Value Shift in Market Research: Only the paranoid survive', ESOMAR Best Paper Overall, *Congress Odyssey,* Athens (Sept. 2010).

6. Havermans, J., 'Knowing everything a customer wants', *Research World,* (Jan. 2006), 18–19.

7. Allen, L. and Green, C., 'Connecting Insight with the Organisation: Knowledge management online', Market Research Society, *Annual Conference* (2006); Fries, J.R., 'Library support for industrial marketing research', *Industrial Marketing Management,* 11 (February 1982), 47–51.

8. Tasgal, A., 'Inspiring Insight through Trends', Market Research Society, *Annual Conference* (2009).

9. Jackson, M., Gider, A., Feather, C., Smith, K., Fry, A., Brooks-Kieffer, J., Vidas, C.D. and Nelson, R., 'Electronic Resources & Libraries, 2nd Annual Conference 2007', *Library Hi Tech News,* 24 (4) (2007), 4–17.

10. Saw, G., Lui, W.W. and Yu, F., '2010: a library odyssey', *Library Management,* 29 (1/2) (2008), 51–66; Tenopir, C., 'Links and bibliographic databases', *Library Journal,* 126 (4) (1 March 2001), 34–35.

11. Lekakos, G., 'It's Personal: Extracting lifestyle indicators in digital television advertising', *Journal of Advertising Research,* 49 (4), (December 2009), 404–18.

12. Bennett, G., Ross, M., Uyenco, B. and Willerer, T., 'Lifestyles of the ad averse: a proposal for an advertising evaluation framework', ESOMAR, *Worldwide Multi Media Measurement (WM3),* Dublin (June 2007).

13. Nyilasy, G. and Reid, L.N., 'The academician-practitioner gap in advertising', *International Journal of Advertising,* 26 (4) (2007), 425–45.

14. Peacock, J. and Bennett, M., 'It can be measured', *Research World* (Sept. 2005), 71.

15. ESOMAR, 'Global Market Research, ESOMAR Industry Report' (2010), 104.

16. Bryant, J.A. and Christensen, L., 'I Want MySpace! Helping an industry innovator (re)innovate', ESOMAR, *Online Research,* Berlin (Oct. 2010).

17. Roberts, A. and Bristowe, L., 'Targeting ad responders', *Admap Magazine,* Issue 486 (Sept. 2007).

18. Comley, P., 'Panel management and panel quality issues – understanding the online panellist', ESOMAR, *Conference on Panel Research,* Budapest (April 2005); Eunkyu, L., Hu, M.Y. and Toh, R.S., 'Are consumer survey results distorted? Systematic impact of behavioural frequency and duration on survey response errors', *Journal of Marketing Research* 37 (1) (February 2000), 125–133.

19. Clancy, K.J., 'Brand confusion', *Harvard Business Review*, 80 (3) (March 2002), 22; Sudman, S., *On the Accuracy of Recording of Consumer Panels II, Learning Manual* (New York: Neal-Schumen, 1981).

20. Sassinot-Uny, L. and Gadeib, A., 'Panel satisfaction index. Quality target for online access panels owners?' ESOMAR, *Panel Research*, Orlando (Oct. 2007).

21. de Jong, K., 'CSI Berlin: The Strange Case of the Death of Panels', ESOMAR, *Online Research*, Berlin, (Oct. 2010).

22. Examples of scanner data applications include González-Benito, O., Martínez-Ruiz, M.P. and Mollá-Descals, A., 'Latent segmentation using store-level scanner data', *Journal of Product & Brand Management*, 17 (1) (2008), 37–47; Lemon, K.W. and Nowlis, S.M., 'Developing synergies between promotions and brands in different price-quality tiers', *Journal of Marketing Research*, 39 (2) (May 2002), 171–185; Chintagunta, P.K., 'Investigating category pricing behaviour at a retail chain', *Journal of Marketing Research*, 39 (2) (May 2002), 141–54.

23. Imms, M., 'So, what are we talking about? What the 50th anniversary collection of conference papers tell us about market research in the UK today', Market Research Society, *Annual Conference*, (2007).

24. Chisnall, P.M., 'Marketing research: state of the art perspectives', *Journal of the Market Research Society*, 44 (1) (1st Quarter 2002), 122–25.

25. Zhang, G.J., Tan, M.O. and Minghui, Z., 'Market Research: The pathway from consumer needs to final products', ESOMAR, *Asia Pacific*, Kuala Lumpur (April 2010).

26. Kachhi, D. and Link, M.W., 'Too Much Information: Does the Internet Dig Too Deep?' *Journal of Advertising Research*, 49 (1) (March 2009), 74–81.

27. Stark, D., 'From social engineering to social networking – privacy issues when conducting research in the web 2.0 world', ESOMAR, *Congress*, Montreux (Sept. 2009).

28. Nancarrow, C., Tinson, J. and Brace, I., 'Consumer savvy and intergenerational effects', *International Journal of Market Research*, 50 (6) (2008), 731–55.

29. Kung, A. and Tse, G., 'The evolving role of in-house market research professionals: From "reactive" to "proactive",' ESOMAR, *Asia Pacific*, Beijing (April 2009).

30. Woodnutt, T. and Owen, R., 'The research industry needs to embrace radical change in order to thrive and survive in the digital era', Market Research Society, *Annual Conference* (2010).

31. Case, S., 'How social media is democratizing research', ESOMAR: *Congress Odyssey*, Athens (Sept. 2010).

4 Qualitative research methods

| Stage 1 |
| Problem definition |

| Stage 2 |
| Research approach developed |

| Stage 3 |
| Research design developed |

| **Stage 4** |
| Fieldwork or data collection |

| Stage 5 |
| Data integrity and analysis |

| Stage 6 |
| Report preparation and presentation |

Qualitative research can offer great insights in understanding the richness, depth and complexity of consumers.

Objectives

After reading this chapter, you should be able to:

1 explain the difference between qualitative and quantitative research;

2 describe why qualitative research is used in marketing research;

3 describe focus group discussions, citing their advantages, disadvantages and applications;

4 describe alternative ways of conducting qualitative research in group settings;

5 describe in-depth interview techniques, citing their advantages, disadvantages and applications;

6 describe projective techniques and compare association, completion, construction and expressive techniques;

7 understand the nature and application of ethnographic approaches;

8 understand the challenges faced by international qualitative researchers;

9 understand the ethical dilemmas faced by qualitative researchers.

10 describe how digital developments offer distinct advantages and challenges for qualitative researchers.

Overview

Researchers may undertake qualitative research to help define a research problem, to support quantitative, descriptive or causal research designs or as a design in its own right. Qualitative research is often used to generate hypotheses and identify variables that should be included in quantitative approaches. It may be used after or in conjunction with quantitative approaches where illumination of statistical findings is needed. In some cases qualitative research designs are adopted in isolation, after secondary data sources have been thoroughly evaluated or even in an iterative process with secondary data sources. In this chapter, we discuss the differences between qualitative and quantitative research and their distinct roles in marketing research. We present reasons for conducting qualitative research and a means to classify methods. This is followed by descriptions and evaluations of the main methods used to conduct qualitative research.

The most widely used qualitative research method is the focus group. The advantages and disadvantages and the manner in which focus groups are planned and conducted is presented. The use of online groups are described and evaluated. The nature of the in-depth interview is evaluated followed by an approach to conduct and in-depth interviewing. The role of the in-depth interviewer is described and the advantages and disadvantages of the approach are summarised. Projective techniques and their link to the use of games in conducting research are evaluated. The applications of these techniques are detailed, followed by an evaluation of their advantages and disadvantages. Ethnographic approaches are described and evaluated. The role of the ethnographer and how the approach has been developed to incorporate visual ethnography and netnography are summarised. There is an overall summary of the relative strengths and weaknesses of qualitative methods under the headings of 'focus groups', 'in-depth interviews', 'projective techniques' and 'ethnographic techniques'.

The considerations involved in conducting qualitative research when researching international markets are discussed. Several ethical issues that arise in qualitative research are identified. Digital developments are changing the manner in which traditional qualitative research techniques are conducted. In addition, a whole array of new qualitative research techniques are emerging. The challenges and opportunities of conducting qualitative research online are presented.

We begin by presenting an example of the use of qualitative research. This example illustrates the use of digital research approaches in a global context. It further shows how theory may be developed by taking theoretical models developed in one geographical location into a wider context. The underlying factors that shape the behaviour of 'Generation Y consumers' can be obtained by using qualitative methods, creating a rich and in-depth understanding for decision makers.

Real research

How cool brands stay hot: branding to Generation Y[1]

The CRUSH model summarises five aspects that are key in developing branding strategies with Generation Y.[2] The model was developed using data from European consumers. The model components are: **Coolness**: What does it mean to be a cool brand for Generation Y? How does a brand achieve a cool status and why should it bother? **Realness**: Brand authenticity is a key aspect that discerns long-term winning brands from fads. With Generation Y, authenticity is attained in ways beyond traditional approaches of claiming origin, heritage or history. **Uniqueness**: A clear positioning based on a sustainable brand DNA increases impact. Generation Y craves anchor brands in a fragmented world. **Self-identification** with the brand: Generation Y only feels emotionally connected with a brand when it feels like a friend to them. This implies that a brand should reflect their diverse lifestyles. **Happiness**: Generation Y brands know how to leverage from positive emotions and avoid arousing negative ones.

MTV Networks wanted to find out if the CRUSH model translated regionally around the world. Could it explain why youth in America, Asia, Africa, and Eastern and Western Europe perceive something as 'cool' or 'likeable'? Exploring the CRUSH dimensions in a qualitative manner helped MTV to shape its brand positioning and focus. In order to do this InSites Consulting (**www.insites.eu**) and MTV Networks (**www.mtv.com**) created 'Crushed Ice', a global online community of influential youth discussing whatever they were observing in their cities over a six-week period. They worked 150 carefully selected urban recruits, aged 18–29 years, living in 15 cities around the world: Amsterdam, Berlin, Cape Town, Dubai, Istanbul, London, Mumbai, New York, Paris, Rio, San Francisco, Shanghai, St Petersburg, Stockholm and Sydney. All participants had to pass a TOEFL test to make sure they could fluently communicate with each other in English. Open ended questions were used to track their leisure time activities, sports, frequently visited websites and social networks as well as devices owned. Half of the participants were studying, the other half were already working. Each of them had to have an active interest in at least one out of the five discussion topics: shopping and fashion; in-home entertainment (movies, games, technology); going out; food and drinks; travel. The participants from all five continents produced 1,589 posts. The community platform consisted of five different rooms and a blog section. The five rooms in the research community were the following: **We Are Room**, where they got to know the participants, the different cities

they were living in and their cultural background; **Crush Room**, where they tried to understand what products, brands and hotspots they were linking to the CRUSH dimensions. The core idea was to understand the reason why something would be perceived a cool, real, unique, like themselves or bringing happiness as well as to detect which consumer trends are related to each of the different components; **Trend Room**, where participants were asked what trends they could name as well as the ones felt to be completely dead; **Brand Room**, in which participants were confronted with ideas thought to be cool or uncool and their critical view was wanted; **Secret Room**: this was a section of the site only accessible to the participants who were selected as being interested and an expert in one of the five discussion topics.

Primary data: qualitative versus quantitative research

Qualitative research
An unstructured, primarily exploratory design based on small samples, intended to provide depth, insight and understanding.

Quantitative research
Research techniques that seek to quantify data and, typically, apply some form of measurement and statistical analysis.

Primary data are originated by the researcher for the specific purpose of addressing the problem at hand. Primary data may be qualitative or quantitative in nature, as shown in Figure 4.1. Dogmatic positions are often taken in favour of either qualitative research or quantitative research. These positions are founded upon which approach is perceived to give the most accurate and useful measurements or understanding of consumers. The extreme stances on this issue mirror each other. Many quantitative researchers are apt to dismiss qualitative studies completely as giving no valid findings, indeed as being little better than journalistic accounts. They assert that qualitative researchers ignore representative sampling, with their findings based on a single case or only a few cases. Equally adamant are some qualitative researchers who firmly reject statistical and other quantitative methods as yielding shallow or completely misleading information. They believe that to understand cultural values and consumer behaviour, especially in its full contextual richness, requires interviewing or intensive field observation.[3]

The arguments between qualitative and quantitative researchers about their relative strengths and weaknesses can be of real practical value. The nature of marketing decision making encompasses a vast array of problems and types of decision maker. This means that seeking a singular and uniform approach to supporting decision makers by focusing on one approach is futile. Defending qualitative approaches for a particular marketing research problem through the positive benefits it bestows and explaining the negative alternatives of a quantitative approach is healthy, and vice versa. Business and marketing decision makers have always used both approaches and will continue to need both.[4]

Figure 4.1

A classification of marketing research data

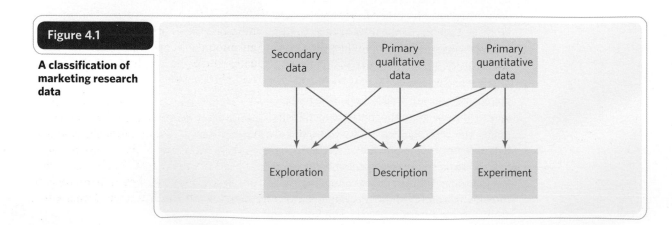

The nature of qualitative research

Qualitative research encompasses a variety of methods that can be applied in a flexible manner. It can enable participants to reflect upon and express their views in a great variety of ways. It can allow researchers to observe consumer behaviour in a great variety of contexts. It seeks to encapsulate the behaviour, experiences and feelings of participants in their own terms and context.[5] Qualitative research is based on at least two intellectual traditions.[6] The first and perhaps most important is the set of ideas and associated methods from the broad area of depth psychology and motivational research.[7] This movement was concerned with the less conscious aspects of the human psyche. It led to a development of methods to gain access to individuals' subconscious and/or unconscious levels. So, while individuals may present a superficial explanation of events to themselves or to others, these methods sought to dig deeper and penetrate the superficial. The second tradition is the set of ideas and associated methods from sociology, social psychology and social anthropology, and the disciplines of ethnography, linguistics and semiology. The emphases here are upon holistic understanding of the world-view of people. The researcher is expected to 'enter' the hearts and minds of those they are researching, to develop an empathy with their experiences and feelings. Both traditions have a concern with developing means of communication between the researcher and those being researched. There can be much interaction between the two broad traditions, which in pragmatic terms allows a wide and rich array of techniques and interpretations of collected data.

Rationale for using qualitative research

It is not always possible, or desirable, to use structured quantitative methods to obtain information from participants or to observe them. Thus, there are several reasons to use qualitative methods. These reasons, either individually or in any combination, explain why certain researchers use qualitative research.

1 *Preferences and/or experience of the researcher.* Just as some researchers enjoy the challenge of using statistical techniques, there are researchers who enjoy the challenges of qualitative methods and the interpretation of diverse types of data. Such researchers have been trained in particular disciplines (e.g. anthropology) that traditionally make use of qualitative research.

2 *Preferences and/or experience of the research user.* Some decision makers are more oriented to receiving support in a qualitative manner. This orientation could come from their training but it could also be due to the type of marketing decisions they have to take. Decision makers working in a creative environment of product design, advertising copy or the development of brand 'personalities', for example, may have a greater preference for data that will feed such design and visually based decisions.

3 *Sensitive information.* Participants may be unwilling to answer or to give truthful answers to certain questions that invade their privacy, embarrass them, or have a negative impact on their ego or status. Techniques that build up an amount of rapport and trust, that allow gentle probing in a manner that suits individual participants, can help researchers get close to participants, and may allow sensitive data to be elicited.

4 *Subconscious feelings.* Participants may be unable to provide accurate answers to questions that tap their subconscious. The values, emotional drives and motivations residing at the subconscious level are disguised from the outer world by rationalisation and other ego defences. For example, a person may have purchased an expensive sports car to overcome feelings of inferiority. But if asked, 'Why did you purchase this sports car?' that person may say, 'I got a great deal', 'My old car was falling apart', or 'I need to impress my customers and clients.' The participants do not have to put words to their deeper emotional drives until researchers approach them!

5   *Complex phenomena.* The nature of what participants are expected to describe may be difficult to capture with structured questions. For example, participants may know what brands of wine they enjoy, what types of music they prefer or what images they regard as being prestigious. They may not be able to clearly explain why they have these feelings or where these feelings are coming from.

6   *The holistic dimension.* The object of taking a holistic outlook in qualitative research is to gain a comprehensive and complete picture of the whole context in which the phenomena of interest occur. In evaluating different forms of consumer behaviour, the researcher seeks to understand the relationship of different contextual environments upon that behaviour. Setting behaviour into context involves placing observations, experiences and interpretations into a larger perspective.[8] This can be done through qualitative observation and interviewing.

7   *Developing new theory.* This is perhaps the most contentious reason for conducting qualitative research. Qualitative researchers may argue that there are severe limitations in conducting experiments upon consumers and that quantitative approaches are limited to elaborating or extending existing theory. The development of 'new' theory through a qualitative approach is called 'grounded theory'.

8   *Interpretation.* Qualitative methods often constitute an important final step in research designs. Surveys often fail to clarify the underlying reasons for a set of findings. Using qualitative methods can help to elaborate and explain underlying reasons in quantitative findings.[9]

Focus group discussions

Focus group
A discussion conducted by a trained moderator among a small group of participants in an unstructured and natural manner.

Moderator
An individual who conducts a focus group interview, by setting the purpose of the interview, questioning, probing and handling the process of discussion.

A **focus group** is a discussion conducted by a trained moderator in a non-structured and natural manner with a small group of participants. A **moderator** leads and develops the discussion. Focus groups are used extensively in new product development, advertising development and image studies. They are so popular that many marketing research practitioners consider this technique synonymous with qualitative research.[10] We describe the salient characteristics of focus groups.[11]

Characteristics

The major characteristics of a focus group are summarised in Table 4.1.

One of the main characteristics and key benefits lies in the amount of creative discussion and other activities that may be generated. Group members have the time to reflect upon the discussion and range of stimuli that may be presented to them. The stimuli may come from other group members and/or from the moderator. Using their intuition and imagination, group members can explain how they feel or behave, in words or other forms of expression that they are comfortable with and using logic that is meaningful to them. The key drawback lies in how intimidating the group scenario may be to certain individuals. Many individuals may be self-conscious in expressing their ideas, feeling they may be ridiculed by others, or they may be shy and unable to express themselves freely in a group. A focus group is generally made up of 6–10 members. Groups of fewer than six are unlikely to generate the momentum and group dynamics necessary for a successful session. Likewise, groups of more than 10 may be too crowded and may not be conducive to a cohesive and natural discussion.[12] Large groups have a tendency to splinter into subgroups as group members compete to get their views across.

A focus group generally should be homogeneous in terms of demographic and socioeconomic characteristics. Commonality among group members avoids interactions and conflicts among group members on side issues.[13] An amount of conflict may draw out issues or get participants to rationalise and defend their views in a number of ways; it can also mean that the discussion does not get stale with everybody agreeing with each other and setting a

Table 4.1	Characteristics of focus groups
Key benefit	Group members 'feed' off each other and creatively reveal ideas that the researcher may not have thought of or dared to tackle
Key drawback	Group members may feel intimidated or shy and may not reveal anything of significance
Group size	6–10
Group composition	Homogeneous, participants pre-screened by questionnaire or through known characteristics
Physical setting	Relaxed, informal atmosphere, 'comfortable' from the perspective of the participants
Stimulating discussion	Use of storyboards, mood boards, products, advertisements, films, music, websites, brochures
Time duration	1.5 to 6 hours
Recording	Audio and visual recording plus notes from observations
Moderator	Observational, interpersonal and communication skills

scenario where genuine disagreement gets stifled. However, major conflicts should and can be avoided by the careful selection of participants. Thus, for many topics, a women's group should not combine married homemakers with small children, young unmarried working women and elderly divorced or widowed women, because their lifestyles may be substantially different. Participants should be carefully screened to meet stated criteria. These criteria are set by the researcher to ensure that participants have had adequate experience with the object or issue being discussed. The most fundamental basis screening of participants is through demographic classification. Common demographic characteristics for determining group composition are: gender, race or ethnicity, age, household location, education level, occupation, income and marital status or family composition. Selecting participants using these characteristics can help increase compatibility but does not guarantee it; their background should be carefully balanced with their experiences.[14] Participants who have already taken part in numerous focus groups should not be included. These so-called professional participants are atypical, and their participation leads to serious validity problems.[15]

The physical setting for the focus group is also important. A relaxed, informal atmosphere helps group members to forget they are being questioned and observed. What is meant by a relaxed, informal atmosphere may change depending upon the type of participant and the subject being tackled. Examples of what 'relaxed and informal' means can include the home of a friend within a particular community, a works café, a village hall, a room in a leisure centre, a meeting room in a hotel or a purpose-built discussion group room. The poor acoustics and hard seats of a works café may not seem relaxed and informal. To group participants, however, it may be the place where they are happy to talk and willing to open up to a moderator. An example of this could be using part of a furniture store to discuss issues around house decoration, furnishings and cleaning or maintaining the home. Such a setting may set a very strong frame of reference to start the focus group and provide lots of stimuli. This example does not mean that all research needs to be conducted *in situ*, but that the technique can be designed to allow the findings from the real and the research environments to inform the overall recommendations.[16] Light refreshments should be served before the session and made available throughout; these become part of the context of relaxation. The nature of these refreshments largely depends upon how long the discussion lasts, the nature of tasks faced by the participants and the ethical viewpoint of the researcher.

Although a focus group may last from one to six hours, duration of one and a half to two hours is typical. When a focus group lasts up to six hours, participants may be performing a series of projective techniques such as building 'mood boards' or 'role playing'. Participants can also be given additional stimuli to discuss such as advertising storyboards and products (new, existing, competitors') to handle and examine. A focus group that lasts for up to six hours will invariably require a break for a meal, but in all circumstances a flow of drinks and snacks should be made available, noting special dietary requirements, e.g. vegan food and drinks.

The lengthy period of discussion in a focus group is needed to establish rapport with the participants, to get them to relax and be in the right frame of mind, and to explore in depth their beliefs, feelings, ideas, attitudes and insights regarding the topics of concern. Focus group discussions are invariably recorded, mostly using audio but often video, for subsequent replay, transcription and analysis. Frequently, where focus groups are conducted in purpose-built studios, decision makers as 'clients' observe the session from an adjacent room using a two-way mirror or through video transmission. However, the existence of the mirror can impact upon everyone's perceptions of what is happening in the discussion. The idea of invisible and unknown people sitting on the other side of the glass can be daunting and inhibiting to participants. Who are they? Why are they there? What are they doing? What are they going to think of me? Participants may not divulge private thoughts, confess to indulgent practices or generally open up if they feel intimidated by the interview process.[17]

The moderator plays a vital role in the success of a focus group. The moderator must establish rapport with the participants and keep the discussion flowing, including the **probing** of participants to elicit insights. Typically, probing differs from questioning in that the probes and the nature of probing are more spontaneous.[18] The moderator may have a central role in the analysis and interpretation of the data. Therefore, the moderator should possess skill, experience, knowledge of the discussion topic, and an understanding of the nature of group dynamics.

Probing
A motivational technique used when asking questions to induce the participants to enlarge on, clarify or explain their answers.

Advantages and disadvantages of focus groups

Focus groups offer several advantages over other data collection techniques. These may be summarised by the ten Ss:[19]

1 *Synergy.* Putting a group of people together will produce a wider range of information, insight and ideas than will individual responses secured privately.

2 *Snowballing.* A bandwagon effect often operates in a group discussion in that one person's comment triggers a chain reaction from the other participants. This process facilitates a very creative process where new ideas can be developed, justified and critically examined.

3 *Stimulation.* Usually after a brief introductory period, the participants want to express their ideas and expose their feelings as the general level of excitement over the topic increases in the group.

4 *Security.* Because the participants' feelings may be similar to those of other group members, they feel comfortable and are therefore willing to 'open up' and reveal thoughts where they may have been reluctant if they were on their own.

5 *Spontaneity.* Because participants are not required to answer specific questions, their responses can be spontaneous and unconventional and should therefore provide an accurate idea of their views.

6 *Serendipity.* Ideas are more likely to arise unexpectedly in a group than in an individual interview. There may be issues that the moderator had not thought of. The dynamics of the group can allow these issues to develop and be discussed. Group members, to great effect, may clearly and forcibly ask questions that the moderator may be reluctant to ask.

7   *Specialisation.* Because a number of participants are involved simultaneously, the use of a highly trained, but expensive, moderator is justified.

8   *Scientific scrutiny.* The group discussion allows close scrutiny of the data collection process in that observers can witness the session and it can be recorded for later analysis. Many individuals can be involved in the validation and interpretation of the collected data, the whole process can be very transparent.

9   *Structure.* The group discussion allows for flexibility in the topics covered and the depth with which they are treated. The structure can match the logical structure of issues from the participants' perspective as well as the language and expressions they are comfortable with.

10 *Speed.* Since a number of individuals are being interviewed at the same time, data collection and analysis can proceed relatively quickly. This advantage has become even more pronounced with the development of e-groups.

Disadvantages of focus groups may be summarised by the five Ms:

1   *Misjudgement.* Focus group results can be more easily misjudged than the results of other data collection techniques. The specific direction of questioning and the ultimate interpretation of findings can be susceptible to the bias of the moderator and other researchers working on a project.

2   *Moderation.* Sometimes focus groups can be difficult to moderate. Much depends upon the 'chemistry' of the group in terms of how group members get on with each other and draw ideas and explanations from each other. The quality of the results depends upon how well the discussion is managed and ultimately on the skills of the moderator.

3   *Messiness.* The unstructured nature of the responses makes coding, analysis and interpretation difficult in comparison with the much more structured approach of quantitative techniques.

4   *Misrepresentation.* Focus group results concentrate on evaluating distinct target groups, describing them and contrasting them to other groups or types of participant. Trying to generalise much wider groups can be misleading.

5   *Meeting.* There are many problems in getting potential participants to agree to take part in a focus group discussion. Even when they have agreed to participate, there are problems in getting focus group participants together at the same time. Running online e-groups has helped to resolve these problems to a great extent and is one of the main factors in the growth of this approach.

Planning and conducting focus groups

The procedure for planning and conducting focus groups is described in Figure 4.2.

Planning begins with an examination of the marketing research problem(s) and objectives. Given the problem definition, the objectives of using focus groups should be clarified. There should be a clear understanding of what information can be elicited and what the limitations of the technique are. The next step is to develop a list of issues, or **topic guide**, that are to be tackled in the focus groups. This list may be a series of specific questions but is more likely to be a set of broad issues that can be developed into questions or probes as the focus group actually takes place. Specific questions may be of help to the moderator who feels that a consistent set of points needs to be presented to different groups in order to allow clear comparisons to be made. Specific questions also act as a 'prop' when the discussion is failing; indeed some group participants may initially feel that their role is to react to specific questions. However,

Topic guide
A list of topics, questions and probes that are used by a moderator to help manage a focus group discussion.

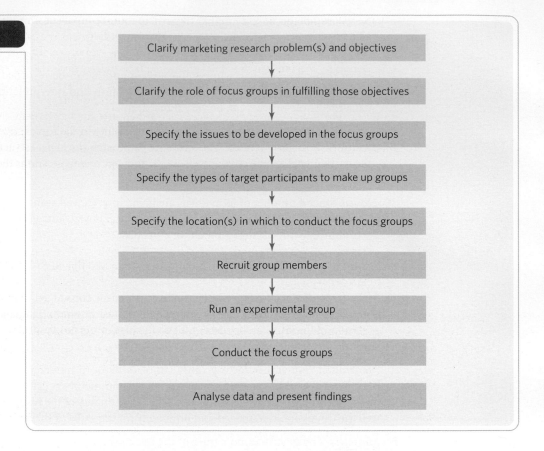

Figure 4.2

Procedure for planning and conducting focus groups

Clarify marketing research problem(s) and objectives

Clarify the role of focus groups in fulfilling those objectives

Specify the issues to be developed in the focus groups

Specify the types of target participants to make up groups

Specify the location(s) in which to conduct the focus groups

Recruit group members

Run an experimental group

Conduct the focus groups

Analyse data and present findings

treating the whole discussion as a means to present set questions may stifle the creativity and spontaneity that are the hallmarks of successful focus groups. The moderator should open the discussion with a general *introductory question* to make participants comfortable with the subject and the purpose of the research. This question should encourage conversation and interaction among the participants. It should not be threatening, it may even question in the third person, i.e. not asking participants what they do or think, and as such it may not be critical to the analysis, though there can be much revealed at this point. The discussion moves on to one or two *transition questions*, which move the discussion towards the key questions and issues. Transition questions help participants to envision the topic in a broader scope. Through these questions, participants become more aware of their fellow participants. Transition questions can ask participants to go into more depth about their experiences and uses of a product, making the connection between the participant and the topic under investigation.[20] The moderator can then move on to the *key questions* developing specific questions, issues and probes that can advance as the moderator tunes into the dynamics of the group. There may be additional, new issues that develop and, indeed, issues that group members do not see as being appropriate, and these can be discussed. The emphasis should be upon an evolution and learning process rather than administering a consistent set of questions.

The types of group members to take part in the discussions are then specified. From this specification, a questionnaire to screen potential participants is prepared. Typical information obtained from the questionnaire includes product familiarity and knowledge, usage behaviour, attitudes towards and participation in focus groups, and standard demographic characteristics. With the types of participants specified, consideration must be taken of what would make them relaxed and comfortable, balanced in both a physical and psychological sense.

Having decided on the location of the focus groups, the actual recruitment of participants progresses. This is one of the most difficult tasks, as potential participants may be sceptical of what may happen at the group, sometimes fearing that they are exposing themselves to a hard-sell campaign of broadband services or home improvements! If participants have attended a focus group beforehand, the process of recruitment is easier, but getting the right types of participant together at the right place and time can prove difficult. With the screening questionnaire, recruitment may take place on a face-to-face basis through street interviews or through database details by email or phone. Even when individuals have said that they will participate in the group, a follow-up is necessary to remind and motivate group members.

Group participants have to be rewarded for their attendance. Usually they enjoy the experience immensely once they are there, but that does not ensure that they attend in the first place. Attendance can be rewarded with cash, a donation to charity or a gift. The following example illustrates the difficulties involved in recruitment and a researcher's creative solution to the problem.

Real research	**So how do you upstage a Ferrari owner?**[21]

Researching an upmarket, socially active audience is difficult at the best of times. The target can be opinionated, demanding, often resistant to research and almost impossible to reach. So, when we got the brief to conduct focus groups among Ferrari, Porsche, top Mercedes and other exotic sports car owners, we were tempted to panic. We knew we could find them, but how could we persuade them to participate? We realised the one thing that would link our target, who were also defined as keen drivers, not just poseurs, was their love of cars and desire to know the latest news about new models (and to try them out if possible). That's why we decided to offer the carrot of a drive around a race and proving track and the opportunity to meet the design and management team at our famous sports car maker. If anything might motivate people who clearly already had sufficient money to indulge a very expensive taste, it should be this package. It worked like a dream, and we had great success getting the right people to come and, more importantly, to participate.

Experimental group
An initial focus group, run to test the setting of the interview, the opening question, the topic guide and the mix of participants that make up the group.

The first focus group to be run should be seen as an **experimental group**. All aspects of running the group should be evaluated. Were the group members relaxed and comfortable in the chosen location, i.e. did the context work as intended? How did they react to the tape recorder, video or two-way mirror, i.e. at what point did they seem to relax and forget that they were being recorded? What types of member interacted well or not, and what issues helped or hindered interaction? How did the introductory and transition questions work in opening up and developing the discussion? How did the topic guide work; were there issues missing or issues that individuals would not tackle? How comfortable was the moderator handling the topics; did they have to interject to liven the discussion? How much did the moderator have to know about the subject to have credibility with the participants? With reflection on these issues, any necessary alterations can be made to the way that the remaining focus groups are administered. There may be very useful information that emerges from the experimental group that can be included in the main analysis. However, if the group does not work well, the information gleaned may be of little use, but the lessons learnt are invaluable in running the remaining groups.

Finally, the focus groups can be actually run. The question arises here of how many groups should be run. Beyond the first experimental group, the number of groups needed can vary. The number of focus groups that should be conducted on a single subject depends on the following factors:

- The extent to which comparisons between different types of participants are sought.
- The types of participant to be targeted and how well they interact in a discussion.
- The geographic spread of participants.
- The time and budget available.

The final stage in planning and conducting focus groups involves the analysis of data (*See* Chapter 10 for more detail). However, at this point there are two essential points to note:

1   *Evolving analysis.* Focus groups can change and develop in terms of the issues discussed and the stimuli used to draw out views from participants. The changes are made as the moderator generates and develops new ideas as each focus group progresses. The moderator makes observations and notes which are part of the total analysis. These help the moderator to decide which issues to probe, which issues to drop and the form of summarising issues that may be presented to groups at certain stages of the discussion.

2   *Not just the narrative.* If the discussion is recorded then transcripts can be produced which can be analysed with proprietary software. These transcripts form a major part of the analysis procedure but the accumulation and reflection upon observations and notes forms a key part of the analysis.

Online focus groups: e-groups

Many focus groups are now run online and may be referred to as an 'e-group'. The fundamental principles of why focus groups are conducted, their management and the data analysis challenges are similar between traditional focus groups and e-groups. Before examining their relative strengths and weaknesses it is worth considering a general description of online focus groups. There is no one generic format for an e-group. As with traditional focus groups, there are many variations and adaptations in e-groups, and their adaptation and use in Marketing Research Online Communities (MROCs) will also be explored. To get some sense of the nature, variation and applications of e-groups, look at the work of the following two leading specialists: VisionsLive (**www.visionslive.com**) and nqual (**www.nqual.com**).

As in the case of traditional focus groups, e-group participation is by invitation only. The participants are pre-recruited and generally come from lists of individuals who have expressed an interest in particular products, services or issues. A screening questionnaire can be administered online to qualify participants. Those who qualify are invited to participate in the e-group and given clear benefits and a reward for their participation. They receive a time, a URL, a room name and a password via email. Before the e-group begins, participants receive information about the discussion that covers such things as how to express emotions when typing. Electronic emotion indicators are produced using keyboard characters and are standard in their use on the Internet. Obvious examples include :-) and :-(for happy and smiling faces. The emotions are usually inserted in the text at the point at which the emotion is felt. Emotions can also be expressed using a different font or colour. There are a wide range of emotions to choose from expressed such as: I'm frowning, I'm laughing to myself, I'm embarrassed, I'm mad now, I'm responding passionately now. These are then followed by responses. Participants can also preview information about the discussion topic by visiting a given website and reading information or downloading and viewing visuals such as television advertisements. Then, just before the e-group begins, participants visit a website where they log on and get some last minute instructions.

When it is time for the discussion, participants move into a web-based chat room. In the chat room, the moderator and participants type to each other in real time. The general practice is for moderators to always pose their questions in capital letters and participants use upper and lower case. Participants are asked to always start their response with the question or issue number, so the moderator can quickly tie the response to the proper question. This makes it fast and easy to transcribe an e-group discussion. A raw transcript is available as soon as the discussion is completed and a formatted transcript can be available within

48 hours (the form of data used depends upon whether the transcript is to be input into qualitative analysis software and is to be built up as the groups progress, and/or is to be read by the client). The whole process of conducting the discussions and uploading transcripts for analysis is much faster than traditional focus groups.

New forms of e-groups continue to emerge. For example, online bulletin boards involve the moderator and participants over an extended period of time, from a few days to a few weeks. Questions and challenges can be slowly fed out over time, allowing the researcher to reflect upon responses that have been received and adapt subsequent questions. Participants can reflect in more depth and respond at their own convenience. Participants may also be given tasks such as collecting and posting visuals and music or offering web links to illustrate ideas and issues. Such an approach can enable an in-depth discussion among 25 or more participants. The extended time period allows participants to react to and build upon each other's ideas in a way that is often not possible during a traditional focus group that lasts even up to 6 hours.

Advantages of e-groups

Participants from all over the country or even the world can take part, and with mobile technology advances, they can physically be anywhere that they are comfortable. Likewise the client or decision maker can observe and comment on the discussion from anywhere. Geographical constraints are removed and time constraints can be lessened. Unlike traditional groups, there is the opportunity to contact participants again at a later date, to revisit issues, or introduce them to modifications in material presented in the original focus group. The Internet and the use of profiled consumers enable the researcher to reach participants that are usually hard to interview: doctors, lawyers, professionals, working mothers and other who are leading busy lives and are not interested in taking part in traditional focus groups.

Moderators may also be able to carry on side conversations with individual participants, probing deeper into interesting areas. Participants may be less inhibited in their responses and can be more likely to fully express their thoughts, especially if they have the facility to reflect and load up images, music or other forms of expression. Many e-groups go well past their allotted time as so many responses are expressed as participants become engaged in the discussion. Finally, as there is no travel, videoing or facilities to arrange, the cost is much lower than traditional groups. Firms are able to keep costs between one-fifth and one-half of the cost of traditional groups.[22]

Disadvantages of e-groups

Only individuals that have access to and know how to use a computer or certain mobile devices can participate in e-groups. The global growth and access to computers means that many types of individual can be accessed, but there remains significant numbers and types that cannot. Since the name of a participant is often private, actually verifying who the participant is and thus whether they fit a target profile is difficult. To overcome this limitation, other traditional methods such as telephone calls are used for the recruitment and verification of participants. This is allow an area where the use of a well managed access panel can help in ensuring the profile of participant is correct for a particular study. Body language, facial expressions, silences, and the tone of voice cannot be observed and electronic emotions cannot capture as full a breadth of emotion as video recording. Another factor that must be considered is the general lack of control over the participant's environment and their potential exposure to distracting external stimuli. Since e-groups could potentially have participants scattered all over the world, researchers and moderators have no idea what else participants may be doing during the discussion. This has to be balanced against the comfort that may be felt by the e-group participant in being able to conduct the discussion in a context where they feel comfortable. Only audio and visual stimuli can be tested. Products cannot be touched (e.g. clothing) or smelled (e.g. perfumes). It may be more difficult to get clients or decision makers involved in e-groups as they can be in observing traditional groups. It is hard to replicate the compelling views of consumers, expressing themselves in an uninhibited manner, of what they feel about a product or service. Table 4.2 presents a summary comparison of e-groups and traditional focus groups.[23]

Table 4.2	Online versus traditional focus groups	
Characteristic	**e-groups**	**Traditional focus groups**
Group size	4 to 8 participants	6 to 10 participants
Group composition	Anywhere in the world	Drawn from a targeted location
Time duration	1 to 1.5 hours – though can last over a week as participants given tasks and come back to the discussion	1.5 to 6 hours
Physical setting	Researcher has little control – but the participant can be in a place that is comfortable to them, especially with the use of mobile technology	Under the control of the researcher
Participant identity	In some circumstances can be difficult to verify	Can be easily verified
Participant attentiveness	Participants can engage in other tasks – not seen by the moderator	Attentiveness can be monitored
Participant recruitment	Easier. Can be recruited online, by email, by access panel, or by traditional means	Recruited by traditional means (telephone, mail, mail panel)
Group dynamics	Limited	Synergistic, snowballing (bandwagon effect)
Openness of participants	Participants can be candid – may be more open with identities hidden to some extent	Participants can be candid as they build up trust of each other. Difficult with sensitive topics
Non-verbal communication	Body language and facial expressions cannot be observed. Some emotions can be expressed	Easy to observe body language and facial expressions. Expression of emotions easier to monitor
Use of physical stimuli	Limited to those that can be displayed online – unless specific engagement tasks given to participants	A variety of stimuli (products, advertising, demonstrations) can be used
Transcripts	Available immediately	Time consuming and expensive to obtain
Observers' communication with moderator	Observers can communicate with the moderator on a split screen	Observers can send messages to the moderator from behind two-way mirrors
Unique moderator skills	Software familiarity, awareness of chat-room slang	Observational
Turnaround time	Can be set up and completed in a few days	Takes many days to organise, administer and analyse
Client travel costs	None	Can be expensive
Client involvement	Limited	High
Basic focus group cost	Much less expensive	More expensive due to facility rental, refreshments, video/audio recording, and transcript preparation

In-depth interviews

In-depth interview
An unstructured, direct, personal interview in which a single participant is probed by an experienced interviewer to uncover underlying motivations, beliefs, attitudes and feelings on a topic.

The meaning of 'in-depth'

An **in-depth interview** is an unstructured, direct, personal interview in which a single participant is probed by an experienced interviewer to uncover underlying motivations, beliefs, attitudes and feelings on a topic.[24] An application of the in-depth interview is illustrated in the following example:

Real research   **Depth interviews and fragrances[25]**

Christian Dior and the research company Repères (**www.reperes.net**) developed an approach that tested consumer reactions to new fragrances and the context in which they are used. This work was particularly aimed at supporting decisions made in the launch of new fragrances. Their exploration was built upon the use of individual in-depth interviews. They felt there were limitations in how consumers could talk about fragrances and so chose metaphors as a way of describing an object using words other than those that consumers may usually employ. A library of images was built that encompassed the broadest array possible of meanings and feelings. Why in-depth interviews? They felt that individual interviews enabled them to go beyond initial reactions and explore the emotional unconscious. This enabled them to explore the whole emotional and imaginary chain underlying the perception of a fragrance. They felt that group discussions would never go as far into perceptions because participants could be restricted in their emotional reactions by the perceptions of other participants. In-depth interviews allowed them to analyse the perceptions of different participants, identifying issues common to all (or to a particular target) vs. those specific to the specific characteristics of each participant.

It is a qualitative interview and as such is based upon conversation, with the emphasis on researchers asking questions and listening, and participants answering.[26] The purpose of most qualitative interviews is to derive meaning through interpretations, not necessarily 'facts' from participant talk. The emphasis should be upon a full interaction to understand the meaning of the participant's experiences and life worlds.[27] In order to tap into these experiences and life worlds, in-depth interviewing involves a certain style of social and interpersonal interaction. In order to be effective and useful, in-depth interviews develop and build upon intimacy; in this respect, they resemble the forms of talking one finds among close friends. They can resemble friendship, and may even lead to long-term friendship. They are also very different from the nature of talking one finds between friends, mainly because the interviewer seeks to use the information obtained in the interaction for some other purpose.[28] As the name implies, in-depth interviewing seeks 'deep' information and understanding.

Going deep into the minds of consumers is a learning process. Researchers make mistakes; they sometimes say the wrong things or upset participants in some way. They learn that their race, age, gender, social class, appearance or voice makes one kind of difference with some participants and another kind of difference with other informants.[29] The lesson from this is that there is no 'ideal' means to conduct the in-depth interview. Researchers learn from their experiences, discovering strengths and playing to them, realising weaknesses and understanding how to compensate for them. In this spirit of experimentation and learning we present a procedure that encapsulates how a researcher may approach the in-depth interview.

Procedure

To illustrate the technique, a scenario is set whereby the researcher is interviewing the marketing director of a cosmetics brand that has successfully sponsored a major sports event. The sponsorship has resulted in many industry awards, increased sales and better employee–employer relations. The researcher wishes to understand why the brand became involved in the sponsorship and how it achieved such success.

The in-depth interview with this busy executive may take from 30 minutes to well over an hour. It may occur on a one-off basis or it may unfold over a number of meetings as more understanding is developed. Once the interviewer has gained access to the marketing director (which can be very problematic; why should they give up valuable time and share commercial knowledge?), the interviewer should begin by explaining the purpose of the interview, showing what both will get out of taking part in the interview and explaining what the process will be like. Beyond the introduction the interviewer may ask the marketing director a general introductory question such as 'What impacts have the industry awards had upon your business?' The interviewer would be expected to have done their homework to know what the awards were, what they were awarded for and who the brand was competing against. This is a very positive feature of the sponsorship experience, and it would be hoped to boost the ego of the marketing director and encourage them to talk freely about the different impacts of the awards. The impact of sponsorship could be upon existing and potential new customers, employees and suppliers. The discussion could then flow into any of these areas. After asking the initial question, the interviewer uses an unstructured format, guided by a topic guide as a reminder of important subject areas to cover. The subsequent direction of the interview is determined by the participant's initial reply, the interviewer's probes for elaboration and the participant's answers.

As with the focus group topic guide and the moderator managing that guide, spontaneity ensures that the process is creative and meaningful to the participant. Suppose that the participant replies to the initial question by saying:

> The award for the 'best use of sponsorship' in the launch of a new product gave us the most satisfaction. It has made us review how we execute all of our new product launches and integrate our different marketing agencies, our employees and supply chains.

The interviewer might then pose a question such as 'Was it the award that initiated the review or would you have done that anyway?' If the answer is not very revealing, e.g. 'We may have', the interviewer may ask a probing question, such as 'what did the award tell you about how you worked as a team?' This question could open up a whole series of issues such as 'trust', 'relationship development' or 'technical support', to name a few. Such an exchange of questions and answers could emerge from a heading of 'Integrating sponsorship with other marketing communications' on the topic guide. The interviewer will keep an eye on the topic guide to ensure that all the important issues are tackled, but the specific wording of the questions and the order in which they are asked is influenced by the participant's replies.

Probing is of critical importance in obtaining meaningful responses and uncovering hidden issues. Probing can be done by asking general questions such as 'Why do you say that?', 'That's interesting, can you tell me more?' or 'Would you like to add anything else?'[30] Probing can search for general issues but also be more specific, an example in the above scenario being 'What does good teamwork mean to you?' One of the main success factors of specific probing is that the researcher understands something about the nature of the subject being researched. This means the researcher appreciates the significance of particular revelations, understands the language (even technical language and jargon in certain areas, like the cosmetics industry) and has credibility with the participant that encourages him or her to open up to the interviewer.

The interviewer must be alert to the issues to go through but also the issues that the participant is willing to talk about, and must listen carefully to and observe which issues fire enthusiasm in the participant. The questions and probes the interviewer puts to participants should follow the interest and logic of the participants, making them feel motivated to respond in a manner that suits them. As with a focus group discussion, the participants should feel comfortable and relaxed, which could mean holding the interview in their office, their home, a bar, a sports club. There have even been experiments using a 'research taxi' in which participants are taken to their destination while they participate in an interview conducted by the researcher-driver and shadowings (observations and interviews) with subway passengers during their home–work commute.[31] In these examples any context in which participants feel at ease can result in a willingness to be more reflective, honest and open. Answering in a manner that suits the participant helps to make the interview more comfortable and relaxed. For a great amount of business research, the in-depth interview is the best way to gain access and to talk to managers. Much of the interviewing takes place in their office at a time that is convenient to them. Researchers can also observe characteristics of the manager in their office environment that can be of help in their analyses. Examples of this could be levels of formality in the workplace, reports and books that the manager has for reference, the manager's use of technology, or the tidiness of the workplace. In the example above where a manager has received a sponsorship award, it could be how that and other awards are displayed, photographs from advertisements, displays of new products. These observations would be entirely based upon the purpose of the study, but the context of the office can be of help to the manager and the researcher. In order to make the above process work, the interviewer should:

1 Do their utmost to develop an empathy with the participant.

2 Make sure the participant is relaxed and comfortable.

3 Be personable to encourage and motivate participants.

4 Note issues that interest the participant and develop questions around these issues.

5 Not be happy to accept brief 'yes' or 'no' answers.

6 Note where participants have not explained clearly enough issues that need probing.

Advantages and challenges of in-depth interviews

In-depth interviews have the following advantages. They can:

1 **Uncover a greater depth** of insights than focus groups. This can happen through concentrating and developing an issue with the individual. In the group scenario, interesting and knowledgeable individuals cannot be solely concentrated upon.

2 **Attribute the responses directly** to the participant, unlike focus groups where it is often difficult to determine which participant made a particular response.

3 **Result in a free exchange** of information that may not be possible in focus groups because there is no social pressure to conform to group response. This makes them ideally suited to sensitive issues, especially commercially sensitive issues.

4 **Be easier to arrange** than the focus group as there are not so many individuals to co-ordinate and the interviewer can travel to the participant.

The following are not necessarily disadvantages, but really the challenges that researchers face when using this very valuable technique:

1 **The lack of structure** makes the results susceptible to the interviewer's influence, and the quality and completeness of the results depend heavily on the interviewer's skills. As with all qualitative techniques, the interviewer needs to develop an awareness of the factors that make them 'see' in a particular way.

2 **The length of the interview**, combined with high costs, means that the number of in-depth interviews in a project tends to be few. If few in-depth interviews can be managed, the researcher should focus upon the quality of the whole research experience. 'Quality' in this context means the qualities that the participant possesses in terms of richness of experience and how relevant the experiences are to the study; the quality of drawing out and getting participants to express themselves clearly and honestly; and the quality of analysis in terms of interpretation of individual participants and individual issues evaluated across all the interviews conducted.

3 **The data obtained can be difficult to analyse and interpret**. Many responses may not be taken at face value; there can be many hidden messages and interpretations in how participants express themselves. The researcher needs a strong theoretical awareness to make sense of the data or the technical means to develop theory if using a grounded theory approach. As well as the transcripts of the interview, additional observations add to the richness and multi-faceted analyses and potential interpretations.

Applications of in-depth interviews

Applying in-depth interviews presents challenges but also many rewards. There are many marketing decisions that can be made with support from researchers using the broad array of techniques under the heading of 'in-depth interviews'. The following summarises the applications:[32]

1 Researching professional people (e.g. finance directors using banking services).

2 Researching children (e.g. attitudes towards a theme park).

3 Researching elite individuals (e.g. wealthy individuals involved in large philanthropic ventures).

4 Detailed probing of participants (e.g. new product development for luxury cars).

5 Discussion of confidential, sensitive or embarrassing topics (e.g. personal hygiene issues).

6 Situations where strong social norms exist and where the participant may be easily swayed by group response (e.g. attitudes of university students towards sports).

7 Detailed understanding of habitual behaviour (e.g. the 'rituals' an individual may go through as they prepare for an evening out).

8 Detailed understanding of complicated behaviour (e.g. the purchase of a second home).

9 Researching competitors who are unlikely to reveal the information in a group setting (e.g. travel agents' perceptions of airline travel packages).

10 Situations where the product consumption experience is sensory in nature, affecting mood states and emotions (e.g. perfumes, bath soap).

In the application of in-depth interviews, the researcher can use other techniques to help maintain the interest of participants, to make the experience more enjoyable for the participants and the researcher alike, and ultimately to draw out the true feelings of participants. A set of techniques that help to achieve all this, which have been applied with great success over many years, is the body of indirect techniques called 'projective techniques'.

Projective techniques

Projective technique

An unstructured and indirect form of questioning that encourages participants to project their underlying motivations, beliefs, attitudes or feelings regarding the issues of concern.

Projective techniques are a category of exercises designed to provoke imagination and creativity that can be used in in-depth interviews. Projective techniques are subject-orientated, non-verbal and indirect self-reporting techniques that have the ability to capture responses from participants in a less structured and more imaginative way than direct questioning. It gets beyond the rational replies participants often make in interview situations, encouraging them to project their underlying motivations, beliefs, attitudes or feelings regarding the issues of concern.[33] They are useful techniques for drawing out emotional values, exploring issues in a non-linear manner or for bypassing participants' rational controls. They also help participants to verbalise unframed, subconscious, low salience or low-involvement attitudes.[34] Viewed as 'face-saving' techniques, projection provides participants with the facility to project their thoughts and feelings on to another person or object (e.g. via completion tests). Projective techniques can enable participants to express feelings and thoughts they would otherwise find difficult to articulate.[35] In applying the techniques, participants can be asked to interpret the behaviour of others rather than to describe their own behaviour. In interpreting the behaviour of others, it is contended that participants indirectly project their own motivations, beliefs, attitudes or feelings into the situation. Thus, the participants' attitudes are uncovered by analysing their responses to scenarios that are deliberately unstructured, vague and ambiguous. The more ambiguous the situation, the more participants project their emotions, needs, motives, attitudes and values, as demonstrated by work in clinical psychology on which projective techniques are based.[36]

As in psychology, these projective techniques are classified as association, completion, construction and expressive. Each of these classifications is discussed below.[37]

Association techniques

Association techniques

A type of projective technique in which participants are presented with a stimulus and are asked to respond with the first thing that comes to mind.

Word association

A projective technique in which participants are presented with a list of words, one at a time. After each word, they are asked to give the first word that comes to mind.

In **association techniques**, an individual is presented with a stimulus and asked to respond with the first thing that comes to mind. Word association is the best known of these techniques. In **word association**, participants are presented with a list of words, one at a time, and encouraged to respond without deliberation to each with the first word that comes to mind. The words of interest, called test words, are interspersed throughout the list, which also contains some neutral, or filler, words to disguise the purpose of the study. The participant's response to each word is recorded verbatim and responses are timed so that participants who hesitate or reason out (defined as taking longer than three seconds to reply) can be identified. The interviewer, not the participant, records the responses.

The underlying assumption of this technique is that association allows participants to reveal their inner feelings about the topic of interest. Responses are analysed by calculating:

1 The frequency with which any word is given as a response.

2 The amount of time that elapses before a response is given.

3 The number of participants who do not respond at all to a test word within a reasonable period.

Those who do not respond at all are judged to have an emotional involvement so high that it blocks a response. It is often possible to classify the associations as favourable, unfavourable or neutral. An individual's pattern of responses and the details of the response are used to determine the person's underlying attitudes or feelings on the topic of interest. There are several variations to the standard word association procedure. Participants may be asked to give the first two, three or four words that come to mind rather than only the first word. This technique can also be used in controlled tests, as contrasted with free association. In controlled tests, participants might be asked, 'Which fashion brands come to mind first when I mention "boring"?' More detailed information can be obtained from completion techniques, which are a natural extension of association techniques.

Completion techniques

Completion technique
A projective technique that requires participants to complete an incomplete stimulus situation.

Sentence completion
A projective technique in which participants are presented with a number of incomplete sentences and are asked to complete them.

Story completion
A projective technique in which participants are provided with part of a story and are required to give the conclusion in their own words.

Construction technique
A projective technique in which participants are required to construct a response in the form of a story, dialogue or description.

Picture response technique
A projective technique in which participants are shown a picture and are asked to tell a story describing it.

Cartoon tests
Cartoon characters are shown in a specific situation related to the problem. Participants are asked to indicate the dialogue that one cartoon character might make in response to the comment(s) of another character.

Expressive technique
A projective technique in which participants are presented with a verbal or visual situation and are asked to relate the feelings and attitudes of other people to the situation.

Role playing
Participants are asked to assume the behaviour of someone else or a specific object.

Third-person technique
A projective technique in which participants are presented with a verbal or visual situation and are asked to relate the beliefs and attitudes of a third person in that situation.

Personification technique
Participants are asked to imagine that the brand is a person and then describe characteristics of that person.

In **completion techniques**, participants are asked to complete an incomplete stimulus situation. Common completion techniques are sentence completion and story completion.[38] **Sentence completion** is similar to word association. Participants are given incomplete sentences and are asked to complete them. Generally, they are asked to use the first word or phrase that comes to mind.

Sentence completion may provide more information about the participants' feelings than word association. Sentence completion is not as disguised as word association however, and many participants may be able to guess the purpose of the study. A variation of sentence completion is paragraph completion, in which the participant completes a paragraph beginning with the stimulus phrase. A further expanded version of sentence completion and paragraph completion is story completion. In **story completion**, participants are given part of a story, enough to direct attention to a particular topic but not to hint at the ending. They are required to give the conclusion in their own words.

Construction techniques

Construction techniques are closely related to completion techniques. Construction techniques require the participants to construct a response in the form of a story, dialogue or description. In a construction technique, the researcher provides less initial structure to the participants than in a completion technique. The two main construction techniques are picture response techniques and cartoon tests.

The roots of **picture response techniques** can be traced to the thematic apperception test (TAT), which consists of a series of pictures of ordinary as well as unusual events. In some of these pictures, the persons or objects are clearly depicted, while in others they are relatively vague. The participant is asked to tell stories about these pictures. The participant's interpretation of the pictures gives indications of that individual's personality. For example, an individual may be characterised as impulsive, creative, unimaginative and so on. The term 'thematic apperception test' is used because themes are elicited based on the subject's perceptual interpretation (apperception) of pictures.

In **cartoon tests**, cartoon characters are shown in a specific situation related to the problem. Participants are asked to indicate what one cartoon character might say in response to the comments of another character. The responses indicate the participants' feelings, beliefs and attitudes towards the situation. Cartoon tests are simpler to administer and analyse than picture response techniques.

Expressive techniques

In **expressive techniques**, participants are presented with a verbal or visual situation and asked to relate the feelings and attitudes of other people to the situation. The participants express not their own feelings or attitudes, but those of others. The main expressive techniques are role playing, the third-person technique and personification.

In **role playing**, participants are asked to play the role or to assume the behaviour of someone else. Participants are asked to speak as though they were someone else, such as another household member with whom they would share a decision or an authority figure. The researcher assumes that participants will project their own feelings into the role.[39]

In the **third-person technique**, participants are presented with a verbal or visual situation and are asked to relate the beliefs and attitudes of a third person rather than directly expressing personal beliefs and attitudes. This third person may be a friend, a colleague, or any person that the researcher chooses. Again, the researcher assumes that the participants will reveal personal beliefs and attitudes while describing the reactions of a third party. Asking an individual to respond in the third person reduces the social pressure to give an acceptable answer.

In the **personification technique**, participants imagine that the brand is a person and then describe characteristics of that person, e.g. their lifestyle, status, demographics, home(s). They can build up layers of this description using words and images from a variety of sources. These descriptions help to uncover and develop the perceived nature of a brand's personality.

Brand personality can also be uncovered using role playing.[40] In a group discussion scenario, participants may be asked to play out the personality of a brand. In an example of researching the personalities of different beer brands, an imaginary setting could be a sports bar after work on a Friday evening. Participants would be individually assigned a brand and asked to role play what they felt to be the personas of brands such as Coors, Guinness, Becks, Stella Artois and Heineken. What the individuals as a brand do, what they say, how they interact with each other in the bar, all allow an expression of personality that straight questioning may not reveal. Video recording of the event, played back to the group, acts as a means to discuss and elicit further meaning of a brand's personality, highlighting any positive and negative associations of the brand.

Advantages and disadvantages of projective techniques

The major advantage of projective techniques is that they may elicit responses that participants would be unwilling or unable to give if they knew the purpose of the study. At times, in direct questioning, the participant may intentionally or unintentionally misunderstand, misinterpret or mislead the researcher. Personal accounts can be more self-conscious and self-justifying than the actions themselves; because they represent the way an individual would like to be judged.[41] This is one of the values of projective techniques which frame the actions as those of 'someone else'. Projective techniques can increase the validity of responses by disguising the purpose. This is particularly true when the issues to be addressed are personal, sensitive or subject to strong social norms. Projective techniques are also helpful when underlying motivations, beliefs and attitudes are operating at a subconscious level.[42]

Projective techniques suffer from many of the disadvantages of unstructured direct techniques, but to a greater extent. These techniques generally require personal interviews with individuals who are experienced interviewers and interpreters; hence they tend to be expensive. Furthermore, as in all qualitative techniques, there can be a risk of interpretation bias. With the exception of word association, all are open-ended techniques, making the analysis and interpretation more problematic.

Some projective techniques such as role playing require participants to engage in what may seem to be unusual behaviour. Certain participants may not have the self-confidence or the ability to express themselves fully with these techniques. In role playing, for example, the skills of acting may make some participants more articulate at expressing their feelings compared with others. The same may be said of techniques where pictures and cartoons are put together and interpreted, in that distinctive skills may make certain participants more adept and comfortable in expressing themselves. To counter this, one could argue that there is a great amount of skill required in articulating ideas and feelings in an open-ended in-depth interview. One could point to fiction writers or poets who are able to encapsulate particular feelings most clearly and succinctly, which again is enormously skilful. With such skill requirements, the disadvantage of the technique lies in the nature of the participants who agree to participate, and how characteristic they may be of distinct target markets.

Applications of projective techniques

Projective techniques are used less frequently than unstructured direct methods (focus groups and in-depth interviews). A possible exception may be word association, which is commonly used to test brand names and occasionally to measure attitudes about particular products, brands, packages or advertisements. As the examples have shown, projective techniques can be used in a variety of situations.[43] The usefulness of these techniques is enhanced when the following guidelines are observed. Projective techniques should be used:

1 Because the required information cannot be accurately obtained by direct questioning.

2 In an exploratory manner to elicit issues that participants find difficult to conceive and express.

3 To engage participants in the subject, by having fun in expressing themselves in interesting and novel ways.

Ethnographic approaches

Ethnography
A research approach based upon the observation of the customs, habits and differences between people in everyday situations.

Ethnography as a general term includes observation and interviewing and is sometimes referred to as participant observation. It is, however, used in the more specific case of a method which requires a researcher to spend a large amount of time observing a particular group of people, by sharing their way of life.[44] Ethnography is the art and science of describing a group or culture. The description may be of a small tribal group in an exotic land or an aluminium smelting plant in Sweden. The task is much like the one taken on by the investigative reporter, who interviews relevant people, reviews records, takes photographs, weighs the credibility of one person's opinions against another's, looks for ties to special interests and organisations and writes the story for a concerned public and for professional colleagues. A key difference between the investigative reporter and the ethnographer, however, is that whereas the journalist seeks out the unusual, the murder, the plane crash, or the bank robbery, the ethnographer writes about the routine daily lives of people. The more predictable patterns of human thought and behaviour are the focus of enquiry.[45]

The origins of ethnography are in the work of nineteenth-century anthropologists who travelled to observe different pre-industrial cultures. Today, ethnography encompasses a much broader range of work, from studies of groups in one's own culture, through experimental writing, to political interventions. Moreover, ethnographers today do not always 'observe', at least not directly. They may work with cultural artefacts such as written texts, online discussions, or the posting of online images. They may study recordings of interactions they have not directly observed,[46] or as in the following example, the observations of teenagers as viewed through photographs taken on their mobile phones.

Real research | Chocolate or mobile?[47]

Ayobamidele Gnädig and Oliver Schieleit are project directors at the German qualitative research agency H.T.P. Concept (**www.htp-concept.de**). They asked teenagers to photo-blog their snacking habits with their mobile phones and saw that many of these were 'boredom relief' moments where they were waiting for trains, buses or friends who were late for an appointment. When they spent time with them, a whole day or just an afternoon, they saw this moment crop up time and again. They also believe they witnessed a change in that these moments were increasingly being filled differently than maybe five or ten years ago. Instead of quickly buying a Mars bar at the nearby kiosk, a young teen was just as likely to spend their time waiting for a bus in writing text messages to their friends. This meant that in some contexts, the text message had become 'top of the mind' over the chocolate bar. Through understanding by observing and not by probing the dynamics, they offered a first step for chocolate brands to develop new ideas, communications and distribution concepts to address this opportunity.

Ethnographic research has the following aims:

- *Seeing through the eyes of others.* Viewing events, actions, norms and values from the per-spective of the people being studied.

- *Description.* Built up in many written and visual forms to provide clues and pointers to the layers of 'reality' experienced by consumers.

- *Contextualism.* Attending to mundane detail to help understand what is going on in a particular context. Whatever the sphere in which the data are being collected, events can be best understood when they are situated in the wider social and historical context.

- *Process.* Viewing social life as involving an interlocking series of events.

- *Avoiding early use of theories and concepts.* Rejecting premature attempts to impose theo-ries and concepts which may exhibit a poor fit with participants' perspectives.

- *Flexible research designs.* Ethnographers' adherence to viewing social phenomena through the eyes of their participants or subjects has led to a wariness regarding the imposition of prior and possibly inappropriate frames of reference on the people they study. This leads to a preference for an open and unstructured research design which increases the possibility of coming across unexpected issues.

Ethnography cannot reasonably be classified as just another single method or technique.[48] In essence, it is a research discipline based upon culture as an organising concept and a mix of both observational and interviewing tactics to record behavioural dynamics. Above all, ethnography relies upon entering participants' natural life worlds, at home, while shopping, at leisure and in the workplace. The researcher essentially becomes a naive visitor in that world by engaging participants during realistic product usage situations in the course of daily life. Whether called on-site, observational, naturalistic or contextual research, ethnographic methods allow marketers to delve into actual situations in which products are used, services are received and benefits are conferred.

One of the key features of all the descriptions and illustrations of forms of ethnography is the context in which the consumer is behaving. The researcher observes people experienc-ing, taking in and reacting to communications, product and services, retail experience, all behaving naturally in the set context. For example in the context of shoppers this does not just mean the retail outlet they visit. The processes of choosing and buying products, of using products or giving them as gifts, of reflecting upon and planning subsequent purchases, are all affected by contextual factors. Context operates on several levels, including the immediate physical and situational surroundings of consumers, as well as language, character, culture and history. Each of these levels can provide a basis for the meaning and significance attached to the roles and behaviour of consumption.

The researcher may observe the consumer acting and reacting in the context of con-sumption. They may observe a shopper spending time reading the labels on cat food, showing different brands to their partner, engaged in deep conversation, pondering, getting frustrated and putting tins back on the shelf. They may see the same shop-per more purposefully putting an expensive bottle of cognac into a shopping trolley without any discussion and seemingly with no emotional attachment to the product. They may want to know what is going on. How may the consumer explain their atti-tudes and motivations behind this behaviour? This is where the interplay of observa-tion and interviewing helps to build such a rich picture of consumers. In questioning the shopper in the above example, responses of 'We think that Rémy Martin cognac is the best' or 'We always argue about which are the prettiest cat food labels' would not be enough. The stories and contexts of how these assertions came to be would be explored. The ethnographer does not tend to take simple explanations for activities that in many circumstances may be habitual to consumers. Ethnographic practice takes a highly critical attitude towards expressed language. It challenges our accepted words at face value, searching instead for the meanings and values that lie beneath the surface. In interviewing situations, typically this involves looking for gaps between expressed and non-verbal communication elements. For example, if actual practices and facial and physical gestures are inconsistent with a participant's expressed attitudes towards the expensive cognac, we are challenged to discover both the reality behind the given answer and the reasons for the 'deception'.

Ethnographic research is also effective as a tool for learning situationally and culturally grounded language, the appropriate words for everyday things as spoken by various age or ethnic groups. Copywriters and strategic thinkers are always pressed to talk about products and brands in evocative and original ways. Ethnography helps act as both a discovery and an evaluation tool.[49] To summarise, ethnographic approaches are useful when the marketing research objectives call for:[50]

1 *High-intensity situations.* To study high-intensity situations, such as a sales encounter, meal preparation and service, or communication between persons holding different levels of authority.

2 *Behavioural processes.* To conduct precise analyses of behavioural processes, e.g. radio listening behaviour, home computer purchasing decisions or home cleaning behaviour.

3 *Memory inadequate.* To address situations where the participant's memory or reflection would not be adequate. Observational methods can stand alone or can complement interviewing as a memory jog.

4 *Shame or reluctance.* To work with participants who are likely to be ashamed or reluctant to reveal actual practices to a group of peers. If they were diabetic, for example, participants may be reluctant to reveal that they have a refrigerator full of sweet snacks, something that an ethnographic observer would be able to see without confronting the subject.

In these applications, the ethnographer is expected to analyse critically the situations observed. The critique or analysis can be guided by theory but in essence the researcher develops a curiosity, thinks in an abstract manner and at times steps back to reflect and see how emerging ideas connect. By reacting to the events and participants as they face them, to draw out what they see as important, ethnographers have the ability to create new explanations and understandings of consumers.

Comparison between qualitative techniques

To summarise comparisons between qualitative techniques, Table 4.3 gives a relative comparison of focus groups, in-depth interviews, projective techniques and ethnographic approaches (qualitative observation). The nature of qualitative research is such that, within the broad categories above, there are numerous variations of the techniques with distinct strengths and weaknesses in eliciting and representing consumer feelings. Really, it is not possible to say that one technique is better or worse than the other. Faced with a given problem, it would seem to be the case of deciding which technique is the most appropriate to represent or understand consumers.[51] What may affect this choice is the confidence that marketing decision makers may have in particular techniques. Thus, for example, any number of arguments may be made for the use of a projective technique as being the best way to tackle indirectly a sensitive issue. If the marketer who has to use the research findings does not believe it to be a trustworthy technique, then other, perhaps less appropriate, techniques may have to be used.

Table 4.3	A comparison of focus groups, in-depth interviews, projective techniques and ethnographic techniques			
Criteria	**Focus groups**	**In-depth interviews**	**Projective techniques**	**Ethnographic techniques**
Degree of structure	Can vary from highly to loosely structured	Can vary from highly to loosely structured	Tends to be loosely structured	Loosely structured though can have a framework to guide observation
Chance to probe individual participants	Low	High	Medium	None when used in isolation and in a covert manner
Moderator bias	Medium	Relatively high	Low to high	None when used in isolation and in a covert manner
Uncovering subconscious information	Low	Medium to high	High	High
Discovering innovative information	High	Medium	Low	Medium
Obtaining sensitive information	Low	Medium	High	High
Involving unusual behaviour or questioning	No	To a limited extent	Yes	Perhaps on the part of the observer

International marketing research

The benefits of qualitative research methods should be clear at this stage. Researchers can develop a deep understanding of consumer experiences and the drivers of their behaviour and aspirations. Capturing the rich context of product, media and shopping behaviour and the manner in which consumers express themselves can support many marketing, branding and design decisions. As well as supporting decisions directly, well crafted qualitative research can help to plan effective and actionable quantitative research. Such a rich and deep understanding of consumers can be paramount in international marketing. Understanding the nuances of language, gestures, symbols and the rich array of expressions in different cultures can be of huge importance in successful international marketing. There are three main challenges in understanding cultures and how they shape and are shaped by consumers in an international context. The first challenge lies in implementing research techniques that in Western cultures may be logical and possible to administer. At one time international qualitative marketing research equated to flying expensive Western focus group moderators around the world. Now, qualitative marketing research has become more adaptive to local cultures, with far more emphasis on training local researchers to adapt and develop techniques that are relevant to participants. The challenge to many international companies was and is to achieve balance between 'local' and 'global', or 'glocal' as it came to be called.[52] The second challenge lies in interpreting what is being expressed by participants.[53] For example, focus groups or ethnographic techniques can be designed with a sound philosophical, theoretical and ethical basis. They can be adapted in how they are delivered for local cultures. However, analysing the data and drawing out the insights can represent a major challenge. It is not just a matter of building a set of transcripts and simply translating them. The quality of communications among researchers can be vital in drawing out the subtleties that can deliver valuable consumer insights. The final challenge lies in the new 'competitors' to traditional forms of qualitative research. The use of qualitative data generated through chat rooms, bulletin boards and other forms of social media are all functions of technological developments. Qualitative moderators often now become part of the 'e-communities' they study to understand them better, blurring the differences between marketing and research. Posted dialogues around a theme, or a brand, can now be content-analysed. Consumers leave a trail of communications, website hits and blogs that can be followed and 'sniffed' for interests, attitudes and unfulfilled needs.[54] Technological developments and how consumers engage with that technology are shaping what qualitative research means and how it can best engage in international communities.

Ethics in marketing research

The essence of qualitative research is that consumers can be examined in great depth. They may be questioned and probed in depth about subjects they hardly reflect upon on a day-to-day basis, never mind talk to strangers about. Great care must be taken not to upset or disturb participants through such intensive questioning. In survey work, reassuring participants that their responses will be confidential can work if there is a demonstrable link between their responses to questions and a means of aggregating all of the findings; making the individual response 'hidden'. In qualitative research, the process is far more intimate and the link between the response and the participant is far more difficult to break. A number of ethical issues related to qualitative research methods should be considered.

One key issue relates to how adversely affected or embarrassed participants may feel in being questioned or observed. What this means largely depends upon the issues being explored and how they are perceived by participants. Some participants may find personal hygiene issues very embarrassing to talk about in a group scenario, but not financial issues. Other individuals may be very frank about their sexual behaviour, while others would be shocked at the notion of talking about sex with a group of strangers. The researchers must get to know how the issues they wish to explore are perceived by their target participants by examining the literature, secondary data and the use of experimentation with different qualitative research methods.

Ethical questions also arise when videoing participants. Regardless of whether or not participants are aware of the use of cameras, at the end of interviews or observations they should be asked to sign a written declaration conveying their permission to use the recording. This declaration should disclose the full purpose of the video, including who will be able to view it. If any participant refuses, the recording should be either destroyed or edited to omit that participant's identity and comments completely. The researcher should be sensitive to the comfort level of the participants, and respect for the participants should warrant restraint. When a participant feels uncomfortable and does not wish to go on, the researcher should not aggressively probe or confront any further. It has also been suggested that participants should be allowed to reflect on all they have said at the end of the interview and should be given the opportunity to ask questions. This may help return the participants to their pre-interview emotional state.

Another major ethical problem that is a research issue and participant specific is the use of alcoholic drinks during interviews. For some participants, relaxing and socialising in a comfortable context, drinking alcohol is very natural. Researchers with experience of running many focus groups would argue that serving alcoholic drinks can help to reduce tension in certain participants and give them the confidence to express their views. Other researchers would argue that this is unethical practice, that in effect the researcher is 'drugging' participants. Whatever the researcher decides is right for the type of participants, the issues they are questioning them about and the context in which the discussion takes place, there are practical problems involved with serving alcohol. Controlling the flow of alcohol and how much is given to certain participants may take attention away from the discussion. If control is not exerted, particular participants may get out of hand and disrupt or even destroy the discussion. Researchers could be accused of not taking reasonable precautions to ensure that participants are in no way adversely affected or embarrassed as a result of the focus group, should the use of alcohol be abused by certain participants.

Digital developments in marketing research

Digital and technological developments present huge opportunities for the qualitative researcher. Such developments are enabling online versions of focus groups, in-depth interviews, games and projective techniques, ethnography applied to virtual communities and the collection of documents, images and other forms of expression in chat rooms and bulletin boards. Online research is enabling the development of traditional qualitative research techniques as well the emergence of new techniques. The advantages and disadvantages of conducting qualitative research online and taking advantage of digital developments may be summarised as follows.[55]

Advantages

- *Extending access to participants.* Provided that potential participants have access to the technology, researchers can cross time and space barriers. They can reach a much wider geographical span of participants, and also populations that are normally hard to reach, especially through the use of mobile devices.

- *Sensitive subjects.* For some participants the sensitivity of the subject being studied may mean that they would not discuss it in a face-to-face manner. The anonymity and distance can help to draw out open and honest views from such participants.

- *Targeted interest groups.* A variety of online formats, such as chat rooms, mailing lists and conferences, focus on specific topics, drawing together geographically dispersed participants who may share interests, experiences or expertise.

- *Cost and time savings.* Issues such as the time and travelling expenses of researchers, the hire of venues and the costs of producing transcripts can make face-to-face interviewing an expensive option for many researchers. Online research dramatically reduces or eliminates many of these costs and thus makes qualitative approaches more accessible to a wider array of companies and decision makers.

- *Handling transcripts.* As interviews or observations are built up through online dialogue, many of the potential biases or mistakes that occur through audio recordings can be eliminated.

Challenges

- *Computer literacy for the researcher.* Applying qualitative research online means that some degree of technical expertise is required of the researcher. The extent of expertise depends upon which techniques are being used. For example, moderators of focus groups online will have to learn about the capabilities of the chosen software for running a focus group. They will also have to learn about the specific skills in making the group experience work well online, perhaps by participating in online research conferences or gaining exposure to alternative discussion practices online.

- *Making contact and recruitment.* Establishing contact online requires a mutual exchange of contact details. There are arrays of techniques that can encourage potential participants to engage in a research project, but in essence the researcher has to develop rapport and trust to gain access to and draw the most out of participants.

- *Interactive skills online.* Even if the researcher develops their skills online, it must be remembered that participants use their technology with varying degrees of expertise – from the naive through to the most sophisticated and cutting-edge user.

- *Losing access.* A key challenge for online studies is to sustain electronic connection with participants for the whole period of the qualitative research process. This is a reminder that, unlike a survey which may be a short, one-off contact with a participant, qualitative techniques may unfold and evolve over time and involve returning to participants as issues develop and theory emerges.

Summary

Qualitative and quantitative research should be viewed as complementary. Unfortunately, many researchers and decision makers do not see this, taking dogmatic positions in favour of either qualitative or quantitative research. The defence of qualitative approaches for a particular marketing research problem, through the positive benefits it bestows and through explaining the negative alternatives of a quantitative approach, should be seen as healthy, as should the defence of quantitative approaches. Decision makers use both approaches and will continue to need both.

In a focus group, participants can portray their feelings and behaviour, using their own language and logic. The value of the technique lies in the unexpected findings that emerge when participants are allowed to express what they really feel. Focus groups are conducted by a moderator in a relaxed and informal manner with a small group of participants. The moderator leads and develops the discussion. An experimental focus group should always be run at the start of any series of discussions. The researcher needs to understand how comfortable target participants feel in the chosen location for discussion, how the opening question works, the topic guide, the probes, the mix of participants and the refreshments. Online developments have seen the e-group emerge as a means to engage with geographically dispersed participants. Such engagement can be conducted in a speedier and cheaper manner than traditional focus groups. Traditional focus groups allow for richer observations of participants and more creative sensory experiences to be evaluated. There is no one absolute correct method to administer a focus group; the researchers should understand the factors that will make the technique work for their particular research problem and the type of participants they have to work with.

In-depth interviewing allows researchers to focus upon individuals with the qualities they deem to be important to their research objectives. With a 'quality individual' the researcher can question and probe to great depth and elicit a quality understanding of that individual's behaviour or feelings. The technique is well suited to tackling commercially and personally sensitive issues. It is also well suited to interviewing children. There are many types of interview that can be applied under the term 'in-depth interview'. They can range from the very open and unstructured to semi-structured exchanges. The application of structure in an in-depth interview can be founded on a theoretical underpinning of how individuals should be questioned and probed.

Projective techniques may be classified as association (word association), completion (sentence completion, story completion), construction (picture response, cartoon tests) and expressive (role playing, third-person, personification) techniques. Projective techniques are particularly useful when participants are unwilling or unable to provide the required information by direct questioning methods.

Ethnography is used to describe a range of methods which require researchers to spend a large amount of time observing a particular group of people, by sharing or immersing themselves in their way of life. The ethnographer is expected to analyse critically the situations they observe. The critique and the analysis can be guided by theory but in essence the researcher develops a curiosity, thinks in an abstract manner and at times steps back to reflect and see how emerging ideas connect. By reacting to the events, narrative, images and other forms of expression and by drawing out what participants see as important, ethnographers have the ability to create new explanations and understandings of consumers.

The qualitative researcher needs to develop an understanding of the interplay between characteristics of the target participants, the issues they will be questioned about and the context in which they will be questioned. Building up this understanding is vital to the success of conducting qualitative research methods in international markets. International qualitative research can reveal the cultural nuances of consumer behaviour, their aspirations, and forms of expression. Such nuances can deliver great opportunities to marketers working in international markets, or indeed in domestic markets where there may be diverse multicultural communities.

When conducting qualitative research, the researcher and their client must respect participants. This should include protecting the anonymity of participants, honouring all statements and promises used to ensure participation, and conducting research in a way not to embarrass or harm participants. With the emergence of techniques that use social media such as ethnography using electronic communities, maintaining an ethical relationship with participants is becoming far more challenging.

Digital developments present huge opportunities for the qualitative researcher. Online versions of traditional forms of qualitative research such as focus groups, semi-structured or in-depth interviews, and ethnographic techniques have been developed to great effect. New qualitative techniques have been developed that add further consumer insights. These developments have the potential to present research to participants as meaningful and enjoyable engagements.

Questions

1   What criticisms do qualitative researchers make of the stance adopted by quantitative researchers, and vice versa?

2   What are the key benefits and drawbacks of conducting focus group discussions?

3   What determines the questions, issues and probes used in a focus group?

4   Why is the focus group moderator so important to the success of a focus group discussion?

5   Describe the purpose and benefits of using stimulus material in a focus group.

6   What is an in-depth interview? Summarise the process of administering an in-depth interview.

7   What are the major advantages of in-depth interviews?

8   Choose any particular application of an in-depth interview and present a case for why you think the technique may work much better than a focus group.

9   What are projective techniques? Under what circumstances should projective techniques be used?

10   What does ethnographic research aim to achieve in the study of consumers?

11   Why may marketing decision makers wish to understand the context of consumption?

12   What limitations are there to conducting qualitative research online, compared with meeting participants face to face?

Exercises

1   An advertising agency has selected three pieces of music that it could use in a new advertising campaign. It has come to you as a researcher to help in making the case for selecting the right piece of music for the campaign. What would be the case for using qualitative research for this task?

2   Visit the website of the Association of Qualitative Research Practitioners (**www.aqrp.co.uk**). Examine the reports and views of contributing practitioners and write a report on what you feel are the latest developments and/or exciting opportunities in the use of focus groups.

3 A cosmetics firm would like to increase its penetration of the student market through a new range of organic and 'ethical' products. Conduct two experimental in-depth interviews with a male and female student. Write a report setting out plans for any subsequent form of in-depth interviews and associated techniques, showing how the experimental interviews have impacted upon these plans.

4 You are a brand manager for Lynx deodorant. You wish to invest in an ethnographic study of young men. Ask another student to play the role of marketing director. What case would you make to the marketing director about the value of investing in an ethnographic study?

5 In a small group discuss the following issues: 'Quantitative research is more important than qualitative research because it generates conclusive findings.' 'The dress, appearance and speech of the moderator create biases in group discussions that cannot be evaluated.' 'Are there any dangers (for researchers and participants) in conducting in-depth studies on issues that participants hardly reflect upon on a day-to-day basis?' 'Projective techniques cannot work well with shy and introverted participants.'

Notes

1. Van den Bergh, J. and Behrer, M. (2011) *How Cool Brands Stay Hot. Branding to Generation Y* (London: Kogan Page).
2. Sbarbaro, S., Van den Bergh, J., Veris, E. and De Ruyck, T., 'We got a crush on you(th)! Influential Gen Y'ers from 15 global cities to learn why something is cool', ESOMAR, *Qualitative*, Vienna (Nov. 2011).
3. Ford, J., Carlson, L. and Kover, A.J., 'Comments – The quant-qual debate: where are we in advertising?' *International Journal of Advertising*, 27 (4) (2008); Alioto, M.F. and Gillespe, D., 'The complex customer: applying qualitative methods in automotive NPD', ESOMAR *Qualitative Research*, Athens (Oct. 2006).
4. Cooper, P., 'We've come a long way', *Research World* (Nov. 2007) 8–11; Cooper, P., 'Consumer understanding, change and qualitative research', *Journal of the Market Research Society*, 41 (1) (January 1999), 3.
5. Kenway, J., 'Keep on moving', *Research* (November 2005), 36.
6. Cooper, P., 'In search of excellence: The evolution and future of qualitative research', ESOMAR, *Annual Congress*, Berlin (Sept. 2007).
7. Sykes, W., 'Validity and reliability in qualitative market research: a review of the literature', *Journal of the Market Research Society*, 32 (3) (1990), 289; De Groot, G., 'Qualitative research: deeply dangerous or just plain dotty?' *European Research*, 14 (3) (1986), 136–141.
8. Truong, Y., 'Personal aspirations and the consumption of luxury goods', *International Journal of Market Research*, 52 (5) (2010), 655–73.
9. Branthwaite, A. and Patterson, S., 'The vitality of qualitative research in the era of blogs and tweeting: An anatomy of contemporary research methods', ESOMAR, *Qualitative Research*, Barcelona, (Nov. 2010).
10. Bloor, M., Frankland, J., Thomas, M. and Robson, K., *Focus Groups in Social Research* (Thousand Oaks, CA: Sage, 2001).
11. Kreuger, R.A. and Casey, M.A., *Focus Groups: A practical guide for applied research*, 3rd edn (Thousand Oaks, CA: Sage, 2000); Drayton, J. and Tynan, C., 'Conducting focus groups – a guide for first-time users', *Marketing Intelligence and Planning*, 6 (1) (1988), 5–9.
12. For more discussion, see Dexter A. and Ngoc Hieu An, B., 'From Bricolage to Pho – Vietnam as a model for global influences and assimilations at meal times', ESOMAR, *Asia Pacific*, Beijing (April 2009); Andrews, M. and Langmaid, R., 'Theory and practice in the large group', Market Research Society, *Annual Conference* (2003); Morgan, D.L., *Planning focus groups* (Thousand Oaks, CA: Sage, 1998), 71–76.
13. Forrest, C., 'Research with a laugh track', *Marketing News*, 36 (5) (4 March 2002), 48; Mazella, G.F., 'Show-and-tell focus groups reveal core bloomer values', *Marketing News*, 31 (12) (9 June 1997), H8.
14. Morgan, D.L. *Planning focus groups* (Thousand Oaks, CA: Sage, 1998), 71–76.
15. MacDougall, C., 'Planning and recruiting the sample for focus groups and in-depth interviews', *Qualitative Health Research*, 11 (1) (January 2001), 117–126; Kahn, H., 'A professional opinion', *American Demographics* (Tools Supplement) (October 1996), 14–19.
16. Gordon, W., 'New life for group discussions', *ResearchPlus* (July 1993), 1.
17. Baskin, M., 'Observing groups', *WARC Best Practice* (Nov. 2010).

18. McPhee, N., 'Is There a Future For "Real" Qualitative Market Research Interviewing in the Digital Age?' ESOMAR, *Congress Odyssey*, Athens (Sept. 2010); Krueger, R.A., *Moderating focus groups* (Thousand Oaks, CA: Sage, 1998), 30.

19. Stokes, D. and Bergin, R., 'Methodology or "methodolatry"? An evaluation of focus groups and depth interviews', *Qualitative Market Research: An International Journal*, 9 (1) (2006) 26–37; Goldsmith, R.E., 'The Focus Group Research Handbook', *The Services Industries Journal*, 20 (3) (July 2000), 214–215; Greenbaum, T.L., *The Handbook for Focus Group Research* (Newbury Park, CA: Sage, 1997).

20. Krueger, R.A., *Developing questions for focus groups* (Thousand Oaks, CA: Sage, 1998), 25.

21. Ellis, R., 'So how do you upstage a Ferrari owner?' *ResearchPlus* (November 1994), 10.

22. Reid, D.J. and Reid, F.J., 'Online focus groups', *International Journal of Market Research*, 47 (2) (2005) 131–62; O'Connor, H. and Madge, C., 'Focus groups in cyberspace: Using the Internet for qualitative research', *Qualitative Market Research*, 6 (2) (2003) 133–43; Kozinets, R.V., 'The field behind the screen: Using netnography for marketing research online communities', *Journal of Marketing Research*, 39 (1) (Feb. 2002).

23. Cheng, C.C., Krumwiede, D. and Sheu, C., 'Online audio group discussions: A comparison with face-to-face methods', *International Journal of Market Research*, 51 (2) (2009) 219–41; Brüggen, E. and Willems, P., 'A critical comparison of offline focus groups, online focus groups and e-Delphi', *International Journal of Market Research*, 51 (3) (2009) 363–81.

24. Supphellen, M., 'Understanding core brand equity: Guidelines for in-depth elicitation of brand associations', *International Journal of Market Research*, 42 (3) (2000); Harris, L.M., 'Expanding horizons', *Marketing Research: A Magazine of Management and Application*, 8 (2) (Summer 1996), 12.

25. Rédier, E. and McClure, S., 'Let the product talk', ESOMAR, *Fragrance Conference*, Paris (Nov. 2007).

26. Kvale, S., *Interviews: An introduction to qualitative research interviewing* (Thousand Oaks, CA: Sage, 1996); Rubin, H.J. and Rubin, I.S., *Qualitative Interviewing: The art of hearing data* (Thousand Oaks, CA: Sage, 1995).

27. Warren, C.A.B., 'Qualitative interviewing', in Gubrium, J.F. and Holstein, J.A. (eds) *Handbook of interview research: Context and method* (Thousand Oaks, CA: Sage, 2002), 83–101.

28. Johnson, J.M., 'In-depth Interviewing', in Gubrium, J.F. and Holstein, J.A. (eds) *Handbook of interview research: Context and method* (Thousand Oaks, CA: Sage, 2002), 104.

29. Schwalbe, M.L. and Wolkomir, M., 'Interviewing men', in Gubrium, J.F. and Holstein, J.A. (eds) *Handbook of interview research: Context and method* (Thousand Oaks, CA: Sage, 2002), 203–220.

30. Schnee, R.K., 'Uncovering consumers' deepest feelings using psychologically probing qualitative research techniques', *Advertising Research Foundation Workshops, Consumer Insights Workshop*, (Oct. 2000); 'Looking for a deeper meaning', *Marketing* (Market Research Top 75 Supplement) (17 July 1997), 16–17.

31. Arnal, L. and Holguin, R., 'Taxis, vans and subways: Capturing insights while commuting', ESOMAR, *Qualitative Research*, Paris, (Nov. 2007).

32. Sharma, A., Pugh, G., 'Serpents with tails in their mouths: A reflexive look at qualitative research', ESOMAR, *Qualitative Research*, Paris, (Nov. 2007); Sokolow, H., 'In-depth interviews increasing in importance', *Marketing News* (13 September 1985), 26.

33. Branthwaite, A., 'Investigating the power of imagery in marketing communication: Evidence-based techniques', *Qualitative Market Research: An International Journal*, 5 (3) (2002) 164–171; Chandler, J. and Owen, M., *Developing brands with qualitative market research*, (Thousand Oaks, CA: Sage, 2002, 86–100; Best, K., 'Something old is something new in qualitative research', *Marketing News*, 29 (18) (28 August 1995), 14.

34. Mariampolski, H., *Qualitative Marketing Research: A comprehensive guide* (Thousand Oaks, Sage, 2001), 206.

35. Boddy, C., 'Projective techniques in market research – valueless subjectivity or insightful reality?' *International Journal of Market Research*, 47 (3) (2005) 239–54.

36. Zaichowsky, J.L., 'The why of consumption: contemporary perspectives and consumer motives, goals, and desires', *Academy of Marketing Science*, 30 (2) (Spring 2002), 179; Levy, S.J., 'Interpreting consumer mythology: Structural approach to consumer behaviour focuses on storytelling', *Marketing Management*, 2 (4) (1994), 4–9.

37. Catterall, M., 'Using projective techniques in education research', *British Educational Research Journal*, 26 (2) (April 2000), 245–56; Kennedy, M.M., 'So how'm I doing?' *Across the Board*, 34 (6) (June 1997), 53–54; Lindzey, G., 'On the classification of projective techniques', *Psychological Bulletin* (1959), 158–168.

38. Grimes, A. and Kitchen, P., 'Researching mere exposure effects to advertising – theoretical foundations and methodological implications', *International Journal of Market Research*, 49 (2) (2007) 191–219.

39. Clarke, B., 'If this child were a car, what sort of car would it be? The global child: Using appropriate projective techniques to view the world through their eyes', ESOMAR, *Qualitative Research*, Cannes (Nov. 2004); Suprenant, C., Churchill, G.A. and Kinnear, T.C. (eds), 'Can role playing be substituted for actual consumption?' *Advances in Consumer Research* (Provo, UT: Association for Consumer Research, 1984), 122–126.

40. Strachan, J. and Pavie-Latour, V., 'Forum – Food for thought: Shouldn't we actually target food advertising more towards kids and not less?' *International Journal of Market Research*, 50 (1) (2008) 13–27.

41. Branthwaite, A. and Patterson, S., 'The vitality of qualitative research in the era of blogs and tweeting: An anatomy of contemporary research methods', ESOMAR, *Qualitative Research*, Barcelona (Nov. 2010).

42. McPhee, N. and Chrystal, G., 'Who's eaten my porridge? Discovering brand image differences', ESOMAR, *Healthcare Conference*, Rome (Feb. 2008); Gill, J. and Johnson, P., *Research Methods for Managers*, 3rd edn (Thousand Oaks, CA: Sage, 2002); Varki, S., Cooil, B. and Rust, R.T., 'Modeling fuzzy data in qualitative marketing research', *Journal of Marketing Research*, 37 (4) (November 2000), 480–89.

43. For more on projective techniques, see Burden, S., 'Emotional . . . but does it sell?' *Admap*, 496 (July/August 2008) 41–42; Clarke, B., 'If this child were a car, what sort of car would it be? The global child: Using appropriate projective techniques to view the world through their eyes', ESOMAR, *Qualitative Research*, Cannes (Nov. 2004); Valentine, V. and Evans, M., 'The dark side of the onion: Rethinking the meaning of "rational" and "emotional" responses', *Journal of the Market Research Society*, 35 (April 1993), 125–44.

44. Angrosino, M., *Doing Ethnographic and Observational Research*, Sage Publications (2007); Travers, M., *Qualitative Research through Case Studies* (London: Sage, 2001), 4.

45. Schensul, J.J., '*Designing and Conducting Ethnographic Research: An Introduction*', AltaMira Press, 2nd edn (2010); Fetterman, D.M., *Ethnography: Step by step* (Thousand Oaks, CA: Sage, 1998), 1.

46. Silverman, D., *Interpreting Qualitative Data: Methods for Analysing Talk, Text and Interaction*, 2nd edn (London: Sage, 2001), 45.

47. Gnädig, A. and Schieleit, O., 'The death of depth: Skimming the surface', *Research World* (Jan. 2006) 44–45.

48. Stewart, A., *The Ethnographer's Method* (Thousand Oaks, CA: Sage, 1998), 5.

49. Mariampolski, H., 'The power of ethnography', *Journal of the Market Research Society*, 41 (1) (January 1999), 81–82.

50. Mariampolski, H., *Qualitative Marketing Research: A comprehensive guide* (Thousand Oaks, CA: Sage, 2001), 52.

51. Branthwaite, A. and Cooper, P., 'A new role for projective techniques', ESOMAR, *Qualitative Research*, Budapest (Oct. 2001), 236–63.

52. Cooper, P., 'In search of excellence: the evolution and future of qualitative research', ESOMAR, *Annual Congress*, Berlin (Sept. 2007).

53. Totman, P., 'Arbiters of Meaning: The hidden role of the interpreter in international qualitative research', ESOMAR, *Qualitative Research*, Barcelona (Nov. 2010).

54. Cooper, P., 'In search of excellence: The evolution and future of qualitative research', ESOMAR, *Annual Congress*, Berlin (Sept. 2007).

55. Mann, C. and Stewart, F., *Internet Communication and Qualitative Research: A Handbook for Researching Online* (London: Sage, 2000), 17–38.

5

Descriptive research design: survey, observation and causal research

Stage 1

Problem definition

Stage 2

Research approach developed

Stage 3

Research design developed

Stage 4

Fieldwork or data collection

Stage 5

Data integrity and analysis

Stage 6

Report preparation and presentation

Because no particular research design is best, a researcher must clearly understand the strengths and weaknesses of all descriptive methods.

Objectives

After reading this chapter, you should be able to:

1 discuss and classify quantitative survey methods and describe the various online, telephone, personal and mail interviewing techniques;

2 identify the criteria for evaluating survey methods;

3 explain and classify the different quantitative observation techniques;

4 identify the criteria for evaluating observation techniques, compare the different techniques, and evaluate which are suited for a particular research project;

5 explain the concept of causality and differentiate two types of validity: internal validity and external validity;

6 discuss the various extraneous variables that can affect the validity of results obtained through experimentation;

7 compare and contrast the use of laboratory versus field experimentation and experimental versus non-experimental designs in marketing research;

8 understand the problems of conducting descriptive research designs in international markets;

9 describe the ethical issues involved in conducting descriptive research designs;

10 appreciate how digital developments are shaping the manner in which descriptive research designs are managed and applied.

Overview

In this chapter, we focus on the major techniques employed in descriptive research designs: surveys, quantitative observation and causal designs. Descriptive research has as its prime objective the description of some phenomena, usually consumer or market characteristics. Survey and quantitative observation techniques are vital techniques in descriptive research designs. Survey techniques may be classified by mode of administration as online, telephone surveys, face-to-face and postal surveys. We describe each of these techniques and present a comparative evaluation of all survey techniques. Then we consider the major observational techniques: personal observation, electronic observation and trace analysis.

We explore the concept of causality, identifying the necessary conditions for this form of description. The role of validity in causal studies is examined, with consideration of the extraneous variables and procedures for controlling them. We present a classification of experimental designs and consider specific designs, along with the relative merits of laboratory and field experiments.

The relative advantages and disadvantages of observation over survey techniques and the considerations involved in conducting survey and observation research when researching international markets are discussed. Several ethical issues that arise in descriptive studies are identified. Many digital developments are shaping how descriptive studies are designed and delivered in manners that are more engaging for participants. Digital developments are also shaping how and what may be observed of consumers.

To begin our discussion, we present an example of a descriptive study that is based upon a causal design to test hypotheses that uses a survey to generate data.

Real research	Consumer consideration of brands they do not remember[1]

In the evaluation of the effectiveness of sports sponsorship, a study examined spectator memorisation of sponsors. To conduct this study, researchers used an experimental research design based upon data collected from face-to-face interviews. The researchers did not expect the conscious memory of sponsors to be strong; however, spectators may have remembered the sponsor brand better than a control group did. Their main hypothesis was that 'There is a conscious memorisation effect of sponsorship, such that (a) recall and (b) recognition of the sponsor brand are higher among spectators of the event (experimental group) than among persons not exposed to the event (control group).' Their data collection took place during an international tennis tournament with the focus on one of the official sponsors. Over four days, face-to-face interviews were conducted with a convenience sample of 584 participants. For the control group (171 persons), interviews took place before spectators entered the stadium. The experimental group (413 persons) were interviewed inside the stadium, after having attended one or several matches. To avoid potential effects due to participant familiarity with the sponsor brand, those participants who recalled being exposed to a sponsor advertisement during the four weeks preceding the event, as well as those who had used the sponsor brand or any of its competitors in the past, were eliminated from the sample. This resulted in 110 usable questionnaires for the control group and 241 usable questionnaires for the experimental group. Of the 241 spectators exposed to the sponsors, 5.8 per cent spontaneously recalled the target brand and 17 per cent recognised the target brand as a sponsor, in support of the main hypothesis. Two hundred remaining spectators who were not conscious of the target brand sponsoring the event revealed significantly higher perceptual implicit memory of the target brand than that among the control group.

SURVEY METHODS

Survey method
A structured questionnaire administered to a sample of a target population, designed to elicit specific information from participants.

Structured data collection
Use of a formal questionnaire that presents questions in a prearranged order.

Fixed-response alternative questions
Questions that require participants to choose from a set of predetermined answers.

The **survey method** of obtaining information is based upon the use of structured questionnaires administered to a sample of a target population. Participants may be asked a variety of questions regarding their behaviour, intentions, attitudes, awareness, motivations, and demographic characteristics. These questions may be asked verbally, in writing or via a computer (including mobile devices). 'Structured' here refers to the degree of standardisation imposed on the data collection process. In **structured data collection**, a formal questionnaire is prepared and the questions are asked in a prearranged order.

The structured-data survey, the most popular data collection method, involves administering a questionnaire. In a typical questionnaire, most questions are **fixed-response alternative questions** that require the participant to select from a predetermined set of responses. The survey method has several advantages. First, the questionnaire can be simple to administer. Second, the data obtained are consistent because the responses are limited to the alternatives stated. The use of fixed-response questions reduces the variability in the results that may be caused by differences in interviewers. Finally, coding, analysis and interpretation of data are relatively simple.[2]

The disadvantages are that participants may be unable or unwilling to provide the desired information. For example, consider questions about motivational factors. Participants may not be consciously aware of their motives for choosing specific brands. Therefore, they may be unable to provide accurate answers to questions about their motives. Participants may be unwilling to respond if the information requested is sensitive or personal. In addition,

Figure 5.1

A classification of survey methods

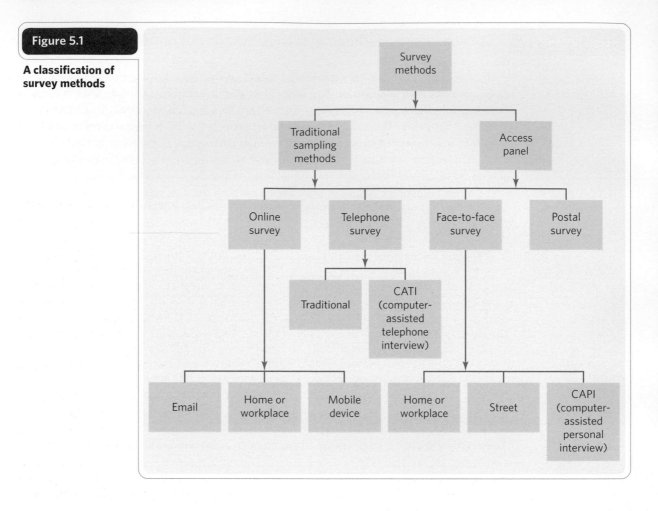

structured questions and fixed-response alternative questions may result in loss of validity for certain types of data such as beliefs and feelings. Finally, wording questions in a consistent manner to all potential survey participants is not easy. The survey imposes the language and logic of the researcher on survey participants. Given this core characteristic of survey techniques, great care must be taken to ensure that the language and logic used in questionnaires are meaningful and valid to target participants. Despite the above disadvantages, the survey approach is by far the most common method of primary data collection in marketing research.[3] Figure 5.1 presents a classification of survey methods.

Survey questionnaires may be administered in four major modes: (1) online surveys, (2) telephone surveys, (3) face-to-face surveys and (4) postal surveys. Online surveys can be conducted via the web on devices in home and offices. The use of mobile devices in administering surveys could be classified as a telephone survey. Whilst many mobile devices are indeed telephones, viewing them solely as a means to conduct a telephone survey misses much of their potential. Mobile devices enable consumers to access audio and video, while communicating via text, email, social media and web browsing. Globally there are more Smartphones in circulation that have great power and functionality and are able to cope with an array of research engagements.[4] We thus classify mobile devices as a form of online survey. Telephone surveys may be further classified as traditional telephone survey and computer-assisted telephone interviews (CATIs). Face-to-face surveys may be conducted in the home or workplace, as street surveys, or as computer-assisted personal interviews (CAPIs). The final major method, postal surveys, takes the form of the traditional hard copy, self-completion survey administered through the post.

Online surveys

Online surveys can be conducted on devices in homes or the workplace, or administered on mobile devices. As a proportion of global spend on marketing research techniques, the use of online surveys has grown consistently over many years, and continues to do so. The survey experience can be designed in a personalised manner, and it can be much cheaper and faster to administer compared to other survey methods.

Email surveys

We begin with email surveys as they can be seen as the forerunner to the massive development of online surveys. Text-based email surveys can be convenient for participants because they require no facilities or expertise beyond those that they use in their day-to-day email communications. They can be conducted online at home, workplace or mobile devices. The survey is written within the body of the email message which is then sent out over the Internet. Participants type the answers to either closed-ended or open-ended questions at designated places, and click on 'reply'. Responses are then data entered and tabulated in the manner of a postal survey or imported with software that interprets the emailed responses and reads the answers directly into a format compatible with the requirements of an analysis package. Email surveys have several limitations, primarily being that they can appear dry and uninteresting.[5] Given the technical limitations of most email systems, questionnaires cannot utilise programmed skip patterns, logic checks or randomisation. The limited intelligence of ASCII text cannot keep a participant from, say, choosing both 'yes' and 'no' to a question where only one response is meaningful. Skipping instructions (e.g. 'If the answer to Question 5 is yes, go to Question 9') must appear explicitly, just as on paper as there is no automated routing. These factors can reduce the quality of data from an email survey and can require much post-survey data cleaning.[6] There are also problems in locating accurate and current email address lists and even if these can be located, given spam protection software, there is no guarantee that an email will reach intended participants. Given the advantages of other online survey methods, the popularity of the email survey is waning.

Online surveys using fixed and mobile devices

Early versions of Internet surveys were labelled as CAWI (computer-assisted web interviews) to follow previous acronyms within the research industry of CATI (Computer Assisted Telephone Interviews) and CAPI (Computer Assisted Personal Interviews). The far simpler term 'online' is used for all Internet surveys hosted on a website. Participants may be recruited online from potential participant databases maintained by either a research agency or a panel management company, or they can be recruited by conventional techniques (telephone, face-to-face or postal). Frequently, participants are not recruited, but those who happen to be visiting a website on which the survey is posted (or other popular websites) are invited to participate in the survey. Either all or every nth web visitor is allowed to participate. Web surveys offer several advantages over email surveys. It is usual to construct buttons, checkboxes and data entry fields that prevent participants from selecting more than one response where only one is intended, or from otherwise typing where no response is required. Skip patterns can be programmed and performed automatically as in CATI or CAPI. It is possible to validate responses as they are entered. Additional survey stimuli such as graphical images, animations and links to other web pages may be integrated into or around the survey. The visual layout and care taken in designing additional stimuli can do much for participant engagement. This can contribute to a higher quality experience for participants, encouraging a more committed response.

Researchers are also conducting online surveys using mobile devices. The Smartphone and tablet offer many possibilities, providing both portability and immediacy for anytime, anywhere data collection. These devices give much potential for researchers to reach and engage with participants who may be difficult to access via other forms of survey, though there remain many challenges.[7] There is a wide variety of mobile devices, from many major manufacturers, in a variety of models. Screen sizes, resolution, processing power, memory, and input modalities vary widely, even between devices of the same manufacturer. Operating systems and application programming environments are also very different.[8] Regardless of the technical challenges, there are a growing number of survey applications using mobile devices.

The following lists summarise the advantages and disadvantages of online surveys:[9]

Advantages

- *Speed*. Compared with other survey methods especially when conducting international research, the time taken to conduct a survey can be reduced to a matter of days rather than weeks. Even if one includes the time taken to contact participants, to establish their willingness to take part in a survey, for them to reply, for the survey to be sent, for it to be completed and then returned, such surveys can be completed relatively quickly.

- *Cost*. Once the electronic questionnaire is designed, it is almost as easy to send it to 10,000 people as to 10, since there are no printing, stationery and postage costs. Preparing data for analysis needs less manual intervention and can be also much cheaper.

- *Quality of response*. A range of design features can be used to make the survey more appealing and interesting. Graphics can be used to create visual and moving forms of scaling to maintain the interest of participants but also to put them in a frame of mind that elicits more from them.

- *Interviewer bias removed*. The method maintains the key advantage of postal surveys in being able to present a consistent form of measurement.

- *Data quality*. Logic and validity checks can be built in thus allowing the development of more personalised questionnaire designs. In areas where open-ended or 'other – please state' responses are required, the participant types in answers ready for analysis.

- *Contacting certain target groups*. Many participants may be reluctant to complete surveys by traditional methods. Much of this reluctance can be attributed to the context of where the survey is administered and how comfortable participants are in these contexts. With the online survey, the participant is largely in control of the context and can respond in circumstances that they feel comfortable with.

Disadvantages

- *Sampling frames*. Access panels usually provide means to access particular types of participant. However, there are major questions surrounding their representativeness and the motivations of panel members.[10] Email directories can help but there can be questions about their currency, accuracy and means of classifying different types of target participant. Another issue is that participants who are recruited through browsing or clicking through banner ads or sources such as Facebook are self-selecting and the researcher does not know whether participants are really representative of a target population. Being able to generalise findings to a particular population becomes difficult with a self-selecting sample.

- *Access to the web*. Though access to the Internet has grown enormously, and continues to grow in even remote and poor communities across the globe, the penetration of households and businesses is still highly variable within and across countries. Much depends upon the characteristics of the type of participant that is being targeted for a survey. Even if they do have access to the Internet, do they have access to the means to engage with the survey in the manner intended by the questionnaire designer?

- *Technical problems*. Depending upon the device that participants use, the questionnaire may 'work' or not as was intended by the designer, this is particularly true with online surveys. Unlike the general homogeneity of computer browsers, virtually no uniform standards exist for the often individually adapted software on mobile devices. Processing power and storage capacity vary more sharply among mobile devices and more restraint is needed in the graphic design of mobile online surveys.[11]

Telephone surveys

Telephone surveys may be categorised as traditional or computer-assisted.

Traditional telephone surveys

Traditional telephone surveys involve phoning a sample of participants and asking them a series of questions, using a paper questionnaire to record the responses. From a central location, a wide geographical area can be covered, including international markets. Given that telephone interviewers cannot give participants any visual prompts, they have to write down answers to any open-ended questions and may have to flick through the questionnaire to find appropriate questions for a particular participant (filtering). Today, this approach is rarely used in commercial marketing research, the more common approach being CATI.

Computer-assisted telephone interviews (CATI)

CATI uses a computerised questionnaire administered to participants over the telephone with a questionnaire on a networked computer or a PC. The main benefit of CATI is the speed of collecting data and analysis. Speed is of the essence in subjects where participant attitudes and behaviour can change quickly. One of the most widespread uses of CATI is for political opinion polls. With CATI, the computer systematically guides the interviewer. Only one question at a time appears on the screen. The computer checks responses for appropriateness and consistency. It uses the responses as they are obtained to personalise the questionnaire. Data collection flows naturally and smoothly. Interviewing time is reduced, data quality is enhanced, and the laborious steps in the data collection process, coding questionnaires and entering data into the computer, are eliminated. Because the responses are entered directly into the computer, interim and update reports on data collection or results can be provided almost instantaneously.

The biggest drawback of CATI lies in participants' willingness to be interviewed by telephone. In a 2003 study participant cooperation by the Council for Marketing and Opinion Research (CMOR) in the USA, only 7 per cent of participants called were willing to answer questions. Across Europe there are several developments that impact upon telephone usage: the percentage of households equipped with a fixed phone is dropping, while the percentage of households equipped with mobile phone access is rising. Additionally, the percentage of mobile-only households is increasing, while the percentage of households that have only fixed phone access is decreasing. There are many factors that make it very difficult to conduct telephone surveys. At times, the technique may be confused in the minds of participants with cold-call selling techniques. To overcome this problem requires interviewers who are trained to reassure participants and to make the interviewing experience worthwhile.

Face-to-face surveys

Face-to-face surveying methods may be categorised as home, workplace, street or computer-assisted.

Home or workplace surveys

In face-to-face home or workplace surveys, participants are interviewed face to face in their 'personal space'. The interviewer's task is to contact the participants, ask the questions and record the responses. In recent years, the use of face-to-face home and workplace surveys has declined due to their high cost. However, there are many situations where they are used because of the reassurances of quality of the interview process, the comfort of the context felt by certain participants and the nature of the questions that are being administered. Face-to-face surveys are used extensively in business-to-business research for participants who cannot be effectively interviewed by telephone or post. Managers being interviewed have the comfort and security of their office and can control the timing and pace of the interview. For the researcher, the big benefit of meeting managers in their office is the ability to build up a rapport, probe and gain the full attention of the manager.

Street surveys

For street surveys, participants are intercepted while they are shopping in city centres or shopping centres. They may be questioned there and then in the street or taken to a specific test facility. In the testing of new product formulations, test facilities are ideal to allow participants the time and context to sample and evaluate products. The technique can also be used to test merchandising ideas, advertisements and other forms of marketing communications. The big advantage of the street survey is that it is more efficient for the participant to come to the interviewer than for the interviewer to go to the participant.[12]

Computer-assisted personal interviews (CAPI)

In CAPI, a computer partially replaces the interviewer. The use of colour, graphical images and on- and off-screen stimuli can all contribute to making the interview process both interesting and stimulating. This method has been classified as a face-to-face survey technique because an interviewer is usually present to guide the participant as needed. CAPI has been used to collect data at test facilities from street surveys, product clinics, conferences and trade shows. It can be used in a kiosk format at locations such as museums or heritage sites to conduct visitor surveys. It may also be used for home or workplace surveys. A major development for marketers, especially in financial services, has been the use of customer satisfaction surveys to guide strategic and operational decisions. With traditional survey techniques, the interviewer may have to carry a huge questionnaire to cope with questions that measure attitudes to a range of banks and a range of services taken from those banks. With CAPI, when a particular bank is chosen, particular questions may be filtered out, and choosing a particular service from that bank can filter out further questions. Questions specific to the participant may then be asked, in all making the interview process far more efficient.

Postal surveys

In the postal survey, questionnaires are mailed to preselected potential participants. A typical mailed package consists of the outgoing envelope, cover letter, questionnaire, return envelope and possibly an incentive. The participants complete and return the questionnaires. There is no verbal interaction between the researcher and the participant in the survey process.[13] There may be an initial contact with potential participants, to establish the correct person to send the questionnaire to, and to motivate them before they receive the survey. Before data collection can begin a sampling frame needs to be compiled so that potential participants can be identified. Therefore, an initial task is to obtain a valid mailing list. Mailing lists can be compiled from telephone directories, customer databases or association membership databases, or can be purchased from publication subscription lists or commercial mailing list companies.[14] Regardless of its source, a mailing list should be current and closely related to the population of interest. With an understanding of characteristics of target participants and what will motivate them to respond honestly, as fully and as quickly as possible, the researcher must also make decisions about the various elements of the postal survey package (see Table 5.1).

Table 5.1	Some decisions related to the postal survey package

Outgoing envelope	Method of addressing; envelope size; colour; postage
Covering letter	Personalisation; sponsorship; type of appeal; signature
Questionnaire	Size, length and content; colour and layout; format and reproduction; participant anonymity
Instructions	As part of covering letter; a separate sheet; alongside individual questions
Return envelope	Whether to include one; type of envelope; postage
Incentives	Feedback of findings; monetary vs. non-monetary; prepaid vs promised amount

A comparative evaluation of survey methods

Not all survey techniques are appropriate in a given situation. Therefore, the researcher should conduct a comparative evaluation to determine which techniques are appropriate. Table 5.2 compares the different survey techniques through a range of criteria. For any particular research project, the relative importance attached to these criteria will vary. These factors may be broadly classified as task, situational and participant factors.

Table 5.2	A comparative evaluation of survey techniques

	Email	Online	Telephone CATI	Home and workplace	Street surveys	CAPI	Postal
Flexibility of data collection	*	****	****	*****	*****	****	*
Diversity of questions	***	****	*	*****	*****	*****	***
Use of physical stimuli	*	***	*	****	*****	*****	***
Sample control	*	**	****	****	****	***	*
Quantity of data	***	****	**	***	***	***	**
Response rate	*	**	***	*****	****	*****	*
Control of data collection environment	*	*	***	****	*****	*****	*
Control of field force	*****	*****	***	*	***	***	*****
Potential for interviewer bias	None	None	***	*****	*****	*	None
Potential to probe participants	*	*	*	*****	***	***	*
Potential to build rapport	*	*	***	*****	****	****	*
Speed	*****	*****	*****	****	***	****	*
Low cost	*****	*****	***	*	**	**	****
Perceived participant anonymity	***	*****	***	*	*	*	*****
Social desirability	*****	*****	***	**	*	****	*****
Obtaining sensitive information	***	***	*	*****	*	***	***
Low incidence rate	***	*****	*****	*	*	*	***
Participant control	*****	****	**	*	*	*	*****

Key: low = *, moderate to low = **, moderate = ***, moderate to high — ****, high = *****

Task factors

The demand that the survey task places upon participants and the data collection process influences the survey method that should be used.

Flexibility of data collection

The flexibility of data collection is determined primarily by the extent to which the participant can interact with the interviewer and the survey questionnaire. The face-to-face survey, whether conducted as a home, workplace or street survey, affords a very high form flexibility of data collection. Because the participant and the interviewer meet face to face, the interviewer can administer complex questionnaires, explain and clarify difficult questions, and even use unstructured techniques.

Diversity of questions

The diversity of questions that can be asked in a survey depends on the degree of interaction the participant has with the interviewer and the questionnaire, as well as the participant's ability actually to see the questions.

Use of physical stimuli

Often it is helpful or necessary to use physical stimuli such as products, product prototypes, commercials or promotional displays during an interview. For the most basic example, a taste test involves tasting a product and answering questions that evaluate the taste. In other cases, photographs, maps or other audio-visual cues are helpful.

Sample control

Sample control
The ability of the survey mode to reach the units specified in the sample effectively and efficiently.

Sample control is the ability of the survey mode to reach participants specified in the sample effectively and efficiently.[15]

Quantity of data

Home and workplace face-to-face surveys allow the researcher to collect relatively large amounts of data. The social relationship between the interviewer and the participant, as well as the home or office environment, can motivate the participant to spend more time in the interview.

Response rate

Response rate
The percentage of the total attempted interviews that are completed.

Survey **response rate** is broadly defined as the percentage of the total attempted interviews that are completed.

Situational factors

In any practical situation, the researcher has to balance the need to collect accurate and high-quality data with the budget and time constraints. The situational factors that are important include control of the data collection environment, control of field force, potential for interviewer bias, potential to probe participants, potential to build rapport, speed and cost.

Control of the data collection environment

The context in which a questionnaire is completed can affect the way that a participant answers questions. An example of this would be the amount of distraction from other people around, noise and temperature. The degree of control a researcher has over the context or environment in which the participant answers the questionnaire differentiates the various survey modes.

Control of field force

Field force
Both the actual interviewers and the supervisors involved in data collection.

The field force consists of interviewers and supervisors involved in data collection. Because they require no such personnel, postal surveys, email and online surveys eliminate most field force challenges.

Potential for interviewer bias

An interviewer can bias the results of a survey by the manner in which they: select participants; ask research questions; pose questions in another way when participants do not understand the question as presented on the questionnaire; probe; and record answers. The extent of the interviewer's role determines the potential for bias.[16]

Potential to probe participants

Although the interviewer has the potential to create bias in the responses elicited from participants, it is balanced somewhat by the amount of probing that can be done. For example, a survey may ask participants which brands of beer they have seen advertised on TV over the past month. A list of brands could be presented to participants and they could simply look at the list and call out the names. What may be important in the survey is what brands they could remember. There may be a first response, of a brand that could be remembered unaided. A simple probe such as 'any others?' or 'any involving sports personalities?' could be recorded as a second response.

Potential to build rapport

Another counter to the bias in the responses elicited from participants by face-to-face surveys is the amount of rapport that can be built up with participants. Rapport may be vital to communicate why the survey is being conducted, with a corresponding rationale for the participant to spend time answering the questions. Beyond motivating participants to take part in a survey is the need for the participant to answer truthfully, to reflect upon the questions properly and not to rush through the questionnaire. Building up a good rapport with participants can be vital to gain a full and honest response to a survey.

Speed

First, there is the speed with which a questionnaire can be created, distributed to participants, and the data returned. Because printing, mailing and data keying delays are eliminated, data can be in hand within hours of writing an online or telephone questionnaire. Data are obtained in electronic form, so statistical analysis software can be programmed to process standard questionnaires and return statistical summaries and charts automatically.

Low cost

For large samples, the cost of online surveys is the lowest. Printing, mailing, keying and interviewer costs are eliminated, and the incremental costs per participant are typically low, so studies with large numbers of participants can be done at substantial savings compared with postal, telephone or face-to-face surveys.[17]

Participant factors

Since surveys are generally targeted at specific participant groups, participant characteristics have to be considered when selecting a survey method. The participant factors that are important include perceived participant anonymity, social desirability, obtaining sensitive information, low incidence rate and participant control.

Perceived participant anonymity

Perceived participant
anonymity
The participants'
perceptions that their
identities will not
be discerned by the
interviewer or researcher.

Perceived participant anonymity refers to the participants' perceptions that their identities will not be discerned by the interviewer or the researcher. Perceived anonymity of the participant is high in postal surveys and online surveys because there is no contact with an interviewer while responding.

Social desirability

Social desirability
The tendency of
participants to give
answers that may not
be accurate but may be
desirable from a social
standpoint.

Social desirability is the tendency of participants to give answers that they feel to be acceptable in front of others, including interviewers. When participants are questioned face to face by an interviewer, they may give an answer that they feel to be 'acceptable' rather than how they really feel or behave.[18]

Obtaining sensitive information

Sensitive information may mean an issue that is personally sensitive, such as the way in which a participant may be classified or the use of hygiene products. What may be deemed 'sensitive' varies enormously between different types of participant. For some participants, asking questions about the type and amount of household cleaning products may be seen as revealing characteristics of their personal cleanliness; they see it as a sensitive issue and would need a lot of reassurance before revealing the truth. Many classification questions in a survey, such as the participant's age, gender, educational or income level, can also be seen as highly sensitive. In business research, characteristics of an organisation's activities may be seen as commercially sensitive.

Low incidence rate

Incidence rate
Refers to the rate of
occurrence or the
percentage of persons
eligible to participate in
a study.

Incidence rate refers to the rate of occurrence or the percentage of persons eligible to participate in the study. Incidence rate determines how many contacts need to be screened for a given sample size requirement. There are times when the researcher is faced with a situation where the incidence rate of survey participants is low. This is generally the case when the 'population' represents a niche or a highly targeted market. Suppose a study was focused upon buyers of new sports cars, specifically to measure and understand characteristics of consumers that aspire to own and could afford a new Audi R8.[19] The incidence of such potential consumers in the wider population would be very low. A lot of wasted effort would be exerted if the 'general population' were to be sampled for a survey. In such cases, a survey method should be selected that can locate qualified participants efficiently and minimise waste.

Participant control

Methods that allow participant control over the interviewing process can solicit greater cooperation and engagement. Two aspects of control are particularly important to participants. The first is control over when to answer the survey, and the flexibility to answer it in parts at different times and even via different modes. The second aspect of control pertains to the ability of the participant to regulate the rate or pace at which they answer the survey.

Other survey methods

We have covered the basic survey methods. Other survey methods are also used, which are variations of these basic methods. The more popular of these other methods are described in Table 5.3.

Table 5.3	Additional survey methods	
Method	**Advantages/disadvantages**	**Comment**
Completely automated telephone surveys (CATS)	Same as CATI	Useful for short, in-bound surveys initiated by participant
Central location interview	Same as street survey	Examples include new product tests, advertising tests, trade shows, conferences
Kiosk-based computer interview	Same as CAPI	Useful in museum, heritage and exhibition sites
Drop-off survey	Same as postal survey, except higher cost and higher response rate	Useful for local-market surveys

Mixed-mode surveys

As is evident from Table 5.2 and the preceding discussion, no survey method is superior in all situations. Depending on such factors as information requirements, budgetary constraints (time and money) and participant characteristics, none, one, two or even all techniques may be appropriate.[20] Remember that the various data collection modes are not mutually exclusive, they can be employed in a complementary fashion to build on each other's strengths and compensate for each other's weaknesses. The researcher can employ these techniques in combination and develop creative twists within each technique. With the growth of the use of email and the Internet as a means of communication, online methods have become the most feasible and popular means of conducting surveys. Where online methods are not appropriate for particular types of participant, a choice can be made by individual participants to select the survey method that they prefer. Many survey analysis packages that include the function of questionnaire design have the ability to formulate the questionnaire into all survey method formats. Mixed-mode designs are increasingly being used for multi-country studies. Depending on the mix of countries being surveyed, face-to-face, CATI or online may be employed, with online being the preferred choice for the US and a growing number of other countries with relatively high Internet penetration. Single mode within country and mixed mode between countries may be the most common mixed-mode design in marketing research.[21] Mixed-mode research offers one of the most serious ways to tackle falling response rates.

Quantitative observation

The recording and counting of behavioural patterns of people, objects and events in a systematic manner to obtain information about the phenomenon of interest.

OBSERVATION TECHNIQUES

Mystery shopper

An observer visiting providers of goods and services as if he or she were really a customer, and recording characteristics of the service delivery.

Quantitative observation techniques are extensively used in descriptive research. Observation involves recording the behavioural patterns of people, objects and events in a systematic manner to obtain information about the phenomenon of interest. The observer does not question or communicate with the people being observed unless they take the role of a **mystery shopper**. Information may be recorded as the events occur or from records of past events. Observational techniques may be structured or unstructured, disguised or undisguised. Furthermore, observation may be conducted in a natural or a contrived environment.[22]

Observation techniques classified by mode of administration

As shown in Figure 5.2, observation techniques may be classified by mode of administration as personal observation, electronic observation and trace analysis.

Personal observation

Personal observation
An observational research strategy in which human observers record the phenomenon being observed as it occurs.

In **personal observation**, a researcher observes actual behaviour as it occurs. The observer does not attempt to control or manipulate the phenomenon being observed but merely records what takes place. For example, a researcher might record the time, day and number of shoppers who enter a shop and observe where those shoppers 'flow' once they are in the shop. This information could aid in designing a store's layout and determining the location of individual departments, shelf locations and merchandise displays.

Electronic observation

Electronic observation
An observational research strategy in which electronic devices, rather than human observers, record the phenomenon being observed.

In **electronic observation**, electronic devices rather than human observers record the phenomenon being observed. The devices may or may not require the participants' direct participation. They are used for continuously recording ongoing behaviour for later analysis.

Of the electronic devices that do not require participants' direct participation, the A.C. Nielsen audimeter is best known. The audimeter is attached to a TV set to record continually the channel to which a set is tuned. Another way to monitor viewers is through the people meter. People meters attempt to measure not only the channels to which a set is tuned but also who is watching.[23] In recent years, there has much interest in collecting and analysing television set-top box (STB) data. As television moves from analogue to digital signals, digital STBs are increasingly more common in homes. Where these are attached to some sort of return path (as is the case in many homes subscribing to cable or satellite TV services), these data can be aggregated and licensed to companies wishing to measure television viewership. Advances in distributed computing make it feasible to analyse these data on a huge scale. Whereas previous television measurement relied on panels consisting of thousands of households, data can now be collected and analysed for millions of households. This holds the promise of providing accurate measurement for much (and perhaps all) of the niche TV content that eludes current panel-based methods in many countries.[24]

There are many electronic observation devices that do require participant involvement. These electronic devices may be classified into five groups: (1) eye tracking monitors, (2) neuromarketing, (3) psycho-galvanometers, (4) voice pitch analysers and (5) devices

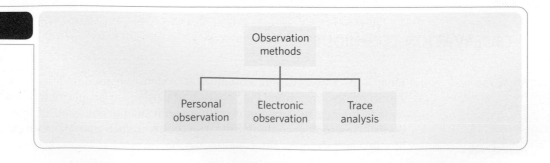

Figure 5.2

A classification of observation methods

Eye tracking equipment
Instruments that record the gaze movements of the eye.

Neuromarketing
The application of neuroscience in marketing, primarily to measure emotions through brain imaging.

Psycho-galvanometer
An instrument that measures a participant's galvanic skin response.

Galvanic skin response
Changes in the electrical resistance of the skin that relate to a participant's affective state.

Voice pitch analysis
Measurement of emotional reactions through changes in the participant's voice.

Response latency
The amount of time it takes to respond to a question.

measuring response latency. Eye tracking equipment – such as oculometers, eye cameras or eye view minuters – records the gaze movements of the eye. These devices can be used to determine how a participant reads an advertisement or views a TV commercial and for how long the participant looks at various parts of the stimulus. Such information is directly relevant to assessing advertising effectiveness.

Neuromarketing is concerned with the direct measurement of the brain's conscious and unconscious responses to marketing stimuli. Typically this involves the measurement of a participant's brain activity through quantitative electroencephalography (qEEG). This measurement is of electrical activity at specific sites across the surface of the brain through sensors affixed to the participant's scalp. Through knowledge of brain function, insight into the mental activity associated with a particular stimulus or study condition can be determined.[25]

The psycho-galvanometer measures galvanic skin response (GSR) or changes in the electrical resistance of the skin.[26] The participant is fitted with small electrodes that monitor electrical resistance and is shown stimuli such as advertisements, packages and slogans. The theory behind this device is that physiological changes such as increased perspiration accompany emotional reactions. Excitement leads to increased perspiration, which increases the electrical resistance of the skin. From the strength of the response, the researcher infers the participant's interest level and attitudes towards the stimuli.

Voice pitch analysis measures emotional reactions through changes in the participant's voice. Changes in the relative vibration frequency of the human voice that accompany emotional reaction are measured with audio-adapted computer equipment.[27]

Response latency is the time a participant takes before answering a question. It is used as a measure of the relative preference for various alternatives.[28] Response time is thought to be directly related to uncertainty. Therefore, the longer a participant takes to choose between two alternatives, the closer the alternatives are in terms of preference. On the other hand, if the participant makes a quick decision, one alternative is clearly preferred. With the increased popularity of computer-assisted data collection, response latency can be recorded accurately and without the participant's awareness. Use of eye tracking monitors, neuromarketing, psycho-galvanometers and voice pitch analysers assumes that physiological reactions are associated with specific cognitive and affective responses. This has yet to be clearly demonstrated. Furthermore, calibration of these devices to measure physiological arousal is difficult, and they are expensive to use. Another limitation is that participants are placed in an artificial environment and know that they are being observed.

Trace analysis

Trace analysis
An approach in which data collection is based on physical traces, or evidence, of past behaviour.

An observation method that can be inexpensive if used creatively is trace analysis. In trace analysis, data collection is based on physical traces, or evidence, of past behaviour. These traces may be left by the participants intentionally or unintentionally. Several innovative applications of trace analysis have been made in marketing research:

- The selective erosion of tiles in a museum indexed by the replacement rate was used to determine the relative popularity of exhibits.
- The number of different fingerprints on a page was used to gauge the readership of various advertisements in a magazine.
- The position of the radio dials in cars brought in for service was used to estimate share of listening audience of various radio stations. Advertisers used the estimates to decide on which stations to advertise.
- The age and condition of cars in a car park were used to assess the affluence of customers.
- The magazines people donated to charity were used to determine people's favourite magazines.

Cookie technology
An identification code stored in the web surfer's browser that identifies a particular user.

- Internet visitors leave traces that can be analysed to examine browsing and usage behaviour through cookie technology.

A comparative evaluation of the observation techniques

A comparative evaluation of the observation techniques is given in Table 5.4. The different observation techniques are evaluated in terms of the degree of structure, degree of disguise, ability to observe in a natural setting, observation bias, measurement and analysis bias, and additional general factors.

Structure relates to the specification of what is to be observed and how the measurements are to be recorded. As can be seen from Table 5.4, personal observation is low, and trace analysis is medium on the degree of structure. Electronic observation can vary widely from low to high, depending on the techniques used. Techniques such as optical scanners are very structured in that the characteristics to be measured – for example, characteristics of items purchased and scanned in supermarket checkouts – are precisely defined. In contrast, electronic techniques, such as the use of hidden cameras to observe children at play with toys, tend to be unstructured.

Personal observation offers a medium degree of disguise because there are limitations on the extent to which the observer can be disguised as a shopper, sales assistant or employee. Trace analysis offers a high degree of disguise because the data are collected 'after the fact': that is, after the phenomenon to be observed has taken place. Some electronic observations such as hidden cameras offer excellent disguise, whereas others, such as the use of eye tracking equipment are very difficult to disguise.

The ability to observe in a natural setting is low in trace analysis because the observation takes place after the behaviour has occurred. Personal observation and audits are excellent on this score because human observers can observe people or objects in a variety of natural settings. Electronic observation techniques vary from low (e.g. use of eye tracking equipment) to high (e.g. use of turnstiles).

Observation bias is low in the case of electronic observation because a human observer is not involved. Observation bias is medium for trace analysis. In this technique, human observers are involved and the characteristics to be observed are not very well defined. The observers typically do not interact with human participants during the observation process, thus lessening the degree of bias. It is high for personal observation due to the use of human observers who interact with the phenomenon being observed.

Trace analysis has a medium degree of data analysis bias as the definition of variables is not very precise. Electronic observation techniques can have a low (e.g. scanner data) to medium (e.g. hidden camera) degree of analysis bias. Unlike personal observation, the bias

Table 5.4	A comparative evaluation of observation techniques		
Criteria	**Personal observation**	**Electronic observation**	**Trace analysis**
Degree of structure	*	* to *****	***
Degree of disguise	***	****	*****
Natural setting	*****	****	*
Observation bias	*****	*	***
Analysis bias	*****	**	***
General remarks	Most flexible	Can be intrusive	Limited traces available

Key: low = *, moderate to low = **, moderate = ***, moderate to high = ****, high = *****

in electronic observation is limited to the medium level due to improved measurement and classification, because the phenomenon to be observed can be recorded continuously using electronic devices.

In addition, personal observation is the most flexible, because human observers can observe a wide variety of phenomena in a wide variety of settings. Some electronic observation techniques, such as the use of eye tracking equipment can be very intrusive, leading to artificiality and bias. Audits using human auditors tend to be expensive. As mentioned earlier, trace analysis is a method that is limited to where consumers actually leave 'traces'. This occurs infrequently and very creative approaches are needed to capture these traces.

Evaluating the criteria presented in Table 5.4 helps to identify the most appropriate observation technique, given the phenomena to be observed, the nature of participants being observed and the context in which the observation occurs. To strengthen the choice of a particular observation technique, it is also helpful to compare the relative advantages and disadvantages of observation versus survey techniques.

Advantages and disadvantages of observation techniques

Other than the use of scanner data, few marketing research projects rely solely on observational techniques to obtain primary data.[29] This implies that observational techniques have some major disadvantages compared with survey techniques. Yet these techniques offer some advantages that can make their use in conjunction with survey techniques most fruitful.

Relative advantages of observation techniques

The greatest advantage of observational techniques is that they permit measurement of actual behaviour rather than reports of intended or preferred behaviour. There is no reporting bias, and potential bias caused by the interviewer and the interviewing process is eliminated or reduced. Certain types of data can be collected only by observation. These include behaviour patterns which the participant is unaware of or unable to communicate. For example, information on babies' and toddlers toy preferences is best obtained by observing babies at play, because they are unable to express themselves adequately. Moreover, if the observed phenomenon occurs frequently or is of short duration, observational techniques may cost less and be faster than survey techniques.

Relative disadvantages of observation techniques

The biggest disadvantage of observation is that the reasons for the observed behaviour may be difficult to determine because little is known about the underlying motives, beliefs, attitudes and preferences. For example, people observed buying a brand of cereal may or may not like it themselves; they may be purchasing that brand for someone else in the household. Another limitation of observation is the extent to which researchers are prepared to evaluate the extent of their own bias, and how this can affect what they observe. In addition, observational data can be time consuming and expensive to collect. It is also difficult to observe certain forms of behaviour such as personal activities that occur in the privacy of the consumer's home. Finally, in some cases such as in the use of hidden cameras, the use of observational techniques may border on being or may actually be unethical. It can be argued that individuals being observed should be made aware of the situation, but this may cause them to behave in a contrived manner.

CAUSALITY

The concept of causality

Causality
Causality applies when the occurrence of X increases the probability of the occurrence of Y.

Experimentation is commonly used to infer causal relationships. The concept of **causality** requires some explanation. The scientific concept of causality is complex. 'Causality' means something very different to the average person on the street than to a scientist.[30] A statement such as 'X causes Y' will have the following meaning to an ordinary person and to a scientist:

Ordinary meaning	Scientific meaning
X is the only cause of Y	X is only one of a number of possible causes of Y
X must always lead to Y	The occurrence of X makes the occurrence of Y more probable (X is a probabilistic cause of Y)
It is possible to prove that X is a cause of Y	We can never prove that X is a cause of Y. At best, we can infer that X is a cause of Y

The scientific meaning of causality is more appropriate to marketing research than is the everyday meaning. Marketing effects are caused by multiple variables and the relationship between cause and effect tends to be probabilistic. Moreover, we can never prove causality (i.e. demonstrate it conclusively); we can only infer a cause-and-effect relationship. In other words, it is possible that the true causal relation, if one exists, will not have been identified. We further clarify the concept of causality by discussing the conditions for causality.

Conditions for causality

Before making causal inferences, or assuming causality, three conditions must be satisfied: (1) concomitant variation, (2) time order of occurrence of variables, and (3) elimination of other possible causal factors. These conditions are necessary but not sufficient to demonstrate causality. No one of these three conditions, or all three conditions combined, can demonstrate decisively that a causal relationship exists.[31] These conditions are explained in more detail in the following sections.

Concomitant variation

Concomitant variation
A condition for inferring causality that requires that the extent to which a cause, X, and an effect, Y, occur together or vary together is predicted by the hypothesis under consideration.

Concomitant variation is the extent to which a cause, X, and an effect, Y, occur together or vary together in the way predicted by the hypothesis under consideration. Evidence pertaining to concomitant variation can be obtained in a qualitative or quantitative manner.

For example, in the qualitative case, the management of a travel company may believe that the retention of customers is highly dependent on the quality of its service. This hypothesis could be examined by assessing concomitant variation. Here, the causal factor X is service level and the effect factor Y is retention level. A concomitant variation supporting the hypothesis would imply that travel companies with satisfactory levels of service would also have a satisfactory retention of customers. Likewise, travel companies with unsatisfactory service would exhibit unsatisfactory retention of customers. If, on the other hand, the opposite pattern was found, we would conclude that the hypothesis was untenable.

Table 5.5	Evidence of concomitant variation between purchase of a skiing holiday and education			
		Purchase of a skiing holiday from a travel company, Y		
		High	*Low*	*Total*
Education, X	*High*	363 (73%)	137 (27%)	500 (100%)
	Low	322 (64%)	178 (36%)	500 (100%)

Table 5.6	Purchase of skiing holiday by income and education			
		Low-income		
		Purchase		
		High	*Low*	*Total*
Education	*High*	122 (61%)	78 (39%)	200 (100%)
	Low	171 (57%)	129 (43%)	300 (100%)
		High-income		
		Purchase		
		High	*Low*	*Total*
Education	*High*	241 (80%)	59 (20%)	300 (100%)
	Low	151 (76%)	49 (24%)	200 (100%)

For a quantitative example, consider a random survey of 1,000 participants questioned on the purchase of a skiing holiday. This survey yields the data in Table 5.5. The participants have been classified into high- and low-education groups based on a median or even split. This table suggests that the purchase of a skiing holiday is influenced by education level. Participants with high education are more likely to purchase a skiing holiday: 73 per cent of the participants with high education have a high purchase level, whereas only 64 per cent of those with low education have a high purchase level. Furthermore, this is based on a relatively large sample of 1,000 participants.

Based on this evidence, can we conclude that high education causes a high purchasing level of skiing holidays? Certainly not! All that can be said is that association makes the hypothesis more tenable; it does not prove it. What about the effect of other possible causal factors such as income? Skiing holidays can be expensive, so people with higher incomes may be more able to afford them. Table 5.6 shows the relationship between the purchase of a skiing holiday and education for different income segments. This is equivalent to holding the effect of income constant. Here again, the sample has been split at the median to produce high- and low-income groups of equal size. Table 5.6 shows that the difference in purchasing levels of a skiing holiday between high- and low-education participants has been reduced considerably. This suggests that the association indicated by Table 5.5 may be spurious. It is possible that considering a third variable will crystallise an association that was originally obscure. The time order of the occurrence of variables provides additional insights into causality.

Time order of occurrence of variables

The time order of occurrence condition states that the causing event must occur either before or simultaneously with the effect; it cannot occur afterwards. By definition, an effect cannot be produced by an event that occurs after the effect has taken place. It is possible, however, for each event in a relationship to be both a cause and an effect of the other event. In other words, a variable can be both a cause and an effect in the same causal relationship. To illustrate, customers who shop frequently in a particular supermarket are more likely to have a store card for that supermarket. In addition, customers who have a loyalty card for a supermarket are likely to shop there frequently.

Consider travel companies and the challenge of retaining their customers. If the quality of their service offering is the cause of retention, then improvements in service must be made before, or at least simultaneously with, an increase in retention. These improvements might consist of training or hiring more staff in their branches. Then, in subsequent months, the retention of customers should increase. Alternatively, retention may increase simultaneously with the training or hiring of additional branch staff. On the other hand, suppose that a travel company experienced an appreciable increase in the level of retaining customers and then decided to use some of that money generated to retrain its branch staff, leading to an improvement in service. In this case, the improved service quality cannot be a cause of increased retention; rather, just the opposite hypothesis might be plausible.

Absence of other possible causal factors

The absence of other possible causal factors means that the factor or variable being investigated should be the only possible causal explanation. Travel company service quality may be a cause of retention if we can be sure that changes in all other factors affecting retention: pricing, advertising, promotional offers, product characteristics, competition and so forth, were held constant or were otherwise controlled.

In an after-the-fact examination of a situation, we can never confidently rule out all other causal factors. In contrast, with experimental designs it is possible to control some of the other causal factors. It is also possible to balance the effects of some of the uncontrolled variables so that only random variations resulting from these uncontrolled variables will be measured. The difficulty of establishing a causal relationship is illustrated by the following example. If you were to design this experiment, imagine trying to pinpoint what 'creativity' means in the context of creating an advertisement.

Real research   **Advertising creativity matters[32]**

A common view is that creativity is a mission of the entire advertising industry, its *raison d'être*. In a frequently cited study,[33] wasteful advertising creativity in advertising agencies, in the form of an abundance of creative ideas, yielded more effective advertisements in the long term. An experiment was undertaken to test the notion of wasteful advertising. The aim was to see whether an abundance of creativity in a single advertisement yielded positive effects. To test their hypotheses, the researchers wished to compare responses between consumers who had been exposed to a more creative versus a less creative advertisement for the same brand with the same message. To do this they chose a 2 (more creative/less creative advertisement) × 2 (perceived creativity before/after) experimental design where participants were randomly assigned to one of the four cells. To avoid stimulus-specific effects, four different brands and accompanying messages were used for a total of 16 experiment cells. All four brands were established and well known in their respective product categories (pain relief, coffee, vodka and condoms). Four pairs of print advertisements were developed, one pair for each brand. Print advertisements usually have three main elements: the brand, text and visuals. In creating test material, the brand and the visuals were kept constant, while the text was varied to communicate the same message In

a more (employing rhetorical figures) or less (without rhetorical figures) creative way. The number of words was kept constant. The participants were recruited from an access panel to represent the adult working population. In total, 1,284 consumers participated in the study, making a cell size of approximately 80 participants. Participants were randomly exposed to one of the stimulus print advertisements online and then directly completed a questionnaire. The results showed that waste in advertising creativity mattered. Rather than improving the functionality of an advertisement and push the message into consumers' minds (which conventional wisdom held to be the major benefit of creativity) an extra degree of creativity may send signals about the advertiser that rub off on consumer perceptions of the brand. More versus less creative advertising signalled greater effort on the advertiser's behalf and was taken as proof of the brand's smartness, and ability to solve problems and develop valuable products. As a result, consumers became more interested in the brand and perceived it to be of higher quality.

The visual characteristics of 'creativity' were not tested in this example which could have had a major impact upon how participants view the creativity of an advert. This does not mean that the experiment has no value, far from it, but it does illustrate the challenges inherent in establishing cause-and-effect relationships. If, as this example indicates, it is difficult to establish cause-and-effect relationships, what is the role of evidence obtained in experimentation?

Evidence of concomitant variation, time order of occurrence of variables, and elimination of other possible causal factors, even if combined, still do not demonstrate conclusively that a causal relationship exists. If all the evidence is strong and consistent, however, it may be reasonable to conclude that there is a causal relationship. Accumulated evidence from several investigations increases our confidence that a causal relationship exists. Confidence is further enhanced if the evidence is interpreted in light of intimate conceptual knowledge of the problem situation. Controlled experiments can provide strong evidence on all three conditions.

Definitions and concepts

Independent variables
Variables that are manipulated by the researcher and whose effects are measured and compared.

In this section, we define some basic concepts and illustrate them using the *Real research* experiment detailed above:

- **Independent variables.** Independent variables are variables or alternatives that are manipulated (i.e. the levels of these variables are changed by the researcher) and whose effects are measured and compared. These variables, also known as treatments, may include price

Test units

Individuals, organisations or other entities whose responses to independent variables or treatments are being studied.

Dependent variables

Variables that measure the effect of the independent variables on the test units.

Extraneous variables

Variables, other than dependent and independent variables, which may influence the results of the experiment.

Experiment

The process of manipulating one or more independent variables and measuring their effect on one or more dependent variables, while controlling for the extraneous variables.

Experimental design

The set of experimental procedures specifying (1) the test units and sampling procedures, (2) the independent variables, (3) the dependent variables, and (4) how to control the extraneous variables.

levels, package designs and advertising themes. In the advertising creativity example, the independent variable was the text used to communicate a message (i.e. 'more' or 'less' creative).

- **Test units.** Test units are individuals, organisations or other entities whose response to the independent variables or treatments is being examined. Test units may include consumers, stores or geographical areas. In the advertising creativity example, the test units were consumers.

- **Dependent variables.** Dependent variables are the variables that measure the effect of the independent variables on the test units. These variables may include sales, profits and market shares. In the advertising creativity example, the dependent variable was a measure of favourable attitudes towards the brand being advertised.

- **Extraneous variables.** Extraneous variables are all variables other than the independent variables that affect the response of the test units. These variables can confound the dependent variable measures in a way that weakens or invalidates the results of the experiment. In the advertising creativity example, product categories, brands, visuals and number of words were extraneous variables that had to be controlled.

- **Experiment.** An experiment is formed when the researcher manipulates one or more independent variables and measures their effect on one or more dependent variables, while controlling for the effect of extraneous variables.[34] The advertising creativity research project qualifies as an experiment based on this definition.

- **Experimental design.** An experimental design is a set of procedures specifying: (1) the test units and how these units are to be divided into homogeneous subsamples, (2) what independent variables or treatments are to be manipulated, (3) what dependent variables are to be measured, and (4) how the extraneous variables are to be controlled.[35]

Validity in experimentation

When conducting an experiment, a researcher has two goals: (1) to draw valid conclusions about the effects of independent variables on the study group, and (2) to make valid generalisations to a larger population of interest. The first goal concerns internal validity, the second external validity.[36]

Internal validity

Internal validity

A measure of accuracy of an experiment. It measures whether the manipulation of the independent variables, or treatments, actually caused the effects on the dependent variable(s).

Internal validity refers to whether the manipulation of the independent variables or treatments actually caused the observed effects on the dependent variables. Thus, internal validity refers to whether the observed effects on the test units could have been caused by variables other than the treatment. If the observed effects are influenced or confounded by extraneous variables, it is difficult to draw valid inferences about the causal relationship between the independent and dependent variables. Internal validity is the basic minimum that must be present in an experiment before any conclusion about treatment effects can be made. Without internal validity, the experimental results are confounded. Control of extraneous variables is a necessary condition for establishing internal validity.

External validity

External validity

A determination of whether the cause-and-effect relationships found in the experiment can be generalised.

External validity refers to whether the cause-and-effect relationships found in the experiment can be generalised. In other words, can the results be generalised beyond the experimental situation, and if so, to what populations, settings, times, independent variables and dependent variables can the results be projected?[37] Threats to external validity arise when the specific set of experimental conditions does not realistically take into account the interactions of other relevant variables in the real world.

It is desirable to have an experimental design that has both internal and external validity, but in marketing research we often have to trade one type of validity for another.[38] To control for extraneous variables, a researcher may conduct an experiment in an artificial environment. This enhances internal validity, but it may limit the generalisability of the results, thereby reducing external validity. For example, pizza restaurants test customers' preferences for new formulations of menu items in test kitchens. Can the effects measured in this environment be generalised to pizza restaurants that may operate in a variety of other environments? (Further discussion on the influence of artificiality on external validity may be found in the section of this chapter on laboratory versus field experimentation.) Regardless of the deterrents to external validity, if an experiment lacks internal validity, it may not be meaningful to generalise the results. Factors that threaten internal validity may also threaten external validity, the most serious of these being extraneous variables.

Extraneous variables

In this section, we classify extraneous variables in the following categories: history, maturation, testing effects, instrumentation, statistical regression, selection bias and mortality.

History

History
Specific events that are external to the experiment but that occur at the same time as the experiment.

Contrary to what the name implies, history (H) does not refer to the occurrence of events before the experiment. Rather, history refers to specific events that are external to the experiment but that occur at the same time as the experiment. These events may affect the dependent variable. The longer the time interval between observations, the greater the possibility that history will confound an experiment of this type.[39]

Maturation

Maturation
An extraneous variable attributable to changes in the test units themselves that occur with the passage of time.

Maturation (MA) is similar to history except that it refers to changes in the test units themselves. These changes are not caused by the impact of independent variables or treatments but occur with the passage of time. In an experiment involving people, maturation takes place as people become older, more experienced, tired, bored or uninterested. Tracking and market studies that span several months are vulnerable to maturation, since it is difficult to know how participants are changing over time.

Maturation effects also extend to test units other than people. For example, consider the case in which the test units are travel companies. Travel companies change over time in terms of personnel, physical layout, decoration, and the range of holidays and services they have to offer.

Testing effects

Testing effects
Effects caused by the process of experimentation.

Testing effects are caused by the process of experimentation. Typically, these are the effects on the experiment of taking a measure on the dependent variable before and after the presentation of the treatment. There are two kinds of testing effects: (1) main testing effect (MT), and (2) interactive testing effect (IT).

Main testing effect
An effect of testing occurring when a prior observation affects a later observation.

The **main testing effect** (MT) occurs when a prior observation affects a later observation. Consider an experiment to measure the effect of advertising on attitudes towards taking a holiday in Egypt. The participants are given a pre-treatment questionnaire measuring background information and attitude towards holidaying in Egypt. They are then exposed to the test advertisement embedded in a TV programme. After viewing the advertisement, the participants again answer a questionnaire measuring, among other things, attitude towards holidaying in Egypt.

Suppose that there is no difference between the pre- and post-treatment attitudes. Can we conclude that the advertisement was ineffective? An alternative explanation might be that the participants tried to maintain consistency between their pre- and post-treatment attitudes. As a result of the main testing effect, post-treatment attitudes were influenced more by pre-treatment attitudes than by the treatment itself. The main testing effect may also be reactive, causing the participants to change their attitudes simply because these attitudes have been measured. The main testing effect compromises the internal validity of the experiment.

Interactive testing effect
An effect in which a prior measurement affects the test unit's response to the independent variable.

In the **interactive testing effect** (IT), a prior measurement affects the test unit's response to the independent variable. Continuing with an advertising experiment, where participants are asked to indicate their attitudes towards taking a holiday in Egypt. As participants become more aware of Egyptian holidays, they are sensitised to Egyptian holidays. They become more likely to pay attention to the test advertisement than are people who were not included in the experiment. The measured effects are then not generalisable to the population; therefore, the interactive testing effects influence the experiment's external validity.[40]

Instrumentation

Instrumentation
An extraneous variable involving changes in the measuring instrument, in the observers or in the scores themselves.

Instrumentation (I) refers to changes in the measuring instrument, in the observers or in the scores themselves. Sometimes measuring instruments are modified during the course of an experiment. In the Egyptian holiday experiment, using a newly designed questionnaire to measure the post-treatment attitudes could lead to variations in the responses obtained.

Statistical regression

Statistical regression
An extraneous variable that occurs when test units with extreme scores move closer to the average score during the course of the experiment.

Statistical regression (SR) effects occur when test units with extreme scores move closer to the average score during the course of the experiment. In the Egyptian holiday advertising experiment, suppose that in a pretest measurement some participants had either very favourable or very unfavourable attitudes towards the country of Egypt. On post-treatment measurement, their attitudes might have moved towards the average. Consumer attitudes change continuously for a wide variety of reasons. Consumers with extreme attitudes have more room for change, so variation may be more likely. This has a confounding effect on the experimental results, because the observed effect (change in attitude) may be attributable to statistical regression rather than to the treatment (test advertisement).

Selection bias

Selection bias
An extraneous variable attributable to the improper assignment of test units to treatment conditions.

Selection bias (SB) refers to the improper assignment of test units to treatment conditions. This bias occurs when selection or assignment of test units results in treatment groups that differ on the dependent variable before the exposure to the treatment condition. If test units self-select their own groups or are assigned to groups on the basis of the researchers' judgement, selection bias is possible.

Mortality

Mortality
An extraneous variable attributable to the loss of test units while the experiment is in progress.

Mortality (MO) refers to the loss of test units while the experiment is in progress. This happens for many reasons, such as test units refusing to continue in the experiment. Mortality confounds results because it is difficult to determine whether the lost test units would respond in the same manner to the treatments as those that remain.

The various categories of extraneous variables are not mutually exclusive; they can occur jointly and also interact with each other. To illustrate, testing–maturation–mortality refers to a situation in which, because of pre-treatment measurement, the participants' beliefs and attitudes change over time and there is a differential loss of participants from the various treatment groups.

Controlling extraneous variables

Confounding variables
Synonymous with extraneous variables, used to illustrate that extraneous variables can confound the results by influencing the dependent variable.

Extraneous variables represent alternative explanations of experimental results. They pose a serious threat to the internal and external validity of an experiment. Unless they are controlled, they affect the dependent variable and thus confound the results. For this reason, they are also called **confounding variables**. There are four ways of controlling extraneous variables: randomisation, matching, statistical control and design control.

Randomisation

Randomisation
A method of controlling extraneous variables that involves randomly assigning test units to experimental groups by using random numbers. Treatment conditions are also randomly assigned to experimental groups.

Randomisation refers to the random assignment of test units to experimental groups by using random numbers. Treatment conditions are also randomly assigned to experimental groups. As a result of random assignment, extraneous factors can be represented equally in each treatment condition. Randomisation is the preferred procedure for ensuring the prior equality of experimental groups,[41] but it may not be effective when the sample size is small because it merely produces groups that are equal on average. It is possible, though, to check whether randomisation has been effective by measuring the possible extraneous variables and comparing them across the experimental groups.

Matching

Matching
A method of controlling extraneous variables that involves matching test units on a set of key background variables before assigning them to the treatment conditions.

Matching involves comparing test units on a set of key background variables before assigning them to the treatment conditions.

Matching has two drawbacks. First, test units can be matched on only a few characteristics, so the test units may be similar on the variables selected but unequal on others. Second, if the matched characteristics are irrelevant to the dependent variable, then the matching effort has been futile.[42]

Statistical control

Statistical control
A method of controlling extraneous variables by measuring the extraneous variables and adjusting for their effects through statistical methods.

Statistical control involves measuring the extraneous variables and adjusting for their effects through statistical analysis. This was illustrated in Table 5.6, which examined the relationship (association) between purchase of skiing holidays and education, controlling for the effect of income. More advanced statistical procedures, such as analysis of covariance (ANCOVA), are also available.

Design control

Design control
A method of controlling extraneous variables that involves using specific experimental designs.

Design control involves the use of experiments designed to control specific extraneous variables. The types of controls possible by suitably designing the experiment are illustrated with the following example.

Experimenting with new products[43]

Controlled-distribution electronic test markets are used increasingly to conduct experimental research on new products. This method makes it possible to create a design that controls for several extraneous factors. The control can allow for the manipulation of variables that can affect the success of new products. In manipulating variables, it is possible to ensure that a new product:

- obtains the right level of supermarket acceptance and all commodity volume distribution;
- is positioned in the correct aisle in each supermarket;
- receives the right number of facings on the shelf;
- has the correct everyday price;
- never has out-of-stock problems;
- obtains the planned level of trade promotion, display and price features on the desired time schedule.

By being able to control these variables, a high degree of internal validity can be obtained.

This example shows that controlled-distribution electronic test markets can be effective in controlling for specific extraneous variables. Extraneous variables can also be controlled by adopting specific experimental designs, as described in the next section.

A classification of experimental designs

Pre-experimental designs
Designs that do not control for extraneous factors by randomisation.

Experimental designs may be classified as pre-experimental, true experimental, quasi-experimental and statistical designs (*see* Figure 5.3).

Pre-experimental designs do not employ randomisation procedures to control for extraneous factors. Examples of these designs include the one-shot case study, the one-group

Figure 5.3

A classification of experimental designs

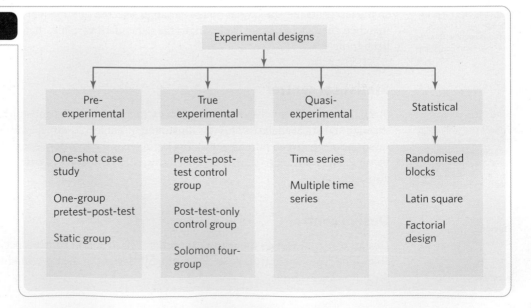

True experimental designs
Experimental designs distinguished by the fact that the researcher can randomly assign test units to experimental groups and also randomly assign treatments to experimental groups.

Quasi-experimental designs
Designs that apply part of the procedures of true experimentation but lack full experimental control.

Statistical designs
Designs that allow for the statistical control and analysis of external variables.

pretest–post-test design and the static group. In **true experimental designs**, the researcher can randomly assign test units to experimental groups and treatments to experimental groups. Included in this category are the pretest–post-test control group design, the post-test-only control group design and the Solomon four-group design. **Quasi-experimental designs** result when the researcher is unable to achieve full manipulation of scheduling or allocation of treatments to test units but can still apply part of the apparatus of the experimentation. Two such designs are time series and multiple time series designs. A **statistical design** is a series of basic experiments that allows for statistical control and analysis of external variables. Statistical designs are classified based on their characteristics and use. The important statistical designs include randomised block, Latin square and factorial.[44]

Laboratory versus field experiments

Field environment
An experimental location set in actual market conditions.

Laboratory environment
An artificial setting for experimentation in which the researcher constructs the desired conditions.

Experiments may be conducted in a laboratory or field environment. A laboratory environment is an artificial one that the researcher constructs with the desired conditions specific to the experiment. The term **field environment** is synonymous with actual market conditions. An example could be in the design of a video game to advertise and portray characteristics of a brand. The experiment could be conducted in a **laboratory environment** where participants sit at computers in a given room to play the tested games. The same experiment could also be conducted in a field environment by allowing the participants to play the games on devices wherever they felt comfortable. The differences between the two environments are summarised in Table 5.7.

Laboratory experiments have the following advantages over field experiments:

- The laboratory environment offers a high degree of control because it isolates the experiment in a carefully monitored environment. Therefore, the effects of history can be minimised.

Table 5.7	Laboratory versus field experiments	
Factor	**Laboratory**	**Field**
Environment	Artificial	Realistic
Control	High	Low
Reactive error	High	Low
Demand artefacts	High	Low
Internal validity	High	Low
External validity	Low	High
Time	Short	Long
Number of units	Small	Large
Ease of implementation	High	Low
Cost	Low	High

- A laboratory experiment also tends to produce the same results if repeated with similar test units, leading to high internal validity.
- Laboratory experiments tend to use a small number of test units, last for a shorter time, be more restricted geographically, and are easier to conduct than field experiments. Hence, they are generally less expensive as well.

Compared with field experiments, laboratory experiments suffer from some main disadvantages:

- The artificiality of the environment may cause reactive error in that the participants react to the situation itself rather than to the independent variable.[45]

Demand artefacts
Responses given because the participants attempt to guess the purpose of the experiment and respond accordingly.

- The environment may cause **demand artefacts**, a phenomenon in which the participants attempt to guess the purpose of the experiment and respond accordingly. For example, while viewing a film clip, the participants may recall pre-treatment questions about the brand and guess that the advertisement is trying to change their attitudes towards the brand.[46]
- Finally, laboratory experiments are likely to have lower external validity than field experiments. Because a laboratory experiment is conducted in an artificial environment, the ability to generalise the results to the real world may be diminished.

It has been argued that artificiality or lack of realism in a laboratory experiment need not lead to lower external validity. One must be aware of the aspects of the laboratory experiment that differ from the situation to which generalisations are to be made. External validity will be reduced only if these aspects interface with the independent variables explicitly manipulated in the experiment, as is often the case in applied marketing research. Another consideration, however, is that laboratory experiments allow for more complex designs than field experiments. Hence, the researcher can control for more factors or variables in the laboratory setting, which increases external validity.[47]

The researcher must consider all these factors when deciding whether to conduct laboratory or field experiments. Field experiments are less common in marketing research than laboratory experiments, although laboratory and field experiments play complementary roles.[48]

Experimental versus non-experimental designs

Three types of research design have been discussed (Chapter 2): exploratory, descriptive and causal. Of these, it may be argued that causal designs are the most appropriate for inferring and measuring cause-and-effect relationships. Although descriptive survey data are often used to provide evidence of 'causal' relationships, these studies do not meet all the conditions required for causality. For example, it is difficult in descriptive studies to establish the prior equivalence of the participant groups with respect to both the independent and dependent variables. On the other hand, an experiment can establish this equivalence by random assignment of test units to groups. In descriptive research, it is also difficult to establish time order of occurrence of variables. In an experiment, however, the researcher controls the timing of the measurements and the introduction of the treatment. Finally, descriptive research offers little control over other possible causal factors.

We do not wish to undermine the importance of descriptive research designs in marketing research. Descriptive research constitutes the most popular research design in marketing research, and we do not want to imply that it should never be used to examine causal relationships. Rather, our intent is to alert the reader to the limitations of descriptive research for examining causal relationships. Likewise, we also want to make the reader aware of the limitations of experimentation.[49] In marketing research terms, it has been used primarily in the field of communications and advertising.[50] However, it has limitations of time, cost and administration of an experiment, with these limitations meaning that experimental techniques have a relatively low penetration into marketing research practice.[51]

Limitations of experimentation

Time

Experiments can be time consuming, particularly if the researcher is interested in measuring the long-term effects of the treatment, such as the effectiveness of an advertising campaign. Experiments should last long enough so that the post-treatment measurements include most or all of the effects of the independent variables.

Cost

Experiments are often expensive. The requirements of experimental group, control group and multiple measurements significantly add to the cost of research.

Administration

Experiments can be difficult to administer. It may be impossible in measuring human activity to control for the effects of the extraneous variables, particularly in a field environment. Field experiments often interfere with a company's ongoing operations, and obtaining cooperation from the retailers, wholesalers and others involved may be difficult. Finally, competitors may deliberately contaminate the results of a field experiment.

International marketing research

The selection of appropriate survey and observation techniques is more challenging in an international context. Given the differences in the economic, structural, informational, technological and socio-cultural environment, the feasibility and popularity of the different survey techniques vary widely. Each individual survey method has its own distinct advantages and disadvantages that the researcher must evaluate. However, if the researcher is designing a survey that is to work in different geographical locations, the additional challenges and opportunities inherent to their selected locations must also be evaluated. Table 5.8 presents a comparative evaluation of the major modes of collecting quantitative data in the context of international marketing research. In this table, the survey techniques are discussed only under the broad headings of online, telephone, face-to-face, and postal surveys. The use of CATI, CAPI, online and the use of access panels depends heavily on the state of technological development in the country. Likewise, the use of street interviewing is contingent upon the dominance of shopping centres in the retailing environment.

Table 5.8	A comparative evaluation of survey techniques for international marketing research

Criteria	Online	Telephone	Face-to-face	Postal
High sample control	−	+	+	−
Difficulty in locating participants at home	+	+	−	+
Inaccessibility of homes	+	+	−	+
Unavailability of a large pool of trained interviewers	+	+	−	+
Large population in rural areas	−	−	+	−
Unavailability of maps	+	+	−	+
Unavailability of current telephone directories	+	−	+	−
Unavailability of mailing lists	+	+	+	−
Low penetration of telephones	−	−	+	+
Lack of an efficient postal system	+	+	+	−
Low level of literacy	−	−	+	−
Face-to-face communication culture	−	−	+	−
Poor access to computers and the Internet	−	+	+	+

Note: A plus denotes an advantage, and a minus denotes a disadvantage.

Ethics in marketing research

Although concerns for the participants' psychological well-being are mild in survey data collection when compared with either qualitative or experimental research, researchers should not place participants in stressful situations. Disclaimers such as 'There are no correct responses; we are only interested in your opinion' can relieve much of the stress inherent in a survey. In many face-to-face survey situations, participants are given a 'thank you booklet' at the end of the interview. As well as saying a genuine thank you for taking part in a survey, the booklet briefly sets out the purpose and benefits of bona fide marketing research. The use of the 'thank you booklet' helps to educate potential participants to distinguish between genuine, professionally conducted marketing research and 'research' conducted as a front for generating sales leads.

Observation of people's behaviour without their consent is often done because informing the participants may alter their behaviour.[52] But this can compromise the privacy of the participants. One guideline is that people should not be observed for research in situations where they would not expect to be observed by the public. Therefore, public places like a shopping centre or a grocery aisle may be fair game. These are places where people observe other people routinely. However, notices should be posted in these areas stating that they are under observation by researchers.

It is often believed that, if participants are aware of the purpose of a research project, they may give biased responses. In these situations, a deliberate attempt is made by the researcher to disguise the purpose of the research. This is often necessary with experimentation, where disguise is needed to produce valid results. Disguising the purpose of the research, however, should not lead to deception. Although this seems like a paradox, one solution is to disclose the possible existence of deception before the start of the experiment and allow the participants the right to redress at the conclusion of the experiment. The following four items should be conveyed: (1) inform participants that in an experiment of this nature a disguise of the purpose is often required for valid results; (2) inform them of the general nature of the experiment and what they will be asked to do; (3) make sure they know that they can leave the experiment at any time; and (4) inform them that the study will be fully explained after the data have been gathered and at that time they may request that their information be withdrawn.

Digital developments in marketing research

There are a growing number of survey applications that are being designed to advance the experience of interviews using mobile devices. There are compelling reasons why researchers see great advantages in the use of mobile devices for marketing research. Entire generations across the globe are being raised to send text messages, surf the web, conduct transactions, and engage in many ways with family, friends, and business associates, all with just a few touches on their mobile devices. These devices represent the next generation for online communication, just as notebook computers replaced desktop computers as they became smaller, lighter and more powerful. However, country to country, the percentage of participants with suitable devices that enable the more data rich forms of survey engagement varies widely. What does not vary is how the mobile device enables researchers to access participants that in the past may have been well out of their reach. In many Western economies, teens, young men, and ethnic populations are among the heaviest users of mobile devices. They are also the hardest to reach via the web or landline phones for survey purposes. Every demographic group is well represented among mobile device users, perhaps better than the representation today found among those with landlines and broadband web-access at home. The portability and accessibility of the mobile device provides the opportunity to make research even more increasingly actionable and closely integrated with marketing campaigns by moving the survey research closer to the point of consumer buying activities. The combined immediacy and portability provided by mobile devices extends the advantages of electronic interviewing to specific challenges confronting researchers today.[53]

The Internet can be a useful vehicle for conducting causal research. Different experimental treatments can be displayed on different websites. Participants can then be recruited to visit these sites and respond to a questionnaire that obtains information on the dependent and extraneous variables. Thus, the Internet can provide a mechanism for controlled experimentation, which may be in a laboratory environment but, and especially with the use of mobile devices, could be a field experiment.

An example of testing the effectiveness of advertisements can be used to illustrate the use of the Internet in causal research. Different advertisements can be posted on different websites. Matched or randomly selected participants can be recruited to visit these sites, with one group visiting only one site. If any pre-treatment measures have to be obtained, participants can answer a questionnaire posted on the site. Then they are exposed to a particular advertisement on that site. After viewing the advertisement, the participants answer additional questions providing post-treatment measures. Control groups can also be implemented in a similar way. Thus, all types of experimental designs that we have considered can be implemented in this manner.

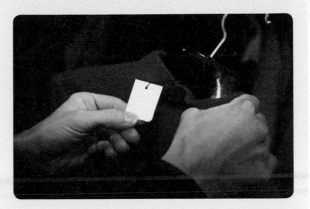

Digital developments are also enabling the development of experiments through virtual test markets and virtual shopping experiences. Experiments in virtual environments can be conducted using mobile devices. They can be designed to be an engaging and enjoyable research experience. With the use of online research communities, experiment treatments can be applied to specific types of participant on a global basis. Virtual experiments can be conducted much quicker and cheaper than conventional marketing research experiments. The following example illustrates why and how Kraft Foods use simulated shopping behaviour to conduct experiments.

Real research   ## Simulated shopping behaviour at Kraft Foods[54]

The task of Kraft Foods Shopper Insight Teams was to gain, accumulate, and synthesize relevant shopper insights that helped innovations, in-store environments and improved differentiation. They recognised that not all available shopper insights were equally reliable, valid and trustworthy. They classified evidence at three levels: Level 1 represented the most valid insights addressing sales-oriented outcomes. Examples included rigorous controlled store tests, test market comparisons, or randomised in-store experiments which clearly and unambiguously identified the key drivers of sales effects in an otherwise tightly controlled test environment, with sufficiently large sample sizes to support robust and generalisable conclusions. Level 2 represented weaker and more indirect methods of scientific investigation, not quite meeting the quality criteria to achieve level 1 evidence. Examples include focus groups, interviews based on retrospective reports of in-store behaviour or smaller-scaled studies without adequate reference standards. Level 3 represented reports that were not based on scientific analysis of shoppers' in-store behaviour. Examples included case studies, anecdotal observations, subjective impressions, expert opinions, and conclusions extrapolated indirectly from other (often undocumented) sources. Gaining Level 1 evidence was challenging as conventional sales-oriented shopper research conducted in physical stores tended to be expensive, time consuming and complex to manage. As a result they turned to virtual shopper simulations as an alternative to traditional tools in shopper research. Simulations provided photo-realistic 3D simulations of product categories and store departments with high-resolution graphics and usually let participants manoeuvre freely through the environment. Shopping behaviour of participants was tracked on a second-to-second basis, yielding detailed information about product contacts and purchases, which, when aggregated to summary metrics, gave estimates of the sales volume and value performance of specific in-store interventions. One of the primary benefits of this approach, beyond considerable savings both in time and increased flexibility, and maximum confidentiality, is experimental control: virtual simulations let researchers completely manipulate both the environment and participants' interaction with it. This approach promises the much sought-after high-quality Level 1 conclusive evidence base to shopper marketing, with unequivocal causal links between directly controllable in-store variables, and their sales impact on shoppers. After some internal validation work, Kraft Foods relied extensively on virtual shopper simulations which have helped them with the missing evidence base for recommendations to shopper marketing, e.g. for optimal shelf placement of our brands, or the positioning of point-of-sale communication inside stores. A by-product of creating virtual store scenarios was the ability to reuse the test material for subsequent presentation and visualisation purposes.

Summary

Three basic means of obtaining primary quantitative data in descriptive research are survey, observation and causal research. Survey involves the direct questioning of participants, observation entails recording participant behaviour, and causal involves the researcher manipulating independent variables in order to measure their effect upon dependent variables.

Surveys involve the administration of a questionnaire and may be classified, based on the method or mode of administration, as (1) online surveys, (2) email surveys, (3) traditional telephone surveys, (4) computer-assisted telephone interviews (CATI), (5) home or workplace face-to-face surveys, (6) street surveys, (7) computer-assisted personal interviews (CAPI), (8) traditional postal surveys. Each method has some general advantages and disadvantages. Although these data collection techniques are usually thought of as distinct and 'competitive', they should not be considered to be mutually exclusive in much the same manner as using quantitative and qualitative techniques should not be considered to be mutually exclusive. It is possible to employ them productively in mixed-mode approaches, especially in conducting surveys across cultures.

The major quantitative observational techniques are personal observation, electronic observation and trace analysis. Compared with surveys, the relative advantages of observational techniques are that they permit measurement of actual behaviour, there is no reporting bias, and there is less potential for interviewer bias. Also, certain types of data can best, or only, be obtained by observation. The relative disadvantages of observation are that very little can be inferred about motives, beliefs, attitudes and preferences, there is a potential for observer bias, most techniques are time consuming and expensive, it is difficult to observe some forms of behaviour, and questions of ethical techniques of observation are far more contentious. Observation is rarely used as the sole method of obtaining primary data, but it can be usefully employed in conjunction with other marketing research techniques to corroborate, validate and enrich analyses and interpretations.

The scientific notion of causality implies that we can never prove that X causes Y. At best, we can only infer that X is one of the causes of Y in that it makes the occurrence of Y probable. Three conditions must be satisfied before causal inferences can be made: (1) concomitant variation, which implies that X and Y must vary together in a hypothesised way; (2) time order of occurrence of variables, which implies that X must precede Y; and (3) elimination of other possible causal factors, which implies that competing explanations must be ruled out. Experiments provide the most convincing evidence of all three conditions. An experiment is formed when one or more independent variables are manipulated or controlled by the researcher and their effect on one or more dependent variables is measured.

In designing an experiment, it is important to consider internal and external validity. Internal validity refers to whether the manipulation of the independent variables actually caused the effects on the dependent variables. External validity refers to the generalisability of experimental results. For the experiment to be valid, the researcher must control the threats imposed by extraneous variables, such as history, maturation, testing (main and interactive testing effects), instrumentation, statistical regression, selection bias and mortality. There are four ways of controlling extraneous variables: randomisation, matching, statistical control and design control.

Experimental designs may be classified as pre-experimental, true experimental, quasi-experimental and statistical designs. An experiment may be conducted in a laboratory environment or under actual market conditions in a real-life setting. Only causal designs encompassing experimentation are appropriate for inferring cause-and-effect relationships. Although experiments have limitations in terms of time, cost and administration, they continue to be popular in marketing, especially in the testing of communications and advertising.

Each individual survey method has its own distinct advantages and disadvantages that the researcher must evaluate. But if the researcher is designing a survey that is to work in different geographical locations, the additional challenges and opportunities inherent to their selected locations must also be evaluated. Participants' well-being should be protected, and they should not face undue stress in being questioned or observed. Participants should not be observed without consent for research in situations where they would not expect to be observed by the public. The ethical issues involved in conducting causal research include disguising the purpose of the experiment. Digital developments in marketing research have fundamentally changed the way that researchers engage with participants, design questionnaires, collect survey data and analyse them. These developments continue with the use of mobile devices to conduct surveys, observations and experiments.

SNAP Learning Edition

The instructions given here work with a Learning Edition of SNAP, available as a download from the SNAP website (**www.snapsurveys.com**). Further details of how you can use SNAP to design your own survey are available on the website that accompanies this text (**www.pearsoned.co.uk/malhotra-euro**). SNAP can design, publish and analyse surveys for the various modes detailed in this chapter, including online, mobile telephone, face-to-face and paper. It can also cope with multi-mode surveys, with participants being offered different options as to how they should complete the questionnaire.

The software has always been developed as an integrated system, so that the simple process of designing a questionnaire automatically creates the database that sits behind the survey. This database then stores the structure of the questionnaire, together with all the replies and this provides the framework for analysis. The benefits of such an approach are that any changes made to the questionnaire at any point, automatically update the database for subsequent analysis.

The survey process is divided into five steps and is summarised below:

1. Create a survey

The starting point is to create the framework for the survey, essentially a title, together with a medium for publishing the questionnaire. SNAP then generates a template that accommodates the specification of the chosen medium.

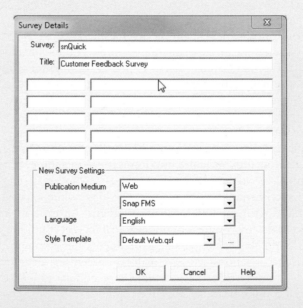

Additional versions of the same questionnaire can then be set up, each with their own style. However, the inherent structure of each version will remain identical, so that if a new question is added to one version, it will automatically be added to all other versions.

2. Design the questionnaire

The next stage is to design the questionnaire. The process is assisted by using SNAP's library of :

- question types
- question styles and
- question wording.

The question types range from multiple choice to free text, together with automated settings for validation purposes.

Question styles range from tick boxes to sliders, and include variation of font style and colours, together with the layout of each question.

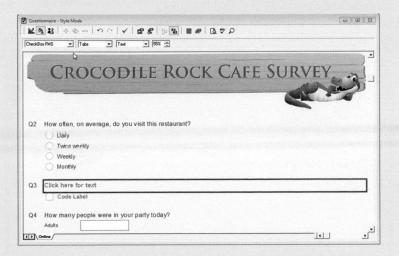

Question wording is available in a series of libraries that can be searched, and various language versions can be accessed.

During the design process, conditions can be preset for the routing or skip-patterns that determine which questions are presented to which participants. This results in a far smoother and more focused experience for the participant. Importantly, it should also reduce the time taken to complete the questionnaire.

3. Publish the questionnaire

Publishing a questionnaire involves the setting of various parameters that control how a questionnaire will appear.

These parameters include the selection of buttons that be selected from a library of different shapes, colours and text. Not all buttons are required on all questionnaires and these can be switched off at will.

Other parameters include margins, validation, progress bars, logos, accessibility, paradata collection, database links, automated alerts and languages.

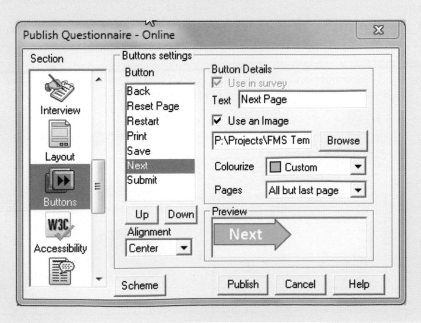

4. Data retrieval

Online surveys are typically self-completion with the participants entering their replies directly. In this situation, data is automatically stored.

Mobile surveys can either be self-completing or be administered by a researcher asking the participant the questions. Whichever way is chosen, the data is stored centrally for analysis and requires little or no editing.

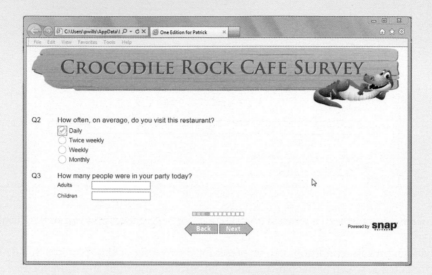

The most labour intensive form of interviewing is the paper survey, whether it is self-completion by the participant, or completed by the interviewer. The data from the paper forms then needs to be transformed into an electronic format, often preceded by a manual coding process for some of the questions, particularly the free-format text questions.

Scanning can generally speed up the process, particularly for questionnaires with a high percentage of tick box questions. Free-format text can always be collected electronically and for certain types of data, such as numbers, postal codes etc., automated coding is possible.

5. Data Analysis

Data can be analysed in many ways within SNAP. There are extensive options for multi-level cross-tabulations and statistics which was traditionally the only form of analysis expected by researchers. Charting technologies have, over the years, both improved the situation in offering more analysis options, but have resulted in many poorly used and positively misleading charts (see Chapter 13). Charts should always be used as a method of presenting results, and not as a method of analysing results.

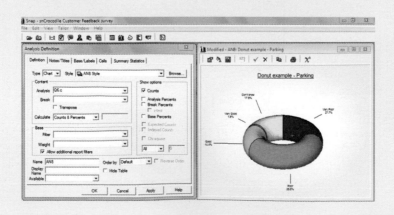

With the rise in text-based data requiring some form of analysis, features such as Word Clouds are now available, offering a dramatic method of analysis text.

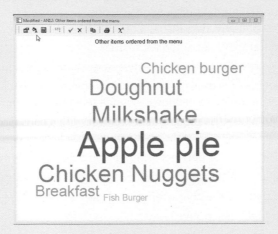

Integrating survey results directly into reports, presentations and dashboards is becoming increasingly common.

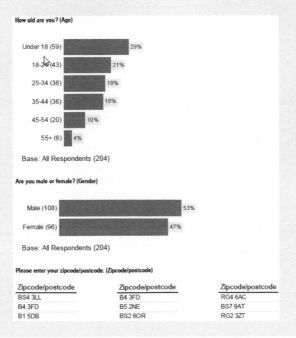

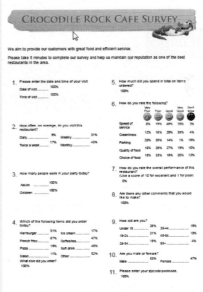

Questions

1 Discuss the dilemma faced by the survey designer who wishes to develop a survey that is not prone to interviewer bias but also sees that interviewer rapport with participants is vital to the success of the survey.

2 Why do interviewers need to probe participants in surveys? What distinguishes survey probing from probing conducted in qualitative interviews?

3 What are the relevant factors for evaluating which survey method is best suited to a particular research project?

4 What are the key advantages of conducting online surveys? Evaluate the potential that online surveys using mobile devices holds for the future.

5 Describe the criteria by which you would evaluate the relative benefits of different observation techniques.

6 What is the difference between qualitative and quantitative observation?

7 Describe a marketing research problem in which both survey and observation techniques could be used for obtaining the information needed.

8 What are the requirements for inferring a causal relationship between two variables?

9 Differentiate between internal and external validity.

10 Describe the various methods for controlling extraneous sources of variation.

11 Compare the characteristics of laboratory and field experimentation.

12 Should descriptive research be used for investigating causal relationships? Why or why not?

Exercises

1 The manager of your educational department has been asked to review which survey method would be the most effective for an evaluation of undergraduate experiences at the end of each academic year. They have come to you to help make a case. Which method would be best and why would it be the best?

2 Locate an online survey, print off the pages and examine the content carefully. What would be the relative advantages of administering the same survey via a street survey? What would a street interviewer need to make this survey effective in a street situation?

3 You have been hired by the campus bookstore to covertly observe students making purchasing decisions while shopping. Spend 30 minutes making these observations and write a report that covers:

(a) How you feel students make their purchasing decisions for books and any other goods available in the shop.

(b) What you feel to be the benefits, limitations and challenges of this approach.

4 You are the marketing research manager for Louis Vuitton (**www.vuitton .com**). The company would like to determine whether it should increase, decrease or maintain the current spend level of advertising. Design a field experiment to address this issue.

5 In a small group discuss the following issues: 'Given the decline in response and cooperation rates to surveys, it would be much better for marketers to invest in quantitative observation techniques and forget conducting surveys' and 'Is it possible to prove causality in any aspects of consumer behaviour?'

Notes

1. Herrmann, J-L., Walliser, B. and Kacha, M., 'Consumer consideration of sponsor brands they do not remember: Taking a wider look at the memorisation effects of sponsorship', *International Journal of Advertising*, 30 (2) (2011), 259–81.

2. Surveys are commonly used in marketing research. See, for example, Rindfleisch, A., Malter, A.J., Ganesan, S. and Moorman, C., 'Cross-sectional versus longitudinal survey research: Concepts, findings and guidelines', *Journal of Marketing Research*, 45 (3) (June 2008), 261–79; Malhotra, N. and McCort, D., 'A cross cultural comparison of behavioural intention models: Theoretical consideration and an empirical investigation', *International Marketing Review*, 18 (3) (2001), 235–69.

3. ESOMAR, 'Global Market Research', ESOMAR Industry Report (2010), 16.

4. Cohen, E. and Jacobs, P., 'How mobile is changing the sociology, psychology and the entertainment/work environment', ESOMAR, *WM3*, Berlin (Oct. 2010).

5. St-Laurent, N., Mathieu, A. and Coderre, F., 'Comparison of the quality of qualitative data obtained through telephone, postal and email surveys', *International Journal of Market Research*, 46 (3) (2004), 349–57; Mann, C. and Stewart, F., *Internet Communication and Qualitative Research: A Handbook for Researching Online* (London: Sage, 2000), 67.

6. Schwartz, M., 'Postal and email "Combos" gain favor with marketers', *B to B*, 87 (2) (11 February 2002), 25; Stevens, J. and Chisholm, J., 'An integrated approach: Technology firm conducts worldwide satisfaction research survey via email, Internet', *Quirk's Marketing Research Review*, 11 (8) (October 1997), 12–13, 64–65.

7. Lavine, S., 'Mobile interviewing – the next frontier of data collection', ESOMAR, *Online Research*, Chicago (Oct. 2009).

8. Zahariev, M., Ferneyhough, C. and Ryan, C., 'Best practices in mobile research', ESOMAR, *Online Research*, Chicago (Oct. 2009).

9. Gorman, J.W., 'An opposing view of online surveying', *Marketing News* (24 April 2000); Johnston, A., 'Welcome to the wired world', *Research* (November 1999), 22–25; Comley, P., 'Will working the web provide a net gain?' *Research* (December 1996), 16.

10. Poynter, R., 'Online research: Stop asking questions and start listening', *Admap* (July/August 2010), 32–34.

11. Hellwig, J. O. and Wirth, T., 'Panel based mobile online research – why mobile online questionnaires contribute to improve data quality,' ESOMAR, *Panel Research*, Dublin (Oct. 2008).

12. Folkman Curasi, C., 'A critical exploration of face-to-face interviewing vs. computer mediated interviewing', *International Journal of Market Research*, 43 (3) (2001) 361–75; Bush, A.J. and Hair, J.E. Jr, 'An assessment of the mall-intercept as a data collection method', *Journal of Marketing Research* (May 1985), 158–67.

13. Manfreda, K.L., Bosnjak, M., Berzelak, J., Haas, I. and Vehovar, V., 'Web surveys versus other survey modes: A meta analysis comparing response rates', *International Journal of Market Research*, 50 (1) (2008) 79–104; Borque,

L., *How to conduct self-administered and mail surveys*, 2nd edn. (Thousand Oaks, CA: Sage, 2002); Brossard, H.L., 'Information sources used by an organisation during a complex decision process: An exploratory study', *Industrial Marketing Management*, 27 (1) (January 1998), 41–50.

14. Schmid, J., 'Assigning value to your customer list', *Catalog Age*, 18 (5) (April 2001), 69; Alan, C.B. and Tse, A.C.B., 'Comparing response rate, response speed and response quality of two methods of sending questionnaires: E-mail vs. mail', *International Journal of Market Research*, 40 (4) (1998); Yoegei, R., 'List marketers head to cyberspace', *Target Marketing*, 20 (8) (August 1997), 54–55.

15. Anolli, L., Villani, D. and Riva, G., 'Personality of people using chat: An on-line research', *CyberPsychology & Behavior*, 8 (1) (Feb. 2005), 89–95; Thompson, S.K., *Sampling* (New York: Wiley, 2002); Childers, T.L. and Skinner, S.J., 'Theoretical and empirical issues in the identification of survey participants', *Journal of the Market Research Society*, 27 (January 1985), 39–53.

16. Graeff, T.R., 'Uninformed response bias in telephone surveys', *Journal of Business Research*, 55 (3) (March 2002), 251; Singer, E., 'Experiments with incentives in telephone surveys', *Public Opinion Quarterly*, 64 (2) (Summer 2000) 171–88; Cannell, C.E., Miller, P.U., Oksenberg, L. and Leinhardt, S. (eds), 'Research on interviewing techniques', in *Sociological Methodology* (San Francisco, CA: Jossey Bass, 1981); Miller, P.U. and Cannell, C.E., 'A study of experimental techniques for telephone interviewing', *Public Opinion Quarterly*, 46 (Summer 1982), 250–69.

17. Fink, A., *How to conduct surveys: A step by step guide*, 3rd edn (Thousand Oaks, CA: Sage, 2005); McMaster, M., 'E-Marketing poll vault', *Sales and Marketing Management*, 153 (8) (August 2001), 25; Fink, A., *A Survey Handbook* (Thousand Oaks, CA: Sage, 1995).

18. Lee, Z. and Sargeant, A., 'Dealing with social desirability bias: An application to charitable giving', *European Journal of Marketing*, 45, 5 (2011).

19. Audi – Born of powerful ideas, European Association of Communications Agencies, Bronze winner (2008).

20. Vicente, P., Reis, E. and Santos, M., 'Using mobile phones for survey research: A comparison with fixed phones', *International Journal of Market Research*, 51 (5) (2009), 613–34; Eva, G. and Jowell, R., 'Conference notes – Prospects for mixed-mode data collection in cross-national surveys', *International Journal of Market Research*, 51 (2) (2009), 267–9.

21. Blyth, B., 'Mixed mode: The only "fitness" regime?' *International Journal of Market Research*, 50 (2) (2008), 241–66.

22. Pettit, R., 'Digital anthropology: How ethnography can improve online research', *Journal of Advertising Research*, 50 (3) (2010) 240–42; Milat, A.J., 'Measuring physical activity in public open space – an electronic device versus direct observation', *Australian & New Zealand Journal of Public Health*, 26 (1) (February 2002), 1; Wilcox, S.B., 'Trust, but verify', *Appliance Manufacturer*, 46 (1) (January 1998), 8, 87.

23. Kasari, H.J., 'People-meter systems in the changing TV climate', *Admap*, 476 (Oct 2006) 55–56; Ephron, E., 'Nielsen's secret passive meter', *Mediaweek*, 10 (36) (18 September 2000).

24. Zigmond, D., Dorai-Raj, S., Interian, Y. and Naverniouk, I., 'Measuring advertising quality on television: Deriving meaningful metrics from audience retention data', *Journal of Advertising Research*, 49 (4) (Dec. 2009), 419–28.

25. Addie, I. and Lewis-Hodgson, D., 'Bioshopping: Revolutionising shopper insight', Market Research Society Annual Conference (2010).

26. For examples of an application of GSR, see Ohme, R.K., Reykowska, D., Wiener, D. and Choromanska, A. 'Analysis of neurophysiological reactions to advertising stimuli by means of EEG and Galvanic Skin Responses measures', *Journal of Neuroscience, Psychology, and Economics*, 2 (1) (2009), 21–31; Anthes, G.H., 'Smile, you're on Candid Computer', *Computerworld*, 35 (49) (3 December 2001), 50.

27. Pullen, J.P., 'Truth down to a science', *ANA Magazine* (Oct. 2006), 78–82; Croal, N.G., 'Moviefone learns to listen,' *Newsweek*, 135 (19) (8 May 2000), 84.

28. Romaniuk, J. and Wight, S., 'The influences of brand usage on response to advertising awareness measures', *International Journal of Market Research*, 51 (2) (2009) 203–218; Haaijer, R., 'Response latencies in the analysis of conjoint choice experiments', *Journal of Marketing Research* (August 2000), 376–82; N. Vasilopoulos, 'The influence of job familiarity and impression management on self-report measure scale scores and response latencies', *Journal of Applied Psychology*, 85 (1) (February 2000), 50.

29. McPhee, N., 'Is there a future for "real" qualitative market research interviewing in the digital age?' ESOMAR, *Congress Odyssey*, Athens (Sept. 2010).

30. Moreno, R. and Martinez, R., 'Causality as validity: Some implications for the social sciences', *Quality & Quantity*, 42 (5) (Oct. 2008) 597–604: Viswanathan, M., *Measurement Error and Research Design* (Thousand Oaks, CA: Sage, 2005); Sobel, M., 'Causal inference in the social sciences', *Journal of the American Statistical Association*, 95 (450) (June 2000).

31. Heckman, J.J., 'The scientific model of causality', *Sociological Methodology*, 35 (1) (2007) 1–98; Gould, G.F. and Gould, J.L., *Chance and Causation: To Experimental Design and Statistica* (New York: W.H. Freeman, 2001); Boruch, R.F., *Randomized Experiments for Planning and Evaluation* (Thousand Oaks, CA: Sage, 1994).

32. Dahlen, M., Törn, F. and Rosengren, S., 'Advertising creativity matters', *Journal of Advertising Research*, 48 (3) (Sept. 2008), 392–403.

33. Gross, I., 'The Creative Aspects of Advertising', *Sloan Management Review*, 14 (1) (1972), 83–109.

34. Viswanathan, M., *Measurement Error and Research Design* (Thousand Oaks, CA: Sage, 2005); Leichty, J., Ramaswamy, V. and Cohen, S.H., 'Choice menus for mass customization: An experimental approach for analyzing customer demand with an application to a web-based information service', *Journal of Marketing Research*, 38 (2) (May 2001), 183–96; Wyner, G.A., 'Experimental design', *Marketing Research: A Magazine of Management and Applications*, 9 (3) (Fall 1997), 39–41; Brown, S.R. and Melamed, L.E., *Experimental Design and Analysis* (Newbury Park, CA: Sage, 1990).

35. Farris, P.W., 'Overcontrol in advertising experiments', *Journal of Advertising Research* (November/December 2000), 73–78.

36. In addition to internal and external validity, there also exist construct and statistical conclusion validity. Construct validity addresses the question of what construct, or characteristic, is in fact being measured (*see* Chapter 7). Statistical conclusion validity addresses the extent and statistical significance of the covariation that exists in the data (*see* Chapters 10–12). See Treadwell, K.R.H., 'Demonstrating experimenter "Ineptitude" as a means of teaching internal and external validity', *Teaching of Psychology*, 35 (3) (Aug. 2008), 184–8; Klink, R.R. and Smith, D.C., 'Threats to the external validity of brand extension research', *Journal of Marketing Research*, 38 (3) (August 2001), 326–35; Campbell, D.T. and Stanley, J.C., *Experimental and Quasi Experimental Designs for Research* (Chicago: Rand McNally, 1966).

37. Blanton, H. and Jaccard, J., 'Representing versus generalizing: Two approaches to external validity and their implications for the study of prejudice', *Psychological Inquiry*, 19 (2) (2008), 99–105; Laurent, G., 'Improving the external validity of marketing models: A plea for more qualitative input', *International Journal of Research in Marketing*, 17 (2) (September 2000), 177; Bordia, P., 'Face-to-face computer-mediated communication: A synthesis of the experimental literature', *Journal of Business Communication*, 34 (1) (January 1997), 99–120; Bowen, D.M., 'Work group research: Past strategies and future opportunities', *IEEE Transactions on Engineering Management*, 42 (1) (February 1995), 30–38; Lynch, J.G. Jr, 'On the external validity of experiments in consumer research', *Journal of Consumer Research*, 9 (December 1982), 225–44.

38. Winer, R., 'Experimentation in the 21st century: The importance of external validity', *Academy of Marketing Science*, 27 (3) (Summer 1999), 349–58; Argyris, C., 'Actionable knowledge: Design causality in the service of consequential theory', *Journal of Applied Behavioural Science*, 32 (4) (December 1966), 390–406; Lynch, J.G. Jr, 'The role of external validity in theoretical research', Calder, B.J., Phillips, L.W. and Tybout, A., 'Beyond external validity', and McGrath, J.E and Brinberg, D., 'External validity and the research process', *Journal of Consumer Research* (June 1983), 109–124.

39. Berger, P. and Maurer, R., *Experimental Design with Applications in Management, Engineering and the Sciences* (Boston, MA: Boston University Press, 2002).

40. Berger, P. and Maurer, R., *Experimental design with applications in management, engineering and the sciences* (Boston: Boston University Press, 2002); Dholakia, U.M. and Morwitz, V.G., 'The scope and persistence of mere-measurement effects: Evidence from a field study of consumer satisfaction measurement', *Journal of Consumer Research*, 29 (2) (2002), 159–67.

41. Small, D.S., Have, T.R.T. and Rosenbaum, P.R., 'Randomization inference in a group-randomized trial of treatments for depression: Covariate adjustment, noncompliance and quantile effects', *Journal of the American Statistical Association*, 103 (481) (March 2008), 271–9; Rosenbaum, P.R., 'Attributing effects to treatment in matched observational studies', *Journal of the American*

Statistical Association, 97 (457) (March 2002), 183–92; Durier, C., Monod, H. and Bruetschy, A., 'Design and analysis of factorial sensory experiments with carry-over effects', *Food Quality and Preference*, 8 (2) (March 1997), 141–9; Nelson, L.S., 'Notes on the use of randomization in experimentation', *Journal of Quality Technology*, 28 (1) (January 1996), 123–6.

42. Glick, R., Guo, X. and Hutchison, M., 'Currency crises, capital-account liberalization and selection bias', *The Review of Economics and Statistics*, 88 (4) (Nov. 2006), 698–714; Rosenbaum, P.R., 'Attributing effects to treatment in matched observational studies', *Journal of the American Statistical Association*, 97 (457) (March 2002), 183–92; Selart, M., 'Structure compatibility and restructuring in judgement and choice', *Organisation Behaviour and Human Decision Processes*, 65 (2) (Feb. 1996), 106–16; Barker Bausell, R., *Conducting Meaningful Experiments* (Thousand Oaks, CA: Sage, 1994).

43. Kim, B., 'Virtual field experiments for a digital economy: A new research methodology for exploring an information economy', *Decision Support Systems*, 32 (3) (January 2002), 215; Chamis, E., 'Auto dealers test online sales in 90-day experiment', *Washington Business Journal*, 19 (11 May 2001), 15; Spethmann, B., 'Choosing a test market', *Brandweek*, 36 (19) (8 May 1995), 42–43; Tarshis, A.M., 'Natural sell-in avoids pitfalls of controlled tests', *Marketing News* (24 October 1986), 14.

44. Other experimental designs are also available. See Borror, C.M., 'Evaluation of statistical designs for experiments involving noise variables', *Journal of Quality Technology*, 34 (1) (January 2002), 54–70; Campbell, D.T. and Russo, M.J., *Social Experimentation* (Thousand Oaks, CA: Sage, 1999); Gunter, B., 'Fundamental issues in experimental design', *Quality Progress*, 29 (6) (June 1996), 105–113.

45. Krishna, A. and Unver, M.U., 'Improving the efficiency of course bidding at Business Schools: Field and laboratory studies', *Marketing Science*, 27 (2) (March/April 2008), 262–82: Dawar, N., 'Impact of product harm crises on brand equity: The moderating role of consumer expectations', *Journal of Marketing Research*, 37 (2) (May 2000), 215–26.

46. Allen, C.T., 'A theory based approach for improving demand artifact assessment in advertising experiments',

Journal of Advertising, 33 (2) (Summer 2004), 63–73; Lane, V.R., 'The impact of ad repetition and ad content on consumer perceptions of incongruent extensions', *Journal of Marketing* (April 2000), 80–91; Perrien, J., 'Repositioning demand artifacts in consumer research', *Advances in Consumer Research*, 24 (1997), 267–71.

47. Ofir, C. and Simonson, I., 'In search of negative customer feedback: The effect of expecting to evaluate on satisfaction evaluations', *Journal of Marketing Research*, 38 (2) (May 2001), 170–82; Laurent, G., 'Improving the external validity of marketing models: A plea for more qualitative input', *International Journal of Research in Marketing*, 17 (2, 3) (September 2000), 177.

48. Blumenschein, K., 'Hypothetical versus real willingness to pay in the health care sector: Results from a field experiment', *Journal of Health Economics*, 20 (3) (May 2001), 441; Alston, R.M. and Nowell, C., 'Implementing the voluntary contribution game: A field experiment', *Journal of Economic Behaviour and Organisation*, 31 (3) (December 1996), 357–68.

49. In some situations, surveys and experiments can complement each other and may both be used. For example, the results obtained in laboratory experiments may be further examined in a field survey. See Johnston, W.J. and Kim, K., 'Performance, attribution, and expectancy linkages in personal selling', *Journal of Marketing*, 58 (October 1994), 68–81.

50. Farris, P.W. and Reibstein, D.J., 'Overcontrol in advertising experiments', *Journal of Advertising Research*, 40 (6) (Nov./Dec. 2000).

51. Ryals, L. and Wilson, H., 'Experimental methods in market research: From information to insight', *International Journal of Market Research*, 47 (4) (2005), 347–66.

52. Phillips, A., 'IJMR Research Methods Forum: "Start listening, stop asking" – Research snoopers and spies – the legal and ethical challenges facing observational research', *International Journal of Market Research*, 52 (2) (2010), 275–81.

53. Lavine, S., 'Mobile interviewing – the next frontier of data collection', ESOMAR, *Online Research*, Chicago (Oct. 2009).

54. Grootenhuis, S. and Treiber, B., 'Incite to action: Encouraging effective utilization of shopper insights in a global context', ESOMAR, *Insights*, Brussels (Feb. 2011).

6 Social media research methods

Stage 1

Problem definition

Stage 2

Research approach developed

Stage 3

Research design developed

Stage 4

Fieldwork or data collection

Stage 5

Data integrity and analysis

Stage 6

Report preparation and presentation

Social media is an additional domain in which to supplement and complement, but not to replace traditional marketing research.

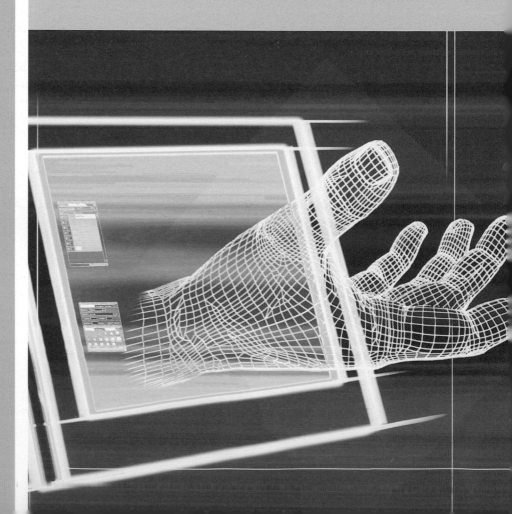

Objectives

After reading this chapter, you should be able to:

1 understand the nature and value of social media research;

2 understand why social media research emerged and how as a body of methods it is developing;

3 describe how social media research can supplement traditional forms of marketing research;

4 describe the difference between active and passive forms of social media research;

5 understand the nature and application of blogging, online research communities and crowdsourcing;

6 understand the challenges and opportunities inherent in conducting social media research in an international context;

7 appreciate the basis of ethical challenges in conducting social media research;

8 appreciate how digital developments are enabling the growth of social media research.

Overview

Millions of people actively engage in social media exchanges across the globe. They actively engage and enjoy discussions, share opinions, images, music and other art forms, meet new people, show off their experiences, likes and dislikes, opinions, values and emotions. Social media facilitates this array of communications, the development of relationships and the building of networks. From the researchers' perspective, social media can reveal characteristics of participants and help create unique consumer insights.

We begin this chapter by describing what social media represents from the researchers' perspective and explain the value it holds in supporting marketing decision making. The emergence of social media research was grounded in the development of Web 2.0 and from this emerged a movement known as 'Research 2.0'. We describe the development of Research 2.0 and how this movement developed. Social media research techniques have distinct benefits, but they may also supplement and change the manner in which traditional forms of marketing research are conducted.

Social media research can be broadly classified into 'active' and 'passive' techniques. We will describe the nature and distinction between 'active' and 'passive' techniques and then illustrate how these are applied in the most popular forms of social media research in marketing. The most widely used social media research techniques will be described and illustrated, with a focus upon what distinctive support they may give to decision makers.

Social media can be experienced in a global context. A key advantage of social media is how it can enable individuals to be brought together from the remotest parts of the world. The communities that may be generated from this reach will be evaluated along with the distinctive international marketing advantages this brings. A key disadvantage of social media is the ethical challenge of conducting research, especially in the context of the well-developed codes of conduct applied in marketing research. Dimensions of the ethical challenge faced by social media researchers will be evaluated. Finally, we will evaluate how digital developments are shaping social media research. The emphasis here will be upon the challenges and development of research techniques that use mobile devices.

We start with an example that illustrates how Philips are developing new marketing research techniques. It illustrates the use of emerging research techniques that can dovetail with traditional marketing research techniques or, in some cases, be a replacement.

Philips' online community[1]

> For companies such as Philips, traditional marketing research methods such as surveys, focus groups and in-depth interviews play an important role in product development and marketing. Philips viewed many of its existing research methods as better suited to the latter stages of concept and product development and wished to develop techniques suited to the 'fuzzy front end' phase of product development. They did not see traditional marketing research as being effective or efficient as they gathered and assimilated exploratory feedback. This feedback Philips saw as more open ended and prone to evolutionary changes as consumers adopt new technology and interact with new brands and one another. They approached this challenge by continuously experimenting with and incorporating new research methods. The new methods helped them bring a new level of consumer insight, but they also brought their own limitations. Ethnographic research proved to be time consuming, expensive and limited in the number of participants it could include. Philips envisioned that an online community would complement the company's existing research initiatives by providing a new, effective tool for uncovering critical insights, including unforseen and unmet needs. Beyond assisting new product development, the community would provide an outlet for other marketing research needs, such as validation of concepts, naming research and studying brand association.

What is social media research?

Social media research
Research based upon the collection of data from social media platforms. It is usually conducted to supplement and support the development of traditional marketing research methods.

Social media networks encompass a great breadth of means by which participants can enjoy and engage in discussions, chat, webcasts, photos, videos, podcasts, animation, surveys, games and virtual worlds. Participants interact with and use social media in many different ways, and in many different contexts. For example, participants form online communities by combining one-to-one (e.g. email and instant messaging), one-to-many (web pages and blogs), and many-to-many (wikis) communication modes. Across the globe, the sheer number and types of participants, and the role that social media plays in their lives has meant that marketers have to understand and engage with this phenomenon. Many brands and marketers, plus the designers that support these brands, have embraced social media to engage with and develop relationships with consumers. Similarly, many researchers have recognised that the user-generated content of social media make them very relevant as a domain for conducting new forms of marketing research. There has emerged a body of researchers that have recognised the many opportunities inherent in social media research. In response to these opportunities, many traditional research methods have been adapted and new methods have been developed. These new methods may be seen as a supplement to traditional forms of marketing research. Engaging with individuals and communities in all the manners that participants engage with social media has opened new avenues for understanding, explaining and predicting the behaviour of consumers in the marketplace. Social media can be used in a variety of marketing research applications including segmentation, idea generation, concept testing, product development, brand launches, pricing and integrated marketing communications. The following example illustrates how easyJet have used social media research to supplement traditional research methods.

Co-creating the future – the easyJet community[2]

> easyJet was one of the first airlines to embrace the opportunity of the Internet. They established a research function in 2006 using an array of traditional research methods to generate consumer insight. They wished to supplement their traditional research methods with a properly conducted online research community. The easyJet Community was

launched in 2008 and consisted of 2000 active participants who had flown with them in the past 12 months. New discussion topics were introduced each week, with members receiving an email inviting them to take part in a specific discussion or even completing a survey. All of those taking part in the community are entered into a monthly prize draw with the chance to win a free pair of return flights to an easyJet destination. Some of the types of research covered with example topic areas include: advertising and brand communications, brand strategy, concept testing and development, customer experience and service delivery, network development, customer understanding, and websites. As well as the breadth of research objectives met by the community, a main benefit for easyJet is the ability to provide findings more quickly than traditional approaches.

There are many advantages in using social media research which will be further developed in relation to traditional marketing research. The key advantages of easyJet's use of social media research are worth noting at this stage:

- **Community** – easyJet created and nurtured a community with members who were happy to engage with others. The context of discussion in a community enabled topics to be developed and challenged over a period of time.
- **Engaging** – new topics were introduced each week to the community. These topics can be set by what the researcher sees as being vital to support marketing decision(s) and/or what is discerned as being interesting and relevant to the community.
- **Rewards** – participants could clearly see tangible incentives for taking part. The intangible rewards lie in the control that participants have in engaging with the community. They can choose if, how and when to respond, and as such they have to be given tasks that they find interesting. They have to be treated with respect.
- **Mixed methods** – surveys could be administered in the community. The focus of the questions set in the survey could emerge from qualitative discussions and/or the posting of images or any art/design representations.
- **Timing and costs** – traditional marketing research methods could be used to generate the knowledge and insight generated in the community, but in comparative terms easyJet's community generated a huge breadth of decision support quickly and cheaply.

The emergence of social media research

The term used in the marketing research industry to describe the development of social media research was Research 2.0 or NewMR. Research 2.0 grew out of the development of Web 2.0. a term first coined by O'Reilly Media (**www.oreilly.com**) in 2004 to describe two interrelated phenomena. The first phenomenon was the growth in websites where users could contribute content to the website, often referred to as user-generated content, or simply UGC. Examples of these types of services included photo sharing sites such as Flckr, video uploaded sites such as YouTube, collaborative projects based on wikis (such as Wikipedia), social networks such as MySpace and Facebook, and blogging. The second phenomenon that was embraced under the term Web 2.0 was the creation of a wide range of tools that made using the web much easier and more rewarding. These tools included such things as AJAX (Asynchronous JavaScript and XML), PHP, and mySQL. With Web 2.0, users were creating content and shaping their experiences and the services they received. During 2004 and 2005, as the term Web 2.0 became increasingly established, the '2.0' label was applied to a wider range of activities, including law, architecture, and even government. In the world of marketing research, the term Research 2.0 came into being in 2006, to reflect a shift away from the old 'command and control' paradigm of marketing research towards a more collaborative approach.

'Command and control' is a term used to summarise what some researchers saw as the limitations of traditional marketing research, especially in the use of surveys. Characteristics of this perspective would include where researchers frame the questions from their own social and cultural perspective and may omit certain topics that participants find important.[3] It would also include the use of the term 'subject' or 'respondent' to describe individuals measured as in the physical sciences (you will note that we use the term 'participant' throughout this book). The term 'respondent' could be seen to denote an individual who simply responds to questions 'commanded' by the researcher. The structure, process and research process could be seen to be 'controlled' by the researcher, i.e. controlled as in the physical sciences. Within this context many researchers argued that the marketing research industry was 'stuck in the 1990s' in that it was using the web merely to conduct the same research online as it would have done offline. It was argued that by not taking full advantage of Web 2.0 capabilities, the marketing research industry was handicapping itself. It was seen to be relying on research methods that only scratched the surface of what consumers thought and felt.[4]

Research 2.0 became a movement that embraced tapping into consumer-generated web data. The benefits of embracing Research 2.0 were seen as:[5]

- **Spontaneous** – enabling access to natural, spontaneous conversations, to consumer agendas, ways of thinking and the subtleties of their language.
- **Heartfelt** – more emotionally rich responses facilitated by the anonymity of the Internet.
- **Cutting edge** – enabling access to more leading-edge and involved consumers – those who wish to articulate views (positive and negative) about brands, products, services and experiences.
- **Immediacy** – enabling feedback in real time as events unfold, rather than when their impact begins to be felt in the marketplace

Research 2.0 was the catalyst to the emergence of new research methods and a critical reflection of how traditional marketing research methods are planned and implemented. It marked a recognition of a shift in respect to the experiences of individuals that researchers wish to measure and understand.[6] This was a move from respondents being 'commanded and controlled' to a more collaborative relationship with participants, researchers and brands sharing a research experience. Social media research has not replaced traditional marketing research; each approach has its own distinctive strengths and challenges and can best be seen as supportive and supplemental. It must be recognised, however, that participant experiences of social media research are shaping the expectations of research participants in terms of how rewarding and engaging research should be. Table 6.1 summarises the distinctive strengths and challenges of traditional marketing research and social research methods.

Of particular note in Table 6.1 is the great body of theory and cases that have supported the development of traditional research methods. There are many new and emerging cases that illustrate the successful use of social media research, but the underpinning sampling, data collection and analytical techniques are still emerging. The same can be said for the ethical challenges in conducting traditional marketing research. Professional research associations such as ESOMAR have taken care to develop and apply codes of practice in order to differentiate bona fide research activities from other data gathering and marketing ventures. Social media research has created a number of ethical challenges. Responses to those challenges are also still emerging. Finally, it is worth noting that even though huge amounts of data may be gathered with sometimes far more individuals represented in comparison to sample surveys, social media research is qualitative in nature. It is primarily exploratory, it embraces and synthesises multifarious forms of data and is organic in terms of how issues and questions emerge and are addressed.

Table 6.1	The relative strengths and challenges of traditional marketing research and social media research methods	
	Strengths	**Challenges**
Traditional marketing research	• Robust theoretical underpinnings to sampling, research methods and data analyses. • Robust development of ethical codes of practice, especially protecting participant anonymity. • Breadth of quantitative and qualitative research methods to measure and understand participants. • Can focus upon specific existing and potential consumers to capture behaviour, attitudes, emotions, aspirations and sensory experiences.	• Gaining access to participants – declining response rates. • Complaints of boring research experiences. This sets challenges to design engaging research. • Debates on the quality of samples used in survey work – especially in the use of access panels. • The costs and time taken to conduct quality research – relative to other forms of data that may support decision makers.
Social media research	• Can reach notoriously difficult to access target participants. • Engaging experiences, technology and context suited to participants. • Participants can express themselves in ways that they are comfortable with. • Speed of capturing a great amount of disparate data.	• Newly developed methods with little theoretical underpinning. • Representativeness – can count incidences of behaviour, but primarily qualitative. • Ethical challenges – participant identities and forms of expression. • Inability to target specific types of participants and/or specific issues.

Active and passive social media research

Listening

Listening involves the evaluation of naturally occurring conversations, behaviours and signals. The information that is elicited may or may not be guided, but it brings the voice of consumers' lives to brands.

Social media research methods can be broadly classified as passive and active[7]. Passive social media research can be seen as an approach akin to observing what is being discussed and displayed in social media. Another term for passive research that is perhaps more commonly used to represent passive social media research is **listening**. Every day, millions of consumers talk about all aspects of their lives online. This wealth of naturally occurring consumer expression offers the opportunity to understand consumers on their terms, using their language and logic. People are talking with one another about their problems, experiences, likes and dislikes, life in general, and their feelings and experiences of brands. They do this using the 'conversational webs' of blogs, forums, social networks, Twitter, communities and wikis. By tuning in to relevant conversations (i.e. by listening), it is argued that more can be learned about consumer attitudes and needs than through traditional 'questioning' methods alone. By listening, researchers may be able to learn more about consumers and prospects by understanding the natural, rich, unfiltered word of mouth around products and service experiences.[8] This approach is illustrated in the following example. Of particular note is how the listening exercise, as a qualitative method, helped to shape the nature and scope of a sample survey.

Real research	## The essentials of listening at Hennessy Cognac[9]

Hennessy (**www.hennessy.com**), the leading cognac brand, discovered a rising trend in links made between their company website and BlackPlanet.com, the largest social network for African-Americans. Digging deeper, Hennessy learned that numbers of BlackPlanet members linked their personal pages to Hennessy's site. Some went further, decorating their pages with borrowed images of Hennessy brands. By listening to signals embedded in linking behaviour, Hennessy had stumbled upon a passionate market they were not aware of. Interested to learn more about these consumers, Hennessy then studied a random sample of BlackPlanet member web pages to understand their themes and use of brand imagery. They also commissioned an online survey with research partner CRM Metrix (**www.crmmetrix.com**) to profile audience attitudes, usage and influence. Hennessy discovered that visions of the Hennessy brand expressed in the member pages 'were not necessarily ours, but this does not make them any less valid'. Recognising the inherent and potential long-term value in BlackPlanet members, Hennessy then sought to learn what would improve the site and make it more interesting and enjoyable. Hennessy went further than just tweaking the site; they asked for and listened to suggestions about 'what would make your experience of drinking Hennessy cognacs more enjoyable?' Realising that BlackPlanet members enjoyed drinking socially and mixing Hennessy into drinks, they added recipes highlighting cognac as an ingredient and offered Hennessy branded e-invitations for parties. Five years after the initial round of responses, the Hennessy site showed the brand's ongoing commitment to listening and evolving the relationship and experience. In 2009, Hennessy's 'Artistry' initiative sponsored musicians and music tours, streamed music and showcased artists. Hennessy also added a social networking component by creating presences on Facebook and YouTube.

In the Hennessey example, researchers did not initially direct specific questions or tasks to participants; they simply observed. The main advantage of this approach is that the 'natural' behaviour of participants and communities can be observed. The main disadvantage is that specific research questions may not be addressed and/or may take an inordinate amount of time to naturally emerge and develop. Researchers that adopt passive social media research observe with specific purposes such as in the following example. In this example, Nivea passively observed the agendas of existing and potential consumers. For Nivea this passive observation was a first stage which would take them on to further stages of collaborative research. Working with targeted participants, Nivea could co-create product improvements and new products.

Real research | **Successful co-creation at Nivea[10]**

Nivea is the best-known brand of the multinational corporation Beiersdorf based in Hamburg, Germany. In order to integrate the voice of customers beyond traditional marketing research techniques like concept tests or focus groups, the Nivea Body Care Division instituted a holistic co-creation approach. Co-creation was aimed to start new product development from scratch at the beginning of the innovation process. The goal was to draw a 'landscape' of the needs, wishes, concerns, consumer language and potential product solutions by users, which are explicitly and implicitly expressed in online communities and social media. Starting out with a broad search, more than 200 online communities, forums and blogs in three languages were screened covering all kinds of consumer tribes that have emerged online. The most relevant and insightful communities and forums on cosmetics, health, lifestyle, fashion, sports and do-it-yourself were observed and analysed in-depth such as **www.beauty24.de**, **www.bubhub.com.au**, **www.badgerandblade.com**, **www.glamour.de**, or **www.undershirtguy.com**. Threads of consumer conversation were retrieved and analysed using qualitative data analysis software. Certain needs, concerns or suggestions for product improvements were repeatedly occurring in consumers' online conversations. Those 'gold nuggets', i.e. fresh, relevant, inspiring and enduring findings, were then aggregated to consumer insights. Product designers joined the research team and helped to interpret and translate the consumer insights into initial products.

Active social media research
May be seen as an approach akin to both observing and engaging in what is being discussed and displayed in social media.

Active social media research may be seen as an approach akin to both observing and engaging in what is being discussed and displayed in social media. Rather than standing back, observing and listening, researchers can join communities and may choose to direct specific questions or tasks to participants. The main advantage of this approach is that researchers can direct participants and communities to address issues and questions that they deem to be important. They can also establish quality standards in how data is collected in much the same way that many qualitative researchers work. The main disadvantage is that specific research issues and questions driven by researchers may not be of interest to participants or communities. Great care has to be taken to protect the values of brands that may be seen as alien to the agendas of particular communities. The following example illustrates an active social research method. Of particular note is how researchers at Weihenstephan have taken care not to discard many of the sound working practices of traditional marketing research.

Real research The Weihenstephan online research community[11]

Weihenstephan is a German dairy company belonging to the international Mueller Dairy Group. Weihenstephan recognised that social media was profoundly changing the basics of interpersonal communication, but they also saw several new challenges for researchers arising from this 'web evolution': discussion groups developed without being previously sampled; answers given to questions that have not been asked yet; well-constructed interviews replaced by dynamic social interaction in virtual communities. As the marketing research industry explores what is 'real' change and what is simply hype regarding 'new research dynamics and methods', new instruments, methods and behaviours are allowing researchers to unlock insights through lots of exciting trial and error procedures. They determined that research using social media needs to be robust, guided and observational. In planning their response to the challenges and opportunities to social media research, Weihenstephan chose a closed online research community, establishing one place for conducting all qualitative and quantitative marketing research. They targeted around 100–150 participants representing various regions in Germany (equal spilt in urban areas of Munich, Stuttgart, Cologne, Berlin and Hamburg). Their community profile ended up with: 80 per cent women, 20 per cent men; a broad age range with 50 per cent aged 20–39 years and 50 per cent aged 40–65 years; broad product usage in dairy market (e.g. milk, butter, yoghurt, cream). Their community worked and several key projects were discussed including: several new concepts and product ideas in existing sub-categories, some preferred flavours for possible line extensions, general attitudes and habits in possible new sub-categories for the brand.

Social media research methods

There is a growing body of passive and active social media research methods. Rather than list and describe this body, we present and illustrate the main approaches. These represent a growing base of case material that describes how different methods are applied and what benefits and challenges are inherent in a selected method. The methods chosen can broadly be categorised as research that utilises blogging, communities and crowdsourcing.

Blogging

Blogging as a research term can represent both passive and active forms of social media research. The use and value of the blog in an active and passive sense can largely be attributed to the great diversity of ways that blogs may be created and presented. The 'blog' can be presented as a piece of writing both short and long, poetry, drawings, still visuals, moving images, music and any combination of these. The blogger may take time to research, edit and articulate their views. They may also produce a blog extremely quickly as a representation of opinions and feelings as they experience them or respond to other blogs. The term used to represent passive research using blogs is **blog and buzz mining**. Such an approach provides the means to observe, track or initiate views in research communities, social networks and anywhere else that people post comments, visuals, music and other forms of art on the Internet. Individual researchers can undertake blog or buzz mining. This can be done by searching the Internet for conversations and postings in an array of blogs that could include Twitter and comments about news stories. Individual researchers do this with a specific set of research objectives to guide their search. Regardless of how many postings researchers gather or how quantitative specific elements of blog analysis may be (e.g. statistics from Twitter analyses), it should be remembered that blog and buzz mining is exploratory and qualitative in nature. The researcher is looking for the juxtaposition of different ideas and forms of expression, emerging patterns and the 'nuggets' of expression that articulate feelings or opinions really well. In addition to the individual researcher addressing specific research objectives, decision makers may turn to specialist research companies that work in blog and buzz mining. An example of such a company is presented in the following example.

Blog and buzz mining
Provide the means to observe, track or initiate views in research communities, social networks and anywhere else that people post comments, visuals, music and other forms of art on the Internet.

Real research	**Buzzmetrics**[12]

Nielsen's Buzzmetrics works like a search engine. It 'listens in' to billions of conversations taking part in blogs, Internet chat rooms, bulletin boards, product rating websites and other places where people share opinions. The content is assimilated into one standardised relational database and then analysed, so that research can be performed. The process delivers three primary offerings. The first is brand audit, looking at how 'word of mouth' works for a brand, at who is talking and what they are saying, who the evangelists and the detractors are, and at the key drivers of negative and positive comment. The second is word of mouth planning in terms of picking up on the key messages emerging and then using the key drivers of positive word of mouth in the brand's marketing activities. The third is a tracking service which monitors the impact of marketing campaigns on the word of mouth around that brand.

This example illustrates that a decision maker working for a brand may use blog and buzz mining for longitudinal purposes, i.e. to view how a series of events unfold and what may be shaping those events. A sense of the impact of specific developments in the marketplace, such as the launch of new product by a competitor, can be monitored. Rapid feedback on the impact of decisions, such as the use of a new celebrity to endorse a brand, can be gathered. As a result, questions can be addressed of what is occurring now for decision makers, and what could be happening through the emergence of specific trends. These questions can be addressed without having to recruit, engage or reward participants.

Whilst blog and buzz mining can save the time and costs associated with interacting with participants, these resource savings cover a major drawback. Researchers may identify particularly interesting participants whose ideas, experiences and forms of articulation they see as being really valuable. Particular issues, points of debate and novel ideas may emerge, but

Participatory blogging

Researcher interaction with individuals in communities and social networks. Individual participants can be targeted and given blogging tasks that relate to specific research objectives.

may be lost if the researcher is unable to interject. Thus there may be individuals and issues that the researcher may wish to question in more depth. The means of response may continue in a blog format and also be in the public domain. When researchers direct questions to develop blogs, they are conducting active social media research. The term used to represent active research using blogs is **participatory blogging**.

The following example illustrates a case of the use of participatory blogging.

Real research　　**Understanding the media habits of government elites**[13]

Hall & Partners (**www.hall-and-partners.com**) use digital technologies to make research more insightful and timely using techniques such as bulletin boards, blog journals, personal videos and collages. The researchers believe that to get close to consumers they have to develop rapport. To achieve this they 'come clean' with participants about what they are trying to find out and ask for their help. This approach has yielded some of their richest insights. In one example, a client wanted to understand the media habits of 'government elites', a small group of powerful people who influence government policy. Having conducted media diaries via bulletin boards with other target participants, the researchers were unsure whether this would work with people with such hectic and demanding schedules. So, after recruiting them, they started sending them emails to establish a personal connection between them and a researcher who would eventually meet them. The response was beyond the researchers' expectations. The participants responded in much greater and much more personal depth through a blog journal via email than they might have done under pressure to complete and return an 'old-fashioned' diary, even if the diary had been online.

Of particular note is what may be deemed as a 'blog' in this context. There is a clear use of narrative and visuals combined to articulate what participants were doing and how they felt. Participants were given a task than may be more engaging than answering direct questions. The outcome of the blogs fed into traditional forms of marketing research, helping to develop and validate the views expressed in the blogs. Finally it is worth noting how the decision makers, especially communications designers, could relate to and find support from the findings of this approach.

It is clear to note from the Hall & Partners case that participatory blogging can enable the researcher to focus in greater depth on research objectives of concern. The blogging exercise can be engaging and enjoyable for participants and the outcomes of great value for decision makers. Researchers can address issues specifically to suit the motivations and characteristics of individual participants. In turn, participants can choose the timing and context of engagement with the blogging task set. In summary, the reasons for tapping into consumer-generated web data through blogging can be seen as being able to access:

- Natural, spontaneous conversations.
- Consumer agendas, ways of thinking and language as opposed to researcher dictated ones.
- More heartfelt, emotionally rich responses facilitated by the anonymity of the Internet.
- A more leading edge and involved sort of consumer.
- An immediacy and topicality of web forums that facilitates feedback in real time, as events unfold.[14]

Communities

Many blogs are delivered, enjoyed and commented upon in a community setting. Communities are spaces where individuals co-exist and share many interests and aspirations. Individuals may share their community in harmony, but for some an element of dissent or debate is an essential characteristic of their membership. In virtual or online communities, members generally have the option to easily join or leave a community, depending upon how well it serves their priorities and interests.

An example of an online community is the parents website Mumsnet (**www.mumsnet.com**). The idea behind this community was to create a website where parents could swap advice about holidays, pushchairs and the previous night's television. Over twelve years it developed into the UK's busiest social network for parents, generating nearly 40 million page views per month and nearly 5 million visits per month. The community that use Mumsnet can view and share a huge breadth of issues, likes, dislikes and concerns that relate to the myriad challenges and joys of bringing up children and being a parent. From a researcher's perspective, there is a huge amount to learn about parents in a passive manner. Individuals within the community may strongly relate to the issues presented and discussed, they could be emotionally charged, supportive and really open. Where there exists a specific problem or challenge (e.g. in the parenting context of coping with a child who is copying unsavoury characteristics of their favourite television character), interested community members can come together to co-create possible solutions or future directions. These forms of expression are what many researchers want from participants in their studies. As such many brands and researchers try to establish communities. These communities are termed market research online communities or MROCs.

Market research online community

A panel of recruited participants who are questioned and observed in a community setting using a variety of research techniques, often over a period of months.

We have presented examples of MROCs earlier in the chapter, in evaluating the cases of Philips, easyjet and Weihenstephan. Online research communities may be devoted to a particular group of individuals, selected countries and/or particular issues. However, given the investment needed to build, maintain and reward a community, many MROCs are built around specific sponsoring brands, as in the earlier examples. A dedicated brand MROC can enable a company to recruit a panel of 'consumer-advisers'. A company and their researchers can engage with members using a variety of quantitative and qualitative techniques, often unfolding over a period of months. The brand MROC establishes a channel that decision makers and designers working for a brand can use to communicate with participants and engage in projects ranging from measuring attitudes, exploration and ethnography, to concept and product development and testing.[15]

Brand MROCs can be seen as a means to address specific research objectives. However, a fundamental difference of the brand MROC compared to other research approaches is the extent to which they feature brand engagement. They actively seek to invite participants to immerse themselves in the world of the brand. This can mean that the aim of an MROC is to develop a relationship with participants to a stage where they become 'critical friends' to the brand, offering continuing 'honest' feedback.[16] It has been argued that that brand MROCs are not just research tools. Some brand MROCs see research being low on the agenda; designing and investing in them to address a wider spectrum of marketing functions.[17] In this wide spectrum of marketing functions, communicating to a brand community can fulfil three distinct purposes.[18] There may be elements of all three purposes fulfilled in an MROC, but a specific purpose may be seen as the main driver. The first would be to create *brand ambassadors*, i.e. by nurturing participants that are seen as thought leaders. With a deep understanding of the values and personality of a brand, plus an emotional commitment to the brand, these participants could be highly persuasive to an array of target markets. The second would be to create *brand analysts*, i.e. by nurturing participants that would test particular concepts and designs. Again, with a deep understanding of the brand, the 'fit' of a new idea to the values of a brand could be tested. This form of testing could be in the use of words, e.g. a new product description; of images, e.g. the use of new celebrity endorsement; of designs, e.g. the look, form and function of a new product. The third would be to create *consumer insight*, i.e. by eliciting characteristics of participants' behaviour, attitudes and emotions. Measuring and understanding characteristics of participants, could work using a breadth of research techniques, allowing participants to reflect and express themselves in a variety of manners.

Where some emphasis of the MROC is towards researching and testing participants, communicating to a community is vital to improve the ultimate quality of research. Every brand has distinctive values, a competitive landscape and potential directions in which it may develop. Participants can enrich their understanding of a brand and appreciate the array of marketing and design decisions that can shape a brands future. With such enrichment and appreciation, participants can respond to research challenges in a most positive manner. They may play with ideas, share particular challenges, and reflect upon solutions. Whatever the primary purpose of a brand MROC, if research is being conducted, there is also a communications challenge to be faced. The following example illustrates the use of a brand MROC designed for the spirits brand Diageo. Of particular note in this example is the care taken to craft communications to participants. Nurturing a sense of community through well-targeted communications was seen as vital to engaging participants, giving them a sense of community and eliciting their views and feelings.

Understanding, embracing and evolving marketing research online communities[19]

Diageo's Altitude Lounge was an online community run by Virtual Surveys (**www.virtualsurveys.com**). Diageo was the world's leading premium drinks business across spirits, wine and beer. Their online community covered five markets: China, Germany, South Korea, the United Kingdom and the United States. Before developing the community they wanted to ensure that they were able to understand the cultural context of the countries in question. This helped them improve how they communicated with participants and learn more about what might motivate them to take part. They took a number of steps to engage with their members.

- Online guide: They created a visual help guide and translated this into all the different languages so it was easier for people to understand how the community worked.
- Native language: They sent emails about topics out in native languages and styled the text so it was a more appropriate way to speak to members in each country.
- Private comments: They made it easier for people to make comments privately by enabling them to reply to their email address with further comments rather than leaving these publically in the discussion.
- Shared results: They offered specific feedback on the concepts they had tested, explaining the impact the research had on Diageo's strategies.
- Incentives: They offered premium alcohol as additional incentives to participation, matching brands to the types of participant taking part.
- Prizes: They conducted country specific prize draws which guaranteed a prize per country.
- User feedback: After the community had been running for four months, they undertook a review of the community with members, asking what they liked about taking part and how they could improve the community.

Diageo saw response rates improve substantially as participants became more interested in taking part in research.

Researchers have recognised the values associated with communities, be they existing online communities, groups within social networks or artificially created communities in MROCs. The key challenge they face in working with communities is one of connecting with participants with integrity. Many communities may be naturally wary of 'outsiders' who may hold questionable values, who observe them, and sometimes aim to shape community agendas. There are examples of researchers locating and engaging with founders or influential 'elders' within communities. Such engagements can build researcher integrity and facilitate more natural conversations. For researchers to properly connect with communities and properly realise their inherent powers of expression, well-planned and targeted communications are vital. The community is clearly a context to conduct research where the previously described stance of 'command and control' would be doomed to fail.[20]

Crowdsourcing

Crowdsourcing
A process of eliciting ideas and developing actions based upon researcher engagement with a large group of self-selecting participants, primarily in online communities.

Crowdsourcing is the act of taking a job traditionally performed by a designated agent (usually an employee) and outsourcing it to an undefined, generally large group of people in the form of an open call.[21] Crowdsourcing has been applied in many areas to perform services, design products and solve problems. In terms of conducting research, crowdsourcing enables ideas to be elicited, and potential insights and actionable solutions based on those insights to be tested and developed. The process of crowdsourcing is a means to draw together the creative thinking and talents of a wide body of individuals. Through the use of online communities, a great breadth and diversity of thinking and talents can be drawn together to generate ideas and actionable solutions.

Perhaps the best known example of the community crowdsourcing is Wikipedia (**http://www.wikipedia.org**). In the English language, this online encyclopedia offers over 3 million articles. The encyclopedia was created and is maintained by participants who freely engage in volunteering their ideas. Every week, thousands of articles are added and edited by a global community of students, professors and subject experts around the world. Wikepedia is not just an example of a crowd creating a body of information that competes with conventional commercial encyclopedias. It is also an example of a community taking ownership of a project by ensuring the validity of information and that the process of validation is within a code of conduct.[22]

In the context of conducting marketing research, crowdsourcing constitutes an active social media research method. Its impact is realised by researchers contacting and engaging self-selecting participants through different online communities, primarily through social media. If these individuals can be inspired by a particular research challenge that they see as being credible, they may spread the word to other individuals within their communities, using for example Facebook or Twitter. As was discussed in the context of communities, well-planned and targeted communications are vital to inspire individuals to want to become part of the crowd and to fully engage in the tasks set for the crowd. Once individuals are drawn into the crowd and become participants, the researcher can achieve the following benefits:

Co-creation
A process by which a group of individuals collaboratively evaluate a challenge and form design solution(s) to best resolve that challenge.

- **Co-creation.** **Co-creation** is a process by which a group of participants collaborate to evaluate the challenges and opportunities inherent in a research task. They can go on to design solutions to those challenges. This group can be really diverse and bring together many different forms of thinking and expression. The nature of debate within this group can develop new, unexpected agendas that can draw in the energy and thinking of new participants. The nature of debate, forms of expression and quality of debate can create a most engaging co-creation experience for participants.

- **Brainstorming**. Traditional brainstorming has been used for several decades, especially in the context of management or marketing issues.[23] Whether formal or informal, the process is the same: participants think of as many ideas as they can and express them; leave the evaluation until later; build on and combine others' ideas; be as imaginative as possible, the wilder the ideas the better. When it works well, ideas flow freely from an interplay that may never have occurred if the group had not brainstormed together.

- **In-depth understanding of issues**. Particular ideas and solutions may be explored in depth. The exploration may occur naturally as different participants are drawn in to explain and illustrate ideas, to present better arguments and to question the ideas and arguments of other participants. Moderators can be used (and may be vital to the success of crowdsourcing in managing debate and contention) to drill down into the source and nature of ideas. Participants can express and illustrate their ideas through a variety of media to include writing, still and moving images or even music.

- **Evaluate emerging insights and proposed actions**. Researchers can build analyses and interpretations of themes that are discussed in a crowd. They can present what they see as the meaning of themes and even what may be seen as an optimum solution to a particular challenge. The popularity of particular solutions may be tested through simple polls through to detailed articulations of what is liked/disliked, will work/not work.

The following example illustrates how crowdsourcing can be used in a research context. As with other social media research, it is worth noting that this example shows how traditional marketing research can be supplemented and developed in a more focused manner.

Real research   **Bristol's adventures in crowdsourcing**[24]

Bristol City Council faced a major challenge in planning their future support for the city; they had to save 20 per cent from their budget. In order to plan these savings they decided to use crowdsourcing techniques. These techniques helped them to communicate the challenge they faced, generate ideas and issues from their citizens and to test the viability of the solutions they devised. They decided to focus the creative energy of their crowd upon urban development in terms of areas that should be 'cherished' or 'changed'. Crowdsourcing helped them to identify areas or things that were valued in Bristol city centre. It also helped them to identify issues with Bristol's central areas and develop solutions that fed into their Central Area Action Plan. Using social media platforms such as Facebook and Twitter, they spread the word that they wanted ideas for Bristol. Participants could make suggestions, upload photos and feedback on other ideas and potential solutions. The Council took great care to make the process engaging, through the use of mapping techniques, presenting ideas that could be voted upon and with strong visual design to communicate results. The process integrated different social media sources, generating 925 comments, which were grouped into 10 main themes. Crowdsourcing worked well for Bristol but did not replace their other means to engage with citizens, primarily conducted through surveys and face-to-face meetings. In partucular they maintained Bristol's Citizens' Panel, neighbourhood forum meetings and public displays and drop-in sessions for consultation around big projects.

The Bristol crowdsourcing project was seen as a great success for the city and was used as an exemplar for other cities wishing to replicate the process and realise the benefits. It must be noted, however, that crowdsourcing has disadvantages. These may be summarised as:

- **Self-selection bias**. This is not particularly a problem associated solely with crowdsourcing. Wherever participants choose to take part in a research project, a number of challenges emerge dependent upon who is drawn in. Even if the crowd is large, notions of representativeness in sample survey terms can be dismissed. It has to be recognised that brainstorming, debating ideas and solutions are primarily qualitative tasks. As such the qualities of participants and the quality of information drawn from them is paramount.

- **Disputes**. Participants may have disagreements about particular ideas and/or the way they express ideas. This is not a problem in itself; the researcher should wish to nurture debate and seek out differences. The problem lies more in how disagreements may develop and are manifested. This is where the role of the moderator is paramount, in just the same manner that a moderator in a focus group maintains order and harmony in debates.

- **Public domain**. The nature of ideas and debate can be difficult to protect. In the case of Bristol City Council, they would have been happy that their ideas and solutions were totally in the public domain. For many brands seeking marketing support through crowdsourcing, ideas that may give them competitive advantage may be easily lost. There may also be issues of who owns the intellectual property rights of particular solutions, especially where these solutions may be design led.

International marketing research

It may seem odd to have a distinct section on international marketing research in a chapter that addresses social media research. It could be argued that a fundamental essence of social media is international or even global in nature. This essence becomes applicable even to brands and research challenges that seemingly focus upon domestic markets. In the Bristol City Council crowdsourcing example presented earlier, it could be argued that designing and developing a city in the UK was a domestic challenge. However, the use of social media could attract participants from an international base: ex-Bristol residents, past visitors, individuals who dream of visiting the city one day and those who may be intrigued with the city's heritage and distinctive characteristics. This illustrates one of the key advantages of social media research, i.e. the ability to reach out to individuals and communities across the globe in novel, engaging ways. Traditional marketing research has always been able to be applied in international markets, but social media research is proving to be of great value in reaching traditionally difficult to get hold of research participants. In additional, social media enables these 'difficult to get hold of participants' to be able to articulate and express themselves in contexts and manners that they are comfortable with.

This key advantage can be illustrated in the context of conducting research in India. With approximately 800 million mobile phone subscribers in India, projected to cross a billion subscribers by 2013, mobile phone based research has a huge potential. This potential can be realised using both traditional and social media research to bridge gaps in knowledge of consumers in a rapidly developing economy. The scheduling of assignments, communication with participants and compilation of data can be facilitated through online platforms and mobile apps for capturing multimedia files. As a consequence of technological developments that enable data from research participants to be collected and integrated in new manners, analyses, interpretations and results can be delivered much more quickly.[25] The impact of the quality of data captured through mobile phones in youth and rural communities in India is illustrated in the following example.

Real research | Mobile in the qualitative space – digital ethnography in India[26]

Anjali Puri, Executive Director at TNS Qualitative Research, (**www.tnsglobal.com/ global/alm/india**), believes that mobile phones have added richness to ethnographic studies. Youth marketers and telecommunications companies were the first to take to incorporating the mobile into traditional ethnographic studies. The approach was to recruit a panel of participants and send them messages to share what they were doing, who they were with, what they were eating and to share pictures of their surroundings, abruptly at different times of the day. Says Anjali:

The biggest advantage of the mobile phone is that it is far less intrusive in the respondents' lives and therefore the data one can collect is a lot more spontaneous and relatively bias free. And, of course, it is possible to capture snapshots of their lives anytime, anywhere.

TNS used mobile phone logs in a rural ethnography study. After establishing initial contact with participants, the study relied on the collection of information from opinion leaders in a village by contact over the mobile phone (in this case largely voice and camera applications) conducted over a period of time. The mobile logs were found to be equally candid and rich in data as the information collected through personal contacts.

Of particular note in this example is the use of the phone in ethnographic studies. Though ethnographic studies may be seen as a traditional form of marketing research, many developments of visual and electronic ethnography are being facilitated by the ability to observe particular individuals in social media domains, in either passive and/or active forms.

Ethics in marketing research

There are a wide range of ethical issues that have emerged as social media research has become more widespread. These may be summarised as:

Theoretical base

Decision makers that use traditional forms of marketing research, may have some sense of the underpinning theories used by researchers. Even if they do not understand (or indeed have any inclination to want to understand) underpinning theories, they may have a level of confidence in research that is built upon a theoretical base that has been peer reviewed and critically developed over a number of decades. How quantitative and qualitative data is captured, how representative samples are drawn, how data is analysed and inferences drawn are areas that have long been scrutinised by practicing researchers and academics. Social media research is in its relative infancy and much more original research needs undertaking to appreciate the full validity and limitations of specific methods. Researchers using social media methods should make sure that decision makers understand the basis of the advice they are given. Where traditional marketing research can supplement and validate social media research, these links should be made clear.

Privacy, security and safety issues

Social media has changed the rules on how 'findable' somebody is. This has enormous implications for privacy and safety. For example, including a literal quote from an online forum in a report may essentially be the same thing as naming the individual, since a search on the quote may return information about the person making it. The discussion about 'what is in the public domain' and what can be used when, where, and how has barely started and will develop rapidly over the next few years.[27] Social media researchers should be able to address questions such as 'If we can collect vast amounts of data passively without the individual being aware of the data trail they are leaving, does that give researchers the right to use it for other purposes?' Some researchers would answer a resounding yes, and see chat rooms, forums and blogs as the ideal setting to conduct unbiased ethnography by 'lurking' at the sites of interest without announcing their presence.[28] Researchers may also consider the impact of the postings on social networking sites. One view within the research community seems to be that postings and blogs are 'published material'. However, bloggers and networkers might not see it in the same way.[29] The following example illustrates the ethical challenges of maintaining and respecting the anonymity of participants. Of particular note is the prediction that these challenges may be taken away from researchers, directly into the hands of decision makers.

Sitting in the chair of King Canute[30]

The use of websites, blog postings, microblogs such as Twitter, photography sites such as Flickr, video sites such as YouTube, social platforms such as MySpace, Facebook, Yahoo and MSN are generating huge qualitative datasets. These are made even more valuable by the use of data aggregators such as FriendFeed (**www.friendfeed.com**). It is possible to tie these separate platforms together and monitor the same person using any or all of these websites. The tools for monitoring and analysing these are also many and varied from cookies which are locked to the individual machine to content searches to pick up every incidence of a particular word used in the last 24 hours to keyword searches which use the keyword tags which blog posters put on their postings so that they can be found more easily. None of these require the permission of the person who has posted the data and there is no sense in which online anonymity can be guaranteed. The industry of mining Internet content bears little resemblance to a marketing research paradigm that gathers samples, validates them and asks participants questions in tried and tested manners. In analysing this difference between an emerging and established research industry, John Griffiths (**www.planningaboveandbeyond.com**) speculates that by 2020 research will be more in the hands of clients or decision makers who will be doing it themselves. Companies will be researching their stakeholders continually without needing to constantly recruit, re-qualify and validate them. Researchers will still be involved but as analysts and insight specialists who 'tune the data' and add value to it.

Digital developments in marketing research

Social media research was founded upon the opportunities afforded by the development of Web 2.0 technologies. As digital developments progress to Web 3.0 technologies and beyond, new techniques will be experimented with, new challenges addressed and new opportunities realised. It would be extremely difficult to predict digital developments in social media research. Such predictions could well be out of date before this book is printed. However, there are three core areas where digital developments are making a major impact upon how social media research is perceived, delivered and experienced. These three areas are **participant engagement**, gamification and mobile devices.

Participant engagement

'Engagement' is the manner in which research participants relate to the process of research, researchers and the topics of study. For a number of years, participant engagement has been seen as central to the future success of the research industry.[31] Falling response rates across most forms of research approaches and markets can be seen as one symptom of a lack of engagement. But beyond gaining initial access to participants lies the less quantifiable challenges of how much they think about, understand and reflect upon the topics

Participant engagement
The manner in which research participants relate to the process of research, researchers and the topics of study.

they are questioned about. To address these challenges, researchers have used many tactics to make the research process more fun, interesting and relevant to individual participants. The inherent nature of social media in terms of it being viewed as a form of entertainment, can facilitate great levels of engagement. Social media participants invest their own time, emotional energy and sometimes money for the privilege to immerse themselves in particular forms of self-development, tasks and relationships. Research processes and experiences that can be embedded into social media experiences present great prospects to access and engage participants. An excellent example of social media engagement lies in the growth of games played at an individual and network level. The principles of successful gaming are being applied to the conduct of research using social media. This movement is known as 'gamification'.

Gamification

Gamification refers to the application of the principles of what are seen as factors of successful gaming, into traditionally non-game processes and experiences such as education and research. This is achieved through the purposeful introduction of mechanisms that are designed to elicit specific, predictable behaviours, whilst simultaneously absorbing individuals in the experience by making it engaging and compelling.[32] Commonly misinterpreted as turning something serious (like filling in one's tax return) into a frivolous game experience, gamification is far more subtle than this. It involves identifying the intrinsic elements that make traditional games motivating and engaging, and building these elements into experiences where they might be missing. Excellent visuals, graphic design and creative questioning can have an impact on the participant experience and thus the quality of information they articulate.[33] Social media researchers would have an aim of making questions and the whole questioning experience more entertaining for participants. This mindset can apply to all forms of data collection, even in survey design. It is relatively simpler to achieve when applied in the context of social media.

Mobile devices

The mobile device is generic term used to refer to a variety of technologies that enable individuals to access data online and interact from wherever they may be. This covers a great breadth of technologies and software beyond mobile phone capabilities. Mobile devices offer great possibilities for researchers to engage participants in a quick and convenient mode that is not limited to a single location or device. They can be used as participants experience brands and services; i.e. the experiential qualities of consumption can be captured in all the ways that participants can articulate their experiences. Mobile devices can be used by research participants to 'tell stories', i.e. to craft and present their lives in words, sounds and images. They can enable participants to portray their feelings as much as their thinking, in a real context. This can yield benefits in terms of speed of response, maintaining participant engagement and the ultimate quality of data.[34]

Many potential research participants are now driven by the innate desire to share their lives, to be in some form of relationship, to participate in an event or an experience with others. They routinely interact with others who may be present not only physically but also virtually. As a result, the mobile device is an intelligent extension of the physical body of the person, and if that person has given appropriate consent, the device can help researchers gain a sense of consumer habits, interests, networks of relationships, and much more. Many individuals have their devices with them at all times and are ready and willing to comment, share and evaluate what they are experiencing, in real-time. This provides researchers with the opportunity to enter into those discussions and get instant, direct feedback and thoughts from individuals.[35]

In addition to the opportunities of proactive engagement of participants, they also offer the ability to collect passive observations of real-time geographic information about participants.[36] Geolocation studies hold great potential for researchers that wish to that builds upon knowledge of the behavioural dimensions that link to participant experiences.

The following example illustrates how digital developments in social media impact upon participant research experiences. Participants can use their mobile devices as an extension of what they may already enjoy, i.e. taking photographs of friends and fashion. With the challenges set to look at fashion and friends in a particular manner, there are clear elements of a game in the research process. Finally, it is clear to see how compelling and engaging this may be for certain participants, especially when compared to interviewing techniques.

Gamification
The application of successful gaming to traditionally non-game processes and experiences.

Mobile device
The mobile device is a generic term used to refer to a variety of technologies that enable individuals to access data online and interact from wherever they may be.

Real research

Visual ethnography at MTV[37]

MTV Networks (**www.mtvne.com**) wanted to understand identity construction among young people. Instead of using a traditional ethnographical approach, they used an alternative approach that combined principles from visual ethnography, nethnography and Research 2.0. Using pictures for observing an individual in their environment is at the core of visual ethnography. In the early days of visual ethnography, pictures were mainly taken by the observer. A new approach has shifted the control towards participants who take their own (self-relevant) pictures. In line with this new approach, they gave full control to the participants. The user-generated ethnography took place in two phases. First, participants got the general instruction to take pictures of all aspects of their life that *they* believed that we should know about in order to get a better understanding of who they were and to get a sense of their daily lives. Next, at several times they received 'special tasks'. These tasks were created to make sure that they collected enough 'relevant observations' in order to help answer the research questions. When creating the special tasks, it was important not to mention the topic of the study directly. Instead they asked each participant to photograph the context where their identity manifests itself. They assigned a special role to clothes and peers. Clothes are one of the main product categories that teenagers use to express their identity. Participants were therefore asked to take pictures of clothes that they wear on several different types of occasions: clothes that they wear at home as a reflection of their personal identity; clothes that represent their social identity; clothes that give insights into their aspirational identity; clothes that they do not want to wear. They applied a similar reasoning for peers. asking participants to take pictures of the friends and people they find important (social identity), others with whom they are not friends but with whom they would like to be friends (aspirational identity), adolescents who they would not like to be friends with (non-group) and others that are different to themselves but still socially acceptable. This last group was included to get a more detailed view on all social groups. To get a better understanding of personal identity, participants were also invited to take pictures of objects that were typical for themselves. Finally, they asked participants to take pictures of the place where they could really be themselves.

Summary

Social media networks encompass a great breadth of means by which participants can enjoy and engage in: discussions, chat, webcasts, photos, videos, podcasts, animation, surveys, games and virtual worlds. Many researchers have recognised that the user-generated content of social media make them very relevant as a domain for conducting new forms of marketing research. Many traditional marketing research methods have been adapted and new methods have been developed. These new methods may be seen as a supplement to traditional forms of marketing research. The key benefits of the use of social media research include: tapping into the energies of communities, delivering engaging research experiences for participants, the ability to capture rich and diverse primarily qualitative data and speedy responses at relatively low costs. The key disadvantages lie in a paucity of theory to underpin the quality of design and implementation of social media research methods. There are also major concerns about the development of appropriate codes of practice to ensure that research is conducted in an ethical manner. Social media research methods can be broadly classified as passive and active. Passive social media research can be seen as an approach akin to observing what is being discussed and displayed in social media. Active social media research can be seen as an approach akin to both observing and engaging in what is being discussed and displayed in social media. Rather than standing back, observing and listening, researchers can join communities and may choose to direct specific questions or tasks to participants.

There is a growing body of passive and active social media research methods. The most widespread methods can broadly be categorised as research that utilise blogging, communities and crowdsourcing. Blogging as a research term can represent both passive and active forms of social media research. The use and value of the blog in an active and passive sense can largely be attributed to the great diversity of ways that blogs may be created and presented. Many blogs are delivered, enjoyed and commented upon in a community setting. Communities are spaces where individuals coexist and share many interests and aspirations. Many brands and researchers try to establish communities. These communities are termed market research online communities or MROCs. A dedicated brand MROC can enable a company to recruit a panel of 'consumer-advisers'. A company and their researchers can engage with members using a variety of quantitative and qualitative techniques, often unfolding over a period of months. Crowdsourcing has been applied in many areas to perform services, design products and solve problems. In terms of conducting research, crowdsourcing enables ideas to be elicited, and potential insights and actionable solutions based on those insights to be tested and developed. The process of crowdsourcing is a means to draw together the creative thinking and talents of a wide body of individuals.

Social media research is proving to be of great value in reaching traditionally difficult to get hold of research participants in a global setting. It enables these 'difficult to get hold of participants' to be able to articulate and express themselves in contexts and manners that they are comfortable with. There are a wide range of ethical issues that have emerged as social media research has become more widespread. Social media research is in its relative infancy and much more original research needs undertaking to appreciate the full validity and limitations of specific methods. Social media has changed the rules on how 'findable' somebody is. This has enormous implications for the privacy and safety of research participants. As digital developments progress to Web 3.0 technologies and beyond, new techniques will be experimented with, new challenges addressed and new opportunities realised. However technologies progress, there are three core areas where digital developments are making a major impact upon how social media research is perceived, delivered and experienced. These three areas are participant engagement, gamification and mobile devices.

Questions

1 Describe the nature of social media research.
2 Evaluate the factors combined to shape the emergence and growth of social media research.
3 Evaluate the ways social media research could supplement traditional forms of marketing research.
4 Evaluate ways social media research could replace traditional forms of marketing research.
5 Describe the nature of active and passive forms of social media research.

6 Discuss the advantages and disadvantages of conducting social media research in a passive manner.

7 What is a participatory blog? What are the distinct advantages of this method?

8 What is a market research online community (MROC)? What are the distinct advantages of this method?

9 What is crowdsourcing? What are the distinct advantages of this method?

10 Discuss the distinctive advantages of conducting social media research in a global context.

11 Discuss the key ethical challenges faced by social media researchers.

12 Describe the main success factors that underpin digital developments in social media research.

Exercises

1 Examine Google Insights for Search at **http://www.google.com/insights/ search/**. Select a brand and break it down into characteristics that can be explored using volume patterns across specific regions, categories and time frames. Write a report that describes your process of observation and the key findings that you believe could be further developed using traditional marketing research methods.

2 Search and evaluate marketing research blogs such as PluggedIn (**http:// pluggedinco.com/blog/**). Write a report on what you would see as the best advice given to run market research online communities (MROCs).

3 Visit the website of research company BrainJuicer (**http://www.brainjuicer .com**). Evaluate the nature of their services and write a report on how their work addresses the agendas of 'engagement', 'gamification' and the use of mobile devices.

4 Imagine that you have been briefed by the Marketing Director of easyJet. They are exploring potential extensions of the easyJet brand and feel that crowdsourcing could be a quick and effective means to generate and test ideas. Write a report that:

    (a) Describes how crowdsourcing could work for easyJet.

    (b) What the advantages and disadvantages of this research method would be.

    (c) A justification of your recommendation to easyJet to progress with crowdsourcing, or not.

5 In a small group discuss the following issues: 'What has been the impact of research participants being more empowered compared to an era when social media was not prevalent?', 'Should all brands actively engage in social media research? What types of brands have less to gain from social media engagement?' and 'What ethical problems do you think participants might raise in relation to geolocation behavioural tracking embedded in their mobile devices?'

Notes

1. Dierikx, R. and Lynch, A., 'Fuelling Philips' innovation engine – continuous ideas and feedback from users', ESOMAR, *Annual Congress*, Montreal (Sept. 2008).

2. Dekkers, S. and Lawrence, G., 'easyJet community – using online communities to co-create the future', ESOMAR, *Panel Research*, Dublin (Oct. 2008).

3. Kearon, J. and Earls, M., 'Me-to-we research', ESOMAR Congress, *Leading the way*, Montreaux (Sept. 2009).

4. Oxley, M. and Light, B., 'Research 2.0: Engage or give up the ghost?' Market Research Conference (2010),

5. Besprosvan, K. and Ovarzun, D., '"Tweetmiotics" – Using Twitter as a consumer centric research tool', ESOMAR *Online Research*, Chicago (Oct. 2009).

6. Poynter, R., 'A taxonomy of new MR', Market Research Society, Annual Conference (2010).

7. Cierpicki, S., Cape, P., Lewis, A., Poynter, R. and Vieira, S., 'What does research 2.0 mean to consumers in Asia Pacific?' ESOMAR, *Asia Pacific Conference*, Beijing (April 2009).

8. Wiesenfeld, D., Bush, K. and Sikdar, R., 'The Value of Listening: Heeding the call of the Snuggie', *Journal of Advertising Research*, 50 (1) (2010).

9. Rappaport, S.D., 'Putting listening to work: The essentials of listening', *Journal of Advertising Research*, 50 (1) (2010) 30–41.

10. Bilgram, V. and Barti, M., 'Successful consumer co-creation: The case of Nivea Body Care', Market Research Society, Annual Conference (2010).

11. Methner, T. and Frank, D., 'Welcome to the House of Research: Achieving new insights and better brand knowledge through courageous ways of collaboration in what is usually a competitive environment', ESOMAR: *Congress Odyssey*, Athens (Sept. 2010).

12. Murphy, D., 'Word perfect', *Research World* (Feb. 2006), 19.

13. Heeg, R., 'The changing face of advertising research', *Research World* (March 2007), 41.

14. Besprosvan, K. and Ovarzun, D., '"Tweetonomics" – Using Twitter as a consumer centric research tool', ESOMAR, *Online Research*, Chicago (Oct. 2009).

15. Kennedy, J. and Verard, L., 'Online community platforms – A macro-overview and case study', ESOMAR, *Online Research*, Chicago (Oct. 2009).

16. Child, P., Fleming, K., Shaw, R. and Skilbeck, T., 'Vive La Difference: Understanding, embracing and evolving MROCs globally', ESOMAR, *Congress Odyssey*, Athens (Sept. 2010).

17. Ewing, T., 'Cultures of collaboration', Market Research Society, Annual Conference (2010).

18. Wilson, D. and Birks, D.F., 'The development of the KubeMatrix™ as a mobile app for Market Research Online Communities', The Association for Survey Computing, 6th International Conference, Bristol (2011).

19. Child, P., Fleming, K., Shaw, R. and Skilbeck, T., 'Vive la difference: Understanding, embracing and evolving MROCs globally', ESOMAR, *Congress Odyssey*, Athens (Sept. 2010).

20. Buckley, N., Hansom, J. and Palmer, A., 'Bloggers as research partners', ESOMAR, *Online Research*, Chicago, (Oct. 2009).

21. Howe, J., *Crowdsourcing: How the power of the crowd is driving the future of business* (Random House Business, 2009).

22. Stokes, R., *eMarketing: The essential guide to digital marketing*, 4th edn (Quirk eMarketing, 2011).

23. Gallupe, R.B. and Cooper, W.H., 'Brainstorming electronically', *Sloan Management Review*, 35 (1) (Fall 1993), 27.

24. McDermott, A. and Higgins, P., 'Bristol's adventures in crowdsourcing', Association for Survey Computing, *Shifting the boundaries of research*, 6th International Conference, Bristol (Sept. 2011).

25. Mukherjee, P. and Mollback-Verbic, P., 'Water Wows: Tapping the unleashed potential of mobile phones', ESOMAR, *Qualitative Research*, Vienna (Nov. 2011).

26. Chakraborty, M. and Arora, S., 'Billion dollar baby: Leveraging mobile technology for research applications in India', ESOMAR, *Asia Pacific*, Kuala Lumpur (April 2010).

27. Poynter, R, A taxonomy of New MR, Market Research Society, Annual Conference (2010).

28. Cooke, M., The new world of Web 2.0 research (Guest editorial) *International Journal of Market Research*, 50, 5, (2008) pp. 570–572.

29. Nairn, A., 'Conference notes – Research ethics in the virtual world', *International Journal of Market Research*, 51 (2) (2009).

30. Griffiths, J., 'Content analytics and the future of market research: The Cloud of Knowing Project', Market Research Society, Annual Conference (2010).

31. Reid, J., Morden, M. and Reid, A., 'Maximizing respondent engagement: The use of rich media', ESOMAR, *Annual Congress*, Berlin (Sept. 2007).

32. Alberts, K. and Findlay, F., 'Gamification: Future or Fail', South African Market Research Association (SAMRA) Conference (2011).

33. Malinoff, B. and Puleston, J., 'How far is too far: Traditional, flash and gamification interfaces, and implications for the future of market research online survey design', ESOMAR, *3D Digital Dimensions*, Miami, (Oct. 2011).

34. Macer, T. (ed.), Denitto, M., Walsh, L. and Martin, P., 'Technology Futures: Perspectives on how technology will transform the market research of tomorrow', Market Research Society, Annual Conference (2009).

35. Johnson, A.J. and Swinton, R., 'Developing second generation mobile research techniques – How mobile research can enhance the enjoyment of media consumption', ESOMAR, *Congress*, Amsterdam (Sept. 2011).

36. Micu, A.C., Dedeker, K., Lewis, I., Moran, R., Netzer, O., Plummer, J. and Plummer, J., 'The shape of marketing research in 2021', *Journal of Advertising Research*, 51 (1) (2011), 213–21.

37. Verhaeghe, A., den Bergh, J.V. and Colin, V., 'Me myself and I: Studying youngsters identity by combining visual ethnography and netnography', ESOMAR, *Qualitative Research*, Instanbul (Nov. 2008).

7

Questionnaire design, measurement and scaling

Participants must find the completion of questionnaires an engaging experience.

Objectives

After reading this chapter, you should be able to:

1   explain the purpose of a questionnaire;

2   describe the process of designing a questionnaire, the steps involved, and guidelines that must be followed at each step;

3   discuss the primary scales of measurement and differentiate nominal, ordinal, interval and ratio scales;

4   classify and discuss scaling techniques as comparative and non-comparative and describe the comparative techniques of paired comparison, rank order, constant sum and Q-sort scaling;

5   describe the non-comparative scaling techniques, distinguish between continuous and itemised rating scales, and explain Likert, semantic differential and Stapel scales;

6   discuss the decisions involved in constructing itemised rating scales;

7   discuss the considerations involved in questionnaire design, measurement and scaling in an international setting;

8   understand the ethical issues involved in questionnaire design, measurement and scaling;

9   appreciate how digital developments are shaping the manner in which questionnaires and scales may be designed, delivered and experienced.

Overview

This chapter discusses the importance of questionnaire design and how researchers must empathise with target participants in order to create effective questionnaires. We describe the objectives of a questionnaire and the steps involved in designing questionnaires. We provide several guidelines for developing effective and engaging questionnaires. We describe the concepts of scaling and measurement and discuss four primary scales of measurement: nominal, ordinal, interval and ratio. We describe and illustrate both comparative and non-comparative scaling techniques. The comparative techniques, i.e. paired comparison, rank order, constant sum and Q-sort scaling, and non-comparative techniques consisting of continuous and itemised rating scales are discussed. We examine the popular itemised rating scales – the Likert, semantic differential and Stapel scales – as well as the construction of multi-item rating scales. The considerations involved in designing questionnaires and scales when researching international markets are discussed. The chapter presents several ethical issues that arise in questionnaire and scale design. We conclude by examining how visual forms of scaling using flash technology can help create more engaging survey experiences for participants.

We begin with an example that illustrates an academic study where characteristics of the questionnaire design could provide an engaging experience for participants.

Real research   ## Brands in songs[1]

The insertion of brands in songs is one of the most ignored forms of product placement. Researchers analysed the memorisation of 17 brands cited in two French songs. The study evaluated perceptions of placement, examining whether the approval of a song and the artist generated a more favourable attitude towards the use of brands. In order to test their hypotheses, an online survey was undertaken. The general principle was to invite participants to listen to two songs, then to question about the brands mentioned. In designing

the survey, the aim was to limit the length of the questionnaire without compromising the quality of the measurement of the variables. The average time required to complete the questionnaire was around 15 minutes. The clarity and the context of the use of the brand involved some subjectivity, and were measured on three-point scales developed by a brand specialist and a linguist. Familiarity with the song, approval or appreciation of the singer, of the song and of the music genre, were variables that participants had no difficulty in understanding, and were therefore measured in a direct manner. The questionnaire was placed on a personal website and designed in the form of three successive web pages. The first screen contained general questions and questions that referred to the participant's interest in music, and it allowed them to listen to the songs. The second screen concerned the knowledge and appreciation of the songs and their singers, and the spontaneous memorisation of the brands. The final screen dealt with the assisted memorisation of brands, the perception of brand placement and with spontaneous memorisation of the brands in several other songs. Compared to a continuous form layout, this presentation on three screens had the advantage of not revealing immediately the length of the questionnaire. It also prevented participants modifying the responses they had already given, and made it possible to keep the object of the study secret until they had listened to the two songs.

Questionnaire definition

Surveys and observation are the two basic methods for obtaining quantitative primary data in descriptive research. Both methods require some procedure for standardising the data collection process so that the data obtained are internally consistent and can be analysed in a uniform and coherent manner. If 40 different interviewers conduct face-to-face interviews or make observations in different parts of the country, the data they collect will not be comparable unless they follow specific guidelines and ask questions and record answers in a standard way. A standardised questionnaire or form will ensure comparability of the data, increase speed and accuracy of recording, and facilitate data integrity and processing.

Questionnaire
A structured technique for data collection consisting of a series of questions, written or verbal, that a participant answers.

A **questionnaire**, whether it is called a schedule, interview form or measuring instrument, is a formalised set of questions for obtaining information from participants. Typically, a questionnaire is only one element of a data collection package that might also include (1) fieldwork procedures, such as instructions for selecting, approaching and questioning participants; (2) some reward, gift or payment offered to participants; and (3) communication aids, such as maps, pictures, music, advertisements and products (as in many online and face-to-face interviews) and return envelopes (in postal surveys).

Any questionnaire has three specific objectives. First, it must translate the information needed into a set of specific questions that participants can and will answer. Developing questions that participants can and will answer and that will yield the desired information is difficult. Two apparently similar ways of posing a question may yield different information. Hence, this objective is most challenging.

Second, a questionnaire must uplift, motivate and encourage the participant to become involved, to cooperate, and to complete the task. Figure 7.1 uses a basic marketing model of

Figure 7.1

Exchange of values between researchers and participants

What the participant may want from the researcher:

- Tangible reward
- Confidentiality
- Interesting subject and experience
- Personal benefits from seeing the research completed
- Social benefits from seeing the research completed
- Being 'chosen' as a participant with expertise on a subject
- Research organisation known for excellence in research
- Rapport and trust

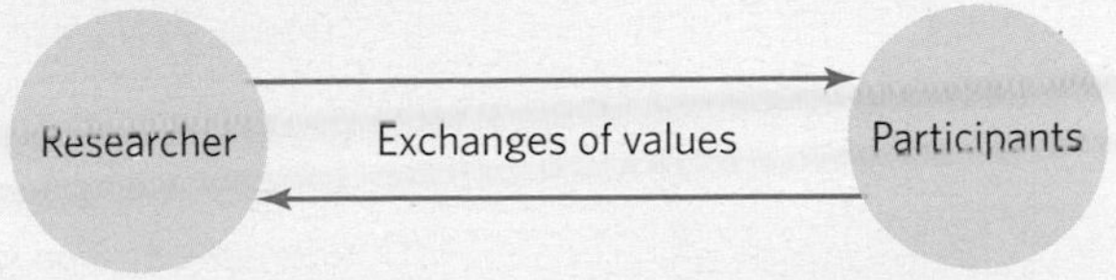

Researcher — Exchanges of values — Participants

What the researcher may want from the participant:

- Honesty
- Takes in reasons for the study
- Follows the instructions in completing the study
- Thinks through the issues before forming an answer
- Social benefits from seeing the research completed
- Says good things about the rationale for marketing research
- Says good things about the research process

exchange of values between two parties to illustrate this point. Before designing any questionnaire or indeed any research technique, the researcher must evaluate 'what is the participant going to get out of this?' In other words, the researcher must have an empathy with target participants and appreciate what they will experience when approached and questioned. Such an appreciation of what participants go through affects the design of how they are approached, the stated purpose of the research, the rewards for taking part and the whole process of questioning and question design.[2]

Not all participants are the same in what they seek from a questionnaire or interview process. In Figure 7.1, some participants may want to see some personal benefit, perhaps a tangible reward, while others may be happy to see the social benefits. Taking care in appreciating what participants expect from the questioning process can nurture responses that have been well thought through, are stated in honesty, and are accurate.

Third, a questionnaire should minimise response error. Response error is defined as the error that arises when participants give inaccurate answers or when their answers are mis-recorded or mis-analysed. A questionnaire can be a major source of response error. Minimising this error is an important objective of questionnaire design.

Questionnaire design process

The great weakness of questionnaire design is a lack of theory. Because there are no scientific principles that guarantee an optimal or ideal questionnaire, questionnaire design is a skill acquired through experience. Therefore, this section presents guidelines and rules to help develop the craft of questionnaire design. Although these guidelines and rules can help researchers avoid major mistakes, the 'fine tuning' of a questionnaire comes from continual creative practice.[3] In order to develop a further understanding of questionnaire design, the process will be presented as a series of steps, as shown in Figure 7.2, and we present guidelines for each step. In practice the steps are interrelated and the development of a questionnaire involves much iteration and interconnection between stages.[4]

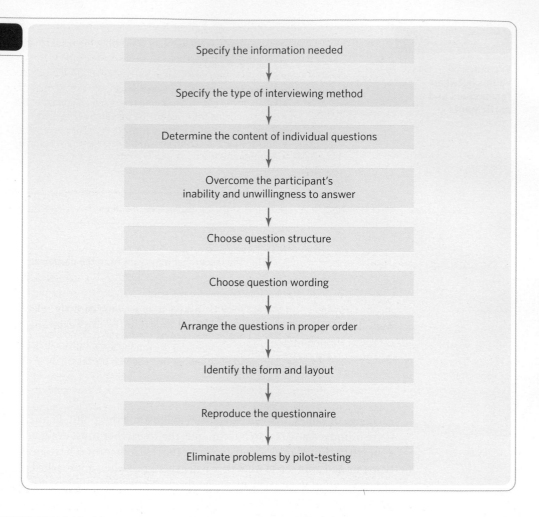

Figure 7.2

Questionnaire design process

Specify the information needed

↓

Specify the type of interviewing method

↓

Determine the content of individual questions

↓

Overcome the participant's inability and unwillingness to answer

↓

Choose question structure

↓

Choose question wording

↓

Arrange the questions in proper order

↓

Identify the form and layout

↓

Reproduce the questionnaire

↓

Eliminate problems by pilot-testing

Specify the information needed

The first step in questionnaire design is to specify the information needed. This is also the first step in the research design process. It is helpful to review the components of the problem and the approach, particularly the research questions, hypotheses and characteristics that influence the research design. It is also vital to have a clear idea of the target participants. The characteristics of participants have a great influence on questionnaire design. The wording and style of questions that may be appropriate for finance directors being surveyed about their IT needs may not be appropriate for retired persons being surveyed about their holiday needs. The more diversified the participant group, the more difficult it is to design a single questionnaire appropriate for the entire group.

Specify the type of interviewing method

An appreciation of how the type of interviewing method influences questionnaire design can be obtained by considering how the questionnaire is administered under each method. Online and postal surveys are self-administered, so the questions must be simple, and detailed instructions must be provided. In online surveys and computer-assisted interviewing (CAPI and CATI), complex skip patterns and randomisation of questions to eliminate order bias can be easily accommodated. In face-to-face interviews, participants may see the questionnaire and interact with the interviewer. Thus, lengthy, complex and varied questions can be asked. In telephone interviews the participants interact with the interviewer, but they do not see the questionnaire. This limits the type of questions that can be asked to short and simple ones. Questionnaires designed for face-to-face and telephone interviews should be written in a conversational style.[5] The type of interviewing method also influences the content of individual questions.

Determine the content of individual questions

Once the information needed is specified and the type of interviewing method decided, the next step is to determine individual question content: what to include in individual questions.

Is the question necessary?

Every question in a questionnaire should contribute to the information needed or serve some specific purpose that will help to elicit desired information from participants. In certain situations, however, questions may be asked that are not directly related to the needed information. It is useful to ask some neutral questions at the beginning of the questionnaire to establish involvement and rapport, particularly when the topic of the questionnaire is sensitive or controversial. Sometimes filter questions are asked to disguise the purpose or sponsorship of the project. Questions unrelated to the immediate problem may sometimes be included to generate client support for the project. At times, certain questions may be duplicated for the purpose of assessing reliability or validity.[6]

Are several questions needed instead of one?

Once we have ascertained that a question is necessary, we must make sure that it is sufficient to get the desired information. Sometimes several questions are needed to obtain the required information in an unambiguous manner. Consider the question 'Do you think Coca-Cola is a tasty and refreshing soft drink?' A yes answer will presumably be clear, but what if the answer is no? Does this mean that the participant thinks that Coca-Cola is not tasty, that it is not refreshing, or that it is neither tasty nor refreshing? Such a question is called a **double-barrelled question**, because two or more questions are combined into one. To obtain the required information, two distinct questions should be asked: 'Do you think Coca-Cola is a tasty soft drink?' and 'Do you think Coca-Cola is a refreshing soft drink?'

Double-barrelled question
A single question that attempts to cover two issues. Such questions can be confusing to participants and result in ambiguous responses.

Another example of multiple questions embedded in a single question is the 'why' question. The 'why' question seems very simple to write in a questionnaire and may be very simple to pose in an interview. It may not be a simple task in responding to such a question as it may tap into many constructs that for the participant may be difficult to conceive and/ or articulate. In the context of a study focusing on cinemas, consider the question 'Why do you like the Odeon cinema?' The possible answers may include: 'I was taken there by my mother and have such happy memories of that visit', 'The Odeon is conveniently located for me to just drop in when I feel like it' and 'It has the best assortment of snacks'. Each answer relates to a different question embedded in the 'why' question. The first tells how the participant first learnt about the Odeon, the second reveals what the participant likes about the Odeon compared with other cinemas, and the third reveals what features of the cinema the participant favours. The three answers are not comparable and any one answer may not be sufficient. Complete information may be obtained by asking two or even more separate questions: 'What do you like about the Odeon compared with other cinemas?' and 'How did you first happen to visit an Odeon cinema?' Most 'why' questions about the use of a product or choice alternative involve two aspects: (1) attributes of the product and (2) influences leading to knowledge of it.[7]

Overcoming the participant's inability and unwillingness to answer

---

Researchers should not assume that participants can provide accurate or well reasoned answers to all questions posed to them (assuming that they are willing to!). The researcher should attempt to overcome the participants' inability to answer. Certain factors limit the participants' ability to provide the desired information. The participants may not be informed, may not remember, or may be unable to articulate certain types of responses.

Is the participant informed?

Participants are often asked about topics on which they are not informed. Marketers and brand designers may have a deep and well informed knowledge of the characteristics that shape their industries and environments. Their target consumers however may have little inclination to spend their time understanding such intricacies. Even if they do wish to understand about issues such as the environmental impact of the use of pesticides in the growth of cotton in a shirt they are considering buying, there may be many complexities that make them uninformed.

Filter question
An initial question in a questionnaire that screens potential participants to ensure they meet the requirements of the sample.

In situations where not all participants are likely to be informed about the topic of interest, **filter questions** that measure familiarity, product use and past experience should be asked before questions about the topics themselves.[8] Filter questions enable the researcher to filter out participants who are not adequately informed. The use of online, CATI and CAPI surveys allows extensive filtering to produce a variety of questionnaire formats that can be tailored to the familiarity, product use and past experiences of participants.

Can the participant remember?

Many things that we might expect everyone to know are remembered by only a few. Test this on yourself. Can you remember what you had for lunch a week ago, or what you were doing a month ago at noon? Further, do you know how many litres of soft drinks you consumed during the last four weeks? Evidence indicates that consumers are particularly poor at remembering quantities of products consumed. In situations where factual data were available for comparison, it was found that consumer reports of product usage exceeded actual usage by 100 per cent or more.[9] Thus, soft drink consumption may be better obtained by asking:

How often do you consume soft drinks in a typical week?

- ○ *Less than once a week*
- ○ *1 to 3 times per week*
- ○ *4 to 6 times per week*
- ○ *7 or more times per week*

Telescoping
A psychological phenomenon that takes place when an individual telescopes or compresses time by remembering an event as occurring more recently than it actually occurred.

The inability to remember leads to errors of omission, telescoping and creation. Omission is the inability to recall an event that actually took place. **Telescoping** takes place when an individual telescopes or compresses time by remembering an event as occurring more recently than it actually occurred.[10] For example, a participant reports three trips to the supermarket in the last two weeks when, in fact, one of these trips was made 18 days ago. Creation error takes place when a participant 'remembers' an event that did not actually occur.

The ability to remember an event is influenced by (1) the event itself, (2) the time elapsed since the event, and (3) the presence or absence of things that would aid memory. We tend to remember events that are important or unusual or that occur frequently. People remember their wedding anniversary and birthday. Likewise, more recent events are remembered better. A fashion shopper is more likely to remember what they purchased on their last shopping trip than what they bought three shopping trips ago.

Research indicates that questions that do not provide the participant with cues to the event, and that rely on unaided recall, can underestimate the actual occurrence of an event. For example, testing whether participants were exposed to a beer advertisement at the cinema could be measured in an unaided manner by questions like 'What brands of beer do you remember being advertised last night at the cinema?' (having established that the participant was at a cinema last night). Naming a brand shows that the participant saw the advert, took in the brand name and could recall it; three different stages. An aided recall approach attempts to stimulate the participant's memory by providing cues related to the event of interest. Thus, the important features to measure may be that the participant saw the advert and took in the brand name – the fact that the participant cannot say the brand name may not affect his or her purchasing intentions. The aided recall approach would list a number of beer brands and then ask 'Which of these brands were advertised last night at the cinema?' In presenting cues, the researcher must guard against biasing the responses by testing out several successive levels of stimulation. The influence of stimulation on responses can then be analysed to select an appropriate level of stimulation.[11]

Is the participant able to articulate?

Participants may be unable to articulate certain types of responses. For example, if asked to describe the 'atmosphere' of a cinema they would prefer to frequent, most participants may be unable to phrase their answers. On the other hand, if the participants are provided with alternative descriptions of cinema atmosphere, they will be able to indicate the one they like the best. If the participants are unable to articulate their responses to a question, they are likely to ignore that question and refuse to respond to the rest of the questionnaire. Thus, participants should be given aids such as pictures, maps and descriptions to help them articulate their responses.

Even if participants are able to answer a particular question, they may be unwilling to do so, because too much effort is required, the situation or context may not seem appropriate for disclosure, no legitimate purpose or need for the information requested is apparent, or the information requested is sensitive.

Effort required of the participants

Most participants are unwilling to devote much effort to providing information. Hence, the researcher should minimise the effort required of the participants.[12] Suppose that the researcher is interested in determining from which shops a participant bought goods on the most recent shopping trip. This information can be obtained in at least two ways. The researcher could ask the participant to list all the items purchased on the most recent shopping trip, or the researcher could provide a list of shops and ask the participant to indicate the applicable ones. The second option is preferable, because it requires less effort from participants.

Context

Some questions may seem appropriate in certain contexts but not in others. For example, questions about personal hygiene habits may be appropriate when asked in a survey sponsored by a health organisation but not in one sponsored by a breakfast cereal manufacturer. Participants are unwilling to respond to questions they consider being inappropriate for the given context. Sometimes, the researcher can manipulate the context in which the questions are asked so that the questions seem appropriate.

Legitimate purpose

Participants are also unwilling to divulge information that they do not see as serving a legitimate purpose. Why should a firm marketing breakfast cereals want to know their age, income and occupation? Explaining why the data are needed can make the request for the information seem legitimate and may increase the participants' willingness to answer. A statement such as 'To determine how the preferences for cereal brands vary among people of different ages, we need information on . . .' can make the request for information seem more legitimate.

Sensitive information

Participants may be unwilling to disclose, at least accurately, sensitive information because this may cause embarrassment or threaten the participants' prestige or self-image, or be seen as too personal and an invasion of privacy. If pressed for the answer, participants may give biased responses; especially during personal interviews.[13] Sensitive topics include money, personal hygiene, family life, political and religious beliefs, and involvement in accidents or crimes. In industrial surveys, sensitive questions may encompass much of what a company does, especially if it reveals strategic activities and plans. The techniques described in the following subsection can be adopted to increase the likelihood of obtaining information that participants are unwilling to give.

Increasing the willingness of participants

Participants may be encouraged to provide information which they are unwilling to give by the following techniques:[14]

1   Place sensitive topics at the end of the questionnaire. By then, initial mistrust has been overcome, rapport has been created, legitimacy of the project has been established, and participants are more willing to give information. In this context, consider how sensitive classification questions such as gender, age and income may be perceived.

2   Preface the question with a statement that the behaviour of interest is common. For example, before requesting information on credit card debt, say, 'Recent studies show that most European consumers are in debt.' This technique describes the use of counter-biasing statements.

3   Ask the question using the third-person technique: phrase the question as if it referred to other people.

4   Hide the question in a group of other questions that participants are willing to answer. The entire list of questions can then be asked quickly.

5   Provide response categories rather than asking for specific figures.[15] Do not ask 'What is your household's annual income?' Instead, ask the participant to indicate an appropriate income category. In face-to-face interviews, give the participants cards that list the numbered choices. The participants then indicate their responses by number.

Choose question structure

A question may be unstructured or structured. We define unstructured questions and discuss their relative advantages and disadvantages and then consider the major types of structured questions: multiple choice, dichotomous and scales.[16]

Unstructured questions

Unstructured questions
Open-ended questions that participants answer in their own words.

Unstructured questions are open-ended questions that participants answer in their own words. They are also referred to as free-response or free-answer questions. The following are some examples:

- What is your occupation?
- What do you think of people who patronise secondhand clothes shops?
- Who is your favourite actor?

Open-ended questions can be good first questions on a topic. They enable the participants to express general descriptions and opinions that can help the researcher interpret their responses to structured questions. They can also be useful as a final question in a questionnaire. After participants have thought through and given all their answers in a questionnaire, there may be other issues that are important to them and that may not have been covered. Having an open-ended question at the end allows participants to express these issues. As well as providing material to help the researcher interpret other responses, the participants have the chance to express what they feel to be important. Unstructured questions have a much less biasing influence on response than structured questions. Participants are free to express any views. Their comments and explanations can provide the researcher with rich insights.

A principal disadvantage in the case of face-to-face interviews is that the potential for bias is high. Whether the interviewers record the answers verbatim or write down only the main points, the data depend on the skills of the interviewers. Recording devices should be used if verbatim reporting is important. Another major disadvantage of unstructured questions is that the coding of responses is costly and time consuming. There is much more use of software to cope with coding open-ended responses. This can be time and cost efficient if the research design employed uses a multiple cross-sectional or longitudinal design, but for the ad hoc survey, such approaches can still be very labour intensive.[17] Implicitly, unstructured or open-ended questions give extra weight to participants who are more articulate.

Pre-coding can overcome some of the disadvantages of unstructured questions. Expected responses are recorded in multiple-choice format, although the question is presented to the participants as an open-ended question. In the case of a face-to-face interview, based on the participant's reply, the interviewer selects the appropriate response category. Because the response alternatives are limited, this approach may be satisfactory when the participant can easily formulate the response and when it is easy to develop pre-coded categories. In general, open-ended questions are useful in exploratory research and as opening or closing questions. They should be chosen with great care as their disadvantages can outweigh their advantages in a large ad-hoc survey.[18]

Structured questions

Structured questions
Questions that pre-specify the set of response alternatives and the response format. A structured question could be multiple choice, dichotomous or a scale.

Structured questions specify the set of response alternatives and the response format. A structured question may be multiple choice, dichotomous or a scale.

Multiple-choice questions In multiple-choice questions, the researcher provides a choice of answers and participants are asked to select one or more of the alternatives given. Consider the following question:

> **Do you intend to buy a new watch within the next six months?**
>
> O *Definitely will not buy*
>
> O *Probably will not buy*
>
> O *Undecided*
>
> O *Probably will buy*
>
> O *Definitely will buy*
>
> *Other (please specify)*
>
> [   ]

Of concern in designing multiple-choice questions are the number of alternatives that should be included and the order of potential responses, known as position bias. The response alternatives should include the set of all possible choices. The general guideline is to list all alternatives that may be of importance and to include an alternative labelled 'other (please specify)', as shown above. The response alternatives should be mutually exclusive.

Order bias (position bias)
A participant's tendency to choose an alternative merely because it occupies a certain position or is listed in a certain order.

Order bias or **position bias** is the participants' tendency to tick an alternative merely because it occupies a certain position or is listed in a certain order. Participants may tend to tick the first or the last statement in a list, particularly the first. For a list of numbers (quantities or prices), there is a bias towards the central value on the list. To control for order bias, with many online or electronic forms of survey, alternative responses or scale items can be positioned randomly for each participant.[19]

Multiple-choice questions overcome many of the disadvantages of open-ended questions because these questions are administered quickly and, where used, interviewer bias is reduced. In self-administered questionnaires, participant cooperation is improved if the majority of the questions are structured. Also, coding and processing of data are much less costly and time consuming. Multiple-choice questions are not without disadvantages. Considerable effort is required to design effective multiple-choice questions. Qualitative techniques may be required to determine the appropriate wording and/or images for response alternatives. It may be difficult to obtain information on alternatives not listed. Even if an 'other (please specify)' category is included, participants tend to choose among the listed alternatives. In addition, showing participants the list of possible answers produces biased responses.[20] There is also the potential for order bias.

Dichotomous question

A structured question with only two response alternatives, such as yes and no.

Dichotomous questions A **dichotomous question** has only two response alternatives, such as yes or no, or agree or disagree. Often, the two alternatives of interest are supplemented by a neutral alternative, such as 'no opinion', 'don't know', 'both' or 'none', as in this example.[21]

The question asked before about intentions to buy a new watch as a multiple-choice question can also be asked as a dichotomous question.

Do you intend to buy a new watch within the next six months?

○ *Yes*

○ *No*

○ *Don't know*

Note that this question could also be framed as a multiple-choice question using response alternatives 'Definitely will buy', 'Probably will buy', 'Probably will not buy', and so forth. The decision to use a dichotomous question should be guided by whether the participants approach the issue as a yes-or-no issue. Although decisions are often characterised as series of binary or dichotomous choices, the underlying decision making process may reflect uncertainty that can best be captured by multiple-choice responses. Another issue in the design of dichotomous questions is whether to include a neutral response alternative. If it is not included, participants are forced to choose between yes and no even if they feel indifferent. On the other hand, if a neutral alternative is included as above, participants can avoid taking a position on the issue, thereby biasing the results.

The general advantages and disadvantages of dichotomous questions are very similar to those of multiple-choice questions. Dichotomous questions are the easiest types of questions to code and analyse, but they have one acute problem. The response can be influenced by the wording of the question. To illustrate, 59.6 per cent of participants in a survey agreed with the statement 'Individuals are more to blame than social conditions for crime and lawlessness in this country'. On a matched sample using an opposing statement, 'Social conditions are more to blame than individuals for crime and lawlessness in this country', 43.2 per cent agreed.[22] To overcome this problem, the question should be framed in one way on one-half of the questionnaires and in the opposite way on the other half. This is referred to as the split-ballot technique.

Scales Scales will be discussed in detail later in this chapter; however, to illustrate the difference between scales and other kinds of structural questions, consider the question about intentions to buy a new watch. One way of framing this using a scale is as follows:

Do you intend to buy a new watch within the next six months?

Definitely will not buy	Probably will not buy	Undecided	Probably will buy	Definitely will buy
1	2	3	4	5

This is only one of several scales that could be used to ask this question (comparative and non-comparative scales will be discussed in detail later).

Choose question wording

Question wording is the translation of the desired question content and structure into words that participants can clearly and easily understand. Deciding on question wording is perhaps the most critical and difficult task in developing a questionnaire. If a question is worded poorly, participants may refuse to answer it or answer it incorrectly. The first condition, known as item non-response, can increase the complexity of data analysis.[23] The second condition leads to response error, discussed earlier. Unless the participants and the researcher assign exactly the same meaning to the question, the results will be seriously biased.[24]

To avoid these problems, we offer the following guidelines:

1 Define the issue.

2 Use ordinary words.

3 Use unambiguous words.

4 Avoid leading or biasing questions.

5 Avoid implicit alternatives.

6 Avoid implicit assumptions.

7 Avoid generalisations and estimates.

8 Use positive and negative statements.

Define the issue

A question should clearly define the issue being addressed. Trainee journalists are cautioned to define issues in terms of who, what, when, where, why and way (the six Ws).[25] Consider the following question:

Which brand of shampoo do you use?

On the surface, this may seem to be a well-defined question, but we may reach a different conclusion when we examine it in terms of 'who', 'what', 'when' and 'where'. 'Who' in this question refers to the participant. It is not clear, though, whether the researcher is referring to the brand the participant uses personally or the brand used by the household. 'What' is the brand of shampoo. But what if more than one brand of shampoo is being used? Should the participant mention the most preferred brand, the brand used most often, the brand used most recently, or the brand that comes to mind first? 'When' is not clear; does the researcher mean last time, last week, last month, last year, or ever? As for 'where', it is implied that the shampoo is used at home, but this is not stated clearly. A better wording for this question would be:

Which brand or brands of shampoo have you personally used at home during the last month? In the case of more than one brand, please list all the brands that apply.

Use ordinary words

Ordinary words should be used in a questionnaire. They should match the vocabulary level of the target participants and/or be supplemented with graphic/visual support to convey issues simply.[26] Even though we may speak the same language as our potential participants, there may be particular colloquialisms and ways of using words and terms they use which we should acquaint ourselves with. When choosing words, bear in mind the intellectual level of the target group of participants, and how comfortable they are with technical terms related to any products or services we are measuring. The researcher may be imposing their language upon participants and that language communicates and puts participants in a particular frame of mind as they answer the questions. Unless that language is meaningful to participants, they will be put in a frame of mind that may not be intended, and be answering different questions from those set. The following example illustrates something of the magnitude of the challenge of using 'ordinary' words in questionnaire design.

Real research | **The forgotten 12 million**[27]

There are the 12 million adults in the UK whose first language is English, but who have a reading and writing age between 9 and 14. This represents almost a third of the adult population. It is a large and diverse audience yet all have literacy issues which in some way limit their lives. Importantly, these people can read and write, they are not illiterate or necessarily interested in improving their skill levels. They may be pretty comfortable as they are, and not publicly acknowledge that they have a problem and may not even be aware of any need to change existing behaviour patterns. Many are likely to feel isolated and defined by their skills deficit and will have almost certainly developed strategies to cover up the fact that they are limited in reading and writing. The implications for research and questionnaire design are considerable. First, individuals will not take part in research that requires reading and writing skills. They are not going to simply volunteer the information that they have literacy issues. They are not going to tell you why they don't come to groups or take part in research. They are just not going to participate. Similarly, they are rarely going to say *'I'm sorry, but the reason I don't want to do that questionnaire is because it's got too many words'*. If they think they are going to look at something complicated, they are just not going to participate. Second, you will not get the most out of them if they do take part. Questionnaires and forms may be completed by the partner or friend of a participant rather than the participant themselves. In short, they and their views will be forgotten. One-third of the adult population – forgotten. Researchers need to consider how the views of these participants may be represented. How can they create a research environment that is more appropriate to their needs and conducive to participation? How can they develop stimulus materials that are effective yet more suited to their needs?

Use unambiguous words

The words used in a questionnaire should have a single meaning that is known to the participants. A number of words that appear to be unambiguous have different meanings for different people.[28] These include 'usually', 'normally', 'frequently', 'often', 'regularly', 'occasionally' and 'sometimes'. Consider the following question:

In a typical month, how often do you visit a boutique?

- ○ *Never*
- ○ *Occasionally*
- ○ *Sometimes*
- ○ *Often*
- ○ *Regularly*

The answers to this question are fraught with response bias, because the words used to describe category labels have different meanings for different participants. Three participants who visit a boutique once a month may tick three different categories: occasionally, sometimes and often. A much better wording for this question would be the following:

In a typical month, how often do you visit a boutique?

- ○ *Less than once*
- ○ *1 or 2 times*
- ○ *3 or 4 times*
- ○ *More than 4 times*

Note that this question provides a consistent frame of reference for all participants. Response categories have been objectively defined, and participants are no longer free to interpret them in their own way. Additionally, all-inclusive or all-exclusive words may be understood differently by various people. Some examples of such words are 'all', 'always', 'any', 'anybody', 'ever', and 'every'. Such words should be avoided. To illustrate, 'any' could mean 'every', 'some', or 'one only' to different participants, depending on how they look at it.

In deciding on the choice of words, researchers should consult a dictionary and thesaurus and ask the following questions:

1 Does the word mean what we intend?

2 Does the word have any other meanings?

3 If so, does the context make the intended meaning clear?

4 Does the word have more than one pronunciation?

5 Is there any word or similar pronunciations that might be confused with this word?

6 Is a simpler word or phrase suggested that may be more meaningful to our target participants?

Avoid leading or biasing questions

Leading question
A question that gives the participant a clue as to what answer is desired or leads the participant to answer in a certain way.

Acquiescence bias (yea-saying)
This bias is the result of some participants' tendency to agree with the direction of a leading question (yea-saying).

A **leading question** is one that clues the participant to what answer is desired or leads the participant to answer in a certain way. Some participants have a tendency to agree with whatever way the question is leading them to answer. This tendency is known as yea-saying and results in a bias called **acquiescence bias**. Consider the following question:

Do you think that patriotic French people should buy imported cars when that would put French workers out of employment?

- ○ *Yes*
- ○ *No*
- ○ *Don't know*

This question would tend to lead participants to a 'No' answer. After all, how could patriotic French people put French people out of work? Therefore, this question would not help determine the preferences of French people for imported versus home manufactured cars.

Bias may also arise when participants are given clues about the sponsor of the project. Participants may tend to respond favourably towards the sponsor. The question 'Is Colgate your favourite toothpaste?' could bias the responses in favour of Colgate. A more unbiased way of obtaining this information would be to ask 'What is your favourite toothpaste brand?'

Avoid implicit alternatives

An alternative that is not explicitly expressed in the options is an implicit alternative. Making an implied alternative explicit may increase the percentage of people selecting that alternative, as in the following two questions:

1   Do you like to fly when travelling short distances?

2   Do you like to fly when travelling short distances, or would you rather drive?

In the first question, the alternative of driving is only implicit, but in the second question it is explicit. The first question is likely to yield a greater preference for flying than the second question.

Questions with implicit alternatives should be avoided unless there are specific reasons for including them. When the alternatives are close in preference or large in number, the alternatives at the end of the list have a greater chance of being selected. To overcome this bias, the split-ballot technique should be used to rotate the order in which the alternatives appear.[29]

Avoid implicit assumptions

Questions should not be worded so that the answer is dependent on implicit assumptions about what will happen as a consequence. Implicit assumptions are assumptions that are not explicitly stated in the question, as in the following example:[30]

1   Are you in favour of increased government spending on protecting the environment?

2   Are you in favour of increased government spending on protecting the environment if it would result in an increase in personal income tax?

Implicit in question 1 are the consequences that will arise as a result of increased spending. There might be a cut in sports sponsorship, rises in personal income tax, a cut in health spending, and so on. Question 2 is a better way to word this question. Question 1's failure to make its assumptions explicit would result in overestimating the participants' support for increased spending on protecting the environment.

Avoid generalisations and estimates

Questions should be specific, not general. Moreover, questions should be worded so that the participant does not have to make generalisations or compute estimates. Suppose that we were interested in households' annual per capita expenditure on clothing. If we asked participants the question:

> What is the annual per capita expenditure on clothing in your household?

they would first have to determine the annual expenditure on clothing by multiplying the monthly expenditure on clothing by 12 or even the weekly expenditure by 52. Then they would have to divide the annual amount by the number of persons in the household. Most participants would be unwilling or unable to perform these calculations. A better way of obtaining the required information would be to ask the participants two simple questions:

> What is the monthly (or weekly) expenditure on clothing in your household?

and

> How many members are there in your household?

The researcher can then perform the necessary calculations.

Use positive and negative statements

Many questions, particularly those measuring attitudes and lifestyles, are presented as statements to which participants indicate their degree of agreement or disagreement. Evidence indicates that the response obtained is influenced by the directionality of the statements: whether they are stated positively or negatively. In these cases, it is better to use dual statements, some of which are positive and others negative. Two different questionnaires could be prepared. One questionnaire would contain half-negative and half-positive statements in an interspersed way. The direction of these statements would be reversed in the other questionnaire.

Arrange the questions in proper order

The order of questions is of equal importance to the wording used in the questions. As noted in the last section, questions communicate and set participants in a particular frame of mind. This frame of mind is set at the start of the questioning process and can change as each question is posed and responded to. It affects how participants perceive individual questions and respond to those questions. As well as understanding the characteristics of language in target participants, questionnaire designers must be aware of the logical connections between questions, as perceived by target participants. The following issues help to determine the order of questions.

Opening questions

The opening questions can be crucial in gaining the confidence and cooperation of participants. These questions should be interesting, simple and non-threatening. Questions that ask participants for their opinions can be good opening questions. They may even be unrelated to the research problem and their responses are not analysed.[31] Though classification questions seem simple to start a questionnaire, issues like age, gender and income can be seen as very sensitive issues. Opening a questionnaire with these questions tends to make participants concerned about the purpose of these questions and indeed the whole survey. They can also give the questionnaire a feel of an 'official form' to be completed (like a national census or a tax form), rather than a positive engagement and experience with a particular topic. However, in some instances it is necessary to qualify participants to determine whether they are eligible to participate in the interview. In this case the qualifying questions serve as the opening questions, and they may have to be classification questions such as the age of the participant.

Type of information

Classification Information
Socio-economic and demographic characteristics used to classify participants.

Identification information
A type of information obtained in a questionnaire that includes name, address and phone number.

The type of information obtained in a questionnaire may be classified as (1) basic information, (2) classification information and (3) identification information. Basic information relates directly to the research problem. Classification information, consisting of socio-economic and demographic characteristics, is used to classify the participants, understand the results, and validate the sample. Identification information includes name, postal address, email address and telephone number. Identification information may be obtained for a variety of purposes, including verifying that the participants listed were actually interviewed and to send promised incentives or prizes. As a general guideline, basic information should be obtained first, followed by classification and finally identification information. The basic information is of greatest importance to the research project and should be obtained first, before risking alienation of the participants by asking a series of personal questions.

Difficult questions

Difficult questions or questions that are sensitive, embarrassing, complex or dull should be placed late in the sequence. After rapport has been established and the participants become involved, they are less likely to object to these questions.

Effect on subsequent questions

Questions asked early in a sequence can influence the responses to subsequent questions. As a rule of thumb, general questions should precede specific questions. This prevents specific questions from biasing responses to the general questions. Consider the following sequence of questions:

Q1: What considerations are important to you in selecting a boutique?
Q2: In selecting a boutique, how important is convenience of its location?

Note that the first question is general whereas the second is specific. If these questions were asked in the reverse order, participants would be clued about convenience of location and would be more likely to give this response to the general question.

Going from general to specific is called the **funnel approach**. The funnel approach is particularly useful when information has to be obtained about participants' general choice behaviour and their evaluations of specific products.[32] Sometimes the inverted funnel approach may be useful. In this approach, questioning starts with specific questions and concludes with the general questions. The participants are compelled to provide specific information before making general evaluations. This approach is useful when participants have no strong feelings or have not formulated a point of view.

Funnel approach
A strategy for ordering questions in a questionnaire in which the sequence starts with the general questions, which are followed by progressively specific questions, to prevent specific questions from biasing general questions.

Logical order

Questions should be asked in a logical order. This may seem a simple rule, but as the researcher takes time to understand participants and how they use language, the researcher should also take time to understand their logic, i.e. what 'logical order' means to target participants. All questions that deal with a particular topic should be asked before beginning a new topic. When switching topics, brief transitional phrases should be used to help participants switch their train of thought.

Branching questions should be designed with attention to logic, making the questionnaire experience more relevant to individual participants.[33] Branching questions direct participants to different places in the questionnaire based on how they respond to the question at hand. These questions ensure that all possible contingencies are covered. They also help reduce interviewer and participant error and encourage complete responses. Skip patterns based on the branching questions can become quite complex. A simple way to account for all contingencies is to prepare a flow chart of the logical possibilities and then develop branching questions and instructions based on it. A flow chart used to assess the use of electronic payments in online clothes purchases is shown in Figure 7.3.

Branching question
A question used to guide an interviewer (or participant) through a survey by directing the interviewer (or participant) to different spots on the questionnaire depending on the answers given.

Figure 7.3

Flow chart for questionnaire design

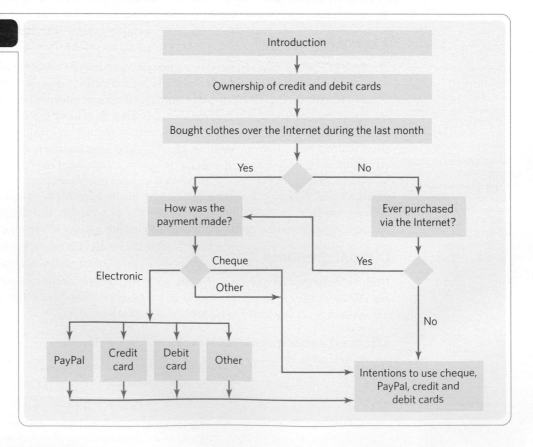

Placement of branching questions is important and the following guidelines should be followed: (1) the question being branched (the one to which the participants are being directed) should be placed as close as possible to the question causing the branching, and (2) the branching questions should be ordered so that the participants cannot anticipate what additional information will be required. Otherwise, the participants may discover that they can avoid detailed questions by giving certain answers to branching questions. For example, the participants should first be asked if they have seen any of the listed advertisements before they are asked to evaluate advertisements. Participants may quickly discover that stating that they have seen an advertisement leads to detailed questions about that advertisement and that they can avoid detailed questions by stating that they have not seen the advertisement.

Identify the form and layout

The format, spacing and positioning of questions can have a significant effect on the results, particularly in self-administered questionnaires.[34] It is good practice to divide a questionnaire into several parts. Several parts may be needed for questions pertaining to the basic information. The questions in each part should be numbered, particularly when branching questions are used. Numbering of questions also makes the coding of responses easier. In addition, if the survey is conducted by post, the questionnaires should preferably be precoded. In **pre-coding**, the codes to enter in the computer can be printed on the questionnaire. Note that when conducting online CATI and CAPI surveys, pre-coding of the questionnaire is built into the questionnaire design software.

Pre-coding
In questionnaire design, assigning a code to every conceivable response before data collection.

With the majority of questionnaires being administered online, researchers should not think of form and structure of a questionnaire in terms of designing a paper or postal survey experience. Such thinking can lead to a dull and monotonous survey experience for online participants. With many people experiencing rich, varied and exciting websites, to then move into a flat, text-based questionnaire experience can be most off-putting. An analogy may be in terms of games technology. Imagine a participant being used to a highly interactive, perhaps 3D games experience, and then being expected to engage with a 'Pong' (one of the earliest arcade video games, a tennis sports game featuring simple two-dimensional graphics). There may be a moment of nostalgia for such an experience but it would be quickly dismissed as being boring and irrelevant.

Reproduce the questionnaire

In the design of an online questionnaire, variations of language, branching, graphics and visuals, the survey experience can be almost tailored to individual participants. Time and money that in the past may have been devoted to the printing of paper based questionnaires can now be avoided and invested in designing the form, layout and look to give participants the most engaging experience. In surveys where there are hard copies of questionnaires (or even in multi-mode surveys where participants have a choice of survey type), how a questionnaire is reproduced for administration can influence the results.

Vertical response columns should be used for individual questions. It is easier for interviewers and participants to read down a single column rather than reading sideways across several columns. Sideways formatting and splitting, done frequently to conserve space, should be avoided. The tendency to crowd questions together to make the questionnaire look shorter should be avoided. Overcrowded questions with little blank space between them can lead to errors in data collection and yield shorter and less informative replies. Moreover, it gives the impression that the questionnaire is complex and can result in lower cooperation and completion rates. Although shorter questionnaires are more desirable than longer ones, the reduction in size should not be obtained at the expense of crowding.

Directions or instructions for individual questions should be placed as close to the questions as possible. Instructions relating to how the question should be administered or answered by the participant should be placed just before the question. Instructions concerning how the answer should be recorded or how the probing should be done should be placed after the question. It is common practice to distinguish instructions from questions by using different typefaces (such as capital, italic or boldfaced letters).

Although colour does not generally influence response rates to questionnaires, it can be employed advantageously in many respects. Colour coding is useful for branching questions. The next question to which the participant is directed is printed in a colour that matches the space in which the answer to the branching question was recorded. The questionnaire should be reproduced in such a way that it is easy to read and answer. The type should be large and clear. Reading the questionnaire should not impose a strain.

In face-to-face interviews and postal surveys, when a printed questionnaire runs to several pages, it should take the form of a booklet rather than a number of sheets of paper clipped or stapled together. Booklets are easier for the interviewer and the participants to handle and do not easily come apart with use. They allow the use of a double-page format for questions and look more professional. Each question should be reproduced on a single page (or double-page spread). Researchers should avoid splitting a question, including its response categories. Split questions can mislead the interviewer or the participant into thinking that the question has ended at the end of a page. This will result in answers based on incomplete questions.

Eliminate problems by pilot-testing

Pilot-testing
Testing the questionnaire on a small sample of participants for the purpose of improving the questionnaire by identifying and eliminating potential problems.

Pilot-testing refers to testing the questionnaire on a small sample of participants to identify and eliminate potential problems as illustrated in the following example.[35]

Re-inventing long haul travel[36]

Air New Zealand worked with Synovate (**www.synovate.com**) to conduct a survey on all areas of designing the flying experience; seats, in-flight entertainment, food and beverage specification, service flow, kitchen design. The actual questionnaire had to be relatively straightforward in structure, but it was critical that the attitudinal statements at the core of the questionnaire were sufficiently discriminatory to separate out what might be quite soft attitudes and feelings. An online questionnaire was piloted on 40 long-haul travellers, who were clearly informed that they were testing the questionnaire. The test questionnaire contained only the attitudinal statements. Participants were asked to pause after each block of attitudinal questions and reflect on whether these statements were clear, easy to understand, and whether they captured the concept of the wider need that Air New Zealand were interested in. Their open-ended responses were reviewed and used to refine the statements. In addition, the participants' actual ratings were analysed to determine whether each statement was sufficiently discriminative across the sample to be useful for segmentation purposes. The final questionnaire included a total of 50 attitudinal statements across the whole long-haul experience.

Even the best questionnaire can be improved by pilot-testing. As a general rule, a questionnaire should not be used in the field survey without adequate pilot-testing. A pilot-test should be extensive. All aspects of the questionnaire should be tested, including question content, wording, sequence, form and layout, question difficulty, and instructions. The participants in the pilot-test should be similar to those who will be included in the actual survey in terms of background characteristics, familiarity with the topic, and attitudes and behaviours of interest.[37] In other words, participants for the pilot-test and for the actual survey should be drawn from the same population.

Pilot-tests are best done by face-to-face interviews, even if the actual survey is to be conducted by online, postal or telephone modes, because interviewers can observe participants' reactions and attitudes. After the necessary changes have been made, another pilot-test could be conducted online, postal or telephone if those modes are to be used in the actual survey. The latter pilot-tests should reveal problems peculiar to the interviewing method. To the extent possible, a pilot-test should involve administering the questionnaire in the environment and context similar to that of the actual survey.

A variety of interviewers should be used for pilot-tests. The project director, the researcher who developed the questionnaire and other key members of the research team should conduct some pilot-test interviews. This will give them a good feel for potential problems and the nature of the expected data. The sample size of the pilot-test is typically small, varying from 15 to 30 participants for the initial testing, depending on the heterogeneity (e.g. a wide array of education levels) of the target population. The sample size can increase substantially if the pilot-testing involves several stages or waves. Editing involves correcting the questionnaire for the problems identified during pilot-testing. After each significant revision of the questionnaire, another pilot-test should be conducted, using a different sample of participants. Sound pilot-testing involves several stages. One pilot-test is a bare minimum. Ideally, pilot-testing should be continued until no further changes are needed.

Finally, the responses obtained from the pilot-test should be analysed. The analysis of pilot-test responses can serve as a check on the adequacy of the problem definition and the data and analysis required to obtain the necessary information. The dummy tables prepared before developing the questionnaire will point to the need for the various sets of data. If the response to a question cannot be related to one of the preplanned dummy tables, either those data are superfluous or some relevant analysis has not been foreseen. If part of a dummy table remains empty, a necessary question may have been omitted. Analysis of pilot-test data helps to ensure that all data collected will be utilised and that the questionnaire will obtain all the necessary data.[38]

Summarising the questionnaire design process

Table 7.1 summarises the questionnaire design process in the form of a checklist.

Table 7.1	Questionnaire design checklist

Step 1: Specify the information needed

1 Ensure that the information obtained fully addresses all the components of the problem.
2 Prepare a set of dummy tables.
3 Have a clear idea of the characteristics and motivations of the target participants.

Step 2: Specify the type of interviewing method

1 Review the type of interviewing method.

Step 3: Determine the content of individual questions

1 Is the question necessary?
2 Are several questions needed instead of one?
3 Do not use double-barrelled questions.

Step 4: Overcome the participant's inability and unwillingness to answer

1 Is the participant informed?
2 If the participant is not likely to be informed, filter questions should be asked before questions about the topics themselves.
3 Can the participant remember?
4 Avoid errors of omission, telescoping and creation.
5 Questions that do not provide the participant with cues can underestimate the actual occurrence of an event.
6 Can the participant articulate?
7 Minimise the effort required of the participant.
8 Is the context in which the questions are asked appropriate?
9 Make the request for information seem legitimate.
10 If the information is sensitive:
    (a) Place sensitive topics at the end of the questionnaire.
    (b) Preface the question with a statement that the behaviour of interest is common.
    (c) Ask the question using the third-person technique.
    (d) Hide the question in a group of other questions that participants are willing to answer.
    (e) Provide response categories rather than asking for specific figures.

Step 5: Choose question structure

1 Open-ended questions are useful in exploratory research and as closing questions.
2 Use structured questions whenever possible.
3 In multiple-choice questions, the response alternatives should include the set of all possible choices and should be mutually exclusive.
4 In a dichotomous question, if a substantial proportion of the participants can be expected to be neutral, include a neutral alternative.
5 Consider the use of the split ballot technique to reduce order bias in dichotomous and multiple-choice questions.
6 If the response alternatives are numerous, consider using more than one question to reduce the information processing demands on the participants.

Step 6: Choose question wording

1 Define the issue in terms of 'who', 'what', 'when' and 'where'.
2 Use ordinary words. Words should match the vocabulary level of the participants.
3 Avoid ambiguous words such as: usually, normally, frequently, often, regularly, occasionally, sometimes, etc.
4 Avoid leading or biasing questions that cue the participant to what the answer should be.

Table 7.1	Continued

5 Avoid implicit alternatives that are not explicitly expressed in the options.

6 Avoid implicit assumptions.

7 Participant should not have to make generalisations or compute estimates.

8 Use both positive and negative statements.

Step 7: Arrange the questions in proper order

1 The opening questions should be interesting, simple and non-threatening.

2 Qualifying questions should serve as the opening questions.

3 Basic Information should be obtained first, followed by classification and finally identification information.

4 Difficult, sensitive or complex questions should be placed late in the sequence.

5 General questions should precede specific questions.

6 Questions should be asked in a logical order.

7 Branching questions should be designed carefully to cover all possible contingencies.

8 The question being branched should be placed as close as possible to the question causing the branching, and the branching questions should be ordered so that the participants cannot anticipate what additional information will be required.

Step 8: Design the form and layout

1 Divide a questionnaire into several parts.

2 Questions in each part should be numbered.

3 If hard copies of the questionnaires are used: coding should be printed on the forms to facilitate manual data entry.

Step 9: Publish the questionnaire

1 The questionnaire should be designed to be visually engaging.

2 Vertical response columns should be used.

3 Grids are useful when there are a number of related questions that use the same set of response categories.

4 The tendency to crowd questions to make the questionnaire look shorter should be avoided.

5 Directions or instructions for individual questions should be placed as close to the questions as possible.

6 If hard copies of the questionnaires are used: a booklet format should be used for long questionnaires; each question should be reproduced on a single page (or double-page spread).

Step 10: Eliminate problems by pilot-testing

1 Pilot-testing should always be done.

2 All aspects of the questionnaire should be tested, including question content, wording, sequence, form and layout, question difficulty, instructions and rewards for taking part in the survey.

3 The participants in the pilot-test should be similar to those who will be included in the actual survey.

4 Begin the pilot-test by using face-to-face interviews.

5 The pilot-test should also be conducted online, postal or telephone if those modes are to be used in the actual survey.

6 A variety of interviewers should be used for pilot-tests.

7 The pilot-test sample size should be small, varying from 15 to 30 participants for the initial testing.

8 After each significant revision of the questionnaire, another pilot-test should be conducted, using a different sample of participants.

9 The responses obtained from the pilot-test should be analysed to check the set up of tables and charts.

10 The responses obtained from the pilot-test should not be aggregated with responses from the final survey.

Measurement and scaling

We begin this section with an example of how the use of different types of scale can give quite different powers of analysis and interpretation.

| Real research | **Numbers, rankings and ratings: Spain is on top** |

According to the international football federation (FIFA) (**www.fifa.com**) post-2010 World Cup rankings, the world champions Spain reigned supreme at the top of the rankings with 1,880 points and the runners-up Holland took second spot with 1,730 points. The top 10 countries were as follows:

Number	Country	March 2011 ranking	Points
1	Argentina	4	1,412
2	Brazil	5	1,411
3	Croatia	8	1,071
4	England	6	1,212
5	Germany	3	1,486
6	Greece	10	1,038
7	Netherlands	2	1,730
8	Portugal	9	1,060
9	Spain	1	1,880
10	Uruguay	7	1,172

Note that the countries have been placed in alphabetical order and that at first glance this gives the impression that South American countries have performed better than European countries. An alphabetical order is used to illustrate the first column 'Number'. The 'number' assigned to denote countries is not in any way related to their football-playing capabilities but simply serves the purpose of identification, e.g. drawing numbered balls to decide which teams may play each other in a competition. This identification number constitutes a nominal scale, which says nothing about the respective performances of the countries. So whilst England is numbered 4 and Germany is numbered 5, this does not reflect the superior performance of Germany.

A much clearer way to present the list would be to place the countries in the order of their ranking, with Spain at the top and Greece at the bottom of the table. The ranking would represent an ordinal scale, where it would be clear to see that the lower the number, the better the performance. But what is still missing from the ranking is the magnitude of differences between the countries.

The only way to really understand how much one country is better than another is to examine the points awarded to each country. The points awarded represent an interval scale. Based on the points awarded, note that only one point separates the closely ranked Argentina (1,412) and Brazil (1,411), or 11 points between Croatia (1,071) and Portugal (1,060), but that the difference between the Netherlands (1,730) ranked at number 2 and Germany (1,486) ranked at number 3 is 244 points.

Measurement

The assignment of numbers or other symbols to characteristics of objects according to certain pre-specified rules.

Measurement means assigning numbers or other symbols to characteristics of objects according to certain pre-specified rules.[39] Note that what we measure is not the object but some characteristic of it. Thus, we do not measure consumers, only their perceptions, attitudes, preferences or other relevant characteristics. In marketing research, numbers are usually assigned for one of two reasons. First, numbers permit statistical analysis of the resulting data. Second, numbers facilitate a universal and transparent communication of measurement rules and results.

The most important aspect of measurement is the specification of rules for assigning numbers to the characteristics. The assignment process must be isomorphic, i.e. there must be one-to-one correspondence between the numbers and the characteristics being measured. For example, the same euro (€) figures can be assigned to households with identical annual incomes. Only then can the numbers be associated with specific characteristics of the measured object, and vice versa. In addition, the rules for assigning numbers should be standardised and applied uniformly. They must not change over objects or time.

Scaling may be considered an extension of measurement. Scaling involves creating a continuum upon which measured objects are located. To illustrate, consider a scale for locating consumers according to the characteristic 'attitude towards visiting a cinema'. Each participant is assigned a number indicating an unfavourable attitude (measured as 1), a neutral attitude (measured as 2) or a favourable attitude (measured as 3). Measurement is the actual assignment of 1, 2 or 3 to each participant. Scaling is the process of placing the participants on a continuum with respect to their attitude towards visiting a cinema. In our example, scaling is the process by which participants would be classified as having an unfavourable, neutral or positive attitude.

Scaling
The generation of a continuum upon which measured objects are located.

Primary scales of measurement

There are four primary scales of measurement: nominal, ordinal, interval and ratio.[40] These scales are illustrated in Figure 7.4, and their properties are summarised in Table 7.2 and discussed in the following sections.

Figure 7.4

An illustration of primary scales of measurement

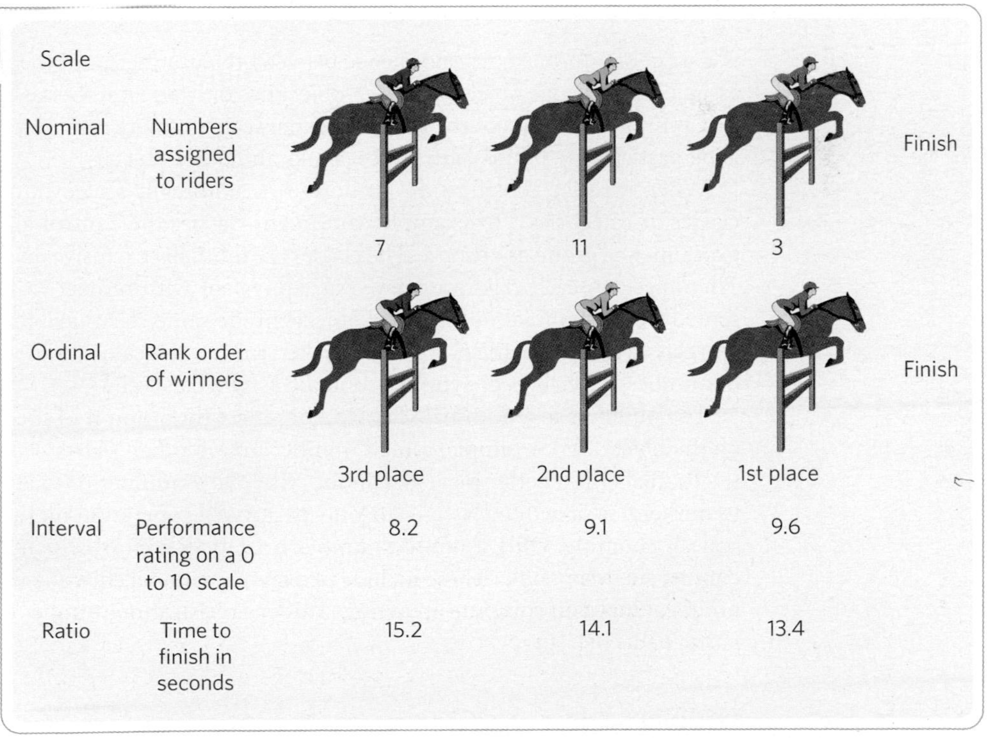

Scale				
Nominal	Numbers assigned to riders	7	11	3	Finish
Ordinal	Rank order of winners	3rd place	2nd place	1st place	Finish
Interval	Performance rating on a 0 to 10 scale	8.2	9.1	9.6	
Ratio	Time to finish in seconds	15.2	14.1	13.4	

Nominal scale

A **nominal scale** is a figurative labelling scheme in which the numbers serve only as labels or tags for identifying and classifying objects. For example, the numbers assigned to the participants in a study constitute a nominal scale; thus a female participant may be assigned a number 1 and a male participant 2. When a nominal scale is used for the purpose of identification, there

Nominal scale
A scale whose numbers serve only as labels or tags for identifying and classifying objects with a strict one-to-one correspondence between the numbers and the objects.

Table 7.2	Primary scales of measurement				
				Permissible statistics	
Scale	Basic characteristics	Common examples	Marketing example	Descriptive	Inferential
Nominal	Numbers identify and classify objects	Student registration numbers, numbers on football players' shirts	Gender classification, types of retail outlet	Percentages, mode	Chi-square, binomial test
Ordinal	Numbers indicate the relative positions of the objects but not the magnitude of differences between them	Rankings of the top four teams in the football World Cup	Ranking of service quality delivered by a number of banks. Rank order of favourite TV programmes	Percentile, median	Rank-order correlation, Friedman ANOVA
Interval	Differences between objects can be compared; zero point is arbitrary	Temperature (Fahrenheit, Celsius)	Attitudes, opinions, index numbers	Range, mean, standard deviation	Product moment correlations, t tests, ANOVA, regression, factor analysis
Ratio	Zero point is fixed; ratios of scale values can be computed	Length, weight	Age, income, costs, sales, market shares	Geometric mean, harmonic mean	Coefficient of variation

is a strict one-to-one correspondence between the numbers and the objects. Each number is assigned to only one object, and each object has only one number assigned to it.

Common examples of the use of nominal scales in marketing research, include characterising participants, brands, attributes, banks and other objects.

When used for classification purposes, the nominally scaled numbers serve as labels for classes or categories. For example, you might classify the control group as group 1 and the experimental group as group 2. The classes are mutually exclusive and collectively exhaustive. The objects in each class are viewed as equivalent with respect to the characteristic represented by the nominal number. All objects in the same class have the same number, and no two classes have the same number. However, a nominal scale need not involve the assignment of numbers; alphabets or symbols could be assigned as well.

The numbers in a nominal scale do not reflect the amount of the characteristic possessed by the objects. For example, a high number on a football player's shirt does not imply that the footballer is a better player than one with a low number or vice versa. The same applies to numbers assigned to classes. The only permissible operation on the numbers in a nominal scale is counting. Only a limited number of statistics, all of which are based on frequency counts, are permissible. These include percentages, mode, chi-square and binomial tests. It is not meaningful to compute an average student registration number or the average gender of participants in a survey.

Ordinal scale

Ordinal scale
A ranking scale in which numbers are assigned to objects to indicate the relative extent to which some characteristic is possessed. Thus, it is possible to determine whether an object has more or less of a characteristic than some other object.

An **ordinal scale** is a ranking scale in which numbers are assigned to objects to indicate the relative extent to which the objects possess some characteristic. An ordinal scale allows you to determine whether an object has more or less of a characteristic than some other object, but not how much more or less. Thus, an ordinal scale indicates relative position, not the magnitude of the differences between the objects. The object ranked first has more of the characteristic as compared with the object ranked second, but whether the object ranked second is a close second or a poor second is not known. Common examples of ordinal scales in marketing research are in the measurement of relative attitudes, opinions, perceptions and preferences. Measurements of this type include 'greater than' or 'less than' judgements from participants.

In an ordinal scale, as in a nominal scale, equivalent objects receive the same rank. Any series of numbers can be assigned that preserves the ordered relationships between the objects. Ordinal scales can be transformed in any way as long as the basic ordering of the objects is maintained.[41]

Interval scale

Interval scale

A scale in which the numbers are used to rank objects such that numerically equal distances on the scale represent equal distances in the characteristic being measured.

In an interval scale, numerically equal distances on the scale represent equal values in the characteristic being measured. An interval scale contains all the information of an ordinal scale, but it also allows you to compare the differences between objects. The difference between any two scale values is identical to the difference between any other two adjacent values of an interval scale. There is a constant or equal interval between scale values. The difference between 1 and 2 is the same as the difference between 2 and 3, which is the same as the difference between 5 and 6. A common example in everyday life is a temperature scale. In marketing research, attitudinal data obtained from rating scales are often treated as interval data.[42]

In an interval scale, the location of the zero point is not fixed. Both the zero point and the units of measurement are arbitrary. Hence, any positive linear transformation of the form $y = a + bx$ will preserve the properties of the scale. Here, x is the original scale value, y is the transformed scale value, b is a positive constant, and a is any constant. Therefore, two interval scales that rate objects A, B, C and D as 1, 2, 3 and 4 or as 22, 24, 26 and 28 are equivalent. Note that the latter scale can be derived from the former by using $a = 20$ and $b = 2$ in the transforming equation.

Because the zero point is not fixed, it is not meaningful to take ratios of scale values. As can be seen, the ratio of D to B values changes from 2:1 to 7:6 when the scale is transformed. Yet, ratios of differences between scale values are permissible. In this process, the constants a and b in the transforming equation drop out in the computations. The ratio of the difference between D and B values to the difference between C and B values is 2:1 in both the scales.

Statistical techniques that may be used on interval scale data include all those that can be applied to nominal and ordinal data in addition to the arithmetic mean, standard deviation, product moment correlations, and other statistics commonly used in marketing research. Certain specialised statistics such as geometric mean, harmonic mean and coefficient of variation, however, are not meaningful on interval scale data.

Ratio scale

Ratio scale

The highest scale. This scale allows the researcher to identify or classify objects, rank order the objects, and compare intervals or differences. It is also meaningful to compute ratios of scale values.

A ratio scale possesses all the properties of the nominal, ordinal and interval scales, and, in addition, an absolute zero point. Thus, in ratio scales possess the characteristic of origin (and distance, order, and description). With ratio scales we can identify or classify objects, rank the objects, and compare intervals or differences. It is also meaningful to compute ratios of scale values. Not only is the difference between 2 and 5 the same as the difference between 14 and 17, but also 14 is seven times as large as 2 in an absolute sense. Common examples of ratio scales in marketing include: sales, costs, market share and number of customers.

Ratio scales allow only proportionate transformations of the form $y = bx$, where b is a positive constant. One cannot add an arbitrary constant, as in the case of an interval scale. An example of this transformation is provided by the conversion of metres to yards ($b = 1.094$). The comparisons between the objects are identical whether made in metres or yards.

All statistical techniques can be applied to ratio data. These include specialised statistics such as geometric mean, harmonic mean and coefficient of variation.

Metric scale

A scale that is either interval or ratio in nature.

The four primary scales discussed above do not exhaust the measurement-level categories. It is possible to construct a nominal scale that provides partial information on order (the partially ordered scale). Likewise, an ordinal scale can convey partial information on distance, as in the case of an ordered metric scale. A discussion of these scales is beyond the scope of this text.[43]

A comparison of scaling techniques

Comparative scales
One of two types of scaling techniques in which there is direct comparison of stimulus objects with one another.

Non-metric scale
A scale that is either nominal or ordinal in nature.

Carryover effects
Where the evaluation of a particular scaled item significantly affects the participant's judgement of subsequent scaled items.

Non-comparative scale
One of two types of scaling techniques in which each stimulus object is scaled independently of the other objects in the stimulus set. Also called monadic scale.

The scaling techniques commonly employed in marketing research can be classified into comparative and non-comparative scales (see Figure 7.5).

Comparative scales involve the direct comparison of stimulus objects. For example, participants may be asked whether they prefer to visit a cinema or a theatre. Comparative scale data must be interpreted in relative terms and have only ordinal or rank order properties. For this reason, comparative scaling is also referred to as **non-metric scaling**. As shown in Figure 7.5, comparative scales include paired comparisons, rank order, constant sum scales, Q-sort and other procedures.

The major benefit of comparative scaling is that small differences between stimulus objects can be detected. As they compare the stimulus objects, participants are forced to choose between them. In addition, participants approach the rating task from the same known reference points. Consequently, comparative scales are easily understood and can be applied easily. Other advantages of these scales are that they involve fewer theoretical assumptions, and they also tend to reduce halo or **carryover effects** from one judgement to another.[44] The major disadvantages of comparative scales include the ordinal nature of the data and the inability to generalise beyond the stimulus objects scaled. For instance, to compare a visit to a pop concert to a cinema or theatre visit, the researcher would have to do a new study. These disadvantages are substantially overcome by the non-comparative scaling techniques.

In **non-comparative scales**, also referred to as monadic or metric scales, each object is scaled independently of the others in the stimulus set. The resulting data are generally assumed to be interval or ratio scaled.[45] For example, participants may be asked to evaluate a cinema visit on a 1 to 6 preference scale (1 = not at all preferred, 6 = greatly preferred). Similar evaluations would be obtained for a theatre visit and a pop concert visit. As can be seen in Figure 7.5, non-comparative scales can be continuous rating or itemised rating scales. The itemised rating scales can be further classified as Likert, semantic differential or Stapel scales. Non-comparative scaling is the most widely used scaling technique in marketing research.

Figure 7.5

A classification of scaling techniques

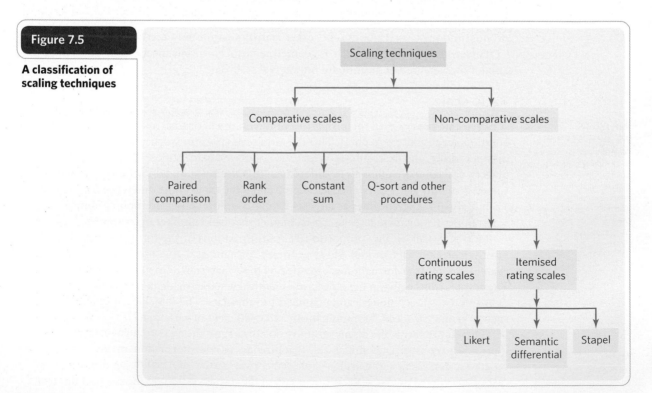

Comparative scaling techniques

Paired comparison scaling

Paired comparison scaling

A comparative scaling technique in which a participant is presented with two objects at a time and asked to select one object in the pair according to some criterion. The data obtained are ordinal in nature.

As its name implies, in **paired comparison scaling** a participant is presented with two objects and asked to select one according to some criterion.[46] The data obtained are ordinal in nature. A participant may state that he or she prefers Belgian chocolate to Swiss, or likes Adidas more than Nike. Paired comparison scales are frequently used when the stimulus objects are physical products.

Figure 7.6 shows paired comparison data obtained to assess a participant's bottled beer preferences. As can be seen, this participant made 10 comparisons to evaluate five brands. In general, with n brands, $[n(n-1)/2]$ paired comparisons include all possible pairings of objects.[47]

Paired comparison data can be analysed in several ways.[48] The researcher can calculate the percentage of participants who prefer one stimulus over another by summing the matrices of Figure 7.6 for all the participants, dividing the sum by the number of participants, and multiplying by 100. Simultaneous evaluation of all the stimulus objects is also possible. Under the assumption of transitivity, it is possible to convert paired comparison data to a rank order.

Transitivity of preference

An assumption made to convert paired comparison data to rank order data. It implies that if Brand A is preferred to Brand B, and Brand B is preferred to Brand C, then Brand A is preferred to Brand C.

Transitivity of preference implies that if Brand A is preferred to B, and Brand B is preferred to C, then Brand A is preferred to C. To arrive at a rank order, the researcher determines the number of times each brand is preferred by summing the column entries in Figure 7.6. Therefore, this participant's order of preference, from most to least preferred, is Carlsberg, Holsten, Stella Artois, Budvar and Grolsch.

Paired comparison scaling is useful when the number of brands is limited, since it requires direct comparison and overt choice. With a large number of brands, however, the number of comparisons becomes unwieldy. Other disadvantages are that violations of the assumption of transitivity may occur, and the order in which the objects are presented may bias the results. Paired comparisons bear little resemblance to the marketplace situation, which involves selection from multiple alternatives. Also participants may prefer one object over certain others, but they may not like it in an absolute sense.[49]

Figure 7.6

Obtaining bottled beer preferences using paired comparisons

Instructions
We are going to present you with 10 pairs of bottled beer brands. For each pair, please indicate which of the two beer brands you prefer.

Recording form

	Holsten	Stella Artois	Grolsch	Carlsberg	Budvar
Holsten		0	0	1	0
Stella Artois	1[a]		0	1	0
Grolsch	1	1		1	1
Carlsberg	0	0	0		0
Budvar	1	1	0	1	
Number of times preferred[b]	3	2	0	4	1

[a] 1 in a particular box means that the brand in that column was preferred over the brand in the corresponding row. 0 means that the row brand was preferred over the column brand.

[b] The number of times a brand was preferred is obtained by summing the 1s in each column.

Rank order scaling

Rank order scaling
A comparative scaling technique in which participants are presented with several objects simultaneously and asked to order or rank them according to some criterion.

In **rank order scaling**, participants are presented with several objects simultaneously and asked to order or rank them according to some criterion. For example, participants may be asked to rank according to overall preference. As shown in Figure 7.7, these rankings are typically obtained by asking the participants to assign a rank of 1 to the most preferred film genre, 2 to the second most preferred, and so on, until a rank of n is assigned to the least preferred genre. Like paired comparison, this approach is also comparative in nature, and it is possible that the participants may dislike the genre ranked 1 in an absolute sense. Furthermore, rank order scaling also results in ordinal data.

Rank order scaling is commonly used to measure attributes of products and services as well as preferences for brands. Compared with paired comparisons, this type of scaling process more closely resembles the shopping environment. It also takes less time and eliminates intransitive responses. If there are n stimulus objects, only $(n - 1)$ scaling decisions need be made in rank order scaling. However, in paired comparison scaling, $[n(n - 1)/2]$ decisions would be required. Another advantage is that most participants easily understand the instructions for ranking. The major disadvantage is that this technique produces only ordinal data.

Finally, under the assumption of transitivity, rank order data can be converted to equivalent paired comparison data, and vice versa. This point was illustrated by examining the 'Number of times preferred' in Figure 7.6. Hence, it is possible to derive an interval scale from rankings using the Thurstone case V procedure.[50]

Figure 7.7

Preference for film genres using rank order scaling

Instructions
Rank the listed film genres in order of preference. Begin by picking out the genre that you like the most and assign it a number 1. Then find the second most preferred genre and assign it a number 2. Continue this procedure until you have ranked all the genres in order of preference. The least preferred genre should be assigned a rank of 10.

No two genres should receive the same rank number

The criterion of preference is entirely up to you. There is no right or wrong answer. Just try to be consistent

Genre	Rank order
Action	
Animated	
Comedy	
Drama	
Factual	
Fantasy	
Light drama	
Romance	
Sci-fi	
Suspense	

Constant sum scaling

Constant sum scaling
A comparative scaling technique in which participants are required to allocate a constant sum of units such as points, euros, chits, stickers or chips among a set of stimulus objects with respect to some criterion.

In **constant sum scaling**, participants allocate a constant sum of units, such as points or euros, among a set of stimulus objects with respect to some criterion. As shown in Figure 7.8, participants may be asked to allocate 100 points to attributes of bottled beers in a way that

Figure 7.8	Instructions

Instructions

Below are eight attributes of bottled beers. Please allocate 100 points among the attributes so that your allocation reflects the relative importance you attach to each attribute. The more points an attribute receives, the more important an attribute is. If an attribute is not at all important, assign it no points. If an attribute is twice as important as some other attribute, it should receive twice as many points.

Note: the figures below represent the mean points allocated to bottled beers by three segments of a target market.

Form

Importance of bottled beer attributes using a constant sum scale

	MEAN POINTS ALLOCATED			
	Attribute	Segment I	Segment II	Segment III
1	Bitterness	8	2	17
2	Hop flavours	2	4	20
3	Fragrance	3	9	19
4	Country where brewed	9	17	4
5	Price	53	5	7
6	High alcohol level	7	60	9
7	Aftertaste	5	0	15
8	Package design	13	3	9
	Sum	100	100	100

reflects the importance they attach to each attribute. If an attribute is unimportant, the participant assigns it zero points. If an attribute is twice as important as some other attribute, it receives twice as many points. The sum of all the points is 100; hence the name of the scale.

The attributes are scaled by counting the points assigned to each one by all the participants and dividing by the number of participants. These results are presented for three groups, or segments, of participants in Figure 7.8. Segment I attaches overwhelming importance to price. Segment II considers a high alcoholic level to be of prime importance. Segment III values bitterness, hop flavours, fragrance and the aftertaste. Such information cannot be obtained from rank order data unless they are transformed into interval data. Note that the constant sum also has an absolute zero; 10 points are twice as many as 5 points, and the difference between 5 and 2 points is the same as the difference between 57 and 54 points. For this reason, constant sum scale data are sometimes treated as metric. Although this may be appropriate in the limited context of the stimuli scaled, these results are not generalisable to other stimuli not included in the study. Hence, strictly speaking, the constant sum should be considered an ordinal scale because of its comparative nature and the resulting lack of generalisability. It can be seen that the allocation of points in Figure 7.8 is influenced by the specific attributes included in the evaluation task.

The main advantage of the constant sum scale is that it allows for fine discrimination among stimulus objects without requiring too much time. It has two primary disadvantages, however. Participants may allocate more or fewer units than those specified. For example, a participant may allocate 108 or 94 points. The researcher must modify such data in some way or eliminate this participant from analysis. Another potential problem is rounding error if too few units are used. On the other hand, the use of a large number of units may be too taxing on the participant and cause confusion and fatigue.[51]

Q-sort and other procedures

Q-sort scaling
A comparative scaling technique that uses a rank order procedure to sort objects based on similarity with respect to some criterion.

Q-sort scaling was developed to discriminate among a relatively large number of objects quickly. This technique uses a rank order procedure in which objects are sorted into piles based on similarity with respect to some criterion. For example, participants are given 100 attitude statements on individual cards and asked to place them into 11 piles, ranging from 'most highly agreed with' to 'least highly agreed with'. The number of objects to be sorted should not be less than 60 nor more than 140; a reasonable range is 60 to 90 objects. The number of objects to be placed in each pile is pre-specified, often to result in a roughly normal distribution of objects over the whole set.

Another comparative scaling technique is magnitude estimation.[52] In this technique, numbers are assigned to objects such that ratios between the assigned numbers reflect ratios on the specified criterion. For example, participants may be asked to indicate whether they agree or disagree with each of a series of statements measuring attitude towards different film genres. Then they assign a number between 0 and to 100 to each statement to indicate the intensity of their agreement or disagreement. Providing this type of number imposes a cognitive burden on the participants.

Verbal protocol
A technique used to understand participants' cognitive responses or thought processes by having them think aloud while completing a task or making a decision.

Another particularly useful procedure (that could be viewed as a very structured combination of observation and depth interviewing) for measuring cognitive responses or thought processes consists of **verbal protocols**. Participants are asked to 'think out loud' and verbalise anything going through their heads while making a decision or performing a task.

Non-comparative scaling techniques

Participants using a non-comparative scale employ whatever rating standard seems appropriate to them. They do not compare the object being rated either with another object or with some specified standard, such as 'your ideal brand'. They evaluate only one object at a time; thus, non-comparative scales are often referred to as monadic scales. Non-comparative techniques consist of continuous and itemised rating scales, which are described in Table 7.3 and discussed in the following sections.

Table 7.3	Basic non-comparative scales			
Scale	**Basic characteristics**	**Examples**	**Advantages**	**Disadvantages**
Continuous rating scale	Place a mark on a continuous line	Reaction to TV advertisements	Easy to construct	Scoring can be cumbersome unless computerised
Itemised rating scales				
Likert scale	Degree of agreement on a 1 (strongly disagree) to 5 (strongly agree) scale	Measurement of attitudes	Easy to construct, administer and understand	More time consuming
Semantic differential scale	Seven-point scale with bipolar labels	Brand product and company images	Versatile	Controversy as to whether the data are interval
Stapel scale	Unipolar 10-point scale, −5 to +5, without a neutral point (zero)	Measurement of attitudes and images	Easy to construct, administered over phone	Confusing and difficult to apply

Continuous rating scale

Continuous rating scale

A measurement scale that has participants rate the objects by placing a mark at the appropriate position on a line that runs from one extreme of the criterion variable to the other. The form may vary considerably. Also called graphic rating scale.

In a **continuous rating scale**, also referred to as a graphic rating scale, participants rate the objects by placing a mark at the appropriate position on a line that runs from one extreme of the criterion variable to the other. Thus, the participants are not restricted to selecting from marks previously set by the researcher. The form of the continuous scale may vary considerably. For example, the line may be vertical or horizontal: scale points, in the form of numbers or brief descriptions, may be provided; and if provided, the scale points may be few or many. Three versions of a continuous rating scale are illustrated in Figure 7.9.

Once the participant has provided the ratings, the researcher divides the line into as many categories as desired and assigns scores based on the categories into which the ratings fall. In Figure 7.9, the participant exhibits a favourable attitude towards the seating at the Odeon cinema. These scores are typically treated as interval data. The advantage of continuous scales is that they are easy to construct; however, scoring may be cumbersome and unreliable. With the increase of computer-assisted personal interviewing (CAPI), kiosk, online and mobile device surveys their use is becoming more frequent. Continuous rating scales can be easily implemented in such surveys. The cursor or point of screen touched in a continuous fashion to select the exact position on the scale that best describes the participant's evaluation. Moreover, the scale values can be automatically scored, thus increasing the speed and accuracy of processing the data.

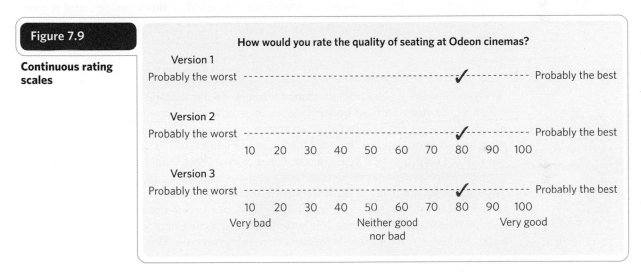

Figure 7.9

Continuous rating scales

Itemised rating scales

Itemised rating scale

A measurement scale having numbers or brief descriptions associated with each category. The categories are ordered in terms of scale position.

In an **itemised rating scale**, participants are provided with a scale that has a number or brief description associated with each category. The categories are ordered in terms of scale position, and the participants are required to select the specified category that best describes the object being rated. Itemised rating scales are widely used in marketing research and form the basic components of more complex scales, such as multi-item rating scales. We first describe the commonly used itemised rating scales – the Likert, semantic differential and Stapel scales – and then examine the major issues surrounding the use of itemised rating scales.

Likert scale

Likert scale

A measurement scale with typically five response categories ranging from 'strongly disagree' to 'strongly agree' that requires participants to indicate a degree of agreement or disagreement with each of a series of statements related to the stimulus objects.

The **Likert scale** is a widely used rating scale that requires the participants to indicate a degree of agreement or disagreement with each of a series of statements about the stimulus objects.[53] Typically, each scale item has five response categories, ranging from 'strongly disagree' to 'strongly agree'. We illustrate with a Likert scale for evaluating attitudes towards a visit to an Odeon cinema.

Figure 7.10

The Likert scale

Instructions
Listed below are different beliefs about the Odeon cinema. Please indicate how strongly you agree or disagree with each by using the following scale:

1 = Strongly disagree, 2 = Disagree, 3 = Neither agree nor disagree, 4 = Agree, 5 = Strongly agree

	1	2	3	4	5
1 I like to visit Odeon cinemas		✓			
2 The Odeon sells poor-quality food		✓			
3 The Odeon presents a wide variety of film genres			✓		
4 I do not like Odeon advertisements				✓	
5 The Odeon charges fair prices				✓	
6 Booking a seat at the Odeon is difficult	✓				
7 The acoustics at Odeon cinemas are excellent				✓	
8 Odeon staff serve their customers very well				✓	
9 The Odeon is a great place for families to enjoy films		✓			

To conduct the analysis, each statement is assigned a numerical score, ranging either from −2 to +2 or from 1 to 5. The analysis can be conducted on an item-by-item basis (profile analysis), or a total (summated) score can be calculated for each participant by summing across items. Suppose that the Likert scale in Figure 7.10 was used to measure attitudes towards the Odeon as well as a local arts based cinema. Profile analysis would involve comparing the two cinema experiences in terms of the average participant ratings for each item. The summated approach is most frequently used and, as a result, the Likert scale is also referred to as a summated scale.[54] When using this approach to determine the total score for each participant on each cinema, it is important to use a consistent scoring procedure so that a high (or low) score consistently reflects a favourable response. This requires that the categories assigned to the negative statements by the participants be scored by reversing the scale. Note that for a negative statement, an agreement reflects an unfavourable response, whereas for a positive statement, agreement represents a favourable response. Accordingly, a 'strongly agree' response to a favourable statement and a 'strongly disagree' response to an unfavourable statement would both receive scores of 5.[55] In the example in Figure 7.10, if a higher score is to denote a more favourable attitude, the scoring of items 2, 4 and 6 will be reversed. The participant to this set of statements has an attitude score of 26. Each participant's total score for each cinema is calculated. A participant will have the most favourable attitude towards a cinema with the highest score. The procedure for developing summated Likert scales is described later in the section on multi-item scales.

The Likert scale has several advantages. It is easy to construct and administer, and participants readily understand how to use the scale, making it suitable for online surveys, kiosk, mobile, mail, telephone or personal interviews. The major disadvantage of the Likert scale is that it takes longer to complete than other itemised rating scales because participants have to read and fully reflect upon each statement.

Semantic differential scale

Semantic differential
A seven-point rating scale with end points associated with bipolar labels.

The **semantic differential** is typically a seven-point rating scale with end points associated with bipolar labels that have semantic meaning. In a typical application, participants rate

Figure 7.11

Semantic differential scale

Instructions
What does visiting an Odeon cinema mean to you? The following sets of opposites summarise characteristics of a visit. Please mark X to indicate what you tend to feel about an Odeon visit.

objects on a number of itemised, seven-point rating scales bounded at each end by one of two bipolar adjectives, such as 'boring' and 'exciting'.[56] We illustrate this scale in Figure 7.11 by presenting a participant's evaluation of a visit to the Odeon cinema on six attributes.

The participants mark the blank that best indicates how they would describe the object being rated.[57] Thus, in our example, an Odeon visit is evaluated as exciting, special, indulgent, cosy, and youthful though noisy. The negative adjective or phrase sometimes appears at the left side of the scale and sometimes at the right. In this example they are mixed and the adjectives of 'youthful' and 'mature' may not readily be classified as positive or negative. By mixing the position of positive and negative adjectives, the tendency of some participants, particularly those with very positive or very negative attitudes, to mark the right- or left-hand sides without reading the labels is controlled.

Individual items on a semantic differential scale may be scored either on a −3 to +3 or on a 1 to 7 scale. The resulting data are commonly analysed through profile analysis. In profile analysis, means or median values on each rating scale are calculated and compared by plotting or statistical analysis. This helps determine the overall differences and similarities among the objects. To assess differences across segments of participants, the researcher can compare mean responses of different segments. Although the mean is most often used as a summary statistic, there is some controversy as to whether the data obtained should be treated as an interval scale.[58] On the other hand, in cases when the researcher requires an overall comparison of objects, such as to determine cinema preference, the individual item scores are summed to arrive at a total score. As in the case of the Likert scale, the scores for the negative items are reversed before summing.

Its versatility makes the semantic differential a popular rating scale in marketing research. It has been widely used in comparing brand, product and company images. It has also been used to develop advertising and promotion strategies and in new product development studies.[59]

Stapel scale

Stapel scale
A scale for measuring attitudes that consists of a single adjective in the middle of an even-numbered range of values.

The **Stapel scale**, named after its developer, Jan Stapel, is a unipolar rating scale with 10 categories numbered from −5 to +5, without a neutral point (zero).[60] This scale is usually presented vertically. Participants are asked to indicate, by selecting an appropriate numerical response category, how accurately or inaccurately each term describes the object.

Itemised rating scale decisions

As is evident from the discussion so far, non-comparative itemised rating scales can take many different forms. The researcher must make six major decisions (see Table 7.4) when constructing any of these scales.

Table 7.4	Summary of itemised rating scale decisions
1 Number of categories	Although there is no single, optimal number, traditional guidelines suggest that there should be between five and nine categories
2 Balanced versus unbalanced	In general, the scale should be balanced to obtain the most objective data
3 Odd or even number of categories	If a neutral or indifferent scale response is possible from at least some of the participants, an odd number of categories should be used
4 Forced versus unforced	In situations where the participants are expected to have no opinion, the accuracy of the data may be improved by a non-forced scale
5 Verbal description	An argument can be made for labelling all or many scale categories. The category descriptions should be located as close to the response categories as possible
6 Physical form	A number of options should be tried and the best one selected

Number of scale categories

Two conflicting considerations are involved in deciding the number of scale categories or response options. The greater the number of scale categories, the finer the discrimination among stimulus objects that is possible. On the other hand, most participants cannot handle more than a few categories. Traditional guidelines suggest that the appropriate number of categories should be between five and nine.[61] Yet there is no single optimal number of categories. Several factors should be taken into account in deciding on the number of categories.

If the participants are interested in the scaling task and are knowledgeable about the objects, many categories may be employed. On the other hand, if the participants are not very knowledgeable or involved with the task, fewer categories should be used. Likewise, the nature of the objects is also relevant. Some objects do not lend themselves to fine discrimination, so a small number of categories are sufficient. Another important factor is the mode of data collection. If telephone interviews are involved, many categories may confuse the participants. Likewise, space limitations may restrict the number of categories in postal questionnaires. If online surveys are used, there is scope for more visual treatment of scale items and categories.

How the data are to be analysed and used should also influence the number of categories. In situations where several scale items are added together to produce a single score for each participant, five categories are sufficient. The same is true if the researcher wishes to make broad generalisations or group comparisons. If, however, individual responses are of interest or if the data will be analysed by sophisticated statistical techniques, seven or more categories may be required. The size of the correlation coefficient, a common measure of relationship between variables, is influenced by the number of scale categories. The correlation coefficient decreases with a reduction in the number of categories. This, in turn, has an impact on all statistical analysis based on the correlation coefficient.[62]

Balanced versus unbalanced scale

Balanced scale
A scale with an equal number of favourable and unfavourable categories.

In a balanced scale, the number of favourable and unfavourable categories is equal; in an unbalanced scale, the categories are unequal.[63] Examples of balanced and unbalanced scales are given in Figure 7.12.

Figure 7.12		

Balanced and unbalanced scales

Balanced scale		**Unbalanced scale**	
Clinique moisturiser for men is:		*Clinique moisturiser for men is:*	
Extremely good		Extremely good	
Very good	✓	Very good	✓
Good		Good	
Bad		Somewhat good	
Very bad		Bad	
Extremely bad		Very bad	

In general, in order to obtain the most objective data, the scale should be balanced. If the distribution of responses is likely to be skewed, however, either positively or negatively, an unbalanced scale with more categories in the direction of skewness may be appropriate. If an unbalanced scale is used, the nature and degree of imbalance in the scale should be taken into account in data analysis.

Odd or even number of categories

With an odd number of categories, the middle scale position is generally designated as neutral or impartial. The presence, position and labelling of a neutral category can have a significant influence on the response. The Likert scale is a balanced rating scale with an odd number of categories and a neutral point.[64]

The decision to use an odd or even number of categories depends on whether some of the participants may be neutral on the response being measured. If a neutral or indifferent response is possible from at least some of the participants, an odd number of categories should be used. If, on the other hand, the researcher wants to force a response or believes that no neutral or indifferent response exists, a rating scale with an even number of categories should be used.

Forced versus non-forced choice

Forced rating scale
A rating scale that forces participants to express an opinion because a 'no opinion' or 'no knowledge' option is not provided.

On **forced rating scales** the participants are forced to express an opinion because a 'no opinion' option is not provided. In such a case, participants without an opinion may mark the middle scale position. If a sufficient proportion of the participants do not have opinions on the topic, marking the middle position will distort measures of central tendency and variance. In situations where the participants are expected to have no opinion, as opposed to simply being reluctant to disclose it, the accuracy of data may be improved by a non-forced scale that includes a 'no opinion' category.[65]

Nature and degree of verbal description

The nature and degree of verbal description associated with scale categories varies considerably and can have an effect on the responses. Scale categories may have verbal, numerical or pictorial descriptions. Furthermore, the researcher must decide whether to label every scale category, label only some scale categories, or label only extreme scale categories. If they are to use pictorial descriptions (which in online surveys may be moving pictures), researchers have to decide whether they are to use labels at all. Providing a verbal description for each scale category may not improve the accuracy or reliability of the data. Yet, an argument can be made for labelling all or many scale categories to reduce scale ambiguity. The category descriptions should be located as close to the response categories as possible.

The strength of the adjectives used to anchor the scale may influence the distribution of the responses. With strong anchors (1 = completely disagree, 7 = completely agree), participants are less likely to use the extreme scale categories. This results in less variable and more peaked response distributions. Weak anchors (1 = generally disagree, 7 = generally agree), in contrast, produce uniform or flat distributions. Procedures have been developed to assign values to category descriptors to result in balanced or equal interval scales.[66]

Table 7.5	Some commonly used scales in marketing				
Construct	Scale descriptors				
Attitude	Very bad	Bad	Neither bad nor good	Good	Very good
Importance	Not at all important	Not important	Neutral	Important	Very important
Satisfaction	Very dissatisfied	Dissatisfied	Neither dissatisfied nor satisfied	Satisfied	Very satisfied
Purchase intent	Definitely will not buy	Probably will not buy	Might or might not buy	Probably will buy	Definitely will buy

Physical form of the scale

A number of options are available with respect to scale form or configuration. Scales can be presented vertically or horizontally. Categories can be expressed by boxes, discrete lines or units on a continuum and may or may not have numbers assigned to them. If numerical values are used, they may be positive, negative or both. Several possible configurations are presented in Figure 7.13.

Figure 7.13

Rating scale configurations

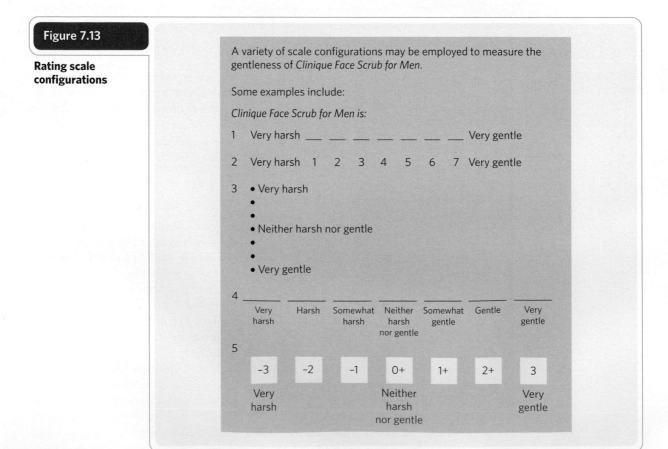

Multi-item scales

Multi-item scale
A multi-item scale consists of multiple items, where an item is a single question or statement to be evaluated.

Construct
A specific type of concept that exists at a higher level of abstraction than do everyday concepts.

A **multi-item scale** consists of multiple items, where an item is a single question or statement to be evaluated. The Likert, semantic differential and Stapel scales presented earlier to measure attitudes toward a visit to an Odeon cinema were examples of multi-item scales. Note that each of these scales has multiple items. The development of multi-item rating scales requires considerable technical expertise.[67] Figure 7.14 presents a sequence of operations needed to construct multi-item scales. The researcher begins by developing the construct of interest. A **construct** is a specific type of concept that exists at a higher level of abstraction than everyday concepts. Examples of such constructs in marketing include 'brand loyalty', 'product involvement' and 'satisfaction'. Next, the researcher must develop a theoretical definition of the construct that establishes the meaning of the central idea or concept of interest. For this we need an underlying theory of the construct being measured. A theory is necessary not only for constructing the scale but also for interpreting the resulting scores. For example, brand loyalty may be theoretically defined as the *consistent repurchase of a brand* prompted by a *favourable attitude toward the brand*. The construct of brand loyalty must be operationalised in a way that is consistent with this theoretical definition. The operational definition specifies which observable characteristics will be measured and the process of assigning value to the construct. For example, in a context of buying fashion items, consumers could be characterised as brand loyal if they exhibit a highly favourable attitude (top quartile) and have purchased the same fashion brand on at least four of the last five purchase occasions.

The next step is to generate an initial pool of scale items. Typically, this is based on theory, analysis of secondary data and qualitative research. From this pool, a reduced set of potential scale items is generated by the judgement of the researcher and other knowledgeable individuals. Some qualitative criterion is adopted to aid their judgement. The reduced set of items may still be too large to constitute a scale. Thus, further reduction is achieved in a quantitative manner.

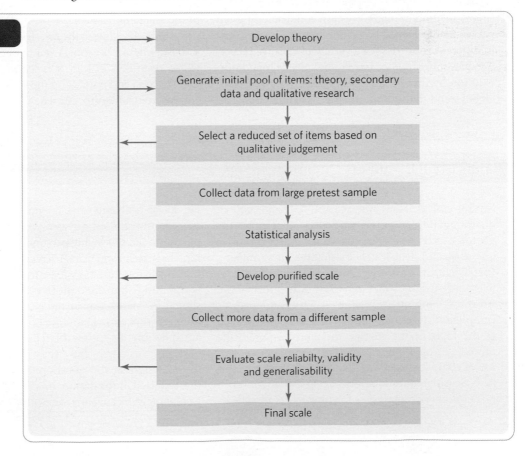

Figure 7.14

Development of a multi-item scale

Develop theory

Generate initial pool of items: theory, secondary data and qualitative research

Select a reduced set of items based on qualitative judgement

Collect data from large pretest sample

Statistical analysis

Develop purified scale

Collect more data from a different sample

Evaluate scale reliabilty, validity and generalisability

Final scale

Data are collected and analysed on the reduced set of potential scale items from a large pretest sample of participants. As a result of statistical analyses, several more items are eliminated, resulting in a purified scale. The purified scale is evaluated for reliability and validity by collecting more data from a different sample. On the basis of these assessments, a final set of scale items is selected. As can be seen from Figure 7.14, the scale development process is an iterative one with several feedback loops.[68]

International marketing research

Questionnaire and scale design should be adapted to specific cultural environments and all efforts made to avoid bias in terms of any one culture. This requires careful attention to each step of the questionnaire design process. The information needed should be clearly specified and form the focus of the questionnaire design. This should be balanced by taking into account any participant differences in terms of underlying consumer behaviour, decision making processes, psychographics, lifestyles and demographic variables. In the context of demographic characteristics, information on marital status, education, household size, occupation, income and dwelling unit may have to be specified differently for different countries, as these variables may not be directly comparable across countries.

Although online surveys may dominate as a survey method in many Western countries, different survey methods may be favoured or more prevalent in different countries for a variety of reasons. Hence, the questionnaire may have to be suitable for administration by more than one mode. Even if there is a global trend that questionnaires have to be designed

to be administered in online surveys, there still remains a need for cultural adaptation of questionnaires. Examples of such adaptation can include the challenges of comprehension and translation. Pilot-testing the questionnaire is complicated in international research because linguistic equivalence must be pilot-tested. The pilot-test data from administering the questionnaire in different countries or cultures should be analysed and the pattern of responses compared to detect any cultural biases.

In designing the scale or response format for international research projects, participants' cultural backgrounds should be taken into account.[69] Researchers should aim is to develop scales that are free of cultural biases. Special attention should be devoted to determining equivalent verbal descriptors in different languages and cultures. The end points of the scale are particularly prone to different interpretations. In some cultures, 1 may be interpreted as best, whereas in others it may be interpreted as worst, regardless of how it is scaled. It is important that the scale end points and the verbal descriptors be employed in a manner consistent with the culture.

Ethics in marketing research

Several ethical issues may have to be addressed in questionnaire design. Of particular concern are the use of overly long questionnaires, asking sensitive questions and deliberately biasing the questionnaire. Participants volunteering their time should not be overburdened by soliciting too much information. An overly long questionnaire may vary in length or completion time depending upon variables such as the topic of the survey, the effort required, the number of open-ended questions, the frequency of use of complex scales and the method of administration. Sensitive questions deserve special attention. A real ethical dilemma exists for researchers investigat-

ing social problems such as poverty, drug use and sexually transmitted diseases such as AIDS, or conducting studies of highly personal products like feminine hygiene products or financial products.[70] When asking sensitive questions, researchers should attempt to minimise the discomfort of the participants. It should be made clear at the beginning of the questionnaire that participants are not obligated to answer any question that makes them uncomfortable.[71]

The researcher has the ethical responsibility of designing the questionnaire so as to obtain the required information in an unbiased manner. Deliberately biasing the questionnaire in a desired direction, e.g. by asking leading questions, cannot be condoned. In deciding the question structure, the most appropriate rather than the most convenient option should be adopted. Also, the questionnaire should be thoroughly pilot-tested before fieldwork

begins. There is also an ethical responsibility to use scales that do not bias findings in any particular direction. This is easy to do by biasing the wording of statements (Likert-type scales), the scale descriptors or other aspects of the scales.

Digital developments in marketing research

Software is widely used to design, create and administer questionnaires, for all survey modes. Although we describe the use of software for the most predominant mode, online surveys, the functions are essentially the same for questionnaires designed for other modes. Questionnaire design software systems helps to automatically perform a variety of tasks such as:

Personalisation. The participant's name and personal responses are automatically inserted into key questions.

Complex branching. Responses to specific questions can trigger routes to other specific questions and sets of responses.

Randomise response choices. The order of presentation of response options in multiple choice questions can be randomised for each participant to control for order bias.

Consistency checks. Inconsistent responses can be identified whilst the interview is in progress so that corrective action can be taken if needed.

Add new response categories as the survey progresses. If many participants give a particular response to an 'Other, please specify' category, that response will be automatically converted into a check-off category and added to the set of pre-specified response options.

In addition, questionnaire software systems have a variety of features that facilitate questionnaire design:

Question list. The user can select a variety of formats from a menu of question types such as open ended, multiple choice, scales, dichotomous questions, numerical. Moreover, one can use buttons, drop-down boxes (closed position or open position), check boxes, or open-ended scrolling text boxes.

Question libraries. The user can select predefined questions or save questions used often in the question library. For example, the question library may contain predefined questions for measuring

satisfaction, purchase intention and other commonly used constructs in marketing.

Questionnaire appearance. The user can select the background colours, graphics and flash applications used in a questionnaire from a range of available templates or create a customised template using the template manager.

Preview. The questionnaire can be previewed as it is developed to examine the content, interactivity, type of questions, branching and background design and make any changes that may be needed.

Publish. The designer can create the HTML questionnaire, post it to a unique web page, create a database to collect the date on the hosting server, and obtain a unique URL to which participants can be directed.

Notification. The designer can create, personalise, send and track email and social media based invitations to participate in the survey.

As each participant completes the survey, the data are transferred online to the data file on the host server. The data can be analysed at any time, even when the survey is running; thus results can be examined in real time.

These features have given questionnaire designers the facility to craft surveys that are far more cost and time efficient in comparison to approaches that depend upon hard copies of questionnaires. They have also enabled designers to create more personalised and appealing surveys for participants. These features, however, are not enough to create questionnaires that are engaging to participants. The following example illustrates how ideas from online game designs can and are being developed for online questionnaires. Such approaches need much pilot-testing and it is not suggested that a questionnaire should be designed to be packed with quizzes, games and flash technology. The intent of this example is to reflect on the experience that participants gain from completing a questionnaire.

Maximising online participant engagement through a game-way research design[72]

Social network sites, in spite of their high engagement levels, use games to further engagement among their participants. Extrapolating the idea to marketing research, ideas from gaming can improve engagement among online survey participants. Creating a fun element to an online survey could motivate participants to put effort into completing a survey without resentment. For example, instead of asking about demographics in a question format, the participant could be allowed to create their own avatar, they could create the person who they are in terms of age, gender, hair colour and dress. This could generate the information sought and at the same time be fun for the participants. Household details could be ascertained by allowing the participant to drag their household members using a cursor, and as they drag each household member on to the screen the participant could be questioned for the details of the member and the appearance of each household member could be customised accordingly. By this, the details of an entire household, its size, number of children, family type, could be generated in one go. Using advanced animation technologies, the participant could upload pictures or capture pictures using the webcam and cartoonise their pictures to use it in the profile of their avatar for the questionnaire. Extending the fun element to give it a sense of 'play' could also be developed. When the participant creates their profile, when they choose a particular option to change the avatar, for example change its dress, they could be allowed to shoot the option from among a set of swinging or bouncing (like a ball) options across the screen. The play element could be extended to other parts of the questionnaire, e.g. in indicating levels of satisfaction for brand X, participants could garland brand X, shower X with roses or applaud, and the negatives could be indicated by punching or throwing tomatoes. The play element could be developed by introducing small puzzles and games in between sections of the questionnaire in the right combination to keep the participant in a playful state of mind.

Summary

A questionnaire has three objectives. It must translate the information needed into a set of specific questions that the participants can and will answer. It must motivate participants to complete the interview. It must also minimise response error. The questionnaire should overcome the participants' inability to answer. Participants may be unable to answer if they are not informed, cannot remember, or cannot articulate the response. The unwillingness of participants to answer must also be overcome. Participants may be unwilling to answer if the question requires too much effort, is asked in a situation or context deemed inappropriate, does not serve a legitimate purpose, or solicits sensitive information. Questions can be unstructured (open-ended) or structured to a varying degree. Structured questions include multiple-choice and dichotomous questions and scales.

Determining the wording of each question involves defining the issue, using ordinary words, using unambiguous words and avoiding dual statements. Leading questions, implicit alternatives, implicit assumptions and generalisations and estimates should be avoided. Once the questions have been worded, the order in which they appear in the questionnaire must be decided. Several considerations should be given to opening questions, type of information, difficult questions, and the effect on subsequent questions. The questions should be arranged in an order that is logical from the participants' perspective.

Measurement is the assignment of numbers or other symbols to characteristics of objects according to set rules. The four primary scales of measurement are nominal, ordinal, interval and ratio. Of these, the nominal scale is the most basic in that the numbers are used only for classifying objects and the only characteristic possessed is description. In the ordinal scale, the numbers indicate the relative position of the objects but not the magnitude of difference between them. The interval scale permits a comparison of the differences between the objects. The highest level of measurement is represented by the ratio scale in which the zero point is fixed.

Scaling techniques can be classified as comparative or non-comparative. Comparative scaling involves a direct comparison of stimulus objects. Comparative scales include paired comparisons, rank order, constant sum and the Q-sort. In non-comparative scaling, each object is scaled independently of the other objects in the stimulus set. The resulting data are generally assumed to be interval or ratio scaled. Non-comparative rating scales can be either continuous or itemised. The itemised rating scales are further classified as Likert, semantic differential or Stapel scales. When using non comparative itemised rating scales, the researcher must decide on the number of scale categories, balanced versus unbalanced scales, an odd or even number of categories, forced versus non-forced choices, the nature and degree of verbal description, and the physical form or configuration.

Questionnaire and scale design should be adapted to specific cultural environments and all efforts made to avoid bias in terms of any one culture. Several ethical issues may have to be addressed in questionnaire design. Of particular concern are the uses of overly long questionnaires, asking sensitive questions and deliberately biasing the questionnaire. Digital developments are enabling questionnaire designers to create more personalised and appealing surveys for participants. By examining participants' online experiences and what engages their interest, questionnaire designers can use digital techniques to enhance their questionnaires and scales.

SNAP Learning Edition

The Questionnaire Design module of SNAP provides the necessary tools both to set up the individual questions in the questionnaire, and also to organise the layout and form of the questionnaire. Further details of how you can use SNAP to design your own survey are available on the website that accompanies this text (**www.pearsoned.co.uk/malhotra-euro**). The software handles all combinations of both structured and unstructured questions.

Any individual survey can involve a different survey mode; this might be online, it might be mobile or it might be a self-completion paper questionnaire. Each mode necessitates a different appearance and SNAP provides a library of predesigned formats for each one.

In addition, since any survey can be multi-mode and involve a combination of survey methods, a facility is available in SNAP to create a different edition of the questionnaire for each mode of interviewing. Behind the selection of various editions sits a database that has been created as the questionnaire has been set up. This database stores the structure of the questionnaire together with the layouts for each of the survey modes.

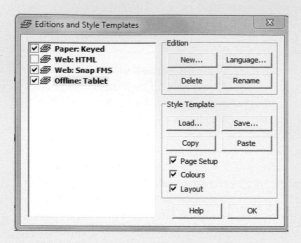

The wording of individual questions has been discussed in this chapter, and SNAP's library of questions can assist by providing a selection of differently phrased questions, many of which have been translated in other languages. These questions can then simply be dragged from the library onto the questionnaire.

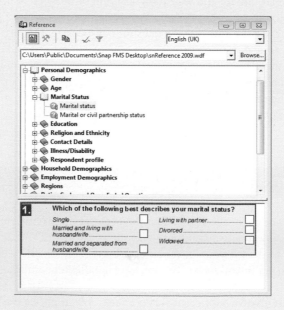

For questions that are to be designed from scratch, the first step is decide on a question type, whether it be open-ended free text, multiple choice, a grid or numeric data. The question types range from multiple choice to free text, together with automated settings for validation as the replies are collected.

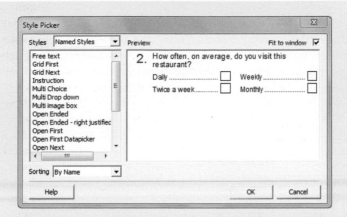

To ensure the flow of a questionnaire and to avoid unnecessary questions being asked, routing/skip patterns can be set up. The conditions can be complex, but essentially each question is only asked if the response to a previous question meets preset criteria.

Once questions have been entered, their sequence can be altered simply by moving them up or down. As the question moves, the numbering is altered, and any routing/skip patterns that have been setup, are automatically recalculated.

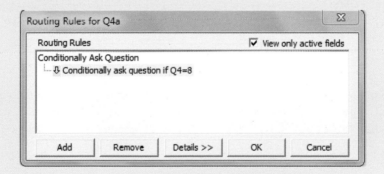

Question styles range from tick boxes to sliders, and include variation of font style and colours, together with the specific layout of each question.

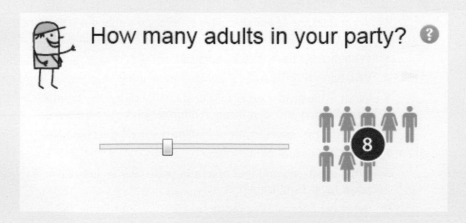

Once a questionnaire has been designed, the next step is the publication. This involves the setting of various parameters that control how a questionnaire appears, such as the shape, colour and text on buttons. Since not all buttons are required on all questionnaires, these can be switched off at will. Other parameters include margins, validation, progress bars, logos, accessibility, paradata collection, database links, automated alerts and languages.

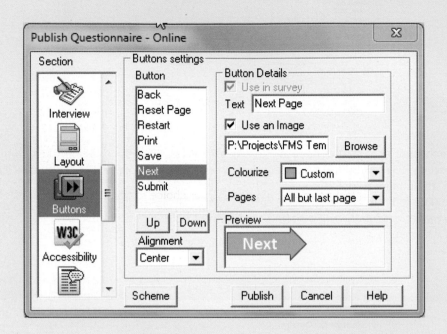

With a questionnaire fully pilot-tested and published, the next stages involve the collection of replies from participants. Chapter 8 covers the creation of a panel of participants for an online survey, and Chapter 9 covers the collection of completed replies for a range of survey methods, including online, mobile and paper.

Questions

1 What is the purpose of a questionnaire?

2 What does the researcher have to offer potential questionnaire participants? Why should this question be considered?

3 What are the advantages and disadvantages of unstructured questions?

4 What are the guidelines available for deciding on question wording?

5 What is the proper order for questions intended to obtain basic, classification and identification information?

6 Describe the issues involved in pilot-testing a questionnaire.

7 What is measurement?

8 What are the advantages of a ratio scale over an interval scale? Are these advantages significant?

9 What is a comparative rating scale?

10   What is a paired comparison? What are the advantages and disadvantages of paired comparison scaling?

11   Describe the semantic differential scale and the Likert scale. For what purposes are these scales used?

12   How does the nature and degree of verbal description affect the response to itemised rating scales?

Exercises

1   Visit the website of one of the online marketing research firms, e.g. **www.hostedsurvey.com**. Choose one of the sample surveys and critically analyse the questionnaire using the principles discussed in this chapter.

2   Heineken beer would like to conduct a survey of 18 to 25-year-old Europeans to determine characteristics of its corporate image. Design a full questionnaire using survey software such as SNAP. Administer this questionnaire in a mode of your choice to 25 fellow students. Write a short report based upon your experience of using the software, the findings you have generated and any limitations you see in the whole process (i.e. how would you do this differently if you were to repeat it?).

3   Develop a constant sum scale to determine preferences for restaurants. Administer this scale to a pilot sample of 20 students to determine their preferences for some of the popular restaurants in your town or city. Based on your pilot, evaluate the efficacy of the scale items you chose, and design new scale items that could be used for a full survey.

4   Design Likert scales to measure the usefulness of the Louis Vuitton Möet Hennessy website. Visit the site at **www.lvmh.com** and rate it on the scales that you have developed. After your site visit, were there any aspects of usefulness that you had not considered in devising your scales, what were they and why were they not apparent before you made your site visit?

5   In a small group discuss the following issues: 'Because questionnaire design is a craft, it is useless to follow a rigid set of guidelines. Rather, the process should be left entirely to the creativity and ingenuity of the researcher'. 'Asking classification questions at the start of a questionnaire only upsets the sensibilities of older participants; young participants are not concerned about where these questions are asked.'

Notes

1. Delattre, E. and Colovic, A., 'Memory and perception of brand mentions and placement of brands in songs', *International Journal of Advertising*, 28 (5) (2009) 807–42.

2. Livin, J., 'Improving response rates in web surveys with default setting: The effects of default on web survey participation and permission', *International Journal of Market Research*, 53 (1) (2011) 75–94; Balabanis, G.,

Mitchell, V.-W. and Heinonen-Mavrovouniotis, S., 'SMS-based surveys: Strategies to improve participation', *International Journal of Advertising*, 26 (3) (2007) 369–85.

3. The founding reference to this subject is Payne, S.L., *The Art of Asking Questions* (Princeton, NJ: Princeton University Press, 1951). See also Lietz, P., 'Research into questionnaire design: A summary of the literature',

International Journal of Market Research, 52 (2) (2010) 249–72; Schrage, M., 'Survey says', *Adweek Magazines' Technology Marketing*, 22 (1) (January 2002) 11; Gillham, B., *Developing a questionnaire* (New York: Continuum International Publishing Group, 2000).

4. These guidelines are drawn from several books on questionnaire design: Dillman, D.A., Smyth, J.D. and Melani, L., *Internet, Mail, and Mixed-Mode Surveys: The Tailored Design Method*, 3rd edn, Wiley (2008); Bradburn, N.M., Sudman, S. and Wansink, B., *Asking Questions: The Definitive Guide to Questionnaire Design – For Market Research, Political Polls, and Social and Health Questionnaires* (Jossey-Bass, 2004); Gillham, B., *Developing a questionnaire* (New York: Continuum International, 2000); Peterson, R.A., *Constructing Effective Questionnaires* (Thousand Oaks, CA: Sage, 2000); Schuman, H. and Presser, S., *Questions and Answers in Attitude Surveys* (Thousand Oaks, CA: Sage, 1996); Fink, A., *How to Ask Survey Questions* (Thousand Oaks, CA: Sage, 1995); Sudman, S. and Bradburn, N.M., *Asking Questions* (San Francisco: Jossey-Bass, 1983).

5. Cierpicki, S., Davis, C., Eddy, C., Lorch, J., Phillips, K., Poynter, R., York, S. and Zuo, B., 'From clipboards to online research communities: A cross-cultural review of respondents' perceptions', ESOMAR, *Congress Odyssey*, Athens (Sept. 2010).

6. Biering, P., Becker, H., Calvin, A. and Grobe, S.J., 'Casting light on the concept of patient satisfaction by studying the construct validity and the sensitivity of a questionnaire', *International Journal of Health Care Quality Assurance*, 19 (3) (2006), 246–58; Clark, B.H., 'Bad examples', *Marketing Management*, 12 (2) (2003), 34–38; Bordeaux, D.B., 'Interviewing – part II: Getting the most out of interview questions', *Motor Age*, 121 (2) (February 2002), 38–40.

7. Bressette, K., 'Deeply understanding the mind to unmask the inner human', ESOMAR, *Qualitative Research*, Marrakech (Nov. 2009); Reynolds, T.J., 'Methodological and strategy development implications of decision segmentation', *Journal of Advertising Research*, 46 (4) (Dec. 2006), 445–61; Healey, B., Macpherson, T. and Kuijten, B., 'An empirical evaluation of three web survey design principles', *Marketing Bulletin*, 16 (May 2005), 1–9; Hess, J., 'The effects of person-level versus household-level questionnaire design on survey estimates and data quality', *Public Opinion Quarterly*, 65 (4) (Winter 2001), 574–84.

8. Alioto, M.F. and Parrett, M., 'The use of "respondent-based intelligent" surveys in cross-national research', ESOMAR, *Latin American Conference*, Sao Paulo, (May 2002), 157–220; Knauper, B., 'Filter questions and question interpretation: Presuppositions at work', *Public Opinion Quarterly*, 62 (1) (Spring 1998), 70–78; Stapel, J., 'Observations: a brief observation about likeability and interestingness of advertising', *Journal of Advertising Research*, 34 (2) (March/April 1994).

9. Braunsberger, K., Gates, R. and Ortinau, D.J., 'Prospective respondent integrity behaviour in replying to direct mail questionnaires: A contributor in overestimating non-response rates', *Journal of Business Research*, 58 (3) (March 2005), 260–67; Lee, E., Hu, M.Y. and Toh, R.S., 'Are consumer survey results distorted? Systematic

impact of behavioural frequency and duration on survey response errors', *Journal of Marketing Research*, 37 (1) (February 2000), 125–133.

10. Wilson, E.J. and Woodside, A.G., 'Respondent inaccuracy', *Journal of Advertising Research*, 42 (5) (Sept./Oct. 2002), 7–18; Gaskell, G.D., 'Telescoping of landmark events: implications for survey research', *Public Opinion Quarterly*, 64 (1) (Spring 2000), 77–89; Menon, G., Raghubir, P. and Schwarz, N., 'Behavioural frequency judgments: An accessibility-diagnosticity framework', *Journal of Consumer Research*, 22 (2) (September 1995), 212–28; Cook, W.A., 'Telescoping and memory's other tricks', *Journal of Advertising Research* (February–March 1987), 5–8.

11. Goodrich, K., 'What's up? Exploring upper and lower visual field advertising effects', *Journal of Advertising Research*, 50 (1) (2010), 91–106.

12. Bednall, D.H.B., Adam, S. and Plocinski, K., 'Ethics in practice: Using compliance techniques to boost telephone response rates', *International Journal of Market Research*, 52 (2) (2010), 155–68.

13. Nancarrow, C. and Brace, I., 'Let's get ethical: Dealing with socially desirable responding online', Market Research Society, *Annual Conference* (2008); Tourangeau, R. and Yan, T., 'Sensitive questions in surveys', *Psychological Bulletin*, 133 (5) (Sept. 2007), 859–83; France, M., 'Why privacy notices are a sham', *Business Week* (18 June 2001), 82.

14. Manfreda, K.L., Bosnjak, M., Berzelak, J., Haas, I. and Vehovar, V., 'Web surveys versus other survey modes: A meta analysis comparing response rates', *International Journal of Market Research*, 50 (1) (2008), 79–104; Hanrahan, P., 'Mine your own business', *Target Marketing* (February 2000), 32; Tourangeau, R. and Smith, T.W., 'Asking sensitive questions: The impact of data collection mode, question format, and question context', *Public Opinion Quarterly*, 60 (20) (Summer 1996), 275–304.

15. Maehle, N. and Supphellen, M., 'In search of the sources of brand personality', *International Journal of Market Research*, 53 (1) (2011), 95–114; Peterson, R.A., 'Asking the age question: A research note', *Public Opinion Quarterly* (Spring 1984), 379–83.

16. Millican, P. and Kolb, C., 'Connecting with Elizabeth: Using artificial intelligence as a data collection aid', Market Research Society, *Annual Conference* (2006); Patten, M.L., *Questionnaire research: A practical guide* (Los Angeles: Pyrczak, 2001); Newman, L.M., 'That's a good question', *American Demographics* (Marketing Tools) (June 1995), 10–13.

17. Esuli, A. and Sebastiani, F., 'Machines that learn how to code open-ended survey data', *International Journal of Market Research*, 52 (6) (2010), 775–800; Popping, R., *Computer-assisted text analysis* (Thousand Oaks, CA: Sage, 2000); Luyens, S., 'Coding verbatims by computers', *Marketing Research: A Magazine of Management and Applications*, 7 (2) (Spring 1995), 20–25.

18. Verhaeghe, A., De Ruyck, T. and Schillewaert, N., 'Join the research – participant-led open-ended questions', *International Journal of Market Research*, 50 (5) (2008), 655–78; Pothas, A.-M., 'Customer satisfaction: Keeping tabs on the issues that matter', *Total Quality Management*, 12 (1) (January 2001), 83.

19. Bellman, S., Schweda, A. and Varan, D., 'The importance of social motives for watching and interacting with digital television', *International Journal of Market Research*, 52 (1) (2010), 67–87.

20. DeMoranville, C.W. and Bienstock, C.C., 'Question order effects in measuring service quality', *International Journal of Research in Marketing*, 20 (3) (2003), 457–66; Singer, E., 'Experiments with incentives in telephone surveys', *Public Opinion Quarterly*, 64 (2) (Summer 2000), 171–88; Schuman, H. and Presser, S., *Questions and Answers in Attitude Surveys* (Thousand Oaks, CA: Sage, 1996).

21. Dolnicar, S., Grün, B. and Leisch, F., 'Quick, simple and reliable: Forced binary survey questions', *International Journal of Market Research*, 53 (2) (2011), 233–54; Blumenschein, K., 'Hypothetical versus real willingness to pay in the health care sector: Results from a field experiment', *Journal of Health Economics*, 20 (3) (May 2001), 441; Herriges, J.A. and Shogren, J.F., 'Starting point bias in dichotomous choice valuation with follow-up questioning', *Journal of Environmental Economics and Management*, 30 (1) (January 1996), 112–31.

22. Albaum, G., Roster, C., Yu, J.H. and Rogers, R.D., 'Simple rating scale formats: Exploring extreme response', *International Journal of Market Research*, 49 (5) (2007); Vriends, M., Wedel, M. and Sandor, Z., 'Split-questionnaire design', *Marketing Research*, 13 (2) (2001), 14–19; Conrad, F.G., 'Clarifying question meaning in a household telephone survey', *Public Opinion Quarterly*, 64 (1) (Spring 2000), 1–27; McBurnett, M., 'Wording of questions affects responses to gun control issue', *Marketing News*, 31 (1) (6 January 1997), 12.

23. Cape, P., Lorch, J. and Piekarski, L., 'A tale of two questionnaires', ESOMAR, *Panel Research*, Orlando (Oct. 2007); Colombo, R., 'A model for diagnosing and reducing non-response bias', *Journal of Advertising Research*, 40 (1/2) (January/April 2000), 85–93; Etter, J.F. and Perneger, T.V., 'Analysis of non-response bias in a mailed health survey', *Journal of Clinical Epidemiology*, 50 (10) (25 October 1997), 1123–28; Omura, G.S., 'Correlates of item non-response', *Journal of the Market Research Society* (October 1983), 321–30.

24. Manfreda, K.L., Bosnjak, M., Berzelak, J., Haas, I. and Vehovar, V., 'Web surveys versus other survey modes. A meta-analysis comparing response rates', *International Journal of Market Research*, 50 (1) (2008), 79–104; Bollinger, C.R., 'Estimation with response error and non-response: Food-stamp participation in the SIPP', *Journal of Business and Economic Statistics*, 19 (2) (April 2001), 129–141.

25. Gillham, B., *Developing a questionnaire* (New York: Continuum International, 2000); Saltz, L.C., 'How to get your news release published', *Journal of Accountancy* 182 (5) (November 1996), 89–91.

26. Reid, J., Morden, M. and Reid, A., 'Maximising respondent engagement: The use of rich media', ESOMAR, *Annual Congress*, Berlin, (Sept. 2007); Couper, M.P., 'Web surveys: A review of issues and approaches,' *Public Opinion Quarterly*, 64 (4) (Winter 2000), 464–94; Edmondson, B., 'How to spot a bogus poll', *American Demographics*, 8 (10) (October 1996), 10–15; O'Brien, J., 'How do market researchers ask questions?' *Journal of the Market Research Society*, 26 (April 1984), 93–107.

27. Cohen, J., 'Reading and writing: The forgotten 12 million', *Market Research Society*, Annual Conference (2006).

28. Snowden, D. and Stienstra, J., 'Stop asking questions: Understanding how consumers make sense of it all', ESOMAR, *Annual Congress*, Berlin (Sept. 2007); Chisnall, P.M., 'Marketing research: State of the art perspectives', *International Journal of Marketing Research*, 44 (1) (First Quarter 2002), 122–5; Abramson, P.R. and Ostrom, C.W., 'Question wording and partisanship', *Public Opinion Quarterly*, 58 (1) (Spring 1994), 21–18.

29. Brinkmann, S., 'Could interviews be epistemic? An alternative to qualitative opinion polling', *Qualitative Inquiry*, 13 (8) (Dec. 2007), 1116–38; Gillham, B., *Developing a questionnaire* (New York: Continuum International, 2000); Adamek, R.J., 'Public opinion and Roe v. Wade: Measurement difficulties', *Public Opinion Quarterly*, 58 (3) (Fall 1994), 409–18.

30. Chen, S., Poland, B. and Skinner, H.A., 'Youth voices: Evaluation of participatory action research', *Canadian Journal of Program Evaluation*, 22 (1) (March 2007), 125; Ouyand, M, 'Estimating marketing persistence on sales of consumer durables in China', *Journal of Business Research*, 55 (4) (April 2002), 337; Jacoby, J. and Szybillo, G.J., 'Consumer research in FTC versus Kraft (1991): A case of heads we win, tails you lose?' *Journal of Public Policy and Marketing*, 14 (1) (Spring 1995), 1–14.

31. Phillips, S. and Hamburger, S., 'A quest for answers: The campaign against Why', ESOMAR, *Annual Congress*, Berlin (Sept. 2007); Galssman, N.A. and Glassman, M., 'Screening questions', *Marketing Research*, 10 (3), (1998), 25–31; Schuman, H. and Presser, S., *Questions and Answers in Attitude Surveys* (Thousand Oaks, CA: Sage, 1996).

32. Rating a brand on specific attributes early in a survey may affect responses to a later overall brand evaluation. For example, see Gendall, P. and Hoek, J., 'David takes on Goliath: An overview of survey evidence in a trademark dispute', *International Journal of Market Research*, 45 (1) (2003), 99–122; Bartels, L.M., 'Question order and declining faith in elections', *Public Opinion Quarterly*, 66 (1) (Spring 2002), 67–79. See also McAllister, I, and Wattenberg, M.P., 'Measuring levels of party identification: Does question order matter?' *Public Opinion Quarterly*, 59 (2) (Summer 1995), 259–68.

33. Watson, P.D., 'Adolescents' perceptions of a health survey using multimedia computer-assisted self-administered interview', *Australian & New Zealand Journal of Public Health*, 25 (6) (December 2001), 520; Bethlehem, J., 'The routing structure of questionnaires', *International Journal of Market Research*, 42 (1) (2000); Willits, F.K. and Ke, B., 'Part-whole question order effects: Views of rurality', *Public Opinion Quarterly*, 59 (3) (Fall 1995), 392–403.

34. Puleston, J. and Sleep, D., 'Measuring the value of respondent engagement – innovative techniques to improve panel quality', ESOMAR, *Panel Research*, Dublin (Oct. 2008).

35. Schlegelmilch, B.B., Diamantopoulos, A. and Reynolds, N., 'Pre-testing in questionnaire design: A review of

the literature and suggestions for further research', *International Journal of Market Research*, 35 (2) (1993), 171–82.

36. Feldhaeuser, H. and Smales, H., 'Flying with the Simpsons: An award winning research paper that helped Air New Zealand reinvent the long haul air travel', ESOMAR, *Asia Pacific*, Melbourne (2011).

37. Blair, J. and Srinath, K.P., 'A note on sample size for behaviour coding pretests', *Field Methods*, 85 (11) (Feb. 2008), 20; Conrad, F. G., 'Clarifying question meaning in a household telephone survey', *Public Opinion Quarterly*, 64 (1) (Spring 2000), 1–27; Diamantopoulos, A., Schlegelmilch, B.B. and Reynolds, N., 'Pre-testing in questionnaire design: The impact of participant characteristics on error detection', *Journal of the Market Research Society*, 36 (Oct. 1994), 295–314.

38. Meir, D., 'The seven stages of effective survey research', *American Marketing Association* (2002); Gillham, B., *Developing a questionnaire* (New York: Continuum International, 2000).

39. Bortholomew, D.J., *Measurement* (Thousand Oaks, CA: Sage, 2006); Wyner, G.A., 'The right side of metrics', *Marketing Management*, 13 (1) (2004) 8–9; Newell, S. J., 'The development of a scale to measure perceived corporate credibility', *Journal of Business Research* (June 2001), 235; Gofton, K., 'If it moves measure it', *Marketing* (Marketing Technique Supplement) (4 September 1997), 17; Nunnally, J.C., *Psychometric Theory*, 2nd edn (New York: McGraw-Hill, 1978), 3.

40. Schuster, C. and Smith, D.A., 'Estimating with a latent class model the reliability of nominal judgments upon which two raters agree', *Educational and Psychological Measurement*, 66 (5) (Oct. 2006), 739; Stevens, S., 'Mathematics, measurement and psychophysics', in Stevens, S. (ed.) *Handbook of Experimental Psychology* (New York: Wiley, 1951).

41. Giovagnoli, A., Marzialetti, J. and Wynn, H.P., 'A new approach to inter-rater agreement through stochastic orderings: The discrete case', *Metrika*, 67 (3) (April 2008), 349–70; Kurpius, S.E., *Testing and measurement*, (Thousand Oaks, CA: Sage, 2002); Moshkovich, H.M., 'Ordinal judgments in multiattribute decision analysis,' *European Journal of Operational Research*, 137 (3) (16 March 2002), 625; Cook, W.D., Kress, M. and Seiford, L.M., 'On the use of ordinal data in data envelopment analysis', *Journal of the Operational Research Society*, 44 (2) (February 1993), 133–140; Barnard, N.R. and Ehrenberg, A.S.C., 'Robust measures of consumer brand beliefs', *Journal of Marketing Research*, 27 (November 1990), 477–84; Perreault, W.D. Jr and Young, F.W., 'Alternating least squares optimal scaling: Analysis of non-metric data in marketing research', *Journal of Marketing Research*, 17 (Feb. 1980), 1–13.

42. Halme, M., 'Dealing with interval scale data in data envelopment analysis', *European Journal of Operational Research*, 137 (1) (February 16, 2002), 22; Lynn, M. and Harriss, J., 'The desire for unique consumer products: A new individual difference scale', *Psychology and Marketing*, 14 (6) (Sept. 1997), 601–16.

43. For a discussion of these scales, refer to Miller, D.C., and Salkind, N.J., *Handbook of Research Design and Social Measurement*, 6th edn (Thousand Oaks, CA: Sage, 2002); Taiwo, A., 'Overall evaluation rating scales: An assessment', *International Journal of Market Research* (Summer 2000), 301–311; Coombs, C.H., 'Theory and methods of social measurement', in Festinger, L. and Katz, D. (eds) *Research Methods in the Behavioral Sciences* (New York: Holt, Rinehart & Winston, 1953).

44. Tellis, G.J., 'Generalizations about advertising effectiveness in markets', *Journal of Advertising Research*, 49 (2) (June 2009), 240–45.

45. There is, however, some controversy regarding this issue. See Louviere, J.J. and Islam, T., 'A comparison of importance weights and willingness-to-pay measures derived from choice based conjoint, constant sum scales and best-worst scaling', *Journal of Business Research*, 61 (9) (Sept. 2008), 903–11; Campbell, D. T. and Russo, M.J., *Social Measurement* (Thousand Oaks, CA: Sage, 2001); Amoo, T., 'Do the numeric values influence subjects' responses to rating scales?' *Journal of International Marketing and Marketing Research* (February 2001), 41.

46. Tavares, S., Cardoso, M. and Dias, J.G., 'The heterogeneous best–worst choice method in market research', *International Journal of Market Research*, 52 (4) (2010), 533–46.

47. It is not necessary to evaluate all possible pairs of objects, however. Procedures such as cyclic designs can significantly reduce the number of pairs evaluated. A treatment of such procedures may be found in Bemmaor, A.C. and Wagner, U., 'A multiple-item model of paired comparisons: Separating chance from latent performance', *Journal of Marketing Research*, 37 (4) (November 2000), 514–24; Malhotra, N.K., Jain, A.K. and Pinson, C., 'The robustness of MDS configurations in the case of incomplete data', *Journal of Marketing Research*, 25 (February 1988), 95–102.

48. For an advanced application involving paired comparison data, see Bemmaor, A.C. and Wagner, U., 'A multiple-item model of paired comparisons: Separating chance from latent performance', *Journal of Marketing Research*, 37 (4) (November 2000), 514 –24.

49. Yvert-Blanchet, N. and Fournier, A., 'Likeability, liking is not enough', ESOMAR, *Fragrance Conference*, Paris (Nov. 2007).

50. Bottomley, P.A., 'Testing the reliability of weight elicitation methods: Direct rating versus point allocation,' *Journal of Marketing Research*, 37 (4) (November 2000), 508–13; Herman, M.W. and Koczkodaj, W.W., 'A Monte Carlo study of pairwise comparison', *Information Processing Letters*, 57 (1) (15 January 1996), 25–29.

51. Chrzan, K. and Golovashkina, N., 'An empirical test of six stated importance measures', *International Journal of Market Research*, 48 (6) (2006), 717–40.

52. Siciliano, T., 'Magnitude estimation', *Quirk's Marketing Research Review* (November 1999); Noel, N.M. and Nessim, H., 'Benchmarking consumer perceptions of product quality with price: An exploration', *Psychology & Marketing*, 13 (6) (September 1996), 591–604; Steenkamp, J.-B. and Wittink, D.R., 'The metric quality of full-profile judgments and the number of attribute levels effect in conjoint analysis', *International Journal of Research in Marketing*, 11 (3) (June 1994), 275–86.

53. Swain, S.D., Weathers, D. and Niedrich, R.W., 'Assessing three sources of misresponse to reversed Likert items', *Journal of Marketing Research*, 45 (1) (Feb. 2008), 116–31;

Bartholomew, D.J., *Measurement* (Thousand Oaks, CA: Sage 2006); Amoo, T. and Friedman, H.H., 'Overall evaluation rating scales: An assessment,' *International Journal of Market Research*, 42 (3) (Summer 2000), 301–310; Albaum, G., 'The Likert scale revisited – an alternative version', *Journal of the Market Research Society*, 39 (2) (April 1997), 331–48; Brody, C.J. and Dietz, J., 'On the dimensionality of 2-question format Likert attitude scales', *Social Science Research*, 26 (2) (June 1997), 197–204; Likert, R., 'A technique for the measurement of attitudes', *Archives of Psychology*, 140 (1932).

54. However, when the scale is multidimensional, each dimension should be summed separately. See Braunsberger, K., Buckler, R.B. and Ortinau, D.J., 'Categorizing cognitive responses: An empirical investigation of the cognitive intent congruency between independent raters and original subject raters', *Journal of the Academy of Marketing Science*, 33 (4) (Sept. 2005), 620–32; Stanton, J.M., 'Issues and strategies for reducing the length of self-report scales,' *Personnel Psychology*, 55 (1) (Spring 2002), 167–94; Aaker, J.L., 'Dimensions of brand personality', *Journal of Marketing Research*, 34 (August 1997), 347–56.

55. Herche, J. and Engelland, B., 'Reversed-polarity items and scale unidimensionality', *Journal of the Academy of Marketing Science*, 24 (4) (Fall 1996), 366–74.

56. Sethi, R., Smith, D.C. and Whan Park, C., 'Cross-functional product development teams, creativity and the innovativeness of new consumer products,' *Journal of Marketing Research*, 38 (1) (Feb. 2001), 73–85; Chandler, T.A. and Spies, C.J., 'Semantic differential comparisons of attributions and dimensions among participants from 7 nations', *Psychological Reports*, 79 (3 pt 1) (December 1996), 747–58.

57. Kurpius, S.E., *Testing and measurement* (Thousand Oaks, CA: Sage, 2002); Miller, D.C. and Salkind, N.J., *Handbook of research design and social measurement*, 6th edn (Thousand Oaks, CA: Sage, 2002); Bearden, W.O. and Netemeyer, R.G., *Handbook of Marketing Scales: Multi-item measures for marketing and consumer behaviour research* (Thousand Oaks, CA: Sage, 1999), 456–464.

58. There is little difference in the results based on whether the data are ordinal or interval; however, see Nishisato, S., *Measurement and multivariate analysis* (New York: Springer-Verlag, 2002); Gaiton, J., 'Measurement scales and statistics: Resurgence of an old misconception', *Psychological Bulletin*, 87 (1980), 567.

59. Swenson, M.,Yu, J.H. and Albaum, G., 'Is a central tendency error inherent in the use of semantic differential scales in different cultures?' *International Journal of Market Research*, 45 (2) (2003), 213–28; Ofir, C., 'In search of negative customer feedback: The effect of expecting to evaluate on satisfaction evaluations', *Journal of Marketing Research* (May 2001), 170–82; Reisenwitz, T.H. and Wimbush, G.J. Jr, 'Over-the-counter pharmaceuticals: Exploratory research of consumer preferences toward solid oral dosage forms', *Health Marketing Quarterly*, 13 (4) (1996), 47–61; Malhotra, S., Van Auken, S. and Lonial, S.C., 'Adjective profiles in television copy testing', *Journal of Advertising Research* (August 1981), 21–25.

60. Brady, M.K., 'Performance only measurement of service quality: A replication and extension', *Journal of Business Research*, 55 (1) (January 2002), 17; Stapel, J., 'About 35 years of market research in the Netherlands', *Markonderzock Kwartaalschrift*, 2 (1969), 3–7.

61. Dawes, J., 'Do data characteristics change according to the number of scale points used?' *International Journal of Market Research*, 50 (1) (2008), 61–77; Anderson, E.W., 'Foundations of the American customer satisfaction index', *Total Quality Management*, 11 (7) (Sept. 2000), 5869–82; Coleman, A.M., Norris, C.E. and Peterson, C.C., 'Comparing rating scales of different lengths – equivalence of scores from 5-point and 7-point scales', *Psychological Reports*, 80 (2) (April 1997), 355–62; Viswanathan, M., Bergen, M. and Childers, T., 'Does a single response category in a scale completely capture a response?' *Psychology and Marketing*, 13 (5) (August 1996), 457–79; Cox, E.P. III, 'The optimal number of response alternatives for a scale: A review', *Journal of Marketing Research*, 17 (November 1980), 407–22.

62. Dawes, J., 'Do data characteristics change according to the number of scale points used? An experiment using 5-point, 7-point and 1-point scales', *International Journal of Market Research*, 50 (1) (2008), 61–104; Coelho, P.S. and Esteves, S.P., 'The choice between a five-point and a ten-point scale in the framework of customer satisfaction measurement', *International Journal of Market Research*, 49 (3) (2007), 313–39; Dodge, Y., 'On asymmetric properties of the correlation coefficient in the regression setting', *The American Statistician*, 55 (1) (February 2001), 51–54; Alwin, D.F., 'Feeling thermometers versus 7-point scales – which are better?' *Sociological Methods and Research*, 25 (3) (February 1997), 318–40.

63. Joshi, A., Tamang, S. and Vashisthaz, H., 'You can't judge a book by its cover! A way to tackle the severe acquiescence bias among Arab respondents', ESOMAR, *Annual Congress*, Montreal (Sept. 2008); Jones, B.S., 'Modeling direction and intensity in semantically balanced ordinal scales: An assessment of Congressional incumbent approval,' *American Journal of Political Science*, 44 (1) (January 2000), 174.

64. Morrel-Samuels, P., 'Getting the truth into workplace surveys,' *Harvard Business Review*, 80 (2) (February 2002), 111; Spagna, G.J., 'Questionnaires: Which approach do you use?' *Journal of Advertising Research* (February–March 1984), 67–70.

65. Kulas, J., Stachowski, A., and Haynes B., 'Middle response functioning in Likert responses to personality items', *Journal of Business and Psychology*, 22 (3) (March 2008), 251–59; McColl-Kennedy, J., 'Measuring customer satisfaction: Why, what and how', *Total Quality Management*, 11 (7) (Sept. 2000), 5883–96.

66. Kruger, J. and Vargas, P., 'Consumer confusion of percent differences', *Journal of Consumer Psychology*, 18 (1) (Jan. 2008), 49–61; Amoo, T., 'Do numeric values influence subjects' responses to rating scales?' *Journal of International Marketing and Market Research* (Feb. 2001), 41; Gannon, K.M. and Ostrom, T.M., 'How meaning is given to rating scales – the effects of response language on category activation', *Journal of Experimental Social Psychology*, 32 (4) (July 1996), 337–60.

67. For an example of a multi-item scale, see Bruner II, G.C. and Kumar, A., 'Attitude toward location based

advertising', *The Journal of Interactive Advertising*, 7 (2) (Spring 2007); Rossiter, J.R., 'The C-OAR-SE procedure for scale development in marketing', *International Journal of Research in Marketing*, 19 (4) (2002), 305–35; Brown, T., 'The customer orientation of service workers: Personality trait effects on self and supervisor-performance ratings', *Journal of Marketing Research*, 39 (1) (February 2002), 110–19.

68. For example, see Kidwell, B., Hardesty, D.M. and Childers, T.L., 'Consumer emotional intelligence: Conceptualisation, measurement and the prediction of consumer decision making', *Journal of Consumer Research*, 35 (1) (June 2008), 154–66; Delgado-Ballester, E., Munuera-Alemán, J.L. and Yagüe-Guillén, M.J., 'Development and validation of brand trust scale', *International Journal of Market Research*, 45 (1) (2003), 35–53; Flynn, L. R. and Pearcy, D., 'Four subtle sins in scale development: Some suggestions for strengthening the current paradigm', *International Journal of Market Research*, 43 (4) (Fourth Quarter 2001), 409–23; King, M.F., 'Social desirability bias: A neglected aspect of validity testing', *Psychology and Marketing*, 17 (2) (Feb. 2000), 79.

69. Van Auken, S., Barry, T.E. and Bagozzi, R.P., 'A cross-country contruct validation of cognitive age', *Journal of the Academy of Marketing Science*, 34 (3) (Summer 2006), 439–55; Page Fisk, A., 'Using individualism and collectivism to compare cultures – a critique of the validity and measurement of the constructs: Comment on Oyserman', *Psychological Bulletin*, 128 (1) (January 2002), 78.

70. Manceau, D. and Tissier-Desbordes , E., 'Are sex and death taboos in advertising? An analysis of taboos in advertising and a survey of French consumer perceptions', *International Journal of Advertising*, 25 (1) (2006), 9–33; Laczniak, G.R. and Murphy, P.E., *Ethical Marketing Decisions: The Higher Road* (Needham Heights, MA: Allyn and Bacon, 1993).

71. Birenbaum-Carmeli, D., Carmeli, Y. and Gornostayev, S., 'Researching sensitive fields: Some lessons from a study of sperm donors in Israel', *International Journal of Sociology and Social Policy*, 28 (11/12) (2008), 425–39; Morris, M.H., Marks, A.S., Allen, J.A. and Peery, N.S., 'Modeling ethical attitudes and behaviours under conditions of environmental turbulence – case of South Africa', *Journal of Business Ethics*, 15 (10) (October 1996), 1119–30.

72. Swahar, G. and Swahar, J., 'Designing innovation: Maximizing online respondent engagement through a game-way research design', ESOMAR, *Innovate*, Barcelona (Nov. 2010).

8

Sampling: design and procedures

Stage 1

Problem definition

Stage 2

Research approach developed

Stage 3

Research design developed

Stage 4

Fieldwork or data collection

Stage 5

Data integrity and analysis

Stage 6

Report preparation and presentation

There is no hope of making scientific statements about a population based on the knowledge obtained from a sample, unless we are circumspect in choosing a sampling method.

Objectives

After reading this chapter, you should be able to:

1 differentiate a sample from a census and identify the conditions that favour the use of a sample versus a census;

2 discuss the sampling design process: definition of the target population, determination of the sampling frame, selection of sampling technique(s), determination of sample size, execution of the sampling process and validating the sample;

3 classify sampling techniques as non-probability and probability sampling techniques;

4 describe the non-probability sampling techniques of convenience, judgemental, quota and snowball sampling;

5 describe the probability sampling techniques of simple random, systematic, stratified and cluster sampling;

6 identify the conditions that favour the use of non-probability sampling versus probability sampling;

7 understand the sampling design process and the use of sampling techniques in international marketing research;

8 identify the ethical issues related to the sampling design process and the use of appropriate sampling techniques;

9 appreciate how digital developments are shaping the manner in which sampling may be designed and executed.

Overview

Sampling is a key component of any research design. Sampling design involves several basic questions:

1 Should a sample be taken?

2 If so, what process should be followed?

3 What kind of sample should be taken?

4 How large should it be?

5 What can be done to control and adjust for non-response errors?

This chapter introduces the fundamental concepts of sampling and the qualitative considerations necessary to answer these questions. We address the question of whether or not to sample and describe the steps involved in sampling, including the use, benefits and limitations of the access panel in sample design. We present the nature of non-probability and probability sampling and related sampling techniques. We discuss the use of sampling techniques in international marketing research and identify the relevant ethical issues. We conclude by examining digital developments that are enabling researchers to design and execute well focused samples, especially in the context of conducting online surveys.

We begin with an example that illustrates a study that used both a census and a simple random sample in measuring the attitudes of physicians and their patients.

Sampling cosmetic surgery consumers[1]

The German Federal Ministry of Food, Agriculture and Consumer Protection funded a study of suppliers and customers of cosmetic surgery. Their study examined market supply, the quality of surgery results and any needs for consumer-oriented political action. The low prevalence of cosmetic surgery made it clear that a multi-mode approach was needed to engage sufficient qualified participants. As the intention of the study was not only to analyse demand but supply as well, the size of the market was estimated by a survey of all physicians and institutions offering cosmetic surgery, i.e. a census. For that purpose, a sampling frame of all suppliers was built. Following that, a questionnaire was sent to 1,712 physicians and institutions covering the number, type, costs and risks of operations as well as age and gender of their patients. Due to mistrust of the physicians, who expected negative consequences by the tax authorities, the response rate was lower than usual (8.8%). In examining demand issues, customer data were collected by a survey of 620 patients from all over Germany who had undergone cosmetic surgery. These patients were selected on a simple random sample basis from the database or sampling frame they compiled. The mix of data collection modes included face-to-face as well as telephone, online and postal surveys.

The random sample, as used in this example, may be seen as an ideal that researchers would prefer to administer. However, researchers have long recognised that they have to compromise between what may be seen as the scientific ideal of sampling and the administrative constraints in achieving that ideal. This balance will be addressed throughout this section. Before we discuss these issues in detail, we address the question of whether the researcher should sample or take a census.

Sample or census

Population

The aggregate of all the elements, sharing some common set of characteristics, that comprise the universe for the purpose of the marketing research problem.

Census

A complete enumeration of the elements of a population or study objects.

Sample

A subgroup of the elements of the population selected for participation in the study.

The objective of most marketing research projects is to obtain information about the characteristics or parameters of a **population**. A population is the aggregate of all the elements that share some common set of characteristics and that comprise the universe for the purpose of the marketing research problem. The population parameters are typically numbers, such as the proportion of consumers who are loyal to a particular fashion brand. Information about population parameters may be obtained by taking a **census** or a **sample**. A census involves a complete enumeration of the elements of a population. The population parameters can be calculated directly in a straightforward way after the census is enumerated. A sample, on the other hand, is a subgroup of the population selected for participation in the study. Sample characteristics, called statistics, are then used to make inferences about the population parameters. The inferences that link sample characteristics and population parameters are estimation procedures and tests of hypotheses.

Table 8.1 summarises the conditions favouring the use of a sample versus a census. Budget and time limits are obvious constraints favouring the use of a sample. A census is both costly and time consuming to conduct. A census is unrealistic if the population is large, as it is for most consumer products. In the case of many industrial products, however, the population is small, making a census feasible as well as desirable. For example, in investigating the use of certain machine tools by Italian car manufacturers, a census would be preferred to a sample. Another reason for preferring a census in this case is that variance in the characteristic of interest is large. For example, machine tool usage of Fiat may vary greatly from the usage of Ferrari. Small population sizes as well as high variance in the characteristic to be measured favour a census.

Table 8.1	Sample versus census		
		Conditions favouring the use of	
Factors		**Sample**	**Census**
1	Budget	Small	Large
2	Time available	Short	Long
3	Population size	Large	Small
4	Variance in the characteristic	Small	Large
5	Cost of sampling errors	Low	High
6	Cost of non-sampling errors	High	Low
7	Nature of measurement	Destructive	Non-destructive
8	Attention to individual cases	Yes	No

If the cost of sampling errors is high (e.g. if the sample omitted a major manufacturer like Ford, the results could be misleading), a census, which eliminates such errors, is desirable. If the cost of non-sampling errors is high (e.g. interviewers incorrectly questioning target participants) a sample, where fewer resources would have been spent, would be favoured.

A census can greatly increase non-sampling error to the point that these errors exceed the sampling errors of a sample. Non-sampling errors are found to be the major contributor to total error, whereas random sampling errors have been relatively small in magnitude.[2] Hence, in most cases, accuracy considerations would favour a sample over a census.

A sample may be preferred if the measurement process results in the destruction or contamination of the elements sampled. For example, product usage tests result in the consumption of the product. Therefore, taking a census in a study that requires households to use a new brand of toothpaste would not be feasible. Sampling may also be necessary to focus attention on individual cases, as in the case of in-depth interviews. Finally, other pragmatic considerations, such as the need to keep the study secret, may favour a sample over a census.

The sampling design process

The sampling design process includes six steps, which are shown sequentially in Figure 8.1. These steps are closely interrelated and relevant to all aspects of the marketing research project, from problem definition to the presentation of the results. Therefore, sample design decisions should be integrated with all other decisions in a research project.[3]

Define the target population

Target population
The collection of elements or objects that possess the information sought by the researcher and about which inferences are to be made.

Element
An object that possesses the information sought by the researcher and about which inferences are to be made.

Sampling unit
An element, or a unit containing the element, that is available for selection at some stage of the sampling process.

Sampling design begins by specifying the **target population**. This is the collection of elements or objects that possess the information sought by the researcher and about which inferences are to be made. The target population must be defined precisely. Imprecise definition of the target population will result in research that is ineffective at best and misleading at worst. Defining the target population involves translating the problem definition into a precise statement of who should and should not be included in the sample.

The target population should be defined in terms of elements, sampling units, extent and time. An **element** is the object about which or from which the information is desired. In survey research, the element is usually the participant. A **sampling unit** is an element, or a unit containing the element, that is available for selection at some stage of the sampling

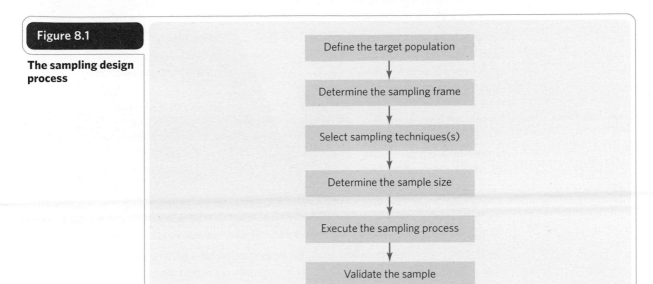

Figure 8.1

The sampling design process

process. Suppose that Clinique wanted to assess consumer response to a new line of lipsticks and wanted to sample females over 25 years of age. It may be possible to sample females over 25 directly, in which case a sampling unit would be the same as an element. Alternatively, the sampling unit might be households. In the latter case, households would be sampled and all females over 25 in each selected household would be interviewed. Here, the sampling unit and the population element are different. Extent refers to the geographical boundaries of the research, and the time refers to the period under consideration.

Defining the target population may not be as easy as it was in this example. Consider a marketing research project assessing consumer response to a new brand of men's moisturiser. Who should be included in the target population? All men? Men who have used a moisturiser during the last month? Men of 17 years of age or older? Should females be included, because some women buy moisturiser for men whom they know? These and similar questions must be resolved before the target population can be appropriately defined.[4] This challenge is further illustrated in the following example.

Real research | **Kiasma: the insightful museum[5]**

Kiasma Museum of Contemporary Art (**www.kiasma.fi**) in Finland is dedicated to contemporary art. Throughout its existence Kiasma has been the most visited museum in Finland. Kiasma's marketing and management team wanted to explore the museum's marketing strategy, contextual development and changes in the external working environment. Research was planned between Kiasma and the media agency Dagmar (**www.dagmar.fi**) with whom they had been working with for over 10 years. One of their first challenges was to establish what the population for the research would be. Would it be the total population for Finland? Kiasma had a public duty to serve the whole population, but it was unfeasible in the context of the research to segment the whole Finnish population, since the museum was located in Helsinki and just pure distance was a hindrance for visiting and/or visiting regularly. The approach they chose was to first gauge the interest in contemporary art in an online panel. The question they posed was a simple 'Are you interested in contemporary art – yes/no?' The result was that a discouraging

33 per cent had an interest in contemporary art. A follow-up question was open-ended, about why the participant was interested or not interested. The results helped them to define a population for their planned survey as 'people living a maximum of 60km from Helsinki, 15–74 years of age and interested in any form of cultural activities, or failing that, are interested in new experiences'. The reasoning behind this was that a person who was interested in at least some form of culture would more easily be persuaded to come to Kiasma.

Determine the sampling frame

Sampling frame
A representation of the elements of the target population that consists of a list or set of directions for identifying the target population.

A **sampling frame** is a representation of the elements of the target population. It consists of a list or set of directions for identifying the target population. Examples of a sampling frame include the telephone directory, an association directory listing the companies in an industry, a customer database, a mailing list on a database purchased from a commercial organisation, a city directory, a map or most frequently in marketing research, an access panel.[6] If a list cannot be compiled, then at least some directions for identifying the target population should be specified, such as random-digit dialling procedures in telephone surveys.

With the growing numbers of individuals, households and businesses, it is possible to compile or obtain a list of population elements, but the list may omit some elements of the population or may include other elements that do not belong. Therefore, the use of a list will lead to sampling frame error.[7]

In some instances, the discrepancy between the population and the sampling frame is small enough to ignore. In most cases, however, the researcher should recognise and attempt to treat the sampling frame error. One approach is to redefine the population in terms of the sampling frame. For example, if a specialist business directory is used as a sampling frame, the population of businesses could be redefined as those with a correct listing in a given location. Although this approach is simplistic, it does prevent the researcher from being misled about the actual population being investigated.[8] Ultimately, the major drawback of redefining the population based upon available sampling frames is that the nature of the research problem may be compromised. Who is being measured and ultimately to whom the research findings may be generalised may not match the target group of individuals identified in a research problem definition. Evaluating the accuracy of sampling frames matches the issues of evaluating the quality of secondary data.

Another way is to account for sampling frame error by screening the participants in the data collection phase. The participants could be screened with respect to demographic characteristics, familiarity, product usage and other characteristics to ensure that they satisfy the criteria for the target population. Screening can eliminate inappropriate elements contained in the sampling frame, but it cannot account for elements that have been omitted. Yet another approach is to adjust the data collected by a weighted scheme to counterbalance the sampling frame error. Regardless of which approach is used, it is important to recognise any sampling frame error that exists, so that inappropriate inferences can be avoided.

Select a sampling technique

Selecting a sampling technique involves several decisions of a broader nature. The researcher must decide whether to use a Bayesian or traditional sampling approach, to sample with or without replacement, and to use non-probability or probability sampling.

In the **Bayesian approach**, the elements are selected sequentially. After each element is added to the sample, the data are collected, sample statistics computed and sampling costs determined. The Bayesian approach explicitly incorporates prior information about population parameters as well as the costs and probabilities associated with making wrong decisions.[9] This approach is theoretically appealing. Yet it is not used widely in marketing research because much of the required information on costs and probabilities is not available. In the traditional sampling approach, the entire sample is selected before data collection begins. Because the traditional approach is the most common approach used, it is assumed in the following sections.

In **sampling with replacement**, an element is selected from the sampling frame and appropriate data are obtained. Then the element is placed back in the sampling frame. As a result, it is possible for an element to be included in the sample more than once. In **sampling without replacement**, once an element is selected for inclusion in the sample, it is removed from the sampling frame and therefore cannot be selected again. The calculation of statistics is done somewhat differently for the two approaches, but statistical inference is not very different if the sampling frame is large relative to the ultimate sample size. Thus, the distinction is important only when the sampling frame is small compared with the sample size.

The most important decision about the choice of sampling technique is whether to use non-probability or probability sampling. Non-probability sampling relies on the judgement of the researcher, while probability sampling relies on chance. Given its importance, the issues involved in this decision are discussed in detail in this chapter.

If the sampling unit is different from the element, it is necessary to specify precisely how the elements within the sampling unit should be selected. With home face-to-face interviews and telephone interviews, merely specifying the address or the telephone number may not be sufficient. For example, should the person answering the doorbell or the telephone be interviewed, or someone else in the household? Often, more than one person in a household may qualify. For example, both the male and female head of household, and even their children, may be eligible to participate in a study examining family leisure-time activities. When a probability sampling technique is being employed, a random selection must be made from all the eligible persons in each household. A simple procedure for random selection is the 'next birthday' method. The interviewer asks which of the eligible persons in the household has the next birthday and includes that person in the sample.

Determine the sample size

Sample size refers to the number of elements to be included in the study. Determining the sample size involves several qualitative and quantitative considerations. Important qualitative factors to be considered in determining the sample size include (1) the importance of the decision, (2) the nature of the research, (3) the number of variables, (4) the nature of the analysis, (5) sample sizes used in similar studies, (6) incidence rates, (7) completion rates, and (8) resource constraints.

In general, for more important decisions, more information is necessary, and that information should be obtained very precisely. This calls for larger samples, but as the sample size increases, each unit of information is obtained at greater cost. The degree of precision may be measured in terms of the standard deviation of the mean, which is inversely proportional to the square root of the sample size. The larger the sample, the smaller the gain in precision by increasing the sample size by one unit. The nature of the research also has an impact on the sample size. For exploratory research designs, such as those using qualitative research, the sample size is typically small. For conclusive research, such as descriptive surveys, larger samples are required. Likewise, if data are being collected on a large number of variables,

---

Bayesian approach
A selection method where the elements are selected sequentially. The Bayesian approach explicitly incorporates prior information about population parameters as well as the costs and probabilities associated with making wrong decisions.

Sampling with replacement
A sampling technique in which an element *can* be included in the sample more than once.

Sampling without replacement
A sampling technique in which an element *cannot* be included in the sample more than once.

Sample size
The number of elements to be included in a study.

Table 8.2	Usual sample sizes used in marketing research studies	
Type of study	**Minimum size**	**Typical range**
Problem identification	500	1,000–2,500 research (e.g. market potential)
Problem-solving research	200	300–500 (e.g. pricing)
Product tests	200	300–500
Test marketing studies	200	300–500
TV, radio, print or online advertising	150	200–300 (per advertisement tested)
Test market audits	10 stores	10–20 stores
Focus groups	6 groups	6–12 groups

i.e. many questions are asked in a survey, larger samples are required. The cumulative effects of sampling error across variables are reduced in a large sample.

If sophisticated analysis of the data using multivariate techniques is required, the sample size should be large. The same applies if the data are to be analysed in great detail. Thus, a larger sample would be required if the data are being analysed at the subgroup or segment level than if the analysis is limited to the aggregate or total sample. Sample size is influenced by the average size of samples in similar studies. Table 8.2 gives an idea of sample sizes used in different marketing research studies. These sample sizes have been determined based on experience and can serve as rough guidelines, particularly when non-probability sampling techniques are used.

Incidence rate refers to the rate of occurrence or the percentage of persons eligible to participate in the study. Incidence rate determines how many contacts need to be screened for a given sample size requirement.[10] For example, suppose that a study of pet ownership targets a sample of households. Of the households that might be approached to see if they qualify, approximately 75 per cent own a pet. This means that, on average, 1.33 households would be approached to obtain one qualified participant. Additional criteria for qualifying participants (e.g. product usage behaviour) will further increase the number of contacts. Suppose that an added eligibility requirement is that the household should have bought a toy for their pet during the last two months. It is estimated that 60 per cent of the households contacted would meet this criterion. Then the incidence rate is $0.75 \times 0.6 = 0.45$. Thus the final sample size will have to be increased by a factor of (1/0.45) or 2.22.

Similarly, the determination of sample size must take into account anticipated refusals by people who qualify. The **completion rate** denotes the percentage of qualified participants who complete the interview.[11] If, for example, the researcher expects an interview completion rate of 80 per cent of eligible participants, the number of contacts should be increased by a factor of 1.25. The incidence rate and the completion rate together imply that the number of potential participants contacted, that is, the initial sample size, should be 2.22×1.25 or 2.78 times the sample size required. In general, if there are c qualifying factors with an incidence of $Q_1 \times Q_2 \times Q_3 \ldots \times Q_c$ each expressed as a proportion, the following are true:

$$\text{Incidence rate} = Q_1 \times Q_2 \times Q_3 \times \ldots \times Q_c$$

$$\text{Initial sample size} = \frac{\text{final sample size}}{\text{incidence rate} \times \text{completion rate}}$$

The number of units that will have to be sampled will be determined by the initial sample size. These calculations assume that an attempt to contact a participant will result in a determination as to whether the participant is eligible. However, this may not be the case. An attempt to contact the participant may be inconclusive as the participant may refuse to answer, not be at home, be busy, or many other reasons. Such instances will further increase the initial sample size. Often

Incidence rate
Refers to the rate of occurrence or the percentage of persons eligible to participate in a study.

Completion rate
The percentage of qualified participants who complete the interview. It enables researchers to take into account anticipated refusals by people who qualify.

a number of variables are used for qualifying potential participants, thereby decreasing the incidence rate. Completion rates are affected by non-response issues.

Finally, the sample size decision should be guided by a consideration of the resource constraints. In any marketing research project, money and time are inevitably limited.

Execute the sampling process

Execution of the sampling process requires a detailed specification of how the sampling design decisions with respect to the population, sampling unit, sampling frame, sampling technique and sample size are to be implemented. Whilst individual researchers may know how they are going to execute their sampling process, once more than one individual is involved, a specification for execution is needed to ensure that the process is conducted in a consistent manner. For example, if households are the sampling unit, an operational definition of a household is needed. Procedures should be specified for empty housing units and for call-backs in case no one is at home.

Validate the sample

Sample validation aims to account for sampling frame error by screening the participants in the data collection phase. Participants can be screened with respect to demographic characteristics, familiarity, product usage and other characteristics to ensure that they satisfy the criteria for the target population. Screening can eliminate inappropriate elements contained in the sampling frame, but it cannot account for elements that have been omitted. The success of the validation process depends upon the accuracy of base statistics that describe the structure of a target population. Once data are collected from a sample, comparisons between the structure of the sample and the target population should be made. Once data have been collected and it is found that the structure of a sample does not match the target population, a weighting scheme can be used.

A classification of sampling techniques

Non-probability sampling
Sampling techniques that do not use chance selection procedures but rather rely on the personal judgement of the researcher.

Sampling techniques may be broadly classified as non-probability and probability (see Figure 8.2). **Non-probability sampling** relies on the personal judgement of the researcher rather than on chance to select sample elements. The researcher can arbitrarily or consciously decide what elements to include in the sample. Non-probability samples may yield good estimates of the population characteristics, but they do not allow for objective evaluation of the precision of the sample results. Because there is no way of determining the probability of selecting any particular element for inclusion in the sample, the estimates obtained are not statistically projectable to the population. Commonly used non-probability sampling techniques include convenience sampling, judgemental sampling, quota sampling and snowball sampling.

Probability sampling
A sampling procedure in which each element of the population has a fixed probabilistic chance of being selected for the sample.

In **probability sampling**, sampling units are selected by chance. It is possible to pre-specify every potential sample of a given size that could be drawn from the population, as well as the probability of selecting each sample. Every potential sample need not have the same probability of selection, but it is possible to specify the probability of selecting any particular sample of a given size. This requires not only a precise definition of the target population but also a general specification of the sampling frame. Because sample elements are selected by chance, it is possible to determine the precision of the sample estimates of the characteristics of interest. **Confidence intervals**, which contain the true population value with a given level of certainty, can be calculated. This permits the researcher to make inferences or projections about the target population from which the sample was drawn. Classification of probability sampling techniques is based on:

Confidence intervals
The range into which the true population parameter will fall, assuming a given level of confidence.

- element versus cluster sampling
- equal unit probability versus unequal probabilities
- unstratified versus stratified selection

- random versus systematic selection
- one-stage versus multistage techniques.

All possible combinations of these five aspects result in 32 different probability sampling techniques. Of these techniques, we consider simple random sampling, systematic sampling, stratified sampling and cluster sampling in depth and briefly touch on some others. First, however, we discuss non-probability sampling techniques.

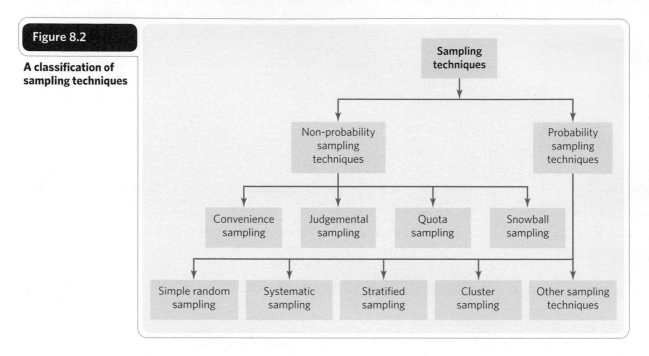

Figure 8.2

A classification of sampling techniques

Non-probability sampling techniques

Figure 8.3 presents a graphical illustration of the various non-probability sampling techniques. The population consists of 25 elements and we have to select a sample of size 5: A, B, C, D and E represent groups and can also be viewed as strata or clusters.

Convenience sampling

Convenience sampling
A non-probability sampling technique that attempts to obtain a sample of convenient elements. The selection of sampling units is left primarily to the interviewer.

Convenience sampling attempts to obtain a sample of convenient elements. The selection of sampling units is left primarily to the interviewer. Often, participants are selected because they happen to be in the right place at the right time. Examples of convenience sampling include: (1) use of students, religious groups and members of social organisations, (2) street interviews without qualifying the participants, (3) some forms of online and email surveys, (4) tear-out questionnaires included in a newspaper or magazine, and (5) journalists interviewing 'people on the street', or on radio or television shows.[12]

Convenience sampling is the least expensive and least time consuming of all sampling techniques. The sampling units are accessible, easy to measure and cooperative. Despite these advantages, this form of sampling has serious limitations. Many potential sources of selection bias are present, including participant self-selection. Convenience samples are not representative of any definable population.[13] Hence, it is not theoretically meaningful to generalise to any population from a convenience sample, and convenience samples are not appropriate for marketing research projects involving population inferences. Convenience samples are not recommended for descriptive or causal research, but they can be used in exploratory research for generating ideas, insights or hypotheses. Convenience samples can

Figure 8.3
A graphical illustration of non-probability sampling techniques

A graphical illustration of non-probability techniques

1 Convenience sampling

A	B	C	D	E	
1	6	11	16	21	Group D happens to assemble at a convenient time and place. So all the elements in this group are selected. The resulting sample consists of elements 16, 17, 18, 19 and 20. Note that no elements are selected from groups A, B, C, E
2	7	12	17	22	
3	8	13	18	23	
4	9	14	19	24	
5	10	15	20	25	

2 Judgemental sampling

A	B	C	D	E	
1	6	11	16	21	The researcher considers groups B, C and E to be typical and convenient. Within each of these groups one or two elements are selected based on typicality and convenience. The resulting sample consists of elements 8, 10, 11, 13 and 24. Note that no elements are selected from groups A and D
2	7	12	17	22	
3	8	13	18	23	
4	9	14	19	24	
5	10	15	20	25	

3 Quota sampling

A	B	C	D	E	
1	6	11	16	21	A quota of one element from each group, A to E, is imposed. Within each group, one element is selected based on judgement or convenience. The resulting sample consists of elements 3, 6, 13, 20 and 22. Note that one element is selected from each column or group
2	7	12	17	22	
3	8	13	18	23	
4	9	14	19	24	
5	10	15	20	25	

4 Snowball sampling

	Selection	Random	Referrals		
A	B	C	D	E	
1	6	11	16	21	Elements 2 and 9 are selected randomly from groups A and B. Element 2 refers elements 12 and 13. Element 9 refers element 18. The resulting sample consists of elements 2, 9 12, 13 and 18. Note that no element is selected from group E
2	7	12	17	22	
3	8	13	18	23	
4	9	14	19	24	
5	10	15	20	25	

be used for pretesting questionnaires, or pilot studies. Even in these cases, caution should be exercised in interpreting the results. Nevertheless, this technique is sometimes used even in large surveys.

Judgemental sampling

Judgemental sampling
A form of convenience sampling in which the population elements are purposely selected based on the judgement of the researcher.

Judgemental sampling is a form of convenience sampling in which the population elements are selected based on the judgement of the researcher. The researcher, exercising judgement or expertise, chooses the elements to be included in the sample because they believe that they are representative of the population of interest or are otherwise appropriate. Common examples of judgemental sampling include: (1) test markets selected to determine the potential of a new product, (2) purchasing professionals selected in business-to-business marketing research because they are considered to be representative of particular companies, (3) product testing with individuals who may be particularly fussy or who hold extremely high expectations, (4) expert witnesses used in court, and (5) boutiques or fashion flagship stores selected to test a new merchandising display system.

Judgemental sampling is inexpensive, convenient and quick, yet it does not allow direct generalisations to a specific population, usually because the population is not defined explicitly. Judgemental sampling is subjective and its value depends entirely on the researcher's judgement, expertise and creativity. It can be useful if broad population inferences are not required. Judgement samples are frequently used in business-to-business marketing research projects, given that in many projects the target population is relatively small.

Quota sampling

Quota sampling
A non-probability sampling technique that is two-stage restricted judgemental sampling. The first stage consists of developing control categories or quotas of population elements. In the second stage, sample elements are selected based on convenience or judgement.

Quota sampling may be viewed as two-stage restricted judgemental sampling that has traditionally been associated with street interviewing. It is now used extensively and with much debate in drawing samples from access panels.[14] The first stage consists of developing control characteristics, or quotas, of population elements such as age or gender. To develop these quotas, the researcher lists relevant control characteristics and determines the distribution of these characteristics in the target population, such as Males 48 per cent, Females 52 per cent (resulting in 480 men and 520 women being selected in a sample of 1,000 participants). Often, the quotas are assigned so that the proportion of the sample elements possessing the control characteristics is the same as the proportion of population elements with these characteristics. In other words, the quotas ensure that the composition of the sample is the same as the composition of the population with respect to the characteristics of interest.

In the second stage, sample elements are selected based on convenience or judgement. Once the quotas have been assigned, there is considerable freedom in selecting the elements to be included in the sample. The only requirement is that the elements selected fit the control characteristics.[15] This technique is illustrated with the following example.

Real research | **How is epilepsy perceived?**

A study was undertaken by the Scottish Epilepsy Association to determine the perceptions of the condition of epilepsy by the adult population in the Scottish city of Glasgow. A quota sample of 500 adults was selected. The control characteristics were gender, age and propensity to donate to a charity. Based on the composition of the adult population of the city, the quotas assigned were as follows:

Propensity to donate		Male 48%		Female 52%		
		Have a flag	No flag	Have a flag	No flag	
Age		50%	50%	50%	50%	Totals
18 to 30	25%	30	30	33	32	125
31 to 45	40%	48	48	52	52	200
46 to 60	15%	18	18	19	20	75
Over 60	20%	24	24	26	26	100
Totals		120	120	130	130	
Totals			240		260	500

Note that the percentages of gender and age within the target population were taken from local census statistics. The percentages of 'propensity to donate' could not be gleaned from secondary data sources and so were split on a 50/50 basis. The interviews were conducted on a Saturday when it was customary to see charity 'flag sellers' operating. One of the hypotheses to be tested in the study was the extent to which those who donated to charities on flag days were more aware of the condition of epilepsy and how to treat

> sufferers. Thus the instruction to interviewers was to split interviews between those who wore the 'flag' that they had bought from a street collector and those who had not bought a flag. It was recognised that this was a crude measure of propensity to donate to a charity but was the only tangible clue that could be consistently observed.

In this example, quotas were assigned such that the composition of the sample mirrored the population. In certain situations, however, it is desirable either to under- or over-sample elements with certain characteristics. To illustrate, it may be desirable to over-sample heavy users of a product so that their behaviour can be examined in detail. Although this type of sample is not representative, nevertheless it may be very relevant to allow a particular group of individuals to be broken down into subcategories and analysed in depth.

Even if the sample composition mirrors that of the population with respect to the control characteristics, there is no assurance that the sample is representative. If a characteristic that is relevant to the problem is overlooked, the quota sample will not be representative. Relevant control characteristics are often omitted because there are practical difficulties associated with including certain control characteristics. For example, suppose a sample was sought that was representative of the different strata of socio-economic classes in a population. Imagine street interviewers approaching potential participants who they believe would fit into the quota they have been set. Could an interviewer 'guess' (from their clothes, accessories, posture?) which potential participants fit into different socio-economic classes, in the same way that they may guess the gender and age of participants? The initial questions of a street interview could establish characteristics of potential participants to see whether they fit a set quota. But given the levels of non-response and ineligibility levels found by such an approach, this is not an ideal solution.

Because the elements within each quota are selected based on convenience or judgement, many sources of selection bias are potentially present. The interviewers may go to selected areas where eligible participants are more likely to be found. Likewise, they may avoid people who look unfriendly or are not well dressed or those who live in undesirable locations. Quota sampling does not permit assessment of sampling error.[16] Quota sampling attempts to obtain representative samples at a relatively low cost. Its advantages are the lower costs and greater convenience to the interviewers in selecting elements for each quota. Under certain conditions, quota sampling obtains results close to those for conventional probability sampling.[17]

Snowball sampling

Snowball sampling

A non-probability sampling technique in which an initial group of participants is selected randomly. Subsequent participants are selected based on the referrals or information provided by the initial participants. By obtaining referrals from referrals, this process may be carried out in waves.

In **snowball sampling**, an initial group of participants is selected, sometimes on a random basis, but more typically targeted at a few individuals who are known to possess the desired characteristics of the target population. After being interviewed, these participants are asked to identify others who also belong to the target population of interest. Subsequent participants are selected based on the referrals. By obtaining referrals from referrals, this process may be carried out in waves, thus leading to a snowballing effect. Even though probability sampling can be used to select the initial participants, the final sample is a non-probability sample. The referrals will have demographic and psychographic characteristics more similar to the persons referring them than would occur by chance.[18]

The main objective of snowball sampling is to estimate characteristics that are rare in the wider population. Examples include users of particular government or social services, such as parents who use nurseries or child minders, whose names cannot be revealed; special census groups, such as widowed males under 35; and members of a scattered minority ethnic group. Another example is research in industrial buyer–seller relationships, using initial contacts to identify buyer–seller pairs and then subsequent 'snowballed' pairs. The major advantage of snowball sampling is that it substantially increases the likelihood of locating the desired characteristic in the population. It also results in relatively low sampling variance and costs.[19] Snowball sampling is illustrated by the following example.

Real research

Sampling horse owners

Dalgety Animal Feeds wished to question horse owners about the care and feeding of their horses. The firm could not locate any sampling frame that listed all horse owners, with the exception of registers of major racing stables. However, the firm wished to contact owners who had one or two horses as it believed this group was not well understood and held great marketing potential. The initial approach involved locating interviewers at horse feed outlets. The interviewers ascertained basic characteristics of horse owners but more importantly they invited them along to focus groups. When the focus groups were conducted, issues of horse care and feeding were developed in greater detail to allow the construction of a meaningful postal questionnaire. As a rapport and trust was built up with those that attended the focus groups, names as referrals were given that allowed a sampling frame for the first wave of participants to the subsequent postal survey. The process of referrals continued, allowing a total of four waves and a response of 800 questionnaires.

In this example, note the non-random selection of the initial group of participants through focus group invitations. This procedure was more efficient than random selection, which given the absence of an appropriate sampling frame would be very cumbersome. In other cases where an appropriate sampling frame exists (appropriate in terms of identifying the desired characteristics in a number of participants, not in terms of being exhaustive – if it were exhaustive, a snowball sample would not be needed), random selection of participants through probability sampling techniques may be more appropriate.

Probability sampling techniques

Probability sampling techniques vary in terms of sampling efficiency. Sampling efficiency is a concept that reflects a trade-off between sampling cost and precision. Precision refers to the level of uncertainty about the characteristic being measured. Precision is inversely related to sampling errors but positively related to cost. The greater the precision, the greater the cost, and most studies require a trade-off. The researcher should strive for the most efficient sampling design, subject to the budget allocated. The efficiency of a probability sampling technique may be assessed by comparing it with that of simple random sampling. Figure 8.4 presents a graphical illustration of the various probability sampling techniques. As in the case of non-probability sampling, the population consists of 25 elements and we have to select a sample of size 5; A, B, C, D and E represent groups and can also be viewed as strata or clusters.

Figure 8.4

A graphical illustration of probability sampling techniques

A graphical illustration of probability sampling techniques

1 Simple random sampling

A	B	C	D	E
1	6	11	16	21
2	7	12	17	22
3	8	13	18	23
4	9	14	19	24
5	10	15	20	25

Select five random numbers from 1 to 25. The resulting sample consists of population elements 3, 7, 9, 16 and 24. Note that there is no element from group C

2 Systematic sampling

A	B	C	D	E
1	6	11	16	21
2	7	12	17	22
3	8	13	18	23
4	9	14	19	24
5	10	15	20	25

Select a random number between 1 and 5, say 2. The resulting sample consists of a population 2, $(2 + 5) = 7$, $(2 + 5 \times 2) = 12$, $(2 + 5 \times 3) = 17$ and $(2 + 5 \times 4) = 22$. Note that all the elements are selected from a single row

3 Stratified sampling

A	B	C	D	E
1	6	11	16	21
2	7	12	17	22
3	8	13	18	23
4	9	14	19	24
5	10	15	20	25

Randomly select a number from 1 to 5 from each stratum, A to E. The resulting sample consists of population elements 4, 7, 13, 19 and 21. Note that one element is selected from each column

4 Cluster sampling (two stage)

A	B	C	D	E
1	6	11	16	21
2	7	12	17	22
3	8	13	18	23
4	9	14	19	24
5	10	15	20	25

Randomly select three clusters, B, D and E. Within each cluster, randomly select one or two elements. The resulting sample consists of population elements 7, 18, 20, 21 and 23. Note that no elements are selected from clusters A and C

Simple random sampling

Simple random sampling (SRS)
A probability sampling technique in which each element has a known and equal probability of selection. Every element is selected independently of every other element, and the sample is drawn by a random procedure from a sampling frame.

In **simple random sampling (SRS)**, each element in the population has a known and equal probability of selection. Furthermore, each possible sample of a given size (n) has a known and equal probability of being the sample actually selected. This implies that every element is selected independently of every other element. The sample is drawn by a random procedure from a sampling frame. This method is equivalent to a lottery system in which names are placed in a container, the container is shaken and the names of the winners are then drawn out in an unbiased manner.

To draw a simple random sample, the researcher first compiles a sampling frame in which each element is assigned a unique identification number. Then random numbers are generated to determine which elements to include in the sample. The random numbers may be generated with a computer routine or a table (see Table 1 in the Appendix of statistical tables). Suppose that a sample of 10 is to be selected from a sampling frame containing 800 elements. This could be done by starting with row 1 and column 1 of Table 1, considering the three rightmost digits, and going down the column until 10 numbers between 1 and 800 have been selected. Numbers outside this range are ignored. The elements corresponding to the random numbers generated constitute the sample. Thus, in our example, elements 480, 368, 130, 167, 570, 562, 301, 579, 475 and 553 would be selected. Note that the last three digits of row 6 (921) and row 11 (918) were ignored, because they were out of range. Using these tables is fine for small samples, but can be very tedious. A more pragmatic solution is to turn to random-number generators in most data analysis packages. For example, in Excel, the Random Number Generation Analysis Tool allows you to set a number of characteristics of your target population, including the nature of distribution of the data, and to create a table of random numbers on a separate worksheet.

SRS has many desirable features. It is easily understood and the sample results may be projected to the target population. Most approaches to statistical inference assume that the data have been collected by SRS. However, SRS suffers from at least four significant limitations. First, it is often difficult to construct a sampling frame that will permit a simple random sample to be drawn. Second, SRS can result in samples that are very large or spread over large geographical areas, thus increasing the time and cost of data collection. Third, SRS often results in lower precision with larger standard errors than other probability sampling techniques. Fourth, SRS may or may not result in a representative sample. Although samples drawn will represent the population well on average, a given simple random sample may grossly misrepresent the target population. This is more likely if the size of the sample is small. For these reasons, SRS is not widely used in marketing research.[20]

Systematic sampling

Systematic sampling
A probability sampling technique in which the sample is chosen by selecting a random starting point and then picking every *i*th element in succession from the sampling frame.

In **systematic sampling**, the sample is chosen by selecting a random starting point and then picking every *i*th element in succession from the sampling frame.[21] The sampling interval, *i*, is determined by dividing the population size *N* by the sample size *n* and rounding to the nearest whole number. For example, there are 100,000 elements in the population and a sample of 1,000 is desired. In this case, the sampling interval, *i*, is 100. A random number between 1 and 100 is selected. If, for example, this number is 23, the sample consists of elements 23, 123, 223, 323, 423, 523, and so on.[22]

Systematic sampling is similar to SRS in that each population element has a known and equal probability of selection. It is different from SRS, however, in that only the permissible samples of size *n* that can be drawn have a known and equal probability of selection. The remaining samples of size *n* have a zero probability of being selected. For systematic sampling, the researcher assumes that the population elements are ordered in some respect. In some cases, the ordering (e.g. alphabetical listing in a telephone directory) is unrelated to the characteristic of interest. In other instances, the ordering is directly related to the characteristic under investigation. For example, credit card customers may be listed in order of outstanding balance, or firms in a given industry may be ordered according to annual sales. If the population elements are arranged in a manner unrelated to the characteristic of interest, systematic sampling will yield results quite similar to SRS.

On the other hand, when the ordering of the elements is related to the characteristic of interest, systematic sampling increases the representativeness of the sample. If firms in an industry are arranged in increasing order of annual sales, a systematic sample will include some small and some large firms. A simple random sample may be unrepresentative because it may contain, for example, only small firms or a disproportionate number of small firms. If the ordering of the elements produces a cyclical pattern, systematic sampling may decrease the representativeness of the sample. To illustrate, consider the use of systematic sampling to generate a sample of monthly sales from the Harrods store in London. In such a case, the sampling frame could contain monthly sales for the last 60 years or more. If a sampling interval of 12 was chosen, the resulting sample would not reflect the month-to-month and seasonal variations in sales.[23]

Systematic sampling is less costly and easier than SRS because random selection is done only once to establish a starting point. Moreover, random numbers do not have to be matched with individual elements as in SRS. Because some lists contain millions of elements, considerable time can be saved, which reduces the costs of sampling. If information related to the characteristic of interest is available for the population, systematic sampling can be used to obtain a more representative and reliable (lower sampling error) sample than SRS. Another relative advantage is that systematic sampling can even be used without knowledge of the elements of the sampling frame. For example, every ith person accessing a website, leaving a shop or passing a point in the street can be intercepted (provided very strict control of the flow of potential participants is exercised). For these reasons, systematic sampling is often employed in online surveys, postal, telephone and street interviews, as illustrated by the following example.

Real research | **Service quality expectations of Hong Kong Chinese shoppers**[24]

Global retailers in the last century have focused on the presumed similarities of consumers across borders, and used the management of product novelty or newness to attract international customers. When novelty and newness fades, however, success moves to a dependence on understanding differences among consumers in different cultures. A study examined how cultural differences affected retail customers' service quality perception in a cultural context distinctly different from Western culture, the Hong Kong Chinese retail supermarket. The key research objective was to examine underlying service quality dimensions of experienced shoppers in two supermarkets. The population was defined as all Chinese shoppers who had previously shopped in the selected PARKnSHOP and Wellcome stores. The sample was a systematic sample using a random start with the selection of Chinese  shoppers occurring as they approached the stores. Each potential participant was qualified by being asked if they had previously shopped at the store with an alternative line of questionning if one did not qualify. A total of 100 interviews were completed at each of four stores for a total of 400 completed interviews.

Stratified sampling

Stratified sampling
A probability sampling technique that uses a two-step process to partition the population into subsequent subpopulations, or strata. Elements are selected from each stratum by a random procedure.

Stratified sampling is a two-step process in which the population is partitioned into subpopulations, or strata. The strata should be mutually exclusive and collectively exhaustive in that every population element should be assigned to one and only one stratum and no population elements should be omitted. Next, elements are selected from each stratum by a random procedure, usually SRS. Technically, only SRS should be employed in selecting the elements from each stratum. In practice, sometimes systematic sampling and other probability sampling procedures are employed. Stratified sampling differs from quota sampling in that the sample elements are selected probabilistically rather than based on convenience or judgement. A major objective of stratified sampling is to increase precision without increasing cost.[25]

The variables used to partition the population into strata are referred to as stratification variables. The criteria for the selection of these variables consist of homogeneity, heterogeneity, relatedness and cost. The elements within a stratum should be as homogeneous as possible, but the elements in different strata should be as heterogeneous as possible. The stratification variables should also be closely related to the characteristic of interest. The more closely these criteria are met, the greater the effectiveness in controlling extraneous sampling variation. Finally, the variables should decrease the cost of the stratification process by being easy to measure and apply. Variables commonly used for stratification include demographic characteristics (as illustrated in the example for quota sampling), type of customer (e.g. credit card versus non-credit card), size of firm, or type of industry. It is possible to use more than one variable for stratification, although more than two are seldom used because of pragmatic and cost considerations. Although the number of strata to use is a matter of judgement, experience suggests the use of no more than six. Beyond six strata, any gain in precision is more than offset by the increased cost of stratification and sampling.

Another important decision involves the use of proportionate or disproportionate sampling. In proportionate stratified sampling, the size of the sample drawn from each stratum is proportionate to the relative size of that stratum in the total population. In disproportionate stratified sampling, the size of the sample from each stratum is proportionate to the relative size of that stratum and to the standard deviation of the distribution of the characteristic of interest among all the elements in that stratum. The logic behind disproportionate sampling is simple. First, strata with larger relative sizes are more influential in determining the population mean, and these strata should also exert a greater influence in deriving the sample estimates. Consequently, more elements should be drawn from strata of larger relative size. Second, to increase precision, more elements should be drawn from strata with larger standard deviations and fewer elements should be drawn from strata with smaller standard deviations. (If all the elements in a stratum are identical, a sample size of one will result in perfect information.) Note that the two methods are identical if the characteristic of interest has the same standard deviation within each stratum.

Disproportionate sampling requires that some estimate of the relative variation, or standard deviation of the distribution of the characteristic of interest, within strata be known. As this information is not always available, the researcher may have to rely on intuition and logic to determine sample sizes for each stratum. For example, large fashion stores might be expected to have greater variation in the sales of some products as compared with small boutiques. Hence, the number of large stores in a sample may be disproportionately large. When the researcher is primarily interested in examining differences between strata, a common sampling strategy is to select the same sample size from each stratum.

Stratified sampling can ensure that all the important subpopulations are represented in the sample. This is particularly important if the distribution of the characteristic of interest in the population is skewed. For example, very few households have annual incomes that allow them to own a second home in another country. If a simple random sample is taken, households that have such a second home may not be adequately represented. Stratified sampling would guarantee that the sample contains a certain number of these households. Stratified sampling combines the simplicity of SRS with potential gains in precision. Therefore, it is a popular sampling technique.

Cluster sampling

Cluster sampling
A two-step probability sampling technique where the target population is first divided into mutually exclusive and collectively exhaustive subpopulations called clusters, and then a random sample of clusters is selected based on a probability sampling technique such as SRS. For each selected cluster, either all the elements are included in the sample, or a sample of elements is drawn probabilistically.

In cluster sampling, the target population is first divided into mutually exclusive and collectively exhaustive subpopulations, or clusters. These subpopulations or clusters are assumed to contain the diversity of participants held in the target population. A random sample of clusters is selected, based on a probability sampling technique such as SRS. For each selected cluster, either all the elements are included in the sample or a sample of elements is drawn probabilistically. If all the elements in each selected cluster are included in the sample, the procedure is called one-stage cluster sampling. If a sample of elements is drawn probabilistically from each selected cluster, the procedure is two-stage cluster sampling. As shown in Figure 8.5, two-stage cluster sampling can be either simple two-stage cluster sampling

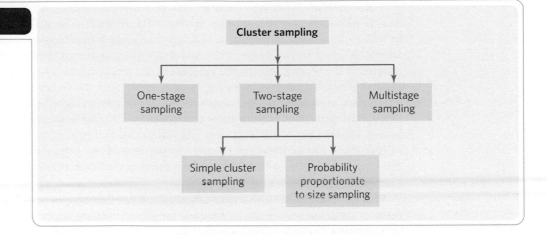

Figure 8.5

Types of cluster sampling

involving SRS or probability proportionate to size sampling. Furthermore, a cluster sample can have multiple (more than two) stages, as in multistage cluster sampling.

The key distinction between cluster sampling and stratified sampling is that in cluster sampling only a sample of subpopulations (clusters) is chosen, whereas in stratified sampling all the subpopulations (strata) are selected for further sampling. The objectives of the two methods are also different. The objective of cluster sampling is to increase sampling efficiency by decreasing costs, but the objective of stratified sampling is to increase precision. With respect to homogeneity and heterogeneity, the criteria for forming clusters are just the opposite of those for strata. Elements within a cluster should be as heterogeneous as possible, but clusters themselves should be as homogeneous as possible. Ideally, each cluster should be a small-scale representation of the population. In cluster sampling, a sampling frame is needed only for those clusters selected for the sample. The differences between stratified sampling and cluster sampling are summarised in Table 8.3.

Area sampling
A common form of cluster sampling in which the clusters consist of geographical areas such as counties, housing tracts, blocks or other area descriptions.

A common form of cluster sampling is **area sampling**, in which the clusters consist of geographical areas, such as counties, housing districts or residential blocks. If only one level of sampling takes place in selecting the basic elements (e.g. if the researcher samples blocks and then all the households within the selected blocks are included in the sample), the design is called one-stage area sampling. If two or more levels of sampling take place before the basic elements are selected (if the researcher samples blocks and then samples households within the sampled blocks), the design is called two-stage (or multistage) area sampling. The distinguishing feature of one-stage area sampling is that all the households in the selected blocks (or geographical areas) are included in the sample.

Table 8.3 **Differences between stratified and cluster sampling**

Factor	Stratified sampling	Cluster sampling (one-stage)
Objective	Increase precision	Decrease cost
Subpopulations	All strata are included	A sample of clusters is chosen
Within subpopulations	Each stratum should be homogeneous	Each cluster should be heterogeneous
Across subpopulations	Strata should be heterogeneous	Clusters should be homogeneous
Sampling frame	Needed for the entire population	Needed only for the selected clusters
Selection of elements	Elements selected from each stratum randomly	All elements from each selected cluster are included

There are two types of two-stage cluster sampling designs, as shown in Figure 8.5. Simple two-stage cluster sampling involves SRS at the first stage (e.g. sampling blocks) as well as the second stage (e.g. sampling households within blocks). This design is called *simple two-stage cluster sampling*. In this design the fraction of elements (e.g. households) selected at the second stage is the same for each sample cluster (e.g. selected blocks). This process was administered in a project that investigated the behaviour of high net worth consumers. A simple random sample of 800 block groups were selected from a listing of neighbourhoods with average incomes exceeding €35,000 in locations ranked in the top half by income according to census data. Commercial database companies supplied head of household names for approximately 95 per cent of the census tabulated homes in the 800 block groups. From the 213,000 enumerated households, 9000 were selected by simple random sampling.[26]

Cluster sampling has two major advantages: feasibility and low cost. In many situations the only sampling frames readily available for the target population are clusters, not population elements. It is often impossible to compile a list of all consumers in a population, given the resources and constraints. Lists of geographical areas, telephone exchanges and other clusters of consumers, however, can be constructed relatively easily. Cluster sampling is the most cost-effective probability sampling technique. This advantage must be weighed against several limitations.[27] Cluster sampling results in relatively imprecise samples, and it is difficult to form clusters in which the elements are heterogeneous, because, for example, households in a block tend to be similar rather than dissimilar.[28] It can be difficult to compute and interpret statistics based on clusters.

Other probability sampling techniques

In addition to the four basic probability sampling techniques, there are a variety of other sampling techniques. Most of these may be viewed as extensions of the basic techniques and were developed to address complex sampling problems. Two techniques with some relevance to marketing research are sequential sampling and double sampling.

Sequential sampling
A probability sampling technique in which the population elements are sampled sequentially, data collection and analysis are done at each stage, and a decision is made as to whether additional population elements should be sampled.

In **sequential sampling**, the population elements are sampled sequentially, data collection and analysis are done at each stage, and a decision is made as to whether additional population elements should be sampled. The sample size is not known in advance, but a decision rule is stated before sampling begins. At each stage, this rule indicates whether sampling should be continued or whether enough information has been obtained. Sequential sampling has been used to determine preferences for two competing alternatives. In one study, participants were asked which of two alternatives they preferred, and sampling was terminated when sufficient evidence was accumulated to validate a preference. It has also been used to establish the price differential between a standard brand and a luxury brand of a consumer durable.[29]

Double sampling
A sampling technique in which certain population elements are sampled twice.

In **double sampling**, also called two-phase sampling, certain population elements are sampled twice. In the first phase, a sample is selected and some information is collected from all the elements in the sample. In the second phase, a subsample is drawn from the original sample and additional information is obtained from the elements in the subsample. The process may be extended to three or more phases, and the different phases may take place simultaneously or at different times. Double sampling can be useful when no sampling frame is readily available for selecting final sampling units but when the elements of the frame are known to be contained within a broader sampling frame. For example, a researcher wants to select households in a given city that consume apple juice. The households of interest are contained within the set of all households, but the researcher does not know which ones they are. In applying double sampling, the researcher would obtain a sampling frame of all households in the first phase. This would be constructed from a directory of city addresses. Then a sample of households would be drawn, using systematic random sampling to determine the amount of apple juice consumed. In the second phase, households that consume apple juice would be selected and stratified according to the amount of apple juice consumed. Then a stratified random sample would be drawn and detailed questions regarding apple juice consumption asked.[30]

Choosing non-probability versus probability sampling

The choice between non-probability and probability samples should be based on considerations such as the nature of the research, relative magnitude of non-sampling versus sampling errors, and variability in the population, as well as statistical and operational considerations (see Table 8.4). For example, in exploratory research, the judgement of the researcher in selecting participants with particular qualities may be far more effective than any form of probability sampling. On the other hand, in conclusive research where the researcher wishes to use the results to estimate overall market shares or the size of the total market, probability sampling is favoured. Probability samples allow statistical projection of the results to a target population.

Table 8.4	Choosing non-probability vs probability sampling	
	Conditions favouring the use of:	
Factors	**Non-probability sampling**	**Probability sampling**
Nature of research	Exploratory	Conclusive
Relative magnitude of sampling and non-sampling errors	Non-sampling errors are larger	Sampling errors are larger
Variability in the population	Homogeneous (low)	Heterogeneous (high)
Statistical considerations	Unfavourable	Favourable
Operational considerations	Favourable	Unfavourable

For some research problems, highly accurate estimates of population characteristics are required. In these situations, the elimination of selection bias and the ability to calculate sampling error make probability sampling desirable. However, probability sampling will not always result in more accurate results. If non-sampling errors are likely to be an important factor, then non-probability sampling may be preferable because the use of judgement may allow greater control over the sampling process.

Another consideration is the homogeneity of the population with respect to the variables of interest. A heterogeneous population would favour probability sampling because it would be more important to secure a representative sample. Probability sampling is preferable from a statistical viewpoint, as it is the basis of most common statistical techniques.

Probability sampling generally requires statistically trained researchers, generally costs more and takes longer than non-probability sampling, especially in the establishment of accurate sampling frames. In many marketing research projects, it is difficult to justify the additional time and expense. Therefore, in practice, the objectives of the study dictate which sampling method will be used.

Uses of non-probability and probability sampling

Non-probability sampling is used in concept tests, package tests, name tests and copy tests where projections to the populations are usually not needed. In such studies, interest centres on the proportion of the sample that gives various responses or expresses various attitudes. Samples for these studies can be drawn using access panels and employing methods such as online surveys, street interviewing and quota sampling. On the other hand, probability sampling is used when there is a need for highly accurate estimates of market share or sales volume for the entire market. National market tracking studies, which provide information on product category and brand usage rates as well as psychographic and demographic profiles of users, use probability sampling.

Summary of sampling techniques

The strengths and weaknesses of basic sampling techniques are summarised in Table 8.5. Table 8.6 describes the procedures for drawing probability samples.

Table 8.5	Strengths and weaknesses of sampling techniques	
Technique	**Strengths**	**Weaknesses**
Non-probability sampling		
Convenience sampling	Least expensive, least time consuming, most convenient	Selection bias, sample not representative, not recommended for descriptive or causal research
Judgemental sampling	Low cost, convenient, not time consuming. Ideal for exploratory research designs	Does not allow generalisation, subjective
Quota sampling	Sample can be controlled for certain characteristics	Selection bias, no assurance of representativeness
Snowball sampling	Can estimate rare characteristics	Time consuming
Probability sampling		
Simple random sampling (SRS)	Easily understood, results projectable	Difficult to construct sampling frame, expensive, lower precision, no assurance of representativeness
Systematic sampling	Can increase representativeness, easier to implement than SRS, sampling frame not always necessary	Can decrease representativeness depending upon 'order' in the sampling frame
Stratified sampling	Includes all important subpopulations, precision	Difficult to select relevant stratification variables, not feasible to stratify on many variables, expensive
Cluster sampling	Easy to implement, cost effective	Imprecise, difficult to compute and interpret results

Table 8.6	**Procedures for drawing probability samples**

Simple random sampling

1　Select a suitable sampling frame.
2　Each element is assigned a number from 1 to N (population size).
3　Generate n (sample size) different random numbers between 1 and N using a software package or a table of simple random numbers (Table 1 in the Appendix of statistical tables). To use Table 1, select the appropriate number of digits (e.g. if $N = 900$, select three digits). Arbitrarily select a beginning number. Then proceed up or down until n different numbers between 1 and N have been selected. Discard 0, duplicate numbers and numbers greater than N.
4　The numbers generated denote the elements that should be included in the sample.

Systematic sampling

1　Select a suitable sampling frame.
2　Each element is assigned a number from 1 to N (population size).
3　Determine the sampling interval i, where $i = N/n$. If i is a fraction, round to the nearest whole number.
4　Select a random number, r, between 1 and i, as explained in simple random sampling.
5　The elements with the following numbers will comprise the systematic random sample:

$r, r + i, r + 2i, r + 3i, r + 4i \ldots r + (n - 1)i$

Stratified sampling

1　Select a suitable sampling frame.
2　Select the stratification variable(s) and the number of strata, H.
3　Divide the entire population into H strata. Based on the classification variable, each element of the population is assigned to one of the H strata.
4　In each stratum, number the elements from 1 to N_h (the population size of stratum h).
5　Determine the sample size of each stratum, n_h, based on proportionate or disproportionate stratified sampling, where

$$\sum_{h=1}^{H} n_h = n$$

6　In each stratum, select a simple random sample of size n_h.

Cluster sampling

We describe the procedure for selecting a simple two-stage sample, because this represents the most commonly used general case.
1　Assign a number from 1 to N to each element in the population.
2　Divide the population into C clusters of which c will be included in the sample.
3　Calculate the sampling interval i, where $i = N/c$. If i is a fraction, round to the nearest whole number.
4　Select a random number, r, between 1 and i, as explained in simple random sampling.
5　Identify elements with the following numbers: $r, r + i, r + 2i, r + 3i, \ldots, r + (c - 1)i$
6　Select the clusters that contain the identified elements.
7　Select sampling units within each selected cluster based on SRS or systematic sampling. The number of sampling units selected from each sample cluster is approximately the same and equal to n/c.
8　If the population of the cluster exceeds the sampling interval i, that cluster is selected with certainty. That cluster is removed from further consideration. Calculate the new proportion size, N^*, the number of clusters to be selected, $c^* (= c - 1)$, and the new sampling interval i^*. Repeat this process until each of the remaining clusters has a population less than the relevant sampling interval. If b clusters have been selected with certainty, select the remaining $c - b$ clusters according to steps 1 to 7. The fraction of units to be sampled from each cluster selected with certainty is the overall sampling fraction n/N. Thus, for clusters selected with certainty, we would select $n_s (n/N)(N_1 + N_2 + \ldots + N_b)$ units. The units selected from clusters selected under two-stage sampling will therefore be $n^* = n - n_s$.

International marketing research

Implementing the sampling design process in international marketing research can be most challenging. For example, developing an appropriate sampling frame can be a difficult task. In many countries, reliable information about the target population may not be available from secondary sources. Government data may be unavailable or highly biased. Population lists may not be available commercially. The time and money required to compile these lists may be prohibitive. The census data available (even for demographics at household level) in some countries has one or more of the following problems: limited availability of variables, outdated data, unreliable data, outdated or unavailable maps. Reliable and updated information from the National Economic Census is not necessarily available for business-to-business, agricultural or industrial studies. It is possible to find many countries where the information at household level is reliable, updated and available online.

Given the lack of suitable sampling frames, the inaccessibility of certain participants, such as women in some cultures, and the dominance of face-to-face interviewing, probability sampling techniques are uncommon in some countries. New modes of data collection such as email, online, SMS, and mobile device have helped to access international participants, facilitated by the use of access panels. With such approaches the validation of survey findings or provision of relevant weighting is not generally feasible, especially in international studies where there may be a lack of valid population data. In international research, the growth of online surveys has caused concern when used with online panels where sampling is usually based upon non-probability methods. What constitutes an adequate sampling frame includes adequate coverage, known probabilities of selection, and being up to date. Access panels with adequate sampling frames, adequate selection/recruitment procedures and adequate controls can provide verifiable research findings.

Ethics in marketing research

The researcher has several ethical responsibilities to both the client and the participants pertaining to sampling.[31] With regard to the client, the researcher must develop a sampling design that best fits the project in an effort to minimise the sampling and non-sampling errors. When probability sampling can be used it should be. When non-probability design such as convenience sampling is used, the limitations of the design should be explicit in any findings that are presented. It is unethical and misleading to treat non-probability samples as probability samples and to project the results to a target population. Appropriate definition of the population and the sampling frame, and application of the correct sampling techniques, are essential if the research is to be conducted and the findings used ethically.

Researchers must be extremely sensitive to preserving the anonymity of the participants when conducting business-to-business research with small populations, particularly when reporting the findings to the client. When the population size is small, it is easier to discern the identities of the participants than when the samples are drawn from a large population. Special care must be taken when sample details are too revealing and when using verbatim quotations in reports to the client. This problem is acute in areas such as employee research. Here a breach of a participant's anonymity can cost the participant a pay rise, a promotion, or their employment. In such situations, special effort should be made to protect the identities of the participants. In such situations, the researcher has the ethical obligation to protect the identities of participants, even if it means limiting the level of sampling detail that is reported to the client and other parties.

Digital developments in marketing research

Sampling techniques commonly used for online surveys may be classified as online intercept (non-random and random), online recruited and other techniques as shown in Figure 8.6. Online recruited techniques can be further classified as panel (recruited or opt-in) or non-panel (list rentals). In online intercept sampling, visitors to a website are intercepted and given an opportunity to participate in a survey. The interception can be made at one or more websites, including high-traffic sites such as Yahoo! In non-random sampling, every visitor is intercepted. This may be meaningful if the website traffic is low, the survey has to be completed in a short time, and little incentive is being offered. However, this results in a convenience sample. Quotas can be imposed to increase representativeness. In random intercept sampling, the software selects visitors at random and a 'pop-up' window asks whether the person wants to participate in the survey. The selection can be made based on simple random or systematic random sampling. If the population is defined as visitors to a particular website, then this procedure results in a probability sample. However, if the population is other than visitors to a particular site, the resulting sample is more similar to a non-probability sample. Nevertheless, randomisation improves representativeness and discourages multiple responses from the same participant.

Online panels function in ways similar to non-online panels and share many of the same advantages and disadvantages. In recruited panels, typically termed as access panels, members can be recruited online or even by traditional means (postal, telephone). Based on the researcher's judgement, certain qualifying criteria can be introduced to pre-screen participants. Participants can be offered incentives such as sweepstake prizes, redeemable points and other types of online currencies. Members typically provide detailed psychographic, demographic, online usage and product consumption information at the time of joining. Opt-in panels operate similarly except that members choose to opt in as opposed to being recruited. To select a sample, the online company sends an email to those panelists who qualify based upon sample specifications given by the researcher. The success of probability sampling techniques depends upon the extent to which the panel is representative of the target population. With panels, highly targeted samples can be achieved, e.g. teenage girls who shop at boutiques more than twice a month.

Non-panel recruited sampling methods can also be used that require potential participants to go online to complete a survey. For example, the Spanish fashion store Zara may hand its customers an invite as they complete a purchase (either in-store or online). This invite directs them to a specific password protected site to respond to a questionnaire. If the population is defined as the company's customers, as in a customer satisfaction survey, and

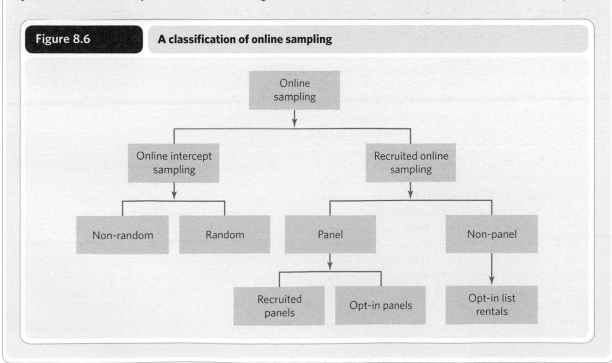

| Figure 8.6 | A classification of online sampling |

a random procedure is used to select participants, a probability sample will be obtained. Other non-panel approaches involve the use of email lists that have been bought from suppliers. Presumably (and great care must be taken in establishing the ethical credentials of such suppliers) these participants have opted in or gave permission for their email addresses to be circulated. Offline techniques such as short telephone screening interviews are also used for recruiting online samples. Many companies routinely collect email addresses in their CRM databases through telephone interactions, product registration cards, on-site registrations, special promotions and competitions.

Summary

Information about the characteristics of a population may be obtained by carrying out either a sample or a census. Budget and time limits, large population size and small variance in the characteristic of interest favour the use of a sample. Sampling is also preferred when the cost of sampling error is low, the cost of non-sampling error is high, the nature of measurement is destructive, and attention must be focused on individual cases. The opposite set of conditions favours the use of a census.

Sampling design begins by defining the target population in terms of elements, sampling units, extent and time. Then the sampling frame should be determined. A sampling frame is a representation of the elements of the target population. It consists of a list of directions for identifying the target population. At this stage, it is important to recognise any sampling frame errors that may exist. The next step involves selecting a sampling technique and determining the sample size. In addition to quantitative analysis, several qualitative considerations should be taken into account in determining the sample size. Execution of the sampling process requires detailed specifications for each step in the sampling process. Finally, the selected sample should be validated by comparing characteristics of the sample with known characteristics of the target population.

Sampling techniques may be classified as non-probability and probability techniques. Non-probability sampling techniques rely on the researcher's judgement. Consequently, they do not permit an objective evaluation of the precision of the sample results, and the estimates obtained are not statistically projectable to the population. The commonly used non-probability sampling techniques include convenience sampling, judgemental sampling, quota sampling and snowball sampling.

In probability sampling techniques, sampling units are selected by chance. Each sampling unit has a non-zero chance of being selected, and the researcher can pre-specify every potential sample of a given size that could be drawn from the population as well as the probability of selecting each sample. It is also possible to determine the precision of the sample estimates and inferences and make projections to the target population. Probability sampling techniques include simple random sampling, systematic sampling, stratified sampling, cluster sampling, sequential sampling and double sampling. The choice between probability and non-probability sampling should be based on the nature of the research, degree of error tolerance, relative magnitude of sampling and non-sampling errors, variability in the population, and statistical and operational considerations.

When conducting international marketing research, it is desirable to achieve comparability in sample composition and representativeness even though this may require the use of different sampling techniques in different countries. It is unethical and misleading to treat non-probability samples as probability samples and to project the results to a target population. The growth of online research has seen a corresponding growth in the use of online panels. Such panels have offered many advantages to researchers wishing to access samples of sufficient size and structure, from across the globe, quickly and relatively cheaply. Such panels create much debate about representativeness, the challenges of working primarily with non-probability samples and the actions required to create probability samples.

SNAP Learning Edition

With the increase in use of online research, there has been a corresponding growth of online panels. One of the major suppliers of such panels is Cint (**www.cint.com**), who have developed Direct Sample, bringing together both owners of online panels and buyers of online samples. SNAP have partnered with Cint to enable SNAP users to access up to 6 million members of research panels worldwide to create a specific panel for any online survey built within SNAP.

Demographic criteria and quota questions are used to specify the type of participants required for any panel. In the example shown, age and gender are the selection criteria, together with the geographical location for selecting the sample, as well as the number of surveys that need to be completed.

A qualifying quota question can then be set, prior to final selection of the panel. The entire process can be completed online with the panel sample being purchased directly from the SNAP shop.

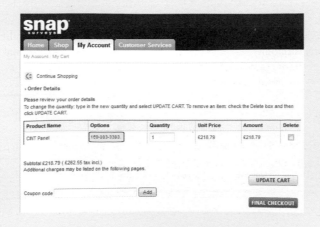

Once the panel has been selected, the survey is then checked by Cint. Once the survey has been approved, Cint then invite the panel to take part in the survey. They follow this up by sending reminders to any panel members who have failed to take the survey at the first invite. SNAP then handles all aspects of the survey, including the checking of quotas.

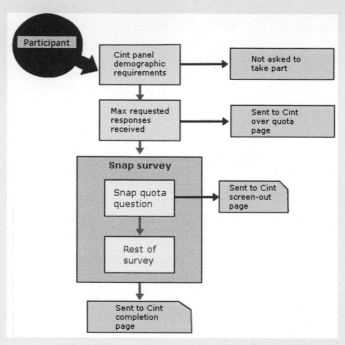

On completion of a survey, the precise combination of quotas may not have been totally met. The final demographics of participants may then need to be adjusted to more closely match the demographics of the target population.

Rim-weighting (also known as 'iterative proportional fitting') uses a mathematical algorithm to help provide an even distribution of results across the entire dataset while balancing certain categories such as age or gender to pre-determined totals. It weights the specified characteristics simultaneously and disturbs each variable as little as possible.

By way of example, in order to weight the sample in the ratio of 50% male and 50% female, but also 20% in each of five age brackets, the algorithm would calculate the correct weighting that needed to be applied to each table entry (combining age and gender).

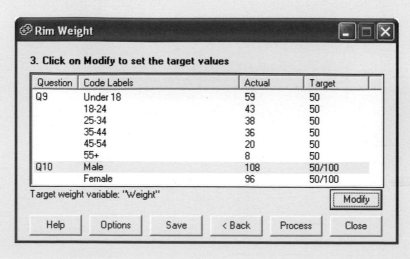

The calculated weight can then be used to specify any form of analysis required.

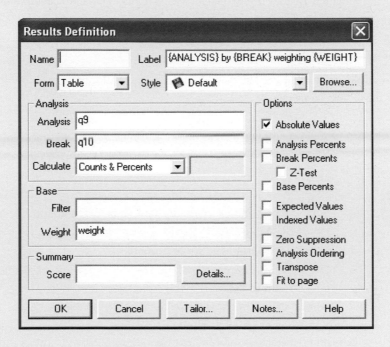

The resulting rim-weighted table will show both the weighted and unweighted totals and the cells will show the values adjusted to the target population.

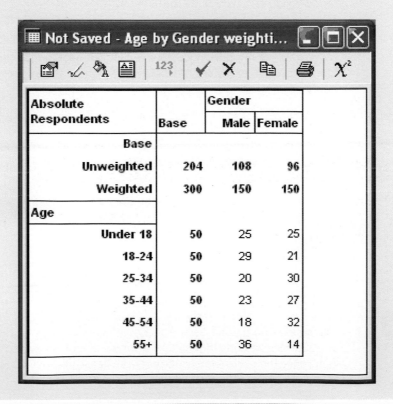

Rim-weighting is a useful tool, but care should be taken if:

- The variables being weighted are too closely related, for example, income bracket and dwelling size.
- The actual values vary too widely from the target, for example, there are 96 male participants and only four females, and the target is to be balanced to 50:50.
- A large number of weights need to be applied.

Chapter 9 provides additional detail on the steps of completing a questionnaire, whether it be for an online, mobile device or a paper survey.

Questions

1 Under what conditions would a sample be preferable to a census? A census preferable to a sample?

2 Describe the sampling design process.

3 How should the target population be defined? How does this definition link with the definition of a marketing research problem?

4 To what extent might the availability of sampling frames determine the definition of a population?

5 Define incidence rate and completion rate. How do these rates affect the determination of the final sample size?

6 How do probability sampling techniques differ from non-probability sampling techniques? What factors should be considered in choosing between probability and non-probability sampling?

7 What is the least expensive and least time consuming of all sampling techniques? What are the major limitations of this technique?

8 What is the major difference between judgemental and convenience sampling? Give examples of where each of these techniques may be successfully applied.

9 Describe snowball sampling. How may the technique be supported by qualitative research techniques?

10 What are the distinguishing features of simple random sampling?

11 Describe stratified sampling. What are the criteria for the selection of stratification variables?

12 Describe the cluster sampling procedure. What is the key distinction between cluster sampling and stratified sampling?

Exercises

1 Examine online databases and secondary data sources to determine all of the airlines operating in the EC. If a survey of airlines was to be conducted to determine their future plans to purchase/lease aeroplanes, would you take a sample or census? Explain why.

2 Visit **www.ralphlauren.com** and collect further secondary data and intelligence to obtain information on the segmentation strategy of Ralph Lauren. As the Vice-President of Marketing for Ralph Lauren, what information would you like to support decisions around an idea to launch a new line of unisex shirts in Europe? Imagine that they had launched these shirts and wanted to determine initial consumer reactions. If non-probability sampling were to be used, which sampling technique would you recommend, and why?

3 Using the website of a major newspaper in your country, search for reports of three recent major surveys. Write a report on the sample sizes used and the extent to which details of precision, confidence levels and any other factors affecting the sample were reported. Note any reporting that sensationalises statistical changes over time that are within the margin of error tolerances.

4 The Alumni Office of your university would like to conduct a survey of on-campus students who are in their final year of study. The office wishes to determine attitudes to joining alumni associations as students progress through further study and their careers. As a consultant you must develop a quota sample. What quota variables would you use? Design a quota matrix. Base this matrix upon your chosen variables and the proportions of these variables within your university.

5 In a small group discuss the following issues: 'Given that many governments use sampling to check the accuracy of various censuses and that non-response rates to censuses are growing, national decennial censuses should be abolished in favour of the use of existing databases and sample surveys.' 'Because non-sampling errors are greater in magnitude than sampling errors, it really does not matter which sampling method is used.' 'The real determinant of sample size is what managers feel confident with; it has little to do with statistical confidence.'

Notes

1. Korczak, D., 'Do I want to be beautiful? Consumer decision making for cosmetic surgery', ESOMAR, *Healthcare Conference*, Rome (Feb. 2008).

2. Kent, R., 'Rethinking data analysis – part one: The limitations of frequentist approaches', *International Journal of Market Research*, 51 (1) (2009), 51–69; Semon, T.T., 'Non-response bias affects all survey research', *Marketing News*, 38, (12) (July 2004), 7; Anon., 'Random sampling', *Marketing News* (16 July 2001), 10; Wilcox, S., 'Sampling and controlling a TV audience measurement panel', *International Journal of Market Research*, 42 (4) (Winter 2000), 413–30; Verma, V. and Le, T., 'An analysis of sampling errors for the demographic and health surveys', *International Statistical Review*, 64 (3) (December 1966), 265–94; Assael, H. and Keon, J., 'Non-sampling vs. sampling errors in sampling research', *Journal of Marketing* (Spring 1982), 114–23.

3. Wywial, J.L., 'Sampling design proportional to order statistic of auxiliary variable', *Statistical Papers*, 49 (2) (April 2008), 277–89; Huizing, L., van Ossenbruggen, R., Muller, M., van der Wal, C., Gerty, Lensvelt-Mulders, J.L.M. and Hubregtse, M., 'Improving panel sampling: Embedding propensity scores and response behaviour in sampling frames', ESOMAR, *Panel Research*, Orlando (Oct. 2007); Anon., 'Random sampling: Bruised, battered, bowed,' *Marketing News*, 36 (5) (4 March 2002), 12; Fink, A., *How to Sample in Surveys* (Thousand Oaks, CA: Sage, 1995); Frankel, M.R., 'Sampling theory', in Rossi, P.H., Wright, J.D. and Anderson, A.B. (eds) *Handbook of Survey Research* (Orlando, FL: Academic Press, 1983), 21–67.

4. Coleman, L., 'Preferences towards sex education and information from a religiously diverse sample of young people', *Health Education*, 108 (1), (2007), 72–91;

Reiter, J.P., 'Topics in survey sampling/finite population sampling and inference: A prediction approach', *Journal of the American Statistical Association*, 97 (457) (March 2002), 357–58; Henry, G.T., *Practical Sampling* (Thousand Oaks, CA: Sage, 1995); Sudman, S., 'Applied sampling', in Rossi, P.H., Wright, J.D. and Anderson, A.B. (eds) *Handbook of Survey Research* (Orlando, FL: Academic Press, 1983), 145–94.

5. Jäntti, S-M. and Järn, C., 'The insightful museum – how to create a customer centred marketing strategy', ESOMAR, *Consumer Insights*, Dubai (Feb. 2009).

6. Körner, T. and Nimmergut, A., 'Using an access panel as a sampling frame for voluntary household surveys', *Statistical Journal of the United Nations*, 21 (2004), 33–52; Cage, R., 'New methodology for selecting CPI outlet samples', *Monthly Labor Review*, 119 (12) (December 1996), 49–83.

7. Wyner, G.A., 'Survey errors', *Marketing Research*, 19 (1) (April 2007), 6–8; Couper, M.P., 'Web surveys: A review of issues and approaches', *Public Opinion Quarterly*, 64 (4) (Winter 2000), 464–94; Smith, W., Mitchell, P., Attebo, K. and Leeder, S., 'Selection bias from sampling frames: Telephone directory and electoral roll compared with door-to-door population census: Results from the Blue Mountain eye study', *Australian & New Zealand Journal of Public Health*, 21 (2) (April 1997), 127–33.

8. For the effect of sample frame error on research results, see Murphy, G.B., 'The effects of organizational sampling frame selection', *Journal of Business Venturing*, 17 (3) (May 2002), 237; Fish, K.E., Barnes, J.H. and Banahan, B.F., III, 'Convenience or calamity', *Journal of Health Care Marketing*, 14 (Spring 1994), 45–49.

9. Kent, R., 'Rethinking data analysis – part two: Some alternatives to frequentist approaches', *International Journal of Market Research*, 51 (2) (2009), 181–202; Bakken, D.G., 'The Bayesain revolution in marketing research', ESOMAR, *Innovate! Conference*, Paris (Feb. 2005).

10. Stevens, C., Jethwani, T. and Renaud, D., 'Online = research nirvana?' ESOMAR, *Conference on Panel Research*, Budapest (April 2005); Lee, K.G., 'Incidence is a key element', *Marketing News* (13 September 1985), 50.

11. Till, A., Souza, F. and Mele, S., 'Right here…right now…location-specific mobile research', ESOMAR, *Annual Congress*, London (Sept. 2006).

12. For an application of convenience sampling, see Schwaiger, M., Sarstedt, M. and Taylor, C.R., 'Art for the sake of the corporation: Audi, BMW Group, Daimler Chrysler, Montblanc, Siemens and Volkswagen help explore the effect of sponsorship on corporate reputations', *Journal of Advertising Research*, 50 (1) (2010), 77–91; Ritchie, L., 'Empowerment and Australian community health nurses work with aboriginal clients: The sociopolitical context', *Qualitative Health Research*, 11 (2) (March 2001), 190–205; Ho, F., Ong, B.S. and Seonsu, A., 'A multicultural comparison of shopping patterns among Asian consumers', *Journal of Marketing Theory and Practice*, 5 (1) (Winter 1997), 42–51.

13. Kerr, G. and Schultz, D., 'Maintenance person or architect? The role of academic advertising research in building better understanding', *International Journal of Advertising*, 29 (4) (2010), 547–68.

14. Huizing, L., van Ossenbruggen, R., Muller, M., van der Wal, C., Lensvelt-Mulders, G.J.L.M. and Hubregtse, M., 'Improving panel sampling: Embedding propensity scores and response behavior in sampling frames', ESOMAR, *Panel Research*, Orlando (Oct. 2007).

15. Thompson, S.K., *Sampling* (New York: Wiley, 2002); Sudman, S., 'Sampling in the twenty-first century', *Academy of Marketing Science Journal*, 27 (2) (Spring 1999), 269–77; Kish, L., *Survey Sampling* (New York: John Wiley, 1965), 552.

16. Curtice, J. and Sparrow, N., 'How accurate are traditional quota opinion polls?' *Journal of the Market Research Society*, 39 (3) (July 1997), 433–48.

17. de Gaudemar, O., 'Benefits and challenges of multi-sourcing – understanding differences between sample sources', ESOMAR, *Panel Research*, Barcelona (Nov. 2006); Getz, P.M., 'Implementing the new sample design for the current employment statistics survey', *Business Economics*, 35 (4) (Oct. 2000), 47–50; Anon., 'Public opinion: Polls apart', *The Economist*, 336 (7927) (12 August 1995), 48; Kalton, G., *Introduction to Survey Sampling* (Beverly Hills, CA: Sage, 1982); Sudman, S., 'Improving the quality of shopping center sampling', *Journal of Marketing Research*, 17 (November 1980), 423–31.

18. For applications of snowball sampling, see Zeng, F., Huang, L. and Dou, W., 'Social factors in user perceptions and responses to advertising in online social networking', *The Journal of Interactive Advertising*, 10 (1) (Fall 2009); Winkler, T. and Buckner, K., 'Receptiveness of gamers to embedded brand messages in advergames: Attitudes towards product placement', *The Journal of Interactive Advertising*, 7 (1) (Fall 2006); Maher, L., 'Risk behaviours of young Indo-Chinese injecting drug users in Sydney and Melbourne', *Australian & New Zealand Journal of Public Health* (Feb. 2001), 50–54; Frankwick, G.L., Ward, J.C., Hutt, M.D. and Reingen, P.H., 'Evolving patterns of organisational beliefs in the formation of strategy', *Journal of Marketing*, 58 (April 1994), 96–110.

19. If certain procedures for listing members of the rare population are followed strictly, the snowball sample can be treated as a probability sample. See Sampath, S., *Sampling Theory and Methods* (Boca Raton, FL: CRC Press, 2000); Henry, G.T., *Practical Sampling* (Thousand Oaks, CA: Sage, 1995); Kalton, G. and Anderson, D.W., 'Sampling rare populations', *Journal of the Royal Statistical Association* (1986), 65–82; Biemacki, P. and Waldorf, D., 'Snowball sampling: Problems and techniques of chain referred sampling', *Sociological Methods and Research*, 10 (November 1981), 141–63.

20. Campbell, C., Parent, M. and Plangger, K., 'Instant innovation: From zero to full speed in fifteen years – How online offerings have reshaped marketing research', *Journal of Advertising Research*, 51 (1) (50th Anniversary Supplement) (2011), 72–86.

21. Lavrakas, P.J., Mane, S. and Laszlo, J., 'Does anyone really know if online ad campaigns are working? An evaluation of methods used to assess the effectiveness of advertising on the Internet', *Journal of Advertising Research*, 50 (4) (2010).

22. When the sampling interval, i, is not a whole number, the easiest solution is to use as the interval the nearest whole number below or above i. If rounding has too great an effect on the sample size, add or delete the extra cases.

23. For an application of systematic random sampling, see Man, Y.S. and Prendergast, G., 'Perceptions of handbills as a promotional medium: An exploratory study', *Journal of Advertising Research*, 45 (1) (March 2005), 124–31; MacFarlane, P., 'Structuring and measuring the size of business markets', *International Journal of Market Research*, 44 (1) (First Quarter 2002), 7–30; Qu, H. and Li, I., 'The characteristics and satisfaction of mainland Chinese visitors to Hong Kong', *Journal of Travel Research*, 35 (4) (Spring 1997), 37–41; Chakraborty, G., Ettenson, R. and Gaeth, G., 'How consumers choose health insurance', *Journal of Health Care Marketing*, 14 (Spring 1994), 21–33.

24. Meng, J., Summey, J.H., Herndon, N.C. and Kwong, K.K., 'On the retail service quality expectations of Chinese shoppers', *International Journal of Market Research*, 51 (6) (2009), 773–96.

25. For applications of stratified random sampling, see Truong, Y., 'Personal aspirations and the consumption of luxury goods', *International Journal of Market Research*, 52 (5) (2010), 655–73; Okazaki, S., 'Social influence model and electronic word of mouth: PC versus mobile Internet', *International Journal of Advertising*, 28 (3) (2009), 439–72; Kjell, G., 'The level-based stratified sampling plan', *Journal of the American Statistical Association*, 95 (452) (December 2000), 1185–91.

26. Opdyke, J.D. and Mollenkamp, C., 'Yes, you are "High Net Worth"', *Wall Street Journal* (May 21, 2002) D1, D3.

27. Zelin, A. and Stubbs, R., 'Cluster sampling: A false economy?' *International Journal of Market Research*, 47 (5) (2005), 501–22

28. Geographic clustering of rare populations, however, can be an advantage. See Laaksonen, S., 'Retrospective two-stage cluster sampling for mortality in Iraq', *International Journal of Market Research*, 50 (3) (2008), 403–17; Rao, P.S., *Sampling methodologies with applications* (Boca Raton, FL: CRC Press, 2001); Carlin, J.B., 'Design of cross-sectional surveys using cluster sampling: An overview with Australian case studies', *Australian & New Zealand Journal of Public Health*, 23 (5) (Oct. 1999), 546–51; Raymondo, J.C., 'Confessions of a Nielsen Housechild', *American Demographics*, 19 (3) (March 1997), 24–27; Sudman, S., 'Efficient screening methods for the sampling of geographically clustered special populations', *Journal of Marketing Research*, 22 (Feb. 1985), 20–29.

29. Sergeant, J. and Bock, T., 'Small sample market research', *International Journal of Market Research*, 44 (2) (2002), 235–44; Walker, J., 'A sequential discovery sampling procedure', *Journal of the Operational Research Society*, 53 (1) (January 2002), 119; Park, J.S., Peters, M. and Tang, K., 'Optimal inspection policy in sequential screening', *Management Science*, 37 (8) (August 1991), 1058–61; Anderson, E.J., Gorton, K. and Tudor, R., 'The application of sequential analysis in market research', *Journal of Marketing Research*, 17 (Feb. 1980), 97–105.

30. For more discussion of double sampling, see Brewer, K., *Design and Estimation in Survey Sampling* (London: Edward Arnold, 2001); Shade, J., 'Sampling inspection tables: Single and double sampling', *Journal of Applied Statistics*, 26 (8) (December 1999), 1020; Baillie, D.H., 'Double sampling plans for inspection by variables when the process standard deviation is unknown', *International Journal of Quality & Reliability Management*, 9 (5) (1992), 59–70; Frankel, M.R. and Frankel, L.R., 'Probability sampling', in Ferber, R. (ed.) *Handbook of Marketing Research* (New York: McGraw-Hill, 1974), 2-230–2-246.

31. Bednall, D.H.B., Adam, S. and Plocinski, K., 'Ethics in practice: Using compliance techniques to boost telephone response rates', *International Journal of Market Research*, 52 (2) (2010), 155–68.

9 Fieldwork and data integrity

The management of fieldwork and data integrity can substantially enhance the quality of data and statistical results.

Objectives

After reading this chapter, you should be able to:

1 describe the survey fieldwork process and explain the selecting, training and supervising of fieldworkers, validating fieldwork and evaluating fieldworkers;

2 discuss the training of fieldworkers in making the initial contact, asking the questions, probing, recording the answers and concluding an interview;

3 discuss supervising fieldworkers in terms of quality control and editing, sampling control, control of cheating and central office control;

4 describe evaluating fieldworkers in areas of cost and time, response rates, quality of interviewing and the quality of data;

5 discuss non-response issues and procedures for improving response rates and adjusting for non-response;

6 discuss the nature and scope of data integrity and the data integrity process;

7 explain questionnaire checking and editing and the treatment of unsatisfactory responses by returning to the field, assigning missing values and discarding unsatisfactory responses;

8 describe the guidelines for coding questionnaires, including the coding of structured and unstructured questions;

9 discuss the data cleaning process and the methods used to treat missing responses: substitution of a neutral value, imputed response, casewise deletion and pairwise deletion;

10 state the reasons for and methods of statistically adjusting data: weighting, variable respecification and scale transformation;

11 describe the procedure for selecting a data analysis strategy and the factors influencing the process;

12 explain the issues related to fieldwork and data integrity when conducting international marketing research;

13 discuss ethical aspects of survey fieldwork and data integrity;

14 appreciate how digital developments are shaping the manner in which the quality of fieldwork and data integrity may be improved.

Overview

The researcher faces two major problems when managing fieldwork operations. First of all, fieldwork should be carried out in a consistent manner so that regardless of who administers a questionnaire, the same process is adhered to. This is vital to allow valid comparisons between all completed questionnaires. Second, fieldworkers to some extent have to approach and motivate potential participants in a manner that sets the correct purpose for a study and motivates the participant to spend time answering the questions properly. This cannot be done in a 'robotic' manner; it requires good communication skills and an amount of empathy with participants, but could be interpreted as a means to bias responses. These two problems may be seen as conflicting, but for the researcher, fieldwork management means resolving these conflicts for each individual data gathering process. This makes survey fieldwork an essential task in the generation of sound research data.

Decisions related to data integrity and analysis should not take place after data have been collected. Before the raw data contained in the questionnaires can be subjected to statistical analysis, they must be converted into a form suitable for analysis. The suitable form and the means of analysis should be considered as a research design is developed. This ensures that the output of the analyses will satisfy the research objectives set for a particular project. The care exercised in the data integrity phase has a direct effect upon the quality of statistical results and ultimately the support offered to marketing decision makers. Paying inadequate attention to data integrity can seriously compromise statistical results, leading to biased findings and incorrect interpretation. Most of the data integrity process and the quality checks inherent in this process are now completed automatically. Online modes which form the majority of surveys have in-built parameters to ensure the quality of data prepared for statistical analysis. Survey software helps researchers to perform quality checks at all stages of data integrity, whatever the mode of collection. With software developments, many researchers will not have to manually intervene in the data integrity process. However, it is important to understand what this process entails and what survey software does to monitor data quality.

We briefly discuss survey fieldwork and data integrity in the context of international marketing research and identify the relevant ethical issues. We conclude by discussing how digital developments in marketing research are enabling more efficient and effective fieldwork and the means to prepare data for statistical analysis. To begin, we present an example that illustrates the role of web portal design in delivering an excellent research experience for survey participants. Managing a positive experience for research participants (and, as in this case, panel members) is vital in ensuring data integrity.

Real research   **GfK's online panel[1]**

The Web Portal is the 'web presence' of an online panel. This is where the panel members go to interact with a research agency and thus is a hugely important aspect of online research. The portal is used to build a relationship with the panel members and retain the high panel retention that is necessary for the quality of continuous research. When communicating with the panel members it is important to retain the personal 'feel'. The GfK website is compared by their panel members with every site they visit, not just those of other research companies. Therefore, the Web Portal had to offer a comparable experience to that offered by, for example, banks and retailers, in terms of functionality and user experience. The system must also be extremely reliable as any problems will have a direct effect on response rates and panel retention. Response levels have been raised to well above the industry average for online access panels, although still below their postal panel peak of 85 per cent. GfK have seen response rates rise directly in line with their increase in the understanding of the differences between the online and offline postal panel. The online panel has a 'core' of panellists from which they experience an 80 per cent response rate. Outside this group there is a continuous influx of panellists who participate for about a year and then drop off. When analysing this against their experience with the postal panels they offered the following lessons.

- Receiving a questionnaire through the post is a much more tangible experience. The questionnaire sits on a 'to-do' pile and this is a constant reminder to complete it. The participant is also able to see the entirety of the questionnaire and can easily make an estimation of the time required to complete it.

- People are much more likely to change their email address than they are to move. It is therefore much easier to lose contact with participants. 'Spam' mailing is a major reason for switching email address and is therefore a major issue for companies running continuous panels.

- The Internet is a rapidly changing environment and it is very easy for panellists to become tired of a website. There are many more distractions for people when they are online. Community sites such as MySpace and Facebook take up increasing amounts of online time. There has also been an increase in entertainment available online, such as gaming and online television services such as the BBC iPlayer.

Taking these factors into account means the panellist communication strategy and incentive schemes are constantly under review. It is always necessary to value the importance of building and maintaining the relationship with the panellists and ensuring they feel valued for the help they provide in conducting the research.

The nature of survey fieldwork

Marketing research data are rarely collected by the persons who design the research. Researchers have two major options for collecting their data: they can develop their own organisations or they can contract with a fieldwork agency. In either case, data collection involves the use of some kind of field force. The field force may operate either from an office (online, telephone, and postal surveys) or in the field (face-to-face interviews at home or a workplace, street interview, CAPI and observation). The fieldworkers who collect the data typically may have little formal marketing research or marketing training. Their training primarily focuses upon the essential tasks of selecting the correct participants, motivating them to take part in the research, eliciting the correct answers from them, accurately recording the answers and conveying those answers for analysis. An appreciation of why these tasks fit into the overall context of conducting marketing research is important, but it is not necessary for the survey fieldworker to be trained in the whole array of research skills.

The growth in online research has changed the nature and emphasis of fieldwork. Traditionally, marketing research used a 'personal attention' approach in which every interviewer focused upon nurturing and addressing each specific participant. Online research has shifted the service design from a personalised to a more 'self-service' approach. Analogous to transactions like self-service petrol stations, company websites, or e-tickets for airlines, the participant becomes a 'partial interviewer' participating in the production of the service. Conducting online research eliminates the bias and the pressure that are usually introduced by the presence of the interviewer in the participant's environment. The intentional or unintentional behaviour and appearance of the interviewer does not influence the participant and how they respond. As a corollary, the participant may provide more truthful answers than would be the case in the presence of another party. Many participants like online research because it puts them in control. For many other participants the 'self-service' form of engaging with researchers is treated with much scepticism. Many participants need to develop a sense of trust, and the benefits of participation need to be clearly promoted by human contact.[2] For these participants, telephone or face-to-face interviews will be required, using traditional forms of fieldwork.

Survey fieldwork and the data collection process

All survey fieldwork involves selecting, training and supervising of persons who collect and manage data.[3] The validation of fieldwork and the evaluation of fieldworkers are also parts of the process. Figure 9.1 represents a general framework for the survey fieldwork and data collection process. Even though we describe a general process, it should be recognised that

Figure 9.1

Survey fieldwork/ data selection process

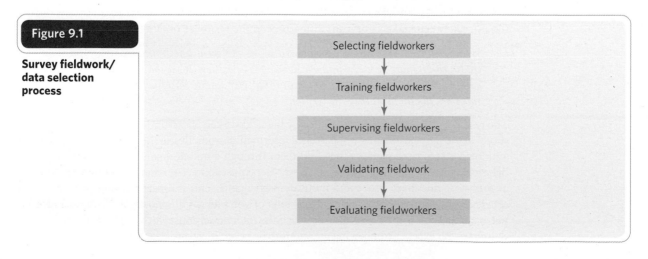

the nature of survey fieldwork can vary widely with the mode of data collection and that the relative emphasis on the different steps will be different for online, telephone, face-to-face and postal surveys.

Selecting survey fieldworkers

The first step in the survey fieldwork process is the selection of fieldworkers. The researcher should (1) develop job specifications for the project, taking into account the mode of data collection; (2) decide what characteristics the fieldworkers should have; and (3) recruit appropriate individuals. Interviewers' background characteristics, opinions, perceptions, expectations and attitudes can affect the responses they elicit.[4]

For example, the social acceptability of a fieldworker to the participant may affect the quality of data obtained, especially in face-to-face interviewing. Researchers generally agree that the appearance and demeanour of the interviewer have a direct impact upon participants' willingness to engage in an interview.

Training survey fieldworkers

Training survey fieldworkers is critical to the quality of data collected. Training may be conducted in person at a central location or, if the interviewers are geographically dispersed, online, by video-conferencing or even by mail. Training ensures that all interviewers administer the questionnaire in the same manner so that the data can be collected uniformly. Training should cover making the initial contact, asking the questions, probing, recording the answers and concluding the interview.[5]

Making the initial contact

The initial contact can result in cooperation or the loss of potential participants.[6] It also sets the potential participant in a 'frame of mind' to answer subsequent questions. Thus interviewers should be trained to make opening remarks that will convince potential participants that their participation is important. They should also motivate potential participants to reflect properly upon the questions posed to them and to answer honestly.

Asking the questions

Even a slight change in the wording, sequence or manner in which a question is asked can distort its meaning and bias the response. Training in asking questions can yield high dividends in eliminating potential sources of bias. Changing the phrasing or order of questions during the interview can make significant differences in the response obtained.

> While we could be faulted for not writing as perfect a questionnaire as we possibly could, still it must be asked in the exact way it is written. It's a challenge for us to try to get the interviewers to be more conversational, but despite this, the field force absolutely must ask questions as they are written![7]

The researcher, who is being represented by the fieldworker, has to understand and 'step into the shoes' of the participants they hope to elicit information from. Researchers impose their language and logic on to participants as they lead them through a questionnaire. If the interviewer is to behave as stated in the above quotation, researchers must appreciate what interviewers go through as they pose questions, probe and motivate participants. This is because asking questions is an art. The subtle smiles, body language and tone of voice all get the most out of the vast array of personalities, intellects and contexts in which the interviewer must work. The art of interviewing develops with experience, allowing questions to be posed in a consistent manner.[8]

The following are guidelines for interviewers in becoming consistent in asking questions:[9]

1 Be thoroughly familiar with the purpose of the questionnaire.

2 Be thoroughly familiar with the structure of the questionnaire.

3 Ask the questions in the order in which they appear in the questionnaire.

4 Use the exact wording given in the questionnaire.

5 Read each question slowly.

6 Repeat questions that are not understood.

7 Ask every applicable question.

8 Follow instructions, working through any filter questions, and probe carefully.

Probing

Probing
A motivational technique used when asking questions to induce the participants to enlarge on, clarify or explain their answers.

Probing is intended to motivate participants to enlarge on, clarify or explain their answers. Probing also helps participants focus on the specific content of the interview and provide only relevant information. Probing should not introduce any bias. An example of the effect of interviewer bias comes from a survey in which one of the authors helped in data analysis (but not in the design of the questionnaire nor management of the whole research process!). The survey related to bread and cake buying habits with one particular question focusing upon 'large cakes' that participants had bought over the previous 12 months. In analysing the data, a percentage of participants had replied '*Christmas cake*'. When analysed further, all the participants who said '*Christmas cake*' had been interviewed by the same interviewer. The conclusion from this analysis was that the interviewer in question had used their own probe in a manner that they would have answered the question, and in their view, to make the interview process work. None of the other interviewers had used this probe, which meant there was an inconsistent approach in eliciting answers from participants. The paradox faced by the survey designers in this example was that the 'rogue' interviewer *may* have used a probe that elicited a true representation of large cake purchasing, the other interviewers consistently failing to draw out a 'true' response.

To help in the process of probing, Table 9.1 provides several examples of the common questions or comments used as probes.[10] Corresponding abbreviations are also provided. The interviewer should record the abbreviations in parentheses next to the question asked.

Table 9.1	Commonly used probes and abbreviations
Standard interviewer's probe	**Abbreviation**
Any other reason?	(AO?)
Any others?	(Other?)
Anything else?	(AE or Else?)
Could you tell me more about your thinking on that?	(Tell more)
How do you mean?	(How mean?)
Repeat question	(RQ)
What do you mean?	(What mean?)
Which would be closer to the way you feel?	(Which closer?)
Why do you feel this way?	(Why?)
Would you tell me what you have in mind?	(What in mind?)

The above list may seem to be simple, but there are hidden dangers. For example, probing '*why*' participants behave in a particular manner or feel about a particular issue takes the interview into the realms of the qualitative interview. Compare the context of the street interview with a short structured questionnaire with the context of the qualitative interview with a questioning approach structured to the participant and where a greater amount of rapport may be developed. The latter scenario is much more conducive to eliciting '*why*' participants behave or feel as they do. The question '*why*' is an example of a seemingly simple question that can create many problems of consistency in fieldwork. In the greater majority of circumstances, '*why*' should be treated as a qualitative issue.

Recording the answers

Although recording participant answers seems simple, several mistakes are common.[11] All interviewers should use the same format and conventions to record the interviews and edit completed interviews. Although the rules for recording answers to structured questions vary with each specific questionnaire, the general rule is to check the box that reflects the participant's answer. The general rule for recording answers to unstructured questions is to record the responses verbatim. The following guidelines help to record answers to unstructured questions:

1 Record responses during the interview.

2 Use the participant's own words.

3 Do not summarise or paraphrase the participant's answers.

4 Include everything that pertains to the question objectives.

5 Include all probes and comments.

6 Repeat the response as it is written down.

Concluding the interview

The interview should not be closed before all the information is obtained. Any spontaneous comments the participant offers after all the formal questions have been asked should be recorded. The interviewer should answer the participant's questions about the project. The participant should be left with a positive feeling about the interview. It is important to thank the participant and express appreciation.

Saying 'thank you' can take many forms. As well as genuinely thanking participants for their cooperation, it serves the purpose of educating participants about the nature and purpose of marketing research, distinguishing marketing research from '**sugging**' and '**frugging**', industry terms for selling or fundraising under the guise of a survey.

Sugging
The use of marketing research to deliberately disguise a sales effort.

Frugging
The use of marketing research to deliberately disguise fundraising activities.

Summary of training issues

To encapsulate the process of interviewer training, the following list summarises the nature and scope of areas in which a marketing research interviewer should be trained:

1 The marketing research process: how a study is developed, implemented and reported.

2 The importance of the interviewer to this process; the need for honesty, objectivity, organisational skills and professionalism.

3 Confidentiality of the participant and the client.

4   Familiarity with marketing research terminology.

5   The importance of following the exact wording and recording responses verbatim.

6   The purpose and use of probing and clarifying techniques.

7   The reason for and use of classification and participant information questions.

8   A review of samples of instructions and questionnaires.

9   The importance of the participant's positive feelings about survey research.

Conversely, researchers should be trained in the 'experience' of gathering data in the field with a practical knowledge of what works in terms of:

- Motivating potential participants to take part in a survey.
- Questions that will elicit the required data.
- Probes that can be consistently applied.
- An interview process that does not confuse or cause boredom in the participant.

The researcher needs to appreciate what the participant and the interviewer go through in the interview process. Without such an understanding, the questionnaires and interview procedures, which seem fine on paper, can lead to very poor-quality data. The following example illustrates the experiences of a 'typical' participant and researcher. Whilst the feelings expressed cannot be generalised to all interview situations, the lesson from this is that the researcher should aim to understand how the target participants and interviewers feel about the process. These feelings must form an integral part of any research design that generates sound and accurate data.

Real research   **How was it for you?[12]**

A participant and an interviewer describe what their interview experiences were like for them.

The participant

'I felt sorry for the interviewer, she was going around all these houses and nobody was in, so I agreed to take part in the survey. The interview did not take that long, only about 10 to 15 minutes, slightly less time than the interviewer said it would. The interviewer was smartly dressed, professional and helpful. She prompted me but did not actually push me. The experience was enjoyable, it was fun, and not a bad way to spend 10 to 15 minutes, although I think that was long enough. I like taking part in a survey if the subject matter is relevant to your life and you feel that your views are being taken into account. I think a lot of women prefer other females (or gay men) to interview them as there is an empathy there, and they might not feel they can be as honest or chatty with men. The age of the interviewer should relate to the subject matter. For example, if you are asking about children, then you should have an interviewer in a mother's age group. I think it is important to actually be in the same position as someone being surveyed. In an interview, you should be honest, do not tell them what you think they want to hear, relax, be friendly and go with the flow. A lot depends on the participant as well as the interviewer. There has to be a bit of banter between the two of you.'

The interviewer

'I do not have a typical day. If I am doing quota sampling I will do around 10 interviews a day. If it is preselected, then I will do 3 to 4 in-depth interviews. But if it's exit interviewing, I can do as many as 20 in a shift. There are pressures to the job sometimes. Getting your quota is like looking for a needle in a haystack. People are much more suspicious, and fewer will open the doors these days. I have interviewed through wrought iron gates, letter boxes, front room windows, and with the chain on the door. For your own safety, you must be aware of where you are and what's around you. Technology has not made my job easier; I feel that interviewing using pen and paper flows better.

My job could be made easier by keeping questionnaires short, and using proper screening questions. The essence is to keep it interesting. The worst thing in the world is when you have got a survey that repeats itself and is boring; huge lists are our worst enemy. All I ask of a participant is that they are honest; they do not have to be articulate or have strong opinions. There are two keys to successful interviewing, smile and be polite at all times, so that it is very hard for people to be rude to you, and be firm and in control of the interview.'

Supervising survey fieldworkers

Supervising survey fieldworkers means making sure that they are following the procedures and techniques in which they were trained. Supervision involves quality control and editing, sampling control, control of cheating and central office control.

Quality control and editing

Quality control of fieldworkers requires checking to see whether the field procedures are being properly implemented.[13] If any problems are detected, the supervisor should discuss them with the fieldworkers and if necessary provide additional training. To understand the interviewers' problems related to a specific study, the supervisors should also do some interviewing. Supervisors should ensure that there are no technical problems in recording and transferring data through electronic means. If a survey is being conducted with hard copies of questionnaires, they should collect and check them daily. They should examine the questionnaires to make sure all appropriate questions have been completed, that unsatisfactory or incomplete answers have not been accepted. Supervisors should also keep a record of hours worked and expenses. This will allow a determination of the cost per completed interview, whether the job is moving on schedule, and whether any interviewers are having problems.

Sampling control

Sampling control
An aspect of supervising that ensures that the interviewers strictly follow the sampling plan rather than select sampling units based on convenience or accessibility.

An important aspect of supervision is **sampling control**, which attempts to ensure that the interviewers are strictly following the sampling plan rather than selecting sampling units based on convenience or accessibility.[14] Interviewers tend to avoid homes, workplaces and people (sampling units) that they perceive as difficult or undesirable. If the sampling unit is not at home, for example, interviewers may be tempted to substitute the next available unit rather than call back. Interviewers sometimes stretch the requirements of quota samples. For example, a 58-year-old person may be placed in the 46–55 category and interviewed to fulfil quota requirements. To control these problems, supervisors should keep daily records of the number of calls made, the number of not-at-homes, the number of refusals, the number of completed interviews for each interviewer, and the total for all interviewers under their control.

Central office control

Supervisors provide quality and cost-control information to the central office so that a total progress report can be maintained. In addition to the controls initiated in the field, other controls may be added at the central office to identify potential problems. Central office control includes tabulation of quota variables, important demographic characteristics and answers to key variables.

Validating survey fieldwork

An interviewer may falsify part of an answer to make it acceptable or may fake answers. The most blatant form of cheating occurs when the interviewer falsifies the entire questionnaire, merely filling in fake answers, either on their own or through the use of friends or family members. Cheating can be minimised through proper training, supervision and by rewarding interviewers properly. Most importantly their work should be validated, which includes recording the names and contact details of participants.[15] Supervisors usually call 10–25 per cent of the participants to enquire whether the fieldworkers actually conducted the interviews. The supervisors ask about the length and quality of the interview, reaction to the interviewer and basic demographic data. The demographic information is cross-checked against the information reported by the interviewers on the questionnaires. The major drawback of this approach is that participants may not trust interviewers with a name and telephone number, perhaps believing that it is to be used in direct marketing to generate a sale.

Evaluating survey fieldworkers

It is important to evaluate survey fieldworkers to provide them with feedback on their performance as well as to identify the better fieldworkers and build a better, high-quality field force. The evaluation criteria should be clearly communicated to the fieldworkers during their training. The evaluation of fieldworkers should be based on the criteria of cost and time, response rates, quality of interviewing and quality of data.[16]

Cost and time

Interviewers can be compared in terms of the total cost (salary and expenses) per completed interview. If the costs differ by city size, comparisons should be made only among fieldworkers working in comparable cities. Fieldworkers should also be evaluated on how they spend their time. Time should be broken down into categories such as actual interviewing, travel and administration.

Response rates

It is important to monitor response rates on a timely basis so that corrective action can be taken if these rates are too low.[17] Supervisors can help interviewers with an inordinate number of refusals by listening to the introductions they use and providing immediate feedback. When all the interviews are over, different fieldworkers' percentage of refusals can be compared to identify the more able interviewers and to help understand what has impacted upon non-response for particular types of participant. Interviewers can be a rich source of understanding why a particular survey works well or not.

Quality of interviewing

To evaluate interviewers on the quality of interviewing, the supervisor must directly observe the interviewing process. The supervisor can do this in person or the fieldworker can record the interview. The quality of interviewing should be evaluated in terms of (1) the appropriateness of the introduction, (2) the precision with which the fieldworker asks questions, (3) the ability to probe in an unbiased manner, (4) the ability to ask sensitive questions, (5) interpersonal skills displayed during the interview, and (6) the manner in which the interview is terminated.

Quality of data

The completed questionnaires of each interviewer should be evaluated for the quality of data. Some indicators of quality data are that (1) the recorded data are legible; (2) all instructions, including skip patterns, are followed; (3) the answers to unstructured questions are recorded verbatim; (4) the answers to unstructured questions are meaningful and complete enough to be coded; and (5) item non-response occurs infrequently.

Errors related to fieldwork

Errors related to fieldwork are non-sampling errors, which consist of non-response and response errors (see Figure 9.2). Response errors can be attributed to the researcher, interviewer or participant. The major sources of error related to fieldwork are interviewer errors, participant errors and non-response errors. Interviewer errors consist of participant selection, questioning, recording and cheating errors. Participant errors consist of inability errors and unwillingness errors. Non-response errors are due to refusals and 'not at home'.

Figure 9.2

Errors related to fieldwork

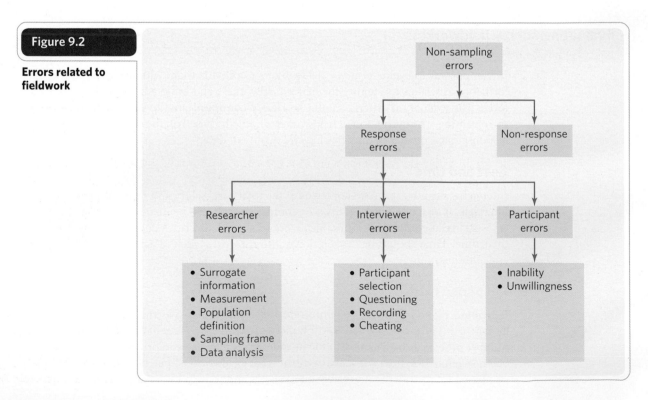

Non-response issues

Non-response error arises when some of the potential participants included in the sample do not respond. This is one of the most significant problems in survey research. Non-participants may differ from participants in terms of demographic, psychographic, personality, attitudinal, motivational and behavioural variables.[18] Evaluating these differences was detailed in the process of sample validation (Chapter 8). For a given study, if the non-participants differ from the participants on the characteristics of interest, the sample estimates can be seriously biased. Higher response rates, in general, imply lower rates of non-response bias, yet response rate may not be an adequate indicator of non-response bias. Response rates themselves do not indicate whether the participants are representative of the original sample.[19] Increasing the response rate may not reduce non-response bias if the additional participants are no different from those who have already responded but do differ from those who still do not respond. As low response rates increase the probability of non-response bias, an attempt should be made to improve the response rate.[20]

This is not an issue that should be considered after a survey approach has been decided and a questionnaire designed. Factors that improve response rates are integral to survey and questionnaire design. The researcher should build up an awareness of what motivates their target participants to participate in a research study. The researchers should ask themselves what their target participants get in return for spending time and effort, answering set questions in a full and honest manner. The following subsection details the techniques involved in improving response rates and adjusting for non-response. There is no definitive formula or theory that explains why non-response occurs nor what to do about it. There have been many practitioner and academic studies about non-response in individual survey modes, in cross-comparisons between modes and in specific contexts e.g. particular countries, participant types and the nature of topic. We continue with ideas to improve non-response, based upon this body of studies. The following example illustrates non-response challenges, comparing different survey modes.

Real research   ## Comparing mobile with fixed phones for surveys[21]

A study targeted at Portuguese adults (age ≥ 15 years) aimed to compare mobile survey with fixed telephone survey methods. The study focused on Internet usage, attitudes towards the Internet, cultural practices and demographics. Two surveys were conducted by the same survey company in order to overcome problems that might confuse the assessment of survey results if multiple sources of data collection were used. There were no conclusive results regarding the performance of mobile phone surveys as opposed to fixed phone surveys in terms of response rates. However, there were several features of mobile phones that could induce lower overall response rates. First, a mobile phone was seen as a personal device and many users may consider receiving a call from strangers on their mobile phone an invasion of their privacy.

The reaction may be a refusal or even a hang-up-without-answering as soon as they see an unfamiliar number on the phone screen. Second, the participant may be more or less willing to cooperate depending on the tariff that has been contracted for the mobile phone. Charging for receiving calls may discourage the acceptance of some calls, namely those from unknown sources. Mobile phones have the advantage of making the person accessible at any time of the day because it is a personal device carried at all times. Those participants who were previously difficult to reach are now reachable thanks to the mobile phone. The time period for contacts can be extended and is not restricted mainly to evenings and weekends; even the holiday period, typically connected with high non-response, may become a good or even a better period to conduct surveys. However, this advantage may become less salient because subscribers, especially lower-income customers, are more likely to turn off their phone and set it to voicemail so as to control the costs incurred by receiving calls.

Improving response rates

The primary causes of low response rates are refusals and not-at-homes, as shown in Figure 9.3.

Refusals   Refusals, which result from the unwillingness or inability of people included in the sample to participate, result in lower response rates and increased potential for non-response bias. Given the potential differences between participants and non-participants, researchers should attempt to lower refusal rates. This can be done by prior notification, incentives, good questionnaire design and administration, follow-up and other facilitators:

- *Prior notification.* In prior notification, potential participants are sent an email, a letter or are telephoned notifying them of the imminent online survey, postal, telephone or face-to-face survey. Prior notification increases response rates, as the participant's attention is drawn to the purpose of a study and the potential benefits, without the apparent 'chore' of the questionnaire. With the potential participant's attention focused upon the purpose and benefits, the chances increase for a greater reception when approached actually to complete a survey.[22]

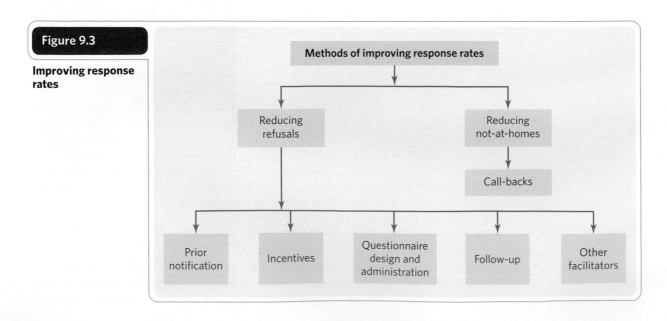

Figure 9.3

Improving response rates

- *Incentives.* Response rates can be increased by offering monetary as well as non-monetary incentives to potential participants. Monetary incentives can be prepaid or promised. The prepaid incentive is included with the survey or questionnaire. The promised incentive is sent to only those participants who complete the survey. The most commonly used non-monetary incentives are premiums and rewards, such as pens, pencils, books and offers of survey results.[23] Prepaid incentives have been shown to increase response rates to a greater extent than promised incentives. The amount of incentive can vary from trivial amounts to tens of euros. The amount of incentive has a positive relationship with response rate, but the cost of large monetary incentives may outweigh the value and quality of additional information obtained.

- *Questionnaire design and administration.* A well-designed questionnaire can decrease the overall refusal rate as well as refusals to specific questions. If the questionnaire and experience of answering the questions are interesting for the participant, using words, logic and visual appeal that are meaningful to them, the response rate can improve. Likewise, the skill used to administer the questionnaire in telephone and face-to-face interviews can increase the response rate. Trained interviewers are skilled in refusal conversion or persuasion. They do not accept a non-response without an additional plea. The additional plea might emphasise the brevity of the questionnaire or importance of the participant's opinion.

- *Follow-up.* Follow-up, or contacting the non-participants periodically after the initial contact, is particularly effective in decreasing refusals in online, SMS and postal surveys. The researcher might send a reminder to non-participants to complete and return the questionnaire. Two or three mailings may be needed in addition to the original one. With proper follow-up, the response rate in postal surveys can be increased to 80 per cent or more. Follow-ups can be done by postcard, letter, telephone, email or face-to-face contacts.[24]

- *Other facilitators.* Personalisation, or sending letters addressed to specific individuals, is effective in increasing response rates, especially when practiced in conjunction with prior notification.[25] The only downside of such an approach is actually obtaining the names and contact details of those to whom a questionnaire should be sent.

Not-at-homes The second major cause of low response rates is not-at-homes. This factor has contributed to the growth of online and mobile surveys. Where telephone and home face-to-face interviews are planned, low response rates can result if the potential participants are not at home when contact is attempted. The likelihood that potential participants will not be at home varies with several factors. People with small children are more likely to be at home. Consumers are more likely to be at home at weekends than on weekdays and in the evening as opposed to during the afternoon. Pre-notification and appointments increase the likelihood that the participant will be at home when contact is attempted. The percentage of not-at-homes can be substantially reduced by employing a series of call-backs, or periodic follow-up attempts to contact non-participants. The decision about the number of call-backs should weigh the benefits of reducing non-response bias against the additional costs. As call-backs are completed, the call-back participants should be compared with those who have already responded to determine the usefulness of making further call-backs. In most consumer surveys, three or four call-backs may be desirable. Although the first call yields the most responses, the second and third calls have a higher response per call. It is important that call-backs be made and controlled according to a prescribed plan.[26]

Adjusting for non-response

Low response rates increase the probability that non-response bias will be substantial. Response rates should always be reported, and, whenever possible, the effects of non-response should be estimated. This can be done by linking the non-response rate to estimated differences between participants and non-participants. Information on differences between the two groups may be obtained from the sample itself. For example, differences found through call-backs could be extrapolated, or a concentrated follow-up could be conducted on a subsample of the non-participants. Alternatively, it may be possible to estimate these differences from other sources.[27] To illustrate, in a survey of owners of vacuum cleaners, demographic and other information may be obtained for participants and non-participants from their guarantee cards. For a postal panel, a wide variety of information is available for both groups from syndicate organisations. If the sample is supposed to be representative of the general population, then comparisons can be made with census figures. Even if it is not feasible to estimate the effects of non-response, some adjustments can still be made during data analysis and interpretation.[28] The strategies available to adjust for non-response error include subsampling of non-participants, replacement, substitution, subjective estimates, trend analysis, simple weighting and imputation.

Subsampling of non-participants   Subsampling of non-participants, particularly in the case of postal surveys, can be effective in adjusting for non-response bias. In this technique, the researcher contacts a subsample of the non-participants, usually by means of telephone, face-to-face interviews or by email. This often results in a high response rate within that subsample. The values obtained for the subsample are then projected to all the non-participants, and the survey results are adjusted to account for non-response. This method can estimate the effect of non-response on the characteristic of interest.

Replacement   In replacement, the non-participants in the current survey are replaced with non-participants from an earlier, similar survey. The researcher attempts to contact these non-participants from the earlier survey and administer the current survey questionnaire to them, possibly by offering a suitable incentive. It is important that the nature of non-response in the current survey be similar to that of the earlier survey. The two surveys should use similar kinds of participants, and the time interval between them should be short. As an example, if a survey is being repeated one year later, the non-participants in the present survey may be replaced by the non-participants in the original survey.

Substitution
A procedure that substitutes for non-participants other elements from the sampling frame who are expected to respond.

Substitution   In substitution, the researcher substitutes for non-participants other elements from the sampling frame who are expected to respond. The sampling frame is divided into subgroups that are internally homogeneous in terms of participant characteristics but heterogeneous in terms of response rates. These subgroups are then used to identify substitutes who are similar to particular non-participants but dissimilar to participants already in the sample. Note that this approach would not reduce non-response bias if the substitutes are similar to participants already in the sample.

Subjective estimates   When it is no longer feasible to increase the response rate by subsampling, replacement or substitution, it may be possible to arrive at subjective estimates of the nature and effect of non-response bias. This involves evaluating the likely effects of non-response based on experience and available information. For example, married adults with young children are more likely to be at home than single or divorced adults or than married adults with no children. This information provides a basis for evaluating the effects of non-response due to not-at-homes in face-to-face or telephone surveys.

Trend analysis
A method of adjusting for non-response in which the researcher tries to discern a trend between early and late participants. This trend is projected to non-participants to estimate their characteristic of interest.

Trend analysis   Trend analysis is an attempt to discern a trend between early and late participants. This trend is projected to non-participants to estimate where they stand on the characteristic of interest.

Weighting
A statistical procedure that attempts to account for non-response by assigning differential weights to the data depending on the response rates.

Weighting   Weighting attempts to account for non-response by assigning differential weights to the data depending on the response rates.[29] For example, in a survey on personal computers, the sample was stratified according to income. The response rates were

85 per cent, 70 per cent and 40 per cent respectively for the high-, medium and low-income groups. In analysing the data, these subgroups are assigned weights inversely proportional to their response rates. That is, the weights assigned would be 100/85, 100/70 and 100/40 respectively for the high-, medium- and low-income groups. Although weighting can correct for the differential effects of non-response, it destroys the self-weighting nature of the sampling design and can introduce complications.[30]

Imputation Imputation involves imputing, or assigning, the characteristic of interest to the non-participants based on the similarity of the variables available for both non-participants and participants.[31] For example, a participant who does not report brand usage may be imputed based on the usage of a participant with similar demographic characteristics. Often there is a high correlation between the characteristic of interest and some other variables. In such cases, this correlation can be used to predict the value of the characteristic for the non-participants.

Imputation
A method to adjust for non-response by assigning the characteristic of interest to the non-participants based on the similarity of the variables available for both non-participants and participants.

The data integrity process

Editing
A review of the questionnaires with the objective of increasing accuracy and precision.

Coding
Assigning a code to represent a specific response to a specific question along with the data record and column position that the code will occupy.

The data integrity process is shown in Figure 9.4. The entire process is guided by the preliminary plan of data analysis that was formulated in the research design phase. The first step is to check for acceptable questionnaires. This is followed by editing, coding and transcribing the data. The data are cleaned and a treatment for missing responses is prescribed. Often, after the stage of sample validation, statistical adjustment of the data may be necessary to make them representative of the population of interest. The researcher should then select an appropriate data analysis strategy. The final data analysis strategy differs from the preliminary plan of data analysis due to the information and insights gained since the preliminary plan was formulated. Data integrity should begin as soon as the first batch of questionnaires is received from the field, while the fieldwork is still going on. Thus, if any problems are detected, the fieldwork can be modified to incorporate corrective action.

Figure 9.4

Data integrity process

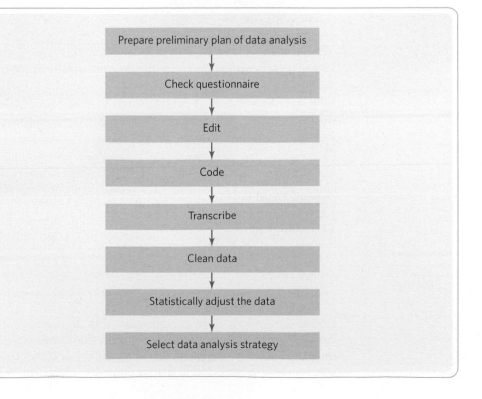

Prepare preliminary plan of data analysis

↓

Check questionnaire

↓

Edit

↓

Code

↓

Transcribe

↓

Clean data

↓

Statistically adjust the data

↓

Select data analysis strategy

Checking the questionnaire

The initial step in questionnaire checking involves reviewing all questionnaires for completion quality, as illustrated in the following example.

Real research   ### Custom cleaning[32]

According to Johan Harristhal of Gfk Custom Research (**www.gfk.com/gfkcr**), completed questionnaires from the field often have many small errors because of the inconsistent quality of interviewing. For example, qualifying responses are not circled, or skip patterns are not followed accurately. These small errors can be costly. When responses from such questionnaires are put on to a computer, Custom Research runs a cleaning program that checks for completedness and logic. Discrepancies are identified on a computer printout, which is checked by the tabulation supervisors. Once the errors are identified, appropriate corrective action is taken before data analysis is carried out. Custom Research has found that this procedure substantially increases the quality of statistical results.

Researchers do not just depend upon error checks at the data entry stage; checks should be made whilst fieldwork is still under way. If the fieldwork was contracted to a data collection agency, the researcher should make an independent check after it is over. A questionnaire returned from the field may be unacceptable for several reasons:

1   Parts of the questionnaire may be incomplete.

2   The pattern of responses may indicate that the participant did not understand or follow the instructions. For example, filter questions may not have been followed.

3   The responses show little variance. For example, a participant has ticked only 4s on a series of seven-point rating scales.

4   The returned questionnaire is physically incomplete: one or more pages is missing.

5   The questionnaire is received after the pre-established cut-off date.

6   The questionnaire is answered by someone who does not qualify for participation.

If quotas or cell group sizes have been imposed, the acceptable questionnaires should be classified and counted accordingly. Any problems in meeting the sampling requirements should be identified, and corrective action, such as conducting additional interviews in the under-represented cells, should be taken where this is possible, before the data are edited. Note that in online surveys, each of the above factors will usually be automatically monitored. Participants may not be allowed to continue with a survey, e.g. leaving gaps in their responses, or an error report will be automatically generated, e.g. when participants have a pattern of responses that demonstrates they have not read instructions or engaged with the survey process.

Editing

Editing is the review of the questionnaires with the objective of increasing accuracy and precision. It consists of screening questionnaires to identify illegible, incomplete, inconsistent or ambiguous responses. Responses may be illegible if they have been poorly recorded. This is particularly common in questionnaires with a large number of unstructured questions.

The replies must be legible if they are to be properly coded. Likewise, questionnaires may be incomplete to varying degrees. A few or many questions may be unanswered.

At this stage, the researcher makes a preliminary check for consistency. Certain obvious inconsistencies can be easily detected. For example, participants in a financial survey may have answered a whole series of questions relating to their perceptions of a particular bank, yet in other questions may have indicated that they have not used that particular bank or even heard of it. Responses to unstructured questions may be ambiguous and difficult to interpret clearly. The answer may be abbreviated, or some ambiguous words may have been used. For structured questions, more than one response may be marked for a question designed to elicit a single response. Suppose that a participant circles 2 and 3 on a five-point rating scale. Does this mean that 2.5 was intended? To complicate matters further, the coding procedure may allow for only a single-digit response.

Treatment of unsatisfactory responses

Unsatisfactory responses are commonly handled by returning to the field to get better data, assigning missing values, and discarding unsatisfactory participants.

Returning to the field Questionnaires with unsatisfactory responses may be returned to the field, where the interviewers recontact the participants. This approach is particularly attractive for business and industrial marketing surveys, where the sample sizes are small and the participants are easily identifiable. The data obtained the second time, however, may be different from those obtained during the original survey. These differences may be attributed to changes over time or differences in the mode of questionnaire administration (e.g. online versus a face-to-face interview).

Assigning missing values If returning the questionnaires to the field is not feasible, the editor may assign missing values to unsatisfactory responses. This approach may be desirable if (1) the number of participants with unsatisfactory responses is small; (2) the proportion of unsatisfactory responses for each of these participants is small; or (3) the variables with unsatisfactory responses are not the key variables.

Discarding unsatisfactory participants In another approach, the participants with unsatisfactory responses are simply discarded. This approach may have merit when (1) the proportion of unsatisfactory participants is small (less than 10 per cent); (2) the sample size is large; (3) the unsatisfactory participants do not differ from satisfactory participants in obvious ways (e.g. demographics, product usage characteristics); (4) the proportion of unsatisfactory responses for each of these participants is large; or (5) responses on key variables are missing. Unsatisfactory participants may differ from satisfactory participants in systematic ways, however, and the decision to designate a participant as unsatisfactory may be subjective. Both these factors bias the results. If the researcher decides to discard unsatisfactory participants, the procedure adopted to identify these participants and their number should be reported.

Coding

Many questionnaire design and data entry software packages code data automatically. Learning how to use such packages or even using spreadsheet packages means that the process of coding is now a much simpler task for the researcher. Many of the principles of coding are based on the days of data processing using 'punched cards' or even, much more recently, DOS files. Whilst there may be many data analysts who could present coherent cases for the use of original forms of data entry, the greater majority of researchers enjoy the benefits of a simpler, speedier and less error-prone form of data entry, using proprietary software packages. Even though the process is mostly automated, it is still important to understand the principles of coding, as reference to the process is made by many professionals in the marketing research industry.

Coding means assigning a code, usually a number, to each possible answer to each question. For example, a question on the gender of participants may be assigned a code of 1 for females and 2 for males. For every individual question in a questionnaire, the researcher decides which codes should be assigned to all its possible answers.

If the question posed has only two possible answers, the codes assigned of 1 or 2 take up one digit space. If the question posed had 25 possible answers such as *'Apart from Formula One, what other sports do you follow on TV or through any other media?'* the possible answers and assigned codes of 1 to 25 would take up two digit spaces. The reason for focusing upon the digit spaces required for any particular question relates to an old convention in marketing research to record the answers from individual questionnaire participants in 'flat ASCII files'. Such files were typically 80 columns wide. The columns would be set out into 'fields', i.e. assigned columns that relate to specific questions. Thus the task for the researcher after assigning codes to individual question responses was to set out a consecutive series of fields or columns. These fields would represent where the answers to particular questions would be positioned in the ASCII file. In each row of a computer file would be the coded responses from individual questionnaire participants. Each row is termed a 'record', i.e. all the fields that make up the response from one participant. All the attitudinal, behavioural, demographic and other classification characteristics of a participant may be contained in a single record.

Table 9.2 shows an extract from a questionnaire designed to elicit an understanding of Formula One television viewing behaviour. Table 9.3 illustrates the answers to these questions

Table 9.2	**Classification questions from the Formula One survey**

Question 1 – Have you watched at least one hour of a Formula One race on television in the 2012 season? (5)

1   Yes
2   No (terminate interview)

Question 2 – Please enter gender (6)

1   Male
2   Female
3   Refused

Question 3 – Please could you tell me how old you are? (7)

1   18–24
2   25–29
3   30–34
4   35–39
5   40–44
6   45–49
7   50–55
8   Refused

Table 9.2	Continued

Question 4 – Out of 19 Formula One Grand Prix held in the 2012 season, how many have you watched on television?   (8)

1		1–2
2		3–4
3		5–6
4		7–9
5		10–12
6		13–15
7		16

Question 5 – Which one Formula One team do you support?
(DO NOT READ OUT AND TICK ONLY ONE.)   (9–10)

01		Don't have a favourite team
02		Don't know
03		Ferrari
04		Force India-Mercedes
05		Lotus-Renault
06		McLaren-Mercedes
07		Mercedes
08		Renault
09		RBR Renault
10		Sauber-Ferrari
11		STR Ferrari
12		Williams Cosworth
13		Virgin Cosworth

Table 9.3	Illustrative computer file held on a flat ASCII file

	Fields					
Records	1–4	5	6	7	8	9–10
Record #1	0001	1	1	2	2	01
Record #11	0011	1	1	3	1	03
Record #21	0021	1	2	7	6	04
Record #2050	2050	1	1	5	4	11

from a selection of participants as set out in codes, fields and records. The classification questions set out in Table 9.2 were placed at the start of the questionnaire, forming the 'screening' part of the questionnaire. It is followed by the first question in the section on 'attitudes and opinions towards F1'.

Question 2 has two possible answers, coded 1 to 2, that take up one digit space (there could be a space for 'Refused' to cope with the very rare occasions where the participants refuse to state their gender and the interviewer cannot discern their gender). Non-response to gender and age questions are usually more prevalent in postal questionnaires.[33] Question 3 has eight possible answers, coded 1 to 8, that take up one digit space. Question 4 has seven possible answers, coded 1 to 7, that take up one digit space. Note that if the actual number of Grands Prix viewed were entered (rather than a category) two digit spaces would be needed. Question 5 has 12 possible answers which are coded 01 to 12, taking up two digit spaces. Note that to the right of each question, is a number in parentheses. These numbers represent the first field positions of each question, as illustrated in Table 9.3.

In Table 9.3, the columns represent the fields and the rows represent the records of each participant. The field space 1–4 is used to record an assigned number to each participant. Table 9.4 illustrates how the same data may be entered using a spreadsheet. Each row represents an individual participant and each column represents the fields required to hold the response to an individual question. Note that there is a column that identifies a specific number attached to each record. Many survey analysis packages record a unique ID for each record so that, as the answers to an individual questionnaire are entered, the ID is automatically updated. However, if a unique ID is attached to each questionnaire before it is sent out (e.g. in a postal survey), the ID may be entered as a distinct field (see column A).

Table 9.4	Example of computer file held on a spreadsheet program					
Records in rows				**Individual fields in columns**		
	A	B	C	D	E	F
	ID	Question 1	Question 2	Question 3	Question 4	Question 5
2	1	1	1	2	2	01
12	11	1	1	3	1	03
22	21	1	2	7	6	04
2051	2050	1	1	5	4	11

Coding is still required to identify the individual responses to individual questions. Spreadsheets are normally wide enough to allow an individual record to be recorded on one line, and they can be set up so that whoever is entering the data can clearly keep track of which questions relate to which columns. Spreadsheets can be used as a format to analyse data in a number of data analysis packages and so are very versatile.

Coding open-ended questions

The coding of structured questions, be they single or multiple choice, is relatively simple because the options are predetermined. The researcher assigns a code for each response to each question and specifies the appropriate field or column in which it will appear; this is termed 'pre-coding'.[34] The coding of unstructured or open-ended questions is more complex; this is termed 'post-coding'. Participants' verbatim responses are recorded on the questionnaire. One option the researcher has is to go through all the completed questionnaires, list the verbatim responses and then develop and assign codes to these responses. Another option that is allowed on some data entry packages is to enter the verbatim responses directly on to the computer, allowing a print-off of the collective responses and codes to be assigned before all of the questionnaires have been entered. The coding process here is similar to the process of assigning codes in the analysis of qualitative data.[35] The verbatim responses to 1,000 questionnaires may generate 1,000 different answers. The words may be different but the essence of the response may mean that 20 issues have been addressed. The researcher decides what those 20 issues are, names the issues and assigns codes from 1–20, and then goes through all the 1,000 questionnaires to enter the code alongside the verbatim response.

The following guidelines are suggested for coding unstructured questions and questionnaires in general.[36] Category codes should be mutually exclusive and collectively exhaustive. Categories are mutually exclusive if each response fits into one and only one category code. Categories should not overlap. Categories are collectively exhaustive if every response fits into one of the assigned category codes. This can be achieved by adding an additional category code of 'other' or 'none of the above'. An absolute maximum of 10 per cent of responses should fall into the 'other' category; the researcher should strive to assign all responses into meaningful categories.

Category codes should be assigned for critical issues even if no one has mentioned them. It may be important to know that no one has mentioned a particular response. For example, a car manufacturer may be concerned about its new website design. In a question 'How did you learn about the new Renault Clio?' key responses such as 'Google' or 'Facebook' should be included as a distinct category, even if no participants gave these answers.

Transcribing

Transcribing data involves keying the coded data from the collected questionnaires into computers. If the data have been collected online or via CATI or CAPI, this step is unnecessary because the data are entered directly into the computer as they are collected. Besides the direct keying of data, they can be transferred by using optical recognition, digital technologies, barcodes or other technologies (see Figure 9.5).

Optical character recognition programs transcribe handwritten text on to computer files. Optical scanning is a data transcribing process by which answers recorded on

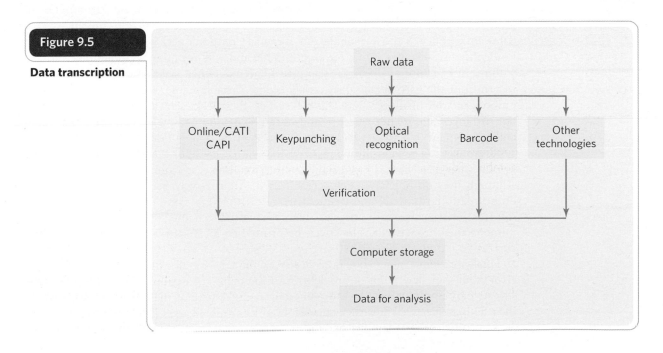

Figure 9.5

Data transcription

computer-readable forms are scanned to form a data record. This requires responses to be recorded in a pre-designated area and for a device to then read that response. A more flexible process is optical mark recognition, where a spreadsheet type of interface is used to read and process forms created by users. These mark-sensed forms are then processed by optical scanners and the data are stored in a computer file. Digital technology has resulted in computerised sensory analysis systems, which automate the data collection process. The questions appear on a computerised grid pad, and responses are recorded directly into the computer using a sensing device. Field interviewers use iPads, notebook computers, PDAs and other handheld devices to record responses, which are then sent via a built-in communication modem, wireless LAN or cellular link directly to another computer in the field or a remote location. Barcodes involve direct machine reading of the codes and simultaneous transcription. Many national censuses use barcodes to identify participants.

Several other technologies may also be used to transcribe the data. Voice recognition and voice response systems can translate recorded voice responses into data files. For example, Microsoft Windows software now includes advanced speech recognition functions and can be used to transcribe data by speaking into a microphone. When online, CATI or CAPI modes are employed and data are verified as they are collected. In the case of inadmissible responses, the computer will prompt the interviewer or participant. In the case of admissible responses, the interviewer or the participant can see the recorded response on the screen and verify it before proceeding.

Cleaning the data

Data cleaning
Thorough and extensive checks for consistency and treatment of missing responses.

Data cleaning includes consistency checks and treatment of missing responses. Even though preliminary consistency checks have been made during editing, the checks at this stage are more thorough and extensive, because they are made by computer.

Consistency checks

Consistency checks
A part of the data cleaning process that identifies data that are out of range, logically inconsistent or have extreme values. Data with values not defined by the coding scheme are inadmissible.

Consistency checks identify data that are out of range or logically inconsistent or have extreme values. Out-of-range data values are inadmissible and must be corrected. For example, participants may be asked to express their degree of agreement with a series of lifestyle statements on a 1–5 scale. Assuming that 9 has been designated for missing values, data values of 0, 6, 7 and 8 would be out of range. Computer packages can be programmed to identify out-of-range values for each variable and will not progress to another variable within a record until a value in the set range is entered. Other packages can be programmed to print out the participant code, variable code, variable name, record number, column number and out-of-range value. This makes it easy to check each variable systematically for out-of-range values. The correct responses can be determined by going back to the edited and coded questionnaire.

Responses can be logically inconsistent in various ways. For example, participants may indicate that they charge long-distance calls to a calling card from a credit card company, although they do not have such a credit card. Alternatively participants might report both unfamiliarity with, and frequent usage of, the very same product. The necessary information (participant code, variable code, variable name, record number, column number and inconsistent values) can be printed to locate these responses and to take corrective action.

Finally, extreme values should be closely examined. Not all extreme values result from errors, but they may point to problems with the data. For example, in the Formula One survey, participants were asked to name the manufacturer of the cars that 'belonged' to their households. Certain participants recorded 10 or more cars. In these circumstances the extreme values can be identified and the actual figure validated in many cases by recontacting the participant.[37]

Treatment of missing responses

Missing responses
Values of a variable that are unknown because the participants concerned provided ambiguous answers to the question or because their answers were not properly recorded.

Missing responses represent values of a variable that are unknown either because participants provided ambiguous answers or because their answers were not properly recorded. Treatment of missing responses poses problems, particularly if the proportion of missing responses is more than 10 per cent. The following options are available for the treatment of missing responses.[38]

1 **Substitute a neutral value.** A neutral value, typically the mean response to the variable, is substituted for the missing responses. Thus, the mean of the variable remains unchanged, and other statistics such as correlations are not affected much. Although this approach has some merit, the logic of substituting a mean value (say 4) for participants who, if they had answered, might have used either high ratings (6 or 7) or low ratings (1 or 2) is questionable.[39]

2 **Substitute an imputed response.** The participants' pattern of responses to other questions is used to impute or calculate a suitable response to the missing questions. The researcher attempts to infer from the available data the responses the individuals would have given if they had answered the questions. This can be done statistically by determining the relationship of the variable in question to other variables based on the available data. For example, product usage could be related to household size for participants who have provided data on both variables. Given that participant's household size, the missing product usage response for a participant could then be calculated. This approach, however, requires considerable effort and can introduce serious bias. Sophisticated statistical procedures have been developed to calculate imputed values for missing responses.[40]

Casewise deletion
A method for handling missing responses in which cases or participants with any missing responses are discarded from the analysis.

3 **Casewise deletion.** In casewise deletion, cases or participants with any missing responses are discarded from the analysis. Because many participants may have some missing responses, this approach could result in a small sample. Throwing away large amounts of data is undesirable because it is costly and time consuming to collect data. Furthermore, participants with missing responses could differ from participants with complete responses in systematic ways. If so, casewise deletion could seriously bias the results.

Pairwise deletion
A method for handling missing responses in which all cases or participants with any missing responses are not automatically discarded; rather, for each calculation, only the cases or participants with complete responses are considered.

4 **Pairwise deletion.** In pairwise deletion, instead of discarding all cases with any missing responses, the researcher uses only the cases or participants with complete responses for each calculation. As a result, different calculations in an analysis may be based on different sample sizes. This procedure may be appropriate when (1) the sample size is large, (2) there are few missing responses, and (3) the variables are not highly related. However, this procedure can produce unappealing or even infeasible results.

The different procedures for the treatment of missing responses may yield different results, particularly when the responses are not missing at random and the variables are related. Hence, missing responses should be kept to a minimum. The researcher should carefully consider the implications of the various procedures before selecting a particular method for the treatment of non-response.

Statistically adjusting the data

Procedures for statistically adjusting the data consist of weighting, variable respecification and scale transformation. These adjustments are not always necessary but can enhance the quality of data analysis.

Weighting

In weighting, each case or participant in the database is assigned a weight to reflect its importance relative to other cases or participants.[41] The value 1.0 represents the unweighted case. The effect of weighting is to increase or decrease the number of cases in the sample that possess certain characteristics.

Weighting is most widely used to make the sample data more representative of a target population on specific characteristics. For example, it may be used to give greater importance to cases or participants with higher quality data. Yet another use of weighting is to adjust the sample so that greater importance is attached to participants with certain characteristics. If a study is conducted to determine what modifications should be made to an existing product, the researcher might want to attach greater weight to the opinions of heavy users of the product. This could be accomplished by assigning weights of 3.0 to heavy users, 2.0 to medium users and 1.0 to light users and non-users. Because it destroys the self-weighting nature of the sample design, weighting should be applied with caution. If used, the weighting procedure should be documented and made a part of the project report.[42] The following example illustrates the use of simple weighting based upon the proportions of age groups in a population.

Real research | **Determining the weight of community centre users**

A postal survey was conducted in the Scottish city of Edinburgh to determine the patron-age of a community centre. The resulting sample composition differed in age structure from the area population distribution as compiled from recent census data. Therefore, the sample was weighted to make it representative in terms of age structure. The weights applied were determined by dividing the population percentage by the corresponding sample percentage. The distribution of age structure for the sample and population, as well as the weights applied, are given in the following table.

Age group	Sample percentage	Population percentage	Weight
13–18	4.32	6.13	1.42
19–24	5.89	7.45	1.26
25–34	12.23	13.98	1.14
35–44	17.54	17.68	1.01
45–54	14.66	15.59	1.06
55–64	13.88	13.65	0.98
65–74	15.67	13.65	0.87
75 plus	15.81	11.87	0.75
Totals	100.00	100.00	

Age groups under-represented in the sample received higher weights, whereas over-represented age groups received lower weights. Thus, the data for a participant aged 13–18 would be overweighted by multiplying by 1.42, whereas the data for a participant aged 75 plus would be underweighted by multiplying by 0.75.

Variable respecification

Variable respecification
The transformation of data to create new variables or the modification of existing variables so that they are more consistent with the objectives of the study.

Variable respecification involves the transformation of data to create new variables or to modify existing variables. The purpose of respecification is to create variables that are consistent with the objectives of the study. For example, suppose that the original variable was product usage, with 10 response categories. These might be collapsed into four categories: heavy, medium, light and non-user. Or the researcher may create new variables that are composites of several other variables. For example, the researcher may create an Index of Information Search (ISS), which is the sum of information new car customers seek from dealers, promotional sources, online and other independent sources. Likewise, one may take the ratio of variables. If the amount of purchases at a clothes shop (X_1) and the amount of purchases where a credit card was used (X_2) have been measured, the proportion of purchases charged to a credit card can be a new variable, created by taking the ratio of the two (X_2/X_1). Other respecifications of variables include square root and log transformations, which are often applied to improve the fit of the model being estimated.

An important respecification procedure involves the use of **dummy variables** for respecifying categorical variables.[43] Dummy variables are also called binary, dichotomous, instrumental or qualitative variables. They are variables that may take on only two values, such as 0 or 1. The general rule is that to respecify a categorical variable with K categories, $K - 1$ dummy variables are needed. The reason for having $K - 1$, rather than K, dummy variables is that only $K - 1$ categories are independent. Given the sample data, information about the Kth category can be derived from information about the other $K - 1$ categories. Consider gender, a variable having two categories. Only one dummy variable is needed. Information on the number or percentage of males in the sample can be readily derived from the number or percentage of females.

Dummy variables
A respecification procedure using variables that take on only two values, usually 0 or 1.

Scale transformation

Scale transformation involves a manipulation of scale values to ensure comparability with other scales or otherwise to make the data suitable for analysis.[44] Frequently, different scales are employed for measuring different variables. For example, image variables may be measured on a seven-point semantic differential scale, attitude variables on a continuous rating scale, and lifestyle variables on a five-point Likert scale. Therefore, it would not be meaningful to make comparisons across the measurement scales for any participant. To compare attitudinal scores with lifestyle or image scores, it would be necessary to transform the various scales. Even if the same scale is employed for all the variables, different participants may use the scale differently. For example, some participants consistently use the upper end of a rating scale whereas others consistently use the lower end. These differences can be corrected by appropriately transforming the data.

Scale transformation
A manipulation of scale values to ensure compatibility with other scales or otherwise to make the data suitable for analysis.

Selecting a data analysis strategy

The selection of a data analysis strategy should be based on the earlier steps of the marketing research process, known characteristics of the data, properties of statistical techniques and the background and philosophy of the researcher. Data analysis is not an end in itself. Its purpose is to produce information that will help address the problem at hand and support effective decision making. The selection of a data analysis strategy must begin with a consideration of the earlier steps in the research process: problem definition (step 1), development of an approach (step 2) and research design (step 3). The preliminary plan of data analysis prepared as part of the research design should be used to facilitate a richer engagement and understanding of meaning that may lie within collected data. Changes in analysis techniques may be necessary in the light of additional information generated in subsequent stages of the research process.

The next step is to consider the known characteristics of the data. The measurement scales used exert a strong influence on the choice of statistical techniques. In addition, the research design may favour certain techniques. For example, analysis of variance is suited for analysing experimental data from causal designs. The insights into the data obtained during data integrity can be valuable for selecting a strategy for analysis.

It is also important to take into account the properties of the statistical techniques, particularly their purpose and underlying assumptions. Some statistical techniques are appropriate for examining differences in variables, others for assessing the magnitudes of the relationships between variables, and still others for making predictions. The techniques also involve different assumptions, and some techniques can withstand violations of the underlying assumptions better than others.

Finally, the researcher's background and philosophy affect the choice of a data analysis strategy. The experienced, statistically trained researcher will employ a range of techniques, including advanced statistical methods. Researchers differ in their willingness to make assumptions about the variables and their underlying populations. Researchers who are conservative about making assumptions will limit their choice of techniques to distribution-free methods. In general, several techniques may be appropriate for analysing the data from a given project.

International marketing research

The selection, training, supervision and evaluation of survey fieldworkers are critical in international marketing research. The quality of local fieldwork agencies can vary a great deal across many countries and so it may be necessary to recruit and train local fieldworkers. The use of local fieldworkers is desirable, because they are familiar with the subtleties of language and culture. They can create an appropriate climate for the interview and sensitivity to the concerns of the participants. Even with these advantages, extensive training may be required and close supervision in order to ensure that the questions are presented as intended. As observed in many countries, local interviewers may help participants with answers and select household or sampling units based on personal considerations rather than the sampling plan. This means that the validation of fieldwork is critical. Proper application of fieldwork procedures can greatly reduce these difficulties and result in consistent and valid findings. International marketing research studies add more complexity regardless of how simple a survey may seem. Collecting data that is comparable between countries may be difficult, but it can be done using some conventional research techniques, with adaptations when needed and/or using mixed mode approaches. Equivalent research procedures enable researchers to detect, analyse and better understand the world's sociocultural differences.

Before analysing the data, the researcher should ensure that the units of measurement are comparable across countries or cultural units. For example, the data may have to be adjusted to establish currency equivalents or metric equivalents. Furthermore, standardisation or normalisation of the data may be necessary to make meaningful comparisons and achieve consistent results.

Ethics in marketing research

Researchers and fieldworkers have an ethical responsibility to respect participants' privacy, feelings and dignity.[45] Moreover, participants should be left with a positive and pleasant experience. These issues should take high priority for researchers in order to elicit the correct responses for a specific project but also more broadly for the health of the marketing research industry. A participant who feels that their trust has been abused, who found an interview to be cumbersome and boring, or who fails to see the purpose of a particular study, is less likely to participate in further marketing research efforts. Collectively, the marketing research industry has the responsibility to look after its most precious assets – willing and honest participants.

Good researchers have an awareness of their responsibilities to fieldworkers and participants. The researcher may take great care in understanding the difficulties of collecting data in the field and go to great pains to ensure that the data gathering process works well for the fieldworker and participant alike. The fieldworker may have been told about the purpose of the study, the purpose of particular questions, the means to select and approach participants and the means to elicit responses correctly from participants. However, fieldworkers may behave in an unethical manner. They may cut corners in terms of selecting the correct participants, posing questions and probes, and recording responses. In such circumstances the fieldworker can cause much damage to an individual study and to the long-term relationship with potential participants. Thus it becomes a vital part of fieldworker training to demonstrate the ethical responsibilities fieldworkers have in collecting data.

Ethical issues that arise during the data integrity and analysis step of the marketing research process pertain mainly to the researcher. While checking, editing, coding, transcribing and cleaning, researchers should try to get some idea about the quality of the data. An attempt should be made to identify participants who have provided data of questionable quality. While analysing the data, the researcher may also have to deal with ethical issues. The assumptions underlying the statistical techniques used to analyse the data must be satisfied to obtain meaningful results. Any departure from these assumptions should be critically examined to determine the appropriateness of the technique for analysing the data at hand.

Digital developments in marketing research

The majority of survey research is now conducted online and the fieldwork related to such approaches occurs in a virtual world. The skills and demands of fieldworkers where there may be no face-to-face, audio or visual contact are different from the more traditional telephone and face-to-face survey techniques. The underlying principles of fieldwork in terms of building a relationship with participants, eliciting data, managing and validating data, remain the same whatever mode of collection is adopted. What differs is the nature of fieldwork tasks. The following example illustrates the administration of a digital diary, that contained survey elements. In evaluating this case, consider what fieldwork means and how quality fieldwork standards could be relevant for the target participants.

Real research	Careers, relationships and bullying[46]

The digital marketing agency Brahms (**www.brassagency .com**) helped to develop a strategy for how the UK Government should communicate online with young people aged 14–19. Their research project required panellists to keep a weekly diary of their lives in order to understand the challenges young people faced over a 6-month period. Paper diary methods were not deemed suitable; cumbersome hard copy documents were not easy to use or sufficiently private. Their solution was to design a bespoke project website to facilitate the diary process. The site was an extranet, effectively a 'walled garden' accessed via a username and password. The panellists could log on and write their entries which would then be visible only to the project team. This ensured privacy, an important consideration as they were keen to make them feel comfortable and to get them to open up and share the details of their lives with the team. Each entry was recorded and the large number of entries could be categorised and analysed with relative ease. The website also allowed the project team to communicate with the panellists should they have any queries. To support participants, a 16-page booklet was created containing all the relevant project information such as the website's URL, the contact details of their moderator, the dates they could expect their incentives once they had completed their blog entries, as well as the relevant Market Research Society information for reference. The aim was that the booklet would act as an aide memoire for the 6-month fieldwork period. As the project progressed, the team needed to get feedback from participants on the hypotheses that the creative team had developed. They felt it important to ensure that the hypotheses were clearly explained, concisely and in a replicable manner ensuring each participant was given the same description in order to be consistent. Brahms created an interactive media player (similar to Windows Media Player) for participants to interact with. This took the form of a chaptered case study video. It was filmed from a central character's perspective showing a young person's decision making process about what career to choose, set over a 6-week summer holiday. Different hypotheses were included in the narrative as she progressed, for example taking part in an online careers fair. As each hypothesis was shown, an 'information point' icon appeared on the player: participants could click on this to find out more about any third-party site being described (e.g. Habbo Hotel) if they were not familiar with it. Presenting ideas in this way was more user-centric, allowing participants a degree of active involvement in the process. They could pause the narrative to ask questions, repeat sections to recap on the ideas or look at an 'information point' where they were unsure about a third-party website being described.

Note in this case how much work would be needed to build and maintain a good relationship with participants, and in this context what materials were designed and 'fed' to participants. This relationship was vital to draw out what participants felt about particular issues, managing this in a consistent manner was a key fieldwork task.

In fieldwork activities where face-to-face or telephone contact is made, online systems can play a valuable role in all the phases of survey fieldwork: selection, training, supervision, validation and evaluation of fieldworkers. Similarly, multimedia capabilities offered by online engagements can be a good supplementary tool for training the fieldworkers in all aspects of interviewing. Training in this manner can complement personal training programmes and add value to the process. Supervision is enhanced by facilitating communication between the supervisors and the interviewers via email and secured chat rooms. Central office control can be strengthened by posting progress reports; quality and cost control information at a secured location on a website, so that it is easily available to all the relevant parties.

Validation of fieldwork, especially for face-to-face and telephone interviews, can be easily accomplished for those participants who have an email address or online access. These participants can be sent a short verification survey by email or asked to visit a website where the survey is posted. Finally, the evaluation criteria can be communicated online to fieldworkers during their training stage, and performance feedback can also be provided to them by using this medium.

Summary

The growth in online research has changed the nature and emphasis of fieldwork. Traditionally, marketing research used a 'personal attention' approach in which every interviewer paid attention to nurturing and addressing each specific participant. Online research has shifted the service design from a personalised to a more 'self-service' approach. Though fieldwork tasks differ between survey modes, especially comparing face-to-face with online approaches, the underlying principles of good fieldwork remains the same. Fieldworkers should be trained in important aspects of fieldwork, including making the initial contact, asking the questions, probing, recording the answers and concluding the interview. Supervising fieldworkers involves quality control and editing, sampling control, control of cheating and central office control. Validating fieldwork can be accomplished by calling 10–25 per cent of those who have been identified as interviewees and enquiring whether the interviews took place. Fieldworkers should be evaluated on the basis of cost and time, response rates, quality of interviewing and quality of data collection.

Fieldwork should be carried out in a consistent manner so that, regardless of who administers a questionnaire, the same process is adhered to. This is vital to allow comparisons between collected data. Fieldworkers to some extent have to approach and motivate potential participants in a manner that sets the correct purpose for a study and motivates the participant to spend time answering the questions properly. This cannot be done in a 'robotic' manner; it requires good communication skills and an amount of empathy with participants. This makes the issue of managing fieldwork an essential task in the generation of sound research data.

Non-response error arises when some of the potential participants included in the sample do not respond. The primary causes of low response rates are refusals and not-at-homes. Refusal rates may be reduced by prior notification, incentives, excellent questionnaire design and administration, and follow-up. The percentage of not-at-homes can be substantially reduced by call-backs. Adjustments for non-response can be made by subsampling non-participants, replacement, substitution, subjective estimates, trend analysis, simple weighting and imputation.

Data integrity begins with a preliminary check of all questionnaires for completeness and interviewing quality. Then more thorough editing takes place. Editing consists of screening questionnaires to identify illegible, incomplete, inconsistent or ambiguous responses. Such responses may be handled by returning questionnaires to the field, assigning missing values or discarding unsatisfactory participants.

The next step is coding. A numeric or alphanumeric code is assigned to represent a specific response to a specific question along with the column position or field that code will occupy. It is often helpful to print off a codebook containing the coding instructions and the necessary information about the variables in the dataset. The coded data are transcribed onto computer memory, disks, other storage devices or entered directly into a data analysis package. For this purpose, keypunching, optical recognition, digital technologies, barcodes or other technologies may be used. Survey design software packages can completely automate the coding process.

Cleaning the data requires consistency checks and treatment of missing responses. Options available for treating missing responses include substitution of a neutral value such as a mean, substitution of an imputed response, casewise deletion and pairwise deletion. Statistical adjustments such as weighting, variable respecification and scale transformations often enhance the quality of data analysis. The selection of a data analysis strategy should be based on the earlier steps of the marketing research process, known characteristics of the data, properties of statistical techniques, and the background and philosophy of the researcher.

Selecting, training, supervising and evaluating fieldworkers is even more critical in international marketing research because the quality of local fieldwork agencies can be highly variable between countries. Ethical issues include making the participants feel comfortable in the data collection process so that their experience is positive. Several ethical issues are related to data processing, particularly the discarding of unsatisfactory responses, violation of the assumptions underlying the data analysis techniques, and evaluation and interpretation of results. The growth of online survey techniques has meant that the nature of participant engagement has changed. The skills and demands of fieldworkers where there may be no face-to-face, audio or visual contact are changing but the underlying principles of quality fieldwork remain the same.

SNAP Learning Edition

Traditionally, most surveys were paper-based and the questionnaires were typically administered by a fieldworker. The completed questionnaires always required a considerable amount of editing, coding and data entry before any analysis could be carried out. With the advent of software such as SNAP, as well as the move to more surveys online, the time from interview to analysis has been considerably reduced.

The very nature of online research has resulted in fewer fieldworker-led surveys and more self-completion surveys. Online surveys can appear far easier to complete, but this is partly due the ability of powerful software programs to design easy-to-complete questionnaires. Powerful edit checks are incorporated at the time of the interview to ensure that only valid data is collected.

Sophisticated routing instructions can also be included in online surveys so that questions can effectively be hidden, avoiding the traditional instructions, such as '*Go to Q4*'. Questions then only appear that are specific to each individual participant. If, for example, a question is displayed that includes an '*Other*' category, a supplementary question can then appear to provide more information relating specifically to that reply. For any participants that don't select '*Other*', the supplementary question will not appear.

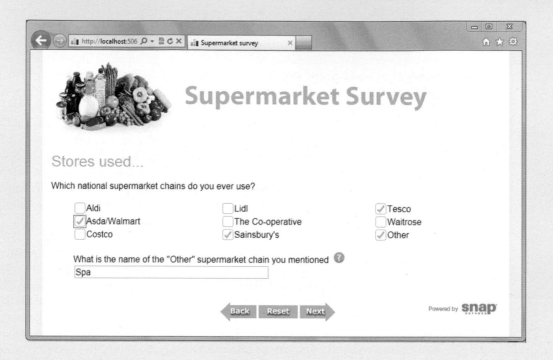

When a specific range of replies are expected for an open-ended question, these can be accommodated by selecting a Source Pattern that has previously been set up. For example, email addresses can automatically be checked to ensure that the origin of the email address ends in either .com, .co.uk, .org etc. Warning messages then appear to the participant if their email address is not of a valid format.

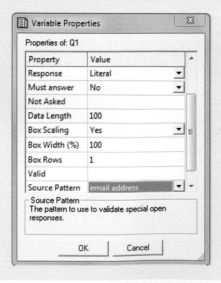

Certain questions are particularly prone to data entry errors, and SNAP provides a library of special-ist keyboards to assist the participant. Dates are one such question, where the format might be day/month/year or month/day/year; the year might be 2 digits or 4 digits and the separators might be a '/' or a '-'. For particular applications, specialist keyboards can be developed to reduce the level of data entry errors.

Online surveys can be more engaging so that the whole experience of completing a survey is more pleasur-able. This enables data of a higher quality to be collected, and a higher response rate achieved from partici-pants. Using the mouse to point at a rating can often be more agreeable than giving a rating from Very Good to Very Poor, or entering a score from 0 to 10.

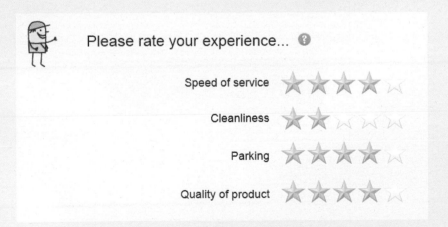

Demographic questions such as location can involve lengthy lists, such as counties or states. Displaying the list in the form of a map can often avoid unnecessary errors of miscoding. A similar approach can be applied in healthcare surveys, displaying parts of the body rather than a long list. Similarly, a car insurance form might work better displaying a diagram of a car, rather than a list of doors and windows etc.

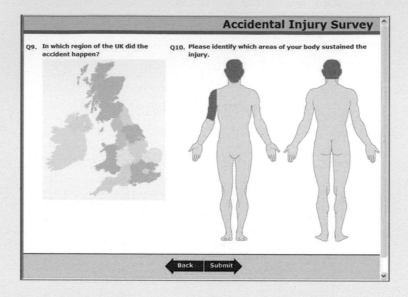

SNAP not only provides design capabilities for online and mobile-based surveys; it also assists in designing professional paper-based questionnaires. Well-designed paper questionnaires can then be set up to be scanned.

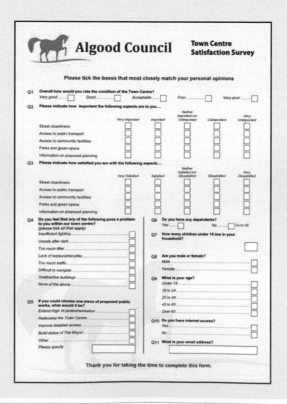

Scanning of paper questionnaires can, in certain circumstances, virtually eliminate all data entry, enabling analysis to be carried as soon as the paper replies have been scanned in. In principle, multi-choice tick box questions are easiest to scan and handwritten open-ended text questions are the most difficult to scan. The decision on whether to scan a questionnaire or key in the replies manually is a function of just how much is required to process the open-ended text, as the interpretation of an individual's handwriting can be difficult.

Once questionnaires have been scanned, SNAP software will automatically generate a computer file for analysis.

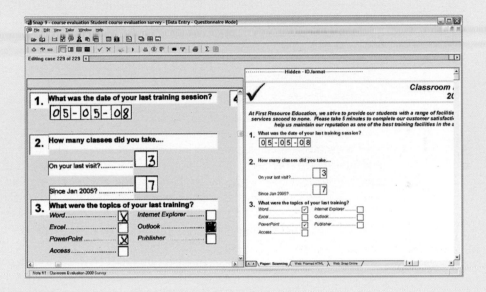

With all the replies collected from a survey, and stored in a computer readable format, analysis can commence. The format of this analysis can be simple or complex and can include a selection of statistical tests. The details of analysis are covered more fully in Chapters 11 and 12.

Questions

1 Why do researchers need to use survey fieldworkers?

2 Describe the survey fieldwork/data collection process.

3 Evaluate what may be done to help interviewers probe correctly and consistently.

4 What is validation of survey fieldwork? How is this done?

5 What strategies are available for adjusting for non-response?

6 Describe the major sources of error related to survey fieldwork.

7 Describe the data integrity process. Why is this process needed?

8 What is the difference between pre-coding and post-coding?

9 What options are available for the treatment of missing data?

10 What kinds of statistical adjustment are sometimes made to the data?

11 Describe the weighting process. What are the reasons for weighting?

12 What considerations are involved in selecting a data analysis strategy?

Exercises

1   Visit the websites of three major marketing research agencies. Evaluate how they present their quality management of fieldwork. Write a report that details what you feel to be the best elements of their respective practices. Note also what additional practices they should be highlighting to reassure potential marketing research buyers and users.

2   In teams of four, design a questionnaire to be used in a street interview. One of the team then takes on the role of the interviewer, the other three to act as participants. Conduct three interviews and video the process. Replay the video and write a report that focuses upon:
    (a) The questionnaire design
    (b) Stopping and motivating participants
    (c) Interviewer instructions
    (d) The consistency of the process
    (e) Ethical issues involved in the process.

3   Visit **www.ettinger.co.uk** and examine online databases, secondary data and intelligence sources to obtain information on the criteria buyers use in selecting luxury leather accessories. Demographic and psychographic data were obtained in a survey designed to explain the choice of luxury leather accessories. What kind of consistency checks, treatment of missing responses, and variable respecification should be conducted on such questions?

4   You are the marketing research manager for AGA (**www.aga-web.co.uk**). AGA has developed a luxury refrigerator and matching freezer at €4,000 each. A European survey was conducted to determine consumer response to the proposed models. The data were obtained by conducting a face-to-face survey at shopping malls in 10 European capital cites. Although the resulting sample of 2,500 is fairly representative on all other demographic variables, it under-represents the upper income households. The marketing research analyst who reports to you feels that weighting is not necessary. Discuss this question with the analyst (a student in your class).

5   In a small group discuss the following issues: 'What makes street interviewing an art?' 'Why do interviewers cheat?' 'Data processing is tedious, time consuming and costly; it should be circumvented whenever possible.'

Notes

1. Van Walwyk, M. and Garland, C., 'Turning the super tanker – the migration from a postal to online methodology', ESOMAR, *Panel Research*, Dublin, (Oct. 2008).

2. Akaoui, J., 'Brand experience on the pitch: How the sponsors fared in the World Cup', *Journal of Advertising Research*, 47 (2) (June 2007), 147–57

3. Guest, G., Bunce, A. and Johnson, L., 'How many interviews are enough? An experiment with data saturation and variability', *Field Methods*, 18 (1) (Feb. 2006), 59–83; Gubrium, J.F. and Holstein, J.A., *Handbook of Survey Research: Context and Method* (Thousand Oaks, CA: Sage, 2000); Frey, J.H. and Oishi, S.M., *How to Conduct Interviews by Telephone and In Person* (Thousand Oaks, CA: Sage, 1995).

4. Dommeyer, C.J., 'The effects of the researcher's physical attractiveness and gender on mail survey response', *Psychology and Marketing*, 25 (1) (Jan. 2008), 47–70; Sacco, J.M., Scheu, C.R. Ryan, A.M. and Schmitt, N., 'An investigation of race and sex similarity effects in interviews: A multilevel approach to relational demography', *Journal of Applied Psychology*, 88 (5) (2003), 852–65; McCombie, S.C., 'The influences of sex of interviewer on the results of an AIDS survey in Ghana', *Human Organization*, 61 (1) (Spring 2002), 51–55; Catina, LA., Binson, D., Canchola, J., Pollack, L.M. *et al.*, 'Effects of interviewer gender, interviewer choice, and item wording on responses to questions concerning sexual behaviour', *Public Opinion Quarterly*, 60 (3) (Fall 1996), 345–75; Coulter, P.B., 'Race of interviewer effects on telephone interviews', *Public Opinion Quarterly*, 46 (Summer 1982), 278–84; Singer, E., Frankel, M.R. and Glassman, M.B., 'The effect of interviewer characteristics and expectations on response', *Public Opinion Quarterly*, 41 (Spring 1983), 68–83.

5. Lai, J. and Shuttles, C., 'Improving cooperation of Asian households through cultural sensitivity training for field interviewers', *Conference Papers* – American Association for Public Opinion Research (2004); Anon., 'Renewing your interviewing skills', *Healthcare Executive*, 17 (1) (Jan./Feb. 2002), 29; Kiecker, P. and Nelson, J.E., 'Do interviewers follow telephone survey instructions?' *Journal of the Market Research Society*, 38 (2) (April 1996), 161–76; Guenzel, P.I., Berkmans, T.R. and Cannell, C.F., *General Interviewing Techniques* (Ann Arbor, MI: Institute for Social Research, 1983).

6. Rogelberg, S.G. and Stanton, J.M., 'Introduction, understanding and dealing with organizational survey non-response', *Organizational Research Methods*, 10 (2) (April 2007), 195–209; Robertson, B., 'The effect of an introductory letter on participation rates using telephone recruitment', *Australian & New Zealand Journal of Public Health*, 24 (5) (October 2000), 552; Feld, K., 'Good introductions save time, money', *Marketing News* 34 (5) (28 Feb. 2000), 19–20; Couper, M.P., 'Survey introductions and data quality', *Public Opinion Quarterly* (Summer 1997), 317–38.

7. Bordeaux, D.B., 'Interviewing Part II: Getting the most out of interview questions', *Motor Age*, 121 (2) (Feb. 2002), 38–40; Anon., 'Market research industry sets up interviewing quality standards', *Management Auckland*, 44 (2) (March 1997), 12.

8. Sethuraman, R., Kerin, R.A. and Cron, W.L., 'A field study comparing online and offline data collection methods for identifying product attribute preferences using conjoint analysis', *Journal of Business Research*, 58 (5) (May 2005), 602–10.

9. This section follows closely the material in *Interviewer's Manual*, rev. edn (Ann Arbor, MI: Survey Research Center, Institute for Social Research, University of Michigan, 1976); Guenzel, P.J., Berkmans, T.R. and Cannell, C.E., *General Interviewing Techniques* (Ann Arbor, MI: Institute for Social Research, 1983).

10. Ting, D.H., 'Further probing of higher order in satisfaction construct' *International Journal of Bank Marketing*, 24 (2/3) (2006), 98–113; Institute for Social Research, University of Michigan, *Interviewer's Manual*, rev. edn (Ann Arbor, MI: Survey Research Center, 1976) 16.

11. Trembly, A.C., 'Poor data quality: A $600 billion issue', *National Underwriter*, 106 (11) (18 March 2002), 48; Anon., 'Market research industry sets up interviewing quality standards', *Management-Auckland*, 44 (2) (March 1997), 12; Morton-Williams, J. and Sykes, W., 'The use of interaction coding and follow-up interviews to investigate comprehension of survey questions', *Journal of the Market Research Society*, 26 (April 1984), 109–27.

12. Park, C., 'How was it for you?' *Research*, Fieldwork Supplement (July 2000), 8–9.

13. Sparrow, N., 'Quality issues in online research', *Journal of Advertising Research*, 17 (2) (June 2007), 179–02; Cri, D. and Micheuax, A., 'From customer data to value: What is lacking in the information chain?' *Journal of Database Marketing and Customer Strategy Management*, 13 (4) (July 2006), 282–99; Pallister, J., 'Navigating the righteous course: A quality issue', *Journal of the Market Research Society*, 41 (3) (July 1999), 327–43; Hurley, R.F. and Laitamaki, J.M., 'Total quality research: Integrating markets and the organization', *California Management Review*, 38 (1) (Fall 1995), 59–78.

14. Sparrow, N., 'What is an opinion anyway? Finding out what people really think?' *International Journal of Market Research*, 53 (1) (2011), 25–39; Czaja, R., Blair, J. and Sebestik, J.P., 'Participant selection in telephone survey: A comparison of three techniques', *Journal of Marketing Research* (August 1982), 381–85.

15. de Jong, K., 'CSI Berlin: The strange case of the death of panels', ESOMAR, *Online Research*, Berlin (Oct. 2010); Frost-Norton, T., 'The future of mall research: Current trends affecting the future of marketing research in malls', *Journal of Consumer Behaviour*, 4 (4) (June 2005), 293–301; Fielding, N.G., *Interviewing: Four volume set* (Thousand Oaks, CA: Sage, 2003); Greengard, S., '50% of your employees are lying, cheating & stealing', *Workforce*, 76 (10) (Oct. 1997), 44–53; Tull, D.S. and Richards, L.F., 'What can be done about interviewer bias?' in Sheth, J. (ed.) *Research in Marketing* (Greenwich, CT: SAT Press, 1980), 143–162.

16. Chapman, D.S. and Rowe, P.M., 'The impact of videoconference technology, interview structure and interviewer gender on interviewer evaluations in the employment interview: A field experiment', *Journal of Occupational and Organizational Psychology*, (Sept. 2001); Johnson, C., 'Making sure employees measure up', *HRMagazine*, 46 (3) (March 2001), 36–41; Pulakos, E.D., Schmitt, N., Whitney, D. and Smith, M., 'Individual differences in interviewer ratings: The impact of standardization, consensus discussion and sampling error on the validity of a structured interview', *Personnel Psychology*, 49 (1) (Spring 1996), 85–102.

17. Manfreda, K.L. Bosnjak, M., Berzelak, J., Haas, I. and Vehovar, V., 'Web surveys versus other survey modes: A meta analysis comparing response rates', *International Journal of Market Research*, 50 (1) (2008) 79–104; Smith, J., 'How to boost DM response rates quickly', *Marketing News*, 35 (9) (23 April 2001), 5; Turley, S.K., 'A case of response rate success', *Journal of the Market Research Society*, 41 (3) (July 1999), 301–309; Edmonston, S., 'Why response rates are declining', *Advertising Age's Business Marketing*, 82 (8) (Sept. 1997), 12.

18. Cooke, M., Johnson, A., Rolfe, G. and Parker, K., 'Association for Survey Computing (ASC): Pizzazz in research; Renewing the rules of engagement', *International Journal of Market Research*, 53 (1) (2011), 115–25 ; Van Kenhove, P., 'The influence of topic involvement on mail-survey response behaviour', *Psychology & Marketing*, 19 (3) (March 2002), 293; Fisher, M.R., 'Estimating the effect of non-response bias on angler surveys', *Transactions of the American Fisheries Society*, 125 (1) (January 1996), 118–26; Martin, C., 'The impact of topic interest on mail survey response behaviour', *Journal of the Market Research Society*, 36 (Oct. 1994), 327–38.

19. Heerwegh, D., 'Effects of personal salutations in email invitations to participate in a web survey', *Public Opinion Quarterly*, 69 (4) (Winter 2005), 588–98; Cummings, S.M., 'Reported response rates to mailed physician questionnaires', *Health Services Research*, 35 (6) (Feb. 2001), 1347–55; Hill, A., Roberts, J., Ewings, P. and Gunnell, D., 'Non-response bias in a lifestyle survey', *Journal of Public Health Medicine*, 19 (2) (June 1997), 203–207; McDaniel, S.W., Madden, C.S. and Verille, P., 'Do topic differences affect survey non-response?' *Journal of the Market Research Society* (January 1987), 55–66.

20. For minimising the incidence of non-response and adjusting for its effects, see Lozar Manfreda, K., Bosnjak, M., Berzelak, J., Haas, I. and Vehovar, V., 'Web surveys versus other survey modes: A meta analysis comparing response rates', *International Journal of Market Research*, 50 (1) (2008), 79–104; Columbo, R., 'A model for diagnosing and reducing non-response bias', *Journal of Advertising Research*, 40 (1/2) (January/April 2000), 85–93; Chen, H.C., 'Direction, magnitude, and implications of non-response bias in mail surveys', *Journal of the Market Research Society*, 38 (3) (July 1996), 267–76.

21. Vicente, P., Reis, E. and Santos, M., 'Using mobile phones for survey research: A comparison with fixed phones', *International Journal of Market Research*, 51 (5) (2009), 613–34.

22. Brennan, M., Benson, S. and Kearns, Z., 'The effect of introductions on telephone survey response rates', *International Journal of Market Research*, 47 (1) (2005), 65–74; Van Kenhove, P., 'The influence of topic involvement on mail-survey response behaviour', *Psychology & Marketing*, 19 (3) (March 2002), 293; Groves, R.M., 'Leverage-saliency theory of survey participation: Description and an illustration', *Public Opinion Quarterly*, 64 (3) (Fall 2000), 299–308; Everett, S.A., Price, J.H., Bedell, A.W. and Telljohann, S.K., 'The effect of a monetary incentive in increasing the return rate of a survey of family physicians', *Evaluation and the Health Professions*, 20 (2) (June 1997), 207–14; Armstrong, J.S. and Lusk, E.J., 'Return postage in mail surveys: A meta-analysis', *Public Opinion Quarterly* (Summer 1987), 233–48; Yu, J. and Cooper, H., 'A quantitative review of research design effects on response rates to questionnaires', *Journal of Marketing Research*, 20 (February 1983), 36–44.

23. Gendall, P. and Healey, B., 'Effect of a promised donation to charity on survey response', *International Journal of Market Research*, 52 (5) (2010), 565–77; Rose, D.S., Sidle, S.D. and Griffith, K.H., 'A penny for your thoughts: Monetary incentives improve response rates for company-sponsored employee surveys', *Organizational Research Methods*, 10 (2) (April 2007), 225–40; Hansen, K.M., 'The effects of incentives, interview length and interviewer characteristics on response rates in a CATI study', *International Journal of Public Opinion Research*, 19 (1) (April 2007), 112–21; Saunders, J., Jobber, D. and Mitchell, V., 'The optimum prepaid monetary incentives for mail surveys', *Journal of the Operational Research Society*, 57 (10) (Oct. 2006), 1224–30; Shaw, M.J., 'The use of monetary incentives in a community survey: Impact on response rates, data, quality and cost', *Health Services Research*, 35 (6) (Feb. 2001), 1339–46.

24. McCarty, C., House, M., Harman, J. and Richards, S., 'Effort in phone survey response rates: The effects of vendor and client controlled factors', *Field Methods*, 18 (2) (May 2006), 172; Zafer Erdogan, B., 'Increasing mail survey response rates from an industrial population: A cost effectiveness analysis of four follow-up techniques', *Industrial Marketing Management*, 31 (1) (Jan. 2002), 65.

25. Ladik, D.M., Carrillat, F.A. and Solomon, P.J., 'The effectiveness of university sponsorship in increasing survey response rate', *Journal of Marketing Theory & Practice*, 15 (3) (July 2007), 263–71; Byrom, J., 'The effect of personalization on mailed questionnaire response rates', *International Journal of Market Research* (Summer 2000), 357–59; Dillman, D.A., Singer, E., Clark, J.R. and Treat, J.L.B., 'Effects of benefits appeals, mandatory appeals, and variations in statements of confidentiality on completion rates for census questionnaires', *Public Opinion Quarterly*, 60 (3) (Fall 1996), 376–89; Gendall, P., Hoek, J. and Esslemont, D., 'The effect of appeal, complexity and tone in a mail survey covering letter', *Journal of the Market Research Society*, 37 (3) (July 1995), 251–68; Greer, T.V. and Lohtia, R., 'Effects of source and paper color on response rates in mail surveys', *Industrial Marketing Management*, 23 (Feb. 1994), 47–54.

26. van Goor, H. and van Goor, A., 'The usefulness of the basic question – procedure for determining non-response bias in substantive variables: A test of four telephone questionnaires', *International Journal of Market Research*, 49 (2) (2007), 221–36.

27. Phillips, A., Curtice, J., Sparrow, N., Whiteley, P., Clarke, H., Sanders, D., Stewart, M. and Moon, N., 'Lessons from the polls: Retrospective views on the performance of the opinion polls conducted in the run-up to the 2010 UK General Election', *International Journal of Market Research*, 5_ _` (2010), 675–96; Groves, R.M., 'Non-repose rates and non-response bias in household surveys', *Public Opinion Quarterly*, 70 (5) (2006), 646–75; Columbo, R., 'A model for diagnosing and reducing non-response bias,' *Journal of Advertising Research*, (Jan./April 2000), 85–93.

28. Abraham, K.G., Maitland, A. and Bianchi, S.M., 'Non-response in the American Time Use Survey', *Public Opinion Quarterly*, 70 (5) (2006), 676–703; Larsen, M.D., 'The psychology of survey response', *Journal of the American Statistical Association*, 97 (457) (March 2002), 358–59; Dey, E.L., 'Working with low survey response rates: The efficacy of weighting adjustments', *Research in Higher Education*, 38 (2) (April 1997), 215–27.

29. De Jong, M.G., Steenkamp, J-B., E.M., Fox, J-P. and Baumgartner, H., 'Using item response theory to measure extreme response style in marketing research: A global investigation', *Journal of Marketing Research*, 45 (1) (Feb. 2008), 104–15; Sobh, R. and Perry, C., 'Research design and data analysis in realism research', *European Journal of Marketing*, 40 (11) (Jan. 2006), 1194; Qin, J., 'Estimation with survey data under non-ignorable non-response or informative sampling', *Journal of the American Statistical Association*, 97 (457) (March 2002), 193–200; Kessler, R.C., Little, R.J. and Grover, R.M., 'Advances in strategies for minimising and adjusting for survey nonresponse', *Epidemiologic Reviews*, 17 (1) (1995), 192–204.

30. Sparrow, N., 'Developing reliable online polls', *International Journal of Market Research*, 48 (6) (2006), 659–80.

31. Groves, R.M. and Peytcheva, E., 'The impact of non-response rates on non-response bias: A meta analysis', *Public Opinion Quarterly*, 72 (2) (Summer 2008), 167–89; Brewer, K., *Design and estimation in survey sampling* (London; Edward Arnold, 2001); Sao, J., 'Variance estimation for survey data with composite imputation and non-negligible sampling fractions', *Journal of American Statistical Association* (March, 1999), 254–65; Drane, J.W., Richter, D. and Stoskopf, C., 'Improved imputation of non-response to mailback questionnaires', *Statistics in Medicine*, 12 (34) (Feb. 1993), 283–88.

32. Trembly, A.C., 'Poor data quality: A $600 billion issue', *National Underwriter*, 106 (11) (18 March 2002), 48; Higgins, K.T., 'Never ending journey', *Marketing Management*, 6 (1) (Spring 1997), 4–7; Harristhal, J., 'Interviewer tips', *Applied Marketing Research*, 28 (Fall 1988), 42–45.

33. Healey, B. and Gendall, P., 'Forum – Asking the age question in mail and online surveys', *International Journal of Market Research*, 50 (3) (2008), 309–17.

34. Schmidt, M., 'Quantification of transcripts from depth interviews, open ended responses and focus groups: Challenges, accomplishments, new applications and perspectives for market research', *International Journal of Market Research*, 52 (4) (2010), 483–509; Jenkins, S., 'Automating questionnaire design and construction', *Journal of the Market Research Society*, 42 (1) (Winter 1999–2000), 79–85; Fink, A., *How to analyze survey data* (Thousand Oaks, CA: Sage, 1995).

35. Esuli, A. and Sebastiani, F., 'Machines that learn how to code open-ended survey data', *International Journal of Market Research*, 52 (6) (2010), 775–800.

36. Kearney, I., 'Measuring consumer brand confusion to comply with legal guidelines', *International Journal of Market Research*, 43 (1) (First Quarter 2001), 85–91; Luyens, S., 'Coding verbatims by computer', *Marketing Research: A Magazine of Management and Applications*, 7 (2) (Spring 1995), 20–25.

37. Albaum, G., Roster, C., Yu, J.H. and Rogers, R.D., 'Simple rating scale formats: Exploring extreme response', *International Journal of Market Research*, 49 (5) (2007).

38. Vicente, P., Reis, E. and Santos, M., 'Using mobile phones for survey research: A comparison with fixed phones', *International Journal of Market Research*, 51 (5) (2009), 613–34; Allison, P.D., *Missing data* (Thousand Oaks, CA: Sage, 2001); Lee, B.-J., 'Sample selection bias correction for missing response observations', *Oxford Bulletin of Economics and Statistics*, 62 (2) (May 2000), 305; Freedman, V.A. and Wolf, D.A., 'A case study on the use of multiple imputation', *Demography*, 32 (3) (August 1995), 459–70; Malhotra, N.K., 'Analysing marketing research data with incomplete information on the dependent variable', *Journal of Marketing Research*, 24 (February 1987), 74–84.

39. A meaningful and practical value should be imputed. The value imputed should be a legitimate response code. For example, a mean of 3.86 may not be practical if only single-digit response codes have been developed. In such cases, the mean should be rounded to the nearest integer. See Allen, N.J., Williams, H., Stanley, D.J. and Ross, S.J., 'Assessing dissimilarity relations under missing data conditions: Evidence from computer simulations', *Journal of Applied Psychology*, 92 (5) (Sept. 2007), 1414–26.

40. Kent, R.A., 'Cases as configurations: Using combinatorial and fuzzy logic to analyse marketing data', *International Journal of Market Research*, 47 (2) (2005), 205–28; Murphy, K.M., 'Estimation and inference in two-step econometric models', *Journal of Business & Economic Statistics*, 20 (1) (Jan. 2002), 88–97; Kara, A., Nielsen, C., Sahay, S. and Sivasubramaniam, N., 'Latent information in the pattern of missing observations in global mail surveys', *Journal of Global Marketing*, 7 (4) (1994), 103–26.

41. Sparrow, N., 'Quality issues on online research', *Journal of Advertising Research*, 47 (2) (June 2007), 179–82.

42. Some weighting procedures require adjustments in subsequent data analysis techniques. See Curtice, J. and Sparrow, N., 'The past matters: Eliminating the pro-Labour bias in British opinion polls', *International Journal of Market Research*, 52 (2) (2010), 169–89; Dawes, J., 'Do data characteristics change according to the number of scale points used?' *International Journal of Market Research*, 50 (1) (2008), 61–77; Tucker, C., Brick, M. and Meekins, B., 'Household telephone service and usage patterns in the United States in 2004: Implications for telephone samples', *Public Opinion Quarterly*, 71 (1) (April 2007), 3–22; Batholomew, D.J., *The analysis and interpretation of multivariate data for social scientists* (Boca Raton, FL: CRC Press, 2002).

43. Labeaga-Azcona, J.M., Lado-Cousté, N. and Martos-Partal, M., 'The double jeopardy loyalty effect using discrete choice models', *International Journal of Market Research*, 52 (5) (2010), 635–54.

44. Dolnicar, S., Grün, B. and Leisch, F., 'Quick, simple and reliable: Forced binary survey questions', *International Journal of Market Research*, 53 (2) (2011), 233–54.

45. Davenport, T.H., Harris, J.G., Jones, G.L. and Lemon, K.N., 'HBR Case Study: The dark side of customer analytics', *Harvard Business Review*, 85 (5) (May 2007), 37; Al-Khatib, J.A., D'Auria Stanton, A. and Rawwas, M.Y.A., 'Ethical segmentation of consumers in developing countries: A comparative analysis', *International Marketing Review*, 22 (2) (2005), 225–46.

46. Shaw, S., 'Communicating creatively: From digital media to stains on the bedroom floor', Market Research Society, *Annual Conference* (2010).

10

Qualitative data analysis

Stage 1
Problem definition

Stage 2
Research approach developed

Stage 3
Research design developed

Stage 4
Fieldwork or data collection

Stage 5
Data integrity and analysis

Stage 6
Report preparation and presentation

Qualitative analysis involves the process of making sense of data that are not expressed in numbers.

Objectives

After reading this chapter, you should be able to:

1 understand the importance of qualitative researchers being able to reflect upon and understand the social and cultural values that shape the way they gather and interpret qualitative data;

2 describe the stages involved in analysing qualitative data;

3 describe the array of data types that qualify as qualitative data;

4 explain the nature and role of coding in the stage of reducing qualitative data;

5 appreciate the benefits of being able to display the meaning and structure that qualitative researchers see in their data;

6 understand why qualitative data analysis pervades the whole process of data gathering and why the stages of analysis are iterative;

7 appreciate the cultural implications of analysing qualitative data collected internationally;

8 understand the ethical implications of the ways that qualitative researchers interpret data;

9 appreciate the strengths and weaknesses of analysing data using qualitative analysis software.

Overview

The application of qualitative techniques is not necessary a pre-defined and structured process. In the majority of instances, qualitative researchers modify their direction as they learn what and who they should focus their attention upon. Data gathering techniques, the nature of participants and the issues explored can change and evolve as a project develops. This chapter starts by examining how researchers reflect upon what happens to the way they perceive and observe as these changes unfold. It discusses how these reflections form a key source of qualitative data to complement the narrative generated from interviews and observations.

The stages involved in a generic process of analysing qualitative data are outlined and described. The first stage of the process involves assembling qualitative data in their rich and varying formats. The second stage progresses on to reducing the data, i.e. selecting, classifying and connecting data that researchers believe to be of the greatest significance. A key element of this stage is the concept of coding. The third stage involves the display of data, i.e. using graphical means to display the meaning and structure that researchers see in the data they have collected. Manual and electronic means of displaying data are discussed. The final stage involves verifying the data. Researchers aim to generate the most valid interpretation of the data they collect, which may be supported by existing theories or through the concept of theoretical sampling. Though these stages seem quite distinct, the reality is that they are iterative and totally interdependent upon each other; the stages unfold in 'waves' to produce an ultimate interpretation that should be of great value to decision makers.

The social and cultural values of qualitative researchers affect how qualitative researchers gather and analyse data. Understanding the social and cultural norms of participants in international environments is discussed. The social and cultural values of researchers affect their interpretation of qualitative data and the ethical implications of not reflecting upon these values are addressed.

The digital applications in the stages of qualitative data collection and analyses are described. There are many distinct advantages to the use of qualitative data analysis software, but many researchers contend that it should be a 'hands-on' process that cannot be mechanised. The arguments from both of these perspectives are presented. To be able to cope with the great amount of data generated from qualitative techniques, a great variety of software packages is available. Examples of analysis software are briefly described followed by website addresses that allow demonstration versions of the software to be downloaded and explored. NVivo, the qualitative data analysis package specifically designed for researchers, is presented.

The qualitative researcher

Self-reflection of social and cultural values

Consider the following advice, addressed at the challenges of diagnosing research problems:

> *A major problem for researchers is that their perception of problems may be reflected through their own social and cultural development. Before defining the problem, researchers should reflect upon their unconscious reference to cultural values . . . The unconscious reference to cultural values can be seen to account for these differences.*[1]

This implies that researchers need to reflect upon their own values and attitudes, the factors that may bias the way they perceive and what they observe. This reflection is just as important in the analysis of qualitative data as it is in the diagnosis of research problems. To illustrate why researchers need to reflect upon what may bias the way they perceive and what they observe, we start this chapter with an example from the world of literature and the treatment of narrative. The example is a précis of an English translation of a Japanese novel; the example could be taken from any novel.

Real research   ## South of the Border, West of the Sun[2]

This novel tells the story of an only child, Hajime, growing up in the suburbs of postwar Japan. His childhood sweetheart and sole companion in childhood was Shimamoto, also an only child. As children they spent long afternoons listening to her father's record collection. When Hajime's family moved away, the childhood sweethearts lost touch. The story moves to Hajime in his thirties. After a decade of drifting he has found happiness with his loving wife and two daughters, and success in running a jazz bar. Then Shimamoto reappears. She is beautiful, intense, enveloped in mystery. Hajime is catapulted into the past, putting at risk all he has at the present.

Imagine that you had been asked to read this novel, but before you read it you were expected to prepare by reading a description of conditions in post-war Japan. From that you may appreciate the significance of a record collection of 15 albums, and how privileged a family may be to own a record player and to have this collection. Imagine someone else being asked to prepare by reading a biography of the author. From that you may appreciate the social and economic conditions of his upbringing, the literature, music and education that he enjoyed. Preparing to read the novel in these two ways may mean that a reader sees very different things in the story. The reader may interpret passages differently, have a different emotional attachment with the conditions and behaviour of the characters, and appreciate the effect of quite subtle events upon the characters.

Put aside any prior reading and imagine a female reader enjoying the book. She may empathise with the main female character Shimamoto and understand her attitudes, values and behaviour in the way that male readers may not be able to comprehend. In the story, Shimamoto suffered from polio as a child, which made her drag her left leg. Imagine a reader who has had to cope with a disability and who may appreciate how as a child one copes with the teasing of young children. The two main characters were 'only children'; imagine the reader who was an only child and who can recall how they would view large families and appreciate the joys, disappointments and array of emotions of being an only child. The list could go on of the different perspectives of the story that may be seen. The reader, with their inherent values and attitudes, may perceive many different things happening in the story. The reader does not normally reflect upon his or her unconscious values and attitudes, but just enjoys the story. In talking to others about the story, the reader may be surprised about how others see it. In watching the film version of the book, the reader may be shocked at the different images the film director presents, images that are very different from the one that resides in their head. Now consider whether there is one ultimate interpretation of the novel, one ultimate 'truth'. It is very difficult to conceive that there is one ultimate interpretation. One may question why anyone would want to achieve such a thing; surely the enjoyment of literature is the ability to have multiple interpretations and 'truths' of a novel.[3]

Narrative for the qualitative researcher

What is the link from the interpretation of a novel to qualitative data analysis in marketing research? Quite simply, the qualitative researcher builds up a narrative and creates a story of the consumers whom decision makers wish to understand. Imagine yourself as a qualitative researcher, supporting decision makers who wish to develop advertisements for an expensive ride-on lawnmower. The key target market they wish to understand is 'wealthy men, over the age of 60, who own a home(s) with at least 1 hectare of garden'. The decisions they face may include the understanding of:

1 What gardening and cutting grass mean to target consumers.

2 How they feel about the experience of buying and using a lawnmower.

3 What relative values (tangible and intangible) are inherent in different brands of lawnmower.

4 What satisfaction they get from the completed job of mowing a large lawn.

5 The nature and qualities of celebrities they admire (who may be used to endorse and use the product in an advertisement).

These questions may be tackled through the use of focus groups. Imagine yourself running these groups. What could you bring to the groups if you have personally gone through the experience of buying an expensive ride-on lawnmower and have gardening and lawnmowing experiences? You may have an empathy with the participants in the same manner as the 'only child' reading of the experiences and emotions of an only child in a story. From this empathy, you may be able to question, probe and interpret the participants' answers really well, drawing an enormous amount from them. Without those experiences you may have to devise ways to 'step into the shoes' of the participants. You may look to the attitudes, values and behaviour of your parents, grandparents or friends for a start, looking for reference points that you are comfortable with, that make sense to you. As you go through a pilot or experimental focus group, you may be surprised by certain participants talking about their lawnmowers as 'friends', giving them pet names and devoting lavish care and attention upon them. Getting an insight into this may mean looking at cases from past research projects or literature from analogous situations such as descriptions of men forming a 'bond' with their cars.

The direction that qualitative researchers take in building up their understanding and ultimately their narrative is shaped by two factors. The first factor is the *theoretical understanding* of the researchers as they collect and analyse the data. This theoretical understanding can be viewed from two perspectives. The first is the use of theory published in secondary data, intelligence and literature. The use of theory from these sources may help researchers to understand what they should focus their attention upon, in their questioning, probing, observations and interpretations. The second is the use of theory from a grounded theory perspective. The researchers may see limitations in existing theory that do not match the observations they are making. These limitations help the researchers to form the focus of their questioning, probing, observations and interpretations.

The second factor that shapes the direction that the researchers take is a *marketing understanding*. In the case of understanding the wealthy male lawnmower owner, the researchers need to understand what marketing decision makers are going to do with the story they create. The researchers need to appreciate the decisions faced in creating an advertisement, building a communications campaign or perhaps changing features of the product. Reference to theoretical and marketing understanding in the researchers helps them to present the most valid interpretation of their story to decision makers. Unlike writing a novel, where the author is happy for the readers to take their own 'truth', researchers are seeking an ultimate interpretation and validity in their story. Achieving a valid interpretation enables the researchers to convey to decision makers a vision or picture of a target market that they can quickly 'step into'. Marketing decision makers, for example, may wish to include a passage of music in an advertisement that the target market has an emotional attachment to, which they find positive and uplifting. With a rich picture or vision of this target market they may be able to choose the right piece of music. The decision makers' cultural and social development may mean that the piece of music is meaningless to them, but you as a researcher have given them the confidence and enabled them to step into the world of the target market.

The researcher's learning as qualitative data

Qualitative researchers have to reflect upon their own social and cultural development, their own attitudes and values to see how these have shaped the narrative and how they shape their interpretation of the narrative. The researchers should recognise their own limitations and the need to develop and learn; in the cases above, this means learning about wealthy men and their relationship with lawnmowers or any target group and their relationships with brands and life experiences. Ultimately they wish to present the most valid story that they see, to have examined the story from many perspectives, to have immersed themselves in the world of their target markets. If you are reading a novel, you may not be inclined to make notes as your reading progresses. You may not make notes of other books to read that may help you to understand the condition of particular characters, or to understand the environment in which they behave. You may not wish to write down the way that you change and learn as you read through the story. A reflection of your unconscious social and cultural values as revealed through your interpretation of the novel may be the last thing you want to do.

As a qualitative researcher you need to do all the above as you build and interpret your story of target consumers. A notebook or diary should be on hand to note new question areas or probes you wish to tackle, and to reflect upon how they have worked. As interviews unfold and you feel your own development and understanding progress, a note of these feelings should be made. As you seek out specific secondary data, intelligence or theory to develop your understanding, you should note why. If you see limitations in existing theories or ideas, you should note why. As an understanding of how decision makers can use the observations that are being made, these should be recorded. Included in these notes should be feelings of failure to ask the right question or probe, emotional states should be noted, of feeling up or down, sad or angry, or nervous.[4] Ultimately the story that emerges in your own notebook should be a revelation of your own social and cultural values. There should be an explicit desire to develop this self-awareness and understand how it has shaped the direction of an investigation and the ultimate story that emerges.

The creation and development of the researcher's notebook is a major part of the narrative that is vital to the successful interpretation of questions and observations of consumers. The key lesson that emerges from the creation and development of the researcher's notebook is that qualitative data analysis is an ongoing process through all stages of data collection, not just when the data have been collected.

> *Analysis is a pervasive activity throughout the life of a research project. Analysis is not simply one of the later stages of research, to be followed by an equally separate phase of 'writing up results'.*[5]

The evolution of questions and probes, deciding who should be targeted for questions and observations and even deciding the context for questioning or observing, means that analysis takes place as data are being gathered.

The process of qualitative data analysis

We go through four perspectives of analysing qualitative data starting with a generic process. Many of the terms used here differ from those linked to specific types of software or to researchers that follow a particular theoretical approach derived from a specific discipline. The generic process outlined is designed to give an understanding of what is involved in qualitative data analysis and how the stages link and interact. The four stages of the generic process are outlined in Figure 10.1. The concept of coding is introduced in this section, a vital concept to understand in all approaches to analysing qualitative data.

Data assembly

Data assembly
The gathering of data from a variety of disparate sources.

Data assembly means the gathering of data from a variety of sources. These would include:

1 Notes taken during or after interviewing or observations.

2 Reflections of researchers, moderators or observers involved in the data collection process.

3 Theoretical support – from secondary data, intelligence or literature sources.

4 Documents produced by or sourced from participants.

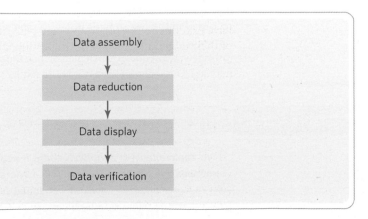

Figure 10.1

Stages of qualitative data analysis

5   Photographs, drawings, diagrams, i.e. still visual images.

6   Audio recordings and transcripts of those recordings.

7   Video recordings.

8   Records made by participants such as mood boards or collages.

Field notes

A log or diary of observations, events and reflections made by a researcher as a study is planned, implemented and analysed.

As discussed in the previous section, the researcher should get into the habit of maintaining a notebook, diary or field notes. As a qualitative investigation evolves in terms of the issues to explore and the participants to target, the researcher goes through a learning process. This learning process means that the researcher may see things differently as interviews or observations progress. Keeping field notes aids the researcher's memory when it comes to the formal process of data analysis and helps enormously in categorising and interpreting collected data. It ultimately helps to generate a 'deeper and more general sense of what is happening'.

In order to make 'deeper and more general sense of what is happening', it is suggested[6] that researchers keep four separate sets of notes in order to systematise the process and thus improve their reliability:

1   Short notes made at the time of observation or interview.

2   Expanded notes made as soon as possible after each session of interviews or observations.

3   A fieldwork journal to record problems and ideas that arise during each stage of fieldwork.

4   A provisional running record of analysis and interpretation.

Data assembly also includes deciding lines of enquiry which should be developed and those that should be dropped. Given that qualitative research is primarily exploratory in nature, questions and probes are not fixed. As an interview or observation takes place, the researcher learns more about an issue and can develop a new question or probe and decide that a question, initially thought to be vital, is no longer relevant. There may be issues that can be compared over a series of interviews or observations, but the whole data collection and data assembly can evolve. Keeping notes is vital as memory alone is fallible, unreliable and potentially biased. Being able to recall, for example, the hesitation in replying to a question displayed by a focus group participant may upon reflection be seen as someone evading the issue. After all the group discussions have been completed and the same question has been posed to others, the interpretation may change to the individual being embarrassed about an issue, primarily through becoming aware of his or her own ignorance. The researchers' notes help them to recall how they were feeling at the point of setting the question, and recall the situation in other groups that gives meaning to a pause that shows up as a quiet spot in an audio or video recording. They may also help the researcher appreciate what is happening when laughter occurs by participants in qualitative techniques. With laughter, the researcher faces the dilemma of interpreting its meaning. Group dynamics, the pitch and intensity of laughter, or even the sly smile that masks a feeling that something is incredibly funny, would need to be recorded in the researcher's notes, to set a vital context to the narrative of any discussion. The same challenges are faced in the following example which deals with the nature of silence in an interview; what does a particular silence mean? The researcher's notes at the time of the silence may hold vital clues to what is being felt by participants but not expressed.

Real research   **Listening to the sounds of silence[7]**

'My depth interview went really badly! It was full of long silences . . . my participants just would not open up!!' This is a cry from researchers who believe that discussions that are not full of verbal give and take have not 'got going'. Many fail to understand that the silence received

in response to the question asked may have told the researcher what they needed to. The way people communicate is deeply linked with the culture, values and norms of a society. If one understands the reason for the silence, one can end up with a far stronger set of findings and interpretations. The following is based on the reflections of over 200 focus group discussions and 100 in-depth interviews conducted in different parts of India by Shobha Prasad (**www.drshti.com**). Silence in India could be based on the social structure between castes. For example, in a study conducted in rural Rajasthan among young men ran into severe issues arising from mingling of castes within the focus group. There were demarcated places where castes were allowed to mingle and communicate; they would talk to each other outdoors but not in inside spaces. It was only when some of the participants were taken out of the group that others opened up to voice their opinions. Language block was occasionally encountered where sessions were conducted in Hindi and participants had differing levels of comfort with the language. In some sessions more educated participants would express themselves in English, creating a sense of inequality in the group. Those who were less educated would then become quiet unless the researcher directly addressed them and tried to draw them back into the discussion. Indians rarely contained strong emotions in silence; they tended to let these feelings out through words. Therefore silence resulting from the two extremes; extreme positive and extreme negative emotion was rare and if it occurred was short lived. 'Extreme delight' was very rarely silent. Extreme negativity tended to result in a short silence which very often just 'broke itself'. The body language accompanying strong negative emotions was very obvious; a closed expression, folded arms, rigid body and refusal to make eye contact. In some cases participants would whisper among themselves. The slightest direct probe was usually adequate to get a verbalisation of these thoughts. The more common causes for silence among both women and men was incomprehension, confusion and feelings of inadequacy, and a lack of confidence. These reasons generally came to light as the session went on, when at some point in response to a probe, participants would admit to have been confused or bewildered.

Unfortunately, the recording and use of field notes or a diary is limited in many qualitative marketing research projects. This may be due to the contents of such notes which could include photographs and other non-verbal data sources. These are unavoidably 'subjective', being what the researcher has chosen to notice. They are developmental, representing the learning and self-reflection that the researcher goes through. The subjective choices are reasoned choices, where issues are deliberately included or excluded. Understanding the reasons for those choices, recognising the learning and self-development that can emerge from these notes, can add so much more depth and greater insight into qualitative data. By developing self-awareness, qualitative researchers can take a more balanced view of the data they collect as they realise many of their own biases and hidden agendas.

Beyond taking notes or keeping a diary, many qualitative techniques make extensive use of material of a semi- or non-verbal nature, generated through participant tasks such as the use of projective techniques. These materials can include drawings, lists, stories, clay models or structures, and collages of photographs, video footage and music. The commonly held view is that it is not these materials that should be analysed but the meanings attached to them by the participants who produced them.[8] These meanings as narrative will have been captured as part of the discussion in recordings or are in the notes of the researcher.[9] The materials themselves would normally be available during analysis, enabling the possibility to notice useful features such as consistencies and differences between participants. They can also be useful in communicating and illustrating findings. Other qualitative researchers go further, taking the view that it is legitimate to 'read' these materials in the absence of the participants who produced them. They would argue that significant and valid meaning can be extracted from them provided they have a strong theoretical basis to drawing their conclusions and meanings.

This relationship between participants' discourse and non-verbal materials mirrors the debate in using photography in ethnographic studies (a common occurrence in qualitative marketing research where participants are given disposable or digital cameras to capture stills or moving images of their experiences). Many significant anthropological ethnographies dating from the mid-1920s onward include photographs relating to the fieldwork. The question that faces anthropologists relates to why photographs may be used in analysis and the relationship, if any, between the photograph and the written text. It is difficult to generalise, but it seems to be the case that photographs have been included in ethnographic reports more for evidential than analytic purposes. The photographs serve essentially presentational and illustrative purposes rather than providing a focus for a more sustained analysis of the visual dimensions of culture.[10] Such perspectives are radically changing as more visual ethnographic techniques gain prominence in qualitative marketing research.[11]

They key feature of the use of photography and visuals is the subtlety of characteristics or events that can be captured and portrayed where words alone may be deficient. This feature has an impact for qualitative researchers for two reasons. The first can be seen from the perspective of qualitative technique participants. Certain participants may not be able to express what they feel about a product, service, advertisement, brand or any design element of their experiences solely using words. They may, however, be able to use visual cues from sources like photographs to represent their feelings. The second can be seen from the perspective of decision makers who use qualitative research findings. Certain marketing decision makers working in visually creative fields such as advertising, product and package design, and branding, work better with visual data compared with words or statistics. They may understand the impact of how consumers feel and will react to their designs through very subtle interpretations of visual data.

Data reduction

Data reduction
The organising and structuring of qualitative data.

Data reduction involves handling the data. This process involves organising and structuring the data. It means having to throw some data away! Imagine a series of 10 focus group discussions and the amount of data that could be collected. There are the memories and notes of the moderator and any other observers who took part, there are the transcripts of what was actually said in interviews, and there may be contributions from participants in the form of mood boards. The transcripts are a vital and for most studies *the* primary data source in qualitative data analysis and much care should be taken in transcribing them. Transferring the dialogue from tape or digital devices can be tortuous as recordings are notoriously 'unclear'. Imagine a focus group in full swing: not every participant takes their turn to speak without talking over other participants, and then they may not speak clearly and loudly enough. As a result it can take a great deal of time to work out what participants actually said and how the questions, responses and ideas connect together. In producing transcripts, it is much better for the researchers to work through the recordings and piece together the components using their notes and memory of events. This is very time consuming, so many researchers use typists to transcribe their recordings of interviews, arguing that their time is better spent reading through and editing transcripts produced in this manner. The use of online software for in-depth interviews and focus groups means that this time-consuming task is eliminated as the transcript is built up as the interview progresses.

Transcripts
'Hard copies' of the questions and probes and the corresponding answers and responses in focus group or in-depth interviews.

The researchers with their transcripts, notes and other supporting material have to decide what is relevant in all these data. Reducing the data involves a process of coding data, which means breaking down the data into discrete chunks and attaching a reference to those chunks of data. Coding is a vital part of coping with qualitative data analysis and, given this importance, the process is discussed in some detail.

Coding data
Breaking down qualitative data into discrete chunks and attaching a reference to those chunks of data.

Coding data Researchers need to be able to organise, manage and retrieve the most meaningful bits of qualitative data that they collect. This is normally done by assigning 'labels' or codes to the data, based upon what the researcher sees as a meaningful categorisation. What happens is that the researcher condenses the great mass of data from a study into analysable units by creating categories from the data.[12] This process is termed the coding of data. Coding is the process of bringing together participants' responses and other data sources into categories that form similar ideas, concepts, themes, or steps or stages in the process. Coding can also enable the categorisation of names, evidence or time sequences. Any hesitations, emotional states or levels of humour can be coded. Indeed, anything that is felt to be revealing in the data can be coded. Data such as a simple response to a question can be coded in many different ways, or placed into many different categories; there is no expectation of mutual exclusivity and data can be recoded as often as is thought necessary.[13]

An illustration of coding is presented using the data presented in the Table 10.1. This table presents the verbatim responses from an open-ended question in a self-completion survey targeted at 12 to 14 year olds. The question asked participants what facilities they would like in a planned new community centre. Though the technique used was quantitative, the survey generated qualitative data and in its much shortened format demonstrates the process that qualitative researchers must go through.

In categorising the responses, the researcher could create codes of '**swimming pool**' or '**disco**' and count the times that these were literally expressed. Alternatively, the researcher could code on the basis of '**sports activities**' or '**recreational activities**' and group together activities such as 'swimming, basketball and snooker' for sports and 'computers, television, discos and tuck shop' for recreational activities. The researcher could code '**indoor activities**' and '**outdoor activities**', or activities that would need supervision and those that would need no supervision. There are many ways that the researcher can categorise the data, it is their choice. Consider how the researcher may cope with the requests for a 'computer room' and 'computers'. Could these be combined under one heading of '**computing**' or would this lose the meaning of having a devoted space, away from other activities that could be noisy and distracting? Consider also how the researcher would cope with the requests for 'stuff for all ages', 'what people will enjoy' and 'all the things people enjoy'. It may seem obvious that a new leisure centre needs to develop facilities that people enjoy and that these may be discarded, but there may be a hint in the first statement of 'stuff for all ages' that may link to the word 'people' used in the two other statements. If the researcher interprets the statements in this way, a category of '**activities to draw in all ages**' could be created; these responses may be seen as tapping into a notion of a leisure centre that is welcoming and not exclusive.

Table 10.1	Teenager requests for facilities at a planned community centre
Requested feature of new community centre	**Gender**
Skate park, death slide, basketball courts, swimming pool	Male
Computer room	Male
Stuff for all ages	Male
Swimming pool	Male
Computers, snooker room	Male
A space for computers, tuck shop	Male
Music, television, up-to-date magazines, pool tables	Female
Music, discos	Female
Swimming pool	Female
Music, pool/snooker, discos	Female
What people will enjoy	Female
All the things people enjoy	Female

| Table 10.2 | **Adult requests for facilities at a planned community centre** |

Requested feature of new community centre	Gender
Regards for residents living nearby, special car parking area to avoid streets nearby being jammed	Male
New centre would soon bring the wrong sort of people; it could form a centre for thugs and crime	Male
Strict rules so as to inconvenience local people living close by as little as possible, e.g. noise	Male
Run and organised well to run functions at affordable prices with dress rules for the lounge and bar	Male
Membership should be given on signature of applicants to a strict set of rules	Male
Emphasis on youth on the estate and run in a way to encourage rather than regiment them	Male
Supervised youth activities, daytime crèche, dance floor, serve coffee/soft drinks for youths	Female
Should be very welcoming and developed for all kinds of people	Female
Active participation by those using the facilities which should give opportunities for the young	Female
To make a safe place for all people of all ages to enjoy	Female
Exterior should be modern. Inside decorated tastefully with nice seats and tables, plenty of hall space	Female
Youth club with a youth leader. Luncheon club for older groups and gentle keep-fit for the elderly	Female

Table 10.2 presents a small selection of the verbatim responses from the same open-ended question in a self-completion survey, this time targeted at adults.

The interesting feature in comparing the statements from the adults with those from the teenagers is how they express themselves in more detail and how they thought beyond specific facilities that make up the leisure centre. These statements were unprompted, so one can imagine how much richer the explanations and justifications would be with an in-depth interview or a focus group. Again, there are many ways that the researcher can categorise the data, perhaps even more than with the teenagers. Categorising these adult statements is not as straightforward as for the teenagers. The researcher could draw out the words '**youth**' or '**rules**' and set these as categories. The researcher could pull out named '**facilities**' such as '**dance floor**' and '**nice seats and tables**' or '**activities**' such as '**youth club**' and '**luncheon club**'. What becomes apparent in reading through the statements (especially with the full set of responses) are implied problems related to issues of parking, the types of people that are attracted or could be attracted, and how 'regimented' or not the centre should be. These are categories or patterns that may be apparent to a researcher, though not explicitly expressed. There may be words expressed that make up the categories, but the words broken down and taken in isolation may lose their impact, if they are just counted.

Table 10.2 illustrates that categorisation into the component words may mean that the contextual material that gives these words meaning can be lost. From the above example, coding can be thought of as a means to:

1 *Retrieve data*, i.e. from the whole mass of data, particular words or statements can be searched for and retrieved to examine the 'fit' with other words or statements.

2 *Organise the data*, i.e. words or statements can be reordered, put alongside each other and similarities and differences evaluated.

3 *Interpret data*, i.e. as words or statements are retrieved and organised in different ways, different interpretations of the similarities and differences can be made.

Coding is a process that enables the researcher to identify what they see as meaningful and to set the stage to draw conclusions and interpret the meaning. Codes are essentially labels to assign meaning to the data compiled during a study.

In broad terms the coding process involves the following stages:

1 *Set up a broad group of coding categories.* These would emerge from an initial reading of the gathered data and the intended purpose of the study. For example, these may be the themes that structured a number of focus group interviews or in-depth interviews.

2 *Work through the data to uncover 'chunks' of data that may be put into brackets or underlined or highlighted.* Codes are usually attached to 'chunks' of varying size, i.e. words, phrases, sentences, paragraphs, an extended story, an image, indeed any component of the collected data, connected or unconnected to a specific context.[14] Sometimes a single sentence or paragraph might be coded into several categories. For example, one paragraph where participants are overtly discussing parking problems at a community centre may also be discussing issues of 'mobility' or 'independence'. Once the start and end of a chunk to be coded is established, a name or number is assigned to it.

3 *Review the descriptions given to the codes.* Working through the data, it may be clear that important themes emerging from the data do not fit into the preset categories or that one theme blurs into two or more separate concepts. At this point new categories have to be set to fit the data. With new categories, the data must then be reviewed and recoded where appropriate. This stage therefore is one of immersion in the data and refining the nature of categories as more meaning is uncovered in the data.

4 *Examine differences between types of participant.* This could be simple demographic comparisons, e.g. to see if there are differences between men and women in how they view independence. The comparisons could be between types of participant that emerge from other codes, e.g. lifestyle aspirations may emerge from the data with groups emerging that may be labelled 'sophisticated minimalists' and 'spiritual warriors'. Comparisons of the behaviour between these emerging groups can be made. Through these comparisons, new insights may emerge about the assigned codes and the descriptors applied to them. New insights may also emerge about the way that participants are described and categorised, combining knowledge of their demographic, geographic, behavioural, psychographic and psychological characteristics.

5 *Develop models of interconnectivity among the coded categories.* This involves basic graphical modelling to explain a sequence of events or a process that the data describe. It could show how categories relate to each other, how participants may be alike or differ and how different contexts impact upon the categories and participants. Again, new insights may emerge about the meaning seen in the data, and the coding process may be further refined.

6 *Iterate between the code descriptions and the developing model.* This stage is again one of immersion in the data, with continual refining of the nature of categories and the structural relationship of those categories. These iterations continue until the researchers have what they believe to be the most valid meaning that they see in the data.

The approach described above can be completed manually or a range of software solutions can be used. The relative advantages and disadvantages of manual or electronic approaches to analysing qualitative data, and especially the iterative process of coding and modelling, are presented later in the text. The point to consider at this stage is that the immersion in the data to draw out meaning is not formulaic, especially as one considers the different types of qualitative data that can be included in analyses. Reducing qualitative data to the essence of meaning as seen by the researchers is a highly creative and subjective process. Given the time that may be allocated to this process, coding can be observed from two perspectives. First, if there is relative little time for the researchers to immerse themselves in the data, it can be thought of as a means to simplify or reduce the mass of data. If an initial broad group of coding categories is kept and their number is relatively small, then the data can be 'stripped down' to a simple general form. This coding approach can be compared directly with simple forms of content analysis.[15] Second, if more time can be afforded, it can be thought of as a means to expand, transform and reconceptualise data, opening up more diverse ideas and analytical possibilities. The general analytical approach is to open up the categories in order to interrogate them further, to try to identify and speculate about further features. Coding here is about going beyond the data, thinking creatively with the data, asking the data questions, and generating theories and frameworks.[16]

Coding is a major process involved in data reduction. The process forces the researchers to focus upon what they believe to be the most valid meaning held in the data. In order to develop that meaning further, the researchers need to communicate their vision to others, to evaluate their interpretations of the data and to reflect upon their own vision. The stage of data display is the means by which researchers communicate their vision of meaning in the data.

Data display

Data display
Involves summarising and presenting the structure that is seen in collected qualitative data.

Data display is an organised, compressed assembly of information that permits conclusion drawing and action.[17] The most frequent form of display for qualitative data in the past has been *extended text*. Such an approach is cumbersome, dispersed and sequential, poorly structured and extremely bulky. The qualitative researcher can resolve these problems with the use of matrices, graphs, charts, networks or 'wordclouds'. All are designed to assemble information into an immediately accessible, compact form so that the analyst can see what is happening and either draw justified conclusions or move on to the next step of analysis the displays suggests may be useful. The creation and use of displays is not an end output of analysis, it is an integral part of the analytic process. For example, designing a matrix as a display involves decisions on what should be displayed in the rows and columns, and deciding what qualitative data, in which form, should be entered in the cells.

Data display also allows a 'public' view of how the researcher has made connections between the different 'data chunks'. Even if others may not have made the same connections and interpret the data in exactly the same manner, the logic of connections should be clear. The display may be in a graphical format, with boxes summarising issues that have emerged and connecting arrows showing the interconnection between issues. Verbatim quotes can be used to illustrate the issues or the interconnections. Pictures, drawings, music or advertisements can also be used to illustrate issues or interconnections. The overall structure allows the decision maker who is to use the analysis to see the general meaning in the collected data. The illustration of issues or interconnections brings that meaning to life.

One of the simplest means to display data is through the use of a spreadsheet. This can be built up and displayed in a manual or electronic format. Table 10.3 presents an example of how a spreadsheet may be set out. This spreadsheet is a sample of all the interviews that may be conducted and the number of issues that may be tackled. The example relates to a bus and tram operator who wishes to understand the attitudes and behaviour of 18 to 25-year-olds related to using public transport. In the columns, details of each interview are presented, and in the final column, notes are made of observations between interviews with a focus on each issue. In the rows, the issues that were discussed in the interviews are presented. These issues may be generated from the topic guide used and/or from the notes of the researcher related to what they see as the emerging issues. The final row details notes of the dynamics of the group, explaining why particular exchanges may be interpreted in a particular way. The analyst cuts and pastes extracts from the transcripts into the relevant cells. With the spreadsheet built up of the reordered transcripts (each focus group may tackle the issues in a different order and with different emphases), comparisons can be made across the columns on particular issues, looking for similarities and differences. Connections between issues can be mapped out with the use of arrows to show the flow of dialogue. The responses from types of participants such as 'city dwellers' or 'suburb dwellers' can be colour coded in order to compare similarities or differences. Different notes, images or any other supplementary material can be pasted on to the spreadsheet to help in the interpretation; all the assembled data can be displayed, or more probably a reduced and coded set of data can be displayed.

Table 10.3	Spreadsheet data display of focus group discourse				
Interviews?	Group 1: 18–25-year-old male car drivers	Group 2: 18–25-year-old female car drivers	Group 3: 18–25-year-old male bus and tram users	Group 4: 18–25-year-old female bus and tram users	Notes on the similarities and differences between groups on issues?
Evening travel	Verbatim discourse taken from the interview that relates to this issue				
Commuting					
Freedom					
Friends					
Notes on the dynamics of individual groups?					

Such a spreadsheet can be built up manually using large sheets of paper from, for example, flip charts, divided into a grid, and the evidence such as chunks of the transcript physically pasted in. This could even be tacked to a large wall allowing the researcher to stand back, reflect, move things about, and add data. The big advantage of this approach is being able to visualise the whole body of data and to move around the data to 'play' with ideas and connections. This works particularly well when there is more than one person working on the analysis and they are drawing ideas and questions out of each other as they relate to the data. The disadvantage is that editing, moving data around and recategorising data can become very cumbersome and messy. This is where electronic means of displaying the data work well. With electronic means, images and notes can be scanned in and added to the transcripts. Changes can be made very easily and quickly in moving data around, recategorising and incorporating new material. Different versions can be easily stored to allow an evaluation of how the thought processes of the researcher have developed. The disadvantage of the approach is that, when attempting to view the data in their entirety, the entire dataset is there but in effect is viewed through a 'window' with a limited field of vision. The 'window' can be readily moved about but the overall perspective is limited.

Another simple means to display data is through the use of a qualitative cross-tabulation. Table 10.4 presents an example of how a crosstabulation may be set out. Again, the example relates to a bus and tram operator who wishes to understand the attitudes and behaviour of 18 to 25-year-olds related to using public transport. The table shows a sample of categories that have been built around issue of 'evening travel'. As the analyst works through the transcripts and codes distinct chunks of data, and with knowledge of who expressed a particular view that is embodied in that chunk, that relationship can be displayed. The table shows that the analyst has established codes to represent views of 'expense', 'personal attacks' 'spontaneity' and 'style'. With a simple classification of participants, in this case by gender, the analyst can display differences in the number of incidences that a specific code emerges. The large differences between males and females in how they brought up the issues 'expense' and 'personal attacks' can help the analyst to explore the data further, or indeed collect more

Table 10.4	Cross-tabulation of emerging categories related to evening travel by gender	
	Gender	
Evening travel	**Male**	**Female**
Expense	16	2
Personal attacks	8	24
Spontaneity	5	5
Style	3	5

data to understand what is creating such divergent attitudes and behaviour. Again, different notes, images or any other supplementary material can be pasted on to the cross-tabulation to help in the interpretation.

The other major means of displaying data is to use flow charts. Figure 10.2 displays a very basic structure of the issues or major categories and subcategories related to how 18 to 25-year-olds view the use of public transport after an evening out.

Visualising the data in this matter can allow the researchers to dip back into the transcripts and their notes to seek alternative ways of connecting evidence and justifying connections. This means that this form of graphic can play a vital role in data reduction and coding, i.e. in making sense of the data, as well as in portraying a final interpretation of the data. Most proprietary qualitative analysis software packages allow data structures to be displayed as in Figure 10.2 but with far more sophisticated features to display structure, differences and supporting evidence. A simple illustration of this in Figure 10.2 is the 'M/F' label attached to categories, used to display behavioural tendencies of male or female participants. With a proprietary qualitative analysis package, quite distinctive structures for participant types may be mapped, with the ability to tap into supporting evidence in actual categories or in the links between categories.[18] Once researchers have displayed what they see as the meaning in the data, they need to demonstrate the credibility of their vision. This involves data verification.

Figure 10.2

Flow chart depicting how 18 to 25-year-olds view public transport

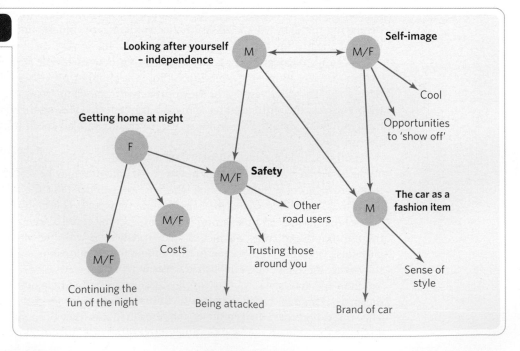

Data verification

Data verification

Involves seeking alternative explanations of the interpretations of qualitative data, through other data sources.

Data verification involves seeking alternative explanations through other data sources and theories. From the start of data collection, qualitative researchers are beginning to decide the meaning of their observations, and noticing regularities, patterns, explanations, possible configurations, causal flows and propositions. The researcher should form these meanings 'lightly', maintaining openness and scepticism, developing conclusions that are embryonic and vague at first, then increasingly explicit and grounded. Final conclusions may not appear until data collection is over, depending upon the volume of data collected in all their forms, the coding, storage and retrieval methods used, and the resource constraints placed upon the researchers. When final conclusions have been drawn, researchers need to demonstrate that they have presented a valid meaning of the data that they have collected. They need to show that the structure or meaning they see is not just a reflection of their own views. This is where the concept of theoretical understanding as discussed at the start of this chapter can help. It is also where the use of the researchers' field notes proves to be invaluable. The use of theory from secondary data, intelligence and the literature can help to guide what may be reasonably expected as a meaning. Other means to verify the data can be through seeking 'similar' research findings and explanations taken from different contexts, different time frames and different researchers.[19] Though the findings from these different scenarios will not be the same, there can be categories that give qualitative researchers the confidence that they are representing a valid view of their participants. This process is illustrated in the following example.

Real research | Ethnographic interpretations[20]

Ethnography generally emphasises deep understanding through a focus on small numbers of participants and getting to know their lifestyles intimately. Interpretations become more robust when researchers openly draw upon information from other sources. As well as using more traditional marketing research sources such as focus groups or surveys other methods can be integrated. To understand what kind of products and services might resonate effectively with Generation Y consumers, researchers from IDEO (**www.ideo.com**) went as deep as they could with individuals, interviewing and observing them in different contexts. They talked to experts: parents, teachers, youth programme leaders and therapists. They held classes at universities made up of students from this generation and collaborated with them to study their own cohort. They engaged individuals who were willing to make mini-documentary videos of their own lives. Combining insight from these various sources and experiences, they were able to reach a deeper understanding around complex areas like identity. They could see how identity played out through their behaviours in co-opting brands, sampling from pop-culture, borrowing from other continents, cultures and time periods. By triangulating methods, their understanding became more nuanced and ultimately more useful as a foundation for relevant innovation.

Triangulation

A process that facilitates the validation of data through cross-verification from more than two sources

Two forms of validation have been suggested as particularly appropriate to the logic of qualitative research.[21] The first is termed 'triangulation', a term derived from navigation, where different bearings give the correct position of an object. **Triangulation** is a process that facilitates the validation of data through cross-verification from more than two sources. In research terms, comparing different kinds of data (e.g. dialogue and photographs, quantitative and qualitative) and different methods (e.g. observations and interviews) allows reflection upon the extent of corroboration, and what may be the causes of any differences.[22] The second is termed 'participant validation'. This involves taking one's findings back to the participants under study. Where the feedback from participants on emergent conclusions is verified by them, there can be more confidence in the validity of the findings.

Qualitative researchers should not just present an interpretation and then seek validation or verification of that perspective. The search for verification is a quest that permeates the whole research process. At face value, data assembly, reduction, display and verification appear to be quite distinct and consecutive stages of data analysis. The reality is that they are iterative and totally interdependent upon each other. As the researchers assemble new data, they should be thinking of means to validate their views, asking questions of different individuals in different ways and recording these thoughts in their field notes. As data are being reduced and coded, the researchers seek different possible explanations and evidence to support categorising, naming and connecting views in a particular manner. The researchers will question their interpretations of words and gestures and their own ways of seeing. This questioning process adds to the verification. The use of data display is a means to communicate to others the meaning and structure that researchers 'see' in qualitative data. The display allows others to understand that vision, to question and evaluate it. The exposure and critique of the vision by other researchers and decision makers further verify the data. Ultimately, such critique can direct the researchers to further data assembly, reduction and display; the stages may unfold in 'waves' to produce an ultimate interpretation of great value to decision makers.

International marketing research

If one were to take the very naive view of qualitative data analysis being to feed data into an analysis package, and to wait for processed data to emerge, then international analysis would focus purely upon issues of language and translation. Such a perspective of qualitative analysis would ignore the context and process of collecting data and the role that these factors play in interpreting the meaning that emerges from interviews and observations. As discussed at the start of this chapter, qualitative researchers need an acute self-awareness of how they 'see' – which affects the way they pose questions and interpret answers.

Consumers in any country use their social and cultural frames of reference to interpret questions posed to them by qualitative researchers and to present a response. Likewise, qualitative researchers use their social and cultural frames to present questions and interpret answers. If the researcher and the participant share the same or similar social and cultural frames of reference, the analysis and interpretation of the data can be relatively straightforward. If the qualitative researcher goes into an international market, there is the potential for big differences in social and cultural frames between the researcher and the researched. The qualitative researcher needs

to develop an understanding of the social and cultural frames of the types of participant in an international market. At the same time, they must have a strong awareness of their own social and cultural frames. Only when qualitative researchers have examined both perspectives can they start to interpret consumer responses.

The process is summarised by qualitative researchers Virginia Valentine and Malcolm Evans as:[23]

> *Consumers give a 'coded' version of the social and cultural relationship with products and brands that drive their 'feelings'. Because language (and language systems) are the medium of culture, the rules of language become the rules of the code. Qualitative research then becomes a matter of working with the code through understanding the rules of language.*

Thus, simple literal translations of transcripts of interviews from international markets entered into a qualitative data analysis package are doomed to failure. The following example examines some of the challenges faced in translating and interpreting Japanese.

Real research **Research insights into Japanese culture**[24]

International researcher Neil Cantle offers the following views of the challenges involved in interpreting Japanese culture. He sees Japanese as a very ambiguous language and this ambiguity, *'Aimai sa'*, is celebrated. Meaning is often implied or understood contextually. Even the simplest of words can be ambiguous. There is even no direct translation for 'yes' or 'no'. The word *'Hai'*, usually understood to mean 'yes' in the West, actually just means 'I have heard you' and a refusal or negative statement is usually implied. Omitting parts of a sentence can also heighten this feeling of ambiguity. In Japanese, the subject, verb and tense do not have to be explicitly stated. Meaning is often interpreted in terms of context and tone. Not finishing sentences and understanding incomplete sentences is an art form to be embraced and practised. Interpreting meaning plays an important part in conversation, and spoken Japanese can be a tricky business even for native speakers. From a research perspective this means that it is very important to find an experienced bilingual and bicultural researcher able not only to interpret what is being said but also to communicate that back to you. It is often remarked that the Japanese do not give much away in body language, facial expressions or gestures, but many Japanese say the same thing about the Westerners. It is almost impossible to learn to interpret Japanese non-verbal communication in a short space of time. Even for native speakers a tilt of the head can mean 'not really' but also 'it's OK'. It is best to ensure a native Japanese speaker interprets this for you.

Understanding the rules of language and understanding oneself are vital for the qualitative researcher to interpret interviews and observations. As the rules of language, with the social and cultural forces that shape those rules, become more alien to the researcher in international markets, the task of analysis and meaningful interpretation becomes more difficult.

Ethics in marketing research

It is interesting to note that within the ESOMAR code of conduct, little reference is made to what is deemed the ethical practice of data analysis, be that quantitative or qualitative. This is understandable, as the chief concern for the marketing research industry is how participants are handled, i.e. the process of eliciting data from them. Care must be taken to ensure that the precious resource of participants is not misled or manipulated. However, with the emergence of social media research techniques, the ability to gather characteristics and views of consumers from multiple sources has generated new ethical challenges.

With quantitative data, there are many established and consistent procedures of analysis. With qualitative data, even though there is a broad framework to manage analysis procedures, there does not exist a body of consistent and established procedures of analysis. The difficulty in establishing consistent procedures lies primarily in the great diversity of data that can be included in the analysis procedure. Go back to the 'Data assembly' subsection to see the types and nature of qualitative data and it is easy to see why this is so. Combining the researcher's notes, transcripts of interviews, pictures, audio and video recordings and mood boards does not lead to a structured process. It is a messy process that owes much to individual patience, creativity and vision. In searching for support of ethical practice to cope with such a 'messy process', there is one area of support that comes from the code of conduct of the Market Research Society in the UK. In its section 'Analysis and reporting of findings', Rules B56 to 58 state:[25]

B.56 Members must ensure that reports and presentations clearly distinguish between facts and interpretation.

B.57 Members must ensure that when interpreting data they make clear which data they are using to support their interpretation.

B.58 Members must ensure that qualitative reports and presentations accurately reflect the findings of the project in addition to the interpretations and conclusions.

The key element of this rule is that the researcher should be explicit about their interpretation of the data collected. This takes us back to the start when we discussed the self-reflection of the social and cultural values of researchers. If qualitative researchers fail or cannot be bothered to reflect upon their own values and cultural norms, their interpretation of qualitative data may be extremely biased. It therefore follows that, for the most valid as well as the most ethical interpretation of qualitative data, researchers must continually reflect and test the extent and effect of their social and cultural values.

Digital developments in marketing research

Qualitative data analysis goes beyond the words in interview transcripts. In an attempt to 'step into the shoes' of target consumers, a whole array of questions, probes, observations, answers and personal notes have to be analysed. As with quantitative data analyses, it is possible to complete qualitative analyses without the aid of a computer. With quantitative analysis, it would be a rare occurrence to analyse data without a computer. With qualitative analysis it is not so rare, many researchers still believe in a 'hands on' immersion in the rich data they have collected. Using the computer should provide speed, memory, ease of data access and the ability to transform and manipulate data in many ways. Overall it should allow a much more efficient and ultimately effective process, as the researcher's effort may be focused upon generating the most effective support for decision makers as quickly as possible rather than upon laborious administrative tasks. The following list summarises qualitative research activities that may be supported by the use of computers:

1 *Field notes.* Making notes before, during and after interviews and observations. Writing and editing these notes if needed as part of a data display to justify a particular interpretation.

2 *Transcripts.* Building up transcripts to represent the discourse in interviews.

3 *Coding.* Attaching keywords to chunks of data or text.

4 *Storage, search and retrieval.* Keeping data in an organised manner, so that relevant segments of data or text can be located, pulled out and evaluated.

5 *Connection.* Linking relevant data segments with each other.

6 *Memos.* Writing up reflective comments that can be 'pasted' on to relevant codes and connections.

7 *Data display.* Placing selected or reduced data in a condensed and organised format using a spreadsheet matrix or network. The display can be part of the development of the analysis or in the final vision produced by the researcher.

8 *Drawing conclusions and verification.* Aiding the researcher to interpret the data display and to test or confirm findings.

9 *Theory building.* Developing systematic and conceptually coherent explanations of findings that are meaningful to marketing decision makers.

10 *Reporting.* Presenting interim and final reports of the findings in a written and oral manner.

Many of these tasks can be performed with readily available word-processing, spreadsheet and presentation packages. Many researchers may be very comfortable using such packages to gather and record data and to present findings. What may be new to many researchers is the use of proprietary software to help with the technical integration of data assembly, reduction, display and verification. Improvements in the functions and power of software that copes with this technical integration occur at a rapid pace. To see examples of different qualitative data analysis packages, download demos and cases and evaluate how applicable they may be to a particular qualitative technique. Visit the following websites:

Qualitative data analysis software	Website
NVivo and XSight	www.qsrinternational.com
Atlas ti	www.atlasti.com
C I SAID	www.code-a-text.co.uk

The following example illustrates why Progressive Sports Technologies (**www.progressivesports. co.uk**) use NVivo and the qualitative techniques that are supported by this software. We recommend that you visit the QSR website to evaluate descriptions of applications and cases of NVivo applications.

Real research　　**Taking sporting equipment to a new standard**[26]

Progressive Sports Technologies Ltd is a UK based sports innovation consultancy that specialises in the research and design of cutting edge fitness equipment for major global sports brands like Nike, Reebok and Speedo. In a research project on elite sporting products, they used NVivo to conduct qualitative data analysis. The sport and fitness sector is a highly competitive industry where athletes and participants search for the latest training advancements in order to gain improved results. Whether training at an elite level or working out for general health and fitness, sporting participants demand goods and services that will better help them achieve their goals. The biggest challenge for sporting manufacturers is working out exactly what elite athletes want from their equipment. Understanding what this elite group wants is more difficult than it sounds. Athletes who are at the top of their game and striving for the smallest improvement in results may not necessarily be able to articulate where they want changes made. Traditionally, sporting equipment designers have first created prototypes of new products and then asked athletes for their feedback, in order to fine tune the equipment. At Progressive, they've turned this process on its head by opening up direct communication channels between their designers and the elite athletes via a new perception study. In Progressive's perception study, detailed interviews were conducted with 25 elite athletes across two countries. By providing the athletes with four distinct products within the same category, such as four very different pairs of running shoes, each participant was asked to describe their perceptions towards the different products in great detail. All interviews were recorded, transcribed and entered into NVivo. The software was used to group all keywords and themes that the athletes were describing. Numerous athletes were tested on multiple days, in different venues and countries. The software was used as an archive of all the testing carried out.

The data files had in the order of 50,000 words relating to the athletes' product perceptions. The software was seen as a huge time saver and allowed Progressive to organise the work in a clear and logical manner. The time saved was huge; the process definitely halved our sorting and evaluation time. In addition, the audio-visual capabilities available in NVivo allowed Progressive to import all files under one umbrella, including sound and movie files for future studies.

Qualitative data analysis packages do not automate the analysis process, nor is that their purpose. The process of coding, as described in the data verification section, depends upon the interpretations made by the researcher. The overall description, model or theory that emerges from the analysis also depends upon interpretations made by the researcher. No analysis package can perform such interpretations. Qualitative data analysis is not formulaic; it requires an approach that gives quick feedback to the researcher on the results of emergent questions. This involves an iterative cycle of reflection and innovation, which means total interaction between the researcher and the computer. Rather than seeing analysis as an automated process, the purpose of software is to aid the researcher to analyse data in a systematic and thorough manner. The researcher seeks patterns, meanings and interconnections in the qualitative data. This can be conducted manually, but by using software the researcher can manipulate the data far more efficiently to help see patterns, meanings and interconnections and ultimately to develop theory. In summary, software packages offer the qualitative researcher the following advantages.

Advantages of computer-assisted qualitative data analysis

1 *Speed*. The speed at which programs can carry out sorting procedures on large volumes of data is fast. This gives the researcher more time to think about the meaning of data, enabling rapid feedback of the results of particular analytic ideas so that new ones can be formulated. Analysis becomes more devoted to creative and intellectual tasks, less immersed in routine.

2 *Rigour*. Rigour adds to the trust placed in research findings. In this context it means counting the number of times things occur as well as demonstrating that negative incidences have been located rather than selecting anecdotes that support a particular interpretation.

3 *Team*. In collaborative research projects where researchers need to agree on the meaning of codes, a check can easily be made of whether team members are interpreting segments in the same way. This is particularly useful as coding moves from the more descriptive and mundane codes to ones that reflect broader theoretical concerns. Researchers can pass coded interviews between them, and compare the results.

4 *Sampling*. It is easy to keep track of who *has* been interviewed, compared with the intentions of who *should* be interviewed. Beyond the sampling of individuals is the concept of theoretical sampling, i.e. the inclusion of events that corroborate or contradict developing theory. As researchers have more time to spend on creative and intellectual tasks, they can develop stronger descriptions and theories and strengthen the validity of their views by ensuring they have sampled sufficient incidences.[27]

It must be reinforced, however, that software packages cannot interpret and find meaning in qualitative data. The programs do facilitate, and in some cases automate, the identification and coding of text. But there is sometimes a false assumption that identification and coding are simple and unproblematic, and critical evaluation and scrutiny of coded segments and code counts are not needed. By facilitating quick analyses which focus on quantitative category relationships, the software may discourage more time-consuming, in-depth interpretations. Thus while the programs are intended as a means of allowing the researcher to stay close to the data, their misuse can have the unintended result of distancing the researcher from the data. As discussed earlier, many decision makers who use qualitative marketing research do not question how analysis is completed, or indeed why it should be completed. The following arguments illustrate the nature of their concerns.[28]

Disadvantages of computer-assisted qualitative data analysis

1 *Mechanistic data analysis.* The computer cannot replace the creative process expected of the qualitative researcher. The researcher can evaluate the interrelated play on particular words, the tone of voice or the gestures of a particular participant. The sensitivity towards these relationships and connections can be lost in a mechanistic search for statements.

2 *Loss of the overview.* The researcher may be seduced into concentrating on the detail of individual chunks of data and assigning codes to the data. This focus may detract from the overall context that is so vital to identify and name chunks of data. Making sense of codes can be greatly facilitated by an ability to visualise the data in their entirety.

3 *Obsession with volume.* Given the ability to manipulate large amounts of data, there may be a push to increase the number of interviews. This may be counterproductive in that the emphasis should be on the interrelated *qualities* of:

- individual participants
- the interview process.

4 *Exclusion of non-text data.* As noted earlier, qualitative 'text' can include notes, observations, pictures and music that make up the total 'picture' or holistic representation of individuals. Many programs were originally designed to cope with the narrative of questions and answers recorded in transcripts. Qualitative analysis software developers have recognised this limitation and have gone to great pains to overcome them, enabling researchers to work with a great breadth of data types. One of the trade-offs faced by software developers in overcoming these limitations is the user-friendliness of their programs compared with the sophistication of being able to manipulate and represent the structure that may lie in multifarious data. As qualitative researchers use and learn how to generate the most from the software, user-friendliness may take a lesser though not ignored role. Experienced qualitative researchers can demand more sophistication to match the realities of coping with qualitative data. For the novice qualitative researcher the packages may seem daunting, but this problem is analogous to an initial exposure to sophisticated survey design packages such as SNAP or statistical packages such as SPSS. In all cases researchers need to appreciate how the software may serve them and work through the examples and cases, to experiment and to build up their knowledge and confidence.

Summary

Qualitative researchers should reflect upon how their social and cultural values affect the way they perceive and observe target participants. These reflections should be built up as field notes as the whole process of data gathering develops and evolves. These notes form a key source of qualitative data to complement the broad array of qualitative data generated from interviews and observations. To successfully draw together a valid interpretation, qualitative data analysis must be set in the context of a theoretical understanding of the issue being researched, and an understanding of the marketing decision makers' use of the findings.

The first stage of the process of analysing qualitative data involves assembling data in their rich and varying formats. The second stage involves reducing the data, i.e. selecting, classifying and connecting data that are believed to be of the greatest significance. A key element of this stage is the concept of coding. The third stage involves displaying data, i.e. using graphical means to display the meaning and structure that a researcher sees in the data collected. The final stage involves verifying the data. The researcher aims to generate the most valid interpretation of these data, which may be supported by existing theories or through the concept of theoretical sampling. The stages of analysis seem quite distinct but in reality they are totally dependent upon each other.

The qualitative researcher needs to develop an understanding of the social and cultural frames of target participants in international markets. At the same time, qualitative researchers must have a strong awareness of their own social and cultural frames. Only when they have examined both perspectives can they effectively interpret consumer responses. There are ethical implications of the extent to which researchers seek the valid interpretations they can make of the qualitative data they have gathered. With the explosion of qualitative data afforded by social media exchanges, the researcher faces new ethical challenges. Consumers may be more open and expressive through social media sources, which can be of great benefit to researchers, but protecting their anonymity represents a great challenge. To be able to cope with the great amount of data generated from qualitative techniques, a great variety of software packages are available. Used correctly, they can facilitate a speedy and rigorous exploration of qualitative data, allowing teams of researchers to perform creative and incisive analyses and interpretations. The main concern with the use of qualitative data analysis packages lies in the potential for them to be mechanistic and to encourage yet more interviews to be completed, sacrificing the quality of data capture.

Questions

1 How may the social and cultural background of researchers affect the way they:
   - gather qualitative data?
   - interpret the whole array of qualitative data they have gathered?
2 What is the significance of a qualitative researcher having a theoretical and marketing understanding of the subject they are researching?
3 Why should a qualitative researcher maintain a field notebook?
4 What may be classified as 'data' when assembling data as part of the data analysis process?
5 What does the word 'coding' mean in the context of qualitative data analysis? What problems do you see associated with the process of coding?
6 What are the advantages and disadvantages of handing over recordings of qualitative interviews to a typist who has taken no part in the interviews?
7 Evaluate the purpose of displaying qualitative data.
8 What advantages and disadvantages do you see in displaying qualitative data in a spreadsheet format?
9 Evaluate 'when' the stage of data verification should occur.
10 Why does the interpretation of qualitative findings have ethical implications?
11 How may different types of software help in the whole process of qualitative data gathering and analysis?
12 Evaluate the main concerns that exist with the use of software in qualitative data analysis.

Exercises

1 You have been given the task of conducting a series of in-depth interviews about luxury cruises targeted at women of 50 years of age and over. What preparatory work could you do to understand characteristics of this subject, the target group and how the target group relates to the subject?

2 You have just started to work for a major qualitative marketing research agency. The CEO notes that her researchers use a great variety of methods to keep field notes, ranging from scrappy notes taken at interviews to detailed diaries. You have been given the task of designing a format of field notes that will incorporate 'short notes made at the time of observation or interview', 'expanded notes made as soon as possible after each session of interviews or observations', 'a fieldwork journal to record problems and ideas that arise during each stage of fieldwork', and 'a provisional running record of analysis and interpretation'. Present the design and the case you would make to other researchers to use your format.

3 You have conducted a series of focus groups with 18 to 21-year-olds about travelling home from evening events. As you complete each group, you ask each participant to send you photographs taken on their mobile phones that record significant events of their journeys home for the forthcoming weekend. What would you do with the images that they send to you?

4 An ethnographic study is planned of young men using Lynx deodorant. You have been asked to compare the relative merits of the qualitative data analysis packages Atlas ti (**www.atlasti.com**) and NVivo (**www .qsrinternational.com**) in terms of coping with the types of data that will be generated and the interpretations that will be performed.

5 In a small group discuss the following issues: 'Quantitative techniques of analysis and data display have no role to play in qualitative data analysis.' 'The reporting of qualitative data analyses can only be of value to creative designers in marketing.'

Notes

1. Malhotra, N.K., Birks, D.F. and Wills, P. *Marketing Research: An Applied Approach*, 4th European Edition (Harlow: Pearson Education, 2012).

2. Murakami, H., *South of the Border, West of the Sun* (London: Harvill, 1999).

3. Interpreting narrative, i.e. the nature and scope of analysing literature is a major subject area in its own right. For a simple introduction into the field see Barry, P., *'An introduction to literary and cultural theory'*, (Manchester University Press, 3rd edn, 2009).

4. For an example of the use of field notes in a qualitative study see: Drenten, J., Okleshen Peters, C. and Boyd Thomas, J., 'An exploratory investigation of the dramatic play of preschool children within a grocery store shopping context', *International Journal of Retail & Distribution Management*, 36 (10) (2009), 831–55; Rubin, H.J. and Rubin, I.S., *Qualitative Interviewing: The art of hearing data* (Thousand Oaks, CA: Sage, 1995), 120.

5. Coffey, A. and Atkinson, P., *Making Sense of Qualitative Data: Complementary Research Strategies* (Thousand Oaks, CA: Sage, 1996), 10–11.

6. Spradley, J.P., *The Ethnographic Interview* (New York: Holt, Rinehart & Winston, 1979).

7. Prasad, S., 'Listening to the sounds of silence', ESOMAR, *Asia Pacific*, Kuala Lumpur (April 2010).

8. Snowden, D. and Stienstra, J., 'Stop asking questions: Understanding how consumers make sense of it all', ESOMAR, *Annual Congress*, Berlin (Sept. 2007); Ereaut, G., *Analysis and Interpretation in Qualitative Market Research* (London: Sage, 2002), 63.

9. Gordon, W. and Langmaid, R., *Qualitative Market Research: A practitioner's and buyer's guide* (Aldershot: Gower, 1988).

10. Ball, M.S. and Smith, G.W.H., *Analyzing visual data* (Newbury Park, CA: Sage, 1992), 9.

11. Verhaeghe, A., Van den Bergh, J. and Colin, V., 'Me myself and I: Studying youngsters' identity by combining visual ethnography and netnography', ESOMAR, *Qualitative Research*, Istanbul (Nov. 2008).

12. Coffey, A. and Atkinson, P., *Making Sense of Qualitative Data* (Thousand Oaks, CA: Sage, 1996), 26.

13. Rubin, H.J. and Rubin, I.S., *Qualitative Interviewing: The art of hearing data* (Thousand Oaks, CA: Sage, 1995), 238.

14. Hubermann, A.M. and Miles, M.B., 'Data management and analysis methods', in Denzin, N.K. and Lincoln, Y.S. (eds) *Handbook of Qualitative Research* (Thousand Oaks, CA: Sage, 1994), 428–44.

15. Weltzer-Ward, L., 'Content analysis coding schemes for online asynchronous discussion', *Campus-Wide Information Systems*, 28 (1) (2011), 56–74; Roberts,

M. and Pettigrew, S., 'A thematic content analysis of children's food advertising', *International Journal of Advertising*, 26 (3) (2007), 357–67; Krippendorf, K., *Content Analysis: An introduction to its methodology* (Beverly Hills, CA: Sage, 1980).

16. Coffey, A. and Atkinson, P., *Making Sense of Qualitative Data: Complementary Research Strategies* (Thousand Oaks, CA: Sage, 1996), 29–30.

17. Miles, M.B. and Huberman, A.M., *Qualitative data analysis: An expanded sourcebook*, 2nd edn (Thousand Oaks, CA: Sage, 1994), 11.

18. This is a very basic overview of the different means to display qualitative data. For a fuller discussion, the following is recommended: Huberman, M. and Miles, M.B., *The Qualitative Researcher's Companion: Classic and Contemporary Readings*, (Thousand Oaks, CA: Sage, 2002); and especially the five chapters devoted to data display in: Miles, M.B. and Huberman, A.M., *Qualitative data analysis: An expanded sourcebook*, 2nd edn (Thousand Oaks, CA: Sage, 1994), 90–244.

19. This process is known as triangulation. For a fuller description of this topic, set in the context of researcher bias, see Schillewaert, N., De Ruyck, T. and Verhaeghe, A., 'Connected research – How market research can get the most out of semantic web waves', *International Journal of Market Research*, 51 (1) (2009), 11–27; Griseri, P., *Management Knowledge: A Critical View* (Basingstoke: Palgrave, 2002), 60–78.

20. Fulton Suri, J. and Gibbs Howard, S., 'Going deeper, seeing further: Enhancing ethnographic interpretations to reveal more meaningful opportunities for design', *Journal of Advertising Research*, 46 (3) (Sept. 2006), 246–50.

21. Silverman, D., *Doing Qualitative Research*, 3rd edn (London: Sage, 2009), 292–310.

22. Patton, M.Q., *Qualitative research and evaluation methods*, 3rd edn (Newbury Park, CA: Sage, 2002).

23. Valentine, V. and Evans, M., 'The dark side of the onion: Rethinking the meanings of "rational" and "emotional" responses', *Journal of the Market Research Society*, 35 (2) (April 1993), 127.

24. Cantle, N., 'Research insights into Japanese culture', *Admap*, 480 (Feb. 2007), 35–37.

25. Code of Conduct, Market Research Society (April 2010), 20.

26. **www.qsrinternational.com/solutions_case-studies_detail.aspx?view=153**, accessed 14 Feb 2012.

27. Schmidt, M., 'Quantification of transcripts from depth interviews, open ended responses and focus groups: Challenges, accomplishments, new applications and perspectives for market research', *International Journal of Market Research*, 52 (4) (2010), 483–509; Seale, C., in Silverman, D., *Doing Qualitative Research: A Practical Handbook* (London: Sage, 2000), 161.

28. Ishmael, G. and Thomas, J.W., 'Worth a thousand words', *Journal of Advertising Research*, 46 (3) (Sept. 2006), 274–78; Packenham, L., 'Can qual research benefit from data-analysis software?' *Admap*, 462 (June 2005), 48–49; Dembrowski, S. and Hanmer-Lloyd, S., 'Computer applications – a new road to qualitative data analysis?' *European Journal of Marketing*, 29 (11) (Nov. 1995), 50; Wolfe, R.A., Gephart, R.P. and Johnson, T.E., 'Computer-facilitated qualitative data analysis: Potential contributions to management research', *Journal of Management*, 19 (3) (Fall 1993), 637.

11 Basic quantitative data analysis

Stage 1

Problem definition

Stage 2

Research approach developed

Stage 3

Research design developed

Stage 4

Fieldwork or data collection

Stage 5

Data integrity and analysis

Stage 6

Report preparation and presentation

Frequency distribution, cross-tabulation and hypothesis testing are the fundamental building blocks of quantitative data analysis. They provide insights into the data, guide subsequent analyses and aid the interpretation of results.

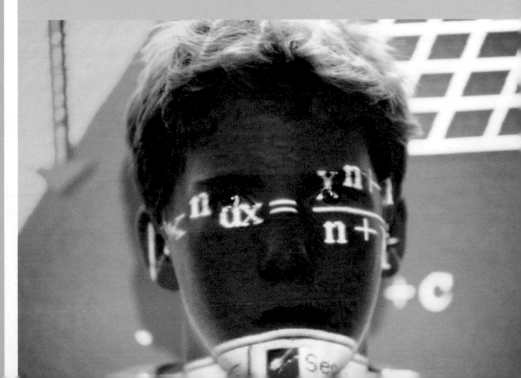

Objectives

After reading this chapter, you should be able to:

1 understand the importance of preliminary data analysis;
2 explain data analysis associated with frequencies;
3 explain data analysis associated with cross-tabulations;
4 understand, discuss and apply data analysis associated with parametric hypothesis testing;
5 understand, discuss and apply data analysis associated with non-parametric hypothesis testing;
6 conduct a preliminary data analysis using SNAP or a similar software.

Overview

Once quantitative data has been prepared for analysis (Chapter 9), the researcher should conduct basic analyses. This chapter describes basic data analyses, including frequency distribution, cross-tabulation and hypothesis testing. First, we describe the frequency distribution and explain how it provides both an indication of the number of out-of-range, missing or extreme values as well as insights into the central tendency, variability and shape of the underlying distribution. Next, we introduce hypothesis testing by describing the general procedure. Hypothesis testing procedures are classified as tests of associations or tests of differences. We consider the use of cross-tabulation for understanding the associations between variables taken two or three at a time. Although the nature of the association can be observed from tables, statistics are available for examining the significance and strength of the association. We present tests for examining hypotheses related to differences based on one or two samples.

Many marketing research projects do not go beyond basic data analysis. These findings are often displayed using tables and graphs (as discussed further in Chapter 13). Although the findings of basic analysis are valuable in their own right, they also provide guidance for conducting multivariate analysis. The insights gained from the basic analysis are also invaluable in interpreting the results obtained from more sophisticated statistical techniques. The following example illustrates the use of a basic data analysis technique in the use of a cross-tabulation and chi-square analysis.

Real research   FIBA Brand Tracker

In 2009, the International Basketball Federation FIBA commissioned IFM Sports Marketing Surveys (**www.sportsmarketingsurveys.com**) to conduct a Brand Health Tracker study. They wished to monitor perceptions of the FIBA brand and FIBA events. They wanted to know what affected the development of their brand. FIBA were particularly interested in how perceptions of basketball differed in the countries under study and whether any differences were statistically significant. IFM Sports Marketing Surveys classified their sample of sports fans based upon the number of games they had watched in the previous year. The following table focuses upon the levels of interest in basketball of

Chinese, Italian, Spanish and UK participants. Cross-tabulation and chi-square analysis provided the following:

Sports fans' level of interest in basketball	Country (absolute numbers of participants, and column %)			
	China	**Italy**	**Spain**	**UK**
Avid	187 (31%)	146 (24%)	83 (15%)	85 (14%)
Occasional	115 (19%)	158 (26%)	226 (41%)	219 (36%)
Low	242 (40%)	238 (39%)	187 (34%)	194 (32%)
None	60 (10%)	67 (11%)	55 (10%)	115 (19%)
Totals	604 (100%)	645 (100%)	609 (100%)	607 (100%)
$x^2 = 145.56$				$p \leq 0.0001$

These results indicate that there was little difference across the four countries in terms of low or no levels of interest in basketball. However, there was a much higher proportion of Chinese and Italians that had an avid interest. UK sports fans had the lowest levels of 'avids' and the highest levels of fans with no interest in basketball. The chi-square test indicated that there were statistically significant differences in levels of interest in basketball across the countries studied.

In order to illustrate the concepts of basic quantitative data analysis, a straightforward example is developed. This example is based upon a small survey that explains Internet usage for personal (non-professional) reasons. Table 11.1 contains data for 30 participants giving the gender (1 = male, 2 = female), familiarity with the Internet (1 = very unfamiliar, 7 = very familiar), Internet usage in hours per week, attitude towards the Internet and towards technology, both measured on a seven-point scale (1 = very unfavourable, 7 = very favourable), and whether the participants have done online shopping or banking (1 = yes, 2 = no). For illustrative purposes, we consider only a small number of observations. As a first step in the analysis, it is important to examine the **frequency distributions** of the relevant variables. This may answer specific questions about the problem or may highlight interesting differences that require further investigation.

Frequency distribution
A mathematical distribution whose objective is to obtain a count of the number of responses associated with different values of one variable and to express these counts in percentage terms.

Table 11.1	Internet usage data						
Participant no.	Gender	Familiarity	Internet usage	Attitude towards Internet	Attitude towards technology	Usage of Internet shopping	Usage of Internet banking
1	1	7	14	7	6	1	1
2	2	2	2	3	3	2	2
3	2	3	3	4	3	1	2
4	2	3	3	7	5	1	2
5	1	7	13	7	7	1	1
6	2	4	6	5	4	1	2
7	2	2	2	4	5	2	2
8	2	3	6	5	4	2	2
9	2	3	6	6	4	1	2

Table 11.1	Continued						
Participant no.	Gender	Familiarity	Internet usage	Attitude towards Internet	Attitude towards technology	Usage of Internet shopping	Usage of Internet banking
10	1	9	15	7	6	1	2
11	2	4	3	4	3	2	2
12	2	5	4	6	4	2	2
13	1	6	9	6	5	2	1
14	1	6	8	3	2	2	2
15	1	6	5	5	4	1	2
16	2	4	3	4	3	2	2
17	1	6	9	5	3	1	1
18	1	4	4	5	4	1	2
19	1	7	14	6	6	1	1
20	2	6	6	6	4	2	2
21	1	6	9	4	2	2	2
22	1	5	5	5	4	2	1
23	2	3	2	4	2	2	2
24	1	7	15	6	6	1	1
25	2	6	6	5	3	1	2
26	1	6	13	6	6	1	1
27	2	5	4	5	5	1	1
28	2	4	2	3	2	2	2
29	1	4	4	5	3	1	2
30	1	3	3	7	5	1	2

Frequency distribution

Researchers often need to answer questions about a single variable. For example:

- How many users of the brand may be characterised as brand loyal?
- What percentage of the market consists of heavy users, medium users, light users and non-users?
- How many customers are very familiar with a new product offering? How many are familiar, somewhat familiar, or unfamiliar with the brand? What is the mean familiarity rating? Is there much variance in the extent to which customers are familiar with the new product?
- What is the income distribution of brand users? Is this distribution skewed towards low-income brackets?

The answers to these kinds of questions can be determined by examining frequency distributions. In a frequency distribution, one variable is considered at a time.

The objective is to obtain a count of the number of responses associated with different values of the variable. The relative occurrence, or frequency, of different values of the variable is expressed in percentages. A frequency distribution for a variable produces a table of frequency counts, percentages and cumulative percentages for all the values associated with that variable. Table 11.2 gives the frequency distribution of familiarity with the Internet. In the table, the first column contains the labels assigned to the different categories of the variable

Table 11.2		Frequency distribution of 'Familiarity with the Internet'			
Value label	**Value**	**Frequency (N)**	**Percentage**	**Valid percentage**	**Cumulative percentage**
Very unfamiliar	1	0	0.0	0.0	0.0
	2	2	6.7	6.9	6.9
	3	6	20.0	20.7	27.6
	4	6	20.0	20.7	48.3
	5	3	10.0	10.3	58.6
	6	8	26.7	27.6	86.2
Very familiar	7	4	13.3	13.8	100.0
Missing	9	1	3.3		
Total		30	100.0	100.0	

and the second column indicates the codes assigned to each value. Note that a code of 9 has been assigned to missing values. The third column gives the number of participants ticking each value. For example, three participants ticked value 5, indicating that they were somewhat familiar with the Internet. The fourth column displays the percentage of participants ticking each value. The fifth column shows percentages calculated by excluding the cases with missing values. If there are no missing values, the fourth and fifth columns are identical. The last column represents cumulative percentages after adjusting for missing values. As can be seen, of the 30 participants who participated in the survey, 10 per cent entered a figure of '5'. If the one participant with a missing value is excluded, this changes to 10.3 per cent. The cumulative percentage corresponding to the value of 5 is 58.6. In other words, 58.6 per cent of the participants with valid responses indicated a familiarity value of 5 or less.

A frequency distribution helps determine the extent of item non-response (1 participant out of 30 in Table 11.1). It also indicates the extent of illegitimate responses. Values of 0 and 8 would be illegitimate responses, or errors. The cases with these values could be identified and corrective action could be taken. The presence of outliers or cases with extreme values can also be detected. For example, in the case of a frequency distribution of household size, a few isolated families with household sizes of nine or more might be considered outliers. A frequency distribution also indicates the shape of the empirical distribution of the variable. The frequency data may be used to construct a histogram, or a vertical bar chart in which the values of the variable are portrayed along the X axis and the absolute or relative frequencies of the values are placed along the Y axis.

Figure 11.1 is a histogram of the frequency data in Table 11.1. From the histogram, one could examine whether the observed distribution is consistent with an expected or assumed distribution.

Figure 11.1

Frequency histogram

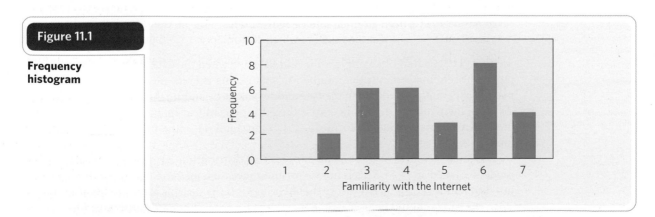

Statistics associated with frequency distribution

A frequency distribution is a convenient way of looking at different values of a variable. A frequency table is easy to read and provides basic information, but sometimes this information may be too detailed and the researcher must summarise it by the use of descriptive statistics. The most commonly used statistics associated with frequencies are measures of location (mean, mode and median), measures of variability (range, interquartile range, variance, standard deviation and coefficient of variation) and measures of shape (skewness and kurtosis).[1]

Measures of location

Measure of location
A statistic that describes a location within a dataset. Measures of central tendency describe the centre of the distribution.

The **measures of location** that we discuss are measures of central tendency because they tend to describe the centre of the distribution. If the entire sample is changed by adding a fixed constant to each observation, then the mean, mode and median change by the same fixed amount.

Mean
The average; that value obtained by summing all elements in a set and dividing by the number of elements.

Mean The **mean**, or average value, is the most commonly used measure of central tendency. The measure is used to estimate the mean when the data have been collected using an interval or ratio scale. The data should display some central tendency, with most of the responses distributed around the mean.

The mean, $\overline{X}$, is given by

$$\overline{X} = \frac{\sum_{i=1}^{n} X_i}{n}$$

where X_i = observed values of the variable X
n = number of observations (sample size).

Generally, the mean is a robust measure and does not change markedly as data values are added or deleted. For the frequencies given in Table 11.1, the mean value is calculated as follows:

$$\overline{X} = (2 \times 2) + (6 \times 3) + (6 \times 4) + (3 \times 5) + (8 \times 6) + (4 \times 7)/29$$
$$= (4 + 18 + 24 + 15 + 48 + 28)/29$$
$$= 137/29$$
$$= 4.724$$

Mode
A measure of central tendency given as the value that occurs with the most frequency in a sample distribution.

Mode The **mode** is the value that occurs most frequently. It represents the highest peak of the distribution. The mode is a good measure of location when the variable is inherently categorical or has otherwise been grouped into categories. The mode in Table 11.2 is 6.

Median
A measure of central tendency given as the value above which half of the values fall and below which half of the values fall.

Median The **median** of a sample is the middle value when the data are arranged in ascending or descending order. If the number of data points is even, the median is usually estimated as the midpoint between the two middle values by adding the two middle values and dividing their sum by 2. The median is the 50th percentile. The median is an appropriate measure of central tendency for ordinal data. In Table 11.2, the middle value is 5, so the median is 5.

The three measures of central tendency for this distribution are different (mean = 4.724, mode = 6, median = 5). This is not surprising, since each measure defines central tendency in a different way. So which measure should be used? If the variable is measured on a nominal scale, the mode should be used. If the variable is measured on an ordinal scale, the median is appropriate. If the variable is measured on an interval or ratio scale, the mode is a poor measure of central tendency. This can be seen from Table 11.2. Although the modal value of 6 has the highest frequency, it represents only 27.6 per cent of the sample. In general, for interval or ratio data, the median is a better measure of central tendency, although it too ignores available information about the variable. The actual values of the variable above and below the median are ignored. The mean is the most appropriate measure of central tendency for interval or ratio data. The mean makes use of all the information available since all of the values are used in computing it. However, it is sensitive to extremely small or extremely large values (outliers). When there are outliers in the data, the mean is not a good measure of central tendency, and it is useful to consider both the mean and the median. In Table 11.2, since there are no extreme values and the data are treated as interval, the mean value of 4.724 is a good measure of location or central tendency. Although this value is greater than 4, it is still not high (i.e. it is less than 5).

Measures of variability

Measure of variability
A statistic that indicates the distribution's dispersion.

The **measures of variability**, which are calculated on interval or ratio data, include the range, interquartile range, variance or standard deviation and coefficient of variation.

Range
The difference between the smallest and largest values of a distribution.

Range The **range** measures the spread of the data. It is simply the difference between the largest and smallest values in the sample:

$$\text{Range} = X_{\text{largest}} - X_{\text{smallest}}$$

As such, the range is directly affected by outliers. If all the values in the data are multiplied by a constant, the range is multiplied by the same constant. The range in Table 11.2 is $7 - 2 = 5$.

Interquartile range
The range of a distribution encompassing the middle 50% of the observations.

Interquartile range The **interquartile range** is the difference between the 75th and 25th percentiles. For a set of data points arranged in order of magnitude, the pth percentile is the value that has p% of the data points below it and $(100 - p)$% above it. If all the data points are multiplied by a constant, the interquartile range is multiplied by the same constant. The interquartile range in Table 11.2 is $6 - 3 = 3$.

Variance
The mean squared deviation of all the values of the mean.

Variance The difference between the mean and an observed value is called the deviation from the mean. The **variance** is the mean squared deviation from the mean. The variance can never be negative. When the data points are clustered around the mean, the variance is small. When the data points are scattered, the variance is large. If all the data values are multiplied by a constant, the variance is multiplied by the square of the constant.

Standard deviation
The square root of the variance.

Standard deviation The **standard deviation** is the square root of the variance. Thus, the standard deviation is expressed in the same units as the data, rather than in squared units. The standard deviation of a sample, s_x is calculated as

$$s_x = \sqrt{\sum_{i=1}^{n} \frac{(X_i - \overline{X})^2}{n - 1}}$$

We divide by $n - 1$ instead of n because the sample is drawn from a population and we are trying to determine how much the responses vary from the mean of the entire population. The population mean is unknown, however; therefore, the sample mean is used instead. The use of the sample mean makes the sample seem less variable than it really is. By dividing by $n - 1$ instead of by n, we compensate for the smaller variability observed in the sample. For the data given in Table 11.1, the variance is calculated as follows:

$$s_x^2 = [2 \times (2 - 4.724)^2 + 6 \times (3 - 4.724)^2 + 6 \times (4 - 4.724)^2 + 3 \times (5 - 4.724)^2 + 8$$
$$\times (6 - 4.724)^2 + 4 \times (7 - 4.724)^2]/28$$
$$= [14.840 + 17.833 + 3.145 + 0.229 + 13.025 + 20.721]/28$$
$$= 69.793/28$$
$$= 2.493$$

The standard deviation, therefore, is calculated as

$$s_x = \sqrt{2.493}$$
$$= 1.579$$

Coefficient of variation
A useful expression in sampling theory for the standard deviation as a percentage of the mean.

Coefficient of variation The **coefficient of variation** is the ratio of the standard deviation to the mean expressed as a percentage, and it is a unitless measure of relative variability. The coefficient of variation, CV, is expressed as

$$\mathrm{CV} = \frac{s_x}{\overline{X}}$$

The coefficient of variation is meaningful only if the variable is measured on a ratio scale. It remains unchanged if all the data values are multiplied by a constant. Because familiarity with the Internet is not measured on a ratio scale, it is not meaningful to calculate the coefficient of variation for the data in Table 11.2. From a managerial viewpoint, measures of variability are important because if a characteristic shows good variability, then perhaps the market could be segmented based on that characteristic.

Measures of shape

In addition to measures of variability, measures of shape are also useful in understanding the nature of the distribution. The shape of a distribution is assessed by examining skewness and kurtosis.

Skewness
A characteristic of a distribution that assesses its symmetry about the mean.

Skewness Distributions can be either symmetric or skewed. In a symmetric distribution, the values on either side of the centre of the distribution are the same, and the mean, mode and median are equal. The positive and corresponding negative deviations from the mean are also equal. In a skewed distribution, the positive and negative deviations from the mean are unequal. **Skewness** is the tendency of the deviations from the mean to be larger in one direction than in the other. It can be thought of as the tendency for one tail of the distribution to be heavier than the other (see Figure 11.2). The skewness value for the data of Table 11.2 is −0.094, indicating a slight negative skew.

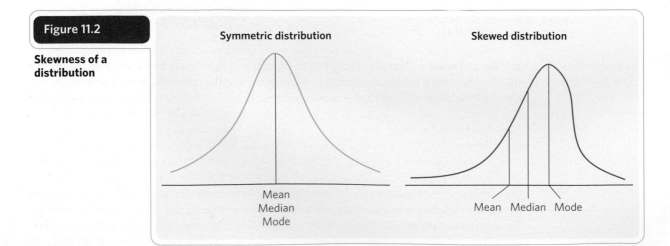

Figure 11.2

Skewness of a distribution

Kurtosis

A measure of the relative peakedness of the curve defined by the frequency distribution.

Kurtosis Kurtosis is a measure of the relative peakedness or flatness of the curve defined by the frequency distribution. The kurtosis of a normal distribution is zero. If the kurtosis is positive, then the distribution is more peaked than a normal distribution. A negative value means that the distribution is flatter than a normal distribution. The value of this statistic for Table 11.2 is -1.261, indicating that the distribution is flatter than a normal distribution. Measures of shape are important because if a distribution is highly skewed or markedly peaked or flat, then statistical procedures that assume normality should be used with caution.

Cross-tabulations

Although answers to questions related to a single variable are interesting, they often raise additional questions about how to link that variable to other variables. To introduce the frequency distribution, we posed several representative marketing research questions. For each of these, a researcher might pose additional questions to relate these variables to other variables. For example:

- How many brand-loyal users are males?
- Is product use (measured in terms of heavy users, medium users, light users and non-users) related to interest in outdoor leisure activities (high, medium and low)?
- Is familiarity with a new product related to age and income levels?
- Is product ownership related to income (high, medium and low)?

Cross-tabulation

A statistical technique that describes two or more variables simultaneously and results in tables that reflect the joint distribution of two or more variables that have a limited number of categories or distinct values.

The answers to such questions can be determined by examining cross-tabulations. A frequency distribution describes one variable at a time, but a cross-tabulation describes two or more variables simultaneously. A cross-tabulation is the merging of the frequency distribution of two or more variables in a single table. It helps us to understand how one variable such as brand loyalty relates to another variable such as gender. Cross-tabulation results in tables that reflect the joint distribution of two or more variables with a limited number of categories or distinct values. The categories of one variable are cross classified with the categories of one or more other variables. Thus, the frequency distribution of one variable is subdivided according to the values or categories of the other variables.

Suppose we are interested in determining whether Internet usage is related to gender. For the purpose of cross-tabulation, participants are classified as 'light' or 'heavy' users. Those reporting five hours or less usage were classified as 'light' users, and the remaining were 'heavy' users. The cross-tabulation is shown in Table 11.3. A cross-tabulation includes a cell for every combination of the categories of the two variables. The number in each cell shows how many participants gave that combination of responses. In Table 11.3, 10 participants were females who reported light Internet usage. The marginal totals in this table indicate that of the 30 participants with valid responses on both variables, 15 reported light usage and 15 were heavy users. In terms of gender, 15 participants were females and 15 were males. Note that this information could have been obtained from a separate frequency distribution for each variable. In general, the margins of a cross-tabulation show the same information as the frequency tables for each of the variables.

Contingency table

A cross-tabulation table. It contains a cell for every combination of categories of the two variables.

Cross-tabulation tables are also called contingency tables. The data are considered to be qualitative or categorical data, because each variable is assumed to have only a nominal scale.[2]

Table 11.3	Gender and Internet usage		
	Gender		
Internet usage	**Male**	**Female**	**Row total**
Light (1)	5	10	15
Heavy (2)	10	5	15
Column total	15	15	

Cross-tabulation is widely used in commercial marketing research because (1) cross-tabulation analysis and results can be easily interpreted and understood by managers who are not statistically oriented; (2) the clarity of interpretation provides a stronger link between research results and managerial action; (3) a series of cross-tabulations may provide greater insights into a complex phenomenon than a single multivariate analysis; (4) cross-tabulation may alleviate the problem of sparse cells, which could be serious in discrete multivariate analysis; and (5) cross-tabulation analysis is simple to conduct and appealing to both qualitative and quantitative researchers.[3] We will discuss cross-tabulation for two and three variables.

Bivariate analysis – two variables

Cross-tabulation with two variables is also known as bivariate cross-tabulation. Consider again the cross-classification of Internet usage with gender given in Table 11.3. Is usage related to gender? It appears to be from Table 11.3. We see that disproportionately more of the participants who are male are heavy Internet users as compared with females. Computation of percentages can provide more insight.

Because two variables have been cross-classified, percentages could be computed either column-wise, based on column totals (Table 11.4), or row-wise, based on row totals (Table 11.5). Which table is more useful?

Table 11.4	Gender and Internet usage – column totals	
	Gender	
Internet usage	**Male**	**Female**
Light (1)	33.3%	66.7%
Heavy (2)	66.7%	33.3%
Column total	100%	100%

Table 11.5	Gender and Internet usage – row totals		
	Gender		
Internet usage	**Male**	**Female**	**Row total**
Light (1)	33.3%	66.7%	100%
Heavy (2)	66.7%	33.3%	100%

The answer depends on which variable will be considered as the independent variable and which as the dependent variable.[4] The general rule is to compute the percentages in the direction of the independent variable, across the dependent variable. In our analysis, gender may be considered as the independent variable and Internet usage as the dependent variable, and the correct way of calculating percentages is shown in Table 11.4. Note that whereas 66.7 per cent of the males are heavy users, only 33.3 per cent of females fall into this category. This seems to indicate that males are more likely to be heavy users of the Internet as compared with females.

Note that computing percentages in the direction of the dependent variable across the independent variable, as shown in Table 11.5, is not meaningful in this case. Table 11.5 implies that heavy Internet usage causes people to be males. This latter finding is implausible. It is possible, however, that the association between Internet usage and gender is mediated by a third variable, such as age or income. This kind of possibility points to the need to examine the effect of a third variable.

Three variables

Often the introduction of a third variable clarifies the initial association (or lack of it) observed between two variables. As shown in Figure 11.3, the introduction of a third variable can result in four possibilities:

1   It can refine the association observed between the two original variables.

2   It can indicate no association between the two variables, although an association was initially observed. In other words, the third variable indicates that the initial association between the two variables was spurious.

3   It can reveal some association between the two original variables, although no association was initially observed. In this case, the third variable reveals a suppressed association between the first two variables: a suppressor effect.

4   It can indicate no change in the initial association.[5]

These cases are explained with examples based on a sample of 1,000 participants. Although these examples are contrived to illustrate specific cases, such sample sizes are not uncommon in commercial marketing research.

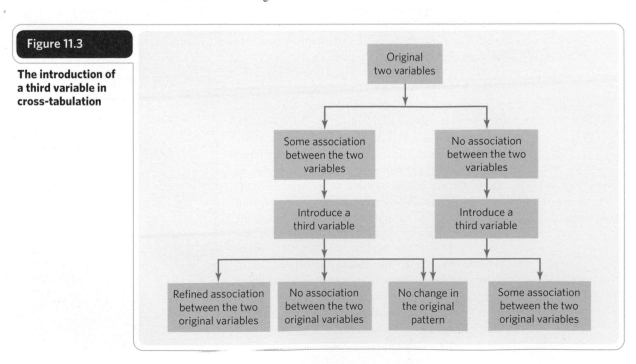

Figure 11.3

The introduction of a third variable in cross-tabulation

Table 11.6	Purchase of luxury branded clothing by marital status	
Purchase of luxury branded clothing	**Marital status**	
	Married	**Unmarried**
High	31%	52%
Low	69%	48%
Column total	100%	100%
Number of participants	700	300

Table 11.7	Purchase of luxury branded clothing by marital status and gender			
Purchase of luxury branded clothing	**Gender**			
	Male marital status		**Female marital status**	
	Married	**Unmarried**	**Married**	**Unmarried**
High	35%	40%	25%	60%
Low	65%	60%	75%	40%
Column total	100%	100%	100%	100%
Number of participants	400	120	300	180

Refine an initial relationship An examination of the relationship between the purchase of luxury branded clothing and marital status resulted in the data reported in Table 11.6. The participants were classified into either high or low categories based on their purchase of luxury branded clothing. Marital status was also measured in terms of two categories: currently married or unmarried. As can be seen from Table 11.6, 52 per cent of unmarried participants fell in the high-purchase category as opposed to 31 per cent of the married participants. Before concluding that unmarried participants purchase more luxury branded clothing than those who are married, a third variable, the buyer's gender, was introduced into the analysis.

The buyer's gender was selected as the third variable based on past research. The relationship between purchase of luxury branded clothing and marital status was re-examined in light of the third variable, as shown in Table 11.7. In the case of females, 60 per cent of the unmarried participants fall in the high-purchase category compared with 25 per cent of those who are married. On the other hand, the percentages are much closer for males, with 40 per cent of the unmarried participants and 35 per cent of the married participants falling in the high-purchase category. Hence, the introduction of gender (third variable) has refined the relationship between marital status and purchase of luxury branded clothing (original variables). Unmarried participants are more likely to fall into the high-purchase category than married ones, and this effect is much more pronounced for females than for males.

Table 11.8	Ownership of expensive cars by education level	
	Education	
Own expensive car	**Degree**	**No degree**
Yes	32%	21%
No	68%	79%
Column total	100%	100%
Number of participants	250	750

Table 11.9	Ownership of expensive cars by education and income levels			
	Income			
	Low-income education		**High-income education**	
Own expensive car	**Degree**	**No degree**	**Degree**	**No degree**
Yes	20%	20%	40%	40%
No	80%	80%	60%	60%
Column total	100%	100%	100%	100%
Number of participants	100	700	150	50

Initial relationship was spurious A researcher working for an advertising agency promoting a car brand costing more than €80,000 was attempting to explain the ownership of expensive cars (see Table 11.8). The table shows that 32 per cent of those with university degrees own an expensive (more than €80,000) car compared with 21 per cent of those without university degrees. The researcher was tempted to conclude that education influenced ownership of expensive cars. Realising that income may also be a factor, the researcher decided to re-examine the relationship between education and ownership of expensive cars in the light of income level. This resulted in Table 11.9. Note that the percentages of those with and without university degrees who own expensive cars are the same for each income group. When the data for the high-income and low-income groups are examined separately, the association between education and ownership of expensive cars disappears, indicating that the initial relationship observed between these two variables was spurious.

General comments on cross-tabulation

More than three variables can be cross-tabulated; the interpretation is quite complex. Also, because the number of cells increases multiplicatively, maintaining an adequate number of participants or cases in each cell can be problematic. As a general rule, there should be at least five expected observations in each cell for the computed statistics to be reliable. Thus, cross-tabulation is an inefficient way of examining relationships when there are more than a few variables. Note that cross-tabulation examines association between variables, not causation. To examine causation, the causal research design framework should be adopted.

The application of hypothesis tests

Basic analysis invariably involves some hypothesis testing. Examples of hypotheses generated in marketing research abound:

- A cinema is being patronised by more than 10 per cent of the households in a city.
- The heavy and light users of a brand differ in terms of psychographic characteristics.
- One hotel has a more 'luxurious' image than its close competitor.
- Familiarity with a restaurant results in greater preference for that restaurant.

Hypothesis testing is based upon principles of statistics such as the concepts of sampling distribution, standard error of the mean or the proportion and the confidence interval. These concepts should be reviewed before proceeding with this section.

As can be seen from Figure 11.4, hypothesis testing can be related to either an examination of associations or an examination of differences. In the application of statistical tests, hypotheses are formulated in an expression about the H_0 − the null hypothesis. In tests of associations the null hypothesis is that there is no association between the variables (H_0: . . . xxx is NOT related to . . . yyy). Tests of associations could relate to the data shown in a cross-tabulation. In tests of differences the null hypothesis is that there is no difference (H_0: . . . xxx is NOT different from . . . yyy). Tests of differences could relate to distributions, means, proportions, medians and rankings.

Figure 11.4

A broad classification of hypothesis testing procedures

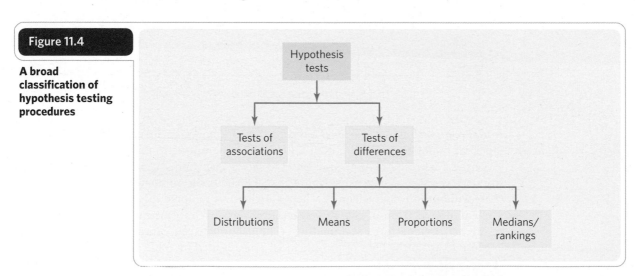

The general approach to hypothesis testing

The following steps are involved in hypothesis testing (Figure 11.5).

1. Formulate the null hypothesis H_0 and the alternative hypothesis H_1.

2. Select an appropriate statistical technique and the corresponding test statistic.

3. Choose the level of significance, α.

4. Determine the sample size and collect the data. Calculate the value of the test statistic.

5. Determine the probability associated with the test statistic under the null hypothesis, using the sampling distribution of the test statistic. Alternatively, determine the critical values associated with the test statistic that divide the rejection and non-rejection regions.

6   Compare the probability associated with the test statistic with the level of significance specified. Alternatively, determine whether the test statistic has fallen into the rejection or the non-rejection region.

7   Make the statistical decision to reject or not reject the null hypothesis.

8   Express the statistical decision in terms of the marketing research problem.

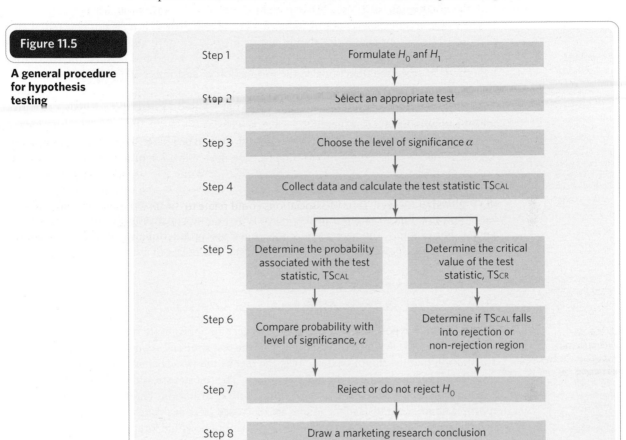

Figure 11.5

A general procedure for hypothesis testing

Step 1: Formulate the hypothesis

Null hypothesis

A statement in which no difference or effect is expected. If the null hypothesis is not rejected, no changes will be made.

Alternative hypothesis

A statement that some difference or effect is expected. Accepting the alternative hypothesis will lead to changes in opinions or actions.

The first step is to formulate the null and alternative hypotheses. A **null hypothesis** is a statement of the status quo, one of no difference or no effect. If the null hypothesis is not rejected, no changes will be made. An **alternative hypothesis** is one in which some difference or effect is expected. Accepting the alternative hypothesis will lead to changes in opinions or actions. Thus, the alternative hypothesis is the opposite of the null hypothesis.

The null hypothesis is always the hypothesis that is tested. The null hypothesis refers to a specified value of the population parameter (e.g. μ, σ, π), not a sample statistic (e.g. $\overline{X}$). A null hypothesis may be rejected, but it can never be accepted based on a single test. A statistical test can have one of two outcomes: that the null hypothesis is rejected and the alternative hypothesis accepted, or that the null hypothesis is not rejected based on the evidence. It would be incorrect, however, to conclude that since the null hypothesis is not rejected, it can be accepted as valid. In classical hypothesis testing, there is no way to determine whether the null hypothesis is true.

In marketing research, the null hypothesis is formulated in such a way that its rejection leads to the acceptance of the desired conclusion. The alternative hypothesis represents the conclusion for which evidence is sought. Taking the opening 'Real research' example, consider an FIBA sponsor, which could be a basketball sportswear brand, considering introducing an online store to complement their physical retail outlets. Given the investment in systems and personnel to make this plan work, it will only be introduced if more than 40 per cent of Internet users shop online. The appropriate way to formulate the hypotheses is

$$H_0: \pi \leq 0.40$$
$$H_1: \pi > 0.40$$

If the null hypothesis H_0 is rejected, then the alternative hypothesis H_1 will be accepted and the new online shopping service introduced. On the other hand, if H_0 is not rejected, then a planned online shopping service should not be introduced until additional supporting evidence is obtained. The test of the null hypothesis is a **one-tailed test** because the alternative hypothesis is expressed directionally: the proportion of customers who express a preference is greater than 0.40.

On the other hand, suppose that the researcher wanted to determine whether the proportion of Internet users who shop via the Internet is different than 40 per cent. Then a **two-tailed test** would be required, and the hypotheses would be expressed as:

$$H_0: \pi = 0.40$$
$$H_1: \pi \neq 0.40$$

In commercial marketing research, the one-tailed test is used more often than a two-tailed test. Typically, there is some preferred direction for the conclusion for which evidence is sought. For example, the higher the profits, sales and product quality, the better. The one-tailed test is more powerful than the two-tailed test. The power of a statistical test is discussed further in step 3.

Step 2: Select an appropriate test

To test the null hypothesis, it is necessary to select an appropriate statistical technique. The researcher should take into consideration how the **test statistic** is computed and the sampling distribution that the sample statistic (e.g. the mean) follows. The test statistic measures how close the sample has come to the null hypothesis. The test statistic often follows a well-known distribution, such as the normal, t, or chi-square distribution. Guidelines for selecting an appropriate test or statistical technique are discussed later in this text. In our example, the z statistic, which follows the standard normal distribution, would be appropriate. This statistic would be computed as follows:

$$z = \frac{p - \pi}{\sigma_p} \quad \text{where} \quad \sigma_p = \sqrt{\frac{\pi(1 - \pi)}{n}}$$

Step 3: Choose the level of significance, α

Whenever we draw inferences about a population, there is a risk that an incorrect conclusion will be reached. Two types of error can occur:

Type I error occurs when the sample results lead to the rejection of the null hypothesis when it is in fact true. In our example, a Type I error would occur if we concluded, based on sample data, that the proportion of customers preferring an online store was greater than 0.40, when in fact it was less than or equal to 0.40. The probability of Type I error (α) is also called the **level of significance**. The Type I error is controlled by establishing the tolerable level of risk of rejecting a true null hypothesis. The selection of a particular risk level should depend on the cost of making a Type I error.

Type II error occurs when, based on the sample results, the null hypothesis is not rejected when it is in fact false. In our example, the Type II error would occur if we concluded, based on sample data, that the proportion of customers preferring an online store was less than or equal to 0.40 when in fact it was greater than 0.40. The probability of Type II error is denoted by β. Unlike α, which is specified by the researcher, the magnitude of β depends on the actual value of the population parameter (proportion). The probability of Type I error (α) and the probability of Type II error (β) are shown in Figure 11.6.

One-tailed test
A test of the null hypothesis where the alternative hypothesis is expressed directionally.

Two-tailed test
A test of the null hypothesis where the alternative hypothesis is not expressed directionally.

Test statistic
A measure of how close the sample has come to the null hypothesis. It often follows a well-known distribution, such as the normal, t, or chi-square distribution.

Type I error
An error that occurs when the sample results lead to the rejection of a null hypothesis that is in fact true. Also called alpha error (α).

Level of significance
The probability of making a Type I error.

Type II error
An error that occurs when the sample results lead to acceptance of a null hypothesis that is in fact false. Also called beta error (β).

Figure 11.6

Type I error (α) and Type II error (β)

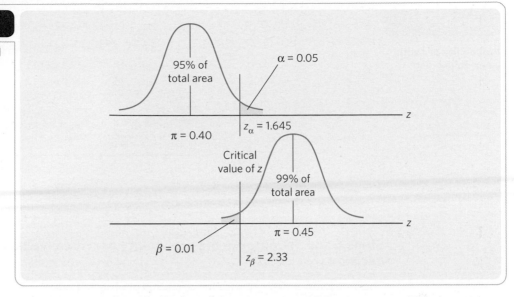

Power of a statistical test	The complement $(1 - \beta)$ of the probability of a Type II error is called the **power of a statistical**

Power of a statistical test

The probability of rejecting the null hypothesis when it is in fact false and should be rejected.

The complement $(1 - \beta)$ of the probability of a Type II error is called the **power of a statistical test**. The power of a test is the probability $(1 - \beta)$ of rejecting the null hypothesis when it is false and should be rejected. Although β is unknown, it is related to α. An extremely low value of α (e.g. 0.001) will result in intolerably high β errors. So it is necessary to balance the two types of errors. As a compromise, α is often set at 0.05; sometimes it is 0.01; other values of α are rare. The level of α along with the sample size will determine the level of β for a particular research design. The risk of both α and β can be controlled by increasing the sample size. For a given level of α, increasing the sample size will decrease β, thereby increasing the power of the test.

Step 4: Collect the data and calculate the test statistic

Sample size is determined after taking into account the desired α and β, errors and other qualitative considerations, such as budget constraints. Then the required data are collected and the value of the test statistic is computed. In our example, 30 users were surveyed and 17 indicated that they shopped online. Thus the value of the sample proportion is $p = 17/30 = 0.567$. The value of σ_p can be determined as follows:

$$\sigma_p = \sqrt{\pi(1 - \pi)/n}$$
$$= \sqrt{0.4 \times 0.6/30}$$
$$= 0.089$$

The test statistic z can be calculated as follows:

$$z = p - \pi/\sigma_p$$
$$= 0.567 - 0.40/0.089$$
$$= 1.88$$

Step 5: Determine the probability or the critical value

Using standard normal tables (Table 2 of the Appendix of statistical tables), the probability of obtaining a z value of 1.88 can be calculated (see Figure 11.7). The shaded area between $-\infty$ and 1.88 is 0.9699. Therefore, the area to the right of $z = 1.88$ is $1.0000 - 0.9699 = 0.0301$. This is also called the **p value** and is the probability of observing a value of the test statistic as extreme as, or more extreme than, the value actually observed, assuming the null hypothesis is true. Alternatively, the critical value of z, which will give an area to the right side of the critical value of 0.05, is between 1.64 and 1.65 and equals 1.645. Note that, in determining the critical value of the test statistic, the area to the right of the critical value is either α or $\alpha/2$. It is α for a one-tailed test and $\alpha/2$ for a two-tailed test.

p value

This is the probability of observing a value of the test statistic as extreme as, or more extreme than, the value actually observed, assuming that the null hypothesis is true.

Figure 11.7

Probability of z with a one-tailed test

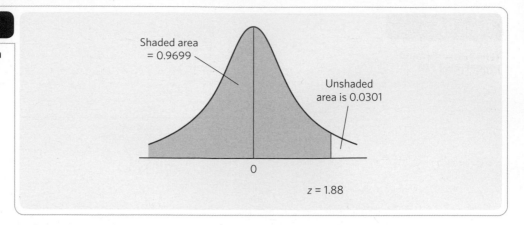

Steps 6 and 7: Compare the probability or critical values and make the decision

The probability associated with the calculated or observed value of the test statistic is 0.0301. This is the probability of getting a p value of 0.567 when $\pi = 0.40$. This is less than the level of significance of 0.05. Hence, the null hypothesis is rejected. Alternatively, the calculated value of the test statistic $z = 1.88$ lies in the rejection region, beyond the value of 1.645. Again, the same conclusion to reject the null hypothesis is reached. Note that the two ways of testing the null hypothesis are equivalent but mathematically opposite in the direction of comparison. If the probability associated with the calculated or observed value of the test statistic (TS_{CAL}) is less than the level of significance (α), the null hypothesis is rejected. If the calculated value of the test statistic is greater than the critical value of the test statistic (TS_{CR}), however, the null hypothesis is rejected. The reason for this sign shift is that the larger the value of TS_{CAL}, the smaller the probability of obtaining a more extreme value of the test statistic under the null hypothesis. This sign shift can be easily seen:

$$\text{if probability of } TS_{CAL} < \text{significance level } (\alpha), \text{ then reject } H_0$$

but

$$\text{if } |TS_{CAL}| > |TS_{CR}|, \text{ then reject } H_0$$

Step 8: Draw the marketing research conclusion

The conclusion reached by hypothesis testing must be expressed in terms of the marketing research problem. In our example, we conclude that there is evidence that the proportion of Internet users who shop online is significantly greater than 0.40. Hence, the recommendation would be to launch the new online store.

Types of hypothesis tests

Parametric tests
Hypothesis testing procedures that assume that the variables of interest are measured on at least an interval scale.

Non-parametric tests
Hypothesis testing procedures that assume that the variables are measured on a nominal or ordinal scale.

Hypothesis tests can be applied to a wide range of data types, and specific tests have been developed for each. They can be broadly classified as parametric or non-parametric, based on the measurement scale of the variables involved. A typology of the types of test is shown in Figure 11.8. **Parametric tests** assume that the variables of interest are measured on at least an interval scale. The most popular parametric test is the t test conducted for examining hypotheses about means. The t test could be conducted on the mean of one sample or two samples of observations. In the case of two samples, the samples could be independent or paired. **Non-parametric tests** assume that the variables are measured on a nominal or ordinal scale. Non-parametric tests based on observations drawn from one sample include the chi-square test, the Kolmogorov–Smirnov test, the runs test and the binomial test. In the

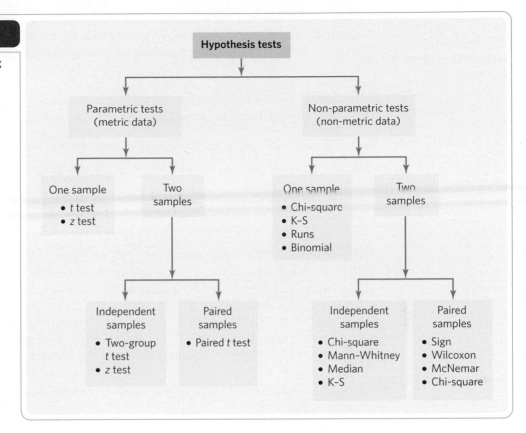

Figure 11.8

Hypothesis testing procedures

case of two independent samples, the chi-square test, the Mann–Whitney U test, the median test and the Kolmogorov–Smirnov two-sample test are used for examining hypotheses about location. These tests are non-parametric counterparts of the two-group t test. For paired samples, non-parametric tests include the Wilcoxon matched-pairs signed-ranks test and the sign test. These tests are the counterparts of the paired t test. In addition, the McNemar and chi-square tests can also be used. Parametric as well as non-parametric tests are also available for evaluating hypotheses relating to more than two samples.

Parametric tests

t test

A univariate hypothesis test using the t distribution, which is used when the standard deviation is unknown and the sample size is small.

t statistic

A statistic that assumes that the variable has a symmetric bell-shaped distribution, that the mean is known (or assumed to be known), and that the population variance is estimated from the sample.

t distribution

A symmetrical bell-shaped distribution that is useful for sample testing ($n < 30$). It is similar to the normal distribution in appearance.

Parametric tests provide inferences for making statements about the means of parent populations. A t test is commonly used for this purpose. This test is based on Student's t statistic. The t statistic assumes that the variable is normally distributed and the mean is known (or assumed to be known) and the population variance is estimated from the sample. Assume that the random variable X is normally distributed, with mean μ and unknown population variance σ^2, which is estimated by the sample variance s^2. Recall that the standard deviation of the sample mean, $\overline{X}$, is estimated as $s_{\overline{X}} = s/\sqrt{n}$. Then $t = (\overline{X} - \mu)/s_{\overline{X}}$ is t distributed with $n - 1$ degrees of freedom.

The t **distribution** is similar to the normal distribution in appearance. Both distributions are bell shaped and symmetric. Compared with the normal distribution, however, the t distribution has more area in the tails and less in the centre. This is because the population variance σ^2 is unknown and is estimated by the sample variance s^2. Given the uncertainty in the value of s^2, the observed values of t are more variable than those of z. Thus, we must go out a larger number of standard deviations from zero to encompass a certain percentage of values from the t distribution than is the case with the normal distribution. Yet, as the number of degrees of freedom increases, the t distribution approaches the normal distribution. In fact, for large samples of 120 or more, the t distribution and the normal distribution are virtually indistinguishable. Table 3 in the Appendix of statistical tables shows selected percentiles of the t distribution. Although normality is assumed, the t test is quite robust to departures from normality.

The procedure for hypothesis testing, for the special case when the t statistic is used, is as follows:

1 Formulate the null (H_0) and the alternative (H_1) hypotheses.

2 Select the appropriate formula for the t statistic.

3 Select a significance level, α, for testing H_0. Typically, the 0.05 level is selected.[6]

4 Take one or two samples and compute the mean and standard deviation for each sample.

5 Calculate the t statistic assuming that H_0 is true.

6 Calculate the degrees of freedom and estimate the probability of getting a more extreme value of the statistic from Table 3 in the Appendix. (Alternatively, calculate the critical value of the t statistic.)

7 If the probability computed in step 6 is smaller than the significance level selected in step 3, reject H_0. If the probability is larger, do not reject H_0. (Alternatively, if the absolute value of the calculated t statistic in step 5 is larger than the absolute critical value determined in step 6, reject H_0. If the absolute calculated value is smaller than the absolute critical value, do not reject H_0.) Failure to reject H_0 does not necessarily imply that H_0 is true. It only means that the true state is not significantly different from that assumed by H_0.[7]

8 Express the conclusion reached by the t test in terms of the marketing research problem.

We illustrate the general procedure for conducting t tests in the following sections, beginning with the one-sample case.

One sample

In marketing research, the researcher is often interested in making statements about a single variable against a known or given standard. Examples of such statements are that the market share for a new product will exceed 15 per cent, at least 65 per cent of customers will like a new package design, and 80 per cent of retailers will prefer a new pricing policy. These statements can be translated to null hypotheses that can be tested using a one-sample test, such as the t test or the z test. In the case of a t test for a single mean, the researcher is interested in testing whether the population mean conforms to a given hypothesis (H_0). For the data in Table 11.1, suppose we wanted to test the hypothesis that the mean familiarity rating exceeds 4.0, the neutral value on a seven-point scale. A significance level of $\alpha = 0.05$ is selected. The hypothesis may be formulated as:

$$H_0: \mu \leq 4.0$$
$$H_1: \mu > 4.0$$
$$t = (\overline{X} - \mu)/s_{\overline{X}}$$
$$s_{\overline{X}} = s/\sqrt{n}$$
$$s_{\overline{X}} = 1.579/\sqrt{29} = 1.579/5.385 = 0.293$$
$$t = (4.724 - 4.0)/0.293 = 0.724/0.293 = 2.471$$

The degrees of freedom for the t statistic to test the hypothesis about one mean are $n - 1$. In this case, $n - 1 = 29 - 1$, or 28. From Table 3 in the Appendix, the probability of getting a more extreme value than 2.471 is less than 0.05. (Alternatively, the critical t value for 28 degrees of freedom and a significance level of 0.05 is 1.7011, which is less than the calculated value.) Hence, the null hypothesis is rejected. The familiarity level does not exceed 4.0.

Note that if the population standard deviation was assumed to be known as 1.5, rather than estimated from the sample, a **z test** would be appropriate. In this case, the value of the z statistic would be

$$z = \frac{\overline{X} - \mu}{\sigma_{\overline{X}}}$$

where

$$\sigma_{\overline{x}} = 1.5/\sqrt{29} = 1.5/5.385 = 0.279$$

and

$$z = (4.724 - 4.0)/0.279 = 0.724/0.279 = 2.595$$

From Table 2 in the Appendix of statistical tables, the probability of getting a more extreme value of z than 2.595 is less than 0.05. (Alternatively, the critical z value for a one-tailed test and a significance level of 0.05 is 1.645, which is less than the calculated value.) Therefore, the null hypothesis is rejected, reaching the same conclusion arrived at earlier by the t test.

The procedure for testing a null hypothesis with respect to a proportion was illustrated earlier in this chapter when we introduced hypothesis testing.

Two independent samples

Several hypotheses in marketing relate to parameters from two different populations: for example, the users and non-users of a brand differ in terms of their perceptions of the brand, high-income consumers spend more on leisure activities than low-income consumers, or the proportion of brand-loyal users in segment I is more than the proportion in segment II. Samples drawn randomly from different populations are termed **independent samples**. As in the case for one sample, the hypotheses could relate to means or proportions.

Means In the case of means for two independent samples, the hypotheses take the following form:

$$H_0: \mu_1 = \mu_2$$
$$H_1: \mu_1 \neq \mu_2$$

The two populations are sampled and the means and variances are computed based on samples of sizes n_1 and n_2. If both populations are found to have the same variance, a pooled variance estimate is computed from the two sample variances as follows:

$$s^2 = \frac{\sum_{i=1}^{n_1}(X_{i_1} - \overline{X}_1)^2 + \sum_{i=1}^{n_2}(X_{i_2} - \overline{X}_2)^2}{n_1 + n_2 - 2} \qquad s^2 = \frac{(n_1 - 1)s_1^2 + (n^2 - 1)s_2^2}{n_1 + n_2 - 2}$$

The standard deviation of the test statistic can be estimated as:

$$s_{\overline{X}_1 - \overline{X}_2} = \sqrt{s^2\left(\frac{1}{n_1} + \frac{1}{n_2}\right)}$$

The appropriate value of t can be calculated as:

$$t = \frac{(\overline{X}_1 - \overline{X}_2) - (\mu_1 - \mu_2)}{s_{\overline{X}_1 - \overline{X}_2}}$$

The degrees of freedom in this case are $(n_1 + n_2 - 2)$.

If the two populations have unequal variances, an exact t cannot be computed for the difference in sample means. Instead, an approximation to t is computed. The number of degrees of freedom in this case is usually not an integer, but a reasonably accurate probability can be obtained by rounding to the nearest integer.[8]

An *F* test of sample variance may be performed if it is not known whether the two populations have equal variance. In this case the hypotheses are:

$$H_0: \sigma_1^2 = \sigma_2^2$$
$$H_1: \sigma_1^2 \neq \sigma_2^2$$

The *F* statistic is computed from the sample variances as follows:

$$F(n_1 - 1), (n_2 - 1) = \frac{s_1^2}{s_2^2}$$

where n_1 = size of sample 1
   n_2 = size of sample 2
   $n_1 - 1$ = degrees of freedom for sample 1
   $n_2 - 1$ = degrees of freedom for sample 2
   s_1^2 = sample variance for sample 1
   s_2^2 = sample variance for sample 2.

As can be seen, the critical value of the *F distribution* depends on two sets of degrees of freedom: those in the numerator and those in the denominator. The critical values of *F* for various degrees of freedom for the numerator and denominator are given in Table 5 of the Appendix of statistical tables. If the probability of *F* is greater than the significance level α, H_0 is not rejected and *t* based on the pooled variance estimate can be used. On the other hand, if the probability of *F* is less than or equal to α, H_0 is rejected and *t* based on a separate variance estimate is used.

Using the data in Table 11.1, suppose we wanted to determine whether Internet usage was different for males as compared with females. A two-independent-samples *t* test can be conducted. The results of this test are presented in Table 11.10. Note that the *F* test of sample variances has a probability that is less than 0.05. Accordingly H_0 is rejected and the *t* test based on the 'equal variances not assumed' should be used. The *t* value is −4.492 and with 18.014 degrees of freedom, this gives a probability of 0.000, which is less than the

F test
A statistical test of the equality of the variances of two populations.

F statistic
The ratio of two sample variances.

F distribution
A frequency distribution that depends upon two sets of degrees of freedom: the degrees of freedom in the numerator and the degrees of freedom in the denominator.

Table 11.10 — **Two independent samples t test**

Summary statistics

	Number of cases	Mean	Standard error mean
Male	15	9.333	1.137
Female	15	3.867	0.435

F test for equality of variances

F value	Two-tail probability
15.507	0.000

t test

Equal variances assumed			Equal variances not assumed		
t value	Degrees of freedom	Two-tail probability	t value	Degrees of freedom	Two-tail probability
−4.492	28	0.000	−4.492	18.014	0.000

significance level of 0.05. Therefore, the null hypothesis of equal means is rejected. Because the mean usage for males (gender = 1) is 9.333 and that for females (gender = 2) is 3.867, males use the Internet to a significantly greater extent than females. We also show the *t* test assuming equal variances because most software packages automatically conduct the *t* test both ways.

Proportions A case involving proportions for two independent samples is also illustrated using the data from Table 11.1, which gives the number of males and females who shop online. Is the proportion of participants who shop online the same for males and females? Table 11.11 shows the frequencies for this question. The proportion is simply calculated by dividing the number by the total for the column, e.g. P_1 = 11/15 or 0.733. The same procedure applies if the proportions are replaced by percentages (i.e. using 73.3 per cent instead of 0.73). However, always check for consistency in your approach.

Table 11.11	Frequency table for online shopping by gender		
	Gender		
Use of Internet for shopping	**Male**	**Female**	**Totals**
Yes	11	6	17
No	4	9	13
Totals	15	15	30

The null and alternative hypotheses are

$$H_0: \pi_1 = \pi_2$$
$$H_1: \pi_1 \neq \pi_2$$

A *z* test is used as in testing the proportion for one sample. In this case, however, the test statistic is given by

$$z = \frac{P_1 - P_2}{s_{\bar{P}_1 - \bar{P}_2}}$$

In the test statistic, the numerator is the difference between the proportions in the two samples, P_1 and P_2. The denominator is the standard error of the difference in the two proportions and is given by

$$s_{\bar{P}_1 - \bar{P}_2} = \sqrt{p(1-p)\left(\frac{1}{n_1} + \frac{1}{n_2}\right)}$$

where

$$p = \frac{n_1 P_1 + n_2 P_2}{n_1 + n_2}$$

A significance level of $\alpha = 0.05$ is selected. Given the data in Table 11.1, the test statistic can be calculated as

$$P_1 - P_2 = (11/15) - (6/15)$$
$$= 0.733 - 0.400 = 0.333$$
$$p = (15 \times 0.733 + 15 \times 0.4)/(15 + 15) = 0.567$$
$$s_{P_1 - P_2} = \sqrt{0.567 \times 0.4333(1/15 + 1/15)} = 0.181$$
$$z = 0.333/0.181 - 1.84$$

Given a two-tail test, the area to the right of the critical value is $\alpha/2$, or 0.025. Hence, the critical value of the test statistic is 1.96. Because the calculated value is less than the critical value, the null hypothesis cannot be rejected. Thus, the proportion of users (0.733) for males and (0.400) for females is not significantly different for the two samples. Note that although the difference is substantial, it is not statistically significant due to the small sample sizes (15 in each group).

Non-parametric tests

Non-parametric tests are used when the independent variables are non-metric. Similar to parametric tests, non-parametric tests are available for testing variables from one sample, two independent samples or two related samples.

Statistics associated with cross-tabulation

In this section we will discuss the statistic commonly used for assessing the statistical significance of cross-tabulated variables. The statistical significance of the observed association is commonly measured by the chi-square statistic.

Chi-square

Chi-square statistic
The statistic used to test the statistical significance of the observed association in a cross-tabulation. It assists us in determining whether a systematic association exists between the two variables.

The **chi-square statistic** (χ^2) is used to test the statistical significance of the observed association in a cross-tabulation. It assists us in determining whether a systematic association exists between the two variables. The null hypothesis, H_0, is that there is no association between the variables. The test is conducted by computing the cell frequencies that would be expected if no association were present between the variables, given the existing row and column totals. These expected cell frequencies, denoted f_e, are then compared with the actual observed frequencies, f_0, found in the cross-tabulation to calculate the chi-square statistic. The greater the discrepancies between the expected and observed frequencies, the larger the value of the statistic. Assume that a cross-tabulation has r rows and c columns and a random sample of n observations. Then the expected frequency for each cell can be calculated by using a simple formula:

$$f_e = \frac{n_r n_c}{n}$$

where n_r = total number in the row
n_c = total number in the column
n = total sample size

For the data in Table 11.3, the expected frequencies for the cells, going from left to right and from top to bottom, are

$$15 \times 15/30 = 7.50, 15 \times 15/30 = 7.50, 15 \times 15/30 = 7.50, 15 \times 15/30 = 7.50$$

Then the value of χ^2 is calculated as follows:

$$\chi^2 = \sum_{all\ cells} \frac{(f_0 - f_e)^2}{f_e}$$

For the data in Table 11.3, the value of χ^2 is calculated as

$$\chi^2 = (5 - 7.5)^2/7.5 + (10 - 7.5)^2/7.5 + (10 - 7.5)^2/7.5 + (5 - 7.5)^2/7.5$$
$$= 0.833 + 0.833 + 0.833 + 0.833$$
$$= 3.333$$

To determine whether a systematic association exists, the probability of obtaining a value of chi-square as large as or larger than the one calculated from the cross-tabulation is estimated. An important characteristic of the chi-square statistic is the number of degrees of freedom (df) associated with it. In general, the number of degrees of freedom is equal to the number of observations less the number of constraints needed to calculate a statistical term. In the case of a chi-square statistic associated with a cross-tabulation, the number of degrees of freedom is equal to the product of number of rows (r) less one and the number of columns (c) less one. That is, $df = (r - 1) \times (c - 1)$.[9] The null hypothesis (H_0) of no association between the two variables will be rejected only when the calculated value of the test statistic is greater than the critical value of the chi-square distribution with the appropriate degrees of freedom, as shown in Figure 11.9.

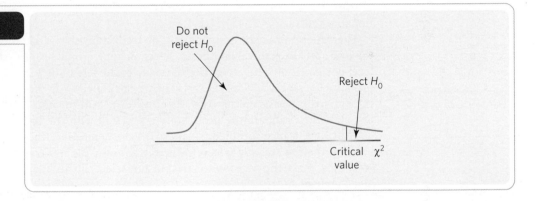

Figure 11.9

Chi-square test of association

Chi-square distribution
A skewed distribution whose shape depends solely on the number of degrees of freedom. As the number of degrees of freedom increases, the chi-square distribution becomes more symmetrical.

The **chi-square distribution** is a skewed distribution whose shape depends solely on the number of degrees of freedom.[10] As the number of degrees of freedom increases, the chi-square distribution becomes more symmetrical. Table 4 in the Appendix of statistical tables contains upper tail areas of the chi-square distribution for different degrees of freedom. In this table, the value at the top of each column indicates the area in the upper portion (the right side, as shown in Figure 11.9) of the chi-square distribution. To illustrate, for 1 degree of freedom, the value for an upper tail area of 0.05 is 3.841. This indicates that for 1 degree of freedom the probability of exceeding a chi-square value of 3.841 is 0.05. In other words, at the 0.05 level of significance with 1 degree of freedom, the critical value of the chi-square statistic is 3.841.

For the cross-tabulation given in Table 11.3, there are $(2 - 1) \times (2 - 1) = 1$ degree of freedom. The calculated chi-square statistic had a value of 3.333. Because this is less than the critical value of 3.841, the null hypothesis of no association cannot be rejected, indicating that the association is not statistically significant at the 0.05 level. Note that this lack of significance is mainly due to the small sample size (30). If instead, the sample size were 300 and each data entry of Table 11.3 were multiplied by 10, it can be seen that the value of the chi-square statistic would be multiplied by 10 and would be 33.33, which is significant at the 0.05 level.

The chi-square statistic should be estimated only on counts of data. When the data are in percentage form, they should first be converted to absolute counts or numbers. In addition, an underlying assumption of the chi-square test is that the observations are drawn independently. As a general rule, chi-square analysis should not be conducted when the expected or theoretical frequency in any of the cells is less than five.

Summary

Basic data analysis provides valuable insights and guides the rest of the data analysis as well as the interpretation of the results. A frequency distribution should be obtained for each variable in the data. This analysis produces a table of frequency counts, percentages and cumulative percentages for all the values associated with that variable. It indicates the extent of out-of-range, missing or extreme values. The mean, mode and median of a frequency distribution are measures of central tendency. The variability of the distribution is described by the range, the variance or standard deviation, coefficient of variation and interquartile range. Skewness and kurtosis provide an idea of the shape of the distribution.

Cross-tabulations are tables that reflect the joint distribution of two or more variables. In cross-tabulation, the percentages can be computed either by column, based on column totals, or by row, based on row totals. The general rule is to compute the percentages in the direction of the independent variable in the columns and the dependent variable in the rows. The independent variable can be thought of as a segmentation variable for which you are interested in the profile description of its different categories. The introduction of a third variable can provide additional insights.

The general procedure for hypothesis testing involves eight steps. Formulate the null and alternative hypotheses, select an appropriate test statistic, choose the level of significance (α), calculate the value of the test statistic, and determine the probability associated with the test statistic calculated from the sample data under the null hypothesis. Alternatively, determine the critical value associated with the test statistic. Compare the probability associated with the test statistic with the level of significance specified or, alternatively, determine whether the calculated value of the test statistic falls into the rejection or the non-rejection region. Accordingly, make the decision to reject or not reject the null hypothesis, and arrive at a conclusion.

Parametric and non-parametric tests are available for testing hypotheses related to differences. In the parametric case, the t test is used to examine hypotheses related to the population mean. Different forms of the t test are suitable for testing hypotheses based on one sample, two independent samples or paired samples. In the non-parametric case, popular one-sample tests include the chi-square test.

The chi-square statistic provides a test of the statistical significance of the observed association in a cross-tabulation.

SNAP Learning Edition

Frequency distributions are perhaps the simplest form of analysis of a survey, presenting both absolute values and percentages for each question/variable selected. Processing one question at a time can be time consuming, and SNAP provides a Summary Report that is essentially a frequency table and a barchart for every single question in a survey.

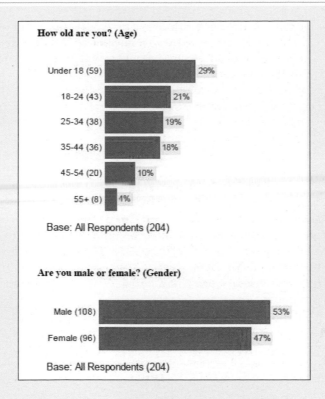

An alternative to the Summary Report is the Questionnaire Report, with the results in either absolute values or percentages presented on a fully designed questionnaire. This format is often easier to understand for non-researchers.

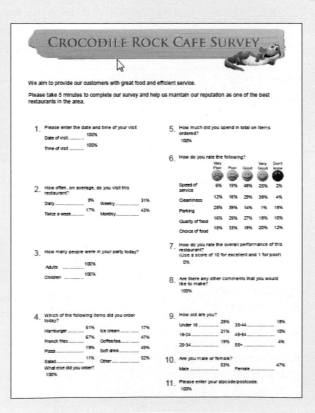

The cross-tabulation is the traditional method of analysing survey data, and for most researchers, it provides the maximum flexibility. At its simplest, it cross-analyses one question against another question, but more typically it is used to cross-analyse each question in the survey against a combination of demographic questions. The results can be presented as absolute values or as a percentage of the row total, column total or overall total.

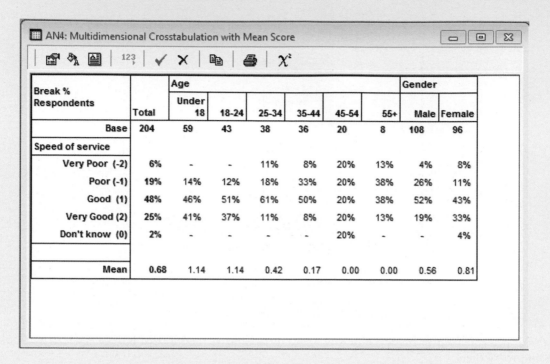

Break % Respondents	Total	Age						Gender	
		Under 18	18-24	25-34	35-44	45-54	55+	Male	Female
Base	204	59	43	38	36	20	8	108	96
Speed of service									
Very Poor (-2)	6%	-	-	11%	8%	20%	13%	4%	8%
Poor (-1)	19%	14%	12%	18%	33%	20%	38%	26%	11%
Good (1)	48%	46%	51%	61%	50%	20%	38%	52%	43%
Very Good (2)	25%	41%	37%	11%	8%	20%	13%	19%	33%
Don't know (0)	2%	-	-	-	-	20%	-	-	4%
Mean	0.68	1.14	1.14	0.42	0.17	0.00	0.00	0.56	0.81

Additional statistical tests, such as confidence levels, significance tests, standard error and deviation can all be added to individual cross-tabulations, and moved to any location above and below the body of the table.

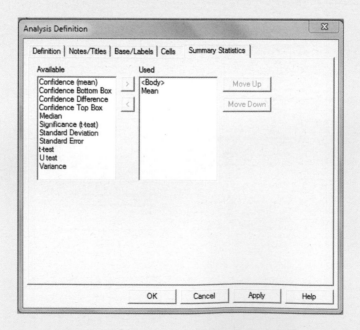

A full range of Descriptive Statistics can be produced by SNAP, simply by selecting an individual variable name. The specific tests can be tailored to only display those results of tests that are required.

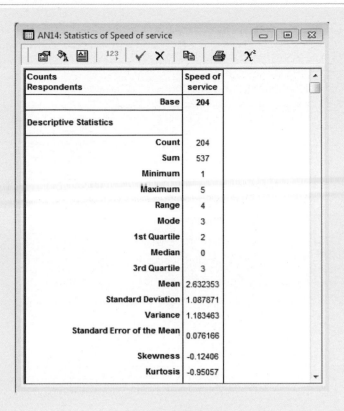

AN14: Statistics of Speed of service

Counts Respondents	Speed of service
Base	204
Descriptive Statistics	
Count	204
Sum	537
Minimum	1
Maximum	5
Range	4
Mode	3
1st Quartile	2
Median	0
3rd Quartile	3
Mean	2.632353
Standard Deviation	1.087871
Variance	1.183463
Standard Error of the Mean	0.076166
Skewness	-0.12406
Kurtosis	-0.95057

Reviewing the results of any question over time can be achieved by generating a variable to divide the date into a number of discrete categories. The median can also be displayed to provide a summary of performance in each quarter.

AN13: Analysis by Year

		Date							
	Total	2011-Q1	2011-Q2	2011-Q3	2011-Q4	2012-Q3	2012-Q1	2012-Q2	2012-Q4
	203	34	34	22	16	16	24	29	28
Speed of service									
Very Poor	43 21%	1 3%	3 9%	1 5%	- -	4 25%	7 29%	11 38%	16 57%
Poor	39 19%	5 15%	5 15%	6 27%	3 19%	2 13%	7 29%	5 17%	6 21%
Good	75 37%	17 50%	16 47%	10 45%	8 50%	7 44%	1 4%	10 34%	6 21%
Very Good	42 21%	10 29%	9 26%	5 23%	5 31%	3 19%	9 38%	1 3%	- -
Don't know	4 2%	1 3%	1 3%	- -	- -	- -	- -	2 7%	- -
Median	Good	Good	Good	Good	Good	Good	Poor	Poor	Very Poor

Tabulations can be carried out in a series of batches, with just a few commands generating a selection of tables. These can be run as a report and either printed or saved as a PDF file.

The range of analyses available within SNAP is very extensive, and further advanced statistical functions of Factor Analysis and Cluster Analysis are covered in Chapter 12.

Questions

1 Describe the procedure for computing frequencies.
2 What measures of location and variability are commonly computed?
3 How is the relative flatness or peakedness of a distribution measured?
4 What is a skewed distribution? What does it mean?
5 What is the major difference between cross-tabulation and frequency distribution?
6 What is the general rule for computing percentages in cross-tabulation?
7 Define a spurious correlation.
8 What is meant by a suppressed association? How is it revealed?
9 Discuss the reasons for the frequent use of cross-tabulations. What are some of the limitations?
10 Present a classification of hypothesis testing procedures.
11 Describe the general procedure for conducting a t test.
12 What is the major difference between parametric and non-parametric tests?

Exercises

1 In each of the following situations, indicate the statistical analysis you would conduct and the appropriate test or test statistic that should be used.

(a) Consumer preferences for Body Shop shampoo were obtained on an 11-point Likert scale. The same consumers were then shown a commercial about the Body Shop. After the commercial, preferences for the Body Shop were again measured. Has the commercial been successful in inducing a change in preferences?

(b) Does the preference for Body Shop shampoo follow a normal distribution?

2 The current advertising campaign for Red Bull would be changed if less than 30 percent of consumers like it.

(a) Formulate the null and alternative hypotheses.

(b) Discuss the Type I and Type II errors that could occur in hypothesis testing.

(c) Which statistical test would you use? Why?

(d) A random sample of 300 consumers was surveyed and 84 participants indicated that they liked the campaign. Should the campaign be changed? Why?

3 An electrical goods chain is having a New Year sale of refrigerators. The number of refrigerators sold during this sale at a sample of 10 stores was:

80   110   0   40   70   80   100   50   80   30

(a) Is there evidence that an average of more than 50 refrigerators per store were sold during this sale? Use $\alpha = 0.05$.

(b) What assumption is necessary to perform this test?

4   In a survey pretest, data were obtained from 45 participants on Benetton clothes. These data are given in the table below, which gives the usage, gender, awareness, attitude, preference, intention and loyalty towards Benetton of a sample of Benetton users. Usage was coded as 1, 2, or 3, representing light, medium or heavy users. Gender was coded as 1 for females and 2 for males. Awareness, attitude, preference, intention and loyalty were measured on a 7-point Likert-type scale (1 = very unfavourable, 7 = very favourable). Note that 5 participants have missing values that are denoted by 9.

Analyse the Benetton data to answer the following questions. In each case, formulate the null and alternative hypotheses and conduct the appropriate statistical test(s).

(a)   Obtain a frequency distribution for each of the following variables and calculate the relevant statistics: awareness, attitude, preference, intention and loyalty towards Benetton.

(b)   Conduct a cross-tabulation of the usage with gender. Interpret the results.

(c)   Does the awareness for Benetton exceed 3.0?

(d)   Do males and females differ in their awareness for Benetton? Their attitude towards Benetton? Their loyalty for Benetton?

(e)   Do the participants in the pretest have a higher level of awareness than loyalty?

(f)   Does awareness of Benetton follow a normal distribution?

(g)   Is the distribution of preference for Benetton normal?

(h)   Assume that awareness towards Benetton was measured on an ordinal scale rather than an interval scale. Do males and females differ in their awareness towards Benetton?

(i)   Assume that loyalty towards Benetton was measured on an ordinal scale rather than an interval scale. Do males and females differ in their loyalty towards Benetton?

(j)   Assume that attitude and loyalty towards Benetton was measured on an ordinal scale rather than an interval scale. Do the participants have a greater awareness of Benetton than loyalty for Benetton?

Number	Usage	Gender	Awareness	Attitude	Preference	Intention	Loyalty
1	3	2	7	6	5	5	6
2	1	1	2	2	4	6	5
3	1	1	3	3	6	7	6
4	3	2	6	5	5	3	2
5	3	2	5	4	7	4	3
6	2	2	4	3	5	2	3
7	2	1	5	4	4	3	2
8	1	1	2	1	3	4	5
9	2	2	4	4	3	6	5
10	1	1	3	1	2	4	5
11	3	2	6	7	6	4	5
12	3	2	6	5	6	4	4
13	1	1	4	3	3	1	1
14	3	2	6	4	5	3	2
15	1	2	4	3	4	5	6
16	1	2	3	4	2	4	2
17	3	1	7	6	4	5	3

Number	Usage	Gender	Awareness	Attitude	Preference	Intention	Loyalty
18	2	1	6	5	4	3	2
19	1	1	1	1	3	4	5
20	3	1	5	7	4	1	2
21	3	2	6	6	7	7	5
22	2	2	2	3	1	4	2
23	1	1	1	1	3	2	2
24	3	1	6	7	6	7	6
25	1	2	3	2	2	1	1
26	2	2	5	3	4	4	5
27	3	2	7	6	6	5	7
28	2	1	6	4	2	5	6
29	1	1	9	2	3	1	3
30	2	2	5	9	4	6	5
31	1	2	1	2	9	3	2
32	1	2	4	6	5	9	3
33	2	1	3	4	3	2	9
34	2	1	4	6	5	7	6
35	3	1	5	7	7	3	3
36	3	1	6	5	7	3	4
37	3	2	6	7	5	3	4
38	3	2	5	6	4	3	2
39	3	2	7	7	6	3	4
40	1	1	4	3	4	6	5
41	1	1	2	3	4	5	6
42	1	1	1	3	2	3	4
43	1	1	2	4	3	6	7
44	1	1	3	3	4	6	5
45	1	1	1	1	4	5	3

5   In a small group discuss the following issues: 'Why waste time doing basic forms of data analysis? Why not just go straight to performing multivariate analyses – whose outputs from most software packages will include basic analyses?' 'Why do managers find cross-tabulations so appealing? What would it take to make managers more appreciative of statistical analyses that go beyond the cross-tabulation?'

Notes

1. See any introductory statistics book for a more detailed description of these statistics; for example, see Berenson, M.L., Levine, D.M. and Krehbiel, T.C., *Basic Business Statistics: Concepts and Applications*, 11th edn (Upper Saddle River, NJ: Prentice Hall, 2009).

2. Excellent discussions of ways to analyse cross-tabulations can be found in Wagner, W.W., *Using SPSS for Social Statistics and Research Methods* (Thousand Oaks, CA: Pine Forge Press, 2007); Denham, B.E., 'Advanced categorical statistics: Issues and applications in communication research', *Journal of Communication*, 52 (1) (March 2002), 162; Hellevik, O., *Introduction to Causal Analysis: Exploring Survey Data by Crosstabulation* (Beverly Hills, CA: Sage, 1984).

3. McKechnie, D.S., Grant, J., Korepina, V. and Sadykova, N., 'Women: Segmenting the home fitness equipment market', *Journal of Consumer Marketing*, 24 (1) (2007), 18–26; Kivetz, R., and Simonson, I., 'Earning the right to indulge: Effort as a determinant of customer preferences toward frequency program rewards', *Journal of Marketing Research*, 39 (2) (May 2002), 155–70; Feick, L.F., 'Analyzing marketing research data with association models', *Journal of Marketing Research*, 21 (Nov. 1984), 376–86.

4. Lenell, W. and Boissoneau, R., 'Using causal-comparative and correlational designs in conducting market research', *Journal of Professional Services Marketing*, 13 (2) (1996), 59–69. See also the classic book by Zeisel, H., *Say It with Figures*, 5th edn (New York: Harper & Row, 1968).

5. Sirkin, R.M., *Statistics for the Social Sciences*, 3rd edn (Thousand Oaks, CA: Sage, 2005); Wright, D.B., *First steps in statistics* (Thousand Oaks, CA: Sage, 2002); Sirkin, R.M., *Statistics for the Social Sciences* (Thousand Oaks, CA: Sage, 1994).

6. Fields, A., *Discovering statistics using SPSS*, 2nd edn (Thousand Oaks, CA: Sage, 2005); Hoenig, J.M., 'The abuse of power: The pervasive fallacy of power calculation for data analysis', *American Statistician*, 55 (1) (Feb. 2001), 19–24; Cowles, M. and Davis, C., 'On the origins of the .05 level of statistical significance', *American Psychologist* (May 1982), 553–58. See also Kotabe, M., Duhan, D.E., Smith, D.K. Jr and Wilson, R.I.D., 'The perceived veracity of PIMS strategy principles in Japan: An empirical inquiry', *Journal of Marketing*, 55 (Jan. 1991), 26–41.

7. Technically, a null hypothesis cannot be accepted. It can be either rejected or not rejected. This distinction, however, is inconsequential in marketing research.

8. The condition when the variances cannot be assumed to be equal is known as the Behrens–Fisher problem. There is some controversy over the best procedure in this case. For an example, see Hulten, B., 'Customer segmentation: The concepts of trust commitment and relationships', *Journal of Targeting, Measurement and Analysis for Marketing*, 15 (4) (Sept. 2007), 256–69; Heilman, C.M., Nakamoto, K. and Rao, A.G., 'Pleasant surprises: Consumer response to unexpected in-store coupons', *Journal of Marketing Research*, 39 (2) (May 2002), 242–52.

9. Higgins, J.J., *Introduction to modern nonparametric statistics*, (Pacific Grove, CA: Duxbury, 2002); Pet, M.A., *Nonparametric Statistics for Health Care Research* (Thousand Oaks, CA: Sage, 1997). For a more extensive treatment, see Lancaster, H.O., *The Chi Squared Distribution* (New York: Wiley, 1969). For a recent application, see Bakir, A., 'Some assembly required: Comparing disclaimers in children's TV advertising in Turkey and the United States', *Journal of Advertising Research*, 49, 1 (March 2009), 93–103.

10. Berenson, M.L., Levine, D.M. and Krehbiel, T.C., *Basic Business Statistics: Concepts and Applications*, 11th edn (Upper Saddle River, NJ: Prentice Hall, 2009).

12 Advanced quantitative data analysis

Stage 1
Problem definition

Stage 2
Research approach developed

Stage 3
Research design developed

Stage 4
Fieldwork or data collection

Stage 5
Data integrity and analysis

Stage 6
Report preparation and presentation

Factor analysis and cluster analysis are multivariate techniques that enable researchers to explore and discover meaning in data. They facilitate the reduction of data and the generation of hypotheses.

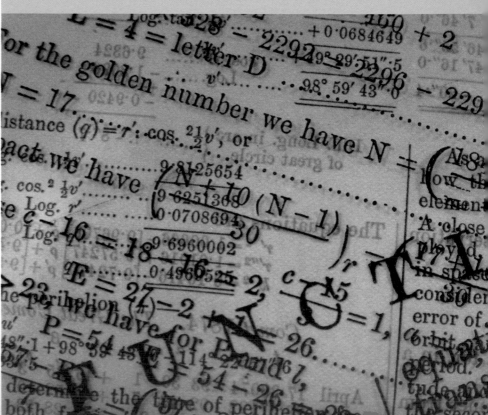

Objectives

After reading this chapter, you should be able to:

1 describe the concept of factor analysis;

2 explain the procedure for conducting factor analysis, including problem formulation, construction of the correlation matrix, selection of an appropriate method, determination of the number of factors, rotation and interpretation of factors;

3 understand the distinction between principal component factor analysis and common factor analysis methods;

4 describe the concept of cluster analysis;

5 explain the procedure for conducting cluster analysis, including formulating the problem, selecting a distance measure, selecting a clustering procedure, deciding on the number of clusters, interpreting clusters and profiling clusters;

6 describe the purpose and methods for evaluating the quality of clustering results and assessing reliability and validity;

7 appreciate how SNAP software is used in factor and cluster analysis.

Overview

Earlier we examined preliminary data analysis procedures and worked through hypothesis testing of parametric and non-parametric data. Here we examine two forms of multivariate data analyses that help researchers to discover meaning in data and formulate hypotheses. We describe the basic concept of factor analysis and give an exposition of the factor model. We also describe the steps in factor analysis and illustrate them in the context of principal components analysis. We then present an application of common factor analysis. The chapter continues with a description of the basic concept of cluster analysis. The steps involved in conducting cluster analysis are discussed and illustrated in the context of hierarchical clustering. Finally, help is provided to appreciate how the SNAP Learning Edition can help with the data analysis challenges presented in this text.

Factor analysis

We begin this section with an example that illustrates an application of factor analysis.

Real research   **Personal alarms**[1]

In a study of personal alarms, women were asked to rate eight personal alarms using the following 15 statements:

1 Feels comfortable in the hand.

2 Could be easily kept in the pocket.

3 Would fit easily into a handbag.

4 Could be easily worn on the person.

5 Could be carried to be very handy when needed.

6   Could be set off almost as a reflex action.

7   Would be difficult for an attacker to take it off me.

8   Could keep a very firm grip on it if attacked.

9   An attacker might be frightened that I might attack him with it.

10   Would be difficult for an attacker to switch off.

11   Solidly built.

12   Would be difficult to break.

13   Looks as if it would give off a very loud noise.

14   An attacker might have second thoughts about attacking me if he saw me with it.

15   I would be embarrassed to carry it around with me.

The question was, 'Could these 15 variables be reduced to a smaller number of derived variables, known as factors, in such a way that too much information was not lost?' Factor analysis enabled these 15 variables to be reduced to four underlying dimensions or factors that women used to evaluate the alarms. Factor 1 seemed to measure a dimension of *size*, on a continuum of small to large. Factor 2 tapped into aspects of the *appearance* of a personal alarm. Factor 3 revealed *robustness* characteristics, with factor 4 related to *hand feel*.

Basic concept

Factor analysis
A class of procedures primarily used for data reduction and summarisation.

Factor analysis is a general name denoting a class of procedures primarily used for data reduction and summarisation. In marketing research, there may be a large number of variables, most of which are correlated and which must be reduced to a manageable level. Relationships among sets of many interrelated variables are examined and represented in terms of a few underlying factors. For example, the image of a fashion brand may be measured by asking participants to evaluate competing fashion brands on a series of items on a semantic differential scale or a Likert scale. These item evaluations may then be analysed to determine the **factors** underlying the image of a fashion brand.

Factor
An underlying dimension that explains the correlations among a set of variables.

In multivariate data analysis techniques such as analysis of variance (ANOVA), multiple regression and discriminant analysis, one variable is considered the dependent or criterion variable, and the others are considered independent or predictor variables. But no such distinction is made in factor analysis. Rather, factor analysis is an **interdependence technique** in that an entire set of interdependent relationships is examined.[2]

Interdependence technique
A multivariate statistical technique in which the whole set of interdependent relationships is examined.

Factor analysis is used in the following circumstances:

1   To identify underlying dimensions, or factors, that explain the correlations among a set of variables. For example, a set of lifestyle statements may be used to measure the psychographic profiles of consumers. These statements may then be factor analysed to identify the underlying psychographic factors as illustrated in the opening example. This is also illustrated in Figure 12.1 based upon empirical analysis, where seven psychographic variables can be represented by two factors. In this figure, factor 1 can be interpreted as homebody vs socialite, and factor 2 can be interpreted as sports vs cinema/theatre.

2   To identify a new, smaller, set of uncorrelated variables to replace the original set of correlated variables in subsequent multivariate analysis (regression or discriminant analysis). For example, the psychographic factors identified may be used as independent variables

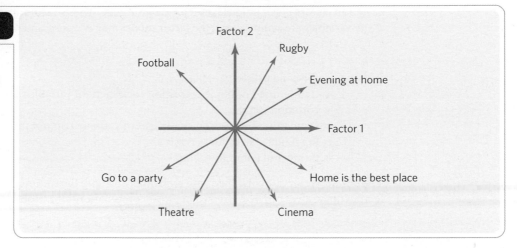

Figure 12.1

Factors underlying selected psychographics and lifestyles

in explaining the differences between loyal and non-loyal consumers. Thus, instead of the seven correlated psychographic variables of Figure 12.1, we can use the two uncorrelated factors, i.e. homebody versus socialite, and sports versus cinema/theatre, in subsequent analysis.

3   To identify a smaller set of salient variables from a larger set for use in subsequent multi-variate analysis. For example, a few of the original lifestyle statements that correlate highly with the identified factors may be used as independent variables to explain the differences between the loyal and non-loyal users.

All these uses are exploratory in nature and, therefore, factor analysis is also called exploratory factor analysis (EFA). Factor analysis has numerous applications in marketing research. For example:

- It can be used in market segmentation for identifying the underlying variables on which to group the customers. New car buyers might be grouped based on the relative emphasis they place on economy, convenience, performance, comfort and luxury. This might result in five segments: economy seekers, convenience seekers, performance seekers, comfort seekers, and luxury seekers.

- In product research, factor analysis can be employed to determine the brand attributes that influence consumer choice. Toothpaste brands might be evaluated in terms of protection against cavities, whiteness of teeth, taste, fresh breath and price.

- In advertising studies, factor analysis can be used to understand the media consumption habits of the target market. The consumers of frozen foods may be heavy viewers of horror films, play a lot of electronic games, and listen to rock music.

- In pricing studies, factor analysis can be used to identify the characteristics of price-sensitive consumers. For example, these consumers might be methodical, economy minded and home centred.

Factor analysis model

Mathematically, factor analysis is somewhat similar to multiple regression analysis in that each variable is expressed as a linear combination of underlying factors. The amount of variance a variable shares with all other variables included in the analysis is referred to as *communality*. The covariation among the variables is described in terms of a small number of common factors plus a unique factor for each variable. These factors are not overtly observed. If the variables are standardised, the factor model may be represented as:

$$X_i = A_{i1}F_1 + A_{i2}F_2 + A_{i3}F_3 + \cdots A_{im}F_m + V_iU_i$$

where X_i = ith standardised variable
A_{ij} = standardised multiple regression coefficient of variable i on common factor j
F = common factor
V_i = standardised regression coefficient of variable i on unique factor i
U_i = the unique factor for variable i
m = number of common factors

The unique factors are correlated with each other and with the common factors.[3] The common factors themselves can be expressed as linear combinations of the observed variables:

$$F_i = W_{i1}X_1 + W_{i2}X_2 + W_{i3}X_3 + \cdots + W_{ik}X_k$$

where F_i = estimate of ith factor
W_i = weight or factor score coefficient
k = number of variables

It is possible to select weights or factor score coefficients so that the first factor explains the largest portion of the total variance. Then a second set of weights can be selected so that the second factor accounts for most of the residual variance, subject to being uncorrelated with the first factor. This same principle could be applied to selecting additional weights for the additional factors. Thus, the factors can be estimated so that their factor scores, unlike the values of the original variables, are not correlated. Furthermore, the first factor accounts for the highest variance in the data, the second factor the second highest, and so on. A simplified graphical illustration of factor analysis in the case of two variables is presented in Figure 12.2. Several statistics are associated with factor analysis.

Figure 12.2

Graphical illustration of factor analysis

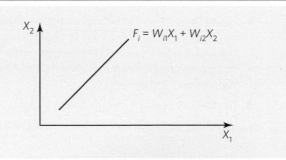

Statistics associated with factor analysis

The key statistics associated with factor analysis are as follows:

Communality. Communality is the amount of variance a variable shares with all the other variables being considered. This is also the proportion of variance explained by the common factors.

Correlation matrix. A correlation matrix is a lower triangular matrix showing the simple correlations, r, between all possible pairs of variables included in the analysis. The diagonal elements, which are all one, are usually omitted.

Eigenvalue. The eigenvalue represents the total variance explained by each factor.

Factor loadings. Factor loadings are simple correlations between the variables and the factors.

Factor loading plot. A factor loading plot is a plot of the original variables using the factor loadings as coordinates.

Factor matrix. A factor matrix contains the factor loadings of all the variables on all the factors extracted.

Factor scores. Factor scores are composite scores estimated for each participant on the derived factors.

Factor scores coefficient matrix. This matrix contains the weights, or factor score coefficients, used to combine the standardised variables to obtain factor scores.

Kaiser–Meyer–Olkin (KMO) measure of sampling adequacy. The Kaiser–Meyer–Olkin (KMO) measure of sampling adequacy is an index used to examine the appropriateness of factor analysis. High values (between 0.5 and 1.0) indicate that factor analysis is appropriate. Values below 0.5 imply that factor analysis may not be appropriate.

Percentage of variance. The percentage of the total variance attributed to each factor.

Residuals. Residuals are the differences between the observed correlations, as given in the input correlation matrix, and the reproduced correlations, as estimated from the factor matrix.

Scree plot. A scree plot is a plot of the eigenvalues against the number of factors in order of extraction.

We describe the uses of these statistics in the next section, in the context of the procedure for conducting factor analysis.

Conducting factor analysis

The steps involved in conducting factor analysis are illustrated in Figure 12.3. The first step is to define the factor analysis problem and identify the variables to be factor analysed. Then a correlation matrix of these variables is constructed and a method of factor analysis is selected. The researcher decides on the number of factors to be extracted and the method of rotation. Next, the rotated factors should be interpreted. Depending on the objectives, the factor scores may be calculated, or surrogate variables selected, to represent the factors in subsequent multivariate analysis. Finally, the fit of the factor analysis model is determined. We discuss these steps in more detail in the following subsections.[4]

Formulate the problem

Formulating the problem includes several tasks. First, the objectives of factor analysis should be identified. The variables to be included in the factor analysis should be specified based on past research (quantitative or qualitative), theory and judgement of the researcher. It is important that the variables be appropriately measured on an interval or ratio scale. An appropriate sample size should be used. As a rough guide, there should be at least four or five times as many observations (sample size) as there are variables.[5] In many marketing research situations, the sample size is small, and this ratio is considerably lower. In these cases, the results should be interpreted cautiously.

To illustrate factor analysis, suppose that the researcher wants to determine the underlying benefits consumers seek from the purchase of toothpaste. A sample of 30 participants were questioned using street interviewing. The participants were asked to indicate their degree of

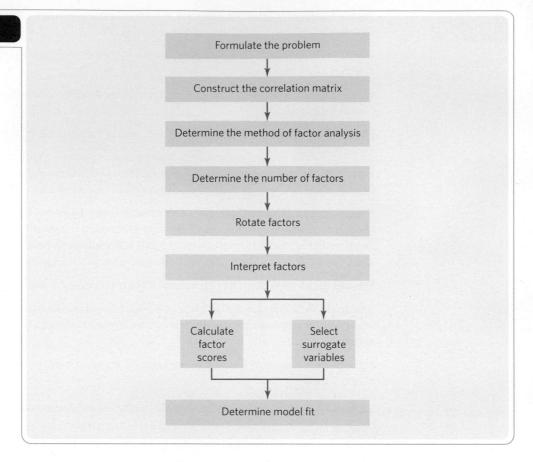

Figure 12.3

Conducting factor analysis

agreement with the following statements using a seven-point scale (1 = strongly disagree, 7 = strongly agree):

V_1 It is important to buy a toothpaste that prevents cavities.
V_2 I like a toothpaste that gives shiny teeth.
V_3 A toothpaste should strengthen your gums.
V_4 I prefer a toothpaste that freshens breath.
V_5 Prevention of tooth decay should be an important benefit offered by a toothpaste.
V_6 The most important consideration in buying a toothpaste is attractive teeth.

The data obtained are given in Table 12.1. For illustrative purposes, we consider only a small number of observations. In actual practice, factor analysis is performed on much larger samples. A correlation matrix was constructed based on these ratings data.

Construct the correlation matrix

The analytical process is based on a matrix of correlations between the variables. Valuable insights can be gained from an examination of this matrix. For factor analysis to be meaningful, the variables should be correlated. In practice, this is usually the case. If the correlations between all the variables are small, factor analysis may not be appropriate. We would also expect that variables that are highly correlated with each other would also highly correlate with the same factor or factors. The correlation matrix, constructed from the data obtained to understand toothpaste benefits, is shown in Table 12.2. There are relatively high correlations among V_1 (prevention of cavities), V_3 (strong gums) and V_5 (prevention of tooth decay). We would expect these variables to correlate with the same set of factors. Likewise, there are relatively high correlations among V_2 (shiny teeth), V_4 (fresh breath) and V_6 (attractive teeth). These variables may also be expected to correlate with the same factors.[6]

Table 12.1	Toothpaste attribute ratings					
Participant number	V_1	V_2	V_3	V_4	V_5	V_6
1	7	3	6	4	2	4
2	1	3	2	4	5	4
3	6	2	7	4	1	3
4	4	5	4	6	2	5
5	1	2	2	3	6	2
6	6	3	6	4	2	4
7	5	3	6	3	4	3
8	6	4	7	4	1	4
9	3	4	2	3	6	3
10	2	6	2	6	7	6
11	6	4	7	3	2	3
12	2	3	1	4	5	4
13	7	2	6	4	1	3
14	4	6	4	5	3	6
15	1	3	2	2	6	4
16	6	4	6	3	3	4
17	5	3	6	3	3	4
18	7	3	7	4	1	4
19	2	4	3	3	6	3
20	3	5	3	6	4	6
21	1	3	2	3	5	3
22	5	4	5	4	2	4
23	2	2	1	5	4	4
24	4	6	4	6	4	7
25	6	5	4	2	1	4
26	3	5	4	6	4	7
27	4	4	7	2	2	5
28	3	7	2	6	4	3
29	4	6	3	7	2	7
30	2	3	2	4	7	2

Table 12.2	Correlation matrix					
Participant	V_1	V_2	V_3	V_4	V_5	V_6
V_1	1.00					
V_2	−0.053	1.00				
V_3	0.873	−0.155	1.00			
V_4	−0.086	0.572	−0.248	1.00		
V_5	−0.858	0.020	−0.778	−0.007	1.00	
V_6	0.004	0.640	−0.018	0.640	−0.136	1.00

Determine the method of factor analysis

Once it has been determined that factor analysis is an appropriate technique for analysing the data, an appropriate method must be selected. The approach used to derive the weights or factor score coefficients differentiates the various methods of factor analysis. The two basic approaches are principal components analysis and common factor analysis. In principal components analysis, the total variance in the data is considered. The diagonal of the correlation matrix consists of unities, and full variance is brought into the factor matrix. **Principal components analysis** is recommended when the primary concern is to determine the minimum number of factors that will account for maximum variance in the data for use in subsequent multivariate analysis. The factors are called *principal components*.

In **common factor analysis**, the factors are estimated based only on the common variance. Communalities are inserted in the diagonal of the correlation matrix. This method is appropriate when the primary concern is to identify the underlying dimensions and the common variance is of interest. This method is also known as *principal axis factoring*. Other approaches for estimating the common factors are also available. These include the methods of unweighted least squares, generalised least squares, maximum likelihood, alpha method and image factoring. These methods are complex and are not recommended for inexperienced users.[7]

In the toothpaste example, the application of principal components analysis is presented in Table 12.3.

Principal components analysis
An approach to factor analysis that considers the total variance in the data.

Common factor analysis
An approach to factor analysis that estimates the factors based only on the common variance. Also called principal axis factoring.

Table 12.3	Results of principal components analysis

Bartlett test of sphericity
Approximate chi-square = 111.314, *df* = 15, significance = 0.00000
Kaiser–Meyer–Olkin measure of sampling adequacy = 0.660

COMMUNALITIES

Variable	Initial	Extraction
V_1	1.000	0.926
V_2	1.000	0.723
V_3	1.000	0.894
V_4	1.000	0.739
V_5	1.000	0.878
V_6	1.000	0.790

INITIAL EIGENVALUES

Factor	Eigenvalue	Percentage of variance	Cumulative percentage
1	2.731	45.520	45.520
2	2.218	36.969	82.488
3	0.442	7.360	89.848
4	0.341	5.688	95.536
5	0.183	3.044	98.580
6	0.085	1.420	100.000

EXTRACTION SUMS OF SQUARED LOADINGS

Factor	Eigenvalue	Percentage of variance	Cumulative percentage
1	2.731	45.520	45.520
2	2.218	36.969	82.488

Table 12.3	Continued

Factor matrix

	Factor 1	Factor 2
V_1	0.928	0.253
V_2	−0.301	0.795
V_3	0.936	0.131
V_4	−0.342	0.789
V_5	−0.869	−0.351
V_6	−0.177	0.871

ROTATION SUMS OF SQUARED LOADINGS

Factor	Eigenvalue	Percentage of variance	Cumulative percentage
1	2.688	44.802	44.802
2	2.261	37.687	82.488

ROTATED FACTOR MATRIX

	Factor 1	Factor 2
V_1	0.962	−0.027
V_2	−0.057	0.848
V_3	0.934	−0.146
V_4	−0.098	0.854
V_5	−0.933	−0.084
V_6	0.083	0.885

FACTOR SCORE COEFFICIENT MATRIX

	Factor 1	Factor 2
V_1	0.358	0.011
V_2	−0.001	0.375
V_3	0.345	−0.043
V_4	−0.017	0.377
V_5	−0.350	−0.059
V_6	0.052	0.395

REPRODUCED CORRELATION MATRIX

Variables	V_1	V_2	V_3	V_4	V_5	V_6
V_1	0.926*	0.024	−0.029	0.031	0.038	−0.053
V_2	−0.078	0.723*	0.022	−0.158	0.038	−0.105
V_3	0.902	−0.177	0.894*	−0.031	0.081	0.033
V_4	−0.117	0.730	−0.217	0.739*	−0.027	−0.107
V_5	−0.895	−0.018	0.859	0.020	0.878*	0.016
V_6	0.057	−0.746	−0.051	0.748	−0.152	0.790*

*The lower left triangle contains the reproduced correlation matrix; the diagonal, the communalities; and the upper right triangle, the residuals between the observed correlations and the reproduced correlations.

Communality
The variance of a measured variance that is explained by the construct on which it loads.

Under 'Communalities', 'Initial' column, it can be seen that the communality for each variable, V_1 to V_6, is 1.0 as unities were inserted in the diagonal of the correlation matrix.

The table labelled 'Initial eigenvalues' gives the eigenvalues. The eigenvalues for the factors are, as expected, in decreasing order of magnitude as we go from factor 1 to factor 6. The eigenvalue for a factor indicates the total variance attributed to that factor. The total variance accounted for by all the six factors is 6.00, which is equal to the number of variables. Factor 1 accounts for a variance of 2.731, which is (2.731/6) or 45.52 per cent of the total variance. Likewise, the second factor accounts for (2.218/6) or 36.97 per cent of the total variance, and the first two factors combined account for 82.49 per cent of the total variance. Several considerations are involved in determining the number of factors that should be used in the analysis.

Determine the number of factors

It is possible to compute as many principal components as there are variables, but in doing so, no parsimony is gained, i.e. we would not have summarised the information nor revealed any underlying structure. To summarise the information contained in the original variables, a smaller number of factors should be extracted. The question is: how many? Several procedures have been suggested for determining the number of factors. These included a priori determination and approaches based on eigenvalues, scree plot, percentage of variance accounted for, split-half reliability and significance tests:

A priori determination. Sometimes, because of prior knowledge, the researcher knows how many factors to expect and thus can specify the number of factors to be extracted beforehand. The extraction of factors ceases when the desired number of factors has been extracted. Most computer programs allow the user to specify the number of factors, allowing for an easy implementation of this approach.

Determination based on eigenvalues. In this approach, only factors with eigenvalues greater than 1.0 are retained; the other factors are not included in the model. An eigenvalue represents the amount of variance associated with the factor. Hence, only factors with a variance greater than 1.0 are included. Factors with a variance less than 1.0 are no better than a single variable because, due to standardisation, each variable has a variance of 1.0. If the number of variables is less than 20, this approach will result in a conservative number of factors.

Determination based on scree plot. A scree plot is a plot of the eigenvalues against the number of factors in order of extraction. The shape of the plot is used to determine the number of factors. Typically, the plot has a distinct break between the steep slope of factors, with large eigenvalues and a gradual trailing off associated with the rest of the factors. This gradual trailing off is referred to as the scree. Experimental evidence indicates that the point at which the scree begins denotes the true number of factors. Generally, the number of factors determined by a scree plot will be one or a few more than that determined by the eigenvalue criterion.

Determination based on percentage of variance. In this approach, the number of factors extracted is determined so that the cumulative percentage of variance extracted by the factors reaches a satisfactory level. What level of variance is satisfactory depends upon the problem. It is recommended that the factors extracted should account for at least 60 per cent of the variance.

Determination based on split-half reliability. The sample is split in half, and factor analysis is performed on each half. Only factors with high correspondence of factor loadings across the two subsamples are retained.

Determination based on significance tests. It is possible to determine the statistical significance of the separate eigenvalues and retain only those factors that are statistically significant. A drawback is that with large samples (size greater than 200) many factors are likely to be statistically significant, although from a practical viewpoint many of these account for only a small proportion of the total variance.

In Table 12.3, we see that the eigenvalue greater than 1.0 (default option) results in two factors being extracted. Our a priori knowledge tells us that toothpaste is bought for two major reasons. The scree plot associated with this analysis is given in Figure 12.4. From the scree plot, a distinct break occurs at three factors. Finally, from the cumulative percentage of variance accounted for, we see that the first two factors account for 82.49 per cent of the variance and that the gain achieved in going to three factors is marginal. Furthermore, split-half reliability also indicates that two factors are appropriate. Thus, two factors appear to be reasonable in this situation.

Figure 12.4

Scree plot

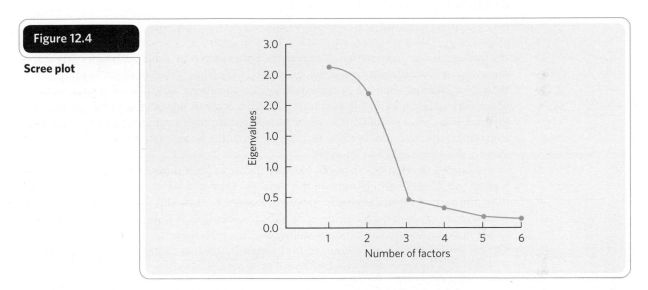

The second column under the 'Communalities' heading in Table 12.3 gives relevant information after the desired number of factors has been extracted. The communalities for the variances under 'Extraction' are different from those under 'Initial' because all of the variances associated with the variables are not explained unless all the factors are retained. The 'Extraction sums of squared loadings' table gives the variances associated with the factors that are retained. Note that these are the same as those under 'Initial eigenvalues'. This is always the case in principal components analysis. The percentage variance accounted for by a factor is determined by dividing the associated eigenvalue by the total number of factors (or variables) and multiplying by 100. Thus, the first factor accounts for $(2.731/6) \times 100$ or 45.52 per cent of the variance of the six variables. Likewise, the second factor accounts for $(2.218/6) \times 100$ or 36.967 per cent of the variance. Interpretation of the solution is often enhanced by a rotation of the factors.

Rotate factors

An important output from factor analysis is the factor matrix, also called the *factor pattern matrix*. The factor matrix contains the coefficients used to express the standardised variables in terms of the factors. These coefficients, the factor loadings, represent the correlations between the factors and the variables. A coefficient with a large absolute value indicates that the factor and the variable are closely related. The coefficients of the factor matrix can be used to interpret the factors.

Although the initial or unrotated factor matrix indicates the relationship between the factors and individual variables, it seldom results in factors that can be interpreted, because

Figure 12.5

Factor matrix before and after rotation

Factors		
Variables	1	2
1	X	
2	X	X
3	X	
4	X	X
5	X	X
6		X

(a) High loadings before rotation

Factors		
Variables	1	2
1	X	
2		X
3	X	
4		X
5	X	
6		X

(b) High loadings after rotation

the factors are correlated with many variables. For example, in Table 12.3, factor 1 is at least somewhat correlated with five of the six variables (absolute value of factor loading greater than 0.3). Likewise, factor 2 is at least somewhat correlated with four of the six variables. Moreover, variables 2 and 5 load at least somewhat on both the factors. This is illustrated in Figure 12.5(a). How should this factor be interpreted? In such a complex matrix, it is difficult to interpret the factors. Therefore, through rotation, the factor matrix is transformed into a simpler one that is easier to interpret.

In rotating the factors, we would like each factor to have non-zero, or significant, loadings or coefficients for only some of the variables. Likewise, we would like each variable to have non-zero or significant loadings with only a few factors, and if possible with only one. If several factors have high loadings with the same variable, it is difficult to interpret them. Rotation does not affect the communalities and the percentage of total variance explained. The percentage of variance accounted for by each factor does change, however. This is seen in Table 12.3 by comparing 'Extraction sums of squared loadings' with 'Rotation sums of squared loadings'. The variance explained by the individual factors is redistributed by rotation. Hence, different methods of rotation may result in the identification of different factors.

The rotation is called **orthogonal rotation** if the axes are maintained at right angles. The most commonly used method for rotation is the **varimax procedure**. This is an orthogonal method of rotation that minimises the number of variables with high loadings on a factor, thereby enhancing the interpretability of the factors.[8] Orthogonal rotation results in factors that are uncorrelated. The rotation is called **oblique rotation** when the axes are not maintained at right angles, and the factors are correlated. Sometimes, allowing for correlations among factors can simplify the factor pattern matrix. Oblique rotation should be used when factors in the population are likely to be strongly correlated.

In Table 12.3, by comparing the varimax rotated factor matrix with the unrotated matrix (entitled 'Factor matrix'), we can see how rotation achieves simplicity and enhances interpretability. Whereas five variables correlated with factor 1 in the unrotated matrix, only variables V_1, V_3 and V_5 correlate highly with factor 1 after rotation. The remaining variables, V_2, V_4 and V_6, correlate highly with factor 2. Furthermore, no variable correlates highly with both the factors. The rotated factor matrix forms the basis for interpretation of the factors.

Orthogonal rotation
Rotation of factors in which the axes are maintained at right angles.

Varimax procedure
An orthogonal method of factor rotation that minimises the number of variables with high loadings on a factor, thereby enhancing the interpretability of the factors.

Oblique rotation
Rotation of factors when the axes are not maintained at right angles.

Interpret factors

Interpretation is facilitated by identifying the variables that have large loadings on the same factor. That factor can then be interpreted in terms of the variables that load high on it. Another useful aid in interpretation is to plot the variables, using the factor loadings as coordinates. Variables at the end of an axis are those that have high loadings on only that factor

Figure 12.6

Factor loading plot

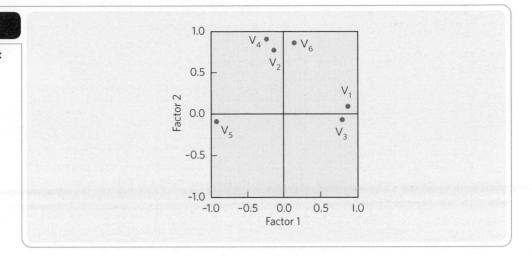

and hence describe the factor. Variables near the origin have small loadings on both the factors. Variables that are not near any of the axes are related to both the factors. If a factor cannot be clearly defined in terms of the original variables, it should be labelled as an undefined or a general factor.

In the rotated factor matrix of Table 12.3, factor 1 has high coefficients for variables V_1 (prevention of cavities) and V_3 (strong gums), and a negative coefficient for V_5 (prevention of tooth decay is not important). Therefore, this factor may be labelled a health benefit factor. Note that a negative coefficient for a negative variable (V_5) leads to a positive interpretation that prevention of tooth decay is important. Factor 2 is highly related with variables V_2 (shiny teeth), V_4 (fresh breath) and V_6 (attractive teeth). Thus factor 2 may be labelled a social benefit factor. A plot of the factor loadings, given in Figure 12.6, confirms this interpretation. Variables V_1, V_3 and V_5 (denoted 1, 3 and 5, respectively) are at the end of the horizontal axis (factor 1), with V_5 at the end opposite to V_1 and V_3, whereas variables V_2, V_4 and V_6 (denoted 2, 4 and 6) are at the end of the vertical axis (factor 2). One could summarise the data by stating that consumers appear to seek two major kinds of benefits from toothpaste: health benefits and social benefits.

Calculate factor scores

Factor scores
Composite scores
estimated for each
participant on the derived
factors.

Following interpretation, factor scores can be calculated, if necessary. Factor analysis has its own stand-alone value. Factor analysis is useful to compute factor scores for each participant that may be used in subsequent multivariate analysis, for example by using cluster analysis to classify different consumer types. A factor is simply a linear combination of the original variables. The factor scores for the ith factor may be estimated as follows:

$$F_i = W_{i1} X_1 + W_{i2} X_2 + W_{i3} X_3 + \cdots + W_{ik} W_k$$

These symbols were defined earlier in the chapter.

The weights or factor score coefficients used to combine the standardised variables are obtained from the factor score coefficient matrix. Most computer programs allow you to request factor scores. Only in the case of principal components analysis is it possible to compute exact factor scores. Moreover, in principal components analysis, these scores are uncorrelated. In common factor analysis, estimates of these scores are obtained, and there is no guarantee that the factors will be uncorrelated with each other. Factor scores can be used instead of the original variables in subsequent multivariate analysis. For example, using the 'Factor score coefficient' matrix in Table 12.3, one could compute two factor scores for each participant. The standardised variable values would be multiplied by the corresponding factor score coefficients to obtain the factor scores.

Select surrogate variables

Surrogate variables
A subset of original variables selected for use in subsequent analysis.

Sometimes, instead of computing factor scores, the researcher wishes to select surrogate variables. Selection of substitute or **surrogate variables** involves singling out some of the original variables for use in subsequent analysis. This allows the researcher to conduct subsequent analysis and to interpret the results in terms of original variables rather than factor scores. By examining the factor matrix, one could select for each factor the variable with the highest loading on that factor. That variable could then be used as a surrogate variable for the associated factor. This process works well if one factor loading for a variable is clearly higher than all other factor loadings. The choice is not as easy, however, if two or more variables have similarly high loadings. In such a case, the choice between these variables should be based on theoretical and measurement considerations. For example, theory may suggest that a variable with a slightly lower loading is more important than one with a slightly higher loading. Likewise, if a variable has a slightly lower loading but has been measured more precisely, it should be selected as the surrogate variable. In Table 12.3, the variables V_1, V_3 and V_5 all have high loadings on factor 1, and all are fairly close in magnitude, although V_1 has relatively the highest loading and would therefore be a likely candidate. However, if prior knowledge suggests that prevention of tooth decay is a very important benefit, V_5 would be selected as the surrogate for factor 1. Also, the choice of a surrogate for factor 2 is not straightforward. Variables V_2, V_4 and V_6 all have comparable high loadings on this factor. If prior knowledge suggests that attractive teeth are the most important social benefit sought from a toothpaste, the researcher would select V_6.

Determine the model fit

The final step in factor analysis involves the determination of model fit. A basic assumption underlying factor analysis is that the observed correlation between variables can be attributed to common factors. Hence, the correlations between the variables can be deduced or reproduced from the estimated correlations between the variables and the factors. The differences between the observed correlations (as given in the input correlation matrix) and the reproduced correlations (as estimated from the factor matrix) can be examined to determine model fit. These differences are called *residuals*. If there are many large residuals, the factor model does not provide a good fit to the data and the model should be reconsidered. In the upper right triangle of the 'Reproduced correlation matrix' of Table 12.3, we see that only five residuals are larger than 0.05, indicating an acceptable model fit.

Cluster analysis

We begin this section with an example that illustrates an application of cluster analysis.

Real research   **Ice cream 'hot spots'[9]**

Häagen-Dazs Shoppe Co.(**www.haagen-dazs.com**), with more than 850 retail ice cream shops in over 50 countries, was interested in expanding its customer base. The objective was to identify potential consumer segments that could generate additional sales. It used geodemographic techniques, which were based upon clustering consumers, using geographic, demographic and lifestyle data. Additional primary data were collected to develop an understanding of the demographic, lifestyle and behavioural characteristics of Häagen-Dazs Shoppe users, which included frequency of purchase, time of day to visit café, day of the week and a range of other product variables. The postcodes or zip codes of participants were also obtained. The participants were then assigned to 40 geodemographic clusters based upon a clustering procedure developed by Nielsen Claritas (**www.claritas.com**). Häagen-Dazs compared its profile of customers with the profile of geodemographic classifications to develop a clearer picture of the types of consumer it was attracting. From this it decided which profiles of consumer or target markets it believed to hold the most potential for additional sales. New products were developed and advertising was established and profiled to target specific consumer types.

Basic concept

Cluster analysis is a class of techniques used to classify objects or cases into relatively homogeneous groups called *clusters*. Objects in each cluster tend to be similar to each other and dissimilar to objects in the other clusters. Cluster analysis is also called *classification analysis* or numerical taxonomy.[10] We are concerned with clustering procedures that assign each object to one and only one cluster.[11] Figure 12.7 shows an ideal clustering situation in which the clusters are distinctly separated on two variables: quality consciousness (variable 1) and price sensitivity (variable 2). Note that each consumer falls into one cluster and there are no overlapping areas. Figure 12.8, on the other hand, presents a clustering situation more likely to be encountered in practice. In Figure 12.8, the boundaries for some of the clusters are not clear cut, and the classification of some consumers is not obvious, because many of them could be grouped into one cluster or another. Groups or clusters are suggested by the data, not defined *a priori*.[12] Cluster analysis has been used in marketing for a variety of purposes, including the following:[13]

- *Segmenting the market.* For example, consumers may be clustered on the basis of benefits sought from the purchase of a product. Each cluster would consist of consumers who are relatively homogeneous in terms of the benefits they seek.[14] This approach is called benefit segmentation.

- *Understanding buyer behaviours.* Cluster analysis can be used to identify homogeneous groups of buyers. Then the buying behaviour of each group may be examined separately, as can happen for example with different types of car buyers. Cluster analysis has been used to identify the kinds of strategies car buyers use to obtain information to support their buying decisions.

- *Identifying new product opportunities.* By clustering brands and products, competitive sets within the market can be determined. Brands in the same cluster compete more fiercely with each other than with brands in other clusters. A firm can examine its current offerings compared with those of its competitors to identify potential new product opportunities.

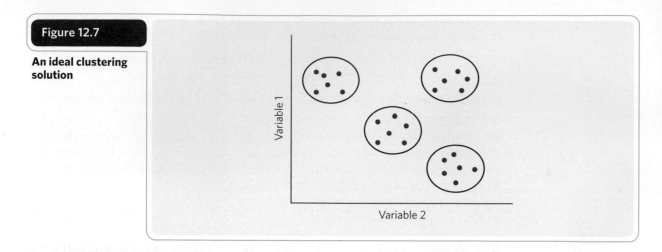

Figure 12.7

An ideal clustering solution

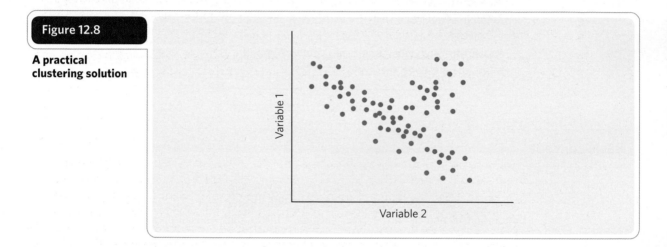

Figure 12.8

A practical clustering solution

- *Reducing data.* Cluster analysis can be used as a general data reduction tool to develop clusters or subgroups of data that are more manageable than individual observations. Subsequent multivariate analysis is conducted on the clusters rather than on the individual observations. For example, to describe differences in consumers' product usage behaviour, the consumers may first be clustered into groups.

Statistics associated with cluster analysis

Before discussing the statistics associated with cluster analysis, it should be mentioned that most clustering methods are relatively simple procedures that are not supported by an extensive body of statistical reasoning. Rather, most clustering methods are heuristics, which are based on algorithms. Thus, cluster analysis contrasts sharply with analysis of variance, regression, discriminant analysis and factor analysis, which are based upon an extensive body of statistical reasoning. Although many clustering methods have important statistical properties, the fundamental simplicity of these methods needs to be recognised.[15] The following statistics and concepts are associated with cluster analysis.

Agglomeration schedule. An agglomeration schedule gives information on the objects or cases being combined at each stage of a hierarchical clustering process.

Cluster centroid. The cluster centroid is the mean values of the variables for all the cases or objects in a particular cluster.

Cluster centres. The cluster centres are the initial starting points in non-hierarchical clustering. Clusters are built around these centres or seeds.

Cluster membership. Cluster membership indicates the cluster to which each object or case belongs.

Dendrogram. A dendrogram, or tree graph, is a graphical device for displaying clustering results. Vertical lines represent clusters that are joined together. The position of the line on the scale indicates the distances at which clusters were joined. The dendrogram is read from left to right. Figure 12.14 later in this chapter is a dendrogram.

Distances between cluster centres. These distances indicate how separated the individual pairs of clusters are. Clusters that are widely separated are distinct and therefore desirable.

Icicle diagram. An icicle diagram is a graphical display of clustering results, so called because it resembles a row of icicles hanging from the eaves of a house. The columns correspond to the objects being clustered, and the rows correspond to the number of clusters. An icicle diagram is read from bottom to top. Figure 12.13 later in this chapter is an icicle diagram.

Similarity/distance coefficient matrix. A similarity/distance coefficient matrix is a lower triangular matrix containing pairwise distances between objects or cases.

Conducting cluster analysis

The steps involved in conducting cluster analysis are listed in Figure 12.9. The first step is to formulate the clustering problem by defining the variables on which the clustering will be based. Then, an appropriate distance measure must be selected. The distance measure determines how similar or dissimilar the objects being clustered are. Several clustering procedures have been developed, and the researcher should select one that is appropriate for the problem at hand. Deciding on the number of clusters requires judgement on the part of the researcher. The derived clusters should be interpreted in terms of the variables used to cluster them and profiled in terms of additional salient variables. Finally, the researcher must assess the reliability and validity of the clustering process.

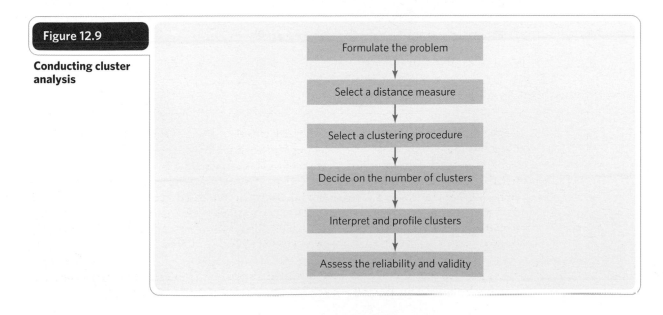

Figure 12.9

Conducting cluster analysis

Formulate the problem

Perhaps the most important part of formulating the clustering problem is selecting the variables on which the clustering is based. Inclusion of even one or two irrelevant variables may distort an otherwise useful clustering solution. Basically, the set of variables selected should describe the similarity between objects in terms that are relevant to the marketing research problem. The variables should be selected based on past research, theory or a consideration of the hypotheses being developed or tested. If cluster analysis is used as an exploratory approach, the researcher naturally exercises their judgement and intuition.

To illustrate, we consider a clustering of consumers based on attitudes towards shopping. Based on past research, six attitudinal variables were identified as being the most relevant to the marketing research problem. Consumers were asked to express their degree of agreement with the following statements on a seven-point scale (1 = disagree, 7 = agree):

V_1 Shopping is fun.
V_2 Shopping is bad for your budget.
V_3 I combine shopping with eating out.
V_4 I try to get the best buys while shopping.
V_5 I don't care about shopping.
V_6 You can save a lot of money by comparing prices.

Data obtained from a pretest sample of 20 participants are shown in Table 12.4. Note that, in practice, clustering is done on much larger samples of 100 or more. A small sample size has been used to illustrate the clustering process.

Table 12.4	Attitudinal data for clustering					
Case number	V_1	V_2	V_3	V_4	V_5	V_6
1	6	4	7	3	2	3
2	2	3	1	4	5	4
3	7	2	6	4	1	3
4	4	6	4	5	3	6
5	1	3	2	2	6	4
6	6	4	6	3	3	4
7	5	3	6	3	3	4
8	7	3	7	4	1	4
9	2	4	3	3	6	3
10	3	5	3	6	4	6
11	1	3	2	3	5	3
12	5	4	5	4	2	4
13	2	2	1	5	4	4
14	4	6	4	6	4	7
15	6	5	4	2	1	4
16	3	5	4	6	4	7
17	4	4	7	2	2	5
18	3	7	2	6	4	3
19	4	6	3	7	2	7
20	2	3	2	4	7	2

Select a distance measure

Because the objective of clustering is to group similar objects together, some measure is needed to assess how similar or different the objects are. The most common approach is to measure similarity in terms of distance between pairs of objects. Objects with smaller distances between them are more similar to each other than are those at larger distances. There are several ways to compute the distance between two objects.[16]

Euclidean distance

The square root of the sum of the squared differences in values for each variable.

The most commonly used measure of similarity is the **Euclidean distance** or its square. The Euclidean distance is the square root of the sum of the squared differences in values for each variable. Other distance measures are also available. The city-block or Manhattan distance between two objects is the sum of the absolute differences in values for each variable. The *Chebychev distance* between two objects is the maximum absolute difference in values for any variable. For our example, we use the squared Euclidean distance.

If the variables are measured in vastly different units, the clustering solution will be influenced by the units of measurement. In a supermarket shopping study, attitudinal variables may be measured on a nine-point Likert-type scale; patronage, in terms of frequency of visits per month and the amount spent; and brand loyalty, in terms of percentage of grocery shopping expenditure allocated to the favourite supermarket. In these cases, before clustering participants, we must standardise the data by rescaling each variable to have a mean of 0 and a standard deviation of 1. Although standardisation can remove the influence of the unit of measurement, it can also reduce the differences between groups on variables that may best discriminate groups or clusters. It is also desirable to eliminate outliers (cases with atypical values).[17]

Use of different distance measures may lead to different clustering results. Hence, it is advisable to use different measures and to compare the results. Having selected a distance or similarity measure, we can next select a clustering procedure.

Hierarchical clustering

A clustering procedure characterised by the development of a hierarchy or treelike structure.

Agglomerative clustering

A hierarchical clustering procedure where each object starts out in a separate cluster. Clusters are formed by grouping objects into bigger and bigger clusters.

Divisive clustering

A hierarchical clustering procedure where all objects start out in one giant cluster. Clusters are formed by dividing this cluster into smaller and smaller clusters.

Linkage methods

Agglomerative methods of hierarchical clustering that cluster objects based on a computation of the distance between them.

Single linkage

A linkage method based on minimum distance or the nearest neighbour rule.

Complete linkage

A linkage method that is based on maximum distance or the farthest neighbour approach.

Select a clustering procedure

Figure 12.10 is a classification of clustering procedures. Clustering procedures can be hierarchical or non-hierarchical, or other procedures. **Hierarchical clustering** is characterised by the development of a hierarchy or treelike structure. Hierarchical methods can be agglomerative or divisive. **Agglomerative clustering** starts with each object in a separate cluster. Clusters are formed by grouping objects into bigger and bigger clusters. This process is continued until all objects are members of a single cluster. **Divisive clustering** starts with all the objects grouped in a single cluster. Clusters are divided or split until each object is in a separate cluster.

Agglomerative methods are commonly used in marketing research. They consist of linkage methods, error sums of squares or variance methods, and centroid methods. **Linkage methods** include single linkage, complete linkage and average linkage. The **single linkage** method is based on minimum distance or the nearest neighbour rule. The first two objects clustered are those that have the smallest distance between them. The next shortest distance is identified, and either the third object is clustered with the first two or a new two-object cluster is formed. At every stage, the distance between two clusters is the distance between their two closest points (see Figure 12.11). Two clusters are merged at any stage by the single shortest link between them. This process is continued until all objects are in one cluster. The single linkage method does not work well when the clusters are poorly defined. The **complete linkage** method is similar to single linkage, except that it is based on the

Figure 12.10

A classification of clustering procedures

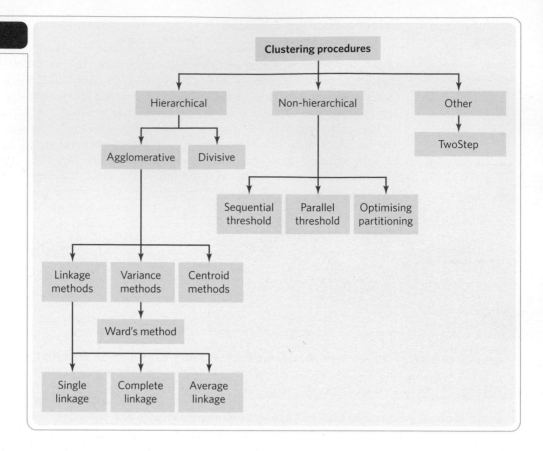

Figure 12.11

Linkage methods of clustering

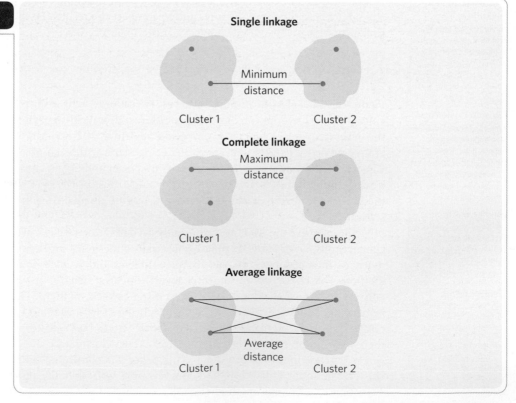

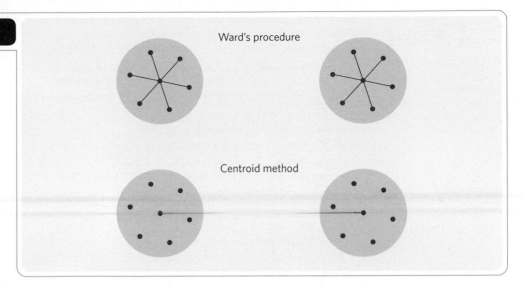

Figure 12.12

Other agglomerative clustering methods

Average linkage

A linkage method based on the average distance between all pairs of objects, where one member of the pair is from each of the clusters.

Variance method

An agglomerative method of hierarchical clustering in which clusters are generated to minimise the within-cluster variance.

Ward's procedure

A variance method in which the squared Euclidean distance to the cluster means is minimised.

Centroid method

A method of hierarchical clustering in which clusters are generated so as to maximise the distances between the centres or centroids of clusters.

Non-hierarchical clustering

A procedure that first assigns or determines a cluster centre and then groups all objects within a pre-specified threshold value from the centre(s).

Sequential threshold method

A non-hierarchical clustering method in which a cluster centre is selected and all objects within a pre-specified threshold value from the centre are grouped together.

Parallel threshold method

A non-hierarchical clustering method that specifies several cluster centres at once. All objects that are within a pre-specified threshold value from the centre are grouped together.

Optimising partitioning method

A non-hierarchical clustering method that allows for later reassignment of objects to clusters to optimise an overall criterion.

maximum distance or the farthest neighbour approach. In complete linkage, the distance between two clusters is calculated as the distance between their two farthest points (see Figure 12.11). The **average linkage** method works similarly. In this method, however, the distance between two clusters is defined as the average of the distances between all pairs of objects, where one member of the pair is from each of the clusters (Figure 12.11). As can be seen, the average linkage method uses information on all pairs of distances, not merely the minimum or maximum distances. For this reason, it is usually preferred to the single and complete linkage methods.

The **variance methods** attempts to generate clusters to minimise the within-cluster variance. A commonly used variance method is **Ward's procedure**. For each cluster, the means for all the variables are computed. Then, for each object, the squared Euclidean distance to the cluster means is calculated (Figure 12.12), and these distances are summed for all the objects. At each stage, the two clusters with the smallest increase in the overall sum of squares within cluster distances are combined. In the **centroid method**, the distance between two clusters is the distance between their centroids (means for all the variables), as shown in Figure 12.12. Every time objects are grouped, a new centroid is computed. Of the hierarchical methods, the average linkage method and Ward's procedure have been shown to perform better than the other procedures.[18]

The second type of clustering procedures, the **non-hierarchical clustering** methods, are frequently referred to as *k*-means clustering. These methods include sequential threshold, parallel threshold and optimising partitioning. In the **sequential threshold method**, a cluster centre is selected and all objects within a pre-specified threshold value from the centre are grouped together. A new cluster centre or seed is then selected, and the process is repeated for the unclustered points. Once an object is clustered with a seed, it is no longer considered for clustering with subsequent seeds. The **parallel threshold method** operates similarly except that several cluster centres are selected simultaneously and objects within the threshold level are grouped with the nearest centre. The **optimising partitioning method** differs from the two threshold procedures in that objects can later be reassigned to clusters to optimise an overall criterion, such as average within-cluster distance for a given number of clusters.

Two major disadvantages of the non-hierarchical procedures are that the number of clusters must be pre-specified and that the selection of cluster centres is arbitrary. Furthermore, the clustering results may depend on how the centres are selected. Many non-hierarchical programs select the first k cases ($k =$ number of clusters) without missing values as initial cluster centres. Thus, the clustering results may depend on the order of observations in the data. Yet non-hierarchical clustering is faster than hierarchical methods and has merit when the number of objects or observations is large. It has been suggested that the hierarchical and non-hierarchical methods be used in tandem. First, an initial clustering solution is obtained using a hierarchical procedure, such as average linkage or Ward's. The number of clusters and cluster centroids so obtained are used as inputs to the optimising partitioning method.[19]

The choice of a clustering method and the choice of a distance measure are interrelated. For example, squared Euclidean distances should be used with Ward's and the centroid methods. Several non-hierarchical procedures also use squared Euclidean distances. In the TwoStep procedure, the Euclidean measure can be used only when all of the variables are continuous.

We will use Ward's procedure to illustrate hierarchical clustering. The output obtained by clustering the data of Table 12.4 is given in Table 12.5. Useful information is contained in the agglomeration schedule, which shows the number of cases or clusters being combined at each stage. The first line represents stage 1, with 19 clusters. Participants 14 and 16 are combined at this stage, as shown in the columns labelled 'Clusters combined'. The squared Euclidean distance between these two participants is given under the column labelled 'Coefficients'. The column entitled 'Stage cluster first appears' indicates the stage at which a cluster is first formed. To illustrate, an entry of 1 at stage 6 indicates that participant 14 was first grouped at stage 1. The last column, 'Next stage', indicates the stage at which another case (participant) or cluster is combined with this one. Because the number in the first line of the last column is 6, we see that, at stage 6, participant 10 is combined with 14 and 16 to form a single cluster. Similarly, the second line represents stage 2 with 18 clusters. In stage 2, participants 6 and 7 are grouped together.

Another important part of the output is contained in the icicle plot given in Figure 12.13. The columns correspond to the objects being clustered; in this case, they are the participants labelled 1 to 20. The rows correspond to the number of clusters. This figure is read from bottom to top. At first, all cases are considered as individual clusters. Since there are 20 participants, there are 20 initial clusters. At the first step, the two closest objects are combined, resulting in 19 clusters. The last line of Figure 12.13 shows these 19 clusters. The two cases, participants 14 and 16, that have been combined at this stage have no blank space separating them. Row number 18 corresponds to the next stage, with 18 clusters. At this stage, participants 6 and 7 are grouped together. Thus, at this stage there are 18 clusters; 16 of them consist of individual participants, and 2 contain two participants each. Each subsequent step leads to the formation of a new cluster in one of three ways: (1) two individual cases are grouped together, (2) a case is joined to an already existing cluster, or (3) two clusters are grouped together.

Another graphic device that is useful in displaying clustering results is the dendrogram (see Figure 12.14). The dendrogram is read from left to right. Vertical lines represent clusters that are joined together. The position of the line on the scale indicates the distances at which clusters were joined. Because many distances in the early stages are of similar magnitude, it is difficult to tell the sequence in which some of the early clusters are formed. It is clear, however, that in the last two stages, the distances at which the clusters are being combined are large. This information is useful in deciding on the number of clusters.

It is also possible to obtain information on cluster membership of cases if the number of clusters is specified. Although this information can be discerned from the icicle plot, a tabular display is helpful. Table 12.5 contains the cluster membership for the cases, depending on whether the final solution contains two, three or four clusters. Information of this type can be obtained for any number of clusters and is useful for deciding on the number of clusters.

Table 12.5	Results of hierarchical clustering

CASE PROCESSING SUMMARY[a,b]

Valid		Missing		Total	
N	%	N	%	N	%
20	100.0	0	0.0	20	100.0

[a] Squared Euclidean distance used.

[b] Ward linkage.

WARD LINKAGE: AGGLOMERATION SCHEDULE

	Clusters combined			Stage cluster first appears		
Stage	Cluster 1	Cluster 2	Coefficients	Cluster 1	Cluster 2	Next stage
1	14	16	1.000	0	0	6
2	6	7	2.000	0	0	7
3	2	13	3.500	0	0	15
4	5	11	5.000	0	0	11
5	3	8	6.500	0	0	16
6	10	14	8.167	0	1	9
7	6	12	10.500	2	0	10
8	9	20	13.000	0	0	11
9	4	10	15.583	0	6	12
10	1	6	18.500	0	7	13
11	5	9	23.000	4	8	15
12	4	19	27.750	9	0	17
13	1	17	33.100	10	0	14
14	1	15	41.333	13	0	16
15	2	5	51.833	3	11	18
16	1	3	64.500	14	5	19
17	4	18	79.667	12	0	18
18	2	4	172.667	15	17	19
19	1	2	328.600	16	18	0

CLUSTER MEMBERSHIP

	Number of clusters		
Case	Four clusters	Three clusters	Two clusters
1	1	1	1
2	2	2	2
3	1	1	1
4	3	3	2
5	2	2	2
6	1	1	1
7	1	1	1
8	1	1	1
9	2	2	2
10	3	3	2
11	2	2	2
12	1	1	1
13	2	2	2
14	3	3	2
15	1	1	1
16	3	3	2
17	1	1	1
18	4	3	2
19	3	3	2
20	2	2	2

Figure 12.13	Vertical icicle plot using Ward's procedure

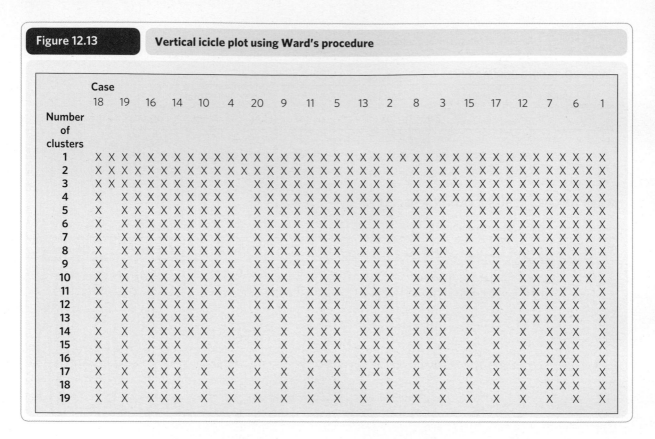

	Case																			
	18	19	16	14	10	4	20	9	11	5	13	2	8	3	15	17	12	7	6	1

Number of clusters

Figure 12.14	

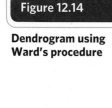

Dendrogram using Ward's procedure

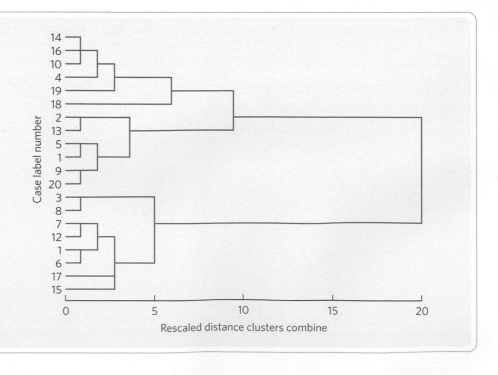

Decide on the number of clusters

A major issue in cluster analysis is deciding on the number of clusters. Although there are no hard and fast rules, some guidelines are available:

1 Theoretical, conceptual or practical considerations may suggest a certain number of clusters. For example, if the purpose of clustering is to identify market segments, decision makers may want a particular number of clusters.

2 In hierarchical clustering, the distances at which clusters are combined can be used as criteria. This information can be obtained from the agglomeration schedule or from the dendrogram. In our case, we see from the agglomeration schedule in Table 12.5 that the value in the 'Coefficients' column suddenly more than doubles between stages 17 (three clusters) and 18 (two clusters). Likewise, at the last two stages of the dendrogram in Figure 12.14, the clusters are being combined at large distances. Therefore, it appears that a three-cluster solution is appropriate.

3 In non-hierarchical clustering, the ratio of total within-group variance to between-group variance can be plotted against the number of clusters. The point at which an elbow or a sharp bend occurs indicates an appropriate number of clusters. Increasing the number of clusters beyond this point is usually not worthwhile.

4 The relative sizes of the clusters should be meaningful. In Table 12.5, by making a simple frequency count of cluster membership, we see that a three-cluster solution results in clusters with eight, six and six elements. If we go to a four-cluster solution, however, the sizes of the clusters are eight, six, five and one. It is not meaningful to have a cluster with only one case, so a three-cluster solution is preferable in this situation.

Interpret and profile clusters

Interpreting and profiling clusters involves examining the cluster centroids. The centroids represent the mean values of the objects contained in the cluster on each of the variables. The centroids enable us to describe each cluster by assigning it a name or label. If the clustering program does not print this information, it may be obtained through discriminant analysis. Table 12.6 gives the centroids or mean values for each cluster in our example. Cluster 1 has relatively high values on variables V_1 (Shopping is fun) and V_3 (I combine shopping with eating out). It also has a low value on V_5 (I don't care about shopping). Hence cluster 1 could be labelled 'fun-loving and concerned shoppers'. This cluster consists of cases 1, 3, 6, 7, 8, 12, 15 and 17. Cluster 2 is just the opposite, with low values on V_1 and V_3 and a high value on V_5; this cluster could be labelled 'apathetic shoppers'. Members of cluster 2 are cases 2, 5, 9, 11, 13 and 20. Cluster 3 has high values on V_2 (Shopping is bad for your budget), V_4 (I try to get the best buys while shopping) and V_6 (You can save a lot of money by comparing prices). Thus, this cluster could be labelled 'economical shoppers'. Cluster 3 is composed of cases 4, 10, 14, 16, 18 and 19.

Table 12.6	Cluster centroids					
	Means of variables					
Cluster number	V_1	V_2	V_3	V_4	V_5	V_6
1	5.750	3.625	6.000	3.125	1.750	3.875
2	1.667	3.000	1.833	3.500	5.500	3.333
3	3.500	5.833	3.333	6.000	3.500	6.000

It is often helpful to profile the clusters in terms of variables that were not used for clustering, such as demographic, psychographic, product usage, media usage or other variables. For example, the clusters may have been derived based on benefits sought. Further profiling may be done in terms of demographic and psychographic variables to target marketing efforts for each cluster. The variables that significantly differentiate between clusters can be identified via discriminant analysis and one-way analysis of variance.

Assess the reliability and validity

Given the several judgements entailed in cluster analysis, no clustering solution should be accepted without some assessment of its reliability and validity. Formal procedures for assessing the reliability and validity of clustering solutions are complex and not fully defensible.[20] Hence, we omit them here. The following procedures, however, provide adequate checks on the quality of clustering results. These are vital if decision makers are to appreciate what constitutes robust clustering solutions:[21]

1   Perform cluster analysis on the same data using different distance measures. Compare the results across measures to determine the stability of the solutions.

2   Use different methods of clustering and compare the results.

3   Split the data randomly into halves. Perform clustering separately on each half. Compare cluster centroids across the two subsamples.

4   Delete variables randomly. Perform clustering based on the reduced set of variables. Compare the results with those obtained by clustering based on the entire set of variables.

Factor analysis and cluster analysis in their various forms are widely used techniques as further illustrated in the following two examples. The first example illustrates an application of cluster analysis in the context of international marketing research. The second example shows how factor analysis can be used in researching ethical evaluations.

Real research   ## Thailand escapists[22]

In a study examining decision making patterns among international tourists, 260 participants provided information on six psychographic orientations: psychological, educational, social, relaxational, physiological, and aesthetic. Cluster analysis was used to group participants into psychographic segments. The results suggested that there were three meaningful segments based upon their lifestyles. The first segment (53 percent) consisted of individuals who were high on nearly all lifestyle scales. This group was called the 'demanders'. The second group (20 percent) was high on the educational scale and was named the 'educationalists', The last group (26 percent) was high on relaxation and low on social scales and was named the 'escapists', Specific marketing strategies were formulated to attract tourists in each segment. In order to recover  from the aftermath of the economic downturn in 2008-09, Thailand made a special effort to reach the 'escapists' as the country with its many relaxation opportunities and natural beauty would appeal the most to these tourists.

| | Real research | **Factors predicting unethical marketing research practices[23]** |

Unethical employee behaviour was identified as a root cause for the global banking and financial mess of 2008–09. If companies want ethical employees, then they themselves must conform to high ethical standards. This also applies to the marketing research industry. In order to identify organisational variables that are determinants of the incidence of unethical marketing research practices, a sample of 420 marketing professionals was surveyed. These marketing professionals were asked to provide responses on several scales, and to provide evaluations of incidence of 15 research practices that have found to pose research ethics problems. One of these scales included 11 items pertaining to the extent that ethical problems plagued the organisation, and what top management's actions were towards ethical situations. A principal components analysis with varimax rotation indicted that the data could be represented by two factors. These two factors were then used in a multiple regression along with four other predictor variables. They were found to be the two best predictors of unethical marketing research practices.

FACTOR ANALYSIS OF ETHICAL PROBLEMS AND TOP MANAGEMENT ACTION SCALES

	Extent of ethical problems within the organisation (Factor 1)	Top management actions on ethics (Factor 2)
1 Successful executives in my company make rivals look bad in the eys of important people in my company.	0.66	
2 Peer executives in my company often engage in behaviours that I considered to be unethical.	0.68	
3 There are many opportunities for peer executives in my company to engage in unethical behaviours.	0.43	
4 Successful executives in my company take credit for the ideas and accomplishment of others.	0.81	
5 In order to succeed in my company, it is often necessary to compromise one's ethics.	0.66	
6 Successful executives in my company are generally more unethical than unsuccessful executives.	0.64	
7 Successful executives in my company look for a 'scapegoat' when they feel they may be associated with failure.	0.78	
8 Successful executives in my company withold information that is detrimental to their self-interest.	0.68	
9 Top management in my company has let it be known in no uncertain terms that unethical behaviours will not be tolerated.		0.73
10 If an executive in my company is discovered to have engaged in unethical behaviour that results primarily in personal gain (rather than corporate gain), he/she will be promptly reprimanded.		0.80
11 If an executive in my company is discovered to have engaged in unethical behaviour that results primarily in corporate gain (rather than personal gain), he/she will be promptly reprimanded.		0.78

	Extent of ethical problems within the organisation (Factor 1)	Top management actions on ethics (Factor 2)
Eigenvalues	5.06	1.17
Percentage of explained variance	46%	11%
Coefficient Alpha	0.87	0.75

To simplify the table, only varimax rotated loadings of 0.40 or greater are reported. Each was rated on a 5-point scale with 1 = 'strongly agree' and 5 = 'strongly disagree'.

Summary

Factor analysis, also called exploratory factor analysis (EFA) is a class of procedures used for reducing and summarising data. Each variable is expressed as a linear combination of the underlying factors. Likewise, the factors themselves can be expressed as linear combinations of the observed variables. The factors are extracted in such a way that the first factor accounts for the highest variance in the data, the second the next highest, and so on. In formulating the factor analysis problem, the variables to be included in the analysis should be specified based on past research, theory and the judgement of the researcher. These variables should be measured on an interval or ratio scale. Factor analysis is based on a matrix of correlation between the variables. In common factor analysis, the factors are estimated based only on the common variance. This method is appropriate when the primary concern is to identify the underlying dimensions and when the common variance is of interest. This method is also known as principal axis factoring.

The number of factors that should be extracted can be determined a priori or based on eigenvalues, scree plots, percentage of variance, split-half reliability or significance tests. Although the initial or unrotated factor matrix indicates the relationships between the factors and individual variables, it seldom results in factors that can be interpreted, because the factors are correlated with many variables. Therefore, rotation is used to transform the factor matrix into a simpler one that is easier to interpret. The most commonly used method of rotation is the varimax procedure, which results in orthogonal factors. If the factors are highly correlated in the population, oblique rotation can be used. The rotated factor matrix forms the basis for interpreting the factors. Factor scores can be computed for each participant that may be used in subsequent multivariate analysis, for example by using cluster analysis to classify different consumer types.

Cluster analysis is used for classifying objects or cases, and sometimes variables, into relatively homogeneous groups. The groups or clusters are suggested by the data and are not defined a priori. The variables on which the clustering is based should be selected based on past research, theory, the hypotheses being tested, or the judgement of the researcher. An appropriate measure of distance or similarity should be selected. The most commonly used measure is the Euclidean distance or its square.

Clustering procedures may be hierarchical or non-hierarchical. Hierarchical clustering is characterised by the development of a hierarchy or treelike structure. Hierarchical methods can be agglomerative or divisive. Agglomerative methods consist of linkage methods, variance methods and centroid methods. Linkage methods are composed of single linkage, complete linkage and average linkage. A commonly used variance method is Ward's procedure. The non-hierarchical methods are frequently referred to as k-means clustering. These methods can be classified as sequential threshold, parallel threshold and optimising partitioning. Hierarchical and non-hierarchical methods can be used in tandem.

The number of clusters may be based on theoretical, conceptual or practical considerations. In hierarchical clustering, the distance at which the clusters are being combined is an important criterion. The relative sizes of the clusters should be meaningful. The clusters should be interpreted in terms of cluster centroids. It is often helpful to profile the clusters in terms of variables that were not used for clustering. The reliability and validity of the clustering solutions may be assessed in different ways.

SNAP Learning Edition

Factor and cluster analysis are both used to discover patterns in data. These patterns are commonly used in marketing research to identify groups of participants who think or behave in particular ways.

A survey generated in SNAP might typically contain a series of questions asking participants to express an opinion on different aspects of a product or service being evaluated. There may be dozens of such questions and spotting trends in such a long list of questions can be difficult; consequently factor analysis is used to reduce the meaning in a list of questions to one of a more manageable size.

The Crocodile survey supplied with SNAP includes a number of attitudinal questions along with several demographic questions, including age, gender and geographical location. The starting point for finding grouping is achieved by running factor analysis on the 5 attitudinal questions (Q6a to Q6e) rating various aspects of the service on a 5-point scale. The most important factors are then determined by selecting the cumulative proportions at a setting of 80%. These factors can then be used as the basis of subsequent analysis.

Factor Analysis Details

Name: FA1 Label: Factor Analysis FA1
Scale: Source: Q6.a to Q6.e
Cutoff Cumulative Proportion ▼ 80% Variables: 5 ☑ Transpose ☐ Varimax

Factor		1	2	3
Label		Food	Speed of Service	Cleanliness
Eigenvalue		1.852128	1.4486	0.810566
Proportion		37.0%	29.0%	16.2%
Cumulative Proportion		37.0%	66.0%	82.2%
Factor Loading	Speed of service	0.351372	0.584706	0.706979
	Cleanliness	0.321525	0.775681	-0.25336
	Parking	0.462932	-0.66482	0.39657
	Quality of food	0.84633	0.065056	-0.17731
	Choice of food	0.833491	-0.24252	-0.24052

A cross-tabulation of just the three most important factors (Food, Service and Cleanliness) can then be carried out against the demographics of age and gender to show mean scores for all combinations.

This shows that the Under-24 category were happier about the food (a positive score) than those 25 and over. It also showed that men were more critical of the cleanliness (a negative score) than the females.

Not Saved - fa1(1) to Fa1(3) by q9 with q10 showing means

Means Respondents	Base	Age						Gender	
		Under 18	18-24	25-34	35-44	45-54	55+	Male	Female
Base	-0.00	0.29	0.27	-0.26	-0.43	0.05	-0.52	-0.05	0.05
Food	-0.00	0.49	0.49	-0.72	-0.70	0.39	-0.56	0.20	-0.22
Speed of Service	0.00	0.49	0.19	0.16	-0.72	-0.30	-1.34	-0.19	0.22
Cleanliness	-0.00	-0.10	0.12	-0.21	0.12	0.07	0.35	-0.14	0.16

A further level of analysis can be achieved by carrying out a *t*-Test using the same variables. An option in SNAP's results definition dialog is selected to include 'Analysis Significance'. The table below now shows the results of *t*-Tests on the mean scores.

With many surveys having up to 50 variables, reducing the list to 6–7 key factors both reduces time and increases the accuracy of interpreting results.

Not Saved - fa1(1) to Fa1(3) by q9 with q10 showing means

Means Analysis Significance Respondents	Base	Age						Gender	
		A. Under 18	B. 18-24	C. 25-34	D. 35-44	E. 45-54	F. 55+	A. Male	B. Female
Base	-0.00	0.29	0.27	-0.26	-0.43	0.05	-0.52	-0.05	0.05
		--CD-F	--CD-F	AB----	AB----	-------	AB----	--	--
Food	-0.00	0.49	0.49	-0.72	-0.70	0.39	-0.56	0.20	-0.22
		--CD-f	--CD-f	AB--E-	AB--e-	--Cd--	ab----	-b	a-
Speed of Service	0.00	0.49	0.19	0.16	-0.72	-0.30	-1.34	-0.19	0.22
		---DeF	---D-F	---D-F	ABC---	a-----	ABC---	-b	a-
Cleanliness	-0.00	-0.10	0.12	-0.21	0.12	0.07	0.35	-0.14	0.16
		-------	--c---	-b----	-------	-------	-------	-b	a-

The key factors developed by using SNAP's factor analysis can then be used as the basis for cluster analysis, in order to identify patterns in the data that may not normally be obvious. Its object is to sort participants into groups, so that members of the same group have similar characteristics and differ from other groups.

The three factors generated in the previous example are input to SNAP's cluster analysis. The number of groups is preset to AUTO, but during the calculations, the software will determine how many identifiable groups or clusters exist. In this example, 6 groups or clusters have been identified.

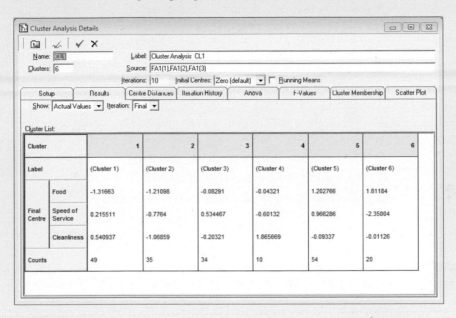

From within this same dialog box, a scatter plot can then be generated based on the six groups that have been identified. By default, these groups are named Cluster 1 to Cluster 6, but the labels can be manually updated to better reflect the participants in that group.

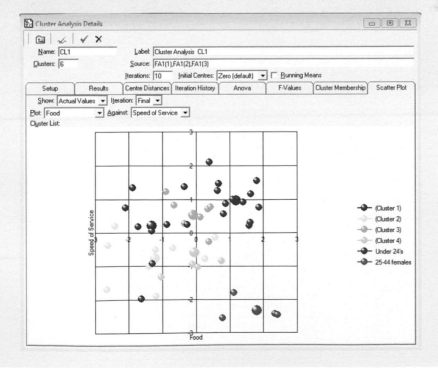

Questions

1 What are the major uses of factor analysis?

2 Briefly define the following: eigenvalue, factor loadings, factor matrix and factor scores.

3 Explain how eigenvalues are used to determine the number of factors.

4 What is a scree plot? For what purpose is it used?

5 Why is it useful to rotate the factors? Which is the most common method of rotation?

6 What guidelines are available for interpreting the factors?

7 What are some of the uses of cluster analysis in marketing?

8 Briefly define the following terms: dendrogram, icicle plot, agglomeration schedule and cluster membership.

9 What is the most commonly used measure of similarity in cluster analysis?

10 Upon what basis may a researcher decide which variables should be selected to formulate a clustering problem?

11 What guidelines are available for deciding the number of clusters?

12 What is involved in the interpretation of clusters?

Exercises

1 In a study of the relationship between household behaviour and shopping behaviour, data on the following lifestyle statements were obtained on a seven-point scale (1 = disagree, 7 = agree):

V_1 I would rather spend a quiet evening at home than go out to a party.
V_2 I always check prices, even on small items.
V_3 Magazines are more interesting than movies.
V_4 I would not buy products advertised on billboards.
V_5 I am a homebody.
V_6 I save vouchers and cash coupons.
V_7 Companies waste a lot of money advertising.

The data obtained from a pretest sample of 25 participants are given below:

No.	V_1	V_2	V_3	V_4	V_5	V_6	V_7
1	6	2	7	6	5	3	5
2	5	7	5	6	6	6	4
3	5	3	4	5	6	6	7
4	3	2	2	5	1	3	2
5	4	2	3	2	2	1	3
6	2	6	2	4	3	7	5
7	1	3	3	6	2	5	7
8	3	5	1	4	2	5	6
9	7	3	6	3	5	2	4
10	6	3	3	4	4	6	5
11	6	6	2	6	4	4	7
12	3	2	2	7	6	1	6
13	5	7	6	2	2	6	1

No.	V_1	V_2	V_3	V_4	V_5	V_6	V_7
14	6	3	5	5	7	2	3
15	3	2	4	3	2	6	5
16	2	7	5	1	4	5	2
17	3	2	2	7	2	4	6
18	6	4	5	4	7	3	3
19	7	2	6	2	5	2	1
20	5	6	6	3	4	5	3
21	2	3	3	2	1	2	6
22	3	4	2	1	4	3	6
23	2	6	3	2	1	5	3
24	6	5	7	4	5	7	2
25	7	6	5	4	6	5	3

  (a) Analyse these data using factor analysis, using the varimax rotation procedure.
  (b) Interpret the factors extracted.
  (c) Calculate factor scores for each participant.
  (d) Examine the model fit.

2 You are a marketing research analyst for a manufacturer of fashion clothing targeted at teenage boys. You have been asked to develop a set of 10 statements for measuring psychographic characteristics and lifestyles that you feel would relate to their fashion personas. The participants would be asked to indicate their degree of agreement with the statements using a seven-point scale (1 = completely disagree, 7 = completely agree). Question 40 students on campus using these scale items. Factor analyse the data to identify the underlying psychographic factors.

3 In a survey pretest, data were obtained from 45 participants on Benetton clothes. These data are given in the table below, which gives the gender, awareness, attitude, preference, intention and loyalty towards Benetton of a sample of Benetton users. Gender was coded as 1 for females and 2 for males. Awareness, attitude, preference, intention and loyalty were measured on a 7-point Likert-type scale (1 = very unfavourable, 7 = very favourable). Note that 5 participants have missing values that are denoted by 9.

Number	Gender	Awareness	Attitude	Preference	Intention	Loyalty
1	2	7	6	5	5	6
2	1	2	2	4	6	5
3	1	3	3	6	7	6
4	2	6	5	5	3	2
5	2	5	4	7	4	3
6	2	4	3	5	2	3
7	1	5	4	4	3	2
8	1	2	1	3	4	5
9	2	4	4	3	6	5
10	1	3	1	2	4	5
11	2	6	7	6	4	5
12	2	6	5	6	4	4

Number	Gender	Awareness	Attitude	Preference	Intention	Loyalty
13	1	4	3	3	1	1
14	2	6	4	5	3	2
15	2	4	3	4	5	6
16	2	3	4	2	4	2
17	1	7	6	4	5	3
18	1	6	5	4	3	2
19	1	1	1	3	4	5
20	1	5	7	4	1	2
21	2	6	6	7	7	5
22	2	2	3	1	4	2
23	1	1	1	3	2	2
24	1	6	7	6	7	6
25	2	3	2	2	1	1
26	2	5	3	4	4	5
27	2	7	6	6	5	7
28	1	6	4	2	5	6
29	1	9	2	3	1	3
30	2	5	9	4	6	5
31	2	1	2	9	3	2
32	2	4	6	5	9	3
33	1	3	4	3	2	9
34	1	4	6	5	7	6
35	1	5	7	7	3	3
36	1	6	5	7	3	4
37	2	6	7	5	3	4
38	2	5	6	4	3	2
39	2	7	7	6	3	4
40	1	4	3	4	6	5
41	1	2	3	4	5	6
42	1	1	3	2	3	4
43	1	2	4	3	6	7
44	1	3	3	4	6	5
45	1	1	1	4	5	3

Consider the following variables: awareness, attitude, preference, intention and loyalty towards Benetton. Cluster the participants based on these variables using hierarchical clustering. How many clusters do you recommend and why?

4   You are a marketing research analyst for a major airline. You have been set the task of determining consumers' attitudes towards budget airlines. Construct a 15-item scale for this purpose. In a group of 5 students, obtain data on this scale and standard demographic characteristics from 25 male and 25 females in your community. These data should then be used to cluster participants and to cluster the 15 variables measuring consumer attitudes to budget airlines.

5   In a small group discuss 'user-friendly statistical packages can create cluster solutions in situations where naturally occurring clusters do not exist' and

identify the uses of factor analysis in each of the following major decision areas in marketing:

(a) Market segmentation

(b) Product decisions

(c) Promotion decisions

(d) Pricing decisions

(e) Distribution decisions

(f) Service delivery decisions.

Notes

1. Magnusson, P.R., 'Benefits of involving users in service innovation', *European Journal of Innovation Management*, 6 (4) (2003), 228–38; Alt, M., *Exploring Hyperspace* (New York: McGraw-Hill, 1990), 74.

2. For a detailed discussion of factor analysis, see Loehlin, J.C., *Latent variable models: An introduction to factor, path, and structural equation analysis* (Mahwah, NJ: Lawrence Erlbaum Associates, 2004); Tacq, J., *Multivariate Analysis Techniques in Social Science Research* (Thousand Oaks, CA: Sage, 1996); Dunteman, G.H., *Principal Components Analysis* (Newbury Park, CA: Sage, 1989). For applications, see Aaker, J.L., 'Dimensions of brand personality', *Journal of Marketing Research*, 34 (August 1997), 347–56; Birks, D.F. and Birts, A.N., 'Service quality in domestic cash management banks', in Birks, D.F. (ed.) *Global Cash Management in Europe* (Basingstoke: Macmillan, 1998), 175–205. See also Cudeck, R. and MacCallum, R.C., *Factor analysis at 100: Historical developments and future directions* (Mahwah, NJ: Lawrence Erlbaum Associates, 2007).

3. See Cudeck, R. and MacCallum, R.C., *Factor analysis at 100: Historical developments and future directions* (Mahwah, NJ: Lawrence Erlbaum Associates, 2007); Pett, M.A., Lackey, N. and Sullivan, J., *Making sense of factor analysis: The use of factor analysis for instrument development in health care research* (Thousand Oaks, CA: Sage, 2006); Ding, A.A., 'Prediction intervals, factor analysis models and high-dimensional empirical linear prediction,' *Journal of the American Statistical Association*, 94 (446) (June 1999), 446–55; Gaur, S., 'Adelman and Morris factor analysis of developing countries', *Journal of Policy Modeling*, 19 (4) (August 1997), 407–15; Lastovicka, J.L. and Thamodaran, K., 'Common factor score estimates in multiple regression problems', *Journal of Marketing Research*, 28 (Feb. 1991), 105–112; Dillon, W.R. and Goldstein, M., *Multivariate Analysis: Methods and Applications* (New York: Wiley, 1984), 23–99.

4. For applications of factor analysis, see Logan, K., 'Hulu .com or NBC? Streaming videos versus traditional TV: A study of an industry in its infancy' *Journal of Advertising Research*, 51 (1) (2011), 276–87' Vanden Bergh, B.G., Lee, M., Quilliam, E.T. and Hove, T., 'The multidimensional nature and brand impact of user-generated ad parodies in social media', *International Journal of Advertising*, 30, (1) (2011), 103–131; Bellman, S., Schweda, A. and Varan, D., 'The importance of social motives for watching and interacting with digital television', *International Journal of Market Research*, 52 (1) (2010), 67–87.

5. Child, D., *The essentials of factor analysis*, 3rd edn (New York: Continuum, 2006); Bartholomew, D.J. and Knott, M., *Latent variable models and factor analysis* (London: Edward Arnold, 1999); Hair J.E. Jr, Anderson, R.E., Tatham, R.L. and Black, W.C., *Multivariate Data Analysis with Readings*, 5th edn (Englewood Cliffs, NJ: Prentice Hall, 1999), 364–419; Basilevsky, A., *Statistical Factor Analysis and Related Methods: Theory and Applications* (New York: Wiley, 1994).

6. Factor analysis is influenced by the relative size of the correlations rather than the absolute size.

7. See Wu, J., DeSarbo, W., Chen, P-J. Fu, Y-Y., 'A latent structure factor analytic approach for customer satisfaction measurement', *Marketing Letters*, 17 (3) (July 2006), 221–37; Henderson, P.W., Giese, J.L. and Cote, J., 'Impression management using typeface design', *Journal of Marketing*, 68 (Oct. 2004), 60–72; Kamakura, W.A. and Wedel, M., 'Factor analysis and missing data', *Journal of Marketing Research*, 37 (4) (Nov. 2000), 490–498; Roberts, J.A. and Beacon, D.R., 'Exploring the subtle relationships between environmental concern and ecologically conscious behavior', *Journal of Business Research*, 40 (1) (Sept. 1997), 79–89; Chatterjee, S., Jamieson, L. and Wiseman, F., 'Identifying most influential observations in factor analysis', *Marketing Science* (Spring 1991), 145–60; Acito, F. and Anderson, R.D., 'A Monte Carlo comparison of factor analytic methods', *Journal of Marketing Research*, 17 (May 1980), 228–36.

8. Other methods of orthogonal rotation are also available. The quartimax method minimises the number of factors needed to explain a variable. The equimax method is a combination of varimax and quartimax.

9. Slavens, R., 'Häagen-Dazs tastes success with Crème de la Crème campaign', *B to B*, 92 (1) (Jan. 2007), 23; Reynolds, E., 'Is Häagen-Dazs shrewd to drop its sexy image?' *Marketing* (6 Sept. 2001), 17; Stuart, L., 'Häagen-Dazs aims to scoop a larger share', *Marketing Week*, 19 (46/2) (21 Feb. 1997), 26.

10. For applications of cluster analysis, see Bassi, F., 'Latent class factor models for market segmentation: An application to pharmaceuticals', *Statistical Methods and Applications*, 16 (2) (Jan. 2007), 279–87; Mathwick, C. and Rigdon, E., 'Play, flow, and the online search experience', *Journal of Consumer Research*, 31 (Sept. 2004), 324–32;

Moe, W.W. and Fader, P.S., 'Modeling hedonic portfolio products: A joint segmentation analysis of music compact disc sales', *Journal of Marketing Research*, 38 (3) (August 2001), 376–88; Arimond, G., 'A clustering method for categorical data in tourism market segmentation research', *Journal of Travel Research*, 39 (4) (May 2001), 391–97; Birks, D.F. and Birts, A.N., 'Cash management market segmentation', in Birks, D.F. (ed.) *Global Cash Management in Europe* (Basingstoke: Macmillan, 1998), 83–109.

11. Overlapping clustering methods that permit an object to be grouped into more than one cluster are also available. See Curry, B., Davies, F., Evans, M., Moutinho, L. and Phillips, P., 'The Kohonen self-organising map as an alternative to cluster analysis: An application to direct marketing', *International Journal of Market Research*, 45 (2) (Feb. 2003), 191–211; Chaturvedi, A., Carroll, J.D., Green, P.E. and Rotondo, J.A., 'A feature based approach to market segmentation via overlapping *k*-centroids clustering', *Journal of Marketing Research*, 34 (August 1997), 370–77.

12. Excellent discussions on the various aspects of cluster analysis may be found in Abonyi, J. and Feil, B., *Cluster Analysis for data mining and system identification* (Basel: Birkhäuser, 2007); Kaufman, L. and Rousseeuw, P.J., *Finding groups in data: An introduction to cluster analysis* (Hoboken, NJ: John Wiley & Sons, 2005); Romsburg, H.C., *Cluster Analysis for Researchers* (Melbourne: Krieger, 2004); Everitt, B.S., Landau, S. and Leese, M., *Cluster Analysis*, 4th edn (Oxford: Oxford University Press, 2001).

13. Ali, J., 'Micro-market segmentation using a neural network model approach', *Journal of International Consumer Marketing* (2001), 7; Douglas, V., 'Questionnaires too long? Try variable clustering', *Marketing News* 29 (5) (27 Feb. 1995), 38; Punj, G. and Stewart, D., 'Cluster analysis in marketing research: Review and suggestions for application', *Journal of Marketing Research*, 20 (May 1983), 134–48.

14. For use of cluster analysis for segmentation, see Tuma, M.N., Decker, R. and Scholz, S.W., 'A survey of the challenges and pitfalls of cluster analysis application in market segmentation', *International Journal of Market Research*, 53 (3) (2011), 391–414; Clark, J., Jones, S., Romanou, E. and Harrison, M., 'Segments, hugs and rock 'n' roll: An attitudinal segmentation of parents and young people', Market Research Society, *Annual Conference* (2009).

15. Caragea, P.C. and Smith, R.L., 'Asymptotic properties of computationally efficient alternative estimators for a class of multivariate normal models', *Journal of Multivariate Analysis*, 98 (104) (August 2007), 1417–40; Sambandam, R., 'Cluster analysis gets complicated', *Marketing Research* (Spring 2003), 16–21; Everitt, B.S., Landau, S. and Leese, M., *Cluster Analysis*, 4th edn (Oxford: Oxford University Press, 2001).

16. For a detailed discussion on the different measures of similarity, and formulae for computing them, see Brandt, C., de Mortanges, C.P., Bluemelhuber, C. and van Riel, A.C.R., 'Associative networks: A new approach to market segmentation', *International Journal of Market Research*, 53 (2) (2011), 189–210; Bradlow, E.T., 'Subscale distance and item clustering effects in self-administered surveys: A new metric', *Journal of Marketing Research* (May 2001), 254–61; Chepoi, V. and Dragan, F., 'Computing a median point of a simple rectilinear polygon', *Information Processing Letters*, 49 (6) (22 March 1994),

281–85; Romsburg, H.C., *Cluster Analysis for Researchers* (Belmont, CA: Lifetime Learning, 1984).

17. For further discussion of the issues involved in standardisation, see Hair, J.E. Jr, Anderson, R.E., Tatham, R.L. and Black, W.C., *Multivariate Data Analysis with Readings*, 5th edn (Englewood Cliffs, NJ: Prentice Hall, 1999), 364–419; Romsburg, H.C., *Cluster Analysis for Researchers* (Melbourne: Krieger, 1990).

18. Everitt, B.S., Landau, S. and Leese, M., *Cluster Analysis*, 4th edn (Oxford: Oxford University Press, 2001); Johnson, R.A. and Wichern, D.W., *Applied Multivariate Statistical Analysis*, 5th edn (Paramus, NJ: Prentice Hall, 2001); Milligan, G., 'An examination of the effect of six types of error perturbation on fifteen clustering algorithms', *Psychometrika*, 45 (Sept. 1980), 325–42.

19. MacLachlan, D.L. and Mulhern, M.G., 'Segment optimization: An empirical comparison', ESOMAR, *Marketing Conference*, Warsaw (Oct. 2004); Everitt, B.S., Landau, S. and Leese, M., *Cluster Analysis*, 4th edn (Oxford: Oxford University Press, 2001); Punj, G. and Stewart, D., 'Cluster analysis in marketing research: Reviews and suggestions for application', *Journal of Marketing Research*, 20 (May 1983), 134–48.

20. For a formal discussion of reliability, validity and significance testing in cluster analysis, see Barnes, S., Bauer, H.H., Neumann, M.M. and Huber, F., 'Segmenting Cyberspace: A customer typology for the Internet', *European Journal of Marketing*, 41 (1/2) (2007), 71–93; Brusco, M.J., Cradit, J.D. and Stahl, S., 'A simulated annealing heuristic for a bicriterion partitioning problem in market segmentation', *Journal of Marketing Research*, 39 (1) (Feb. 2002), 99–109; Chen, H.-M., 'Using clustering techniques to detect usage patterns in a web-based information system', *Journal of the American Society for Information Science and Technology*, 52 (11) (Sept. 2001), 888; Dibbs, S. and Stern, P., 'Questioning the reliability of market segmentation techniques', *Omega*, 23 (6) (Dec. 1995), 625–36; Funkhouser, G.R., 'A note on the reliability of certain clustering algorithms', *Journal of Marketing Research*, 30 (Feb. 1983), 99–102; Klastorin, T.D., 'Assessing cluster analysis results', *Journal of Marketing Research*, 20 (Feb. 1983), 92–98; Arnold, S.J., 'A test for clusters', *Journal of Marketing Research*, 16 (Nov. 1979), 545–51.

21. Bottomley, P. and Nairn, A., 'Blinded by science: The managerial consequences of inadequately validated cluster analysis solutions,' *International Journal of Market Research*, 46 (2) (2004), 171–87.

22. Hyde, K.F., 'Contemporary information search strategies of destination-naïve international vacationers', *Journal of Travel and Tourism Marketing*, 21 (2/3) (2006), 63–76; Brown, T. J., Qu, H. and Rittichainuwat, B.N., 'Thailand's international travel image: Mostly favourable', *Cornell Hotel and Restaurant Administration Quarterly*, 42 (2) (April 2001), 85–95.

23. Rittenburg, T., Valentine, S. and Faircloth, J., 'An ethical decision making framework for competitor intelligence gathering', *Journal of Business Ethics*, 70 (3) (Feb. 2007), 235–45; Akaah, I.P and Riordan, E.A., 'The incidence of unethical practices in marketing research: An empirical investigation', *Journal of the Academy of Marketing Science*, 18 (1990), 143–52.

24. Although F-values can be used as an indicator of how many cluster groups should be specified, it is not advisable to rely exclusively on this measure.

13 Report preparation and presentation

Stage 1

Problem definition

Stage 2

Research approach developed

Stage 3

Research design developed

Stage 4

Fieldwork or data collection

Stage 5

Data integrity and analysis

Stage 6

Report preparation and presentation

Managers should find reports easy to understand, be confident in the findings, and be clear about the action they should take, based on the researcher's approach, insight and integrity.

Objectives

After reading this chapter, you should be able to:

1 discuss the basic requirements of report preparation, including report format, report writing, graphs and tables;

2 discuss the nature and scope of the oral presentation;

3 describe the approach to the marketing research report from a decision maker's perspective;

4 explain the reason for follow-up with decision makers and describe the assistance that should be given to decision makers and the evaluation of the research project;

5 understand the report preparation and presentation process in international marketing research;

6 identify the ethical issues related to the interpretation and reporting of the research process and findings;

7 appreciate how digital developments are shaping the manner in which reports may be designed, delivered and experienced.

Overview

Here we describe the importance of report preparation and presentation and outline the process of producing written and oral presentations. We provide guidelines for report preparation, including report writing and preparing tables and graphs. We discuss the nature and characteristics of successful oral research presentations. Research follow-up, including assisting decision makers and evaluating the research process, is described. The special considerations for report preparation and presentation in international marketing research are discussed, and relevant ethical issues are identified. We conclude by examining how digital developments can help in the design of more engaging reports for research users and decision makers.

We begin with an example of how the BMW Group devised an innovative and engaging means to convey the findings of a large complex study. This case illustrates that researchers have to go beyond just feeding decision makers with research findings, to find a reporting format that is relevant, engaging, and credible to decision makers.

Real research	Visualising future consumers[1]

A client approached BMW Group Designworks (**www.bmwgroup.com**) with the following brief:

> Devise a method to transfer 2,000 pages of research content, communicating very new consumer environments in under an hour to 15,000 corporate knowledge workers.

The research they were asked to communicate represented a very large study on changes in consumer behaviour in the future. As part of the study, researchers created text-based scenarios around personas from different age segments, and tested the communication impact on a small sample of the target audience. They designed four short films to act as 'visual management summaries', communicating the most important five to seven points for different future timeframes. Another 40–50 supporting points per timeframe were woven into dialogue or communicated visually in set, action sequences, costume design, or graphic effects. The four films were digitised and integrated into an interactive CD-ROM, acting as 'visual hooks' to get viewers engaged with the data. The CD-ROM contained the entire body of research for reference, and was organised to parallel the structural aspects of the key points. The films were structured as interviews with consumers typical of an age and timeframe. Set against black backgrounds for neutrality, the characters answered questions in a way that implied an off-screen narrator, delivering the audience observations on their behaviours and values. As the characters talked, their observations were shown in live action scenes, which were cut into the studio footage. When a key point was reached, it was punctuated either through sound (a narrated voice over), visuals (graphic overlays) or pacing (shift in flow). They used a variety of techniques to juxtapose the present and the future in these films. The work was tested iteratively during development to ensure the general approach and the specific techniques were creating the intended impact and increased retention. They searched for techniques that had transferability, and tested these on sample members of development and marketing teams including engineers, general managers, researchers, designers and financial controllers.

Importance of the report and presentation

For the following reasons, the report and its presentation are important parts of the marketing research project:

1 They are the tangible products of the research effort. After the project is complete and decisions have been made, there is little documentary evidence of the project other than the written report. The report serves as a historical record of the project.

2 Management decisions are guided by the report and the presentation. If the first five stages in the project are carefully conducted but inadequate attention is paid to the sixth stage, the value of the project to decision makers will be greatly diminished.

3 The involvement of many decision makers in a research project is limited to the written report and the oral presentation. These individuals evaluate the quality of the entire project on the quality of the report and presentation.

4 Decision makers' decision to undertake marketing research in the future or to use the particular research supplier again will be influenced by the perceived usefulness of the report and the presentation.

The above factors of importance seem self evident, but many researchers fail to heed this advice. The following quote encapsulates the environment in which researchers have to engage decision makers.

> *In today's ever more complex and fragmenting business environment one thing is clear. Everyone is time pressured, low attention spans are prevalent and if you have something to say, often you have to say it clearly and concisely. And just to make things even more difficult, real 'face time' with clients is at a premium and importantly the synopsis of a research study is most often widely distributed and communicated in a written form primarily by email and the dreaded PowerPoint.*[2]

There has long been criticism of how researchers fail to appreciate the needs of decision makers and engage them in presenting reports. It has been argued that the barriers between researchers and decision makers have grown due to the following factors:[3]

- **Overload**. Decision makers can be overloaded with marketing research, which can mean large numbers of presentations and meetings every month. As well as marketing research, there is an increasing amount of other data that decision makers have to deal with, including financial reports, information systems data, corporate news feeds and other intelligence sources.

- **Pace of work**. The pace of work has increased; this is driven in part by personal technology, adoption of other countries' working practices and also by increased competition. Distractions add to this pace with a 'Blackberry culture' meaning that decision makers get easily distracted with exacerbated short attention spans.
- **Quality**. Researchers making presentations of variable quality; sometimes they are too long (100-page presentations are still being produced), sometimes they are badly presented, sometimes they are not very easy to understand and lack a point of view and/or insight – and sometimes they are just plain boring.

Researchers need to appreciate the context and manner in which decision makers use information. Based upon this appreciation, they need to address the quality of their written (be that digital or hard copy) reports and their oral presentations. If decision makers view researchers responsible for poor quality presentations that do not address their needs and/or engage them, their credibility can be seriously harmed.

Preparation and presentation process

To develop high quality presentations, we begin by examining the report preparation and presentation process; this is illustrated in Figure 13.1. The process begins by interpreting the results of data analysis in the light of the marketing research problem, approach, research design and fieldwork. Instead of merely summarising the quantitative and/or qualitative analyses, the researcher should present the findings in such a way that they can be used directly as input into decision making. Wherever appropriate, conclusions should be drawn and recommendations made. The researcher should aim to make the recommendations actionable.

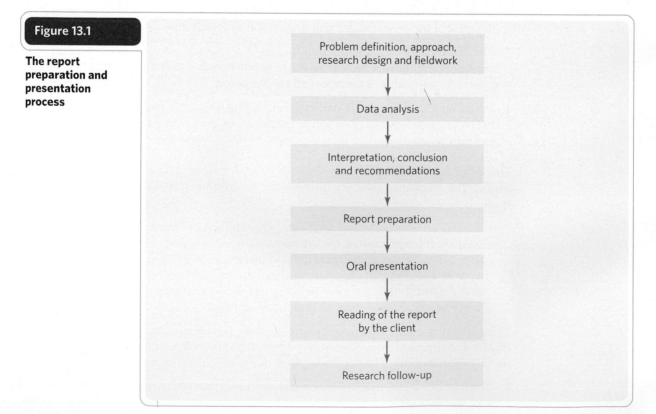

Figure 13.1

The report preparation and presentation process

Before writing the report, the researcher should discuss the major findings, conclusions and recommendations with the key decision makers. These discussions play a major role in ensuring that the report meets the decision makers' needs and is ultimately accepted. These discussions should confirm specific dates for the delivery of the written report and other data.

The entire marketing research project should be summarised in a single written report or in several reports addressed to different readers. Generally, an oral presentation supplements the written documents. Decision makers should be given an opportunity to read the report. After that, the researcher should take the necessary follow-up actions. The researcher should assist decision makers in understanding the report, help in interpretations of the findings that can affect their implementation, offer to undertake further research and reflect upon the research process to evaluate its overall worth.

Report preparation

Researchers differ in the way they prepare a research report. The personality, background, expertise and responsibility of the researcher, along with the decision maker to whom the report is addressed, interact to give each report a unique character. Yet there are guidelines for formatting and writing reports and designing tables and graphs.[4]

Report format

Report formats are likely to vary with the researcher or the research firm conducting the project, the decision makers for whom the project is being conducted, and the nature of the project itself. Hence, the following is intended as a guide from which the researcher can develop a format for the research project at hand. Most research reports include the following elements:

1 Submission letter

2 Title page

3 Table of contents

   (a) Main sections

   (b) List of tables

   (c) List of graphs

   (d) List of appendices

   (e) List of exhibits

4 Executive summary

   (a) Summary of prime objectives

   (b) Major findings

   (c) Conclusions and recommendations

5 Problem definition

   (a) Background to the problem

   (b) Statement of the marketing problem

   (c) Statement of the research objectives – information needs

6 Approach to the problem and research design

   (a) Type of research design

   (b) Data collection from secondary sources

   (c) Data collection from primary sources

7 Data analysis

   (a) Research design

   (b) Plan of data analysis and means of interpreting results

8 Results

9 Conclusions and recommendations

10 Limitations and caveats

11 Appendices

   (a) Letter of authorisation

   (b) Questionnaire development and pretesting

   (c) Questionnaires, forms, interview guides

   (d) Sampling techniques, including error and confidence levels

   (e) Fieldwork

   (f) Lists including contact individuals and organisations.

This format closely follows the earlier stages of the marketing research process. The results may be presented in several chapters of the report. For example, in a domestic or international survey, data analysis may be conducted for the overall sample and then the data for each geographical region may be analysed separately. If so, the results from each analysis may be presented in a separate chapter.

Submission letter A formal report generally contains a letter of submission that delivers the report to decision makers and summarises the researcher's overall experience with the project, without mentioning the findings. The letter should also identify the need for further action on the part of decision makers, such as implementation of the findings or further research that should be undertaken.

Title page The title page should include the title of the report, information (name, address and telephone number) about the researcher or organisation conducting the research, the name of the decision makers for whom the report was prepared, and the date of release. The title should encapsulate the nature of the project with a tone that is meaningful to the target decision makers, not one of technical 'research-speak'.

Table of contents The table of contents should list the topics covered and the appropriate page numbers. In most reports, only the major headings and subheadings are included. The table of contents is followed by a list of tables, a list of graphs, a list of appendices and a list of exhibits.

Executive summary The executive summary is of vital importance in a report. In many instance this may be the only portion of the report that decision makers read. The summary should concisely describe the problem, approach and research design that was adopted. A summary section should be devoted to the major results, conclusions and recommendations. The executive summary should be written after the rest of the report has been written.

Problem definition The problem definition section of the report gives the background to the problem. This part summarises elements of the marketing and research problem diagnosis. Key elements of any discussions with decision makers, industry experts and initial secondary data analyses are presented. Having set this context for the whole project, a clear statement of the marketing decision problem(s) and the marketing research problem(s) should be presented.

Approach to the problem and research design The approach to the problem section should discuss the broad approach that was adopted in addressing the problem. This section should summarise the theoretical foundations that guided the research, any analytical models formulated, research questions, hypotheses and the factors that influenced the research design. The research design should specify the details of how the research was conducted, preferably with a graphical presentation of the stages undertaken, showing the relationships between stages. This should detail the methods undertaken in the data collection from secondary and primary sources. These topics should be presented in a non-technical, easy-to-understand manner. The technical details should be included in an appendix. This section of the report should justify the specific methods selected.

Data analysis The section on data analysis, be it quantitative or qualitative, should describe the plan of data analysis and justify the data analysis strategy and techniques used. The techniques used for analysis should be described in simple, non-technical terms, with examples to guide the reader through the interpretations.

Results The results section is normally the longest part of the report and may entail several chapters. It may be presented in any of the following ways:

1 *Forms of analysis.* For example, in a health care marketing survey of hospitals, the results were presented in four chapters. One chapter presented the overall results, another examined the differences between geographical regions, a third presented the differences between for-profit and non-profit hospitals, and a fourth presented the differences according to bed capacity. Often, results are presented not only at the aggregate level but also at the subgroup level (market segment, geographical area, etc.).

2 *Forms of data collection.* For example, a study may contain significant elements of secondary data collection and analyses, a series of focus group interviews and a survey. The results in such circumstances may be best presented by drawing conclusions from one method before moving on to another method. The conclusions derived from focus groups, for example, may need to be established to show the link to a sample design and questions used in a survey.

3 *Objectives.* There may be a series of research objectives whose fulfilment may incorporate a variety of data collection methods and levels of analysis. In these circumstances the results combine methods and levels of analyses to show connections and to develop and illustrate emerging issues.

The results should be organised in a coherent and logical way. Choosing whether to present by *forms of analysis, forms of data collection,* or *objectives* helps to build that coherence and logic. The presentation of the results should be geared directly to the components of the marketing research problem and the information needs that were diagnosed in the initial research brief and proposal. The nature of the information needs and characteristics of the recipients of the report ultimately determine the best way to present results.

Conclusions and recommendations Presenting a mere summary of the quantitative or qualitative findings is not enough for most marketing research users. The researcher should interpret the results in light of the problem being addressed to arrive at major conclusions. Based on the results and conclusions, the researcher may make recommendations to decision makers. Sometimes, researchers are not asked to make recommendations because they research only one area and do not understand the bigger picture of a sponsoring organisation.

The researcher may not have been fully involved in the diagnosis of the marketing and research problems, in which case the researcher's interpretations may not fit into the context that the decision maker understands.

In any research project there are many approaches that can be taken to analyse the data. This can result in a potential overabundance of data (quantitative and/or qualitative), and distilling the 'meaning' from the data and presenting this in a clear report can result in much of the original meaning or richness being lost.[5] To maintain the meaning or richness, the researcher should strive to understand the nature of the decision making process that is being supported. Only then can sound interpretations of the collected data be made.

Limitations and caveats All marketing research projects have limitations caused by time, budget and other organisational constraints. Furthermore, the research design adopted may be limited in terms of the various types of errors, and some of these may be serious enough to warrant discussion. This section should be written with great care and a balanced perspective. On the one hand, the researcher must make sure that decision makers do not rely too heavily on the results or use them for unintended purposes, such as projecting them to unintended populations. On the other hand, this section should not erode decision makers' confidence in the research or unduly minimise its importance.

Appendices At the end of the report, documents can be compiled that may be used by different readers to help them to understand characteristics of the research project in more detail. These should include the letter of authorisation to conduct the research; this authorisation could include the agreed research proposal. Details that relate to individual techniques should be included relating to questionnaires, interview guides, sampling and fieldwork activities. The final part of the appendix should include lists of contacts, references used and further sources of reference.

Report writing

Readers A report should be written for a specific reader or readers: namely, the decision makers who will use the results. The report should take into account the readers' technical sophistication and interest in the project as well as the circumstances under which they will read the report and how they will use it.[6]

Technical jargon should be avoided unless the researcher is absolutely sure of the technical abilities and demands of the readers of a report. As expressed by one expert, 'The readers of your reports are busy people; and very few of them can balance a research report, a cup of coffee, and a dictionary at one time.'[7] Instead of technical terms such as maximum likelihood, heteroscedasticity and non-parametric, researchers should try to use descriptive explanations. If some technical terms cannot be avoided, definitions should be presented in a glossary or appendix. When it comes to marketing research, decision makers would rather live with a problem they cannot solve than accept a solution they cannot understand. Often the researcher must cater to the needs of several audiences with different levels of technical sophistication and interest in the project. Such conflicting needs may be met by including different sections in the report for different readers or separate reports entirely.

Easy to follow The report should be easy to follow.[8] It should be structured logically and written clearly. The material, particularly the body of the report, should be structured in a manner so that the reader can easily see the inherent connections and linkages. Headings should be used for different topics and subheadings for subtopics. A logical organisation also leads to a coherent report. Clarity can be enhanced by using well-constructed sentences that are short and to the point. The words used should express precisely what the researcher wants to communicate. Difficult words, slang and clichés should be avoided. An excellent check on the clarity of a report is to have two or three people who are unfamiliar with the project read it and offer critical comments. Several revisions of the report may be needed before the final document emerges.

Presentable and professional appearance The look of a report is important. The report should be professionally reproduced with quality paper, typing and binding for hard copies, and with skilful graphic design and the use of appropriate visuals for online reports. The typography should be varied. Variation in type size and skilful use of white space can greatly contribute to the appearance and readability of the report. However, a balance should be sought with styles of variation. Too much variation can lead to confusion; variation is only useful if it aids understanding.

Objective Objectivity is a virtue that should guide report writing. Researchers can become so fascinated with their project that they overlook their 'objective' role. The report should accurately present the research design, results and conclusions of the project, without slanting the findings to conform to the expectations of management. Decision makers are unlikely to receive with enthusiasm a report that reflects unfavourably on their judgement or actions. Yet the researcher must have the courage to present and defend the results objectively.

Reinforce text with tables, graphs and visuals It is important to reinforce key information in the text with tables, graphs, pictures, maps and other visual devices. Visual aids can greatly facilitate communication and add to the clarity and impact of the report. Guidelines for tabular and graphical presentation are discussed later.

Reinforce tables, graphs and visuals with text Conversely it is important to illustrate tables, graphs and visuals with verbatim quotes from questionnaires and interviews. Quotes can bring to life the meaning in tables, graphs and visuals and, used carefully, can make the reading of the report far more interesting than a solid body of statistics.

Conciseness A report should be concise. Anything unnecessary should be omitted. If too much information is included, important points may be lost. Avoid lengthy discussions of common procedures. However, brevity should not be achieved at the expense of completeness.

Drawing together the above considerations in writing a good report can be challenging. There can be a delicate balance between keeping a report short and concise against superficiality and not addressing specific information needs of decision makers. The following list should focus the mind of the report writer as it encapsulates typical mistakes that can make good research ineffective[9]:

- *The order in the report is based on the order of the questionnaire.* Typically, a report such as this has no beginning or end and has to be completely rewritten by the buyer before it can be used by anybody else in the organisation.
- *The report does not discriminate between relevant subgroups but only shows totals.* The need to go back and ask for more, deeper analysis (sometimes for more money) can be a great factor of annoyance.
- *The report contains too much research jargon,* so that any reader outside the profession can only guess at its meaning.
- *The report contains tables with too many figures.* In the end, there is only confusion. For researchers, the percentages derived from their data files have meaning, but not so for the reader.
- *The report doesn't distinguish between different audiences* in the organisation buying the research.

- *The vast majority of reports are still prepared and delivered on 'paper'* (including virtual paper like Word, PowerPoint or PDF documents). In a modern day business environment, with its fast pace decision making, research information on 'paper' can be too difficult to find and penetrate. Decision makers need the right information at the right time and have no time to wait or to search through reports.

Guidelines for tables

Statistical tables are a vital part of the report and deserve special attention. We illustrate the guidelines for tables using data from a Formula One Racetrack study conducted by IMF Sports Marketing Surveys (**www.sportsmarketingsurveys.com**). Table 13.1 presents the findings from three questions. The rows in Table 13.1 show groupings of Formula One viewing habits. The columns in Table 13.1 present gender and age groupings of the participants.

The numbers in parentheses in the following paragraphs refer to the numbered sections of the table.

Title and number Every table should have a number (1a) and title (1b). The title should be brief yet clearly descriptive of the information provided. Arabic numbers are used to identify tables so that they can be referenced in the text.[10]

Arrangement of data items The arrangement of data items in a table should emphasise the most significant aspect of the data. For example, when the data pertain to time, the items should be arranged by appropriate time period. When order of magnitude is most important, the data items should be arranged in that order (2a). If ease of locating items is critical, an alphabetical arrangement is most appropriate.

Basis of measurement The basis or unit of measurement should be clearly stated (3a). In Table 13.1, the total sample size is shown and the subsample sizes of the different ways of classifying participants. The main body of data is shown in percentages. The % signs would normally be removed, with a note to tell the reader that the main body is based upon column percentages or row percentages, or percentages related to the total sample size.

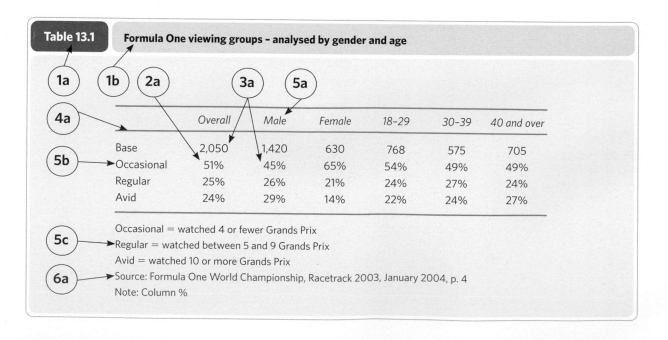

Table 13.1   Formula One viewing groups – analysed by gender and age

	Overall	Male	Female	18–29	30–39	40 and over
Base	2,050	1,420	630	768	575	705
Occasional	51%	45%	65%	54%	49%	49%
Regular	25%	26%	21%	24%	27%	24%
Avid	24%	29%	14%	22%	24%	27%

Occasional = watched 4 or fewer Grands Prix
Regular = watched between 5 and 9 Grands Prix
Avid = watched 10 or more Grands Prix
Source: Formula One World Championship, Racetrack 2003, January 2004, p. 4
Note: Column %

Leaders, rulings and spaces The reader's eye should be guided to be able to read across the table clearly. This can be achieved with ruled lines (4a), alternate shaded rows, or white spaces with dotted lines leading from the row headings to the data.

Explanations and comments: headings, stubs and footnotes Explanations and comments clarifying the table can be provided in the form of captions, stubs and footnotes. Designations placed over the vertical columns are called headings (5a). Designations placed in the left-hand column are called stubs (5b). Information that cannot be incorporated in the table should be explained by footnotes (5c). Letters or symbols should be used for footnotes rather than numbers. The footnotes that are part of the original source should come after the main table, but before the source note.

Sources of the data If the data contained in the table are secondary, the source of data should be cited (6a).

Guidelines for graphs

As a general rule, graphical aids should be employed whenever practical. Graphical display of information can effectively complement the text and tables to enhance clarity of communication and impact.[11] As the saying goes, a picture is worth a thousand words. The guidelines for preparing graphs are similar to those for tables. Therefore, this section focuses on the different types of graphical aids.[12] We illustrate several of these using a variety of data sources.

Geographic and other maps Geographic and other maps, such as product positioning maps, can communicate relative location and other comparative information. Maps can portray customer locations and types, potential consumers, location of competitors, road networks to show consumer flows, and other facilities that may attract consumers to certain locations.

Pie chart

A round chart divided into sections.

Round or pie charts In a **pie chart**, the area of each section, as a percentage of the total area of a circle, reflects the percentage associated with the value of a specific variable. Pie charts are very useful in presenting simple relative frequencies in numbers or percentages. A pie chart is not useful for displaying relationships over time or relationships among several variables. As a general guide, a pie chart should not contain more than seven sections.[13] Figure 13.2 shows the percentages of different forms of travel to work. Greater care must be taken with 3D pie charts as the relative sizes of the pie segments can become distorted.

Line chart

A chart that connects a series of data points using continuous lines.

Line charts A **line chart** connects a series of data points using continuous lines. This is an attractive way of illustrating trends and changes over time. Several series can be compared

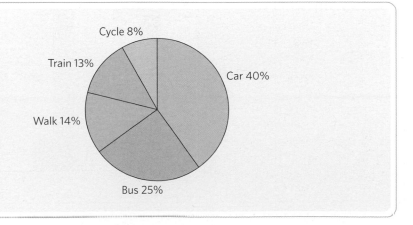

Figure 13.2

Pie chart shows the percentage of different form of travel to work

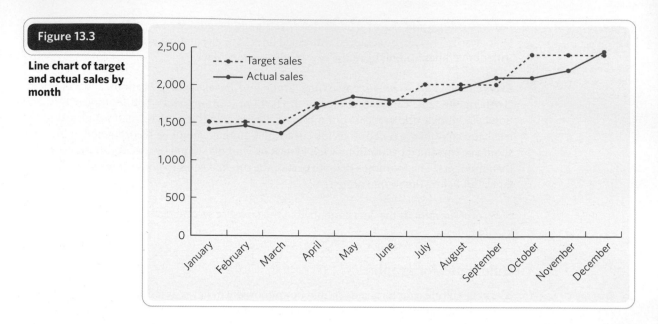

Figure 13.3

Line chart of target and actual sales by month

on the same chart, and forecasts, interpolations and extrapolations can be shown. If several series are displayed simultaneously, each line should have a distinctive colour or form (see Figure 13.3).[14]

Histograms and bar charts A **bar chart** displays data in various bars that may be positioned horizontally or vertically. Bar charts can be used to present absolute and relative magnitudes, differences and change (see Figure 13.4). A **histogram** is a vertical bar chart in which the height of the bar represents the relative or cumulative frequency of occurrence of a specific variable. Other variations on the basic bar chart include the stacked bar chart (Figure 13.5) and the 3D cluster bar chart (Figure 13.6). Stacked and cluster bar charts can work well with a few data items presented, to represent differences qualitatively between groups. As noted with pie charts, 3D charts should be used with great caution as they can distort the message and confuse an audience. Most graphics packages have a great array of 3D options; however, there are few circumstances where they can be used to present data in a clear and unbiased manner.

Bar chart
A chart that displays data in bars positioned horizontally or vertically.

Histogram
A vertical bar chart in which the height of the bar represents the relative or cumulative frequency of occurrence.

Figure 13.4

Bar chart of preferred fast food by age

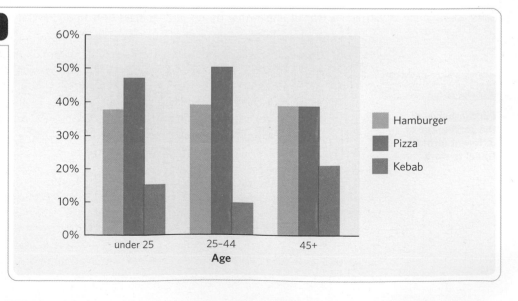

Figure 13.5

Stacked bar chart of the rating aspects of service

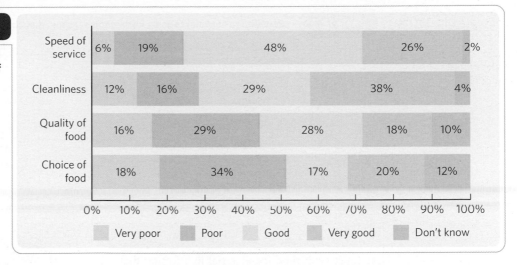

Figure 13.6

The 3D cluster bar chart of preferred fast food by age

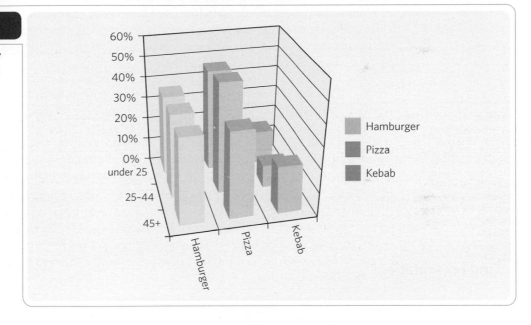

Schematic figures and flow charts Schematic figures and flow charts take on a number of different forms. They can be used to display the steps or components of a process, as in Figure 13.1. They can also be of great value in presenting qualitative data analyses by representing the nature and interconnection of ideas that have been uncovered (see Chapter 10). Another useful form of these charts is classification diagrams. Examples of classification charts for classifying secondary data were provided earlier in the text (Figures 3.1 to 3.4). An example of a flow chart for questionnaire design was also given earlier (Figure 7.3).[15]

Report distribution

The marketing research report should be distributed to appropriate personnel who may use (or influence the use of) the findings in different ways. The report could be distributed in a variety of formats including hard copy and electronic, static and interactive. Increasingly, research reports are being published or posted directly online. Normally these reports are not located in publicly accessible areas but in locations that are protected by passwords or on intranets. The various presentation, word-processing and spreadsheet packages have

Table 13.2	Percentage of projects using each mode of report distribution 2010	
Microsoft PowerPoint		53%
Acrobat PDF		21%
Microsoft Excel		20%
Microsoft Word		16%
Online static reports		16%
Interactive analysis		10%
Printed tables		8%
Digital dashboards		6%

the capacity to produce material in a format that can be posted directly online. There are a number of advantages to publishing reports online. These reports can incorporate all kinds of multimedia presentations, including graphs, pictures, animation, audio and full-motion video as illustrated in the opening case of this chapter. The dissemination is immediate and the reports can be accessed by authorised persons online on a global basis. These reports can be electronically searched to identify materials of specific interest.

Table 13.2 presents a rank order preference for the use of different formats to present reports. This table is based upon an annual study of how research companies use different software applications in the research process. PowerPoint slides have been the outright most popular means to deliver reports for many years, for companies in all parts of the world and of all sizes. The use of hard copy and static reports forms the majority of report distribution. The use of interactive analysis and digital dashboards are relatively low. These report formats enable decision makers to interrogate findings, juxtapose research findings with other essential business data and dig deeper into data to discover and tailor findings to suit their needs.[16]

Digital dashboard
A portal that enables a decision maker to tailor and focus upon business data and analyses. Its visual design is akin to the car dashboard, enabling the user to quickly assimilate key metrics.

Oral presentation

The entire marketing research project should be presented to the decision makers of the organisation that has commissioned the research (bearing in mind this may be in-house). This presentation will help decision makers understand and accept the written report. Any preliminary questions that decision makers may have can be addressed in the presentation. Because many decision makers form their first and lasting impressions about the project based on the oral presentation, its importance cannot be overemphasised.[17]

The key to an effective presentation is preparation. A written script or detailed outline should be prepared following the format of the written report. The presentation must be geared to the audience. This audience may physically be in the same room as the researcher(s) and/or they may be at remote locations through video conferencing. Wherever the audience is located, the researcher should determine the backgrounds, interests and involvement of those in the project, as well as the extent to which they are likely to be affected by it. The presentation should be rehearsed several times before it is made. Visual aids such as tables and graphs should be displayed with a variety of media. Flip charts mounted on an easel enable the researcher to manipulate numbers, graphically represent ideas or respond in a spontaneous manner. They are particularly useful in communicating answers to technical questions. Visual aids can also be drawn on the pages in advance, and the speaker flips through the pages during the presentation. Although not as flexible, magnetic boards and felt boards allow for rapid presentation of previously prepared material. Overhead and high definition projectors can present simple charts as well as complex overlays produced by the successive additions of new images and even certain objects to the screen. The use of presentation packages such as PowerPoint are of obvious immense help as illustrated by their prominence in use in Table 13.2. However, the presenter must not lose sight of the message, must not just think that the audience has to be 'talked to' and must put every effort into engaging their audience. The value of 'performance' in presenting research findings is illustrated in the following example.

Real research

A cunning plan was formed . . .[18]

In presenting the findings of a study for the Swiss Bank UBS (**www.ubs.com**), Spring Research (**www.springresearch.co.uk**) delivered a one-day workshop which brought together 30+ stakeholders from Publicis, Starcom (UBS's media partner) and UBS teams. This grouping brought together a broad mix of experience and creativity. Spring wanted to hold the session in a

climate where people felt confident about themselves and could work well with one another. They picked a comfortable, relaxed hotel in Zurich that allowed freedom of movement. Spring arrived early to dress the room with insights, images and stories of individuals that took part in the research as they wanted the environment to act as a stimulus. All workshop participants were given a HNWI (high net worth individual, the type of participant the research project had focused upon) in advance of the session and asked to spend time thinking about this person's needs, wants and desires. The workshop began with objectives for the day and a quick introduction on the state of the market. They then asked the workshop participants to really get into the minds of the HNWIs. Each was asked to get into character and split into teams of eight people. In their teams, each individual was asked to introduce themselves before being interviewed by a journalist from 'The Examiner' (a fake national newspaper) who was tasked with finding out as much as possible about them and their colleagues. Each team was then asked to put together a 'front page story' that would give the world the inside scoop on the audiences' lives. Each team was then asked to present their story to the rest of the group. As well as the individual consumer profiles, they put together verbatim comments and six short films to bring to life individuals and key themes. There was some reluctance about role playing before the event, but for many it ended up being the most rewarding element as they really got themselves into the minds of the people they wanted most to reach. The level of involvement generated through this approach ensured greater ownership and commitment to the outcomes of the research from UBS and Publicis Starcom and really helped introduce consumer insight directly into the 'bloodstream' of each organisation. It also enabled Spring to fast track ideas as the right people were in attendance, so the session worked as an effective means of taking key decision makers on a journey which led to consensus and an agreed forward direction which was able to be acted on immediately.

Research follow-up

After the presentation of research findings, decision makers should be given time to read the report in detail. This means that there are two other tasks for the researchers after the oral presentation. The researcher should help decision makers understand and implement the findings and take follow-up action. Second, while it is still fresh in the researcher's mind, the entire marketing research project should be evaluated. The following example illustrates how these tasks are managed in the relationship between Motorola and the research company GfK.

Real research	Dedicated staffing at Motorola and GfK to ensure focus on the 'debrief'[19]

An approach to ensuring proper post-presentation follow-up and action planning is to 'staff' for it, i.e. build the action-planning function into the research organisation to foster and support the client. Motorola has built a follow-up capability into its research organisation by having a staff of 'consultants' whose primary responsibility is servicing their respective key client groups. These 'consultants' are not only responsible for following up and ensuring results are properly understood and used, but also for synthesising research across studies. The result of this new structure for Motorola has been greater research mileage, impact, visibility, and more satisfied research users. It also off-loads the research manager who must move back to the 'implementing' mode – next project, next country – from the often time consuming, yet critical, follow-ups and post-presentation analysis. It has the effect of essentially splitting the project responsibilities, so that the same level of energy and effort that were placed on set-up and execution are devoted to delivering the results and planning action steps. The same structure is mirrored at GfK, from the supplier side. The research teams of the different projects provide professional research execution in terms of planning and executing global research, as well as in preparing the final presentation. However, there is an additional insights team which consists of two functions: a 'consultant' responsible for analysis and insight generation; and a 'synergy' manager responsible for learning across all studies, in all stages of the process – from planning, to executing, to delivering the results. The insight team at GfK explores different sources to create valuable insight not only from one single project, but from all they know about the specific topic under consideration. This team prepares the basis for actionable output. It understands what Motorola knows already, and where gaps exist. It also supports workshops and meetings with internal stakeholders, and prepares the results that address a special need of a certain audience. It also can support the Motorola consultants within the workshops and meetings to generate actions out of the findings, by applying workshop techniques and thus being a kind of 'process-enabler'.

Assisting decision makers

After the decision makers have read the report in detail, several questions may arise. Parts of the report, particularly those dealing with technical matters, may not be understood and the researcher should provide the help needed. Sometimes the researcher helps implement the findings. Often, the researcher will be retained to help with the selection of a new product or advertising agency, development of a pricing policy, market segmentation or other marketing actions. An important reason for management follow-up is to discuss further research projects. For example, the researcher and decision makers may agree to repeat the study after two years. Where possible and as illustrated in the Motorola–GfK example, the researcher should also aim to make links between the findings of a project and other studies. By reviewing 'historical' findings in the context of current issues, project findings can be seen as more valid and decision makers may increase their trust in the process.[20] Finally, the researcher should help decision makers to make the information generated in the marketing research project a part of the firm's decision support system. Ad hoc marketing research should be seen as a significant component of an ongoing link and understanding of target consumers. A key element of researchers being able to assist marketing decision makers is the level of trust that exists between the two parties. The nature of personal interaction between managers and researchers is very important in creating trust in the researcher and consequently in the results of the research. The quality of personal interaction affects decision makers' perceptions of the overall quality of the report itself. Trust between the decision maker and the researcher has been found to influence the perceived quality of user–researcher interactions, the level of researcher involvement, the level of user commitment to the relationship and the level of market research utilisation.[21]

Evaluation of the research project

Although marketing research is scientific, which may seem to imply a rigid, systematic process, it clearly involves creativity, intuition and personal judgement. Hence, every marketing research project provides an opportunity for learning, and the researcher should critically evaluate the entire project to obtain new insights and knowledge. The key question to ask is: 'Could this project have been conducted more effectively or efficiently?' This question, of course, raises several more specific questions. Could the problem have been defined differently so as to enhance the value of the project or reduce the costs? Could a different approach have yielded better results? Was the research design that was used the best? How about the method of data collection? Should an SMS survey have been used instead of an online survey? Was the sampling plan employed the most appropriate? Were the sources of possible design error correctly anticipated and kept under control, at least in a qualitative sense? If not, what changes could have been made? How could the selection, training and supervision of fieldworkers be altered to improve data collection? Was the data analysis strategy effective in yielding information useful for decision making? Were the conclusions and recommendations appropriate and useful? Was the report adequately written and presented? Was the project completed within the time and budget allocated? If not, what went wrong? The insights gained from such an evaluation will benefit the researcher and the subsequent projects conducted.

International marketing research

The guidelines presented earlier in this chapter apply to international marketing research, although report preparation may be complicated by the need to prepare reports for decision makers with distinctive organisational roles in different countries and in different languages. In such a case, the researcher should prepare different versions of the report, each geared to specific readers. The different reports should be comparable, although the formats may differ. The guidelines for oral presentation are also similar to those given earlier, with the added proviso that the presenter should be sensitive to cultural norms. For example, making jokes, which is frequently done in many countries, is not appropriate in all cultures (which may also include particular organisational cultures).

Most marketing decisions are made from facts and figures arising out of marketing research. But these figures and how they have been arrived at have to be credible to decision makers. The subjective experience and gut feeling of managers could vary widely across countries, necessitating that different recommendations be made for implementing the research findings in different countries. This is particularly important when making innovative or creative recommendations such as in advertising campaigns.

Ethics in marketing research

Report preparation and presentation involves many issues relating to research integrity. These issues include defining the research problem to suit hidden agendas, ignoring pertinent data, compromising the research design, deliberately misusing statistics, falsifying figures, altering research results, misinterpreting the results with the objective of supporting a personal or corporate point of view, and withholding information.[22] A survey of 254 researchers found that 33 per cent believed that the most difficult ethical problems they face encompass issues of research integrity. The researcher must address these issues when preparing the report and presenting the findings. The dissemination of research results to management and other stakeholders, as may be appropriate, should be honest, accurate and complete. The researcher should aim to be objective throughout the research process.

Ethical challenges are also faced when research procedures and analyses do not reveal anything new or significant. For example, the chi-square analysis may reveal that there is no association between observed variables (Chapter 11). Ethical dilemmas can arise in these instances if the researcher nevertheless attempts to form an association from such analyses. The researchers are being paid for their expert interpretation of data, and can nothing meaningful be said?

Like researchers, decision makers also have the responsibility for full and accurate disclosure of the research findings and are obligated to employ these findings honourably. For example, consumers can be negatively affected by a client who distorts the research findings to develop a biased advertising campaign that makes brand claims that have not been substantiated by marketing research. Ethical issues also arise when client firms, such as fast-food brands, use marketing research findings as a foundation to formulate questionable communications and marketing campaigns.

Digital developments in marketing research

One of the main challenges of writing and making oral presentations of research reports lies in engaging managers, decision makers and other users/influencers. Engagement means that these individuals will take the time and space to read, watch, listen to the intended message. It means they will appreciate the integrity of the researcher and their professionalism in conducting and delivering the research. To achieve engagement, researchers have to compete against many other demands on the time and space of decision makers, but at their disposal are myriad digital developments and creative means of communication. We have illustrated examples of digital developments in presenting findings through creative communications at BMW Group Designworks and Spring Research working with UBS. The following example illustrates the communication challenges faced by researchers with a complex and dispersed audience. It shows how they used the distinctive skills of researchers and their views of the real insights in a study, matched with the communication skills of digital marketers.

Real research	Animated information graphics video – *Meet Ryan and Maria*[23]

A digital marketing team undertook a study to support the development of a strategy for how the UK government should communicate online with young people aged 14–19. When the research was complete, the project presented several reporting challenges. Feedback to the client had to combine 11 overlapping work streams from a range of disciplines (qualitative, quantitative, ethnographic, secondary and academic). Furthermore, a diverse range of client audiences needed to be engaged, including: the commissioning client team who were spread across four locations; two layers of senior departmental colleagues; a government ministerial audience; and an additional audience of interested third parties. In addition to the geographical dispersion of the audiences it was anticipated that many would have little prior knowledge of the project. Another challenge was the time available to present findings; for example, in one case they had a five-minute meeting slot in which to summarise six months of work. In responding to these challenges the researchers' aim was to tailor the information to meet the needs of each audience as clearly as possible. Video was considered at an early stage due to the likely need to describe the project to a number of other audiences over the course of the project's lifetime. The creative team produced a five-minute animated information graphics video called *Meet Ryan and Maria* demonstrating how two digital natives navigate between the real and virtual worlds seamlessly, demonstrating some of the places they go and the possible role advice from government could play in this journey. The video was complete with music, voiceover and used a hand animation technique. It helped to communicate complex ideas persuasively in a short space of time and was produced in a range of formats which could be easily shared among client audiences.

As in the above example, the technology may be there and a good relationship between researchers and visual designers to make a big impact on report and presentation dynamics. However, those regularly on either side of the marketing research debrief know that the pressures of timetable and budget do not always allow for this. They know that quantitative-based presentations are not regularly given this kind of treatment, and that the balance of time between thinking and physically charting is often awry. There may be few chances to extend timetables, or to make budgets magically increase; so a change of mindset is required, to enable better use to be made of the time and money that is available.[24]

Given the ability to search electronically and tailor reports online, research findings are now becoming more 'pull' oriented, as opposed to the 'push' orientation of a printed report. The 'pull' orientation means that decision makers and other research users can conduct analyses to suit their needs, sometimes working with raw data. Beyond the researchers' presentation of the focus and findings of a study, many

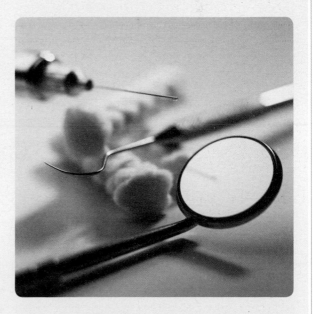

interactive reporting formats enable users to create their own unique reports. Using database-driven technology and reporting software it is possible to have a completely interactive experience that allows data interrogation through the specification of questions, filters, cross-tabulations and even applied weighting.[25] The use of digital dashboards with their flexibility in terms of presenting both quantitative and qualitative data represents a major development in how research findings are presented and used.

The 'push' orientation, i.e. the static report, is the most popular form of reporting, as detailed in Table 13.2. The interpretation that a researcher may generate will continue to be written, but can now be accessed as a result of a search, instigation of a link, or even just rolling the mouse pointer over an icon. The basic structure of a website, and the ease with which it is possible to navigate around a large amount of information, ensures that decision makers can quickly find exactly what they want. It is also possible to have index areas constantly visible on the screen to ensure that areas of information contained within a single report, or indeed multiple reports, can be accessed quickly. With mobile technology, such access can be at any time and any place, and the report reader can immerse themselves in a report in the environment and context that really suits them.

Examples of how marketing research reports online are making decision makers' lives easier are:[26]

- Reporting and interrogating real-time data (not just from online interviews but from CATI and CAPI data).

- Creating automated report formats – as illustrated in the following example.

Real research — Automated reporting for dental practices

Researchers are facing a dilemma: how to provide clients with powerful reporting with cost effective pricing. In developing their custom Patient Experience System for dental practitioners, SNAP Surveys was faced with providing complex reporting for each of several thousand dental practices (**www.snapsurveys.com/dental**). Each client required an individual interpretation of the results of the survey of their clients, an indication of how they performed when benchmarked against other dental practices, and an action plan based on the results of the survey. These requirements would normally be handled by an experienced research team, but with a resulting cost . . .

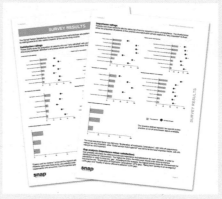

SNAP Surveys developed a fully automated reporting system that was triggered at the completion of the survey, and generated a custom report highlighting areas where the practice was performing well and where there was room for improvement. An executive summary was generated automatically together with an individual list of actions based on the performance of the individual dental practice. Results from the individual dental practice were then automatically benchmarked against national average results with practice results in green and benchmark results in red.

- Linking different research projects' reports together to create a more detailed overview.
- Building charts and tables by adding different elements (such as confidence limits and explanation of chart movements).
- Applying rules to the reporting to ensure the robustness of the presented results.

- Applying complex modelling calculations and processes to data as they are made available.

Though these benefits are clear, as illustrated in Table 13.2, the use of interactive and online marketing research reports is still primarily 'locked' into static presentations, and there is some way to go to realise these benefits.

Summary

Report preparation and presentation is the final step in the marketing research project. This process begins with interpretation of data analysis results and leads to conclusions and recommendations. Next, the formal report is written and an oral presentation made. After decision makers have read the report, the researcher should conduct a follow-up, assisting management and undertaking a thorough evaluation of the marketing research project.

For the researcher, the oral presentation is usually considered the end of what could have been months of long hours, exhausting travel, and intense data analysis, all in search of the valuable insights. The presentation is delivered and the researcher may see it is finally over, and their mindset moves on to the next project. For the receiver of the research report, this may be just the beginning. The researcher may have delivered some provocative insights and thought they had considered every possible angle. Reports, however, can raise more questions, and decision makers may want more details.[27] The researcher has to consider how they assist decision makers to get the most out of reports and presentations. They also have to learn from the experience of presenting their findings, in order to plan more creative, efficient and effective research in the future.

In international marketing research, report preparation may be complicated by the need to prepare reports for decision makers in different countries and in different languages. Several ethical issues are pertinent, particularly those related to the interpretation and reporting of the research process and findings to decision makers and the use of these results by management. Digital developments in marketing research are enabling reports and presentations to be delivered in far more engaging and relevant formats. With the use of mobile technology, this can mean that research users can access reports and presentations anywhere and at any time. The uses of digital dashboards in marketing research are facilitating new ways to present reports. Digital dashboards can enable research data to be interrogated and juxtaposed with performance data from across an organisation.

The final example presents a metaphor of the use of the guitar in supporting presentations. It is a final reminder that digital developments that facilitate professional presentations can never replace the creative skills of conveying the story and impact of a piece of research upon a decision making situation.

Real research | My paradigm is the guitar[28]

Developments in modern technology have had a profound impact on the art of business presentation. There is no doubt that the standard of visualisation in presentations has improved immeasurably, but has the presentation itself? Technically good presentations are becoming commonplace, perhaps even predictable. Predictability precedes boredom.

Presenters spend too much time creating a slide show and not enough on their performance. Presenters have forgotten to plan their personal involvement and the involvement of their audience.

My paradigm is the guitar. The guitar represents a tool that supports presentation, but that can never do the performance for you. From my own experience as a guitarist, presentations and gigs have many parallels. You have to prepare diligently, and have a good plan for the progress of the performance. You should know your material. You must be able to excite the audience and get them involved. You must be able to improvise and respond to requests. You should have a good guitar, but the good guitar on its own won't carry the day. You will.

SNAP Learning Edition

Once the analysis phase of a survey project is complete, the next stage is the Reporting. Analysed data can be presented in SNAP in a number of different formats.

Charting technologies have, over the years, improved the situation in offering more analysis options, and used carefully they can be a useful tool to present the results to third parties. The range of SNAP charts includes horizontal and vertical bars, line and pie charts, gantt charts and scatter plots, as well as radar and polar charts. The results can either be printed or exported to office products such as Word and Powerpoint.

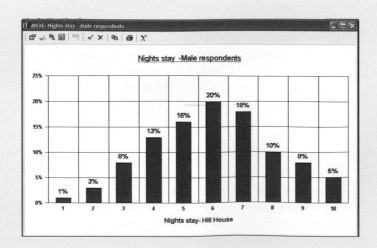

Open-ended text should, wherever possible, be reported, and in specific cases can provide a level of analysis. SNAP's List reporting details the text for any combination of questions and can be reported along-side other demographical data.

With a rise in the requirement for text-based data analysis, features such as Word Clouds provide a unique method of combining both reporting and analysis, with the software automatically adjusting the font size and colour according the number of occurrences of a word or phrase. Word Clouds have instant impact and work well in any form of presentation or report.

SNAP's Smart Reporting provides a facility to go beyond the traditional tables and charts, enabling full and detailed reports. Benchmark reporting can be included as well as dashboards.

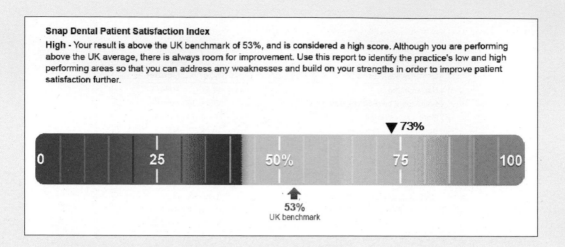

Interpretation of the results in the form of narrative normally requires time from a researcher to look through each set of analyses, and can only be accomplished once all the data has been received. Smart Reporting can be preconfigured to set all the conditional checks for each of the conclusions and recommendations, enabling reporting to be carried automatically, and should an interim report need to be generated, this causes no problems at all.

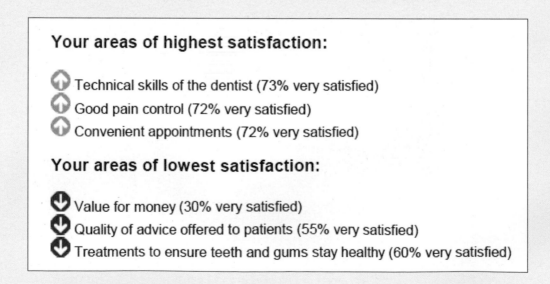

Smart Reporting does require a skill level to generate all the conditional checks for the reporting, and to format all the analyses in advance, but it does generate a layout that is very readable for non-researchers.

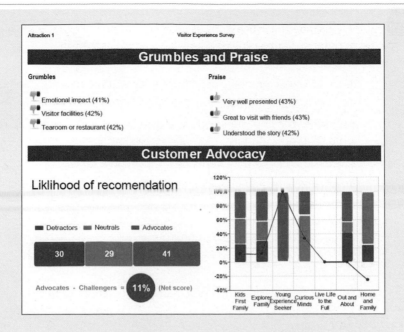

In many situations, multiple versions of a report are required, for perhaps each of 100 store locations nationally. Each of the individual store's report might contain benchmarking against other regional stores, as well as benchmarking against national store data. Smart Reporting reduces the workload enormously and a single command can be run to generate each of the 100 reports, with each report containing perhaps 40–50 pages.

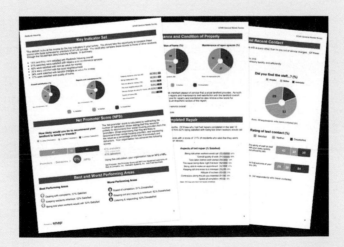

From Chapter 5 through to Chapter 13, we have included information on SNAP that demonstrates the relevance and impact of using the software in effective research design. We have provided an insight into the power of the software, to show how professional surveys can be designed, published and experienced. We have then considered the extensive options to produce tables, charts and statistical analyses, finally generating engaging reports that can be readily understood by researchers and non-researchers alike. Further details of how you can use SNAP to design your own survey are available on the website that accompanies this text (**www.pearsoned.co.uk/malhotra-euro**).

Questions

1 Describe the process of report preparation.
2 Why is the quality of report presentation vital to the success of a marketing research project?
3 Describe a commonly used format for writing marketing research reports.
4 Why is the 'limitations and caveats' section included in the report?
5 Discuss the importance of objectivity in writing a marketing research report.
6 Describe the guidelines for report writing.
7 How should the data items be arranged in a table?
8 What are the advantages and disadvantages of presenting data using 3D charts?
9 What is the purpose of an oral presentation? What guidelines should be followed in an oral presentation?
10 To what extent should researchers interpret the information they present in a report?
11 Describe the evaluation of a marketing research project in retrospect.
12 Graphically represent the consumer decision making process described in the following paragraph:

The consumer first becomes aware of the need. Then the consumer simultaneously searches for information from several sources: retailers, advertising, word of mouth, and independent publications. After that a criterion is developed for evaluating the available brands in the marketplace. Based on this evaluation, the preferred brand is selected.

Exercises

1 Obtain a copy of an old marketing research report (many marketing research agencies or companies that have commissioned research will provide copies of old reports for educational purposes). Evaluate the ways in which you could improve the structure and style of presentation in this report.

2 Prepare an oral presentation of the report above, to be targeted at senior marketing managers. Deliver your presentation to a group of fellow students (role playing the managers) and ask them to critique the presentation.

3 Visit **www.confirmit.com** to evaluate the formats of reports used by this company. How does the format of their automated reports compare to the one in this book?

4 You are a researcher preparing a report for a high-tech firm on 'The demand potential for digital cameras in Europe'. Develop a format for your report. How is that format different from the one given in this book? Discuss the format and purposes of each section with your boss (role played by a student in your class).

5 In a small group discuss the following issues: 'Writing reports is an art. Presenting reports is an art. Reading reports is an art. It is all a matter of art.' 'Writing a report that is concise and yet complete is virtually impossible as these two objectives are conflicting.'

Notes

1. Bernstein, A., Robin, L. and Zych, M., 'The art of research narratives – impact through entertainment', ESOMAR, *Annual Congress*, London (Sept. 2006).

2. Saxton, G. and Davidson, A., 'The business of storytelling with qualitative research', Market Research Society, *Annual Conference* (2009).

3. Johnston, A., 'It's engagement, but is it research? Effectively engaging decision makers', ESOMAR, *Qualitative Research*, Istanbul (Nov. 2008).

4. Few, S., *Show Me the Numbers: Designing Tables and Graphs to Enlighten* (Analytics Press, 2004); Tufte, E.R., *Visual Explanations: Images and Quantities, Evidence and Narrative* (Cheshire, CT: Graphic, 1997); Fink, A., *How to Report on Surveys* (Thousand Oaks, CA: Sage, 1995).

5. Birks, D.F., 'Market research', in Baker, M.J. (ed.) *The Marketing Book*, 3rd edn (Oxford: Butterworth–Heinemann, 1994), 262.

6. Keys, T. Jr, 'Report writing', *Internal Auditor*, 53 (4) (August 1996), 65–66.

7. Anon., 'What you say', *Advertising Age*, 79 (14) (April 2008), 4; Wolcott, H.F., *Writing up qualitative research*, 2nd edn (Thousand Oaks, CA: Sage, 2001); Britt, S.H., 'The writing of readable research reports', *Journal of Marketing Research* (May 1971), 265. See also Mort, S., *Professional Report Writing* (Brookfield, IL: Ashgate, 1995); Shair, D.I., 'Report writing', *HR Focus*, 71 (2) (Feb. 1994), 20.

8. Anon., 'New international aims for young readers with quick response codes in news stories', *Marketing Week*, 31 (11), (March 2008), 13; Low, G.S., 'Factors affecting the use of information in the evaluation of marketing communications productivity', *Academy of Marketing Science Journal*, 29 (1) (Winter 2001), 70–88; Boland, A., 'Got report-o-phobia? Follow these simple steps to get those ideas onto paper', *Chemical Engineering*, 103 (3) (March 1996), 131–32.

9. van Meel, I. and Rietberg, J., 'Information a la carte – The need to select, prepare and present', ESOMAR, *Congress*, Montreux (Sept. 2009).

10. Tanase, G., 'Real-life data mart processing', *Intelligent Enterprise*, 5 (5) (8 March 2002), 22–24; Wilson, L.D., 'Are appraisal reports logical fallacies?' *Appraisal Journal*, 64 (2) (April 1996), 129–33; Leach, J., 'Seven steps to better writing', *Planning*, 59 (6) (June 1993), 26–27; Ehrenberg, A.S.C., 'The problem of numeracy', *American Statistician*, 35 (May 1981), 67–71.

11. Wallgren, A., Wallgren, B., Persson, R., Jorner, U. and Haaland, J.A., *Graphing Statistics and Data* (Thousand Oaks, CA: Sage, 1996); Tufte, E.R., *Visual Display of Quantitative Information* (Cheshire, CT: Graphic, 1992).

12. Dean, J., 'High-powered charts and graphs', *Government Executive*, 34 (1) (Jan. 2002), 58; Kauder, N.B., 'Pictures worth a thousand words', *American Demographics* (Tools Supplement) (November/December 1996), 64–68.

13. Gutsche, A.M., 'Visuals make the case', *Marketing News*, 35 (20) (24 Sept. 2001), 21–22; Hinkin, S., 'Charting your

course to effective information graphics', *Presentations*, 9 (11) (Nov. 1995), 28–32.

14. Lee, M., 'Its all in the charts', *Malaysian Business* (1 Feb. 2002), 46; Chen, M.T., 'An innovative project report', *Cost Engineering*, 38 (4) (April 1996), 41–45; Zelazny, G., *Say It with Charts*, 3rd edn (Homewood, IL: Business One Irwin, 1996).

15. Clarke III, I., Flaherty, T.B. and Yankey, M., 'Teaching the visual learner: The use of visual summaries in marketing education', *Journal of Marketing Education*, 28 (3) (Dec. 2006), 216–26; Anon., 'Flow chart', *B-to-B*, 87 (4) (8 April 2002), 16; Johnson, S. and Regan, M., 'A new use for an old tool', *Quality Progress*, 29 (11) (Nov. 1996), 144; Parr, G.L., 'Pretty-darned-quick flowchart creation', *Quality* (August 1996), 62–63.

16. Macer, T. and Wilson, S., *GlobalPark Annual Market Research Software Survey 2010*, Seventh annual survey (2011).

17. Bendzko, A. and Ricketts, A., 'No more death by research debrief: Innovative ways to convert insights into action', ESOMAR, *Annual Congress*, Berlin (Sept. 2007); Desiderio, L., 'At the sales presentation: Ask and listen', *ID*, 38 (4) (April 2002), 55; McConnell, C.R., 'Speak up: The manager's guide to oral presentations', *Health Care Manager*, 18 (3) (March 2000), 70–77; Verluyten, S.P., 'Business communication and intercultural communication in Europe: The state of the art', *Business Communication Quarterly*, 60 (2) (June 1997), 135–43.

18. Hamburger, S. and Lawry, P., 'Storytelling with international millionaires – a creative approach to research', ESOMAR, *Annual Congress*, Montreal (Sept. 2008).

19. Bendzko, A. and Ricketts, A., 'No more death by research debrief: Innovative ways to convert insights into action', ESOMAR, *Annual Congress*, Berlin (Sept. 2007).

20. Eshpeter, B., 'Communicating research findings: Eight common pitfalls', *Imprints* (January 2004), 8–9.

21. Niven, A. and Imms, M., 'Connecting with clients: Re-thinking the debrief', Market Research Society, *Annual Conference* (2006); Moorman, C., Deshpande, R. and Zaltman, G., 'Factors affecting trust in market research relationships', *Journal of Marketing*, 57 (Jan. 1993), 81–101; Deshpande, R. and Zaltman, G., 'Factors affecting the use of market research information: A path analysis', *Journal of Marketing Research*, 19 (Feb. 1982), 25.

22. Liebman, M., 'Beyond ethics: Companies deal with legal attacks on marketing practices', *Medical Marketing and Media*, 37 (2) (Feb. 2002), 74–77; Giacobbe, R.W., 'A comparative analysis of ethical perceptions in marketing research: USA vs Canada', *Journal of Business Ethics*, 27 (3) (Oct. 2000), 229–45; Milton-Smith, J., 'Business ethics in Australia and New Zealand', *Journal of Business Ethics*, 16 (14) (Oct. 1997), 1485–97; Chonko, L.B., *Ethical Decision Making in Marketing* (Thousand Oaks, CA: Sage, 1995).

23. Shaw, S., 'Communicating creatively: From digital media to stains on the bedroom floor', Market Research Society, *Annual Conference* (2010).

24. Swan, N. and Cathcart, B., 'Tell the truth and shame the devil: How can the discipline of journalism improve insight and research?' Market Research Society, *Annual Conference* (2010).

25. Macer, T., 'On your marks, get set…' *Research in Business* (May 2006), 7–8: Macer, T., 'PowerPoint slammed as research results delivery device', *Research* (May 2006), 14.

26. Hummerston, A., 'Net reporting comes of age', *Research* (May 2000), 36.

27. Bendzko, A. and Ricketts, A., 'No more death by research debrief: Innovative ways to convert insights into action', ESOMAR, *Annual Congress*, Berlin (Sept. 2007).

28. Willetts, N.J., 'Going live', *Marketing Week* (13 November 1997), 47–48.

14 International marketing research

Stage 1

Problem definition

Stage 2

Research approach developed

Stage 3

Research design developed

Stage 4

Fieldwork or data collection

Stage 5

Data integrity and analysis

Stage 6

Report preparation and presentation

The global impact of social media and digital developments demand an international research mindset from all marketing researchers.

Objectives

After reading this chapter, you should be able to:

1   develop a framework for conducting international marketing research;
2   explain in detail the marketing, governmental, legal, economic, structural, informational and technological, and socio-cultural environmental factors and how they have an impact on international marketing research;
3   describe characteristics of the use of secondary data, qualitative techniques, online, telephone, face-to-face and postal survey methods in different countries;
4   discuss how to establish the equivalence of scales and measures, including construct, operational, scalar and linguistic equivalence;
5   describe the processes of back translation and parallel translation in translating a questionnaire into a different language;
6   discuss the ethical considerations in international marketing research;
7   appreciate how digital developments are shaping the manner in which international marketing research is planned and administered.

Overview

This chapter starts by evaluating the need for international marketing research. It then discusses the environment in which international marketing research is conducted, focusing on the marketing, governmental, legal, economic, structural, informational and technological, and socio-cultural environment.[1] Although illustrations of how the six steps of the marketing research process should be implemented in an international setting have been presented in earlier chapters, here we bring together characteristics of secondary data, qualitative techniques, survey methods, scaling techniques and questionnaire translation. Relevant ethical issues in international marketing research are identified. We conclude by examining how digital developments can help in the design and administration of international marketing research. We begin with an example that illustrates how an online survey enabled an understanding of consumer values across six nations.

Real research   A measure of global brands[2]

Research company Fresh Intelligence (**www.freshintelligence.com**) used cross-cultural communication theory (a combination of anthropology, sociology and psychology) to underpin a study of values across international markets. They developed a list of 22 values that described a wide range of attitudes towards personal and social well-being. They worded values in such a way that they could be attributed both to a consumer personally and to a brand. Their online survey was conducted with 3000 participants over the age of 18, with 500 participants in each country (samples representative to each country by age, gender, regions; industry exclusions). The countries picked differed greatly in their history and current position in the world. All of them were large and very attractive markets. The researchers chose three developing and promising economies: Brazil, Russia and China representing the BRIC block; and three developed prosperous countries: Canada, US and Australia. These countries had some core similarities and strong differences in their values. They saw, for example, that feeling safe, secure and protected was among the top five values across all six countries, and it was the highest value in the US, Canada and Russia. The most economically wealthy countries valued hard work the most: the US, Canada and China. Three others, Russia, Brazil and Australia, seemed to put more value on the other side of work–life balance: only these countries had 'family' in their top three values; hard work was not a priority at all. Only China highly valued both hard work and family. All countries except for Brazil included being responsible, reliable and trustful in their top five values.

What is international marketing research?

The term 'international marketing research' can be used very broadly. It denotes research for true international products (international research), research carried out in a country other than the country of the research-commissioning organisation (overseas research), research conducted in all important countries where a company may have existing and/or potential consumers (multinational research), and research conducted in and across different cultures (cross-cultural research). The last category of cross-cultural research does not have to cross national boundaries. Many countries have a vast array of ethnic groups, giving the researcher many challenges in understanding consumers in these groups within their home country. The following example is a brief illustration of the array of problems faced by researchers working in India.

Real research **Engaging with Indian consumers[3]**

The Indian consumer market is at once both a tremendous opportunity and a great challenge. Heading towards 2020, it has been argued that India will grow in economic stature from a 50 million 'middle class' to 600 million. Moving to higher levels of urbanisation, with the youngest median age population in the world, and an active workforce, the aggregate demand for consumer goods from this massive middle class will outstrip that of almost every other country in the world. What makes India different and often a puzzle is its sometimes surprising dissimilarity to other eastern countries, and its amazing diversity. With more than 5,000 towns and 600,000 villages spread across 28 states, India's people speak over 17 major languages and 844 dialects and practice eight religions.

The example above supports the contention that, in research approach, there is no difference between domestic and international marketing research. In other words, researchers have to adapt their techniques to their target participants, and the subtle cultural differences within a country offer the same challenges as the much more apparent differences over thousands of kilometres.

A framework for international marketing research

Conducting international marketing research can be more complex than conducting domestic marketing research. Although the basic six-step framework for domestic marketing research is applicable, the environment prevailing in the countries, cultural units or international markets that are being researched influences the way the six steps of the research process should be performed. Figure 14.1 presents a framework for conducting international marketing research.

The differences in the environments of countries, cultural units or overseas markets should be considered when conducting international marketing research. These differences may arise in the marketing, governmental, legal, economic, structural, informational and technological, and socio-cultural environments, as shown in Figure 14.1.

Figure 14.1

A framework for international marketing research

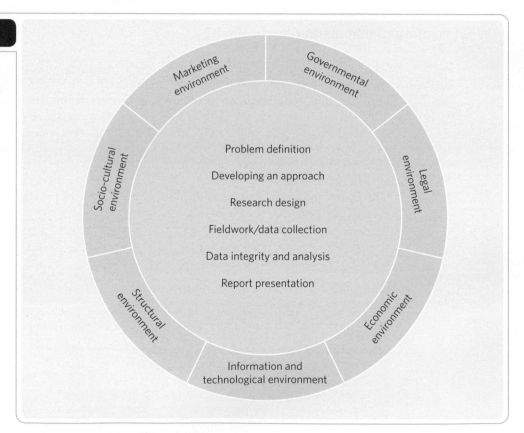

Marketing environment

Governmental environment

Legal environment

Economic environment

Information and technological environment

Structural environment

Socio-cultural environment

Problem definition

Developing an approach

Research design

Fieldwork/data collection

Data integrity and analysis

Report presentation

Marketing environment

The role of marketing in economic development varies in different countries. For example, many developing countries are frequently oriented towards production rather than marketing. Demand typically exceeds supply, and there is little concern about customer satisfaction, especially when the level of competition is low. In assessing the marketing environment, the researcher should consider the variety and assortment of products available, pricing policies, government control of media and the consumer attitudes towards advertising, the efficiency of the distribution system, the level of marketing effort undertaken, and the unsatisfied needs and behaviour of consumers. For example, surveys conducted in Europe usually involve questions on the variety and selection of merchandise. These questions would be inappropriate in some African countries, which are characterised by shortage economies. Likewise, questions about pricing may have to incorporate bargaining as an integral part of the exchange process. Questions about promotion should be modified as well. With viral advertising, an extremely important promotion may be implemented or viewed across different countries. However, certain themes, words and illustrations used in Europe are taboo in some countries. This is illustrated in the following example which describes characteristics of research in the Middle East.

<table>
<tr><td>**Real research**</td><td>**Tackling the acquiescence bias among Arab participants[4]**</td></tr>
</table>

Among the numerous sources of measurement error, the ones that have the strongest influence on the quality of responses are 'acquiescence bias' and 'social desirability bias'. Acquiescence bias is a systematic bias caused by some participants tending to agree with whatever is presented to them. Such a bias may be caused by either participants or interviewers being overly friendly during interviews. Although the Arab culture is very diverse and kaleidoscopic from several perspectives, there are still some traits that make it suitable to be seen in a unified

way. Politeness is at the core of interaction between Arabs. It is quite common to see an Arab express a heartfelt greeting to a total stranger. Such a gesture is just one of the various ways an Arab exhibits politeness. 'Being agreeable' is important too. In a business meeting, for instance, in response to a proposal or a viewpoint, it is unlikely that an Arab would evince outright disagreement in the very first instance. This is, in fact, analogous to the inability of an Arab participant to express a negative reaction in the context of a survey involving assessment of product concepts. An Arab would rather subtly suggest an alternative point of view or move the discussion to another topic than express dissent. In addition, being polite is in accord with being a good host. A guest at one's home is treated with deference and every attempt is made to please and serve their needs. In surveys done in the Middle East, most interviews are done face-to-face at the participant's place of residence. In such a scenario, it is easy to see why a participant treats the interviewer as a guest, and exhibits behaviour that is seen as fitting for a good host. A negative response to a product concept would thus be seen as equivalent of being disagreeable and, hence, impolite. In effect, the participant would rather say that the concept is likely to be acceptable than say that it will not succeed.

Governmental environment

An additional relevant factor is the governmental environment. The type of government has a bearing on the emphasis on public policy, regulatory agencies, government incentives and penalties, and investment in government enterprises. Some governments, particularly in developing countries, do not encourage overseas competition. High tariff barriers create disincentives to the efficient use of marketing research approaches. Also, the role of government in setting market controls, developing infrastructure and acting as an entrepreneur should be carefully assessed. The role of government is also crucial in many developed countries, where government has traditionally worked with industry towards a common national industrial policy. At the tactical level, the government determines tax structures, tariffs and product safety rules and regulations, often imposing special rules and regulations on overseas multinationals and their marketing practices. In many countries, the government may be an important member of the distribution channel. The government purchases essential products on a large scale and then sells them to consumers, perhaps on a rationed basis.

Legal environment

The legal environment encompasses common law, overseas law, international law, transaction law, antitrust, bribery and taxes. From the standpoint of international marketing research, particularly salient are laws related to the elements of the marketing mix. Product laws include those dealing with product quality, packaging, warranty and after-sales service, patents, trademarks and copyright. Laws on pricing deal with price fixing, price discrimination, variable pricing, price controls and retail price maintenance. Distribution laws relate to exclusive territory arrangements, type of channels, and cancellation of distributor or wholesaler agreements. Likewise, laws govern the type of promotional methods that can be employed. Although all countries have laws regulating marketing activities, some countries have only a few laws that are loosely enforced and others have many complicated laws that are strictly enforced. In many countries the legal channels are clogged and the settlement of court cases is prolonged. In addition, home-country laws may also apply while conducting business or marketing research in overseas countries.

Economic environment

Economic environmental characteristics include economic size (gross domestic product, or GDP); level, source and distribution of income; growth trends; and sectoral trends. A country's stage of economic development determines the size, the degree of modernisation and the standardisation of its markets. Consumer, industrial and commercial markets become more standardised and consumers' work, leisure and lifestyles become more homogenised by economic development and advances in technology.

Informational and technological environment

Elements of the informational and technological environment include information and communication systems, access to broadband, broadband speeds, the prevalence and use of mobile devices, the use of other electronic equipment, energy, production technology, science and invention. Advances in science and technology have made disproportionate impacts on consumers across the globe. It would be a mistake to generalise about the impact of information and technology on developing economies and on particular rural consumers. The following example illustrates the progress made in developing economies in terms of information and technology. Understanding such progress in individual target communities is vital for international researchers.

Real research   **Moving straight to a mobile infrastructure[5]**

It is important not to oversimplify the term 'developing markets'. Developing markets should also not be treated as a single 'region'. There are many points of cultural, economic, social and technological difference in every country and even within some countries. While a piecemeal transport infrastructure in many developing countries can make travel challenging for researchers, particularly in rural areas, there is evidence that many developing countries are ahead of the developed world in implementing mobile communications infrastructure. This is particularly true in Africa, where more than 600 million people now have mobile phones. It is a mistake to assume that developed markets are simply behind the pace of change in marketing research, simply because they have not progressed from door-to-door interviewing to computer assisted telephone interviewing (CATI) or online research. While face-to-face surveys will remain important in these markets, it will not be the only method of data collection. Cambodia, for example, has very limited fixed-line coverage for telecoms because of the dark years under the Khmer Rouge and subsequent Vietnamese occupation, but it has bypassed the development of fixed-line communications (now around one per 100 people) and moved straight to a mobile infrastructure (currently around 30 per 100 people). The situation is the same across Africa and many other developing countries and signifies a different evolution in the development of technology that can be used for data capture in research to that for developed countries. Mobile phones are embedded into the daily lives of people throughout the developing world. Research across seven sub-Saharan African countries revealed that 7 out of 10 people first experience the Internet via mobile, and for 6 out of 10 people it remains the main mode of access.

Structural environment

Structural factors relate to transportation, communication, utilities and infrastructure. Personal contact with participants may be difficult for a variety of reasons in individual countries. Based on geography alone, national samples in China and Indonesia are really challenging. China is predominantly rural and Indonesia consists of several thousand islands. There are creative research designs that enable participants to be accessed in remote communities where travel and infrastructure make research expensive and time consuming. Such a design is illustrated in the following example.

Real research   **Smart and non-Smart phones in developing markets[6]**

In China, TNS (**www.tnsglobal.com**) and MobileMeasure (**www.mobile-measure.com**) successfully ran qualitative and quantitative projects in both urban and rural settings using non-Smart Java-enabled phones. The TNS research team used MobileMeasure's TPV platform (a Text, Photo and Video blogging application). This enabled them to effectively bring qualitative and quantitative research to life without actually having to absorb substantial additional travel and moderation costs, particularly when researching in multiple remote locations. TPV worked on both Smart and non-Smart (Java-enabled phones), facilitating a far more representative sample and rising to the challenge of conducting cost-effective qualitative and quantitative research in 'lower tier' cities and towns and remote and out of the way areas. Through its partnership with MobileMeasure, TNS was able to have research participants use their non-Smart (Java-enabled phones) to blog text and upload photos and videos real time, capturing 'in-the-moment' behaviour instantly. The TNS moderators were provided with a data online dashboard. They were often located remotely in other parts of the country, but could monitor the live feeds coming in. Additionally they could comment, communicate and elicit responses from the group or individual participants in real time or in a pre-planned manner, all done remotely. On average TNS recorded 20–25 text blogs per week, 18–25 photos per week and 3–5 videos per week per participant, highlighting the validity and robustness of this technique and its natural fit with participants' daily lives.

Socio-cultural environment

Socio-cultural factors include values, literacy, language, religion, communication patterns, and family and social institutions. Relevant values and attitudes towards progress, time, achievement, work, authority, wealth, scientific method, risk, innovation and change could be considered here. In India, as noted earlier, there are 17 major languages and more than 844 dialects. India is divided into linguistic states. The country can be described as a mini-Europe, each state like a separate country within Europe, with its own language and cultural peculiarities. A survey which even approaches national representation in scope will generally be printed in at least 12 languages.[7]

Each country's environment is unique, so international marketing research must take into consideration the environmental characteristics of the countries or overseas markets involved. The following example illustrates how dangerous terms such as the 'Asian market' may be for international marketers.

Real research   ## Diversities in the ASEAN region[8]

Many marketing commentators evaluating prospects in Asia focus on the two countries with the biggest populations and economic growth rates, China and India. It is easy to miss other rich and dynamic economies in the ASEAN (Association of South-East Asian Nations) region: Indonesia, Malaysia, Thailand, Singapore, the Philippines and Vietnam, as well as a collection of smaller countries. This is one of the world's most dynamic sub-regions with a combined young, literate population of 575 million and an average GDP growth rate consistently above 6 per cent. However, there is no South-East Asian mind-set; it is a complex sub-region. The region may be viewed as immensely diverse, from the social acceptance of power and wealth inequalities in Indonesia, through to the strict, risk-averse Thais and a clear gender disparity in the Philippines. An acute understanding of cultural, historical and political differences will pay dividends to anyone operating across these markets. Marketers should apply the 'one-size-fits-all' mentality with great caution. There are some common themes that bring together the people of the ASEAN region, one of them being a thirst for digital technology. Filipinos are among the most avid blog readers on the planet, second only to the South Koreans. Thais spend the longest time talking on the phone of any nation in Asia. The region does not have a digital lifestyle in the western image yet. What we see in the ASEAN countries is people longing to connect with the outside world and finding a platform for self-expression.

For companies that wish to expand into large geographical regions, the challenges in the above example can cause problems. Should they invest in research into every country or even regions within countries, or will these be prohibitive in time and cost terms? If they cannot manage to research individual countries in a region, which countries should they focus upon? Researching from the security of a key market may miss subtleties that local researchers would be quick to pick up on. Another benefit of local researchers is that desk research and their knowledge can help to fill in many gaps. The ideal is to have a multi-country project, coordinated from one location with local suppliers building out individual country knowledge within a common framework. The research approach should ensure quality control and consistency, and it should lead to actionable and global strategic recommendations, with all local markets represented. Such a maxim is fine, provided that international researchers can demonstrate the potential returns from such an investment, which is inherently very difficult to achieve.

The extent to which companies may invest in research targeted at individual countries may be evaluated in terms of not only the potential returns and idiosyncrasies of that country, but also the complexities of implementing research techniques that will work well. To help understand the problems of implementing international marketing research, we provide additional details for implementing secondary data, qualitative techniques, survey methods, measurement and scaling techniques and questionnaire translation.[9]

Secondary data

The topic of secondary data was covered in detail earlier in the text (Chapter 3). An example of a secondary data source of great use in international marketing research is presented in the following example.

Real research | **Roper Reports Worldwide[10]**

Each year since 1997, GfK Roper Consulting (**www.gfkamerica.com**) has conducted over 30,000 face-to-face surveys with consumers aged 13+ years, across the world's leading markets. It aims to be representative of the national populations in North America and Western Europe, and of the urban population in other countries. The Roper Reports Worldwide study does not cover all countries but 22 megacities (population over 10 million and listed in order of size): Tokyo, Seoul, Mexico City, New York City, Mumbai, Delhi, Sao Paulo, Los Angeles, Shanghai, Osaka, Cairo, Kolkata, Jakarta, Guangzhou, Buenos Aires, Beijing, London, Paris, Istanbul, Rio de Janeiro, Moscow and Bangkok. The study is founded upon key factors that drive consumer behaviour in general and in the megacity, namely: (1) *Personal values:* With the blurring of age and gender, marketers are putting more emphasis on understanding the personal values of their consumers. (2) *Geography:* While globalisation is making lifestyles more similar around the world, life and consumer priorities still differ from one country to another. (3) *Life-stage/demographics:* While differences between consumers of different ages and genders is eroding, life-stage can play an important role in driving consumers' needs and product choices. (4) *Lifestyles:* Personal values show us the things that people aspire to; it is also important to understand the lifestyles that people actually lead. The two are not the same. (5) *Attitudes and behaviour:* How consumers relate to a specific product category, in terms of attitudes and behaviours.

It is worth recalling where secondary data can support the research process, especially given some of the difficulties of conducting primary research in international markets. Secondary data can help to:

1 Diagnose the research problem.

2 Develop an approach to the problem.

3 Develop a sampling plan.

4 Formulate an appropriate research design (e.g. by identifying the key variables to measure or understand).

5 Answer certain research questions and test some hypotheses.

6 Interpret primary data with more insight.

7 Validate qualitative research findings.

Obtaining secondary data on international markets to gain support for the above is much simpler with the advent of the Internet. Online resources can allow access to international markets which in the past may have required travel to the country and a great amount of time-consuming searching. Judicious use of online resources does not mean that the international researcher will automatically gain support in the above seven areas. There may still be little or no secondary data that relate to the issues we wish to research in an international market, especially when new product/market opportunities are being explored. For what data we can obtain, the principles of evaluating secondary data, as set out in Table 3.1, still apply. Conducting an evaluation of the nature, specifications, accuracy, currency and dependability may be far more difficult in international markets. The process and specifications of research conducted in international markets may not be explicit; one may need a deep understanding of conducting primary research in a country to understand why data have been collected in a particular manner. Language is also a major issue, not only in reading and interpreting data, but in the definitions used in measurements. Finally, secondary research from a target country may have been heavily influenced by political forces. The researcher may need to be aware of such influences in order to interpret and make use of the findings.

Qualitative methods

There are differences between European and American researchers in their approach to focus groups. In general terms, an American approach can be seen as far more structured and tends to be a foundation for subsequent surveys, while the European approach tends to be more evolutionary and exploratory. The question of the perspective from which one plans and conducts qualitative research is not really important until other researchers or moderators from international markets become involved in the process. As well as the training and thinking of researchers who plan and administer focus groups, there can be cultural differences in how participants engage in the technique. The resultant output of focus groups across cultures in international markets may not match the expectations of the decision maker who will be supported by the research.

Decision makers often require global answers to develop global marketing campaigns, yet data are often single-market related and cannot be easily interpreted across various countries. Researchers can be wary of using varying methods across different countries and cultures. They recognise that more control in the design and implementation of research is needed and that many forms of bias can emerge when working across cultures. However, there are many examples of where qualitative research is practiced to great effect, especially in understanding subtle cultural nuances. An example of such an approach lies in semiotics, which has great potential in supporting communication strategies for global brands entering developing markets. This visually based approach plays a critical part in the development of cross-cultural communications. It helps brands to keep up with rapid and culturally revolutionary change, especially in countries such as the Brazil, Russia, India and China. In developing markets this involves tracking richer and more nuanced patterns of cultural diversity. Individual developing markets live with and increasingly celebrate their own inner diversity (India, for example, being as internally diverse as Europe), while global diversity simultaneously sweeps in. For the international researcher, developing overseas markets has become ripe for semiotics to be disseminated and practiced by local research experts.[11]

Another example of an increasing use of qualitative research in international marketing research is in the use of social media research techniques, especially the use of marketing research online communities. From around 2005 in the United States, Canada, the United Kingdom and other parts of Western Europe, and in other parts of the world including Australia and New Zealand, online research communities have flourished. The technique provides primarily qualitative consumer insight on development topics in products, services, brands and communications.[12] An online research community is a group of people who have been provided with an online environment in which to interact with each other (and the client and researcher) about topics related to a research interest. Typically, they are constructed in content management systems (e.g. Community Server), which provide functionality such as forums, blogging, polls, personal spaces, videos and email contact mechanisms. The reasons for setting them up are to: monitor key issues within a market; tap into leading-edge consumers/innovators within a market; have a group of consumers available throughout a development process; genuinely collaborate in a two-way direction with consumers; easily monitor issues in many markets around the globe; have a cost-effective way to research many issues. There have been some well-documented case studies of successful multinational communities but most are run completely in English. Running successful communities, in situations where multicultural effects are larger or in multiple languages, presents many challenges though there are companies and researchers developing such approaches.[13] The following example illustrates some of the challenges in administering online research communities for international marketing research.

| Real research | **The global marketing research online community[14]** |

The application of marketing research online communities (MROCs) around the world is still an emerging discipline but a number key principles of their success are emerging. A natural assumption with a multi-country community is to segment it by language alone. This is for both pragmatic reasons where there is a direct cost when needing to translate, but also because this is the most visible differentiator. However, because two countries share a language, it does not mean they will naturally share ideals, beliefs or cultural terms of reference. The social interactions between a brand or representatives of a brand are more important for the success of an MROC than the interactions between participants. Conversations flourish only if there is a two-way flow. Emphasising the fact that feedback will be given to the community and how their input will help shape decisions is the primary message that should be presented through the life cycle of a community. One of the biggest challenges practitioners and clients using MROCs face is the need to embrace this conversational stance. Typically MROCs are moderated everyday, asking questions, posting discussions, and probing answers. This moderation needs to cater to the specific needs of participants and be pitched in a way that is easily understood. The moderator has a role in policing, providing technical support and answering other queries. Moderation is challenging in many ways. Content must be clear and concise, broad to encourage debate, specific as to not be ambiguous, but not leading. The number of questions in any one topic can be limited. Moderators need to be sensitive to misunderstanding from participants, and clarify meaning or context of questions. By understanding the specific online behaviour of the target audience a moderator can make the question interesting to the participants and remain in tune with the client's objectives. A good moderator will be able to act intuitively and reflect the needs of participants. The moderator becomes an interpreter in the widest sense of the word. While language is a start point, it is not the destination. They must understand their community and preferably show similar behaviours to those they are talking to in the community. Moderators need to understand 'the way things work' online in that country. By understanding the background to any conversation the moderator is able to add a greater understanding to the research. The right moderator not only adds to the knowledge of a particular country, but will also add to the knowledge of the community, not only as a group but sometimes even as individuals. It is also important for a moderator to be culturally sensitive and in a position to understand and acknowledge that social norms and simple points of reference are different both between and sometimes within countries.

This example also illustrates the essence of qualitative research in terms of exploring through rewording, of adapting an interview until sense is made. In international marketing research this calls for linguistic skills and a cultural awareness matching native speakers in any target country. This may not be a solution that is feasible for all international research projects. Depending upon the array of countries to be researched, recruiting researchers with the relevant linguistic skills may not be possible, but it is the best alternative should local research companies not exist or be considered to be of poor quality. Good-quality local researchers should be sought out, because, even if researchers with the relevant linguistic abilities are available, there are other cultural nuances that can affect the trust, rapport and comfort of qualitative research participants. Often participants are unfamiliar with the process or simply do not trust the researcher.

In general, patience and sensitivity are required to overcome cultural problems in conducting qualitative research in international markets.[15] An excellent working relationship with a local research company can be absolutely vital to success and in many cultures can only be achieved by developing a personal relationship. Listening to the advice of local research companies will also enhance sensitivity to participants. Patience is expressed by a preparedness to lengthen the research schedule, extra care in translation, pretests of wording and tact, and respect for participants and local researchers. Whether shaped by European or American paradigms or even any emerging paradigm that underpins social media research, good qualitative research should be open and a learning process. This openness and learning should be shared among decision makers, the researchers coordinating research activities and local researchers working in individual countries. All parties should clearly understand the premises for exploring particular issues, probing certain individuals and the bases for interpreting data. In qualitative international marketing research, where there may be confusion about the premises for the whole approach, there is a much greater need for openness between all parties involved.

Survey methods

The following sections discuss the major interviewing methods in light of the challenges of conducting international research.[16]

Online surveys

The vast majority of survey research is conducted online. This pattern has generally occurred across the globe, with countries like Canada, Japan, The Netherlands and Germany leading the way with high proportions of their research spend being devoted to online surveys. The primary benefits of reducing costs and the time needed to generate results are clear. It also is able to reach participants in places and at times where they are spending significant parts of their lives.[17] When considering the relative cost per interview it must far and away be the largest single source of quantitative research data in the world. Online research has distinct advantages in all applications including international research, overseas research, multinational research, and cross-cultural research. However, there is a body of criticism of the approach and alternatives mooted that are based upon social media research methods.

Online access panels remain the predominant sampling source for online research projects. The key concern for the owners of online panels is to acquire and maintain a critical mass of members who are motivated to repeatedly participate in online surveys.[18] For researchers, however, as more projects come online questions have been asked about the rigour, reliability, generalisability and inter-changeability of panel sources. The quality of online surveys has been criticised as clients and researchers try to improve response rates, create representative samples, and identify weak participants. Online access panels are not random samples of any definable population but sources of convenience samples. The extent to which they are comparable to each other is dependent on recruitment sources used and these can vary across different countries. In classical sampling theory they suffer from frame errors, and sometimes very substantial ones.[19] As dominant as the online survey and access panel is, it has been argued that people active in social networks do not tend to become members of panels, and vice versa.[20] This means that using social media research methods are no better than access panels at gaining representative views of target participants. Mixing various online research methods (beyond well-documented mixed-mode surveys) could well be the future for international researchers, as illustrated in the following example.

Real research | **Fusing contemporary research methods at Danone**[21]

Danone (**www.danone.com**) wanted to understand the use of water in daily life and highlight consumer expectations for water consumption in general. In order to investigate water consumption from different angles, a 'fusion research' design was implemented. Fusion research is a research design where multiple (contemporary) research methods are combined in order to study a certain research question from different angles. The divide between taking data from more traditional and new sources is analogous to the divide between a walled garden and a wild garden. In the 'walled garden' where everything is controlled, traditional survey research can be used among research communities with questions posed and answer received. In the 'wild garden'

social media netnotgraphy among natural communities can be used to generate spontaneous private but anonymous conversations, with far less controls. Such a hybrid brought great benefits to the Danone study: using the social web for better, faster recruitment, employing better survey vocabulary, inspiring and insightful data, and a happier, more open, conversational style of discourse between researchers and participants.

Telephone surveys and CATI

In the 1990s, telephone surveys were the dominant mode of survey data collection in countries with extensive telephone coverage. For some years, telephone surveys have ran second to online surveys in terms of global research spend.[22] This move can be attributed to the strengths of online surveys but also to some of the weaknesses of traditional telephone surveys as the use of mobile devices has grown. The development of mobile communications and especially Smartphones has meant a move away from the telephone coverage configuration that enabled traditional telephone surveys to be conducted. This has impacted upon national surveys and even more so on international surveys using the telephone. Although the type of phone access varies greatly from country to country, across Europe there have been significant developments in telephone arrangements: the percentage of households equipped with a fixed phone has fallen, while the percentage of households equipped with mobile phone access has risen. In addition, the percentage of mobile-only households has increased, while the percentage of households that have only fixed phone access has decreased. In countries such as Finland, Italy, Portugal, Belgium and Slovenia, fixed phone coverage has already been overtaken by mobile phone coverage. There seems to be a tendency to a widespread generalisation of the phenomenon to other countries. International researchers need to understand the distribution and use of phone types in any particular country that they plan a telephone survey. Mobile phone users are different from fixed phone users. Mobile surveys offer the possibility of covering segments of the population that own only a mobile phone and is therefore excluded from current fixed phone surveys. However, mobile phone-based surveys pose technical, cost and ethical issues that are distinct from those associated with fixed phone surveys. Not all mobile phones are the same and we have used the convention of the term 'mobile device' to cover a great breadth of mobile communications. An example within this term is the use of the Smartphone. Not all mobile phones are Smartphone's and the term itself has no single accepted definition. What is clear, is that the number of people across the globe owning such devices is growing rapidly. Surveys are already being completed on Smartphones though there may be great limitations in their consistent use within a country, never mind in international research, given the challenges of using techniques such as Flash technology.[23]

Demographic differences between fixed phone and mobile phone users may become less prevalent as mobile phone dissemination increases globally and extends to specific subgroups. In general (and there are good individual examples that demonstrate the reverse) mobile phone samples tend to over-represent younger people, employed people in urban and thriving economies, and to under-represent people living in smaller households, those with lower educational levels and rural economies. As with online surveys on an international basis, researchers need to improve survey quality, such as using multiple-mode surveys or switching to new methods altogether. Mixed phone designs may be easier to deal with if there is evidence that conducting an interview over a fixed phone or over a mobile phone has no influence on how the participants come up with their answers.[24]

Street surveys

In the 1980s, street surveys replaced the telephone for the bulk of consumer research and replaced home surveys for advertising research. The context of the street, the mall or the shopping centre offered the advantages of easy access to large groups of relatively homogeneous populations and allowed researchers to explain, test and control complex material including visuals. Because of the presence of a trained interviewer, attitudes, opinions, and beliefs and secondary claims and meanings could be probed with additional open-end and closed-end questions. Since the late 1990s, the street survey has been replaced by the use of online surveys for a significant percentage of consumer and advertising studies.[25] However, in many countries, with low Internet and telephone penetration or with comparatively low literacy rates, the street survey still offers the best and predominant means to conduct surveys.

This should not imply that the technique is 'relegated' to use in developing economies. There are still many survey challenges, where the quota sample enables a large and well-structured sample, and where the street survey captures complex views 'of the moment'. This is illustrated in the following example of a multinational research project.

Real research	**Emotional tennis**[26]

Many brands invest in sports events, essentially to benefit from the visibility they offer. Emotions felt by spectators are crucial in the sponsorship relationship between brands and consumers. By comparing emotions felt by spectators during the French and Australian Open tennis tournaments, a study wished to assess how emotions shaped the preliminary step of sponsorship effectiveness; the appreciation of the event. The study focused on the French and Australian Opens. There was no doubt that these two events were marketed differently and attended by different people, but it was felt that the universality of the emotional phenomenon should elicit similar emotional responses. To test their hypotheses and allow for comparisons, two identical data collections were held during Roland Garros (French) 2008 (N1 = 437) and the Australian Open 2009 (N2 = 375). Data was collected during the first five days of each event, using a street survey technique. Each construct was measured using previously validated multi-item scales after three independent judges had translated them from English to French. Their findings revealed that positive emotions were felt twice as intensely as negative emotions, meaning that spectators' emotional experience was globally positive at both events.

Provided that the environment of the street allows a survey to be conducted, the street survey is an excellent means to identify and interview individuals where there are poor or non-existent sampling frames. Given the congestion in many major international cities, the locations where interviews will be conducted have to be carefully selected. However, this does not differ from planning and conducting street surveys in 'home' markets. As with home and workplace surveys, the differences lie in the culture of approaching someone in the street and their willingness to divulge information to a stranger.

Home and workplace face-to-face surveys

Home and workplace face-to-face surveys require a large pool of qualified interviewers and are time consuming and costly. However, when one considers the quality of rapport that can be built up between the interviewer and participant, the amount of probing and the quality of audio-visual stimuli that can be used, there are clear benefits that can outweigh the costs. In many areas of business-to-business marketing research, the only means to contact certain managers may be through the face-to-face survey, held in their workplace. In many countries, this approach may be the only means to reach particular participants and/or the only context in which they feel relaxed, open and are willing to give truthful responses to questions. Given the costs and time needed to conduct such interviews, there has been a growth of the use of ethnography and observational techniques to supplement interviews.

Postal surveys

Because of their low cost, postal surveys continue to be used in most developed countries where literacy is high and the postal system is well developed. At 4 per cent, postal surveys globally constitute the lowest form of quantitative data collection. Sweden (15 per cent) Finland (14 per cent) Norway (14 per cent) and Japan (14 per cent) constitute the highest levels

Construct equivalence
A type of equivalence that deals with the question of whether the marketing constructs have the same meaning and significance in different countries.

Conceptual equivalence
A construct equivalence issue that deals with whether the interpretation of brands, products, consumer behaviour and the marketing effort are the same in different countries.

of postal surveys worldwide.[27] In many parts of Africa, Asia and South America, the use of postal surveys and postal panels is low because of illiteracy and the large proportion of population living in rural areas. In a study of past, present and future marketing research techniques in China, researchers reported rare occasions when they had good results with postal surveys. Participants did not seem to have as much enthusiasm in responding to a postal survey and taking the trouble to post it back, especially when the survey was commercial in nature.[28] However, there are still many survey situations where sampling challenges can be properly addressed and where participants are happy to complete a hard copy questionnaire in a time and space that suits their circumstances. Postal surveys are, typically, more effective in business-to-business international marketing research, although it can be a major challenge to identify the appropriate participant within each firm and to personalise the address.

Measurement and scaling

Functional equivalence
A construct equivalence issue that deals specifically with whether a given concept or behaviour serves the same role or function in different countries.

Category equivalence
A construct equivalence issue that deals specifically with whether the categories in which brands, products and behaviour are grouped are the same in different countries.

Operational equivalence
A type of equivalence that measures how theoretical constructs are operationalised in different countries to measure marketing variables.

In international marketing research, it is critical to establish the equivalence of scales and measures used to obtain data from different countries. As illustrated in Figure 14.2, this requires an examination of construct equivalence, operational equivalence, scalar equivalence and linguistic equivalence.[29]

Construct equivalence deals with the question of whether the marketing constructs (e.g. opinion leadership, customer satisfaction and brand loyalty) have the same meaning and significance in different countries. It focuses on the basic conceptual definition of the underlying construct. In many countries, the number of brands available in a given product category is limited. In some countries, the dominant brands have become generic labels symbolising the entire product category. Consequently, a different perspective on brand loyalty may have to be adopted in these countries.

Construct equivalence comprises conceptual equivalence, functional equivalence and category equivalence. **Conceptual equivalence** deals with the interpretation of brands, products, consumer behaviour and marketing effort. For example, sales promotion techniques are an integral component of marketing effort throughout Europe. On the other hand, in countries with shortage economies, where the market is dominated by the sellers, consumers view sales with suspicion because they believe that the product being promoted is of poor quality. **Functional equivalence** examines whether a given concept or behaviour serves the same role or function in different countries. For example, in many developing countries, bicycles are predominantly a means of transportation rather than of recreation. Marketing research related to the use of bicycles in these countries must examine different motives, attitudes,

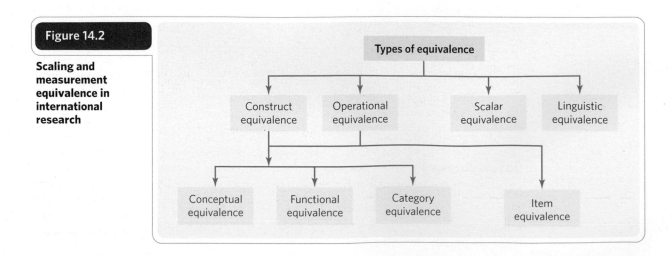

Figure 14.2

Scaling and measurement equivalence in international research

behaviours and even different competing products than such research would in Europe. Category equivalence refers to the category in which stimuli such as products, brands and behaviours are grouped. In Europe, the category of the principal shopper may be defined as either the male or female head of household. This category may be inappropriate in countries where routine daily shopping is done by a domestic servant. Furthermore, the category 'household' itself varies across countries.

Operational equivalence concerns how theoretical constructs are operationalised to make measurements. In Europe, leisure may be operationalised as playing golf, tennis or other sports, watching TV, or basking in the sun, for example. This operationalisation may not be relevant in countries where people do not play these sports or do not have round-the-clock TV transmission. Lying in the sun is generally not normal behaviour in countries with very hot climates.

Measurement equivalence deals with the comparability of responses to particular (sets of) items. Measurement equivalence includes configural (structural), metric (measurement unit) and scalar equivalence. Configural equivalence concerns the relationships of measured items to the latent constructs. Technically, configural equivalence implies that the patterns of factor loadings should be the same across countries or cultural units. Metric equivalence refers to the unit of measurement; the factor loading should be the same. Metric equivalence suggests that the survey instruments (questionnaires) are measuring the same constructs to the same extent in different countries or cultures.

Scalar equivalence refers to equivalence of both the unit of measurement and the constant in the equation between the construct and the items measuring the construct (the intercept). The distinction is important because for some purposes (e.g., comparing structural relationships across groups) both metric and scalar equivalence are needed. Finally, linguistic equivalence refers to both the spoken and the written language forms used in scales, questionnaires and interviewing. The scales and other verbal stimuli should be translated so that they are readily understood by participants in different countries and have equivalent meaning.[30]

Questionnaire translation

Questionnaires may have to be translated for administration in different cultures. Frequent use is made of direct translation, in which a bilingual translator translates the questionnaire directly from a base language to the participant's language. If the translator is not fluent in both languages and is not familiar with both cultures, however, direct translation of certain words and phrases may be flawed. Procedures like back translation and parallel translation have been suggested to avoid these errors. In back translation, the questionnaire is translated from the base language by a bilingual speaker whose native language is the language into which the questionnaire is being translated. This version is then retranslated back into the original language by a bilingual whose native language is the initial or base language. Translation errors can then be identified. Several repeat translations and back translations may be necessary to develop equivalent questionnaires, and this process can be cumbersome and time consuming.[31]

An alternative procedure is parallel translation. A committee of translators, each of whom is fluent in at least two of the languages in which the questionnaire will be administered, discuss alternative versions of the questionnaire and make modifications until consensus is reached. In countries where several languages are spoken, the questionnaire should be translated into the language of each participant subgroup. It is important that any non-verbal stimuli (pictures and advertisements) also be translated using similar procedures. The following example illustrates some of the challenges and importance of translation in research.

Measurement equivalence

Deals with the comparability of responses to particular (sets of) items. Measurement equivalence includes configural (structural), metric (measurement unit) and scalar equivalence.

Configural equivalence

Concerns the relationships of measured items to the latent constructs and implies that the patterns of factor loadings should be the same across countries or cultural units.

Metric equivalence

Refers to the unit of measurement; the factor loading should be the same.

Scalar equivalence

The demonstration that two individuals from different countries with the same value on some variable will score at the same level on the same test. Also called metric equivalence.

Linguistic equivalence

The equivalence of both spoken and written language forms used in scales and questionnaires.

Back translation

A translation technique that translates a questionnaire from the base language by a translator whose native language is the one into which the questionnaire is being translated. This version is then retranslated back into the original language by someone whose native language is the base language. Translation errors can then be identified.

Parallel translation

A translation method in which a committee of translators, each of whom is fluent in at least two languages, discuss alternative versions of a questionnaire and make modifications until consensus is reached.

Taking the people's temperature – right across Europe[32]

Eurobarometer measures public opinion across Europe on behalf of the European Commission. First published in 1974, it runs twice a year, in spring and autumn, and now surveys some 25,000 participants in each wave. The objectives set by the EC for the Eurobarometer are threefold. First, to evaluate the activities of the European Commission and indicate how the public might welcome a particular proposition, e.g. nuclear energy. Second, to measure how European public opinion has changed over a period of time. Third, to observe and anticipate public attitudes towards important events directly or indirectly linked to the development of the EU. One of the most challenging steps of the Eurobarometer is to ensure that question meaning is the same across all countries surveyed, taking into account specific national and cultural differences. For example, in France, the phrase 'mobile phone' is translated as 'téléphone mobile'. In French-speaking Belgium, that would mean 'wireless handset'. To address such issues, TNS (**www.tnsglobal.com**) always starts with a bilingual (English/French) version of the initial questionnaire. From this point, a meeting takes place to review the quality of the bilingual version to check if the meaning of each question is clear for all countries. A final bilingual version of the questionnaire is then made available so that each country can carry out its translation into the local language(s). The translations are carried out, working from the final questionnaire by two different translators. After this, all questionnaires are back translated into English or French by external experts. Any differences between the back-translated version and the original are immediately identified and reviewed.

Ethics in marketing research

Ethical responsibilities for marketing research conducted internationally are very similar to those for research conducted domestically. In conducting marketing research across Europe (and indeed globally), ESOMAR produce codes of conduct that guides professional practice that protects the interests of all research stakeholders. In general, for each of the six stages of the marketing research design process, the same four stakeholders (client, researcher, participant and public) should act honourably and respect their responsibilities to one another. For individual countries, a key development in honourable practice lies in the development of professional associations. The ESOMAR website lists these associations should there be any specific operational and ethical concern related to conducting research in that country.

International research has become more commonplace and possible with the advent of digital and social media. The marketing and research opportunities are immense but as consequence, new confidentiality and ethical concerns have emerged. Social networking, blogging, online communities and web 2.0 technologies offer innovative ways of engaging participants, but introduce new privacy and legal issues for researchers to manage. These issues include identity theft, harassment, defamation of character, and maintaining client confidentiality. At the same time, technological advances in computing power, mobile devices and storage media carry many benefits, but they too add risk that must be mitigated. Protecting participant privacy and client confidentiality has never been as challenging for researchers as it is in a digital world. Regulators and the public are quick to pounce when privacy breaches occur.[33] There are a number of institutions, both government and non-government (including professional research associations), that are attempting to support participants in protecting their privacy. This has and will continue to have a major impact on the way in which the researcher will be able to contact and engage with participants, as well as what type of information can be collected and shared with the business world.[34] One of the biggest ethical challenges facing international researchers given the global impact of digital and social media lies in differentiating marketing research from other data gathering practices.

Digital developments in marketing research

Digital development in marketing research can be extensively used in all aspects of international research. These uses parallel those discussed around specific techniques in earlier chapters and hence will not be repeated here. Of particular note, however, are social media and online research developments that can be used to communicate with participants and marketing decision makers anywhere in the world. The nature of that communication, in its openness in forms of expression and reach into distant communities, has given a new dimension to international marketing research. For example, the online survey overcomes geographic boundaries and differences in postal systems to solicit responses from around the world. Research using mobile devices can facilitate engaging with specialist target groups that in the past may have been difficult or even impossible to reach. Online research can also enhance the quality of data supplied to participants, generating more meaningful and relevant responses. The environmental characteristics of international markets detailed in this chapter present a formidable research task, especially when first learning about a country. Providing that the researcher has strong critical facilities, the sheer mass of data available online can provide great insight into particular countries or cultures. Material can be accessed quickly and anywhere to help shape an understanding of the different environmental contexts of a target country. This is particularly relevant in tracking down secondary data sources that may not be available in the home country of a researcher.

Summary

With the globalisation of markets, international marketing research is burgeoning rapidly. As well as the technical requirements of conducting successful marketing research as outlined in this text, the researcher has to cope with new cultures and languages in targeted international markets. Given the array of ethnic groups within most European countries, the challenges of understanding new cultures and languages can exist within a 'home' country.

The environment prevailing in the international markets being researched influences all six steps of the marketing research process. Important aspects of this environment include the marketing, governmental, legal, economic, structural, informational and technological, and socio-cultural environment.

In collecting data from different countries, it is desirable to use techniques with equivalent levels of reliability rather than the same method. Repeating identical techniques across borders may result in subtle cultural and linguistic differences being ignored, which may have a great effect upon the nature and quality of data that are generated. It is critical to establish the equivalence of scales and measures in terms of construct equivalence, operational equivalence, scalar equivalence and linguistic equivalence. Questionnaires used should be adapted to the specific cultural environment and should not be biased in favour of any one culture or language. Back translation and parallel translation are helpful in detecting translation errors.

The ethical concerns facing international researchers are similar in many ways to the issues confronting domestic researchers. International research has become more commonplace and possible with the advent of digital and social media. The marketing and research opportunities are immense but as consequence, new confidentiality and ethical concerns have emerged. Digital development in marketing research can be extensively used in all aspects of international research. These developments are used to communicate with participants and marketing decision makers anywhere in the world. They have brought an openness in forms of expression and reach into distant communities and have given a new dimension to international research.

Questions

1 Evaluate the meaning of 'international' from the perspective of the researcher.

2 What characteristics distinguish international marketing research from domestic marketing research?

3 Describe the aspects of the environment of each country that should be taken into account in international marketing research.

4 What is meant by the informational and technological environment? How do the variables comprising the informational and technological environment influence international marketing research?

5 What is meant by the socio-cultural environment? How do the variables comprising the socio-cultural environment influence international marketing research?

6 How should the researcher evaluate secondary data obtained from international markets?

7 Describe the factors that may influence the approach to qualitative methods in different countries.

8 Select a country and use environmental characteristics to illustrate why CATI works particularly well as a survey technique.

9 Select a country and use environmental characteristics to illustrate why home surveys do not work particularly well as a survey technique.

10 Select a country and use environmental characteristics to illustrate why online surveys work particularly well as a survey technique.

11 How should the equivalence of scales and measures be established when the data are to be obtained from different countries or cultural units?

12 What problems are involved in the direct translation of a questionnaire into another language?

Exercises

1 Obtain a copy of an old marketing research report that has been conducted in the country where you are studying (many marketing research agencies or companies that have commissioned research will provide copies of old reports for educational purposes). Evaluate how the research would have been conducted if the same project were conducted in Malaysia.

2 Compile data on the GDP, level of literacy and percentage of households with telephones for 20 different countries. Using a proprietary statistics package, run a regression analysis with GDP as the dependent variable and the other two variables as the independent variables. Interpret your results.

3 Visit the website of the Spanish fashion company Zara at **www.zara.com**. What can you learn about the company's international marketing efforts? Write a report on what you see as their main international marketing research challenges.

4 You are the Marketing Research Director of Unilever (**www.unilever.com**). What challenges do you see in researching markets for household products

in the Far East? Prepare a report for the Unilever Board in Europe making the case for a higher investment in marketing research in this region.

5   In a small group discuss the following issues: 'Some marketing strategists have argued that a standardised marketing strategy should be adopted for all international markets. Does this imply that the research design and techniques should be standardised no matter where the research is being conducted?' 'Given the huge cultural diversity that exists in many parts of Europe, should researchers have a mindset of 'home' and 'international' markets?'

Notes

1. See de Jong, M.G., Steenkamp, J-B. E.M., Fox, J-P. and Baumgartner, H., 'Using item response theory to measure extreme response style in marketing research: A global investigation', *Journal of Marketing Research*, 45 (1) (Feb. 2008), 104–105; Denton, T., 'Indexes of validity and reliability for cross-societal measures', *Cross Cultural Research*, 42 (2) (May 2008), 118; Ross, R.H., Broyles, S.A. and Leingpibul, T., 'Alternative measures of satisfaction in cross-cultural settings', *The Journal of Product and Brand Management*, 17 (2) (2008), 82; Malhotra, N.K., 'Cross-cultural marketing research in the twenty-first century', *International Marketing Review*, 18 (3) (2001), 230–34; Douglas, S.P., 'Exploring new worlds: The challenge of global marketing', *Journal of Marketing*, 65 (1) (Jan. 2001), 103–107; Malhotra, N.K., Agarwal, J. and Peterson, M., 'Cross-cultural marketing research: Methodological issues and guidelines', *International Marketing Review*, 13 (5) (1996), 7–43.

2. Churkina, O. and Sandler, C., 'Glocalization – a measure of global brands: Adaptation to local cultures', ESOMAR, *Asia Pacific*, Melbourne, (2011).

3. Gupta, S. and Samanta, R., 'Of heads and hearts and cultures apart! How a billion minds consume communication', ESOMAR, *Asia Pacific Conference*, Singapore (April 2008).

4. Joshi, A., Tamang, S. and Vashisthaz, H., 'You can't judge a book by its cover! A way to tackle the severe acquiescence bias among Arab participants', ESOMAR, *Annual Congress*, Montreal (Sept. 2008).

5. Worthington, P., 'Research in developing markets: Upwardly mobile', *Admap* (July/August 2010), 28–29.

6. Williams, N. and Fergusson, J., 'Bridging the digital divide in qualitative research in emerging markets: Smart Qual using Smart and non-Smart phones in developing markets', ESOMAR, *Asia Pacific*, Melbourne (2011).

7. Hutton, G., 'If you board the Asian bus, better mind your language', *ResearchPlus* (Feb. 1996), 9.

8. Young, M., 'Popularity of mobile and blogs is an untapped opportunity in ASEAN', *Admap*, South East Asia Supplement (Feb. 2009), 6–7.

9. See Cho, H.J., Jin, B. and Cho, H., 'An examination of regional differences in China by socio-cultural factors', *International Journal of Market Research*, 52 (5) (2010),

613–33; Craido, A.R. and Craido, J.R., 'International marketing research: Opportunities and challenges in the 21st century', *Advances in International Marketing*, 17 (2007), 1–13; James, D., 'Dark clouds should part for international marketers', *Marketing News*, 36 (1) (Jan. 11 2002), 9–10.

10. Chiarelli, N., 'Megacities as the new frontiers – a global consumer lifestyle study', ESOMAR, *Annual Congress*, Montreal (Sept. 2008).

11. Evans, M. and Shivakumar, H., 'Insight, cultural diversity, revolutionary change: Joined up semantic thinking for developing markets', ESOMAR, *Congress Odyssey*, Athens, (Sept. 2010).

12. Cierpicki, S., Alexander, D., Alchin, S., Brunton, C. and Poynter, R., 'It works for us but does it work for them? How online research communities work for consumers invited to participate', ESOMAR, *Online Research*, Chicago (Oct. 2009).

13. Comley, P., 'Online research communities – a user guide', *International Journal of Market Research*, 50 (5) (2008), 679–94.

14. Child, P., Fleming, K., Shaw, K. and Skilbeck, T., 'Vive La Difference: Understanding, embracing and evolving MROCs globally', ESOMAR, *Congress Odyssey*, Athens (Sept. 2010).

15. Zimmerman, A.S. and Szenberg, M., 'Implementing international qualitative research: Techniques and obstacles', *Qualitative Market Research: An International Journal*, 3 (3) (2000), 158–64.

16. Chisnall, P.M., 'International Marketing Research', *International Journal of Marketing Research*, 49 (1) (2007), 133–35; Hsieh, M-H., 'Measuring global brand equity using cross national survey data', *Journal of International Marketing*, 12 (2) (2004), 28–57; Malhotra, N.K., 'Cross-cultural marketing research in the twenty-first century', *International Marketing Review*, 18 (3) (2001), 230–34; Douglas, S.P., 'Exploring new worlds: The challenge of global marketing', *Journal of Marketing*, 65 (1) (Jan. 2001), 103–107.

17. ESOMAR, '*Global Market Research*, ESOMAR Industry Report (2010), 29.

18. Brüggen, E., Wetzels, M., de Ruyter, K. and Schillewaert, N., 'Individual differences in motivation to participate in

online panels: The effect on response rates and response quality perceptions', *International Journal of Market Research*, 53 (3) (2011).

19. de Jong, K., 'CSI Berlin: The strange case of the death of panels', ESOMAR, *Online Research*, Berlin (Oct. 2010).

20. de Jong, K., 'Ready or Not', in *Global Market Research*, ESOMAR Industry Report (2010), 30.

21. Baskin, M., 'Online research: Now and next – peak panel, gamification and digividuals', *Warc Exclusive* (March 2011); De Ruyck, T., Verhaeghe, A. and Rogeaux, M., 'Exploring the world of water: Fusing contemporary research methods', ESOMAR, *Congress Odyssey*, Athens (Sept. 2010).

22. ESOMAR, 'Global Market Research, *ESOMAR Industry Report* (2010) 29.

23. de Jong, K., 'CSI Berlin: The strange case of the death of panels', ESOMAR, *Online Research*, Berlin, (Oct. 2010).

24. Vicente, P., Reis, E. and Santos, M., 'Using mobile phones for survey research: A comparison with fixed phones', *International Journal of Market Research*, 51 (5) (2009), 613–34.

25. Maronick, T., 'Pitting the mall against the Internet in advertising research completion: Internet panels are more popular. Are they more effective?' *Journal of Advertising Research*, 51 (1) (2011), 321–31.

26. Bal, C., 'Understanding sport-related emotions in sponsorship', *Admap* (Nov. 2009), 45–47.

27. ESOMAR, *Global Market Research*, ESOMAR Industry Report (2010), 103.

28. Fine, B., Ellis, R.S. and Xu, D., 'Research methodologies in China – past, present and future', ESOMAR, *Asia Pacific*, Beijing (April 2009).

29. Giannakopoulou, C., Siomkos, G. and Vassilikopoulou, A., 'The input of psychology in methodological considerations of cross cultural marketing research', *European Journal of Scientific Research*, 20 (2) (April 2008), 249–54; Sharma, S. and Weathers, D., 'Assessing generalisability of scales used in cross-national research', *International Journal of Research in Marketing*, 20 (3) (2003), 287–95; Baumgartner, H. and Steenkamp, J-B. E.M., 'Response styles in marketing research: A cross-national investigation', *Journal of Marketing Research*, 38

(2) (2001), 143–46; Myers, M.B., 'Academic insights: An application of multiple-group causal models in assessing cross cultural measurement equivalence', *Journal of International Marketing*, 8 (4) (2000), 108–121; Malhotra, N.K., Agarwal, J. and Peterson, M., 'Cross-cultural marketing research: Methodological issues and guidelines', *International Marketing Review*, 13 (5) (1996), 7–43.

30. Denton, T., 'Indexes of validity and reliability for cross-sectional measures', *Cross-Cultural Research*, 42 (2) (May 2008), 118; Wong, N., Rindfliesch, A., Burroughs, J.E., Steenkamp, J-B. E.M. and Bearden, W.O., 'Do reverse-worded items confound measures in cross-cultural consumer research? The case of the material values scale', *Journal of Consumer Research*, 30 (1) (2003), 72–91; Thorne, L., 'The sociocultural embeddedness of individuals' ethical reasoning in organisations (cross cultural ethics)', *Journal of Business Ethics*, 35 (1) (Jan. 2002), 1–13; McDonald, G., 'Cross-cultural methodological issues in ethical research', *Journal of Business Ethics*, 27 (1/2) (Sept. 2000), 89–104.

31. de Jong, M.G., Steenkamp, J-B. E.M., Fox, J-P. and Baumgartner, H., 'Using item response theory to measure extreme response style in marketing research: A global investigation', *Journal of Marketing Research*, 45 (1) (Feb. 2008), 104–105; Behling, O. and Law, K.S., *Translating Questionnaires and other research instruments: Problems and solutions* (Thousand Oaks, CA: Sage, 2000); Malhotra, N.K. and McCort, D., 'A cross-cultural comparison of behavioural intention models: Theoretical consideration and an empirical investigation', *International Marketing Review*, 18 (3) (2001), 235–69.

32. Whiteside, S., 'The international communications market: A summary of Ofcom research into global media brands', *Warc Exclusive* (Dec. 2008); De Voogd, L. and Carballo, M., 'Taking the temperature', *Research* (Jan. 2006), 38–39.

33. Stark, D., 'From social engineering to social networking – Privacy issues when conducting research in the web 2.0 world', ESOMAR, *Research Congress*, Montreux (Sept. 2009).

34. Alioto, M.F., 'The researcher as Renaissance man: The creation of modern skill sets', ESOMAR, *Annual Congress*, Berlin (Sep. 2007).

Appendix: Statistical tables

| Table 1 | | Simple random numbers | | | | | | | | | | | |

Line/col.	(1)	(2)	(3)	(4)	(5)	(6)	(7)	(8)	(9)	(10)	(11)	(12)	(13)	(14)
1	10480	15011	01536	02011	81647	91646	69179	14194	62590	36207	20969	99570	91291	90700
2	22368	46573	25595	85393	30995	89198	27982	53402	93965	34095	52666	19174	39615	99505
3	24130	48390	22527	97265	76393	64809	15179	24830	49340	32081	30680	19655	63348	58629
4	42167	93093	06243	61680	07856	16376	39440	53537	71341	57004	00849	74917	97758	16379
5	37570	39975	81837	16656	06121	91782	60468	81305	49684	60072	14110	06927	01263	54613
6	77921	06907	11008	42751	27756	53498	18602	70659	90655	15053	21916	81825	44394	42880
7	99562	72905	56420	69994	98872	31016	71194	18738	44013	48840	63213	21069	10634	12952
8	96301	91977	05463	07972	18876	20922	94595	56869	69014	60045	18425	84903	42508	32307
9	89579	14342	63661	10281	17453	18103	57740	84378	25331	12568	58678	44947	05585	56941
10	85475	36857	53342	53988	53060	59533	38867	62300	08158	17983	16439	11458	18593	64952
11	28918	69578	88231	33276	70997	79936	56865	05859	90106	31595	01547	85590	91610	78188
12	63553	40961	48235	03427	49626	69445	18663	72695	52180	20847	12234	90511	33703	90322
13	09429	93969	52636	92737	88974	33488	36320	17617	30015	08272	84115	27156	30613	74952
14	10365	61129	87529	85689	48237	52267	67689	93394	01511	26358	85104	20285	29975	89868
15	07119	97336	71048	08178	77233	13916	47564	81056	97735	85977	29372	74461	28551	90707
16	51085	12765	51821	51259	77452	16308	60756	92144	49442	53900	70960	63990	75601	40719
17	02368	21382	52404	60268	89368	19885	55322	44819	01188	65255	64835	44919	05944	55157
18	01011	54092	33362	94904	31273	04146	18594	29852	71685	85030	51132	01915	92747	64951
19	52162	53916	46369	58586	23216	14513	83149	98736	23495	64350	94738	17752	35156	35749
20	07056	97628	33787	09998	42698	06691	76988	13602	51851	46104	88916	19509	25625	58104
21	48663	91245	85828	14346	09172	30163	90229	04734	59193	22178	30421	61666	99904	32812
22	54164	58492	22421	74103	47070	25306	76468	26384	58151	06646	21524	15227	96909	44592
23	32639	32363	05597	24200	13363	38005	94342	28728	35806	06912	17012	64161	18296	22851
24	29334	27001	87637	87308	58731	00256	45834	15398	46557	41135	10307	07684	36188	18510
25	02488	33062	28834	07351	19731	92420	60952	61280	50001	67658	32586	86679	50720	94953
26	81525	72295	04839	96423	24878	82651	66566	14778	76797	14780	13300	87074	79666	95725
27	29676	20591	68086	26432	46901	20849	89768	81536	86645	12659	92259	57102	80428	25280
28	00742	57392	39064	66432	84673	40027	32832	61362	98947	96067	64760	64584	96096	98253
29	05366	04213	25669	26422	44407	44048	37937	63904	45766	66134	75470	66520	34693	90449
30	91921	26418	64117	94305	26766	25940	39972	22209	71500	64568	91402	42416	07844	69618
31	00582	04711	87917	77341	42206	35126	74087	99547	81817	42607	43808	76655	62028	76630
32	00725	69884	62797	56170	86324	88072	76222	36086	84637	93161	76038	65855	77919	88006
33	69011	65795	95876	55293	18988	27354	26575	08625	40801	59920	29841	80150	12777	48501
34	25976	57948	29888	88604	67917	48708	18912	82271	65424	69774	33611	54262	85963	03547
35	09763	83473	73577	12908	30883	18317	28290	35797	05998	41688	34952	37888	38917	88050
36	91567	42595	27959	30134	04024	86385	29880	99730	55536	84855	29088	09250	79656	73211
37	17955	56349	90999	49127	20044	59931	06115	20542	18059	02008	73708	83517	36103	42791
38	46503	18584	18845	49618	02304	51038	20655	58727	28168	15475	56942	53389	20562	87338
39	92157	89634	94824	78171	84610	82834	09922	25417	44137	48413	25555	21246	35509	20468
40	14577	62765	35605	81263	39667	47358	56873	56307	61607	49518	89656	20103	77490	18062
41	98427	07523	33362	64270	01638	92477	66969	98420	04880	45585	46565	04102	46880	45709

▶

Line/col.	(1)	(2)	(3)	(4)	(5)	(6)	(7)	(8)	(9)	(10)	(11)	(12)	(13)	(14)
42	34914	63976	88720	82765	34476	17032	87589	40836	32427	70002	70663	88863	77775	69348
43	70060	28277	39475	46473	23219	53416	94970	25832	69975	94884	19661	72828	00102	66794
44	53976	54914	06990	67245	68350	82948	11398	42878	80287	88267	47363	46634	06541	97809
45	76072	29515	40980	07391	58745	25774	22987	80059	39911	96189	41151	14222	60697	59583
46	90725	52210	83974	29992	65831	38857	50490	83765	55657	14361	31720	57375	56228	41546
47	64364	67412	33339	31926	14883	24413	59744	92351	97473	89286	35931	04110	23726	51900
48	08962	00358	31662	25388	61642	34072	81249	35648	56891	69352	48373	45578	78547	81788
49	95012	68379	93526	70765	10592	04542	76463	54328	02349	17247	28865	14777	62730	92277
50	15664	10493	20492	38301	91132	21999	59516	81652	27195	48223	46751	22923	32261	85653
51	16408	81899	04153	53381	79401	21438	83035	92350	36693	31238	59649	91754	72772	02338
52	18629	81953	05520	91962	04739	13092	97662	24822	94730	06496	35090	04822	86774	98289
53	73115	35101	47498	87637	99016	71060	88824	71013	18735	20286	23153	72924	35165	43040
54	57491	16703	23167	49323	45021	33132	12544	41035	80780	45393	44812	12515	98931	91202
55	30405	83946	23792	14422	15059	45799	22716	19792	09983	74353	68668	30429	70735	25499
56	16631	35006	85900	98275	32388	52390	16815	69293	82732	38480	73817	32523	41961	44437
57	96773	20206	42559	78985	05300	22164	24369	54224	35083	19687	11052	91491	60383	19746
58	38935	64202	14349	82674	66523	44133	00697	35552	35970	19124	63318	29686	03387	59846
59	31624	76384	17403	53363	44167	64486	64758	75366	76554	31601	12614	33072	60332	92325
60	78919	19474	23632	27889	47914	02584	37680	20801	72152	39339	34806	08930	85001	87820
61	03931	33309	57047	74211	63445	17361	62825	39908	05607	91284	68833	25570	38818	46920
62	74426	33278	43972	10119	89917	15665	52872	73823	73144	88662	88970	74492	51805	99378
63	09066	00903	20795	95452	92648	45454	69552	88815	16553	51125	79375	97596	16296	66092
64	42238	12426	87025	14267	20979	04508	64535	31355	86064	29472	47689	05974	52468	16834
65	16153	08002	26504	41744	81959	65642	74240	56302	00033	67107	77510	70625	28725	34191
66	21457	40742	29820	96783	29400	21840	15035	34537	33310	06116	95240	15957	16572	06004
67	21581	57802	02050	89728	17937	37621	47075	42080	97403	48626	68995	43805	33386	21597
68	55612	78095	83197	33732	05810	24813	86902	60397	16489	03264	88525	42786	05269	92532
69	44657	66999	99324	51281	84463	60563	79312	93454	68876	25471	93911	25650	12682	73572
70	91340	84979	46949	81973	37949	61023	43997	15263	80644	43942	89203	71795	99533	50501
71	91227	21199	31935	27022	84067	05462	35216	14486	29891	68607	41867	14951	91696	85065
72	50001	38140	66321	19924	72163	09538	12151	06878	91903	18749	34405	56087	82790	70925
73	65390	05224	72958	28609	81406	39147	25549	48542	42627	45233	57202	94617	23772	07896
74	27504	96131	83944	41575	10573	03619	64482	73923	36152	05184	94142	25299	94387	34925
75	37169	94851	39117	89632	00959	16487	65536	49071	39782	17095	02330	74301	00275	48280
76	11508	70225	51111	38351	19444	66499	71945	05422	13442	78675	84031	66938	93654	59894
77	37449	30362	06694	54690	04052	53115	62757	95348	78662	11163	81651	50245	34971	52974
78	46515	70331	85922	38329	57015	15765	97161	17869	45349	61796	66345	81073	49106	79860
79	30986	81223	42416	58353	21532	30502	32305	86482	05174	07901	54339	58861	74818	46942
80	63798	64995	46583	09785	44160	78128	83991	42865	92520	83531	80377	35909	81250	54238
81	82486	84846	99254	67632	43218	50076	21361	64816	51202	88124	41870	52689	51275	83556
82	21885	32906	92431	09060	64297	51674	64126	62570	26123	05155	59194	52799	28225	85762
83	60336	98782	07408	53458	13564	59089	26445	29789	85205	41001	12535	12133	14645	23541
84	43937	46891	24010	25560	86355	33941	25786	54990	71899	15475	95434	98227	21824	19535
85	97656	63175	89303	16275	07100	92063	21942	18611	47348	20203	18534	03862	78095	50136
86	03299	01221	05418	38982	55758	92237	26759	86367	21216	98442	08303	56613	91511	75928
87	79626	06486	03574	17668	07785	76020	79924	25651	83325	88428	85076	72811	22717	50585
88	85636	68335	47539	03129	65651	11977	02510	26113	99447	68645	34327	15152	55230	93448
89	18039	14367	61337	06177	12143	46609	32989	74014	64708	00533	35398	58408	13261	47908
90	08362	15656	60627	36478	65648	16764	53412	09013	07832	41574	17639	82163	60859	75567
91	79556	29068	04142	16268	15387	12856	66227	38358	22478	73373	88732	09443	82558	05250
92	92608	82674	27072	32534	17075	27698	98204	63863	11951	34648	88022	56148	34925	57031
93	23982	25835	40055	67006	12293	02753	14827	23235	35071	99704	37543	11601	35503	85171
94	09915	96306	05908	97901	28395	14186	00821	80703	70426	75647	76310	88717	37890	40129
95	59037	33300	26695	62247	69927	76123	50842	43834	86654	70959	79725	93872	28117	19233
96	42488	78077	69882	61657	34136	79180	97526	43092	04098	73571	80799	76536	71255	64239
97	46764	86273	63003	93017	31204	36692	40202	35275	57306	55543	53203	18098	47625	88684
98	03237	45430	55417	63282	90816	17349	88298	90183	36600	78406	06216	95787	42579	90730
99	86591	81482	52667	61582	14972	90053	89534	76036	49199	43716	97548	04379	46370	28672
100	38534	01715	94964	87288	65680	43772	39560	12918	80537	62738	19636	51132	25739	56947

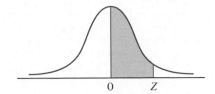

Table 2		Area under the normal curve								

Z	.00	.01	.02	.03	.04	.05	.06	.07	.08	.09
0.0	.0000	.0040	.0080	.0120	.0160	.0199	.0239	.0279	.0319	.0359
0.1	.0398	.0438	.0478	.0517	.0557	.0596	.0636	.0675	.0714	.0753
0.2	.0793	.0832	.0871	.0910	.0948	.0987	.1026	.1064	.1103	.1141
0.3	.1179	.1217	.1255	.1293	.1331	.1368	.1406	.1443	.1480	.1517
0.4	.1554	.1591	.1628	.1664	.1700	.1736	.1772	.1808	.1844	.1879
0.5	.1915	.1950	.1985	.2019	.2054	.2088	.2123	.2157	.2190	.2224
0.6	.2257	.2291	.2324	.2357	.2389	.2422	.2454	.2486	.2518	.2549
0.7	.2580	.2612	.2642	.2673	.2704	.2734	.2764	.2794	.2823	.2852
0.8	.2881	.2910	.2939	.2967	.2995	.3023	.3051	.3078	.3106	.3133
0.9	.3159	.3186	.3212	.3238	.3264	.3289	.3315	.3340	.3365	.3389
1.0	.3413	.3438	.3461	.3485	.3508	.3531	.3554	.3577	.3599	.3621
1.1	.3643	.3665	.3686	.3708	.3729	.3749	.3770	.3790	.3810	.3830
1.2	.3849	.3869	.3888	.3907	.3925	.3944	.3962	.3980	.3997	.4015
1.3	.4032	.4049	.4066	.4082	.4099	.4115	.4131	.4147	.4162	.4177
1.4	.4192	.4207	.4222	.4236	.4251	.4265	.4279	.4292	.4306	.4319
1.5	.4332	.4345	.4357	.4370	.4382	.4394	.4406	.4418	.4429	.4441
1.6	.4452	.4463	.4474	.4484	.4495	.4505	.4515	.4525	.4535	.4545
1.7	.4554	.4564	.4573	.4582	.4591	.4599	.4608	.4616	.4625	.4633
1.8	.4641	.4649	.4656	.4664	.4671	.4678	.4686	.4693	.4699	.4706
1.9	.4713	.4719	.4726	.4732	.4738	.4744	.4750	.4756	.4761	.4767
2.0	.4772	.4778	.4783	.4788	.4793	.4798	.4803	.4808	.4812	.4817
2.1	.4821	.4826	.4830	.4834	.4838	.4842	.4846	.4850	.4854	.4857
2.2	.4861	.4864	.4868	.4871	.4875	.4878	.4881	.4884	.4887	.4890
2.3	.4893	.4896	.4898	.4901	.4904	.4906	.4909	.4911	.4913	.4916
2.4	.4918	.4920	.4922	.4925	.4927	.4929	.4931	.4932	.4934	.4936
2.5	.4938	.4940	.4941	.4943	.4945	.4946	.4948	.4949	.4951	.4952
2.6	.4953	.4955	.4956	.4957	.4959	.4960	.4961	.4962	.4963	.4964
2.7	.4965	.4966	.4967	.4968	.4969	.4970	.4971	.4972	.4973	.4974
2.8	.4974	.4975	.4976	.4977	.4977	.4978	.4979	.4979	.4980	.4981
2.9	.4981	.4982	.4982	.4983	.4984	.4984	.4985	.4985	.4986	.4986
3.0	.49865	.49869	.49874	.49878	.49882	.49886	.49889	.49893	.49897	.49900
3.1	.49903	.49906	.49910	.49913	.49916	.49918	.49921	.49924	.49926	.49929
3.2	.49931	.49934	.49936	.49938	.49940	.49942	.49944	.49946	.49948	.49950
3.3	.49952	.49953	.49955	.49957	.49958	.49960	.49961	.49962	.49964	.49965
3.4	.49966	.49968	.49969	.49970	.49971	.49972	.49973	.49974	.49975	.49976
3.5	.49977	.49978	.49978	.49979	.49980	.49981	.49981	.49982	.49983	.49983
3.6	.49984	.49985	.49985	.49986	.49986	.49987	.49987	.49988	.49988	.49989
3.7	.49989	.49990	.49990	.49990	.49991	.49991	.49992	.49992	.49992	.49992
3.8	.49993	.49993	.49993	.49994	.49994	.49994	.49994	.49995	.49995	.49995
3.9	.49995	.49995	.49996	.49996	.49996	.49996	.49996	.49996	.49997	.49997

Each entry represents the area under the standard normal distribution from the mean to Z.

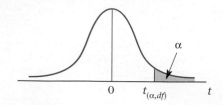

Table 3	t distribution

Degrees of freedom	Upper tail area					
	.25	.10	.05	.025	.01	.005
1	1.0000	3.0777	6.3138	12.7062	31.8207	63.6574
2	0.8165	1.8856	2.9200	4.3027	6.9646	9.9248
3	0.7649	1.6377	2.3534	3.1824	4.5407	5.8409
4	0.7407	1.5332	2.1318	2.7764	3.7469	4.6041
5	0.7267	1.4759	2.0150	2.5706	3.3649	4.0322
6	0.7176	1.4398	1.9432	2.4469	3.1427	3.7074
7	0.7111	1.4149	1.8946	2.3646	2.9980	3.4995
8	0.7064	1.3968	1.8595	2.3060	2.8965	3.3554
9	0.7027	1.3830	1.8331	2.2622	2.8214	3.2498
10	0.6998	1.3722	1.8125	2.2281	2.7638	3.1693
11	0.6974	1.3634	1.7959	2.2010	2.7181	3.1058
12	0.6955	1.3562	1.7823	2.1788	2.6810	3.0545
13	0.6938	1.3502	1.7709	2.1604	2.6503	3.0123
14	0.6924	1.3450	1.7613	2,1448	2.6245	2.9768
15	0.6912	1.3406	1.7531	2.1315	2.6025	2.9467
16	0.6901	1.3368	1.7459	2.1199	2.5835	2.9208
17	0.6892	1.3334	1.7396	2.1098	2.5669	2.8982
18	0.6884	1.3304	1.7341	2.1009	2.5524	2.8784
19	0.6876	1.3277	1.7291	2.0930	2.5395	2.8609
20	0.6870	1.3253	1.7247	2.0860	2.5280	2.8453
21	0.6864	1.3232	1.7207	2.0796	2.5177	2.8314
22	0.6858	1.3212	1.7171	2.0739	2.5083	2.8188
23	0.6853	1.3195	1.7139	2.0687	2.4999	2.8073
24	0.6848	1.3178	1.7109	2.0639	2.4922	2.7969
25	0.6844	1.3163	1.7081	2.0595	2.4851	2.7874
26	0.6840	1.3150	1.7056	2.0555	2.4786	2.7787
27	0.6837	1.3137	1.7033	2.0518	2.4727	2.7707
28	0.6834	1.3125	1.7011	2.0484	2.4671	2.7633
29	0.6830	1.3114	1.6991	2.0452	2.4620	2.7564
30	0.6828	1.3104	1.6973	2.0423	2.4573	2.7500
31	0.6825	1.3095	1.6955	2.0395	2.4528	2.7440
32	0.6822	1.3086	1.6939	2.0369	2.4487	2.7385
33	0.6820	1.3077	1.6924	2.0345	2.4448	2.7333
34	0.6818	1.3070	1.6909	2.0322	2.4411	2.7284
35	0.6816	1.3062	1.6896	2.0301	2.4377	2.7238
36	0.6814	1.3055	1.6883	2.0281	2.4345	2.7195
37	0.6812	1.3049	1.6871	2.0262	2.4314	2.7154
38	0.6810	1.3042	1.6860	2.0244	2.4286	2.7116
39	0.6808	1.3036	1.6849	2.0227	2.4258	2.7079
40	0.6807	1.3031	1.6839	2.0211	2.4233	2.7045

Degrees of freedom	Upper tail area					
	.25	.10	.05	.025	.01	.005
41	0.6805	1.3025	1.6829	2.0195	2.4208	2.7012
42	0.6804	1.3020	1.6820	2.0181	2.4185	2.6981
43	0.6802	1.3016	1.681 1	2.0167	2.4163	2.6951
44	0.6801	1.3011	1.6802	2.0154	2.4141	2.6923
45	0.6800	1.3006	1.6794	2.0141	2.4121	2.6896
46	0.6799	1.3002	1.6787	2.0129	2.4102	2.6870
47	0.6797	1.2998	1.6779	2.0117	2.4083	2.6846
48	0.6796	1.2994	1.6772	2.0106	2.4066	2.6822
49	0.6795	1.2991	1.6766	2.0096	2.4049	2.6800
50	0.6794	1.2987	1.6759	2.0086	2.4033	2.6778
51	0.6793	1.2984	1.6753	2.0076	2.4017	2.6757
52	0.6792	1.2980	1.6747	2.0066	2.4002	2.6737
53	0.6791	1.2977	1.6741	2.0057	2.3988	2.6718
54	0.6791	1.2974	1.6736	2.0049	2.3974	2.6700
55	0.6790	1.2971	1.6730	2.0040	2.3961	2.6682
56	0.6789	1.2969	1.6725	2.0032	2.3948	2.6665
57	0.6788	1.2966	1.6720	2.0025	2.3936	2.6649
58	0.6787	1.2963	1.6716	2.0017	2.3924	2.6633
59	0.6787	1.2961	1.6711	2.0010	2.3912	2.6618
60	0.6786	1.2958	1.6706	2.0003	2.3901	2.6603
61	0.6785	1.2956	1.6702	1.9996	2.3890	2.6589
62	0.6785	1.2954	1.6698	1.9990	2.3880	2.6575
63	0.6784	1.2951	1.6694	1.9983	2.3870	2.6561
64	0.6783	1.2949	1.6690	1.9977	2.3860	2.6549
65	0.6783	1.2947	1.6686	1.9971	2.3851	2.6536
66	0.6782	1.2945	1.6683	1.9966	2.3842	2.6524
67	0.6782	1.2943	1.6679	1.9960	2.3833	2.6512
68	0.6781	1.2941	1.6676	1.9955	2.3824	2.6501
69	0.6781	1.2939	1.6672	1.9949	2.3816	2.6490
70	0.6780	1.2938	1.6669	1.9944	2.3808	2.6479
71	0.6780	1.2936	1.6666	1.9939	2.3800	2.6469
72	0.6779	1.2934	1.6663	1.9935	2.3793	2.6459
73	0.6779	1.2933	1.6660	1.9930	2.3785	2.6449
74	0.6778	1.2931	1.6657	1.9925	2.3778	2.6439
75	0.6778	1.2929	1.6654	1.9921	2.3771	2.6430
76	0.6777	1.2928	1.6652	1.9917	2.3764	2.6421
77	0.6777	1.2926	1.6649	1.9913	2.3758	2.6412
78	0.6776	1.2925	1.6646	1.9908	2.3751	2.6403
79	0.6776	1.2924	1.6644	1.9905	2.3745	2.6395
80	0.6776	1.2922	1.6641	1.9901	2.3739	2.6387
81	0.6775	1.2921	1.6639	1.9897	2.3733	2.6379
82	0.6775	1.2920	1.6636	1.9893	2.3727	2.6371
83	0.6775	1.2918	1.6634	1.9890	2.3721	2.6364
84	0.6774	1.2917	1.6632	1.9886	2.3716	2.6356
85	0.6774	1.2916	1.6630	1.9883	2.3710	2.6349
86	0.6774	1.2915	1.6628	1.9879	2.3705	2.6342
87	0.6773	1.2914	1.6626	1.9876	2.3700	2.6335
88	0.6773	1.2912	1.6624	1.9873	2.3695	2.6329
89	0.6773	1.2911	1.6622	1.9870	2.3690	2.6322
90	0.6772	1.2910	1.6620	1.9867	2.3685	2.6316
91	0.6772	1.2909	1.6618	1.9864	2.3680	2.6309
92	0.6772	1.2908	1.6616	1.9861	2.3676	2.6303
93	0.6771	1.2907	1.6614	1.9858	2.3671	2.6297
94	0.6771	1.2906	1.6612	1.9855	2.3667	2.6291

Degrees of freedom	Upper tail area					
	.25	.10	.05	.025	.01	.005
95	0.6771	1.2905	1.6611	1.9853	2.3662	2.6286
96	0.6771	1.2904	1.6609	1.9850	2.3658	2.6280
97	0.6770	1.2903	1.6607	1.9847	2.3654	2.6275
98	0.6770	1.2902	1.6606	1.9845	2.3650	2.6269
99	0.6770	1.2902	1.6604	1.9842	2.3646	2.6264
100	0.6770	1.2901	1.6602	1.9840	2.3642	2.6259
110	0.6767	1.2893	1.6588	1.9818	2.3607	2.6213
120	0.6765	1.2886	1.6577	1.9799	2.3578	2.6174
130	0.6764	1.2881	1.6567	1.9784	2.3554	2.6142
140	0.6762	1.2876	1.6558	1.9771	2.3533	2.6114
150	0.6761	1.2872	1.6551	1.9759	2.3515	2.6090
α	0.6745	1.2816	1.6449	1.9600	2.3263	2.5758

For a particular number of degrees of freedom, each entry represents the critical value of t corresponding to a specified upper tail area α.

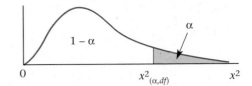

| Table 4 | | Chi-square distribution | | | | | | | | | | |

Degrees of freedom	Upper tail area (α)											
	.995	.99	.975	.95	.90	.75	.25	.10	.05	.025	.01	.005
1			0.001	0.004	0.016	0.102	1.323	2.706	3.841	5.024	6.635	7.879
2	0.010	0.020	0.051	0.103	0.211	0.575	2.773	4.605	5.991	7.378	9.210	10.597
3	0.072	0.115	0.216	0.352	0.584	1.213	4.108	6.251	7.815	9.348	11.345	12.838
4	0.207	0.297	0.484	0.711	1.064	1.923	5.385	7.779	9.488	11.143	13.277	14.860
5	0.412	0.554	0.831	1.145	1.610	2.675	6.626	9.236	11.071	12.833	15.086	16.750
6	0.676	0.872	1.237	1.635	2.204	3.455	7.841	10.645	12.592	14.449	16.812	18.548
7	0.989	1.239	1.690	2.167	2.833	4.255	9.037	12.017	14.067	16.013	18.475	20.278
8	1.344	1.646	2.180	2.733	3.490	5.071	10.219	13.362	15.507	17.535	20.090	21.955
9	1.735	2.088	2.700	3.325	4.168	5.899	11.389	14.684	16.919	19.023	21.666	23.589
10	2.156	2.558	3.247	3.940	4.865	6.737	12.549	15.987	18.307	20.483	23.209	25.188
11	2.603	3.053	3.816	4.575	5.578	7.584	13.701	17.275	19.675	21.920	24.725	26.757
12	3.074	3.571	4.404	5.226	6.304	8.438	14.845	18.549	21.026	23.337	26.217	28.299
13	3.565	4.107	5.009	5.892	7.042	9.299	15.984	19.812	22.362	24.736	27.688	29.819
14	4.075	4.660	5.629	6.571	7.790	10.165	17.117	21.064	23.685	26.119	29.141	31.319
15	4.601	5.229	6.262	7.261	8.547	11.037	18.245	22.307	24.996	27.488	30.578	32.801
16	5.142	5.812	6.908	7.962	9.312	11.912	19.369	23.542	26.296	28.845	32.000	34.267
17	5.697	6.408	7.564	8.672	10.085	12.792	20.489	24.769	27.587	30.191	33.409	35.718
18	6.265	7.015	8.231	9.390	10.865	13.675	21.605	25.989	28.869	31.526	34.805	37.156
19	6.844	7.633	8.907	10.117	11.651	14.562	22.718	27.204	30.144	32.852	36.191	38.582
20	7.434	8.260	9.591	10.851	12.443	15.452	23.828	28.412	31.410	34.170	37.566	39.997
21	8.034	8.897	10.283	11.591	13.240	16.344	24.935	29.615	32.671	35.479	38.932	41.401
22	8.643	9.542	10.982	12.338	14.042	17.240	26.039	30.813	33.924	36.781	40.289	42.796
23	9.260	10.196	11.689	13.091	14.848	18.137	27.141	32.007	35.172	38.076	41.638	44.181
24	9.886	10.856	12.401	13.848	15.659	19.037	28.241	33.196	36.415	39.364	42.980	45.559
25	10.520	11.524	13.120	14.611	16.473	19.939	29.339	34.382	37.652	40.646	44.314	46.928
26	11.160	12.198	13.844	15.379	17.292	20.843	30.435	35.563	38.885	41.923	45.642	48.290
27	11.808	12.879	14.573	16.151	18.114	21.749	31.528	36.741	40.113	43.194	46.963	49.645
28	12.461	13.565	15.308	16.928	18.939	22.657	32.620	37.916	41.337	44.461	48.278	50.993
29	13.121	14.257	16.047	17.708	19.768	23.567	33.711	39.087	42.557	45.722	49.588	52.336
30	13.787	14.954	16.791	18.493	20.599	24.478	34.800	40.256	43.773	46.979	50.892	53.672
31	14.458	15.655	17.539	19.281	21.434	25.390	35.887	41.422	44.985	48.232	52.191	55.003
32	15.134	16.362	18.291	20.072	22.271	26.304	36.973	42.585	46.194	49.480	53.486	56.328
33	15.815	17.074	19.047	20.867	23.110	27.219	38.058	43.745	47.400	50.725	54.776	57.648
34	16.501	17.789	19.806	21.664	23.952	28.136	39.141	44.903	48.602	51.966	56.061	58.964
35	17.192	18.509	20.569	22.465	24.797	29.054	40.223	46.059	49.802	53.203	57.342	60.275
36	17.887	19.233	21.336	23.269	25.643	29.973	41.304	47.212	50.998	54.437	58.619	61.581
37	18.586	19.960	22.106	24.075	26.492	30.893	42.383	48.363	52.192	55.668	59.892	62.883
38	19.289	20.691	22.878	24.884	27.343	31.815	43.462	49.513	53.384	56.896	61.162	64.181
39	19.996	21.426	23.654	25.695	28.196	32.737	44.539	50.660	54.572	58.120	62.428	65.476
40	20.707	22.164	24.433	26.509	29.051	33.660	45.616	51.805	55.758	59.342	63.691	66.766

Degrees of freedom	Upper tail areas (α)											
	.995	.99	.975	.95	.90	.75	.25	.10	.05	.025	.01	.005
41	21.421	22.906	25.215	27.326	29.907	34.585	46.692	52.949	56.942	60.561	64.950	68.053
42	22.138	23.650	25.999	28.144	30.765	35.510	47.766	54.090	58.124	61.777	66.206	69.336
43	22.859	24.398	26.785	28.965	31.625	36.436	48.840	55.230	59.304	62.990	67.459	70.616
44	23.584	25.148	27.575	29.787	32.487	37.363	49.913	56.369	60.481	64.201	68.710	71.893
45	24.311	25.901	28.366	30.612	33.350	38.291	50.985	57.505	61.656	65.410	69.957	73.166
46	25.041	26.657	29.160	31.439	34.215	39.220	52.056	58.641	62.830	66.617	71.201	74.437
47	25.775	27.416	29.956	32.268	35.081	40.149	53.127	59.774	64.001	67.821	72.443	75.704
48	26.511	28.177	30.755	33.098	35.949	41.079	54.196	60.907	65.171	69.023	73.683	76.969
49	27.249	28.941	31.555	33.930	36.818	42.010	55.265	62.038	66.339	70.222	74.919	78.231
50	27.991	29.707	32.357	34.764	37.689	42.942	56.334	63.167	67.505	71.420	76.154	79.490
51	28.735	30.475	33.162	35.600	38.560	43.874	57.401	64.295	68.669	72.616	77.386	80.747
52	29.481	31.246	33.968	36.437	39.433	44.808	58.468	65.422	69.832	73.810	78.616	82.001
53	30.230	32.018	34.776	37.276	40.308	45.741	59.534	66.548	70.993	75.002	79.843	83.253
54	30.981	32.793	35.586	38.116	41.183	46.676	60.600	67.673	72.153	76.192	81.069	84.502
55	31.735	33.570	36.398	38.958	42.060	47.610	61.665	68.796	73.311	77.380	82.292	85.749
56	32.490	34.350	37.212	39.801	42.937	48.546	62.729	69.919	74.468	78.567	83.513	86.994
57	33.248	35.131	38.027	40.646	43.816	49.482	63.793	71.040	75.624	79.752	84.733	88.236
58	34.008	35.913	38.844	41.492	44.696	50.419	64.857	72.160	76.778	80.936	85.950	89.477
59	34.770	36.698	39.662	42.339	45.577	51.356	65.919	73.279	77.931	82.117	87.166	90.715
60	35.534	37.485	40.482	43.188	46.459	52.294	66.981	74.397	79.082	83.298	88.379	91.952

For a particular number of degrees of freedom, each entry represents the critical value of χ^2 corresponding to a specified upper tail area, α.

For larger values of degrees of freedom (df), the expression $z = \sqrt{2\chi^2} - \sqrt{2(df) - 1}$ may be used and the resulting upper tail area can be obtained from the table of the standardised normal distribution.

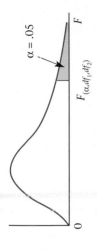

$\alpha = .05$

$F_{(\alpha, df_1, df_2)}$

Table 5 — F distribution

Numerator df_1

Denominator df_2	1	2	3	4	5	6	7	8	9	10	12	15	20	24	30	40	60	120	∞
1	161.4	199.5	215.7	224.6	230.2	234.0	236.8	238.9	240.5	241.9	243.9	245.9	248.0	249.1	250.1	251.1	252.2	253.3	254.3
2	18.51	19.00	19.16	19.25	19.30	19.33	19.35	19.37	19.38	19.40	19.41	19.43	19.45	19.45	19.46	19.47	19.48	19.49	19.50
3	10.13	9.55	9.28	9.12	9.01	8.94	8.89	8.85	8.81	8.79	8.74	8.70	8.66	8.64	8.62	8.59	8.57	8.55	8.53
4	7.71	6.94	6.59	6.39	6.26	6.16	6.09	6.04	6.00	5.96	5.91	5.86	5.80	5.77	5.75	5.72	5.69	5.66	5.63
5	6.61	5.79	5.41	5.19	5.05	4.95	4.88	4.82	4.77	4.74	4.68	4.62	4.56	4.53	4.50	4.46	4.43	4.40	4.36
6	5.99	5.14	4.76	4.53	4.39	4.28	4.21	4.15	4.10	4.06	4.00	3.94	3.87	3.84	3.81	3.77	3.74	3.70	3.67
7	5.59	4.74	4.35	4.12	3.97	3.87	3.79	3.73	3.68	3.64	3.57	3.51	3.44	3.41	3.38	3.34	3.30	3.27	3.23
8	5.32	4.46	4.07	3.84	3.69	3.58	3.50	3.44	3.39	3.35	3.28	3.22	3.15	3.12	3.08	3.04	3.01	2.97	2.93
9	5.12	4.26	3.86	3.63	3.48	3.37	3.29	3.23	3.18	3.14	3.07	3.01	2.94	2.90	2.86	2.83	2.79	2.75	2.71
10	4.96	4.10	3.71	3.48	3.33	3.22	3.14	3.07	3.02	2.98	2.91	2.85	2.77	2.74	2.70	2.66	2.62	2.58	2.54
11	4.84	3.98	3.59	3.36	3.20	3.09	3.01	2.95	2.90	2.85	2.79	2.72	2.65	2.61	2.57	2.53	2.49	2.45	2.40
12	4.75	3.89	3.49	3.26	3.11	3.00	2.91	2.85	2.80	2.75	2.69	2.62	2.54	2.51	2.47	2.43	2.38	2.34	2.30
13	4.67	3.81	3.41	3.18	3.03	2.92	2.83	2.77	2.71	2.67	2.60	2.53	2.46	2.42	2.38	2.34	2.30	2.25	2.21
14	4.60	3.74	3.34	3.11	2.96	2.85	2.76	2.70	2.65	2.60	2.53	2.46	2.39	2.35	2.31	2.27	2.22	2.18	2.13
15	4.54	3.68	3.29	3.06	2.90	2.79	2.71	2.64	2.59	2.54	2.48	2.40	2.33	2.29	2.25	2.20	2.16	2.11	2.07
16	4.49	3.63	3.24	3.01	2.85	2.74	2.66	2.59	2.54	2.49	2.42	2.35	2.28	2.24	2.19	2.15	2.11	2.06	2.01
17	4.45	3.59	3.20	2.96	2.81	2.70	2.61	2.55	2.49	2.45	2.38	2.31	2.23	2.19	2.15	2.10	2.06	2.01	1.96
18	4.41	3.55	3.16	2.93	2.77	2.66	2.58	2.51	2.46	2.41	2.34	2.27	2.19	2.15	2.11	2.06	2.02	1.97	1.92
19	4.38	3.52	3.13	2.90	2.74	2.63	2.54	2.48	2.42	2.38	2.31	2.23	2.16	2.11	2.07	2.03	1.98	1.93	1.88
20	4.35	3.49	3.10	2.87	2.71	2.60	2.51	2.45	2.39	2.35	2.28	2.20	2.12	2.08	2.04	1.99	1.95	1.90	1.84
21	4.32	3.47	3.07	2.84	2.68	2.57	2.49	2.42	2.37	2.32	2.25	2.18	2.10	2.05	2.01	1.96	1.92	1.87	1.81
22	4.30	3.44	3.05	2.82	2.66	2.55	2.46	2.40	2.34	2.30	2.23	2.15	2.07	2.03	1.98	1.94	1.89	1.84	1.78
23	4.28	3.42	3.03	2.80	2.64	2.53	2.44	2.37	2.32	2.27	2.20	2.13	2.05	2.01	1.96	1.91	1.86	1.81	1.76
24	4.26	3.40	3.01	2.78	2.62	2.51	2.42	2.36	2.30	2.25	2.18	2.11	2.03	1.98	1.94	1.89	1.84	1.79	1.73
25	4.24	3.39	2.99	2.76	2.60	2.49	2.40	2.34	2.28	2.24	2.16	2.09	2.01	1.96	1.92	1.87	1.82	1.77	1.71
26	4.23	3.37	2.98	2.74	2.59	2.47	2.39	2.32	2.27	2.22	2.15	2.07	1.99	1.95	1.90	1.85	1.80	1.75	1.69
27	4.21	3.35	2.96	2.73	2.57	2.46	2.37	2.31	2.25	2.20	2.13	2.06	1.97	1.93	1.88	1.84	1.79	1.73	1.67
28	4.20	3.34	2.95	2.71	2.56	2.45	2.36	2.29	2.24	2.19	2.12	2.04	1.96	1.91	1.87	1.82	1.77	1.71	1.65
29	4.18	3.33	2.93	2.70	2.55	2.43	2.35	2.28	2.22	2.18	2.10	2.03	1.94	1.90	1.85	1.81	1.75	1.70	1.64
30	4.17	3.32	2.92	2.69	2.53	2.42	2.33	2.27	2.21	2.16	2.09	2.01	1.93	1.89	1.84	1.79	1.74	1.68	1.62
40	4.08	3.23	2.84	2.61	2.45	2.34	2.25	2.18	2.12	2.08	2.00	1.92	1.84	1.79	1.74	1.69	1.64	1.58	1.51
60	4.00	3.15	2.76	2.53	2.37	2.25	2.17	2.10	2.04	1.99	1.92	1.84	1.75	1.70	1.65	1.59	1.53	1.47	1.39
120	3.92	3.07	2.68	2.45	2.29	2.17	2.09	2.02	1.96	1.91	1.83	1.75	1.66	1.61	1.55	1.50	1.43	1.35	1.25
∞	3.84	3.00	2.60	2.37	2.21	2.10	2.01	1.94	1.88	1.83	1.75	1.67	1.57	1.52	1.46	1.39	1.32	1.22	1.00

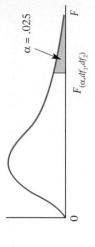

$\alpha = .025$

Numerator df_1

Denominator df_2	1	2	3	4	5	6	7	8	9	10	12	15	20	24	30	40	60	120	∞
1	647.8	799.5	864.2	899.6	921.8	937.1	948.2	956.7	963.3	968.6	976.7	984.9	993.1	997.2	1001	1006	1010	1014	1018
2	38.51	39.00	39.17	39.25	39.30	39.33	39.36	39.37	39.39	39.40	39.41	39.43	39.45	39.46	39.46	39.47	39.48	39.49	39.50
3	17.44	16.04	15.44	15.10	14.88	14.73	14.62	14.54	14.47	14.42	14.34	14.25	14.17	14.12	14.08	14.04	13.99	13.95	13.90
4	12.22	10.65	9.98	9.60	9.36	9.20	9.07	8.98	8.90	8.84	8.75	8.66	8.56	8.51	8.46	8.41	8.36	8.31	8.26
5	10.01	8.43	7.76	7.39	7.15	6.98	6.85	6.76	6.68	6.62	6.52	6.43	6.33	6.28	6.23	6.18	6.12	6.07	6.02
6	8.81	7.26	6.60	6.23	5.99	5.82	5.70	5.60	5.52	5.46	5.37	5.27	5.17	5.12	5.07	5.01	4.96	4.90	4.85
7	8.07	6.54	5.89	5.52	5.29	5.12	4.99	4.90	4.82	4.76	4.67	4.57	4.47	4.42	4.36	4.31	4.25	4.20	4.14
8	7.57	6.06	5.42	5.05	4.82	4.65	4.53	4.43	4.36	4.30	4.20	4.10	4.00	3.95	3.89	3.84	3.78	3.73	3.67
9	7.21	5.71	5.08	4.72	4.48	4.32	4.20	4.10	4.03	3.96	3.87	3.77	3.67	3.61	3.56	3.51	3.45	3.39	3.33
10	6.94	5.46	4.83	4.47	4.24	4.07	3.95	3.85	3.78	3.72	3.62	3.52	3.42	3.37	3.31	3.26	3.20	3.14	3.08
11	6.72	5.26	4.63	4.28	4.04	3.88	3.76	3.66	3.59	3.53	3.43	3.33	3.23	3.17	3.12	3.06	3.00	2.94	2.88
12	6.55	5.10	4.47	4.12	3.89	3.73	3.61	3.51	3.44	3.37	3.28	3.18	3.07	3.02	2.96	2.91	2.85	2.79	2.72
13	6.41	4.97	4.35	4.00	3.77	3.60	3.48	3.39	3.31	3.25	3.15	3.05	2.95	2.89	2.84	2.78	2.72	2.66	2.60
14	6.30	4.86	4.24	3.89	3.66	3.50	3.38	3.29	3.21	3.15	3.05	2.95	2.84	2.79	2.73	2.67	2.61	2.55	2.49
15	6.20	4.77	4.15	3.80	3.58	3.41	3.29	3.20	3.12	3.06	2.96	2.86	2.76	2.70	2.64	2.59	2.52	2.46	2.40
16	6.12	4.69	4.08	3.73	3.50	3.34	3.22	3.12	3.05	2.99	2.89	2.79	2.68	2.63	2.57	2.51	2.45	2.38	2.32
17	6.04	4.62	4.01	3.66	3.44	3.28	3.16	3.06	2.98	2.92	2.82	2.72	2.62	2.56	2.50	2.44	2.38	2.32	2.25
18	5.98	4.56	3.95	3.61	3.38	3.22	3.10	3.01	2.93	2.87	2.77	2.67	2.56	2.50	2.44	2.38	2.32	2.26	2.19
19	5.92	4.51	3.90	3.56	3.33	3.17	3.05	2.96	2.88	2.82	2.72	2.62	2.51	2.45	2.39	2.33	2.27	2.20	2.13
20	5.87	4.46	3.86	3.51	3.29	3.13	3.01	2.91	2.84	2.77	2.68	2.57	2.46	2.41	2.35	2.29	2.22	2.16	2.09
21	5.83	4.42	3.82	3.48	3.25	3.09	2.97	2.87	2.80	2.73	2.64	2.53	2.42	2.37	2.31	2.25	2.18	2.11	2.04
22	5.79	4.38	3.78	3.44	3.22	3.05	2.93	2.84	2.76	2.70	2.60	2.50	2.39	2.33	2.27	2.21	2.14	2.08	2.00
23	5.75	4.35	3.75	3.41	3.18	3.02	2.90	2.81	2.73	2.67	2.57	2.47	2.36	2.30	2.24	2.18	2.11	2.04	1.97
24	5.72	4.32	3.72	3.38	3.15	2.99	2.87	2.78	2.70	2.64	2.54	2.44	2.33	2.27	2.21	2.15	2.08	2.01	1.94
25	5.69	4.29	3.69	3.35	3.13	2.97	2.85	2.75	2.68	2.61	2.51	2.41	2.30	2.24	2.18	2.12	2.05	1.98	1.91
26	5.66	4.27	3.67	3.33	3.10	2.94	2.82	2.73	2.65	2.59	2.49	2.39	2.28	2.22	2.16	2.09	2.03	1.95	1.88
27	5.63	4.24	3.65	3.31	3.08	2.92	2.80	2.71	2.63	2.57	2.47	2.36	2.25	2.19	2.13	2.07	2.00	1.93	1.85
28	5.61	4.22	3.63	3.29	3.06	2.90	2.78	2.69	2.61	2.55	2.45	2.34	2.23	2.17	2.11	2.05	1.98	1.91	1.83
29	5.59	4.20	3.61	3.27	3.04	2.88	2.76	2.67	2.59	2.53	2.43	2.32	2.21	2.15	2.09	2.03	1.96	1.89	1.81
30	5.57	4.18	3.59	3.25	3.03	2.87	2.75	2.65	2.57	2.51	2.41	2.31	2.20	2.14	2.07	2.01	1.94	1.87	1.79
40	5.42	4.05	3.46	3.13	2.90	2.74	2.62	2.53	2.45	2.39	2.29	2.18	2.07	2.01	1.94	1.88	1.80	1.72	1.64
60	5.29	3.93	3.34	3.01	2.79	2.63	2.51	2.41	2.33	2.27	2.17	2.06	1.94	1.88	1.82	1.74	1.67	1.58	1.48
120	5.15	3.80	3.23	2.89	2.67	2.52	2.39	2.30	2.22	2.16	2.05	1.94	1.82	1.76	1.69	1.61	1.53	1.43	1.31
∞	5.02	3.69	3.12	2.79	2.57	2.41	2.29	2.19	2.11	2.05	1.94	1.83	1.71	1.64	1.57	1.48	1.39	1.27	1.00

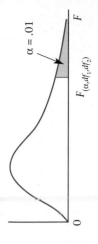

$\alpha = .01$

$F_{(\alpha, df_1, df_2)}$

Numerator df_1

Denominator df_2	1	2	3	4	5	6	7	8	9	10	12	15	20	24	30	40	60	120	∞
1	4052	4999.5	5403	5625	5764	5859	5928	5982	6022	6056	6106	6157	6209	6235	6261	6287	6313	6339	6366
2	98.50	99.00	99.17	99.25	99.30	99.33	99.36	99.37	99.39	99.40	99.42	99.43	99.45	99.46	99.47	99.47	99.48	99.49	99.50
3	34.12	30.82	29.46	28.71	28.24	27.91	27.67	27.49	27.35	27.23	27.05	26.87	26.69	26.60	26.50	26.41	26.32	26.22	26.13
4	21.20	18.00	16.69	15.98	15.52	15.21	14.98	14.80	14.66	14.55	14.37	14.20	14.02	13.93	13.84	13.75	13.65	13.56	13.46
5	16.26	13.27	12.06	11.39	10.97	10.67	10.46	10.29	10.16	10.05	9.89	9.72	9.55	9.47	9.38	9.29	9.20	9.11	9.02
6	13.75	10.92	9.78	9.15	8.75	8.47	8.26	8.10	7.98	7.87	7.72	7.56	7.40	7.31	7.23	7.14	7.06	6.97	6.88
7	12.25	9.55	8.45	7.85	7.46	7.19	6.99	6.84	6.72	6.62	6.47	6.31	6.16	6.07	5.99	5.91	5.82	5.74	5.65
8	11.26	8.65	7.59	7.01	6.63	6.37	6.18	6.03	5.91	5.81	5.67	5.52	5.36	5.28	5.20	5.12	5.03	4.95	4.86
9	10.56	8.02	6.99	6.42	6.06	5.80	5.61	5.47	5.35	5.26	5.11	4.96	4.81	4.73	4.65	4.57	4.48	4.40	4.31
10	10.04	7.56	6.55	5.99	5.64	5.39	5.20	5.06	4.94	485	4.71	4.56	4.41	4.33	4.25	4.17	4.08	4.00	3.91
11	9.65	7.21	6.22	5.67	5.32	5.07	4.89	4.74	4.63	4.54	4.40	4.25	4.10	4.02	3.94	3.86	3.78	3.69	3.60
12	9.33	6.93	5.95	5.41	5.06	4.82	4.64	4.50	4.39	4.30	4.16	4.01	3.86	3.78	3.70	3.62	3.54	3.45	3.36
13	9.07	6.70	5.74	5.21	4.86	4.62	4.44	4.30	4.19	4.10	3.96	3.82	3.66	3.59	3.51	3.43	3.34	3.25	3.17
14	8.86	6.51	5.56	5.04	4.69	4.46	4.28	4.14	4.03	3.94	3.80	3.66	3.51	3.43	3.35	3.27	3.18	3.09	3.00
15	8.68	6.36	5.42	4.89	4.56	4.32	4.14	4.00	3.89	3.80	3.67	3.52	3.37	3.29	3.21	3.13	3.05	2.96	2.87
16	8.53	6.23	5.29	4.77	4.44	4.20	4.03	3.89	3.78	3.69	3.55	3.41	3.26	3.18	3.10	3.02	2.93	2.84	2.75
17	8.40	6.11	5.18	4.67	4.34	4.10	3.93	3.79	3.68	3.59	3.46	3.31	3.16	3.08	3.00	2.92	2.83	2.75	2.65
18	8.29	6.01	5.09	4.58	4.25	4.01	3.84	3.71	3.60	3.51	3.37	3.23	3.08	3.00	2.92	2.84	2.75	2.66	2.57
19	8.18	5.93	5.01	4.50	4.17	3.94	3.77	3.63	3.52	3.43	3.30	3.15	3.00	2.92	2.84	2.76	2.67	2.58	2.49
20	8.10	5.85	4.94	4.43	4.10	3.87	3.70	3.56	3.46	3.37	3.23	3.09	2.94	2.86	2.78	2.69	2.61	2.52	2.42
21	8.02	5.78	4.87	4.37	4.04	3.81	3.64	3.51	3.40	3.31	3.17	3.03	2.88	2.80	2.72	2.64	2.55	2.46	2.36
22	7.95	5.72	4.82	4.31	3.99	3.76	3.59	3.45	3.35	3.26	3.12	2.98	2.83	2.75	2.67	2.58	2.50	2.40	2.31
23	7.88	5.66	4.76	4.26	3.94	3.71	3.54	3.41	3.30	3.21	3.07	2.93	2.78	2.70	2.62	2.54	2.45	2.35	2.26
24	7.82	5.61	4.72	4.22	3.90	3.67	3.50	3.36	3.26	3.17	3.03	2.89	2.74	2.66	2.58	2.49	2.40	2.31	2.21
25	7.77	5.57	4.68	4.18	3.85	3.63	3.46	3.32	3.22	3.13	2.99	2.85	2.70	2.62	2.54	2.45	2.36	2.27	2.17
26	7.72	5.53	4.64	4.14	3.82	3.59	3.42	3.29	3.18	3.09	2.96	2.81	2.66	2.58	2.50	2.42	2.33	2.23	2.13
27	7.68	5.49	4.60	4.11	3.78	3.56	3.39	3.26	3.15	3.06	2.93	2.78	2.63	2.55	2.47	2.38	2.29	2.20	2.10
28	7.64	5.45	4.57	4.07	3.75	3.53	3.36	3.23	3.12	3.03	2.90	2.75	2.60	2.52	2.44	2.35	2.26	2.17	2.06
29	7.60	5.42	4.54	4.04	3.73	3.50	3.33	3.20	3.09	3.00	2.87	2.73	2.57	2.49	2.41	2.33	2.23	2.14	2.03
30	7.56	5.39	4.51	4.02	3.70	3.47	3.30	3.17	3.07	2.98	2.84	2.70	2.55	2.47	2.39	2.30	2.21	2.11	2.01
40	7.31	5.18	4.31	3.83	3.51	3.29	3.12	2.99	2.89	2.80	2.66	2.52	2.37	2.29	2.20	2.11	2.02	1.92	1.80
60	7.08	4.98	4.13	3.65	3.34	3.12	2.95	2.82	2.72	2.63	2.50	2.35	2.20	2.12	2.03	1.94	1.84	1.73	1.60
120	6.85	4.79	3.95	3.48	3.17	2.96	2.79	2.66	2.56	2.47	2.34	2.19	2.03	1.95	1.86	1.76	1.66	1.53	1.38
∞	6.63	4.61	3.78	3.32	3.02	2.80	2.64	2.51	2.41	2.32	2.18	2.04	1.88	1.79	1.70	1.59	1.47	1.32	1.00

For a particular combination of numerator and denominator degrees of freedom, each entry represents the critical value of F corresponding to a specified upper tail area α.

Glossary

A

Active social media research May be seen as an approach akin to both observing and engaging in what is being discussed and displayed in social media.

Agglomerative clustering A hierarchical clustering procedure where each object starts out in a separate cluster. Clusters are formed by grouping objects into bigger and bigger clusters.

Alternative hypothesis A statement that some difference or effect is expected. Accepting the alternative hypothesis will lead to changes in opinions or actions.

Acquiescence bias (yea-saying) This bias is the result of some participants' tendency to agree with the direction of a leading question (yea-saying).

Analytical model An explicit specification of a set of variables and their interrelationships designed to represent some real system or process in whole or in part.

Analytical services Companies that provide guidance in the development of research design.

Area sampling A common form of cluster sampling in which the clusters consist of geographical areas such as counties, housing tracts, blocks or other area descriptions.

Association techniques A type of projective technique in which participants are presented with a stimulus and are asked to respond with the first thing that comes to mind.

Audit A data collection process derived from physical records or performing inventory analysis. Data are collected personally by the researcher, or by representatives of the researcher, and are based on counts usually of physical objects rather than people.

Average linkage A linkage method based on the average distance between all pairs of objects, where one member of the pair is from each of the clusters.

B

Back translation A translation technique that translates a questionnaire from the base language by a translator whose native language is the one into which the questionnaire is being translated. This version is then retranslated back into the original language by someone whose native language is the base language. Translation errors can then be identified.

Balanced scale A scale with an equal number of favourable and unfavourable categories.

Bar chart A chart that displays data in bars positioned horizontally or vertically.

Bayesian approach A selection method where the elements are selected sequentially. The Bayesian approach explicitly incorporates prior information about population parameters as well as the costs and probabilities associated with making wrong decisions.

Bibliographic databases Databases composed of citations to articles in journals, magazines, newspapers, marketing research studies, technical reports, government documents and the like. They often provide summaries or abstracts of the material cited.

Blog and buzz mining Provide the means to observe, track or initiate views in research communities, social networks and anywhere else that people post comments, visuals, music and other forms of art on the Internet.

Branching question A question used to guide an interviewer (or participant) through a survey by directing the interviewer (or participant) to different spots on the questionnaire depending on the answers given.

Branded marketing research products Specialised data collection and analysis procedures developed to address specific types of marketing research problems.

Broad statement of the problem The initial statement of the marketing research problem that provides an appropriate perspective on the problem.

C

Carryover effects Where the evaluation of a particular scaled item significantly affects the participant's judgement of subsequent scaled items.

Cartoon tests Cartoon characters are shown in a specific situation related to the problem. Participants are asked to indicate the dialogue that one cartoon character might make in response to the comment(s) of another character.

Casewise deletion A method for handling missing responses in which cases or participants with any missing responses are discarded from the analysis.

Category equivalence A construct equivalence issue that deals specifically with whether the categories in which brands, products and behaviour are grouped are the same in different countries.

Causal research A type of conclusive research where the major objective is to obtain evidence regarding cause-and-effect (causal) relationships.

Causality Causality applies when the occurrence of X increases the probability of the occurrence of Y.

Census A complete enumeration of the elements of a population or study objects.

Centroid method A method of hierarchical clustering in which clusters are generated so as to maximise the distances between the centres or centroids of clusters.

Chi-square distribution A skewed distribution whose shape depends solely on the number of degrees of freedom. As the number of degrees of freedom increases, the chi-square distribution becomes more symmetrical.

Chi-square statistic The statistic used to test the statistical significance of the observed association in a cross-tabulation. It assists us in determining whether a systematic association exists between the two variables.

Classification information Socio-economic and demographic characteristics used to classify respondents.

Cluster sampling A two-step probability sampling technique where the target population is first divided into mutually exclusive and collectively exhaustive subpopulations called clusters, and then a random sample of clusters is selected based on a probability sampling technique such as SRS. For each selected cluster, either all the elements are included in the sample, or a sample of elements is drawn probabilistically.

Co-creation A process by which a group of individuals collaboratively evaluate a challenge and form design solution(s).

Coding Assigning a code to represent a specific response to a specific question along with the data record and column position that the code will occupy.

Coding and data entry services Companies whose primary service offering is their expertise in converting completed surveys or interviews into a usable database for conducting statistical analysis.

Coding data Breaking down qualitative data into discrete chunks and attaching a reference to those chunks of data.

Coefficient of variation A useful expression in sampling theory for the standard deviation as a percentage of the mean.

Cohort analysis A multiple cross-sectional design consisting of surveys conducted at appropriate time intervals. The cohort refers to the group of participants who experience the same event within the same interval.

Common factor analysis An approach to factor analysis that estimates the factors based only on the common variance. Also called principal axis factoring.

Communality The variance of a measured variance that is explained by the construct on which it loads.

Comparative scales One of two types of scaling technique in which there is direct comparison of stimulus objects with one another.

Complete linkage A linkage method that is based on maximum distance or the farthest neighbour approach.

Completion rate The percentage of qualified participants who complete the interview. It enables researchers to take into account anticipated refusals by people who qualify.

Completion technique A projective technique that requires particpants to complete an incomplete stimulus situation.

Conceptual equivalence A construct equivalence issue that deals with whether the interpretation of brands, products, consumer behaviour and the marketing effort are the same in different countries.

Conclusive research A research design characterised by the measurement of clearly defined marketing phenomena.

Concomitant variation A condition for inferring causality that requires that the extent to which a cause, X, and an effect, Y, occur together or vary together is predicted by the hypothesis under consideration.

Confidence intervals The range into which the true population parameter will fall, assuming a given level of confidence.

Configural equivalence Concerns the relationships of measured items to the latent constructs and implies that the patterns of factor loadings should be the same across countries or cultural units.

Confounding variables Synonymous with extraneous variables, used to illustrate that extraneous variables can confound the results by influencing the dependent variable.

Consistency checks A part of the data cleaning process that identifies data that are out of range, logically inconsistent or have extreme values. Data with values not defined by the coding scheme are inadmissible.

Constant sum scaling A comparative scaling technique in which participants are required to allocate a constant sum of units such as points, euros, chits, stickers or chips among a set of stimulus objects with respect to some criterion.

Construct A specific type of concept that exists at a higher level of abstraction than do everyday concepts.

Construct equivalence A type of equivalence that deals with the question of whether the marketing constructs have the same meaning and significance in different countries.

Construction technique A projective technique in which participants are required to construct a response in the form of a story, dialogue or description.

Contingency table A cross-tabulation table. It contains a cell for every combination of categories of the two variables.

Continuous rating scale A measurement scale that has participants rate the objects by placing a mark at the appropriate position on a line that runs from one extreme of the criterion variable to the other. The form may vary considerably. Also called graphic rating scale.

Convenience sampling A non-probability sampling technique that attempts to obtain a sample of convenient elements. The selection of sampling units is left primarily to the interviewer.

Cookie technology An identification code stored in the web surfer's browser that identifies a particular user.

Cross-sectional design A type of research design involving the collection of information from any given sample of population elements only once.

Cross-tabulation A statistical technique that describes two or more variables simultaneously and results in tables that reflect the joint distribution of two or more variables that have a limited number of categories or distinct values.

Crowdsourcing A process of eliciting ideas and developing actions based upon researcher engagement with a large group of self-selecting participants, primarily in online communities.

Customer database A database that details characteristics of customers and prospects that can include names and addresses, geographic, demographic and buying behaviour data.

Customised services Companies that tailor research procedures to best meet the needs of each client.

D

Data assembly The gathering of data from a variety of disparate sources.

Data cleaning Thorough and extensive checks for consistency and treatment of missing responses.

Data display Involves summarising and presenting the structure that is seen in collected qualitative data.

Data reduction The organising and structuring of qualitative data.

Data verification Involves seeking alternative explanations of the interpretations of qualitative data, through other data sources.

Demand artefacts Responses given because the participants attempt to guess the purpose of the experiment and respond accordingly.

Dependent variables Variables that measure the effect of the independent variables on the test units.

Descriptive research A type of conclusive research that has as its major objective the description of something, usually market characteristics or functions.

Design control A method of controlling extraneous variables that involves using specific experimental designs.

Dichotomous question A structured question with only two response alternatives, such as yes and no.

Digital dashboard A portal that enables a decision maker to tailor and focus upon business data and analyses. Its visual design is akin to the car dashboard, enabling the user to quickly assimilate key metrics.

Directory databases Databases that provide information on individuals, organisations and services.

Divisive clustering A hierarchical clustering procedure where all objects start out in one giant cluster. Clusters are formed by dividing this cluster into smaller and smaller clusters.

Double-barrelled question A single question that attempts to cover two issues. Such questions can be confusing to participants and result in ambiguous responses.

Double sampling A sampling technique in which certain population elements are sampled twice.

Dummy variables A respecification procedure using variables that take on only two values, usually 0 or 1.

E

Editing A review of the questionnaires with the objective of increasing accuracy and precision.

Electronic observation An observational research strategy in which electronic devices, rather than human observers, record the phenomenon being observed.

Element An object that possesses the information sought by the researcher and about which inferences are to be made.

Ethnography A research approach based upon the observation of the customs, habits and differences between people in everyday situations.

Euclidean distance The square root of the sum of the squared differences in values for each variable.

Experiment The process of manipulating one or more independent variables and measuring their effect on one or more dependent variables, while controlling for the extraneous variables.

Experimental design The set of experimental procedures specifying (1) the test units and sampling procedures, (2) the independent variables, (3) the dependent variables, and (4) how to control the extraneous variables.

Experimental group An initial focus group, run to test the setting of the interview, the opening question, the topic guide and the mix of participants that make up the group.

Exploratory research A research design characterised by a flexible and evolving approach to understand marketing phenomena that are inherently difficult to measure.

Expressive technique A projective technique in which participants are presented with a verbal or visual situation and are asked to relate the feelings and attitudes of other people to the situation.

External data Data that originate outside the organisation.

External suppliers Outside marketing research companies hired to supply marketing research services.

External validity A determination of whether the cause-and-effect relationships found in the experiment can be generalised.

Extraneous variables Variables, other than dependent and independent variables, which may influence the results of an experiment.

Eye tracking equipment Instruments that record the gaze movements of the eye.

F

F distribution A frequency distribution that depends upon two sets of degrees of freedom: the degrees of freedom in the numerator and the degrees of freedom in the denominator.

F statistic The ratio of two sample variances.

F test A statistical test of the equality of the variances of two populations.

Factor An underlying dimension that explains the correlations among a set of variables.

Factor analysis A class of procedures primarily used for data reduction and summarisation.

Factor scores Composite scores estimated for each participant on the derived factors.

Field environment An experimental location set in actual market conditions.

Field force Both the actual interviewers and the supervisors involved in data collection.

Field notes A log or diary of observations, events and reflections made by a researcher as a study is planned, implemented and analysed.

Field services Companies whose primary service offering is their expertise in collecting data for research projects.

Filter question An initial question in a questionnaire that screens potential participants to ensure they meet the requirements of the sample.

Fixed-response alternative questions Questions that require participants to choose from a set of predetermined answers.

Focus group A discussion conducted by a trained moderator among a small group of participants in an unstructured and natural manner.

Forced rating scale A rating scale that forces participants to express an opinion because a 'no opinion' or 'no knowledge' option is not provided.

Frequency distribution A mathematical distribution whose objective is to obtain a count of the number of responses associated with different values of one variable and to express these counts in percentage terms.

Frugging The use of marketing research to deliberately disguise fundraising activities.

Full-service suppliers Companies that offer a full range of marketing research activities.

Full-text databases Databases that contain the complete text of secondary source documents comprising the database.

Functional equivalence A construct equivalence issue that deals specifically with whether a given concept or behaviour serves the same role or function in different countries.

Funnel approach A strategy for ordering questions in a questionnaire in which the sequence starts with the general questions, which are followed by progressively specific questions, to prevent specific questions from biasing general questions.

G

Galvanic skin response Changes in the electrical resistance of the skin that relate to a participant's affective state.

Gamification The application of successful gaming to traditionally non-game processes and experiences.

Graphical models Analytical models that provide a visual picture of the relationships between variables.

H

Hierarchical clustering A clustering procedure characterised by the development of a hierarchy or treelike structure.

Histogram A vertical bar chart in which the height of the bar represents the relative or cumulative frequency of occurrence.

History Specific events that are external to the experiment but that occur at the same time as the experiment.

Hypothesis An unproven statement or proposition about a factor or phenomenon that is of interest to a researcher.

I

Identification information A type of information obtained in a questionnaire that includes name, address and phone number.

Implicit alternative An alternative that is not explicitly expressed.

Implicit assumption An assumption that is not explicitly stated in a question.

Imputation A method to adjust for non-response by assigning the characteristic of interest to the non-participants based on the similarity of the variables available for both non-participants and participants.

Incidence rate Refers to the rate of occurrence or the percentage of persons eligible to participate in a study.

Independent samples The samples are independent if they are drawn randomly from different populations.

Independent variables Variables that are manipulated by the researcher and whose effects are measured and compared.

In-depth interview An unstructured, direct, personal interview in which a single participant is probed by an experienced interviewer to uncover underlying motivations, beliefs, attitudes and feelings on a topic.

Instrumentation An extraneous variable involving changes in the measuring instrument, in the observers, or in the scores themselves.

Interactive testing effect An effect in which a prior measurement affects the test unit's response to the independent variable.

Interdependence technique A multivariate statistical technique in which the whole set of interdependent relationships is examined.

Internal data Data available within the organisation for whom the research is being conducted.

Internal validity A measure of accuracy of an experiment. It measures whether the manipulation of the independent variables, or treatments, actually caused the effects on the dependent variable(s).

Interquartile range The range of a distribution encompassing the middle 50% of the observations.

Interval scale A scale in which the numbers are used to rank objects such that numerically equal distances on the scale represent equal distances in the characteristic being measured.

Itemised rating scale A measurement scale having numbers or brief descriptions associated with each category. The categories are ordered in terms of scale position.

J

Judgemental sampling A form of convenience sampling in which the population elements are purposely selected based on the judgement of the researcher.

K

k-sample median test A non-parametric test used to examine differences among more than two groups when the dependent variable is measured on an ordinal scale.

Kurtosis A measure of the relative peakedness of the curve defined by the frequency distribution.

L

Laboratory environment An artificial setting for experimentation in which the researcher constructs the desired conditions.

Leading question A question that gives the participant a clue as to what answer is desired or leads the participant to answer in a certain way.

Level of significance The probability of making a Type I error.

Lifestyles Distinctive patterns of living described by the activities people engage in, the interests they have, and the opinions they hold of themselves and the world around them.

Likert scale A measurement scale with typically five response categories ranging from 'strongly disagree' to 'strongly agree' that requires participants to indicate a degree of agreement or disagreement with each of a series of statements related to the stimulus objects.

Limited-service suppliers Companies that specialise in one or a few phases of a marketing research project.

Line chart A chart that connects a series of data points using continuous lines.

Linguistic equivalence The equivalence of both spoken and written language forms used in scales and questionnaires.

Linkage methods Agglomerative methods of hierarchical clustering that cluster objects based on a computation of the distance between them.

Listening Listening involves the evaluation of naturally occurring conversations, behaviours and signals. The information that is elicited may or may not be guided, but it brings the voice of consumers' lives to brands.

Longitudinal design A type of research design involving a fixed sample of population elements measured repeatedly. The sample remains the same over time, thus providing a series of pictures that, when viewed together, vividly illustrate the situation and the changes that are taking place.

M

Main testing effect An effect of testing occurring when a prior observation affects a later observation.

Market research reports and advisory services Companies that provide off-the-shelf reports as well as data and briefs on a range of markets, consumer types and issues.

Marketing decision problem The problem confronting the marketing decision maker, which asks what the decision maker needs to do.

Marketing research The function that links the consumer, customer and public to the marketer through information – information used to identify and define marketing opportunities and problems; generate, refine, and evaluate marketing actions; monitor marketing performance; and improve understanding of marketing as a process. Marketing research specifies the information required to address these issues, designs the method for collecting information, manages and implements the data collection process, analyses the results, and communicates the findings and their implications.

Marketing research online community A panel of recruited participants who are questioned and observed in a community setting using a variety of research techniques, often over a period of months.

Marketing research problem A problem that entails determining what information is needed and how it can be obtained in the most feasible way.

Marketing research process A set of six steps which define the tasks to be accomplished in conducting a marketing research study. These include problem definition, developing an approach to the problem, research design formulation, fieldwork, data integrity and analysis, and report generation and presentation.

Matching A method of controlling extraneous variables that involves matching test units on a set of key background variables before assigning them to the treatment conditions.

Mathematical models Analytical models that explicitly describe the relationship between variables, usually in equation form.

Maturation An extraneous variable attributable to changes in the test units themselves that occur with the passage of time.

Mean The average; that value obtained by summing all elements in a set and dividing by the number of elements.

Measure of location A statistic that describes a location within a dataset. Measures of central tendency describe the centre of the distribution.

Measure of variability A statistic that indicates the distribution's dispersion.

Measurement The assignment of numbers or other symbols to characteristics of objects according to certain pre-specified rules.

Measurement equivalence Deals with the comparability of responses to particular (sets of) items. Measurement equivalence includes configural (structural), metric (measurement unit) and scalar equivalence.

Media panels A data gathering technique composed of samples of participants whose TV viewing behaviour is automatically recorded by electronic devices, supplementing the purchase information recorded in a diary or blog.

Median A measure of central tendency given as the value above which half of the values fall and below which half of the values fall.

Metric equivalence Refers to the unit of measurement; the factor loading should be the same.

Metric scale A scale that is either interval or ratio in nature.

Missing responses Values of a variable that are unknown because the participants concerned provided ambiguous answers to the question or because their answers were not properly recorded.

Mobile device The mobile device is a generic term used to refer to a variety of technologies that enable individuals to access data online and interact from wherever they may be.

Mode A measure of central tendency given as the value that occurs with the most frequency in a sample distribution.

Moderator An individual who conducts a focus group interview, by setting the purpose of the interview, questioning, probing and handling the process of discussion.

Mortality An extraneous variable attributable to the loss of test units while the experiment is in progress.

Multi-item scale A multi-item scale consists of multiple items, where an item is a single question or statement to be evaluated.

Multiple cross-sectional design A cross-sectional design in which there are two or more samples of participants, and information from each sample is obtained only once.

Mystery shopper An observer visiting providers of goods and services as if they were really a customer, and recording characteristics of the service delivery.

N

Neuromarketing The application of neuroscience in marketing, primarily to measure emotions through brain imaging.

Nominal scale A scale whose numbers serve only as labels or tags for identifying and classifying objects with a strict one-to-one correspondence between the numbers and the objects.

Non-comparative scale One of two types of scaling techniques in which each stimulus object is scaled independently of the other objects in the stimulus set. Also called monadic scale.

Non-hierarchical clustering A procedure that first assigns or determines a cluster centre and then groups all objects within a pre-specified threshold value from the centre.

Non-metric scale A scale that is either nominal or ordinal in nature.

Non-parametric tests Hypothesis testing procedures that assume that the variables are measured on a nominal or ordinal scale.

Non-probability sampling Sampling techniques that do not use chance selection procedures but rather rely on the personal judgement of the researcher.

Non-response error A type of non-sampling error that occurs when some of the participants included in the sample do not respond. This error may be defined as the variation between the true mean value of the variable in the original sample and the true mean value in the net sample.

Non-sampling error An error that can be attributed to sources other than sampling and that can be random or non-random.

Null hypothesis A statement in which no difference or effect is expected. If the null hypothesis is not rejected, no changes will be made.

Numeric databases Databases containing numerical and statistical information that may be important sources of secondary data.

O

Objective evidence Perceived to be unbiased evidence, supported by empirical findings.

Oblique rotation Rotation of factors when the axes are not maintained at right angles.

Omnibus survey A distinctive form of survey that serves the needs of a syndicated group. The omnibus survey targets particular types of participants such as those in specific geographic locations, e.g. Luxembourg residents, or consumers of particular types of products, e.g. business air travellers. With that target group of participants, a core set of questions can be asked, with other questions added as syndicate members wish.

One-tailed test A test of the null hypothesis where the alternative hypothesis is expressed directionally.

Online community providers Build online research communities where researchers can employ a wide variety of quantitative and qualitative techniques to connect to consumers.

Online databases Databases that can be accessed, searched and analysed via the Internet.

Online focus groups and streaming Provide platforms for running online focus groups and streaming the results.

Online services Companies which specialise in the use of the Internet to collect, analyse and distribute marketing research information.

Operational data Data generated about an organisation's customers, through day-to-day transactions.

Operational equivalence A type of equivalence that measures how theoretical constructs are operationalised in different countries to measure marketing variables.

Optimising partitioning method A non-hierarchical clustering method that allows for later reassignment of objects to clusters to optimise an overall criterion.

Order bias (position bias) A participant's tendency to choose an alternative merely because it occupies a certain position or is listed in a certain order.

Ordinal scale A ranking scale in which numbers are assigned to objects to indicate the relative extent to which some characteristic is possessed. Thus, it is possible to determine whether an object has more or less of a characteristic than some other object.

Orthogonal rotation Rotation of factors in which the axes are maintained at right angles.

P

p value This is the probability of observing a value of the test statistic as extreme as, or more extreme than, the value actually observed, assuming that the null hypothesis is true.

Paired comparison scaling A comparative scaling technique in which a participant is presented with two objects at a time and asked to select one object in the pair according to some criterion. The data obtained are ordinal in nature.

Pairwise deletion A method for handling missing responses in which all cases or participants with any missing responses are not automatically discarded; rather, for each calculation, only the cases or participants with complete responses are considered.

Panel A sample of participants who have agreed to provide information at specified intervals over an extended period.

Panel providers Provide access to consumer, B2B and specialist panels of participants alongside scripting and hosting surveys.

Paradigm A set of assumptions consisting of agreed upon knowledge, criteria of judgement, problem fields and ways to consider them.

Parallel threshold method A non-hierarchical clustering method that specifies several cluster centres at once. All objects that are within a pre-specified threshold value from the centre are grouped together.

Parallel translation A translation method in which a committee of translators, each of whom is fluent in at least two languages, discuss alternative versions of a questionnaire and make modifications until consensus is reached.

Parametric tests Hypothesis testing procedures that assume that the variables of interest are measured on at least an interval scale.

Participant engagement The manner in which research participants relate to the process of research, researchers and the topics of study.

Participatory blogging Researcher interaction with individuals in communities and social networks. Individual participants can be targeted and given blogging tasks that relate to specific research objectives.

Perceived participant anonymity The participants' perceptions that their identities will not be discerned by the interviewer or researcher.

Personal observation An observational research strategy in which human observers record the phenomenon being observed as it occurs.

Personification technique Participants are asked to imagine that the brand is a person and then describe characteristics of that person.

Picture response technique A projective technique in which participants are shown a picture and are asked to tell a story describing it.

Pie chart A round chart divided into sections.

Pilot-testing Testing the questionnaire on a small sample of particpants for the purpose of improving the questionnaire by identifying and eliminating potential problems.

Population The aggregate of all the elements, sharing some common set of characteristics, that comprise the universe for the purpose of the marketing research problem.

Power of a statistical test The probability of rejecting the null hypothesis when it is in fact false and should be rejected.

Pre-coding In questionnaire design, assigning a code to every conceivable response before data collection.

Pre-experimental designs Designs that do not control for extraneous factors by randomisation.

Primary data Data originated by the researcher specifically to address the research problem.

Principal components analysis An approach to factor analysis that considers the total variance in the data.

Probability sampling A sampling procedure in which each element of the population has a fixed probabilistic chance of being selected for the sample.

Probing A motivational technique used when asking questions to induce the participants to enlarge on, clarify or explain their answers.

Problem definition A broad statement of the general problem and identification of the specific components of the marketing research problem.

Problem identification research Research undertaken to help identify problems that are not necessarily apparent on the surface, yet exist or are likely to arise in the future.

Problem-solving research Research undertaken to help solve marketing problems.

Projective technique An unstructured and indirect form of questioning that encourages participants to project their underlying motivations, beliefs, attitudes or feelings regarding the issues of concern.

Psycho-galvanometer An instrument that measures a participant's galvanic skin response.

Psychographics Quantified profiles of individuals based upon lifestyle characteristics.

Purchase panels A data gathering technique in which participant's record their purchases, either online, in a diary or in a blog.

Q

Q-sort scaling A comparative scaling technique that uses a rank order procedure to sort objects based on similarity with respect to some criterion.

Qualitative research An unstructured primarily exploratory design based on small samples, intended to provide depth, insight and understanding.

Quantitative observation The recording and counting of behavioural patterns of people, objects and events in a systematic manner to obtain information about the phenomenon of interest.

Quantitative research Research techniques that seek to quantify data and, typically, apply some form of measurement and statistical analysis.

Quasi-experimental designs Designs that apply part of the procedures of true experimentation yet lack full experimental control.

Questionnaire A structured technique for data collection consisting of a series of questions, written or verbal, that a participant answers.

Quota sampling A non-probability sampling technique that is two-stage restricted judgemental sampling. The first stage consists of developing control categories or quotas of population elements. In the second stage, sample elements are selected based on convenience or judgement.

R

Random sampling error The error because the particular sample selected is an imperfect representation of the population of interest. It may be defined as the variation between the true mean value for the sample and the true mean value of the population.

Randomisation A method of controlling extraneous variables that involves randomly assigning test units to experimental groups by using random numbers. Treatment conditions are also randomly assigned to experimental groups.

Range The difference between the smallest and largest values of a distribution.

Rank order scaling A comparative scaling technique in which participants are presented with several objects simultaneously and asked to order or rank them according to some criterion.

Ratio scale The highest scale. This scale allows the researcher to identify or classify objects, rank order the objects, and compare intervals or differences. It is also meaningful to compute ratios of scale values.

Reporting Offers research companies reporting solutions that seek to engage clients in oral and electronic presentations beyond conventional reporting methods such as hard-copy reports and PowerPoint.

Research brief A document produced by the users of research findings or the buyers of a piece of marketing research. The brief is used to communicate the perceived requirements of a marketing research study.

Research design A framework or blueprint for conducting the marketing research project. It specifies the details of the procedures necessary for obtaining the information needed to structure or solve marketing research problems.

Research proposal The official layout of the planned marketing research activity.

Research questions Refined statements of the specific components of the problem.

Response error A type of non-sampling error arising from participants who do respond but who give inaccurate answers or whose answers are mis-recorded or mis-analysed. It may be defined as a variation between the true mean value of the variable in the net sample and the observed mean value obtained in the market research project.

Response latency The amount of time it takes to respond to a question.

Response rate The percentage of the total attempted interviews that are completed.

Role playing Participants are asked to assume the behaviour of someone else or a specific object.

Runs test A test of randomness for a dichotomous variable.

S

Sample A subgroup of the elements of the population selected for participation in the study.

Sample control The ability of the survey mode to reach the units specified in the sample effectively and efficiently.

Sample size The number of elements to be included in a study.

Sampling control An aspect of supervising that ensures that the interviewers strictly follow the sampling plan rather than select sampling units based on convenience or accessibility.

Sampling frame A representation of the elements of the target population that consists of a list or set of directions for identifying the target population.

Sampling unit An element, or a unit containing the element, that is available for selection at some stage of the sampling process.

Sampling with replacement A sampling technique in which an element *can* be included in the sample more than once.

Sampling without replacement A sampling technique in which an element *cannot* be included in the sample more than once.

Scalar equivalence The demonstration that two individuals from different countries with the same value on some variable will score at the same level on the same test. Also called metric equivalence.

Scale transformation A manipulation of scale values to ensure compatibility with other scales or otherwise to make the data suitable for analysis.

Scaling The generation of a continuum upon which measured objects are located.

Scanner data Data obtained by passing merchandise over a laser scanner that reads the UPC from the packages.

Scanner panels Scanner data where panel members are identified by an ID card, allowing information about each panel member's purchases to be stored with respect to the individual shopper.

Scanner panels with pay TV The combination of a scanner panel with manipulations of the advertising that is being broadcast by pay TV companies.

Secondary data Data collected for some purpose other than the problem at hand.

Selection bias An extraneous variable attributable to the improper assignment of test units to treatment conditions.

Semantic differential A seven-point rating scale with end points associated with bipolar labels.

Semiotics The study of signs in the context of consumer experience.

Sentence completion A projective technique in which participants are presented with a number of incomplete sentences and are asked to complete them.

Sequential sampling A probability sampling technique in which the population elements are sampled sequentially, data collection and analysis are done at each stage, and a decision is made as to whether additional population elements should be sampled.

Sequential threshold method A non-hierarchical clustering method in which a cluster centre is selected and all objects within a pre-specified threshold value from the centre are grouped together.

Simple random sampling (SRS) A probability sampling technique in which each element has a known and equal probability of selection. Every element is selected independently of every other element, and

the sample is drawn by a random procedure from a sampling frame.

Single cross-sectional design A cross-sectional design in which one sample of participants is drawn from the target population and information is obtained from this sample once.

Single linkage A linkage method based on minimum distance or the nearest neighbour rule.

Skewness A characteristic of a distribution that assesses its symmetry about the mean.

Snowball sampling A non-probability sampling technique in which an initial group of participants is selected randomly. Subsequent participants are selected based on the referrals or information provided by the initial participants. By obtaining referrals from referrals, this process may be carried out in waves.

Social desirability The tendency of respondents to give answers that may not be accurate but may be desirable from a social standpoint.

Social media research Research based upon the collection of data from social media platforms. It is usually conducted to supplement and support the development of traditional marketing research methods.

Software providers Provide software packages that create platforms to script, host and analyse surveys, or Software as a Service (SaaS) options.

Special-purpose databases Databases that contain information of a specific nature, e.g. data on a specialised industry.

Specific components of the problem The second part of the marketing research problem definition that focuses on the key aspects of the problem and provides clear guidelines on how to proceed further.

Standard deviation The square root of the variance.

Stapel scale A scale for measuring attitudes that consists of a single adjective in the middle of an even-numbered range of values.

Statistical control A method of controlling extraneous variables by measuring the extraneous variables and adjusting for their effects through statistical methods.

Statistical designs Designs that allow for the statistical control and analysis of external variables.

Statistical regression An extraneous variable that occurs when test units with extreme scores move closer to the average score during the course of the experiment.

Story completion A projective technique in which participants are provided with part of a story and are required to give the conclusion in their own words.

Stratified sampling A probability sampling technique that uses a two-step process to partition the population into subsequent subpopulations, or strata. Elements are selected from each stratum by a random procedure.

Structured data collection Use of a formal questionnaire that presents questions in a prearranged order.

Structured questions Questions that pre-specify the set of response alternatives and the response format. A structured question could be multiple choice, dichotomous or a scale.

Substitution A procedure that substitutes for non-participants other elements from the sampling frame who are expected to respond.

Sugging The use of marketing research to deliberately disguise a sales effort.

Surrogate variables A subset of original variables selected for use in subsequent analysis.

Survey method A structured questionnaire administered to a sample of a target population, designed to elicit specific information from participants.

Surveys Interviews with a large number of participants using a questionnaire.

Syndicated services Companies that collect and sell common pools of data designed to serve information needs shared by a number of clients.

Syndicated sources (services) Information services offered by marketing research organisations that provide information from a common database to different firms that subscribe to their services.

Systematic sampling A probability sampling technique in which the sample is chosen by selecting a random starting point and then picking every ith element in succession from the sampling frame.

T

t **distribution** A symmetrical bell-shaped distribution that is useful for sample testing ($n < 30$). It is similar to the normal distribution in appearance.

t **statistic** A statistic that assumes that the variable has a symmetric bell-shaped distribution, that the mean is known (or assumed to be known), and that the population variance is estimated from the sample.

t **test** A univariate hypothesis test using the *t* distribution, which is used when the standard deviation is unknown and the sample size is small.

Target population The collection of elements or objects that possess the information sought by the researcher and about which inferences are to be made.

Telescoping A psychological phenomenon that takes place when an individual telescopes or compresses time by remembering an event as occurring more recently than it actually occurred.

Test statistic A measure of how close the sample has come to the null hypothesis. It often follows a well-known distribution, such as the normal, *t*, or chi-square distribution.

Test units Participants, organisations or other entities whose responses to independent variables or treatments are being studied.

Testing effects Effects caused by the process of experimentation.

Theory A conceptual scheme based on foundational statements, or axioms, that are assumed to be true.

Third-person technique A projective technique in which participants are presented with a verbal or visual situation and are asked to relate the beliefs and attitudes of a third person in that situation.

Topic guide A list of topics, questions and probes that are used by a moderator to help manage a focus group discussion.

Total error The variation between the true mean value in the population of the variable of interest and the observed mean value obtained in the marketing research project.

Trace analysis An approach in which data collection is based on physical traces, or evidence, of past behaviour.

Transcripts 'Hard copies' of the questions and probes and the corresponding answers and responses in focus group or in-depth interviews.

Transitivity of preference An assumption made to convert paired comparison data with rank order data. It implies that if Brand A is preferred to Brand B, and Brand B is preferred to Brand C, then Brand A is preferred to Brand C.

Trend analysis A method of adjusting for non-response in which the researcher tries to discern a trend between early and late participants. This trend is projected to non-participants to estimate their characteristic of interest.

Triangulation A process that facilitates the validation of data through cross-verification from more than two sources.

True experimental designs Experimental designs distinguished by the fact that the researcher can randomly assign test units to experimental groups and also randomly assign treatments to experimental groups.

Two-tailed test A test of the null hypothesis where the alternative hypothesis is not expressed directionally.

Type I error An error that occurs when the sample results lead to the rejection of a null hypothesis that is in fact true. Also known as alpha error (α).

Type II error An error that occurs when the sample results lead to acceptance of a null hypothesis that is in fact false. Also known as beta error (β).

U

Unstructured questions Open-ended questions that participants answer in their own words.

V

Variable respecification The transformation of data to create new variables or the modification of existing variables so that they are more consistent with the objectives of the study.

Variance The mean squared deviation of all the values of the mean.

Variance method An agglomerative method of hierarchical clustering in which clusters are generated to minimise the within-cluster variance.

Varimax procedure An orthogonal method of factor rotation that minimises the number of variables with high loadings on a factor, thereby enhancing the interpretability of the factors.

Verbal models Analytical models that provide a written representation of the relationships between variables.

Verbal protocol A technique used to understand participants' cognitive responses or thought processes by having them think aloud while completing a task or making a decision.

Voice pitch analysis Measurement of emotional reactions through changes in the participant's voice.

Volume tracking data Scanner data that provide information on purchases by brand, size, price and flavour or formulation.

W

Ward's procedure A variance method in which the squared Euclidean distance to the cluster means is minimised.

Weighting A statistical procedure that attempts to account for non-response by assigning differential weights to the data depending on the response rates.

Word association A projective technique in which participants are presented with a list of words, one at a time. After each word, they are asked to give the first word that comes to mind.

Z

z test A univariate hypothesis test using the standard normal distribution.

Index